D1369579

SOVIET INSTITUTIONS,
THE INDIVIDUAL
AND SOCIETY

SOVIET INSTITUTIONS

THE INDIVIDUAL

AND SOCIETY

By

KAREL HULICKA
Professor of History
State University of New York at Buffalo

and

IRENE M. HULICKA
Professor of Psychology
D'Youville College

THE CHRISTOPHER PUBLISHING HOUSE

BOSTON, MASSACHUSETTS

COPYRIGHT © 1967

BY THE CHRISTOPHER PUBLISHING HOUSE

Library of Congress Catalog Card Number 67-13544

PRINTED IN

THE UNITED STATES OF AMERICA

JN
6515
1967
H8

To

Charles and Our Students

477160

TABLE OF CONTENTS

PREFACE

Most students, who do not specialize in Soviet studies, can afford the time to take no more than one or two courses on the Soviet Union. Therefore, the majority of books and courses on the Soviet Union deal rather exclusively with one or two major topics such as Soviet government and politics, economics, history or law. Hence the student or reader acquires fairly detailed information about one or two aspects of the Soviet system, but learns relatively little about a number of other important topics. During twenty years of lecturing on the Soviet economy, government and politics of the U.S.S.R. and History of Russia and the Soviet Union, the senior author has been told by many people, students and non-students alike, that they would like to have an interdisciplinary course or a book on the U.S.S.R. which describes and discusses a wide variety of Soviet institutions and practices. We, therefore, decided to undertake the task of writing such a book. It proved to be a rather formidable task to discuss in one book, as we have, Marxist-Leninist ideology, the government and politics of the U.S.S.R., the economy, agriculture, the judicial system, foreign policy, youth organizations, social welfare measures, education, the family, religion, goals for the future communist society and prospects for the attainment of these goals, along with a number of other topics. The task was made immeasurably more difficult because the system about which we are writing has been in a constant state of flux; no sooner would a chapter be written than a major change in policy or organization would be announced in the U.S.S.R. It is recognized that even while the manuscript is in press, some of the details are becoming outdated; no book on the U.S.S.R. can be completely up-to-date. We have, however, attempted to present general principles and approaches so that, even if some of the details change, the reader will be able to gain an overall understanding of the operation of the Soviet system.

In writing this book, we encountered a number of difficulties, in addition to those associated with the changing nature of the system about which we were writing. Of these, one of the most troublesome was the fact that some people subscribe to the belief that if one does not unequivocally condemn everything about the Soviet system, one is somehow "unpatriotic." To give a *carte blanche* condemnation of the Soviet system would be unscholarly; to concede that not all aspects of the system are deplorable does not signify admiration. Because of the rather prevalent antagonism to the Soviet system in the West, we also realize that by presenting Soviet statements and viewpoints, sometimes without immediate critical analysis, we might run the risk of being accused of subscribing to these views; yet had we criticized and condemned every statement by party and state officials, the book would have been so long and so cluttered with condemnations that the reader would probably have learned little from it except that the Soviet system is "bad."

Although in writing this book we have relied heavily on original sources, the views of Western authors have been taken into consideration, and have naturally greatly influenced the authors. Thus we are deeply indebted to the broad community of scholars of Soviet affairs. Specific references are made to a number of the Western authors whose work and viewpoints influenced our conclusions; because of space limitations and the general nature of their influence, the majority of books by Western authors are listed in the Bibliography rather than in the chapter reference lists. On the advice of our publisher, all Soviet and other non-English titles and the names of all foreign publishers have been translated into English. In the preparation of this book, translations of Soviet articles in the *Current Digest of the Soviet Press* (C.D.S.P.), *Problems of Economics* and *Soviet Law and Government* were invaluable. Although the major Soviet publications were available to us, through the above publications we were able to make use of material that would not otherwise have been available. Appreciation is also expressed to the Research Foundation of the State University of New York and to the Graduate School of the State University of New York at Buffalo for financial support. Naturally, the authors assume full responsibility for the views expressed in this book.

It is hoped that this book will meet the needs of those people who want to be informed about many aspects of the Soviet system, but do not have the time to read several books on the U.S.S.R. In addition to serving as a text for general survey courses on the Soviet Union, this book can also be used as a supplement to other texts and/or as reference material for a variety of courses, including social studies, economics, history, law, comparative government, foreign policy, sociology and education.

K. H.
I. M. H.

INTRODUCTION

Events in the Soviet Union during the last five decades constitute one of the most fascinating and, in some respects, one of the most depressing social experiments in the history of mankind. In 1917 the minority Bolshevik Party seized political power in Russia. Since then, under the guise of Marxist-Leninist ideology, the leaders of the Bolshevik Party (later renamed the Communist Party of the Soviet Union—the C.P.S.U.) have used terrorism, coercion, repression, persuasion, token rewards and promises of a magnificent future in their attempt to restructure the society, first into socialism and eventually into communism. Socialism has purportedly been achieved; communism, according to the leaders of the C.P.S.U., will be achieved in the foreseeable future.

Soviet-style socialism, the leaders of the C.P.S.U. maintain, constitutes a form of social organization infinitely superior to any form of social organization which has existed heretofore in the history of mankind. One of the sources of its alleged superiority is the public ownership of the means of production which, it is claimed, has totally eliminated economic exploitation of man by man. Soviet spokesmen assert that under socialism class distinctions are eradicated; class struggle is eliminated; all citizens have equal social opportunities in all spheres; a fairer system of distribution, based on need as well as work, is possible; and a higher and more profoundly democratic form of political organization emerges. Soviet-style socialism is, however, according to party leaders, only a portent of better things to come.

In the early sixties Khrushchev announced that the process of transition from socialism to communism had already begun. Under communism, according to the Party Program, "all sources of public wealth will gush forth abundantly," the material needs of all members of society will be satisfied fully, and all people will work gladly and selflessly for the good of society, since the well-being of the individual and society will be inextricably and harmoniously linked. All class barriers are to disappear, and in the classless society full social equality in every sense of the word is to prevail. Distribution is to be based exclusively on need, and labor for the good of society is to become a "prime vital necessity" of life. Because of efficient organization and high productive capacity, each individual is to have ample time for personal development and to participate in public self-government. The new society is to be composed of highly cultured, public-spirited individuals who will be fully capable of public self-administration; the state and the state apparatus will become superfluous and eventually wither away.

No communist leader, Soviet or otherwise, wants to limit the benefits of the "earthly communist paradise" to one country only. "All the peoples of the globe," according to a Soviet spokesman, "are moving toward it (communism) and will eventually come to it."[1] All communist leaders ascribe to the ultimate goal of establishing communist societies throughout the world. In fact, no society can aspire to achieve communism in its most complete form unless all societies adopt communist goals and the communist style of social organization. The messianic zeal of communist party members and the world-domination goal of the communist doctrine are among the most cogent reasons for the public in societies which are not sympathetic to communist ideology to be fully informed about communist doctrines, techniques, goals and appeal.

Around the turn of the century when the first Marxist organizations were still in their infancy, a Russian scholar argued wisely that "to defeat what is false in socialism, we must recognize what is true in it."[2] His advice is equally appropriate today. Most governments and citizens in the Western world reject Soviet-style socialism and communism, and are strongly motivated to curb the expansion of the communist movement. In any struggle it is advantageous to know the strengths as well as the weaknesses of the opposing system. If a firm and effective stand is to be taken against communism and against the style of life which the Soviet and other communist leaders would, if given a chance, impose upon mankind, it is necessary to know the adversary fully. The majority of Westerners are probably firmly convinced that communism and the Soviet Union are "bad," and of these, most—but by no means all, could probably provide a certain amount of highly realistic justification for the negative evaluation. But what proportion of those who condemn communism could provide reasonably authentic explanations for the fact that communism apparently has a positive appeal for millions of people? The almost certain fact that a very significant proportion of the people who are sympathetic to communism are totally ignorant of its negative features does not justify lack of or one-sided information on the part of the citizens of the Western world. Responsible citizens and scholars must address themselves soberly to the question of what it is that communism offers or promises which at least some thoughtful scholars, some politicians, some national leaders—particularly in newly independent states, and some working people find more attractive than what is offered by the ideology of the Western world. Full awareness of the features of communist ideology and practice which appeal to others can contribute appreciably to the effectiveness of measures designed to counter the spread of Marxism.

In addition to describing and analyzing the structure and functions of Soviet governmental, economic and social institutions, this book presents material which is intended to enable the reader to understand the appeal value of communist ideology and practice for persons who live in the "socialist bloc" and for persons whom communist leaders are attempting to influence. Occasionally Soviet interpretations and certain commendable aspects of the Soviet social system or Marxism-Leninism might be over-emphasized. If this does happen, the underlying motivation is the authors' desire to arm the reader with knowledge about the strengths of the system and the ideology which are in competition with Western ideology and the Western way of life and with some insight into the insidious techniques which Soviet leaders use in their attempt to win converts. The authors' respect for the intelligence of American college students and other readers allows them to assume that they will not interpret presentations of Soviet statements about Marxist-Leninist ideology, Soviet official positions and Soviet arguments justifying their positions and policies, as manifestations of a pro-Soviet or pro-communist bias. To present the position of another does not signify agreement with it. The authors further assume that readers will recognize when they are quoting Soviet sources or paraphrasing Soviet positions, and will agree that no matter how much they might want to do so, they cannot with justification rewrite the Party Program or the speeches of Khrushchev or Brezhnev or otherwise modify Soviet statements, policies, goals or claims. It is, of course, well-established that there are frequently wide discrepancies between Marxist-Leninist ideology and Soviet practice, between what Soviet leaders say and do, and between claimed accomplishments and stark reality. Unfortunately, persons and nations most susceptible to Soviet influence have greater access to statements about the lofty theory and about the claims and promises of Soviet leaders than to information about Soviet reality. The attempts of governments, agencies and individuals to disseminate information about the negative features of Soviet ideology and practice would perhaps be more effective if they were designed specifically to counter the positive appeal of Soviet propaganda. To paraphrase the Russian scholar, to defeat what is undesirable in socialism, we must recognize what actually is and what appears to be desirable in it.

Since knowledge of Soviet ideology, *as it is presented by Soviet theoreticians,* is required if its impact on citizens of the U.S.S.R. and individuals elsewhere is to be understood, the major portion of the first chapter will be devoted to a presentation of relevant features of Marxist-Leninist ideology *as it is taught in the Soviet Union.* At this point, Marxist-Leninist ideology will be presented without critical comment since to criticize Marxism-Leninism would violate the decision to present the ideology as it is presented in the U.S.S.R. The following presentation differs markedly from Soviet statements in one crucial respect: although it includes the Marxist critique of capitalism because the critique is an integral part of the Marxist-Leninist theory, it excludes most of the scathing criticism of Western ideologies and practices which constitute a major portion of almost all Soviet theoretical pronouncements. It is, however, important to keep in mind that Soviet citizens are given completely inaccurate and highly derogatory information about the ideology and practices of Western societies. They are told over and over again that Marxist-Leninist ideology and Soviet practices are infinitely superior to their counterparts in the West. Soviet leaders particularly enjoy to present and emphasize internal problems in the United States, such as prolonged strikes, racial discrimination and unemployment, as "irrefutable evidence of the rottenness" of Western society and of the superiority of the Soviet system. Furthermore, in the Soviet Union, unlike in some societies, no competing ideologies are tolerated. Marxism-Leninism is presented as the correct ideology which must be understood and accepted by all citizens.

REFERENCES

1 V. Ivanov, V. Pchelin and M. Sakov, "The Party's Growing Role in the Building of Communism," *Kommunist,* No. 17, Nov., 1959, pp. 3-20. (C.D.S.P., Vol. XII, No. 1, pp. 3-7)

2 Quoted in Harold J. Berman, *Justice in Russia,* (Cambridge, Mass.: Harvard University Press, 1950), p. 94.

SOVIET INSTITUTIONS,
THE INDIVIDUAL
AND SOCIETY

Chapter I

MARXIST-LENINIST IDEOLOGY

Marxist-Leninist Conception of History

Marxism-Leninism as it is taught in the U.S.S.R. is a doctrine based on Lenin's interpretation and elaboration of theories developed by Karl Marx and Friedrich Engels.[1] Lenin's interpretation, in turn, is adapted selectively by the leaders of the C.P.S.U. to fit the exigencies of the present. Interpretations of the teachings of Marx, Engels and Lenin have varied widely with the interpreter. Many persons who consider themselves to be Marxists or Marxists-Leninists do not agree with the Soviet interpretations of Marxism-Leninism. Therefore, it is necessary to emphasize that in subsequent sections terms such as Marxists, Marxists-Leninists, Marxism-Leninism, etc., refer exclusively to Soviet positions or interpretations.

Marxism-Leninism is a thoroughly materialistic, deterministic, atheistic theory which encompasses history, economics, politics, social development, philosophy and ethics. It is materialistic in the sense that it is based on the assumption that the material basis of nature is primary and that thought and consciousness are the property of matter. Theories of idealistic philosophers, such as Berkeley, Leibnitz and Hegel who proposed that nature is in some way the creation of the mind or spirit, are rejected *in toto*. Marxism-Leninism is, however, not materialistic in the sense that exclusive emphasis is placed on material prosperity. On the contrary, leaders who are guided by Marxist-Leninist ideology have required people under their control to forego even basic material necessities so that eventually the "ideal" society might be established. Marxism-Leninism is rigidly atheistic and deterministic in that it completely rejects all religions, and all theories about God or the supernatural, and assumes that all phenomena are necessary consequences of antecedent conditions. One of the claims of its proponents is that Marxism-Leninism is the only theory which has "correctly" applied the concept of objective causality to provide an understanding of historical development and social organization.

Materialist dialectics, as developed by Marx and Engels, is purported to provide a completely adequate, inclusive, deterministic explanation for all change and development, including physical, biological, chemical, ideo-

3

logical and social changes. Their dialectical approach could be described as a materialistic transformation and extension of the idealistic dialectics of Hegel, who held that the development of ideas follows the dialectical form of thesis, antithesis and synthesis. Each idea, Hegel said, embodies a partial truth which is opposed by a contradictory idea which also embodies a partial truth. In the ensuing conflict of ideas, a new and higher idea, which embodies a new, but still partial, truth emerges. It in turn generates a new opposite and a new conflict. Thus each synthesis becomes a thesis in terms of which a new struggle is established. The process continues until finally a synthesis is reached which embodies the whole truth. Marx and Engels objected vehemently to the idealistic basis of Hegelian dialectics. They maintained, however, that by adopting the "correct" materialistic position they were able to reveal through application of the dialectical process that the motive force or the source of all development is the contradictory nature of reality.

According to materialist dialectics, any developing thing has within it the embryo of something else, its own antithesis or negating element, which prevents it from remaining inert and immutable. All development, whether it be in nature, thought, human life, or forms of social organization, depends on the "struggle" or opposition of mutually exclusive tendencies or qualities. The struggle of opposite forces leads eventually to the resolution of the contradiction through a radical qualitative change in which old forms are destroyed and new forms emerge. Development through dialectical negation is the basis for progress. Engels wrote:

> "In the eyes of dialectic philosophy, nothing is established for all time, nothing is absolute or sacred. On everything and in everything it sees the stamp of inevitable decline; nothing can resist it save the unceasing process of formation and destruction, the unending ascent from the lower to the higher . . . ."[2]

Marx and Engels concentrated particularly on applying the principles of materialist dialectics to an analysis of the development of forms of social organization. This segment of their doctrine is commonly called historical materialism. The thesis that all social changes and political revolutions are based on economic factors is a major tenet of historical materialism. Engels stated:

> "The materialistic concept of history starts from the proposition that the production of the means to support human life, and next to production, the exchange of things produced is the basis of all social structure; that in every society that has appeared in history, the manner in which wealth is distributed and society is divided into classes or orders is dependent on what is produced, how it is produced, and how the products are exchanged. From this point of view, the final causes of all social changes and political revolutions are to be sought, not in men's brains, not in man's insight into eternal truth and justice, but in changes in the modes of production and exchange. They are to be sought, not in the *philosophy,* but in the *economics* of each particular epoch."[3]

According to Marxist analysis, mankind is divided into classes on the basis of ownership or non-ownership of the means of production. Those who own the means of production are able to exploit those who do not, and this economic exploitation of man by man is a primary reason for human misery. *Class struggle,* that is, the struggle between the exploited and the exploiter, has served as the historical mechanism for dialectical change in human organization. It is maintained that in all societies, with the exception of primitive tribal groups and societies structured on the communist ideal, *production relations* have been characterized by the exploitation of people involved in the process of production for the benefit of the people who own the means of production. Typically, throughout history *productive forces*—the instruments of production and the people who conduct the production process on the basis of a certain amount of experience—have improved gradually. Each newly developed skill, technique and instrument serves as a basis for further development, and people gain new production experience in the process of adapting actively to their environment. *Production relations,* however, remain relatively static because those who benefit from the established production relationship resist change and protect their favorable position by legal and political measures. When contradictions between the developing productive forces and the static production relations become extreme, members of the oppressed class, i.e., those engaged directly in the productive process, rise against their oppressors, i.e., the owners of the means of production, and a new form of production relations is established which is temporarily in harmony with the production forces. However, as the production forces again develop while the production relations remain unchanged, new contradictions emerge and a new struggle ensues. Thus, each newly emerging social structure carries within itself its own antithesis or negating elements.

Marx described the history of society in terms of a series of socio-economic formations: primitive-communal, slavery, feudalism, capitalism and finally socialism, the first stage of communism. In the primitive-communal system, there was no private property, the few known instruments of production could be produced by anyone, and the low level of production made economic exploitation of man by man virtually impossible. However, with the gradual development of productive forces through new skills and new tools, social division of labor developed. Production exceeded subsistence requirements and private ownership of property was introduced. With these features the way was open for the introduction of new social relations involving exploitation.

With the development of slavery, society was divided into antagonistic classes, the slaves and the slave owners. Because production forces were poorly developed, the value of exploitation lay in reducing the consumption of the slaves to a bare minimum. During this period production forces developed—slaves built ships, dams, irrigation ditches, etc., and some slave owners devoted themselves to the arts and sciences. To cope with the opposition evoked by the brutal exploitation of the slaves and to maintain the rights of the exploiting class, the state, an instrument of coercion, was developed. The exploiters, because of an abundance of cheap labor, did little to improve the instruments of production, and the working class, being denied the fruits of its labor, sometimes even destroyed rather than improved the tools. Eventually the system was so fraught with contradictions that change was inevitable; a combination of slave uprisings, attacks from barbarians, and the internal weaknesses of the system resulted in a social revolution, the replacement of slavery by feudalism.

Under feudalism, Marx said, production relations were determined by ownership of the means of production, chiefly the land, by the feudal lords. The serfs were bound to the soil and obliged to work for their economic masters, but many of them were permitted to possess small personal holdings. There was a significant impetus to the development of productive forces in agriculture, the crafts and trade, because the direct producers were able to benefit to a certain extent from their own work. Class struggle, based on antagonistic relations between the ruling feudal lords and the oppressed peasants and craftsmen, was reflected in the political and ideological superstructure of society. Each feudal lord maintained an armed force and condemned and punished as he saw fit within his own estates. Rigid social barriers impeded movement from one social strata to another within the feudal hierarchy. Finally, the growing contradiction between the development of production forces and the static production relations precipitated revolutionary changes, and the capitalist phase emerged gradually. Scientific and technical developments which augmented productivity, the establishment of large factories which required a "free" labor market, and overseas trade added impetus to the change.

According to Marx, production relations under capitalism are characterized by the private ownership of the means of production by a small capitalist class that exploits the much larger working class, which is forced to sell its labor power because it is deprived of the means of production. He defined capitalism as a system of society in which the instruments of production are operated for the private profit of those who own them by means of the labor of workers. Although Marx and Engels indicted capitalism as a system of exploitation in which class relations are irreconcilably antagonistic, they conceded that in some respects, particularly with reference to development of production forces, capitalism constituted a significant improvement over feudalism. The bourgeoisie as "the product of a long course of development, of a series of revolutions in the modes of production and exchange" initially played "a most revolutionary role in

history" and capitalism "created more massive and more colossal productive forces than all preceding generations together."[4] Marx attributed the
remarkable development of production forces under capitalism primarily
to the massive exploitation of the workers. He argued that for "exploitation veiled by religious and political illusions," capitalism has substituted
"naked, shameless, direct, brutal exploitation" and "has left no other bond
between man and man than naked self-interest, than callous 'cash payment'."[5]

The growth of capitalism, he stated, required the development of the
modern working class, the proletariat, "a class of laborers who live only so
long as they find work and find work only so long as their labor increases
capital."[6] The capitalist does not require physical force to compel the
workers to produce, Marx concluded, because the workers must sell their
labor "voluntarily" or starve to death. Under capitalism "the worker
exists for the process of production instead of the process of production
existing for the worker."[7]

Marxist economic doctrine, elaborated chiefly in the three volumes of
Capital, is primarily a critique of capitalism rather than a blueprint for
the development of the more perfect form of social organization which
Marx predicted. The essential elements of the Marxist critique of capitalism are summarized without comment in the subsequent paragraphs. Marx
argued that profit is the only goal of production under capitalism and
that the traditional formula for commodity circulation C-M-C (Com-
modity-Money-Commodity), the sale of one commodity for the purpose of
buying another, has been transformed by capitalist entrepreneurs into the
formula M-C-M (Money-Commodity-Money), the purchase of a commodity for the purpose of selling it at a profit. In order to produce "surplus
value," the source of profit, the capitalist entrepreneur must be able to purchase "a commodity whose use value has the peculiar quality of being a
source of value." Surplus value cannot derive from the vicissitudes of the
market or advances in prices, for mutual losses and gains of buyers and
sellers must eventually cancel themselves out, nor can it derive from the
circulation of commodities, since this represents an exchange of equivalents
rather than an increase in value. The value of a commodity is defined as the
amount of "socially necessary" labor required for its production. Socially
necessary labor time, of course, varies with factors such as skill, technological
conditions and intensity of effort.

The source of profit or surplus value under capitalism, according to
Marx, is human labor power, since human labor power possesses the unique
characteristic of being able to create more value than its own market value.
Under capitalism the worker is forced to sell his labor on the market like
any other commodity where its market value is determined by the socially
necessary labor time requisite for its production—that is, the cost of main-

taining the worker and his family. Although labor has the property of being able to produce more than is required for its own subsistence, the capitalist pays only the market value for labor. Thus, if in one-half day a worker is able to produce the value which is required for his subsistence and replacement, he will be paid only for the value of his labor in that half day, since the capitalist attempts to maintain wages at subsistence level. However, since the capitalist purchased labor hours, the worker is required to engage in production for the additional half day, and the capitalist appropriates the value that is produced by the labor during that time. *Surplus value,* that is, the difference between the value created during the period of socially necessary labor and that created during the total labor hours, is a measure of the workers' "exploitation." Profit, including rent and interest, derives solely from the surplus value created by the workers.

Marx maintained that the capitalist mode of production, because of irreconcilable contradictions, carries within it the seeds of its own destruction. An essential feature of capitalism is the extortion of surplus value from the workers by the capitalists. The capitalist constantly attempts to maximize profits by increasing surplus value. Techniques include decreasing wages and increasing working hours if labor is not sufficiently strong to protect itself, and increasing the efficiency of workers so that the value of their wages may be produced in a shorter time. This, combined with the spur of competition, requires the use of newer and more complex machinery, plant expansion, and other forms of capital accumulation, which the capitalist is able to introduce because he has appropriated surplus value from the workers. However, unless the capitalist is able to use such measures as increasing the intensity of exploitation, depressing wages below their value, getting cheaper raw materials from abroad and expanding the foreign market, the rate of profit will fall as the ratio between capital investment and investment in labor decreases because profit is derived solely from the surplus value of labor.[8]

Marx conceded that wages may increase during periods of expansion because of a labor shortage, but even under these circumstances, he claimed, the capitalist appropriates a disproportionate share of the increased output, and thus the difference in positions of the laborer and the capitalist is widened. During periods of expansion, the needs of economic growth are met by increasing the absolute supply of labor through more extensive exploitation —overwork, the use of unskilled labor, and the employment of women and children. However, as capital accumulation proceeds, the greater investment in machinery may result in a proportionately decreased need for labor, or concurrently opportunities for employment may increase less rapidly than the number of workers available for employment. Hence there is created a "vast industrial reserve army" which "during periods of stagnation and average prosperity weighs down the active labor army; during periods of over production and paroxysm, it holds its pretensions in check. Relative surplus population is therefore the pivot upon which the law of supply and demand works."[9] Thus an army of unemployed permits the capitalists to overwork the employed, and at the same time the ranks of the unemployed are swelled by overwork of the employed.

One of the contradictions within capitalism, Marx asserted, is its inability to develop at a constant rate. Crises or depressions are inevitable, since capitalistic expansion results in the production of more commodities than can be purchased by the masses with the limited purchasing power which is allotted to them by their economic masters. The ultimate cause of all economic crises, Marx argued, is the poverty of the masses. Economic crises appear in the form of overproduction of commodities, difficulties in finding markets, reduced prices and a sharp curtailment of production. During the crises, unemployment increases markedly, wages are cut, credit facilities break down and people are ruined, particularly small entrepreneurs. Depressions reduce the number of capitalists, reduce the value of previously accumulated capital, increase the army of unemployed, and worsen the lot of the masses who are available for still greater exploitation by those capitalists who survived the depression and eventually initiate another period of economic expansion. With repetitions of the expansion-depression cycle, society becomes increasingly divided into two classes, a small and extremely wealthy capitalist class and the great mass of the population which has been forced into economic subjugation.

Thus, Marx argued, capitalism, like its predecessors, is fraught with internal contradictions which will eventually result in its destruction. Capitalism cannot stabilize itself because constant expansion is indispensable but unattainable. Periods of expansion can sometimes be extended through imperialism, colonialism, and on occasion, war, but ultimately crises are unavoidable and invariably worsen the lot of the masses. The powerful capitalists have attempted to safeguard their favored position by a superstructure of laws and institutions which serve to impede forces operating for change. However, according to Marx, the internal contradictions within the system, the disharmony between production relations and productive forces, and the exploitation of the majority of mankind by the few, make the downfall of capitalism and the emergence of a new social order inevitable. The rise and fall of capitalism is held to be a necessary outgrowth of the operation of laws of materialist dialectics. As in the past, class struggle is to serve as the mechanism for dialectical change. The *Communist Manifesto* summarizes the historical process as follows:

"The history of all hitherto existing society is the history of class struggles. Freeman and slave, patrician and plebeian, lord and serf, guild master and journeyman, in a word, oppressor and oppressed, stood in constant opposition to one another, carried on an uninterrupted, now hidden, now open fight, a fight that each time ended, either in a revolutionary reconstitution of society at large or in the common ruin of the contending classes . . . for modern bourgeois society . . . has established new classes, new conditions of oppression, new forms of struggle in place of the old ones. . . . Society as a whole is more and more splitting up into two great hostile camps, into two great classes directly facing each other—the bourgeoisie and the proletariat."[10]

Marx concluded that capitalism cannot be reformed, and therefore must be destroyed. To the proletariat he assigned the task of destruction. Predicting the ultimate destruction of capitalism, he wrote:

"Along with the constantly diminishing number of magnates of capital who usurp and monopolize all advantages of this process of transformation, grows the mass of misery, oppression, slavery, degradation, exploitation; but with this too grows the revolt of the working class, a class always increasing in numbers, and disciplined, united, organized by the very mechanism of the process of capitalist production itself. The monopoly of capital becomes a fetter upon the mode of production, which has sprung up and flourished along with, and under it. Centralization of the means of production and socialization of labor at last reach a point where they become incompatible with their capitalist integument. The integument is burst asunder. The knell of capitalist private property sounds. The expropriators are expropriated."[11]

Marx and Engels, however, assumed that the new form of social organization which would be established after the proletariat had destroyed capitalism would differ from all preceding societies in that production relations would not be based on private ownership of the means of production, and exploitation of man by man would be eliminated. Engels asserted:

". . . the history of these class struggles form a series of evolutions in which, nowadays, a stage has been reached where the exploited and oppressed class—the proletariat—cannot attain emancipation from the sway of the exploiting and ruling class—the bourgeoisie—without at the same time, and once and for all, emancipating society at large from all exploitation, oppression, class distinctions and class struggles."[12]

Thus, according to the Marxists, capitalism will finally be destroyed by the workers who will rise against their capitalist oppressors, achieve political supremacy, assume ownership of the means of production and operate them in a new social economy, in which the misery caused by the inexorable functioning of capitalism will be eliminated; every man will receive a just share of the value produced by his own labor; and labor, resources, science and technology will be used to advance human welfare.

Marxists offer the theory of class struggle as an explanation for the motivation underlying significant events and changes in all societies based on economic exploitation. According to their analysis, class structure is determined by production relations; religion, color, geographical location, language, education, etc., are extraneous variables, some of which, such as education, may be affected by class status, but which do not determine class status. Lenin stated:

"Classes are large groups of people which differ from each other by the place which they occupy in a historically determined system of social production, by their relation (in most cases fixed and formulated by law) to the means of production, by their role in the social organization of labor, and consequently by the dimensions and mode of acquiring the share of social wealth of which they dispose. Classes are groups of people one of which can appropriate the labor of another owing to the different places they occupy in a definite system of social economy."[13]

The two basic classes in capitalist societies, according to the Marxists, are the capitalists and the wage workers. In addition, there are other classes and sub-classes, such as landlords, peasants, petty bourgeoisie and the intelligentsia, which on the basis of self-interest, ally themselves more strongly with one or the other of the basic classes. Capitalist society is purportedly characterized by irreconcilable antagonistic contradictions between the bourgeoisie and the working class. According to materialist dialectics, the bourgeoisie, which was originally a progressive class, becomes increasingly reactionary, and impedes social progress in its own self-interest. Concurrently, the working class, which was created and even organized by capitalist production, becomes increasingly angered by its exploitation, and will eventually, the Marxists predict, be the instrument of the destruction of the capitalist system.

Marxists argue that the antagonistic contradictions between the goals of the wage workers and the owners of the means of production provide the basis for a prolonged conflict, the outcome of which is inevitable victory for the working class. However, impressive barriers impede the progress of the workers toward their "ultimate victory." One of these barriers is the state which, Marx claimed, was evolved as a technique for one class to dominate another and to keep the exploited class within a given framework of production. In the primitive communal system, before classes had evolved, the state was unnecessary and the affairs of society were managed directly by its members. However, Marx argued, with the advent of private ownership and the consequent economic inequalities, decisions affecting the whole society could no longer be based on agreement of all or even the majority of the members of society. Decisions that would meet with the approval of the exploiting class would be to the disadvantage of the exploited class. Members of the exploiting classes were able to preempt all positions of power. Since decisions were made for the benefit of the small, powerful minority, the exploiting classes had to create instruments of coercion, such as the army, courts, police and prisons to supplement their economic power to maintain positions of dominance. Thus, Marx concluded that the state results from the irreconcilability of class contradictions, and is an instrument of exploitation for the ruling class, an instrument for the suppression and coercion of the exploited. The state and the ideological and political superstructure support the dominant position of the ruling class and the old production relations. The exploiting class never voluntarily relinquishes its property and power, the sources of its privileged position.

The conflict between production forces and production relations, which forms the basis for class conflict, develops gradually in an evolutionary manner, but can be resolved only by a revolutionary transformation of production relations. What is required, according to Marx, is a revolution which transfers political power from the obsolete ruling class to the class which embodies the new production relations. Only after the formerly exploited class acquires political power can the necessary changes in economic and social relations be introduced. Thus, Marx argued, the working class cannot achieve the goal of freeing itself and all mankind from exploitation as long as the bourgeoisie monopolizes political power and has at its service a powerful state, with all its related institutions, to suppress the strivings of the working class. The working class, to achieve the goals assigned to it by Marx and Engels, must preempt political power.

A second major barrier to the materialization of the ultimate goals of the working class, according to the Marxists, is that the working class, without assistance, is not fully aware of its necessary objectives and of the course which must be followed to achieve these objectives. The working class, like all classes, strives to materialize its interests, but it tends to concentrate on a one-sided and insufficient struggle in the economic sphere, neglecting or at least not giving the necessary priority to struggle in the political and ideological spheres. Marxists do not belittle the importance of the economic struggle by the working class to improve wages, working hours, working conditions, etc., through trade union organizations, strikes and other techniques. Even under capitalism, they concede, economic struggle offers definite possibilities for improving the lot of the working class. More important, since the need to protect immediate economic interests is comprehensible to all workers, the economic struggle is considered to be valuable in that it involves a large proportion of workers, requires the formation of workers' organizations, educates the workers in class consciousness and prepares them for the anti-capitalist movement. However, the Marxists argue, economic struggle alone is totally insufficient because it does not affect the foundations of the capitalist system and therefore cannot free society from exploitation. Real progress is held to be possible only when the struggle extends beyond the immediate interests of the workers and matures into an ideological and political struggle.

Marxist theory stresses that ideological advances require that the workers realize that the capitalist system is a form of exploitation which must be eradicated, that the interests of workers of all nations are identical and that progress must be achieved through the efforts of the working class. The required class consciousness, the awareness of identity of interests within classes and fundamental contradictions of interests between classes, is developed to a certain extent in the process of a day-to-day struggle for improvement, including economic improvement. However, the working class, without guidance, is not automatically cognizant of the ultimate source of its oppression, of all the necessary components of its long-range goals, and of all that must be involved in attaining its goals. Marxists contend that the working class must have a scientific theory to direct its liberating efforts, in order that the operation of the "objective laws of history" might be facilitated. The required theory, Marxism-Leninism, is supposed to reveal with "scientific accuracy" the basic interest of the working class, that is, the need to free itself from exploitation; the necessary technique, that is, the revolutionary destruction of capitalism and the building of socialism; and the fundamental techniques of the working-class movement.

Although Marxists contend that the workers' movement requires the joint operation of ideological, political and economic forms of struggle, at certain phases of the movement one form of struggle may have priority over the others. Thus, during the initial phase of the movement, economic gains by the workers are mere palliatives, and the primary importance of economic struggle is its contribution to the development of the class consciousness of the workers and its organization of the workers for eventual political action. Purportedly, the higher the level of revolutionary consciousness of the masses, the more quickly and efficiently the problems of society are solved. Ideological preparation is considered to be a prerequisite for necessary political action. Although Marxists consider that the spiritual life of society is a reflection of its material being, i.e., that ideas do not exist independently from matter, they do not deny that ideas, aspirations and other mental phenomena influence historical and social events. On the contrary, since ideas originate in the requirements of social development, they can in turn influence the course of social development, because those ideas which correspond to the current needs of social life eventually reach the consciousness of the broad masses who embody them into a *cause*. Ideas then become a material force through which people are united, organized and stimulated to engage in definite practical actions. At any given time, social consciousness is composed of conflicting ideas with the new serving as an impetus to change and the old fostering adherence to the *status quo*. Old ideology dies slowly because it is maintained by tradition, habit and the institutions and organs of power controlled by the reactionary dominant class. Without the mobilizing, organizing and transforming influence of new ideas, society would progress but slowly, if at all, in the development of its material life. Thus Marxists accord primary importance to the ideological struggle which is designed to make the masses more aware of their exploitation and its causes, to develop their class consciousness and their hatred of capitalists and capitalism, to inspire them to attempt to build a more nearly perfect society, to tell them how that more nearly perfect society should be organized, to show them how to go about building the new society and to convince them that they must undertake the revolutionary task. Thus, ideological struggle paves the way for the initiation of political action. However, according to Marxist dogma, the ideological struggle must continue unabated long after a successful political revolution because social consciousness changes slowly, reactionary ideology and the vacillations of the masses pose a constant threat, and the goals of the ideological struggle vary from one phase of social development to another.

Marxists consider political revolution to be the highest stage of the working class struggle. The goal of the political struggle is to transfer state power from the capitalists to the working people who need it to accomplish the complex construction tasks of the socialist revolution. The goal of the socialist revolution, the Marxists say, is to relieve all mankind from exploitation and oppression. This goal, they contend, cannot be achieved unless private ownership and capitalist production relations are replaced by socialist ownership of the means of production and socialist production relations. Since the bourgeois state protects the obsolete production relations, the working class must destroy the capitalist state, appropriate state power and introduce the new and higher form of production relations. Initially, the working class must retain state power in a new form in order to protect the gains of the revolution against reactionary forces. Marx and Engels predicted, however, that the state, which they described as fundamentally an organ of coercion and oppression, would become superfluous under the new and eminently fair-to-all socialist relations, and would eventually "wither away."

Marxists contend that the ideological and political struggle of the working class must be led by a political party of the proletariat—a Marxist-Leninist party, and that it is preferable that all the working people of all nations unite in the struggle to overthrow capitalism. Since the working people of all nations did not cooperate, modern Marxists concede that the working-class revolution may occur at different times in different nations, but cling stubbornly to the prediction that eventually political power in all states will be preempted by the workers. A Marxist-Leninist party is considered indispensable since it, guided by the "scientific" theory of Marxism-Leninism, is able to guide and accelerate the ideological struggle, direct and select the appropriate times and techniques for political action, and take leadership in the construction of a new society. The political struggle, the Marxists maintain, requires that the workers oppose not only their own capitalist employers, but also the bourgeois state which protects the interests of the capitalist class. The struggle may be waged by political strikes, demonstrations, election campaigns, armed uprisings, or by any technique which permits progress toward the essential goal—the overthrow of capitalism and the control of state power by the proletariat. Although the form of the revolution may vary from a peaceful transfer of power through parliamentary techniques, which Marxists believe is possible under exceptionally favorable circumstances, to the more usual form, armed uprising, it must always result, the Marxists say, in the establishment of the dictatorship of the proletariat.

Although Marx and Engels indicated that the proletariat needed an independent political party for the revolutionary transformation from capitalism to socialism, it was Lenin who most deeply influenced the structure and functioning of the Communist Party as it developed in the Soviet Union. Lenin taught that the party had to assume the leading role in the working-class movement, and at the same time had to propagate a militant class consciousness among the workers so that they would fight as a united force against their class enemies, the exploiters, and the state which provided a superstructure to protect the exploiters. Lenin wrote:

> "Only a political party of the working class, i.e., a Communist Party, is capable of uniting, educating and organizing such a vanguard of the proletariat and the whole mass of the working people, a vanguard which alone is able to resist the inevitable traditions and relapses of trade unionist narrowness or trade union prejudices amidst the proletariat, and to lead all the joint activities of the whole proletariat, i.e., to lead the proletariat politically and through it to lead all the masses of the working people."[14]

He held that only a political party characterized by its "irreconcilability with capitalism" is able to lead the working class to effect the required revolutionary reconstruction of society. This position is echoed by contemporary communists who state:

> "The communists are waging an active struggle for the abolition of capitalism, for a revolutionary transformation of capitalist society, for they hold that the taking of political power by the working class and the establishment of the dictatorship of the proletariat are essential conditions for this transformation."[15]

Marxism-Leninism teaches that the revolutionary dictatorship of the proletariat is necessary to bring about the required transformation. Lenin stated that the term "dictatorship of the proletariat" means that

> ". . . only a definite class, namely that of urban and industrial workers in general, is able to lead the whole mass of the toilers and the exploited in the struggle for the overthrow of the yoke of capital, in the process of this overthrow, in the struggle to maintain and consolidate the victory, in the work of creating the new socialist social system, in the whole struggle for the complete abolition of classes."[16]

Contemporary Soviet theoreticians define the dictatorship of the proletariat as ". . . power in the hands of the working people, led by the working class and having as its aim the building of socialism."[17]

Marxism-Leninism teaches that the dictatorship of the proletariat is a historical necessity during the transition period because as long as the remnants of the exploiting classes and the economic conditions for their existence continue, there will always be danger of attempts to restore the old regime. Reactionary classes inevitably resist revolutionary transformations and during the early phases of the revolution, the former exploiters are aided by tradition, the vacillation of the masses, their own superior education, organizational and productive experience, the remnants of their economic power, foreign support and a number of other factors. If a firm and unswerving dictatorship of the proletariat is not established, which does not hesitate to use force against the former oppressors if necessary, the probability of a successful counter-revolution is great. However, according to Marxism-Leninism, the primary strength of the dictatorship of the proletariat is not its willingness to eradicate oppression by force; rather it is strong because it is a power which expresses the people's will and is applied by the people themselves. In fact, Lenin described it as "the dictatorship of the vast majority" which survived because "it enjoyed the confidence of the vast masses."[18] Soviet citizens are taught that suppression is the chief function of an exploiting, i.e., capitalist state, but in the proletarian dictatorship, suppression of the exploiters is merely an unfortunate necessity; the chief function of the proletarian state is reorganization of economic, social and political life along socialist lines. Marxists-Leninists claim that unless political power is seized and the dictatorship of the proletariat is established, there can be no victory for socialism. Merely to recognize the existence of class struggle or to attempt to institute economic reform is insufficient. Lenin wrote ". . . only he is a Marxist who *extends* the recognition of class struggle to the dictatorship of the proletariat."[19] Therefore, according to the Marxists, the dictatorship of the proletariat is an absolute necessity during the initial stage of socialist construction. However, as economic, social and political relations within society are changed under the dictatorship of the proletariat, its *raison d'être* purportedly disappears. Khrushchev stated:

> "The working class is the only class in history which does not entertain the purpose of perpetuating its own domination. When the conditions which gave rise to its dictatorship disappear, when the tasks which society could accomplish solely with its help are consummated, the state gradually develops under the leadership of the working class, into a nationwide organization of all the working people of socialist society."[20]

Marxists assert that the working class will not attempt to perpetuate its domination over society because it has no vested interest, such as private ownership of the means of production, to protect. Under the dictatorship of the proletariat, society is supposed to progress from one composed of classes with conflicting interests to one composed of friendly classes with similar interests, and eventually into a classless society. Under these circumstances, since class conflict will purportedly be eliminated, and the basic interests of all members of society will be identical, the proletariat should be able to relinquish its dictatorial functions, and all members of society should work cooperatively toward the materialization of common goals. The state, which the Marxists say functions primarily as an organ of oppression and coercion, will become superfluous because in a classless, harmonious society, there should be no need for oppression or coercion. Consequently, as society progresses from what the Marxists consider to be a lower to a higher stage, the functions of the state are to change and to decrease, until eventually the state can "wither away" because it is no longer needed.

Marxists contend that as society evolves from a lower to a higher form of social organization, i.e., from capitalism through socialism to communism, democratic practices also evolve through several progressive stages. Low in the Marxist hierarchy of democratic practices is bourgeois democracy under which, they say, the masses have formal political rights which are of little value to them because the entire structure of society is designed to serve the interests of the privileged classes. They argue that equality of political rights without corresponding equality of opportunity in economic and social spheres is impossible and that therefore the political rights granted to the masses under capitalism are largely formal and non-functional. The dictatorship of the proletariat allegedly allows for the operation of a higher form of democracy in that political power is used for the benefit of the formerly oppressed majority, i.e., all working people, rather than for the benefit of the privileged minority. However, it is admitted that even proletarian democracy falls short of perfection for a number of objective reasons: oppression of a minority including the former privileged classes and other dissenters is required for the establishment of the new social order; the necessary social and economic equality cannot be established instantaneously without adequate preparation which includes restructuring the entire economic and social basis of society; the political and social consciousness of the people is not sufficiently developed to warrant their full democratic participation in all phases of social life; the most adequate forms of political life have not been developed, etc. Therefore, the initial period after the proletariat, under the leadership of the party, attains political power is essentially one of preparation for the ultimate expansion of democratic practices in economic and social spheres as well as in politics. One of the tasks of the dictatorship of the proletariat is to establish firmly the superstructure of socialism and to prepare conditions for the emergence of socialist democracy under which all citizens purportedly have equal political rights and freedoms, and more important, according to the statements of Soviet leaders, equal rights and opportunities in social and economic spheres so that political rights can be functional and real rather than mere formalities. The dictatorship of the proletariat is a class concept. When classes are eliminated entirely, or even before that, when only friendly classes which share common goals remain, the need for the dictatorship of the proletariat allegedly disappears. Only then, and only under socialism, the Marxists claim, can genuine political equality be achieved.

The Marxist analysis stresses that materialization of the changes which they predict and deem desirable requires the elimination of antagonistic relations between classes. Since class conflict is purportedly based primarily on the economic exploitation of one class by another, the Marxists attend particularly to the elimination of the economic basis for classes and for exploitation. Their solution, in theory, is very simple. People are divided into classes, they say, on the basis of the ownership or non-ownership of the means of production. The owners of the means of production are able to appropriate the surplus value of the labor of the propertyless workers who have no choice but to sell their labor for what the owners of the means of production will pay for it. Class conflict develops because the workers, deeply resentful of their exploitation, strive to improve their material well-being, and the owners of the means of production simultaneously strive to strengthen and extend their advantage over the workers. The solution, the Marxists say, is for the workers to rise against the owners of the means of production, to gain control over the state which protects the propertied class and to expropriate the means of production which will be given to and operated for the benefit of society as a whole. When the means of production are owned by and operated for the benefit of all members of society, there can be no economic basis for classes, or class conflict, the Marxists say, since one group of people cannot exploit another. Thus, the Marxists argue, public ownership of the means of production will eliminate classes, class conflict and antagonistic contradictions which impede maximum use of production potential. This, they say, will pave the way for the establishment of a society in which harmonious relations prevail, and each individual gives to society "according to his ability" and is rewarded by society "according to his need."

Marx and his followers, particularly those who have actually attempted to restructure society according to the Marxist pattern, realized that no society could be transformed instantaneously from one "beleaguered" with class conflict and oppression to a classless harmonious society in which the resources of society are used for the good of all. In Marxist terms, the transfer of political power to the proletariat and the transfer of the ownership of the means of production to society requires a revolutionary or "leap-like" step, but the elimination of classes, class interests, class conflicts and the development of an identity of interest between society and all its members necessarily proceed in a gradual, evolutionary manner. Marx himself was so preoccupied with analyzing and presenting the evils of capitalism that he paid relatively less attention to the problems of transition from capitalism to communism and to the structure of the new communist society. His program for the transformation of society after the proletariat has attained political power is outlined in the *Communist Manifesto*.

"The proletariat will use its political supremacy to wrest, by degrees, all capital from the bourgeoisie, to centralize all instruments of production in the hands of the state,—that is, of the proletariat organized as a ruling class;

and to increase the total productive forces as rapidly as possible. Of course, in the beginning, this cannot be effected except by means of despotic inroads on the rights of property, and on the conditions of bourgeois production; by means of measures, therefore which appear economically insufficient and untenable, but which in the course of movement outstrip themselves, necessitate further inroads upon the old social order, and are unavoidable as a means of revolutionizing the mode of production.

"These measures will, of course, be different in different countries. Nevertheless in the most advanced countries the following will be pretty generally applicable: 1. Abolition of property in land and application of all rents of land to public purposes. 2. A heavy progressive or graduated income tax. 3. Abolition of all rights of inheritance. 4. Confiscation of property of all emigrants and rebels. 5. Centralization of credit in the hands of the state, by means of a national bank with state capital and exclusive monopoly. 6. Centralization of the means of communication and transport in the hands of the state. 7. Extension of factories and instruments of production owned by the state; the bringing into cultivation of waste lands, and the improvement of the soil generally in accordance with a common plan. 8. Equal liability of all to labor. Establishment of industrial armies, especially for agriculture. 9. Combination of agriculture with manufacturing industries, gradual abolition of the distinction between town and country by a more equable distribution of the population over the country. 10. Free education for all children in public schools. Abolition of child factory labor in its present form. Combinations of education with industrial production, etc."[21]

He conceded that even after capitalism is destroyed, deductions will have to be made from the value of what workers produce to replace the means of production, to expand production by capital accumulation, to cover the costs of administration, to support those unable to work and to provide a reserve to cover exigencies such as poor harvests and natural catastrophies.[22] Apart from the necessary deductions to the common fund, Marx contended that in the new society

". . . the individual producer receives back from society . . . exactly what he gives to it. . . . He receives a certificate from society that he has furnished such and such an amount of labor (after deducting his labor for the common fund) and with this certificate he draws from the social stock of means of consumption as much as the same amount of labor costs. The same amount of labor which he has given to society in one form, he receives back in another."[23]

Marx recognized that this system of distribution would result in inequalities, since value of the labor of workers would necessarily vary as a function of education, experience, natural talent and intensity of effort, and because the consumption needs of a man with several dependents would be greater than that of a worker who had to support only himself on the basis of his labor value. Therefore, the system of distribution outlined above was to be applied only during the transition period. Marx held that

"In a higher phase of communist society, after the enslaving subordination of individuals under division of labor, and therewith also the antithesis between mental and physical labor, has vanished; after labor, from a mere means of life, has itself become the prime necessity of life; after the productive forces have also increased with the all-round development of the individual and all the springs of cooperative wealth flow more abundantly—only then can the narrow horizon of bourgeois rights be fully left behind and society inscribe on its banners: from each according to his ability to each according to his needs."[24]

Marxists assert that when society assumes ownership of the means of production, the economic basis for classes is removed. However, classes, class conflict and inequalities do not disappear automatically. As long as distribution is according to labor rather than according to need, economic inequalities will obviously prevail. These economic inequalities are, however, purported to be vastly different from the economic inequalities which exist under capitalism because they are not based on exploitation of one class by another, and do not carry the potential for future exploitation. In spite of the economic inequalities which arise from distribution according to labor, this mode of distribution is supposed to facilitate the development of the classless society. Marxists recognize many barriers to the establishment of a classless society, even after the economic basis of society changes. Chief among these are the aspirations of the former exploiting class and their unwillingness to relinquish their favored positions, the advantages which they retain such as superior education and training, their experience in the positions of power, tradition, habit and traditional subservience on the part of the masses. Therefore, the Marxists contend that class struggle continues long after the dictatorship of the proletariat is established. In fact, the existence of class struggle is one of the major reasons for the necessity of the dictatorship. Gradually, however, Marxists believe, antagonistic contradictions between classes are removed as the combined result of the radically changed production relations and methods of distribution, oppression of the former exploiters, education, modification of traditions, depletion of the ranks of the old die-hards through death, etc. Eventually only two or perhaps three classes remain, the workers, the peasants and the intelligentsia, which Stalin classified as a stratum of the worker and peasant classes, rather than as a separate class. When this stage is reached, the difference between the workers and peasants are held to be of a non-antagonistic nature in that goals and aspirations of both classes are to be identical, and class conflict is to have been eliminated. Finally, at a higher phase of society, all people, workers, peasants and intelligentsia alike, are to be members of one vast classless society, in which the interests of each individual and of society as a whole form an identity; each individual works for the good of society and society attends equally to the needs of each individual.

Marxists maintain that the socialist revolution differs from all previous revolutions in several respects. First, it is claimed that while previous revolutions merely substituted one form of exploitation for another, the socialist revolution ends exploitation, leads eventually to the abolition of classes, removes all forms of oppression and marks the beginning of true brotherhood and equality among people, the establishment of eternal peace and the complete social regeneration of humanity. Second, the socialist revolution is inspired and led by the working class and the gains accrue to them and eventually to all members of society. Finally, whereas the main tasks of previous revolutions were destructive, the destruction of obsolete capitalist relations by the socialist revolution is merely a necessary prerequisite for the accomplishment of constructive socio-economic goals—the establishment of a fundamentally different and allegedly higher social order.[25]

Marxism-Leninism teaches that each individual must assume responsibility for and play an active role in the materialization of communist goals. It is argued that the exploiting classes have, in an attempt to justify the right of an elite minority to oppress the majority, consistently belittled the role of the masses who have been portrayed as a dull-witted mob, capable only of submitting to the will of others, unable to influence the course of events and therefore predestined to submit obediently to poverty and oppression. The exploiters, the Marxists contend, have used religion, as well as economic exploitation and state institutions, as a tool to help them to maintain the subservient position of the masses. Religious teachings, such as the impossibility of attaining happiness on this earth, that man's destiny is to toil and pray, that the next world will provide the reward for humility and obedience, and that the wrath of God and the torment of hell will be the lot of those who were not meek and humble in the face of oppression, the Marxists argue, are intended to force the masses to accept their lowly lot meekly and complacently. Marxists, of course, state categorically that the hope for happiness or the fear of punishment beyond the grave is ridiculous; man lives but once and should value and try to improve life on earth; God is non-existent; the world is operated entirely by objective laws without any supernatural intervention whatsoever. They emphasize that the masses are not destined to play a lowly, subservient role; on the contrary, historical necessity finds its main expression through the masses who contribute the force that plays the determining role in social development.

Marxists-Leninists point to areas in which the masses have played a decisive role in the development of society. The material items necessary for existence and the material basis for the progressive development of society are provided by the production activities of the masses. In all struggles for national liberation, defensive wars and social revolutions, the masses constitute the chief driving force. Brains and talent are not a class privilege; the preponderance of great cultural and scientific contributions which have been made by members of the propertied class is explicable on the basis of the extensive economic and political techniques which have been used to exclude working people from mental, scientific and cultural activities in order to maintain the supremacy of the ruling class. Nevertheless, in the early stages of cultural development, basic contributions were made by the working people, and even in modern times an amazing number of scientific and cultural advances have been made by members of the exploited class, in spite of dire oppression. However, the Marxists say, the political effect of the masses is significantly submerged in an exploiting society during peaceful periods; the ruling class at all times attempts to reduce the political activities of the masses to a safe minimum and uses the power of the state and spiritual coercion to accomplish its goals. The influence of the masses over political life, a field of class conflict between the exploiters and the exploited, is determined by the level of their struggle against their oppressors, which in turn varies with factors such as organization, class consciousness and awareness of goals. Only after the exploiters have been overthrown can the workers determine policy.

Marxists point out that some kind of organization is necessary for any class to govern, and each class organization requires leaders to formulate policy and to direct the activities of its members. A revolutionary organization is particularly in need of skillful, experienced and energetic leaders. Although leadership is an objective necessity in the historical process, the driving and creative force in social development is determined by the struggle of large social groups, classes and masses, not by the leaders. The activities of all people proceed under definite social conditions which determine the objective laws of development and the tasks which confront society. No man, no matter how powerful, can negate the laws of history or reverse their effect. Marxists say that certain men may be classified as great because of their clear recognition of the tasks of the class that is fighting for progress, and because they organize and lead the people toward the materialization of goals. However, leaders are not the creators or instigators of events or mass movements; they can function only with the support of the masses and in relation to the activities of the masses, class struggle and social need.

Soviet leaders, in the aftermath of the attack on the Stalin cult, have been reemphasizing the Marxist-Leninist theory on the decisive role of the masses. A Soviet theorist stated recently:

"The creativity of the popular masses and their participation in administering the country is a basic question of the Marxist-Leninist world view, of the practices of communist construction and of the life of Soviet society. The Party has resolutely condemned the disdainful attitude toward the working people that was implanted during the Stalin cult period. . . . Stalin rendered lip service to the decisive role of the popular masses in history, but when it came to deeds he regarded ordinary people as the mechanical executors of a leader's instructions, of his will. Marxists-Leninists cannot agree with such a position. It is basically hostile to our world view and to the nature of Soviet man. The Soviet people are the free creators of their own life who make conscious use of the laws of history. They are the true masters in society while all the public figures who organize the activity of the masses are without exception only their trusted agents and are always and in everything accountable to the people. The C.P.S.U. Central Committee and the entire Party firmly follow the course of comprehensively developing socialist democracy and they emphasize that organizations and public figures are only the servants of the people and the executors of their will."[26]

Obviously, a great discrepancy exists between Marxist-Leninist theory, faithfully reiterated by Soviet leaders, and Soviet practice; in reality, the people are the servants of the party leaders and have no choice but to execute their will.

The cult of the individual, or the expression of excessive admiration for and subservience to a leader, is considered to be alien to Marxism-Leninism and harmful to the cause of the working masses. It allows the masses to assume that their tasks in the class struggle and the struggle for the establishment of socialism can be accomplished by someone else, and that instead of thinking, initiating, creating and actively influencing the course of events, they need only passively carry out the instructions of an all-wise leader. In addition to undermining the desire of the masses to show initiative and develop their creative activities, the cult of the individual makes it impossible for them to do so by destroying the "profound democracy which is inherent in the socialist movement." However, it is conceded that true leaders of the working class, maintaining close ties with the people and wisely directing their struggle, have an important function in history and deserve the admiration of and respect of the people. A Soviet spokesman commented:

". . . the Communist Party recognizes the important role of the leaders in the communist and workers' movement and the necessity of upholding and strengthening their authority. Marxism-Leninism considers it inadmissible to confuse the cult of the individual with the earned authority of leaders who properly interpret the objective laws of development, who fight for the basic interests of the working people and who lean upon the collective and on the practical revolutionary experience of the masses."[27]

Thus Marxists-Leninists state that they have discarded the myth that society owes everything to a handful of elite and claim to have demonstrated that the masses play a decisive role in the development of society. Realization of their role in history purportedly awakens the consciousness of the masses, makes them realize that they must not depend upon a "savior" or on fate to free them from oppression, inspires them to struggle for emancipation, gives them faith in victory and courage to remold society in accordance with the aspirations of the majority of mankind, the workers themselves.

Adherents of Marxism-Leninism consider that one of the major contributions of the theory is the insight which it provides into the nature of human freedom. They claim that all pre-Marxists had completely erroneous notions about freedom, since their positions were derived from false premises. Religious fatalists held that man's fate is predetermined by God; metaphysical materialists considered that man is completely subject to the laws of nature, and hence has no freedom; many idealists held that man is completely free, since the world is derived from consciousness. Marxists maintain that it is incorrect to assume that man is completely free or that he has no freedom. According to dialectical materialism, man can neither revoke, modify nor act independently of the objective laws of the development and operation of nature, society and thought. However, by knowing the laws, man can utilize them in his own interest and herein lies his freedom. Engels wrote: "Freedom is the recognition of necessity. Necessity is blind only in so far as it is not understood."[28] Marxists argue that before Marx, Engels and Lenin revealed to mankind the objective laws which govern the development of human society, social development was characterized by spontaneity because people were unable to see the social consequences of their own acts; that is, the laws were operating as they always have and will, but because people did not know the laws, they were not able to apply them to manipulate social development. Now, Marxists-Leninists say, mankind knows the objective laws, and no longer is it necessary to submit blindly to impinging social forces; mankind can make use of the laws to restructure society into a higher phase and through the very use of the laws, mankind is able to enjoy one form of freedom. Moreover, by applying the laws to form the type of society advocated by the Marxists, it is claimed that mankind will be able to enjoy a higher form of social freedom than has heretofore existed. According to Khrushchev:

> "The criterion of real freedom and happiness is a social system which frees man from the yoke of exploitation, gives him broad democratic liberties and the opportunity to live in fitting conditions, a system that inspires him with confidence in the morrow, unfetters his individual abilities and talents and makes him feel that his labor is for the good of society. . . . The Soviet people are demonstrating what the really free man is capable of."[29]

This then is a simplified synopsis of what Soviet people are taught. It could be summarized as follows: capitalism is decadent, fraught with contradictions, doomed to destruction; capitalism must be destroyed because it is an eminently unjust system in which the masses are exploited and oppressed for the benefit of the few who own the means of production; the only praiseworthy feature in capitalist society is the production efficiency of the leading states, but even so, the U.S.S.R. will, Soviet leaders say, soon take the lead in production efficiency. The Soviet people are told that because Soviet society has been shaped and built according to the principles of Marxism-Leninism and under the guidance of the Communist Party, the Soviet social order is already vastly superior to the capitalist social order in all fundamental respects. They are informed that among their many advantages are greater equality, a fairer system of distribution, more freedom, particularly in social and economic spheres, but also in political spheres, a higher form of democracy and a more glorious prospect for the future. It is conceded that some, and perhaps even a majority, of workers in some capitalist states currently enjoy a higher standard of living, but Soviet citizens are assured that they will have the highest standard of living in the world in the near future. Soviet citizens are encouraged to pity the "poor, oppressed, exploited" workers who live in capitalist states, under the "yoke of capitalist oppression." Although Soviet citizens are informed that they are at present the most fortunate of mankind, it is conceded to them that they do indeed have to put up with a few inconveniences so that eventually the more nearly perfect social order might emerge in all its glory. They are promised a glorious future to compensate for past sacrifices and current inconveniences. They are warned, however, that they must strive consciously, unselfishly, actively, diligently and unceasingly to carry out the dictates of Marxism-Leninism, to implement the Marxist-Leninist program of the party, to build a magnificent communist society in which "all sources of public wealth will gush forth abundantly, and the great principle 'From each according to his ability, to each according to his need' will be implemented."[30]

Soviet citizens are thoroughly indoctrinated with the Marxist-Leninist version of the communist utopia which excludes economic exploitation and oppression of man by man, and promises abundance for all. They are likewise thoroughly indoctrinated with the Marxist critique of capitalism. Marx, however, was criticizing nineteenth century capitalist societies and failed to predict developments such as the tremendous strength of trade unions and government regulations which have served to eradicate, mitigate or even reverse some of what he considered to be the most reprehensible features of capitalism. Thus to a large extent the evils which Soviet citizens are taught are inherent in capitalist society are greatly overexaggerated or even nonexistent. Life in Western societies is described to Soviet citizens in a grossly biased manner; isolated examples which can be described in an unfavorable manner are treated as major and everyday occurrences. They are told next to nothing about the positive features of Western political systems.

Within the U.S.S.R., it is not permissible to subject Marxist-Leninist theory to critical evaluation. Soviet citizens are expected to accept Marxism-Leninism in the form that it is presented to them by their party leaders as the undisputed and indisputable truth. The complete unwillingness to consider and evaluate alternative theories, or to permit critical evaluation of Marxism-Leninism is, of course, an indication of an awareness of weakness, an awareness by the party leaders that the theory to which they profess devotion is not without flaws, and that the position which they have preempted in society is not justified on the basis of the theory. Even the most devoted Marxist would, if he were to be completely honest with himself, surely be forced to admit that though Marx, Engels and Lenin left a rich intellectual legacy, some of their pronouncements and conclusions were unfounded, ambiguous, conflicting, and even erroneous and that their blueprint for the future of mankind should, at the very least, be subjected to critical evaluation.

Whether or not one accepts the Marxist ideal for the restructuring of society and of economic, political, social and human relations, Marxist-Leninist theory cannot be described, even by the most ardent Marxist, as a completely coherent, internally consistent, logically sound and practical guide to action. If Marxism-Leninism, as a theory, were to be evaluated unemotionally, entirely independent from biases determined by approval or disapproval of Marxist-Leninist goals for society, it would probably be rated as not much better or not much worse than other social theories. However, few people consider Marxist-Leninist ideology from the point of view of formal theory construction. Rather, Marxism-Leninism is evaluated on the basis of the goals which it prescribes for mankind and the techniques which it advocates for the materialization of the goals. The majority of mankind, including most Westerners and probably a goodly number of Soviet citizens, do not prescribe to the Soviet interpretation of the Marxist-Leninist ideals for society, and are repulsed by Soviet-style techniques for achieving the ideals. Millions of people, some of whom may sympathize to a certain degree with the goals of Marxism-Leninism, have been profoundly shocked by the cruel, repressive techniques which Soviet leaders have adopted, purportedly in accordance with Marxist-Leninist theory, in their attempts to propel Soviet society toward materialization of these goals. Soviet citizens, however, regardless of how they feel about Marxist-Leninist goals for society, and Soviet-style Marxist-Leninist techniques for achieving these goals, have no choice but to act as if the goals and techniques are unequivocally correct.

The major point, however, is not what is wrong with Marxist-Leninist theory or the Marxist-Leninist ideal, but rather the fact that a wide gulf exists between the theory and its application in the U.S.S.R. Subsequent chapters will describe innumerable examples of discrepancies between the theoretical pronouncements and actual practice in the Soviet Union. At this point a few examples will be sufficient. Marxist-Leninist theory upholds democratic principles, but the U.S.S.R. has evolved into a rigid dictatorship in which the masses are denied a choice of form of government and are ruled by one or at best a few party leaders. The Marxist-Leninist program was designed to eradicate economic exploitation; each individual was to be awarded the full market value for his labor, minus necessary deductions for capital construction, defense and administration. In the U.S.S.R. the worker's reward for his labor is in fact considerably lower than in any other highly industrialized state, since the leaders have deemed it expedient to emphasize the production of producer goods rather than consumer goods. Marxist-Leninist ideology honors the freedom of the individual; yet the needs of the masses of the people are subordinated to the needs of the state. The top leadership, without consulting the people, decides what needs will be given priority. Subsequently, the people are told that the decisions, which might be highly unpalatable to them, were based exclusively on considerations of what is best for their welfare. According to Marxism-Leninism, the masses are the creators of history, but according to Soviet practice, the masses need omniscient parents, the top party leadership, to make all decisions. Soviet leaders have constantly maintained that a system of law and justice based on Marxist-Leninist ideology is eminently fair and far superior to its counterpart in all capitalist states. Yet contemporary Soviet leaders who, during the Stalin era, boasted about the Soviet judicial practices, now admit that during the preceding decades there were hundreds of thousands of unjustified arrests and tens of thousands of unjustified executions or long-term imprisonments.

When Soviet officials do admit that the system is not working as well as it should according to the theory, they make it clear that neither the theory nor the leaders who are holding the reins of power are at fault. Marxist-Leninist theory, and party leaders as long as they are in power, are infallible; the theory and the dictates of the leaders are, however, sometimes misinterpreted or inefficiently implemented by underlings. Minor party, governmental and managerial officials are blamed for anything that goes wrong. The myth of the infallibility of a particular leader, however, tends to dissipate when the leader dies or is demoted. Until Stalin was safely entombed, he was lauded as the infallible interpreter and implementor of Marxist-Leninist ideology. During his era Marxist-Leninist ideology was purportedly applied with complete faithfulness, and the welfare of the masses was purportedly of paramount importance. Since Stalin's denunciation by Khrushchev in 1956, leading party officials, who during Stalin's lifetime had praised both Stalin and the entire Soviet system to the hilt, admitted that Stalin had made numerous errors and that millions of people had been treated unjustly, thereby indicating that much of what they had said previously had been nothing but prevarication. Stalin, the erstwhile god-like leader, was demoted to the position of a convenient scapegoat responsible for the errors and the malfunctioning of the system in the past. During the Khrushchev era, official Soviet pronouncements suggested that the Marxist-Leninist program was being implemented with maximum efficiency, that the democratic tenets of Marxism-Leninism were sacred and that everything was being done for the sake of the people. The minor malfunctionings of the system which were occasionally admitted were attributed exclusively to the inefficiency or lack of political astuteness of individuals below the top leadership. Khrushchev, like Stalin, was an infallible interpreter of Marxist-Leninist ideology. However, in October, 1964, Khrushchev was demoted from his pinnacle of power by the very men who only a few days previously had made public statements lauding their "dear Nikita Sergeyevich." The full truth about the Khrushchev era is not yet known. One thing is certain: shocking discrepancies exist between Soviet description of how their system operates and reality, and between the promises of Marxism-Leninism and actual practices in the U.S.S.R. In most societies discrepancies exist between ideology and practice, since theory and ideology may be considered ideals toward which the society is striving. However, discrepancies between ideology and reality and between official pronouncements of policy and actual policy of the magnitude which exist in the U.S.S.R. are rare.

Impact on the Individual and Society

Marxist-Leninist theory, along with criticisms of capitalism and praise for socialism, is taught to every Soviet citizen—in the schoolroom and lecture hall, in youth organizations and party groups, on the job, via television, radio, press and by all possible techniques. All official reports and scientific documents must adhere to and preferably propagate historical and dialectical materialism. From the cradle to the grave, the Soviet people are enveloped in Marxist-Leninist ideology. Soviet leaders are not content with merely exposing people to the ideology. The people are expected to know, understand, believe in and live by Marxist-Leninist principles.

What does Marxist-Leninist theory mean to the people of the Soviet Union? The reactions of the people to Marxist-Leninist ideology are, of course, confounded by their perception of the discrepancies between theoretical pronouncements and Soviet practices, and by their evaluation of the concrete advantages and disadvantages which have accrued to them as a result of the development of Soviet-style socialism. Naturally, also, the impact of the ideology itself, apart from its practical application or misapplication, varies from individual to individual.[31] The individual who has a firm belief in the truth and essential rightness of Marxism-Leninism is affected by it very differently from the one who merely pays the necessary lip service to it. Persons with strong religious convictions, and there are many such persons in the U.S.S.R., are affected differently from those who accept the Marxist-Leninist contention that religion is used by the exploiters as a tool to maintain the oppression of the exploited classes. In general, the reactions of persons who lived under Tsarism are different from those who have been brought up under the present regime, but within the former group there are vast differences. Among the older generation are zealous revolutionaries who fought selflessly for what they believed to be a great and worthy cause; of course, death and the Stalin purges have greatly thinned the ranks of the original revolutionaries, and it is probable that of those few who remain, many are deeply disillusioned when they compare what they believed they were fighting for with the dictatorial, oppressive system which has emerged in the U.S.S.R. Others among the older people may have a nostalgic attitude toward "the good old days," some because of resistance to change, and some because they may actually have had a more comfortable existence prior to the Bolshevik revolution. Still others who have enjoyed an increase in economic and social status may be wholehearted devotees of Marxist-Leninist ideology and the Soviet way of life. Young people who have lived under no other system, and have only very distorted ideas about other social ideologies and other social orders may, depending on their degree of intellectual curiosity and their satisfaction or dissatisfaction with the current situation, accept Soviet ideology and the Soviet system as "normal" and good, chafe under the imposed restrictions, wonder about life elsewhere, etc. The reactions of members of minority national groups are no doubt influenced by the intensity of national feeling and the amount of current freedom and oppression in comparison to conditions under Tsarism. The attitudes of individuals and relatives of individuals who have been subjected to illegal arrests and imprisonment, and officials who have been required to make illegal arrests must, for example, be very different from the attitudes of those to whom the regime has accorded high economic and social status. In short, the attitude of a specific individual toward Marxism-Leninism and its specific effect on him is dependent upon a multitude of factors. However, few if any individuals in the U.S.S.R. are unaffected by Marxist-Leninist ideology, over and above the fact that the society in which they live purportedly operates on the basis of the goals and techniques specified by the ideology.

What are some of the characteristics of this ideology which affects the lives of millions of people? Perhaps the most important characteristic is that Marxism-Leninism, as it is presented to the Soviet people, is an optimistic ideology.[32] Soviet theorists claim that "Only Marxist philosophy, the Marxist-Leninist theory, shows mankind the majestic goal of its liberating struggle, discloses the path of unlimited social progress and gives people historical optimism, confidence in the morrow"[33] and that "Marxism-Leninism placed mankind in the correct, accurately computed historical orbit leading to the bright communist future."[34] Among other things, Marxism promises the end of all exploitation, the liberation of society from all forms of oppression and from social-class enslavement, genuine equality and brotherhood among people, complete social justice, the establishment of eternal peace, the complete social regeneration of humanity, and material abundance for all with time freed from the production of necessities to be devoted to science, the arts, recreation and other pleasurable activities. Marxist-Leninist promises in regard to abundance, equality, freedom, democracy and peace correspond to the needs and desires of the Soviet masses. Marxism-Leninism is taught to the Soviet people in a manner designed to gain their respect, devotion and understanding. The individual is permitted to feel that his personal and collective efforts and sacrifices are directed toward a better life for himself, or if not for himself, at least for his children and grandchildren, and perhaps for all mankind. Soviet citizens who accept Marxist-Leninist goals and believe that Marxist-Leninist techniques will result ultimately and in the not too distant future in the materialization of the goals have strong reasons to strive diligently for their fulfillment. The manner in which the theory is presented to the people is designed to build up their confidence in and hope for the future, while the Communist Party provides the rigid discipline necessary for the present.

Marxism-Leninism is presented to the Soviet people as an inclusive doctrine which serves as a guide to action and explains historical and social development, the development and functioning of consciousness, politics, economics, ethics, religion, the role of the individual and the masses in society, and in fact, almost every major problem which has been attended to by great thinkers throughout the centuries. The theory is sufficiently broad, vague and ambiguous that Soviet leaders are able to adapt it to fit every practical situation which arises and every change in policy which they see fit to introduce. Soviet leaders, who are skillful propagandists par excellence, have in Marxist-Leninist theory an extremely convenient and malleable tool. Each time that the Soviet people are told that they must make new sacrifices, or that the fulfillment of promises will be delayed, their leaders are able to use Marxist-Leninist theory to justify the unpopular decisions and to relate current sacrifices to the promised magnificent future. Even the mass arrests, imprisonments and executions which were so common in the 1930's were justified on the basis of Marxism-Leninism, since all victims were purportedly "enemies of the people" who were obstructing progress toward the communist ideal. The leaders themselves are not to be held responsible for the introduction of highly unpopular or repressive measures; they are merely "correctly" interpreting the methods prescribed by Marx and Lenin to achieve Marxist-Leninist goals. From time to time a new policy has been introduced which is the diametric opposite of its predecessor; Soviet leaders have, however, been able to use Marxist-Leninist theory equally well to justify both policies, each in turn.

The essential correctness of Marxism-Leninism is never to be questioned in the U.S.S.R. Anyone who would dare to propose an alternative doctrine or to suggest that another social doctrine has certain valuable attributes or that Marxism-Leninism is in some respects erroneous would be guilty of a serious offence. It is sometimes conceded that the doctrine may require elaboration and expansion, but the basic principles are held to be fundamentally true and correct. Thinkers in the U.S.S.R. not only need not, but in fact, must not concern themselves with evaluating the relative merits of alternative doctrines. They are, however, encouraged to devote their energies to developing techniques and methods for the more complete materialization of Marxist-Leninist goals. The grand design for the socialist, and eventually the communist, society has been outlined. Minor modifications in the plan, and in techniques for materializing the plan with reference to the concrete situation are permissible. To these ends Soviet thinkers are permitted to address themselves. It may be assumed that at least some Soviet intellectuals are not completely satisfied to be relegated to the role of technicians in the construction of a new social order, especially since they were not consulted about the original design, nor do they have the right to an opinion about the correctness of the basic techniques which are used to build the new social order.

Soviet leaders take care to present Marxist-Leninist theory in a manner which is acceptable and intelligible to the masses. Marxism-Leninism dignifies the common working man. To him it assigns a significant role in past, present and future social development. For him it plans a utopian society. A favorite party slogan is "Everything for the sake of man, for the benefit of man."[35] The dominant role of the propertied class in science and the arts is explained in a manner by no means belittling to the working people. Physical labor, usually performed by the working class, is held to be no less important than mental work which in the main has been performed by the propertied class. The distinction between physical and mental labor is to be destroyed. The working people are told that they, not individual leaders, are the driving force in all major social changes: ". . . it is the people who are the chief motive force in the historical process . . . the Communist Party has been able to perform its vanguard role and score great victories thanks to its indissoluble ties with the working class and with the broad masses of the people."[36] At the same time the working people are permitted to participate in the development of techniques and innovations to speed up the materialization of Marxist-Leninist goals; the new socialist and communist society is to emerge because of their efforts. Thus Marxism-Leninism assigns to the working masses a position of unparalleled importance along with tasks of unparalleled difficulty.

Oppressed groups, people who have been treated as inferior by those higher on the social and economic ladder, people who have been exploited by others and denied privileges enjoyed by others because of factors external to themselves stand to gain by the Marxist-Leninist promise that classes will be abolished. Traditionally, the minority privileged classes have been admired, emulated or resented by the masses of people. The equalization, the democratization, the promise that each person is to be judged and rewarded on the basis of his own qualities and accomplishments rather than primarily on the basis of the social and economic status of his forefathers appeals to the majority of people who, in most social systems, would not be members of the most privileged classes.

The firm materialist basis of Marxism-Leninism, apart from its rejection of an all-powerful Deity, has an appeal for the practical working classes that an idealistic philosophy could not have. Materialism corresponds to their usual mode of thought. However, the complete disparagement and rejection of all religious beliefs is another matter. The Soviet people have been told that they must no longer believe in God or in any supernatural Being or Power. For religious faith they must substitute faith in Marxism-Leninism; instead of having faith in a supernatural Being, they are told that they must have faith in man and in society guided by Marxist-Leninist principles. They are taught that they can and must achieve what they previously believed God would do for them, that they, not a supernatural force, are responsible for their destiny, that instead of dreaming about a non-existent hereafter, they must strive for happiness and well-being on this earth, goals which were unattainable by the masses under other systems, but can be attained by all if Marxism-Leninism is fully practiced. The disruptive effect of the attack on religious beliefs has, no doubt, been partially mitigated by the substitute faith in Marxism-Leninism and by scientific developments which have facilitated acceptance of some of the anti-religious aspects of Marxism-Leninism. However, it is probable that a large number of Soviet citizens experience either an acute conflict because they can neither completely reject long-established religious beliefs nor completely accept Marxist-Leninist ideology, or a psychological emptiness because they have no faith of any kind. Marxism-Leninism teaches that no longer need man feel he is the pawn of an impersonal deity or the helpless victim of circumstances beyond his control. However, there is ample evidence to suggest that many Soviet citizens feel that they are the helpless victims of their own social order or the pawns of the impersonal party dictatorship. Those who accept the substitute offered for religion are bound to an unceasing struggle to accomplish what had hitherto been considered to be controlled by supernatural forces. To assume for oneself, even in part, the role hitherto attributed to God requires courage, endurance, persistence, effort and extensive faith in oneself and one's fellow man. Failures can no longer be blamed on fate or on the will of God. Each person and society as a whole must assume responsibility for failures and because of this responsibility must strive even more diligently for success. In many respects, the Marxist-Leninist substitute for religion makes more stringent demands on the individual than any major religion. Those individuals who, in spite of all anti-religious propaganda, have maintained their religious beliefs face many difficulties in the Soviet Union. Public affirmation of their faith marks them as persons who have not fully understood or accepted Marxism-Leninism; hence either their intelligence or their loyalty to the common cause may be considered questionable. In their attempts to instill in their children their own religious faith, they meet numerous obstacles, the most significant of which is, of course, Marxist-Leninist ideology which is taught to all children through many avenues. Strong social pressures converge to brand the religious Soviet citizen as reactionary, disloyal or unintelligent.

Thus Marxism-Leninism as taught to Soviet citizens is a comprehensible, optimistic, anti-religious doctrine which dignifies the common man and promises a glorious future. It is presented as the absolute "truth." Moreover, this "truth" is presented in such a way as to make sensible heroes out of those who accept it, believe in it, and govern their actions by it, while those who oppose it are deemed unwise, misled, unpatriotic, selfish or reactionary.

The theory, considered apart from Soviet reality, may be in certain respects uplifting. Many intelligent, serious people in all walks of life and from many nations have been inspired by the theory and have willingly made great self-sacrifices in an attempt to remold society in accordance with its dictates. But the theory and Soviet reality are, in many respects, very widely separated. A very large proportion of Soviet citizens must be painfully aware of the wide discrepancies between theoretical pronouncements and bleak reality. One can only imagine the depths of the cynicism, the feelings of helplessness, the hostility or despair which must be experienced by people who believe in the correctness of Marxist-Leninist goals for society, but deplore the oppressive techniques which have been used in the U.S.S.R. under the protective guise of Marxism-Leninism, and the even greater frustration of those who reject Marxism-Leninism *in toto*. It is conceivable that to many the discrepancies between Marxist-Leninist ideology and the reality of the Soviet system might be more demoralizing than the bleak reality would have been without the theory.

REFERENCES

1 For a good overview of the historical development of communism see R. N. Carew Hunt, *The Theory and Practice of Communism,* (New York: Macmillan Co., 1959).

2 Friedrich Engels, quoted in M. Oakeshott, *Social and Political Doctrines of Contemporary Europe,* (New York: Cambridge University Press, 1950), p. 104.

3 Friedrich Engels, *Ludwig Feuerbach,* (New York: International Publishers, 1935), p. 28.

4 Karl Marx and Friedrich Engels, *The Communist Manifesto,* edited by Samuel H. Beer, (New York: Appleton-Century-Crofts, Inc., 1955), pp. 11-14.

5 *Ibid.,* p. 12.

6 *Ibid.,* p. 16.

7 Karl Marx, quoted in M. Oakeshott, *Social and Political Doctrines of Contemporary Europe, op. cit.,* p. 120.

8 Karl Marx, *Capital,* (Moscow: Foreign Languages Publishing House, 1959), Vol. 3, pp. 272-81.

9 *Ibid.,* Vol. 1, p. 639.

10 Marx and Engels, *The Communist Manifesto, op. cit.,* pp. 9-10.

11 Marx, *Capital, op. cit.,* Vol. 1, p. 763.

12 Marx and Engels, *The Communist Manifesto, op. cit.,* Friedrich Engels, Preface to the English Edition of 1888, pp. 5-6.

13 V. I. Lenin, *Works,* (Moscow: Foreign Languages Publishing House, 1952), Vol. 29, p. 388.

14 *Ibid.,* Vol. 32, p. 222.

15 *Fundamentals of Marxism-Leninism, Manual,* (Moscow: Foreign Languages Publishing House, 1961), p. 410.

16 Lenin, *Works, op. cit.,* Vol. 29, p. 387.

17 *Fundamentals of Marxism-Leninism, op. cit.,* p. 625.

18 Lenin, *Works, op. cit.,* Vol. 31, p. 325.

19 *Ibid.,* Vol. 25, p. 384.

20 N. S. Khrushchev, *Report on the Program of the Communist Party of the Soviet Union,* (New York: Crosscurrents Press, 1961), Vol. 2, p. 107.

21 Marx and Engels, *The Communist Manifesto, op. cit.,* pp. 31-2.

22 Karl Marx, *Critique of the Gotha Programme,* (New York: International Publishers, 1938), pp. 6-8.

23 *Ibid.,* p. 8.

24 *Ibid.,* p. 10.

25 Cf. *Fundamentals of Marxism-Leninism, op. cit.,* pp. 207-9.

26 D. Chesnokov, "The November Plenary Session of the Party Central Committee and Questions of State Construction," *Kommunist,* No. 2, Jan., 1963, pp. 11-20. (C.D.S.P., Vol. XV, No. 10, pp. 27-8)

27 "On the Forthcoming Publication of Multivolume History of the C.P.S.U.," *Pravda,* June 22, 1962, pp. 2-4; June 24, 1962, pp. 2-3.

28 Friedrich Engels, *Anti-Dühring,* quoted in M. Oakeshott, *Social and Political Doctrines of Contemporary Europe, op. cit.,* p. 103.

29 N. S. Khrushchev, *Report of the Central Committee of the C.P.S.U. to the Twenty-Second Congress of the Communist Party of the Soviet Union,* (New York: Crosscurrents Press, 1961), p. 135.

30 Khrushchev, *Report on the Program of the Communist Party of the Soviet Union, op. cit.,* p. 33.

31 Cf. Barrington Moore, *Soviet Politics—The Dilemma of Power,* (Cambridge, Mass.: Harvard University Press, 1951), pp. 402-25.

32 Cf. Donald G. MacRae, "The Intellectual and Emotional Factors in Communist Affiliation," in Howard R. Swearer and Richard P. Longaker, *Contemporary Communism, Theory and Practice,* (Belmont, Cal.: Wadsworth, 1963), pp. 30-5.

33 "Peaceful Coexistence Does Not Mean Slackening of the Ideological Struggle," *Kommunist,* No. 8, May, 1962, pp. 60-8.

34 Khrushchev, *Report on the Program of the Communist Party of the Soviet Union, op. cit.,* p. 121.

35 Khrushchev, *Report of the Central Committee of the C.P.S.U. to the Twenty-Second Congress of the Communist Party of the Soviet Union, op. cit.,* p. 120.

36 "On the Forthcoming Publication of Multivolume History of the C.P.S.U.," *op. cit.,* pp. 2-3.

CHAPTER II

THE COMMUNIST PARTY OF THE SOVIET UNION

Rise to Power

The Communist Party of the Soviet Union (C.P.S.U.) is an elitist organization, which is dominated by a few leaders who attempt to exercise complete control over all aspects of Soviet society.[1] The party was able to seize and maintain its extraordinary amount of power because of a number of circumstances including the decadence of Russian Tsarism, the autocratic bureaucratic organization which it inherited, the Russian social-political heritage, the general discontent which permeated Russian society, the weakness, lack of wisdom and ineffectiveness of its opponents, and to a very large extent, because of the genius of Lenin, the leader of the revolutionary Bolsheviks. Parenthetically, it might be pointed out that in many respects the dictatorship by the leadership of the Communist Party constitutes an extension of the autocratic theories and practices of Tsarism.

The official political doctrine prevailing in Russia at the beginning of the twentieth century was that Divine Power had vested in the Tsar authority to govern the Russian masses and the subjugated minorities of the empire. The Tsar's power, like God's omnipotence, was not subject to restrictions. Since he was divinely inspired, his will was the source of all laws, justice, morality and truth. As God's representative, the Tsar was sacrosanct. Obedience to his command was a mandate from heaven for all his subjects. This doctrine, which was an anachronism in the nineteenth century, persisted in Russia because the Tsarist state suppressed all forms of political expression that were at variance with the autocratic doctrine on which it based its authority, and because the Tsar was too conceited and politically blind to compromise with the principles of democracy.

Agents of the bureaucratic, autocratic apparatus represented the authority of the Tsar in every town and village. The bureaucrats, unlike their counterparts in democratic countries, were in no way responsible to the people. They had little or no interest in the needs of the populace, and were often arbitrary, contemptuous and brutal, especially in dealing with the peasants. After the assassination of Tsar Alexander II in 1881, additional arbitrary power was granted to the bureaucrats: large areas were placed under martial law; suspected revolutionaries were subjected to administrative declaration of guilt by the bureaucrats; individuals were forbidden to practice their professions and many were deported to Siberia without judicial procedure and without even being told the reason for deportation. The Tsar used the uniformed and secret police and the armed forces as instruments to maintain the status quo. The individual was helpless in the Tsarist police state.[2] Many individuals, who would have been responsible citizens if they had been permitted to participate in governmental affairs, were pushed by the system from moderate to radical positions which did not preclude the use of revolutionary and terroristic methods.

Tsarist autocracy was supported by those groups within the population which benefited from maintaining the stability of the established order: The nobility and the large landowners, the upper echelons of the ecclesiastical hierarchy, the Tsarist bureaucrats and the police force. However, even within these groups there were some individuals who opposed Tsarism. Included among the opponents were members of the nobility who resented their exclusion from a meaningful sharing of political power, and some of the intelligentsia who had been influenced by western liberalism and were keenly aware of legitimate forces for social change. In addition, many members of the privileged classes were disturbed or disgusted by the Tsar's ineffective leadership.

Among the masses, discontent prevailed. Industrial workers chafed under long working hours, low wages, poor conditions of work and few legitimate opportunities for redress of grievances through trade union activities. The peasants who comprised the bulk of the population had particularly strong reasons to feel bitter toward the regime and to demand a change. Although serfdom had been abolished in 1861, the emancipation decree had merely authorized an improved status for the peasants but did not guarantee it. Landowners retained huge tracts of the best land for their own use, and demanded unreasonably high prices for the small parcels of land which the former serfs were permitted to purchase. The high price of the land, low prices for agricultural produce and low yields because of outmoded farming techniques, made it impossible for the majority of the peasants to pay for the land which they so urgently desired. The economic and social plight of the peasants tended to deteriorate progressively, and concurrently their resentment toward the regime and the propertied classes increased. As the discontent of the masses of workers and peasants grew, an increasingly powerful, potential revolutionary force was available for use by any revolutionary group which could convince the masses that the proposed changes would be to their advantage.

During the latter part of the nineteenth and the early part of the twentieth centuries forces within the empire which sought to weaken or destroy the autocratic power of the Tsar gained momentum. After a revolutionary outburst in 1905, precipitated by the defeat of the Tsarist army in the Russo-Japanese war, the Tsar, who feared a widespread revolutionary movement, issued a Manifesto which promised freedom of speech, freedom of assembly, unbiased suffrage and a representative legislative assembly (the Duma). Although the Manifesto temporarily inhibited demands for a more radical solution, it soon became apparent that the Tsar did not intend to adhere to the concessions which circumstances had made it expedient for him to grant. The failure of the Tsar to keep his promises, the steadily worsening condition of the masses and the ineffective leadership which the autocracy provided in World War I all contributed to the fomenting of revolutionary activities.

Well before the turn of the century, conspiratory groups and societies, in the main spearheaded by intellectuals, had been meeting secretly to discuss techniques to effect the changes that were deemed necessary. In the absence of a climate of political freedom, all societies that were critical of the regime and sought to effect constitutional modifications, economic reform and social progress had to meet clandestinely. Many political dissenters met under the guise of literary discussion groups. Literary works were treated with considerable leniency by Tsarist authorities and even Karl Marx's *Das Kapital* circulated freely in Russia because the authorities considered that Marx's program for the future was nothing more than a utopian dream. Initially most of the groups which opposed the regime were loosely organized intellectual movements rather than political parties. Of these, the Populist movement constituted the parent trunk from which developed nihilist, anarchist, liberal and socialist groups of all types.[3] After the assassination of Tsar Alexander II by a fanatical anarchist in 1881, a campaign of persecution was launched against all Populists and radicals in an attempt to eradicate all political conspiracy. Many of the conspirators fled to Western Europe where they came into direct contact with the Marxist movement.

In 1897 several of the principal branches of the Populist movement united to form the Socialist Revolutionary Party which sought to establish a peasant program of agrarian socialism. In 1898 the Russian Marxists, under the leadership of Plekhanov and Lenin, established the Russian Social Democratic Labor Party (R.S.D.L.P.). The Marxists directed their revolutionary appeal to industrial workers who, though few in numbers, were conveniently grouped in large cities. They predicted a rapid industrialization of Russia with a corresponding increase in the number of workers who could be welded into a class conscious proletariat to supply the mass base for a revolution against capitalism and Tsarist autocracy.

Almost immediately, disagreements emerged among the Russian Marxists about techniques to materialize the political and social transformation which was deemed necessary. The "Legal Marxists" argued that instead of taking overt political action against the state, the workers should cooperate with the bourgeoisie in the development of industries and the establishment of capitalism. Another faction, which Lenin labelled the Economists, argued that the goal of the working class movement was practical labor reforms which could be achieved through strong trade unions. The Economists preferred to leave political activity and particularly political revolution to the middle class liberals, with whom they shared the goal of constitutional and representative government. Since the goals and approaches of these groups were at variance with the tenets of Lenin's interpretation of Marxism, they were soon demoted from leading positions in the Russian Social Democratic Labor Party which was controlled by revolutionaries such as Plekhanov, Akselrod, Zasulich, Potresov and particularly Lenin.

In 1903 the R.S.D.L.P. was subdivided into two factions, the Bolsheviks and the Mensheviks, which for the following 15 years, until the Bolsheviks asserted final and complete dominance, pursued policies of combined cooperation and opposition, rapprochement and divergence. The names, Bolshevik and Menshevik, derived from a situation which arose at the Second Congress of the R.S.D.L.P. which was held in London in 1903. The faction led by Lenin was initially outnumbered and outvoted, but after the withdrawal from the Congress of the Economists and the Bundists (a group which claimed to represent the Jewish proletariat), it was able to dominate the Congress, elect its representatives to the central party organs and force adoption of its program. Thereafter, Lenin's faction, with more ingenuity than justification, called itself the Bolsheviks (the majority men) and its opponents within the party the Mensheviks (the minority men).

Reasons for the split within the party included differences of opinion about revolutionary tactics and about the composition and operation of the party. Both factions agreed that the revolution would have to proceed through two phases, an initial bourgeois democratic revolution and a subsequent socialist revolution. The Mensheviks favored an alliance with liberal bourgeois forces in the struggle for the overthrow of autocracy, and the materialization of limited objectives such as constitutional liberties, social legislation and universal suffrage. They argued that this type of cooperation was appropriate during a period of capitalistic growth and industrialization which they held to be a necessary prerequisite for a successful socialist revolution. Lenin's preferred strategy was to form a temporary alliance with the peasantry rather than with the bourgeoisie. He contended:

"The proletariat must carry to completion the democratic revolution by allying to itself the mass of the peasantry, in order to crush by force the resistance of the autocracy and to paralyze the instability of the bourgeoisie. The proletariat must accomplish the socialist revolution by allying to itself the mass of the semi-proletarian elements of the population in order to crush by force the resistance of the bourgeoisie and to paralyze the instability of the peasantry and the petty bourgeoisie."[4]

He argued that the interests of the proletariat and the liberal bourgeoisie were fundamentally incompatible and that, whereas it was appropriate to profit from the strivings of the bourgeoisie, an alliance would be dangerous because the bourgeoisie might be able to gain and maintain control over the movement. Because the peasantry was weak and poorly organized, he felt that it was both safe and advantageous to affiliate the interests of the working class and the peasantry temporarily, to promise to assist the peasants to achieve some of their goals, and subsequently, when the proletariat would be in a stronger position, to treat the peasant bourgeoisie as a class enemy.

As to the nature of the party, Lenin advocated a small elitist party of dedicated revolutionaries who would operate in strict subordination to the central leadership; this core group would serve as the leading vanguard for the masses of workers who would aid the party without belonging to it.[5] The Mensheviks, on the other hand, favored giving party membership to anyone who believed in and was willing to support the party program. Although the Mensheviks embraced the concept of centralized leadership, they argued that rank and file party members should not be denied the right to discuss and, on occasion, to influence party policy. Thus, the Mensheviks advocated a relatively democratic, mass-based party organization, while the Bolsheviks under Lenin, advocated a small, elitist organization of revolutionaries strictly subordinated to the central leadership. Lenin argued:

> "Broad democracy in party organization, amidst the gloom of autocracy . . . is nothing more than a *useless and harmful toy*. It is a useless toy because, as a matter of fact, no revolutionary organization has ever practiced *broad* democracy, nor could it, however much it desired to do so. It is a harmful toy because any attempt to practice 'broad democratic principles' will simply facilitate the work of the police in making big raids; it will perpetuate the prevailing primitiveness, divert the thoughts of practical workers from the serious and imperative task of training themselves to become professional revolutionaries to that of drawing up detailed 'paper' rules for election systems."[6]

Lenin's arguments concerning the danger of a large, relatively democratic organization had definite practical validity during the period of political conspiracy. However, despite the fact that the conditions which partially justified his position have long since changed, the practices which he advocated have continued to this day.

In 1902 Lenin outlined what he conceived to be the necessary tactical approach of the party in his pamphlet, *What Is To Be Done?* He gave primary importance to the development of an organized, disciplined, elitist Marxist Party to guide the masses in a struggle for socialism. Second, he deemed it absolutely essential to undermine the influence of factions which repudiated political revolutionary activities and favored action through trade unions as a primary method for improving the welfare of the working class. Third, he argued that every revolutionary situation which might occur in Russia should be transformed by the party into a bid for total power. Until 1917, in spite of numerous intra-party conflicts and extended periods of exile, Lenin forged doggedly toward the materialization of these goals. He demonstrated a remarkable knack for manipulating any objective situation to facilitate progress toward the party goals which he designated, and he always worked on the assumption that the end justified the means. Lenin held that the party had to propagate militant class consciousness among the workers, leading them to feel overwhelming hatred for the state as well as for their employers. Strikes and workers' demonstrations were valued as a technique to train the workers to fight as a unified force against their class enemies and the state which protected these enemies. Lenin asserted that although the workers might believe that their goal was improved working conditions, the chief goal of the labor movement was to prepare an army of proletarian fighters who would support the party when it issued the call for revolution. Each success achieved by the labor movement was to be used by the party to encourage the workers to increase their demands and combativeness, and to enlist greater support for the working class movement. Great efforts were to be made to arouse and maintain the revolutionary spirit of the masses of workers and peasants.

Since the policies determined by the party were to be implemented by the masses, their support was imperative. To obtain the required support, Lenin advocated improved working conditions and standards of living for the workers and agreed that the party should openly support the desire of the peasants to seize land from the gentry and the nobility. However, he refused to support a pledge to give the peasants title to the land, and rejected the idea of sharing power with the peasants after a successful revolution; the proletarian party was to monopolize all power in the name of the workers and peasants. Thus, while many Russian Marxists contended that the revolutionary government should be a democratic coalition, as early as 1902 Lenin insisted that the proletarian party should maintain exclusive leadership over the workers' state. The dictatorship of the proletariat was to be characterized by a single party rule.[7]

In March, 1917, autocracy was overthrown by a revolutionary movement which was not sponsored or lead by any political party. The revolution started spontaneously in Petrograd with large scale demonstrations of workers. The workers were joined by large numbers of people angered by food shortages and inflation. Workers' strikes followed. The army joined the demonstrators, disarmed the Tsarist police and armed the workers. Relatively little blood was shed because no force in the entire empire was willing to fight for autocracy. The revolutionary movement spread rapidly and was victorious in all parts of Russia. The Tsar had no choice but to abdicate.

A Provisional Government was formed after a conference between the leaders of the Duma and the Soviets of Workers' and Soldiers' Deputies, which had been established on an elective basis during the height of the revolutionary activity. The leaders of the Duma had not participated in the revolution and agreed to form a government only to prevent chaos. Without the broad support of the revolutionary masses which could be obtained only through cooperation with the Soviets, the Duma would have been powerless. With the approval of the Soviets, the Provisional Government legalized workers' strikes and guaranteed broad civil liberties, legal equality and amnesty for political prisoners. It promised that a Constituent Assembly, elected by universal, equal and secret vote, would determine the form of government and draft a new constitution. The promised measures of reform were not to be postponed because of the existence of war conditions. The Provisional Government was liberal and moderate. After Tsarism was overthrown, Russia began to move toward the formation of a democratic republic. However, a combination of factors including Russia's involvement in World War I, the skill of the Bolshevik leaders, especially Lenin, and the poor judgment and mistakes of the Bolshevik opponents prevented the development of a democratic republic.

After the March or Bourgeois Revolution, Lenin argued that the major task for the Bolsheviks was to overthrow the Provisional Government. He decided that although the workers' and soldiers' deputies to the Soviets were predominantly Mensheviks and Social Revolutionaries, the unstructured nature of the Soviets would permit the Bolsheviks to weld them into a powerful weapon against the Provisional Government. His strategy was to discredit the Provisional Government and simultaneously to discredit the Mensheviks and the Social Revolutionaries within the Soviets. The task was not difficult. The Provisional Government, instead of being free to attend to important internal matters, fulfilled the obligations of the Tsarist government to the Allies by continuing the Russian war efforts. A separate peace with Germany, convocation of the Constituent Assembly and the long overdue land reform might have insured the transformation of Russia into a democratic republic. The absence of these conditions were assets to the Bolsheviks. Progressive inflation worsened the situation of the workers. The peasants, angered that the land reform should be delayed because of nebulous democratic principles, did not trust the government and started to seize the land of large estates. Soldier peasants, loathe to miss the opportunity to expropriate land, deserted the army by thousands. The Bolsheviks under Lenin's guidance fully supported the large scale demoralization. They issued slogans which expressed the most urgent desires of the masses: "Peace for the soldiers, bread for the cities (workers), and land for the peasants." Lenin's appeal to and support from the masses exceeded that of all other Bolshevik, Menshevik and Social Revolutionary leaders. Because of his power over the masses, the majority of the Bolsheviks supported Lenin's radical revolutionary program. He advocated immediate action through the Soviets to appropriate the power of the "bourgeois" Provisional Government, and insisted that action was required before the "bourgeoisie" had time to consolidate their power and to establish a democratic republic.

During the summer of 1917 a few demonstrations against the Provisional Government were staged. Almost no section of the population was satisfied. The peasants chafed against the long delayed land reforms; there was major dissatisfaction about the conduct of the war; increased inflation, unemployment caused by lack of materials, and hunger made demands from the workers for improvement inevitable. The Bolsheviks made skillful use of the dissatisfaction to discredit all opponents. Also, by this time, the Bolsheviks had obtained a majority in the Soviets of Petrograd, Moscow and several other large cities. By November, 1917, Lenin was able to convince the majority of his colleagues that the time was ripe for a Bolshevik revolution. Two leading Bolsheviks, Kamenev and Zinoviev, opposed the decision and publicized the forthcoming action. Nevertheless, the Bolsheviks, with help from the Petrograd Military Revolutionary Committee, the Petrograd Garrison and the Soviets, were able to wrest power from the Provisional Government with a minimum of bloodshed and fighting. In fact, after the Bolsheviks seized the capital, Petrograd, the city looked so normal that many people did not realize that another revolution had occurred. Moscow fell a few days later and the rest of the country followed without much resistance. Rival governments, which were set up in a few regions inhabited by minority groups, were ousted within a relatively short time by the Bolsheviks with the help of the Red Army.

The Bolshevik Party, by no means one of the largest of the Russian political parties, was able to seize power because of a complex of factors which included wide-spread, long-standing and legitimate dissatisfaction among most sections of the population, the existence of a state of war, the weakness of the opponents of Bolshevism, Lenin's superior leadership, discipline within the party, skillful use of the dissatisfaction of the population, promises of egalitarianism and the use of attractive slogans which expressed the desires of the people. Although the ultimate goals of the revolution were derived from Marx's theory, the techniques of the revolution were not. Mass support for the revolution derived from dissatisfaction with the current situation, and the hope that the Bolshevik promises would be fulfilled. The majority of workers and peasants, far from being devotees of the Marxist theory, had never even heard of Marx. The success of the revolution cannot be attributed to Marx's theory.

After the overthrow of the Provisional Government, the All-Russian Congress of Soviets, dominated by the Bolsheviks and left-wing Social Revolutionaries, proclaimed the transfer of power to the Soviets. The Council of

Commissars, a new and solidly Bolshevik government with Lenin as chairman, was formed. Since one of the Bolshevik promises had been convocation of a Constituent Assembly, Lenin agreed reluctantly to hold elections. He realized that the Bolsheviks could not attain majority status in an elected assembly, and that the assembly would attempt to replace the Soviets, a revolutionary institution. His predictions were correct. Bolsheviks held only slightly over one-fifth of the seats in the Constituent Assembly, which was formed on the basis of a relatively free election. However, because of their control over the revolutionary movement, the Bolsheviks were able to present the Constituent Assembly with two equally unacceptable alternatives. The Assembly could make itself superfluous by supporting the Bolshevik dominated Soviet government, or could bring about its own annihilation by opposing it. The Assembly acted in accordance with the second alternative. It met only twice in January, 1918, before it was dispersed by the Red Guards. The potential for democratic practices, legal procedures and majority decisions was replaced by the revolution with its own laws. For a very short time, the Bolsheviks found it expedient to permit members of other "leftist" parties to participate minimally in the affairs of state. However, under Lenin's leadership, the Bolsheviks proceeded rapidly to consolidate their dictatorship and to rid themselves of all real or potential opposition. By 1922, as a result of the arrest, imprisonment or execution of the leaders of rival parties, the consolidation of the one-party dictatorship was virtually completed. Never, since the election of the impotent Constituent Assembly in 1917, have the electorate of the U.S.S.R. had the right to choose between political parties.

Party Organization

PRINCIPLES

A distinction must be made between the professed principles and operative practices of the Communist Party of the Soviet Union. Since Lenin's time, party leaders have typically paid lip service to democratic principles and have maintained that the C.P.S.U. and its handmaiden, the Soviet Government, operate on a higher level of democracy than can be attained by any non-socialist form of political organization. Professed organizational and operative principles of the C.P.S.U. such as democratic centralism, inner-party democracy, collective leadership and criticism and self-criticism convey the impression that the C.P.S.U. is a democratic organization in which the party leaders are responsible to the party members who elect them, and free discussion of competing ideas prevails. In actual practice, the C.P.S.U. is a highly undemocratic organization which is controlled by the dictatorial grip of sometimes one, sometimes a few, top leaders. As is often the case in the U.S.S.R., a wide gulf exists between lofty theory and dreary practice.

Marx and Engels indicated that the proletariat needed an independent political party for the revolutionary transformation from capitalism and socialism, and in 1847 they participated in the establishment of the first communist organization—the Communist League. However, it was Lenin who most deeply influenced the structure and functioning of the Communist Party as it developed in the Soviet Union, and in fact, in all other states, since the C.P.S.U. has served as a model for all other Communist Parties. The fundamental principles of party policy and tactics, the organizational principles and the norms of internal functioning, were formulated by Lenin.

Lenin was adamant that the party should be an elitist group organized in terms of democratic centralism and strict intra-party discipline. His emphasis on elitism has already been mentioned. In 1902 he argued that the party should be

". . . a small compact core, consisting of reliable, experienced, hardened workers, with responsible agents in the principal districts and connected by the rule of strict secrecy with the organizations of revolutionaries . . . that the organization must consist chiefly of persons engaged in revolutionary activities as a profession."[8]

The elitist principle is still operative: the Party Statutes describe the C.P. S.U. as the "militant, tested vanguard of the Soviet people, uniting on a voluntary basis the most socially conscious part of the working class, collective farm peasantry and intelligentsia of the U.S.S.R."

Lenin maintained that "Absolute centralism and the strictest discipline of the proletariat constitute one of the fundamental conditions for victory over the bourgeoisie."[9] According to current Party Statutes, democratic centralism, "the guiding principle of the organizational structure of the Party," is defined as:

". . . election of all Party executives from bottom to top, periodic accountability of Party bodies to their Party organizations and to higher bodies; strict Party discipline and subordination of the minority to the majority; and the unconditionally binding nature of the decisions of higher bodies upon lower ones." (Rule 19)

These provisions, if implemented fully, would provide a democratic basis for the functioning of the party. The rules convey the impression that: party leaders at all levels are the elected representatives of the party membership; the power of the leaders derives from their status as representatives of the members; the leadership is responsible to the members; and if the leadership ceased to express the will of the majority of members, it would be replaced by a process of democratic elections. However, the democratic essence of these provisions is flagrantly violated. The rank and file members have no voice whatsoever in the selection of the top party leadership. The most powerful position in the Communist Party of the Soviet Union, the First Secretary of the Central Committee, has typically been acquired on the basis of a naked struggle for power. Stalin attained his dictatorial position by forming an alliance with first one and then another group of potential rivals, always using the temporary alliance to remove other sources of opposition or other rivals by execution, deportation or demotion, and at the same time, arranging that loyal supporters be assigned to strategic positions. During the mid-1950's Khrushchev apparently used the techniques of his predecessor to "pack" the Central Committee of the C.P.S.U. with delegates who could be counted on to vote for him. He was then able to claim that his election to the top position in the party was based on the "democratic principles of the party." His election, however, appears to have involved clever manipulation in a situation in which democratic principles were completely submerged. Although many details are not available at this time, it is probable that Khrushchev's demotion in October, 1964 was the result of a *coup d'état* that had been planned carefully by a handful of top ranking party leaders—the members of the Presidium and the Secretariat. Even the members of the Central Committee who were convened with haste to approve the decision of the Presidium were given no advance warning that Khrushchev was to be stripped of his power. The rank and file party members were not consulted in any way about Khrushchev's dismissal and had no voice in the selection of his successors.

Although elections are held more or less regularly in accordance with the statutory provisions, it is a well-established policy that all officers and delegates to higher party conclaves must be approved for reliability and suitability by the higher party organization. Higher party organizations, in effect, exercise a veto power over the "free election" of delegates and officers. Not infrequently, higher party officials designate the delegates and officers which lower party organizations are expected to ratify by election. Lower party organizations have the statutory right to remove their own officers and delegates but approval by a higher party organization is mandatory. In form only are the party elections from the bottom to the top.

The Party Statutes approved by the Twenty-Second Congress (1961) incorporated one totally new feature—"the principle of systematic turnover of the membership of Party bodies and continuity of leadership" (Rule 25). Not less than one quarter of the membership of the Central Committee of the C.P.S.U. and its Presidium are to be newly elected at each regular election, and as a rule, Presidium members shall not be elected for more than three successive terms. However, outstanding party leaders "by virtue of their recognized authority and high political, organizational or other abilities" may be successively elected to executive bodies for a longer period, provided that they are re-elected by not less than three-quarters of the votes cast in secret ballot. At least one third of the members of the Central Committees of Union Republics and of the territory and province committees, and one-half of the members of the lower party committees must be newly elected at each regular election. Members of the executive committees of the intermediate party organizations may not be re-elected for more than three successive terms while in the primary party organizations only two terms are permitted. Special exceptions may also be made for highly qualified individuals at these levels.

Khrushchev indicated that these changes were designed to facilitate the promotion of talented young people to leading party posts, to enable the party to root out leaders who organize "family circles" and engage in "mutual concealment of short-comings and mistakes in work," and "to provide a guarantee against any recurrence of the cult of the personality."[10] In addition, since it allows a larger number of members to attain temporary positions of prestige within the party, the move is designed to affect the initiative of members and their overall enthusiasm for the party. The party leaders have apparently had good reason to be concerned about the establishment of "family circles." Because higher level party officials exercise full authority over the selection of delegates to or officers of any party congress or organization, officials at each level have ample opportunity to fill the key positions under their jurisdiction with trusted supporters.

Superficially, it might appear that the new rules provide a mechanism through which even top ranking party officials such as Secretaries of the Central Committee and members of the Presidium could be voted out of office. However, the probability of such an event is infinitesimal, since the real locus of power is retained by the upper echelon of leaders, and particularly by the First Secretary. The decision to remove or demote a high ranking party official is ordinarily the prerogative of the First Secretary, or at best, the decision is made by members of the Secretariat and the Presidium. Party members lower in the hierarchy have no voice whatsoever in such decisions. Successive re-elections of top leaders can always be justified by virtue of their outstanding qualities. The late Kozlov pointed out that the principle of the systematic renewal of party organs must be linked closely with the principle of continuity of leadership because "without a more or less steady group of leaders, the continuity of leadership or the transfer of accumulated experience cannot be insured."[11] On the other hand, the principle of systematic renewal could be used effectively by strong leaders at all levels in the hierarchy to cast aside inefficient, unreliable or potentially threatening members of the party apparatus, and to keep junior party officials completely subservient to the leaders whose decision determines who is to be re-elected. In all respects the real power of the C.P.S.U. is preempted by the top leader or leaders of the party. The Statutes adopted by the Twenty-Second Party Congress are more democratic in form than the Statutes which they replaced. However, the C.P.S.U. has never operated as a democratic organization, and it is improbable that the new democratic statutory features will appreciably increase the *de facto* practice of democracy.

The rule that party officials at a lower level are held accountable to party officials at a higher level is upheld. Lower level party leaders and organizations are required to report to and carry out the orders of higher level party leaders. However, the rule that party officials are accountable to the organization which "elected" them amounts, in practice, merely to the fact that officials report their decisions to their respective organizations. Members of the party organization are expected, or rather required, to approve and enforce the policy decisions of the leadership. Under no circumstances, however, may the party members reject or even criticize the decisions of the party leaders.

The principle of democratic centralism emphasizes party discipline and the subordination of the minority to the majority. This aspect of the principle probably corresponds fairly closely to reality, although it seems likely that most members have learned that to express no opinion is preferable to the expression of one which does not agree with the "majority opinion" i.e. the opinion of the party leadership. Party spokesmen maintain that before a decision is adopted all members are completely free to express diverse and even conflicting opinions. The concept of inner-party democracy is described in Rule 27 of the Party Statutes which states:

> "The free and businesslike discussion of questions of Party policy in individual Party organizations or in the Party as a whole is the inalienable right of the Party member and an important principle of inner-Party democracy. Only on the basis of inner-Party democracy can criticism and self-criticism be developed and Party discipline, which must be conscious and not mechanical, be strengthened."

However, a word of caution is added in the same rule.

> "Broad discussion, especially discussion on an All-Union scale, of questions of Party policy must be carried out in such a way as to ensure the free expression of the views of Party members and *to prevent the possibility of attempts to form factional groupings destructive to Party unity or of attempts to split the Party.*" (italics added)

Thus, even within the statement of the guaranteed right for free discussion the provision is added that the discussion is to be free only within the limits prescribed by the party leaders. A certain amount of freedom and initiative is permissible with respect to discussions of techniques and approaches to implement the party program. Critical freedom, however, is the right of only those who command the party apparatus. Fear of being purged has destroyed most of the initiative of Soviet communists. Conformity and passive acceptance of the dictates of superiors in the party hierarchy characterizes party affairs.

Since the party leadership brooks no competition, the development of factions within the party is not tolerated. However, within the upper echelons of party leadership, it is inevitable that there must be a considerable amount of discussion, exchange of opinion and even violent disagreement.

Because the party leaders maintain an absolute monopoly of political power in the U.S.S.R., they formulate all major programs and policies which are to be implemented by all governmental, economic, social and cultural agencies, and even determine the organizational structure within which policies are to be implemented and goals are to be attained. Since the party cannot work toward the materialization of all its goals simultaneously, all major policy decisions must reflect a compromise with respect to party values and priorities, and in the formulation of any major policy decision, alternative proposals must be considered. Compromises must be made with reference to conflicting interests, both within the party and within society as a whole. Undoubtedly there are genuine differences of opinion based on personal interpretations of party or public welfare concerning the relative priority of different goals and the effectiveness of alternative techniques for the materialization of a selected goal. The personal status of individual leaders within the party hierarchy is inevitably affected when one goal is given priority or one technique is selected at the expense of another. It may be assumed that spokesmen for different political lines support or reflect the interests of different subgroups within society and that a considerable amount of jockeying for power, give-and-take and exchange of concessions occurs. It might be suggested that in the freer atmosphere which has developed since Stalin's demise, groups or cliques within the party tend to articulate the interests of various subsections of the population in a manner somewhat analogous to that of separate political parties in a multiparty system. The analogy cannot, of course, be carried too far because, among other reasons, subsections within the party and the population have no direct technique through which they can give or withhold support from party spokesmen, and stringent limitations on freedom of discussion still exist. However, pressure for the removal of some of these limitations must be fairly strong because at the Twenty-Second Party Congress Khrushchev found it necessary to publicly reject a demand by "certain comrades" that the party rule against factionalism be abolished.

Soviet leaders have provided almost no information about the actual process of reaching a decision within the ruling ranks of the party. The top organs of the party serve as the major arena for political conflict, and it may be assumed that policy decisions in this arena, as in all organizations in which unanimity is virtually impossible, are affected by the balance of power within the party leadership, sincere interest in the welfare of the party or society, compromises between conflicting interests and a multitude of other factors. However, because the party attempts to present itself as a unified, purposeful organization, the existence of intra-party disagreements is usually glossed over in the party press, and the decisions of the party leaders are purported to be unanimous. The impression of unanimity has been disrupted when it has been necessary to make public the outcome of a power struggle, and Khrushchev occasionally announced that some of his colleagues had opposed decisions which were made under his sponsorship.

Subordinates within the party are expected to provide automatic ratification for the decisions of their superiors. Once a decision is adopted, each member is required to strive unconditionally to implement it, even if in the privacy of his own thoughts he opposes it. Party discipline also requires that members refrain from discussing intra-party questions outside the party. The most realistic portion of the definition of democratic centralism is the statement that the decisions of higher bodies are absolutely binding upon lower bodies. In this case practice corresponds to the professed principle. The C.P.S.U. is a rigidly hierarchical organization, in which all subordinates are unconditionally obligated to carry out the policy directives and decisions which are the exclusive prerogative of the central command.

The principle of collective leadership is posited as one of the major functional norms of the C.P.S.U. The Party Statutes include a scathing condemnation of the dictatorial practices associated with one-man leadership. Rule 28 states:

> "The highest principle of Party leadership is collectivity of leadership— the indispensable condition of the normal functioning of Party organizations, the correct rearing of cadres and the development of the activeness and initiative of Communists. The cult of the individual and the violations of inner-Party democracy connected with it cannot be tolerated in the Party. . . . Collective leadership does not absolve officials of individual responsibility for matters entrusted to them."

During the Stalin era, propaganda conveyed the impression that all major decisions were based on the collective agreement of the top party leaders. Subsequently, it was openly admitted that Stalin had blatantly violated the principle of collective leadership. Khrushchev, during his period of primacy, attempted to convey the impression that he always consulted with his party colleagues. Apparently, until shortly before his dismissal, he, unlike Stalin, relied primarily on persuasion backed by authority rather than on terroristic methods to obtain support for his policy. However, the praise which colleagues and subordinates heaped on Khrushchev until his demotion was so reminiscent of the adulation of Stalin that Khrushchev, himself, saw the need to proclaim publicly the leading role of collective leadership. He stated:

> "In many speeches at the Congress, and not infrequently in our press, special emphasis is laid on my person in discussing the activities of the Central Committee. My role is stressed in carrying out the most important measures of the party and the government. Now, I appreciate the kind sentiments guiding these comrades. May I, however, emphasize most emphatically that everything said about me should be addressed to the Central Committee of our Leninist Party, to the Presidium of the Central Committee. Not a single major measure, not a single responsible speech has been made on anyone's personal instructions, but is the result of collective discussion and collective decisions. . . ."[12]

Khrushchev's public proclamation of the dominant role of the Central Committee might have been nothing more than a propaganda move designed to "prove" that he adhered to the principle of collective leadership. Because of the rigid party discipline, it would have been possible for him to terminate personal praise by issuing an order to that effect. Whether or not he typically allowed other members of the top party leadership to participate extensively in the formulation of major policies, he apparently liked to "tolerate" the praise.

Obviously, no one man could take responsibility for all major policy decisions in the U.S.S.R. The top leaders have access to advice and consultation from the most qualified experts in all areas of endeavor. According to the principle of collective leadership, alternative policies formulated on the basis of expert advice are evaluated carefully by the top party leaders, and after due deliberation, a consensus is attained, which, as indicated previously, may have required a number of concessions and compromises. This is apparently what happens when no one leader has attained a position of dominance. However, when one leader is able to entrench himself as the number one man of the party, as Khrushchev did, he can short circuit the decision-making process by imposing his decision on the entire group of leaders before a consensus is reached. Under these circumstances, the vote of one person within the leadership group carries much more weight than that of the other members, and the principle of collective leadership becomes an empty farce. Several lines of evidence suggest that toward the end of his career Khrushchev demonstrated progressive proclivity toward violating the collective leadership principle. To date, no single individual in the post-Khrushchev leadership seems to have attained a position of marked dominance, and hence, the decisions of the new leadership may, at least temporarily, reflect collective agreement.

Soviet spokesmen point to the requirement that party members engage freely in criticism and self-criticism as a manifestation of profound inner-party democracy. Criticism of others, and to a lesser extent, self-criticism are indeed commonly practiced. Public statements by ranking party officials frequently contain a scathing denunciation of the work of lower-level party officials. Letters from rank-and-file party members containing harsh criticisms of the work of local party functionaries are often published. Criticism is indeed tolerated and even encouraged, but only within carefully circumscribed limits. It is permissible to criticize lower level party functionaries for bureaucratic inefficiency, lack of devotion to duty, errors, behavior unbecoming to a communist, ineffective implementation of party decisions and faulty interpretation of Marxism-Leninism or the party line. However, criticism of the activities and decisions of the top party leader is not allowed. After the de-Stalinization movement and after Khrushchev's dismissal, the rank and file members were, of course, permitted to reiterate the criticisms directed by the new leaders to the erstwhile infallible party dictators. The regime, the current party leadership and the current party line are completely out of bounds for criticism. Such criticism, or criticism which could be considered as the germ of a proposal for an alternative platform, would be categorized as counter-revolutionary agitation, and would be considered a criminal offense. Thus, party members are encouraged to offer only those criticisms which meet with the approval of the party leaders, and which have the potential to facilitate the materialization of centrally determined party policies.

The policy of criticism and self-criticism contributes relatively little to the democratic operation of the C.P.S.U. However, it does serve the party in a number of ways. It provides the rank and file members with a safe and acceptable outlet for frustrations which must inevitably develop with respect to the operation of the party, and at the same time, it suggests to them that their vigilance and their recommendations are of crucial importance in the attainment of party goals. Fear of open criticism helps to force lower level party functionaries and members to adhere more strictly to party policy and to perform party duties more efficiently. It directs the attention of high level party officials to the negligence or inefficiency of subordinates and consequently facilitates the manning of party posts with efficient and reliable people. It also protects the myth of the infallibility of the high level leadership, because if the affairs of the party are not running smoothly in a particular sphere, criticism can always be directed toward scapegoats lower in the hierarchy. Finally, it provides one of the channels through which the party leadership is able to inform itself about the tensions, frustrations and aspirations of the rank and file party members.

The party leadership stresses that one of its most important operative principles is the maintenance of close links with the masses of the people. Lenin wrote:

> ". . . it is not enough to call ourselves the 'vanguard', the advanced detachment, we must act like one; we must act in such a way that *all* the other detachments shall see us and be obliged to admit that we are marching in the vanguard."13

Consequently, all party members are exhorted to develop close, basic continuous ties with the masses by working with them in trade unions, youth, peasant, cultural and all other organizations. Such close links are deemed necessary to determine the needs and interests of the masses, to find ways to serve them, to educate them and to convince them of the value of the communist program. The party states that without knowledge of the level of experience and class consciousness of the masses, it might surge too far ahead of them and lose their support. Although the party is to take into account the needs and aspirations of the masses in its formulation of policy, it must be prepared to lead the masses rather than to be unduly influenced by them. According to Stalin:

> "The Party cannot be a real party if it limits itself to registering what the masses of the working class feel and think, if it drags at the tail of the spontaneous movement, if it is unable to overcome the inertia and political indifference of the spontaneous movement, if it is unable to rise above the momentary interests of the proletariat, if it is unable to elevate the masses to the level of the class interests of the proletariat. The Party must stand at the head of the working class; it must see farther than the working class; it must lead the proletariat. . . ."14

In practice, this means that party members must be active in all organizations. At every meeting of every organization, party members must be prepared to ensure that all policy decisions conform fully with the current party line. They must, moreover, utilize every opportunity to convince the masses of the correctness of party policies, to encourage the masses to participate actively in the struggle to materialize party goals and to educate the masses and raise their level of class consciousness. According to the Party Statutes, "the Party directs the great creative activity of the Soviet people and imparts an organized, planned and scientific character to their struggle to achieve the ultimate goal, the victory of communism . . . the Party exists for and serves the people." Thus, the party claims to act for the people and in their name, although the people have never been given the opportunity to delegate to the party the right to act for them.

The Communist Party maintains a tight monopoly over all political life in the country. Stalin defended the party dictatorship by arguing that multiple parties are necessary only in a society that is divided into antagonistic classes, so that each class may be represented by its chosen delegates. He maintained that by 1936 antagonistic social classes had been abolished in the Soviet Union, and that since the two remaining "friendly classes," the workers and peasants, were both represented in the Communist Party, there was no need for dual or multiple parties. Politics to Marxists-Leninists is a struggle among classes, not a choice of alternatives. Stalin asserted that it is incorrect to describe the one-party rule as undemocratic because the Communist Party represents the majority of the people and governs in the interest of the people. His reply to Western criticisms included the countercharge that Western bourgeois parties represent merely the propertied minority and govern in the interest of the bourgeoisie and the middle class. Stalin, of course, failed to take into consideration the proposition that competition among political parties is a prerequisite for the majority to be able to express a consensus. Moreover, the assertion that the majority of Soviet workers and peasants freely support the policy of the party is an unsubstantiated hypothesis, not a verified fact.

Even the most unbiased and objective observer could not legitimately describe the C.P.S.U. as a democratic organization, either in its relationship to the Soviet people or in the relationship between the leadership and membership. The party has permeated all aspects of Soviet society and is omnipotent in all organized groups. It has, indeed, established close ties with the people so that it is reasonably cognizant of their desires, aspirations and complaints. Nevertheless, it functions predominantly as an elitist vanguard. The party imposed its absolute rule upon the people by right of victory in the Bolshevik Revolution and the subsequent civil war. Its ability to maintain its power has depended largely, but not exclusively, on coercive measures such as armed might, terrorism, and the speedy suppression of all real and potential opposition and on its control over the selection of the elite in all spheres of activity.

As the people's vanguard, it is the party which decides what is good for the country and the people. Not only does the party paternalistically lead the people by the hand toward the goals which it has set for them, but likewise the small core of party leaders treat the party membership much as a general staff treats the officers and troops under its command. Party decisions and policies are established by the top leadership, and sometimes, at least in the past, by one supreme leader alone. Party members do not enter into the deliberations of the party elite, nor are they permitted to criticize the decisions and policies. Very often, however, they are given the opportunity to give unanimous ratification of the decisions of their superiors. Through a centralized chain of command rigid discipline is imposed by the party apparatus upon the membership.

The C.P.S.U. is authoritarian, paternalistic, elitist and totalitarian. Although it represents a minority of Soviet citizens, it has preempted all power for itself. Its members are not permitted to have extra-party loyalties or interests which might conflict with party obligations. Not only party members, but all Soviet citizens must submit to personal hardships and sacrifices to carry out the dictates of the party. The authority of the party over the lives of all Soviet citizens is virtually complete. Party control and guidance encompasses every political, economic, social, cultural and scientific aspect of life in the U.S.S.R. All forms of human behavior come under the scrutiny of the party, which may act independently of governmental administration as well as through it to regulate private as well as public life.

Organization of the Party

The Communist Party of the Soviet Union is a hierarchical, pyramidical organization. At the peak of the pyramid is the All-Union party organization (the C.P.S.U.) to which all lower organizations are subordinate and subservient. Each of the fifteen Union Republics with the exception of the Russian Soviet Federated Socialist Republic (R.S.F.S.R.) has its own party organization (e.g. The Communist Party of the Ukrainian S.S.R.) which is responsible for implementing the decisions of the All-

Union organization, and for supervising all lower party organizations within the Union Republic. Party affairs within the R.S.F.S.R. are under the jurisdiction of the Russian Bureau of the C.P.S.U. In some, but not all, of the Union Republics, party organizations are established at the territorial or regional levels. These intermediate organizations are responsible to the party organization of the Union Republic and in turn are responsible for city and district party organizations within their territory. City or district party organizations are established throughout the U.S.S.R. In areas in which territorial or regional organizations are not established, the city and district organizations are responsible directly to the party organization of the Union Republic. At the local level are the primary party organizations which are supervised by district or city organizations.

The major features of the organizational structure of the C.P.S.U. have remained essentially unchanged since they were established under Lenin's direction. Sub-units within the overall organizational framework have, however, been changed from time to time in accordance with the exigencies of the situation. The structure of the party is designed to serve a variety of purposes, the most important of which is to provide the leaders of the party with a disciplined, efficient, broadly-based organization through which their instructions can flow downward and be accepted and implemented immediately. The party leaders need representatives at all lower levels who can be trusted to fulfill their orders. The all-encompassing nature of the party's control over society, the magnitude of the territory and the millions of people who are subject to party control make it imperative for the party leaders to delegate supervisory functions to chosen representatives, who are held responsible within a limited sphere or area for the fulfillment of the orders of the party leaders. The broad base of the party pyramid, composed of well-disciplined party members who are closely supervised by their party superiors, enables the leadership to consolidate its control over all key positions in Soviet society. Members of the party hierarchy are available at all levels to ensure that the dictates of the party leadership are understood and acted upon by all members of the governmental hierarchy and by all administrators and economic managers. The structure of the party thus provides the party leaders with spokesmen at all levels, and perhaps no less important, observers who are required to report through the party chain of command any deviation from party policy on the part of any organization, individual or official. Through the lower level party organizations, the influence of the party on non-party members is greatly enhanced, since party members are directed to ensure that no decision is made by any group or organization which is not consistent with party policy. The hierarchical structure of the party organization is, in brief, designed to provide the party leaders with a disciplined, reliable mechanism to ensure that orders are understood and implemented at all levels of society, to inform the leaders of developments which require their attention and to consolidate the absolute control of the party.

The major organizational units of the party at each of the levels of party organization are outlined in Figure 1. The structure and functions of each of these units will be described in subsequent sections. At each of the levels of the party organization (All-Union, Union Republic, territorial or regional, city or district, and primary), the highest organ, according to Party Statutes, is the Party Congress, the Party Conference or the Party Meeting. Members of a Conference at a lower level in the hierarchy elect delegates to the Conference or Congress at the next level in the hierarchy. At each level, a committee and/or bureau is selected by the members or delegates to make decisions for the party organization when the Conference or Congress is not in session. At the lower levels a party secretary and at the higher levels a Secretariat is responsible for carrying out the day to day work of the organization.

In its general outline, the party organization is relatively democratic in structure. Nominally, election proceeds upward from the broad base of the primary organizations to the All-Union Party Congress. Likewise, the executive organs at each level are nominally elected by and responsible to their parent Conference or Congress which is composed of duly elected representatives of the party members. However, within the C.P.S.U., the Western democratic tradition which holds that elected representatives are responsible to their electorate has been reversed. In reality, lower organs in the C.P.S.U. are responsible and subordinate to the higher organs which they have allegedly elected; the executive organs, rather than being guided by the instructions of the Conferences and Congresses, actually guide and direct the decisions and activities of elected representatives of the party membership.

All-Union Party Organization

THE CONGRESS OF THE COMMUNIST PARTY OF THE SOVIET UNION

The All-Union Party Congress is described by the Party Statutes as the "supreme organ" of the C.P.S.U. The Party Congress is to be convened by the Central Committee not less often than once every four years; it may be convened earlier at the discretion of the Central Committee or on the request of at least one third of the party membership represented at the preceding Party Congress (Rule 31). During the interval from 1939 to 1952, when the Congress was supposed to be convened at least once every three years, not one Congress was held. Although war is a legitimate excuse, the party did not convene a Congress until seven years after the termination of hostilities. Stalin's successors have been somewhat more scrupulous than he was in ordering the convocation of the Party Congress.

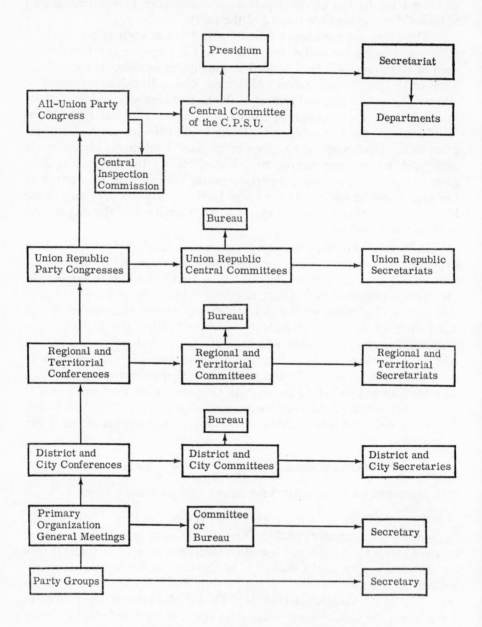

Figure 1. Organization of the Communist Party of the Soviet Union

The norms of representation at the Party Congress are fixed by the Central Committee. At the Nineteenth and Twentieth Party Congresses each voting delegate represented 5,000 party members, and at the extraordinary Twenty-First Party Congress in 1959 there was one delegate per 6,000 members. However, "consistently implementing the line calling for the development of inner-party democracy, the Party Central Committee . . . considerably broadened the norms of representation at the Twenty-Second Party Congress."[15] A total of 4,813 delegates were elected, including 4,408 voting delegates and 405 delegates with an advisory vote, each of whom represented 2,000 members or candidate members of the party. At the Twenty-Second Congress there were three and one-half times as many delegates as there were at each of the three preceding Congresses.[16]

The election of delegates to the Congress, as to all party bodies, is by secret ballot. The Statutes specify, "In elections, all party members have the unrestricted right to challenge candidates and to criticize them. Voting must be on individual candidates" (Rule 24). Whether this right is exercised depends on circumstances and the leadership of the party. The most important question is how the list of nominees is established. According to the *U.S.S.R. Illustrated Monthly,* the procedure is as follows:

> "At a regional conference or congress a nominating committee composed of representatives of the delegations from the primary organizations is established. This committee usually numbers from 150 to 300 depending on size of the congress or conference. After discussion and conferences with the delegations, a preliminary combined list of nominees is submitted to the congress or conference where the delegates have unlimited right to accept, reject and substitute candidates. Each nominee is discussed individually to determine who is to be left on the list. A majority vote is necessary for the candidate to be listed on the ballot. There is no restriction on the number of candidates on the ballot but the number elected cannot exceed the established norm of representation. Those nominees receiving the largest number of votes are declared elected with the provision that each one must be approved by at least half of the assembled delegates."[17]

What is not included in the preceding description of the procedure of electing delegates to a Congress is the manipulation and control by party officials of names to be listed on the ballots. The assumption that the relatively democratic electoral principles of the Party Statutes are violated frequently is upheld by letters from party members which have been published in the Soviet press. Although the following excerpts from letters do not refer to the election of delegates to an All-Union Party Congress, they describe undemocratic procedures which permeate electoral practices at all levels of the party organization. A party member described the nomination procedure this way:

> "Before the report and election meeting, the old party bureau prepares a list of candidates for the new bureau and instructs individual party members to nominate the chosen candidates at the meeting. After the communists, who have been so instructed, have nominated the candidates, a motion is immedi-

ately made to 'close nominations'. It should also be taken into account that the chairman of the meeting (also chosen ahead of time in many cases), makes every effort to obstruct the nomination of other candidates."[18]

Another party member complained:

". . . Comrade Podolsky, secretary of the party bureau and director of the administration, who was presiding at the meeting, spoke for the old party bureau in offering a list of seven candidates for the new party bureau. When the communists at the meeting attempted to add to the proffered list, all the candidates they named were rejected by the chairman under some excuse or other.

"Everything had been written down ahead of time by Comrade Podolsky —who would be nominated and by whom. We were ordered to vote for people who, in the majority of cases, were suitable to Comrade Podolsky. And if these orders had not been given the results of the elections, the list of candidates, and the way the meeting was run would have been different."[19]

Why the party has permitted the publication of letters which reveal the violation of the Party Statutes is not certain. Although it is remotely possible that the establishment of real elections is contemplated, it is more likely that letters such as these are designed to convey the false impression that manipulations are rare and when they do occur are not condoned by the leadership. In actuality, the manipulation of elections is unimportant with reference to policy formulation because all major decisions are made by the top party leaders rather than by the elected representatives of the party members.

To be elected to the All-Union Party Congress is considered to be a distinction and a reward. The party arranges to have all sections of the population represented, and the Credential Commission makes detailed statistical reports on age, occupation, education, nationality, sex and length of party membership of the delegates. The breadth of representation is used as a technique to enhance popular support for the party program.

According to the Statutes, the Congress, as the highest body of the C.P.S.U., elects the Central Committee and the Central Inspection Committee; hears and approves the reports of these committees and other central organizations; reviews, amends and approves the Program and Statutes of the Party; determines the line of the party on questions of domestic and foreign policy, and considers and decides major questions of communist construction (Rule 33). In theory, the delegates are free to criticize the leadership and its policies, to formulate new policies and to insist on their adoption, and to elect whom they choose to lead the party. These democratic potentials have never materialized. Because of the size and infrequent meetings of the Congress, and especially because of the autocratic practices of the party leadership, the delegates are convened primarily to be informed of the party line and of the decisions of the leadership. Since the Fifteenth Party Congress, when Stalin consolidated his dictatorship, free debate and spontaneous discussion have fallen into desuetude and all proposals of the party leadership have been adopted unanimously. The Congress has become a rubber stamp sounding board for the supreme party leadership.

THE CENTRAL COMMITTEE

Between sessions of the All-Union Party Congress, the Central Committee functions as the supreme organ of the Communist Party. The Party Statutes vest extraordinary authority in the Central Committee:

> "In the intervals between congresses the Central Committee of the Communist Party of the Soviet Union directs the entire work of the Party and local Party bodies; selects and places executive cadres; directs the work of central state organizations and public organizations of the working people through the Party groups within them; creates various agencies, institutions and enterprises of the Party and directs their work; appoints the editorial boards of central newspapers and magazines that function under its control; and distributes the funds of the Party budget and supervises its implementation (Rule 35)."

A plenary session of the Central Committee must be held not less than once every six months and extraordinary meetings may be called by the Presidium or the First Secretary. Membership of the Central Committee is fixed by the Party Congress. The Twenty-Second Party Congress in 1961 elected the largest Central Committee in the history of the party, consisting of 175 full members and 155 candidate members. Of these, almost two thirds had not previously been members of the Central Committee. Thus, the new "principle of systematic turn-over" was implemented. Most of the members of the Central Committee are party functionaries or high officials of the state bureaucracy. Usually included are: secretaries of the principal party organizations throughout the U.S.S.R., the Chairman and Vice-Chairmen of the Council of Ministers of the U.S.S.R. and other important officials of the governments of the U.S.S.R. and the Union Republics, leading members of the Presidium of the Supreme Soviet, military, and diplomatic leaders, trade union, youth organization and party publicists and eminent scientists and artists. Again, an attempt is made to represent all sections of the population. The Statutes point out that a member or candidate member of the Central Committee must by his entire activity justify the high trust placed in him by the party. If he has sullied his honor and dignity he cannot remain a member. He may be removed from membership if two-thirds of the members of the Central Committee vote by secret ballot in favor of his removal (Rule 26). The top party leadership apparently instructs the Central Committee to remove members who, for one reason or another, have failed to maintain the favor of the leadership. Thus, after Khrushchev's dismissal, his son-in-law, A. I. Adzhubei was removed from the Central Committee because of "mistakes in his work."[20]

The Central Committee is an organ of the party not of the state;

nevertheless the party leadership issues through the Central Committee general directives and resolutions that assume the character of legal ordinances when they are co-signed by the Chairman of the Council of Ministers or the Chairman of the Presidium of the Supreme Soviet. The Central Committee elects a Presidium, Secretariat and Control Committee and delegates specific responsibilities to each of these organs. It is held responsible for all party actions taken by these subdivisions and in theory has the power to reverse their decisions, change their membership and to resolve internal disputes within or between these organs.

In addition to the fact that the top echelon of the party leadership has preempted the power of the party, the Central Committee is too large a body to function effectively as a policy making organ. During the Stalin regime it, like the Congress, served merely to ratify the policy directives and changes announced by the party leadership. However, in June, 1957 at an extraordinary session, a Central Committee, which contained a strong pro-Khrushchev element, was able to overrule the Presidium. Thus, Khrushchev used the Central Committee to purge the Presidium of the "antiparty" majority which had attempted to curb his power. The Central Committee met more frequently and made decisions of greater importance under Khrushchev than under Stalin. However, except during times of intra-party conflict, such as the struggle for party leadership which followed Stalin's death and, to a somewhat lesser extent, the developments which resulted in Khrushchev's dismissal, the Central Committee, like its parent body, the Congress, serves primarily to ratify and legitimatize the decisions of the party leadership through approval by an elected body of the party. The major organs which operate under the nominal supervision of the Central Committee are summarized in Figure 2. The two most important organs of the Central Committee, the Presidium and the Secretariat, exercise the real powers of the Central Committee in its name. In reality, the Central Committee is the instrument of the Presidium and the Secretariat, rather than the reverse.

THE PRESIDIUM

The Presidium of the Central Committee of the Communist Party was established by the Nineteenth Party Congress in 1952 to replace the Political Bureau (Politburo) and the Organizational Bureau (Orgburo). It serves as the permanent executive organ of the party and in the name of the Central Committee directs all other organs of the party in all matters of policy. The number of members has varied from twenty-five voting members and eleven candidates in 1952 to eleven full members and five candidates in 1961, and ten full members and six candidates in 1964. Members of the Presidium are invariably top ranking party officials. Usually included among the Presidium members are the First Secretary of the

C.P.S.U.; Secretaries of the C.P.S.U.; the Chairman and one or more Vice-Chairmen of the U.S.S.R. Council of Ministers; the Chairman of the Presidium of the U.S.S.R. Supreme Soviet; and the incumbents in other ranking party or governmental posts.[21] Although members of the Presidium are formally "elected" by the Central Committee, it is almost certain that the slate designated by the dominant party leader or leaders is automatically ratified. Thus, the man or men at the very top of the party hierarchy select new candidates to be admitted into the "upper inner-circle" and on occasion, remove colleagues from this pinnacle of power. A number of Commissions or Bureaus are established by the Presidium, as indicated in Figure 2. The exact number and the titles of these organs have varied from time to time. Usually major responsibility for the conduct of a Bureau or Commission is assigned to the Presidium member who acts as a specialist in that area. Among the organs of the Presidium, one of the largest is the Bureau for the R.S.F.S.R. and its subordinate Bureaus for Party Organs, Agriculture, Industry, etc. The R.S.F.S.R., the Russian Union Republic, is unique in that it does not have a discrete Union Republic party organization. This uniqueness in party structure derives chiefly from the dominant role which the R.S.F.S.R., as the largest and most populous Union Republic, plays in the affairs of the C.P.S.U. In a sense, the C.P.S.U. is the party organization of the R.S.F.S.R. The Bureau for the R.S.F.S.R., which operates under the jurisdiction of the Presidium of the Central Committee of the C.P.S.U., coordinates and directs the work of subordinate party organizations, and supervises the economic, ideological and educational work of the party within the R.S.F.S.R.

The Party-State Control Committee was established in November, 1962 by joint action of the Presidium of the Central Committee, and the U.S.S.R. Council of Ministers. It is a unified organ of party and state control with subordinate branches established by the corresponding agencies at all party and governmental levels. The tasks of the Party-State control agencies include:

> "Rendering assistance to the party and the state in the fulfillment of the C.P.S.U. program, in organizing a systematic check on the execution of party and government directives, in the further improvement of the guidance of communist construction and in the observance of party and state discipline and socialist legality."[22]

This reorganization is purportedly based on Lenin's teaching that there should be a constant and unified system of party and state control which involves the participation of broad masses. Reports in the Soviet press indicate that since its establishment, the Party-State Control Committee has been extremely active in investigating cases of embezzlement, speculation, mismanagement in housing distribution, shortcomings in plan fulfillment, and unnecessary inefficiency in economic management.

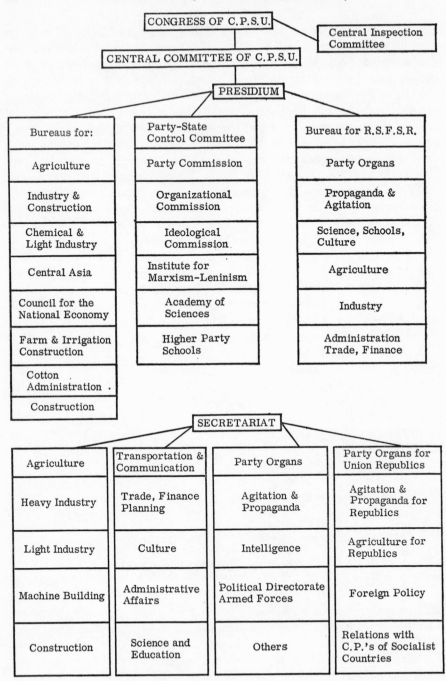

Figure 2. The Central Organs of the C.P.S.U.

The Party Commission is a truncated successor to the Party Control Committee which was abolished when the Party-State Control Committee was established in 1962. Its chief functions are the enforcement of party discipline, and the evaluation of appeals from party members with reference to expulsion from the party and party penalties which have been imposed by lower party organs. The appellate function is apparently not meaningless; it was reported that between the Twenty-First and Twenty-Second Party Congresses over 70,000 appeals had been examined and over 15,000 persons had been restored to party ranks, including a large number expelled from the party in the past owing to unfounded political charges."[23]

The fact that the Presidium has Bureaus for Agriculture, Industry, Construction and other branches of the economy is a demonstration of the close control which the party finds it expedient to exercise over the economy. The Bureau for Central Asia was established primarily because of economic problems in the Central Asian Union Republics. One of the most important Commissions of the Presidium is the Ideological Commission, which is invariably headed by one of the leading ideologists of the party. In conjunction with the Academy of Sciences, the party schools, the Institute of Marxism-Leninism, and the media of communication which operate under its supervision, it guides the ideological work of the party.

The Presidium usually meets once a week, or even more often at the discretion of its chairman. It deliberates on matters of high policy affecting the state as well as the party. Its communiques are considered to be politically binding on the government as well as on all party organs. The extent to which the Presidium exercises real power depends largely on whether the party leader has been able to preempt the locus of power and on his personality. Under Stalin all power was concentrated in the hands of the great dictator and even the Presidium, composed of the inner circle of party leaders, was powerless. Stalin announced his plans to his colleagues and they meekly agreed even when they disapproved. During the period of "collective leadership" from 1953 to 1957, real power was exercised by the Presidium. From 1957 until October, 1964, Khrushchev, who occupied the positions of Chairman of the Presidium, First Secretary of the C.P.S.U., and Chairman of the Council of Ministers of the U.S.S.R., held the locus of both party and state power. Although during much of this period he probably had the support of most of his colleagues on the Presidium on most matters, and was probably usually able to obtain consensus in the interest of party unity, his successors have indicated that on a number of occasions he acted in an arbitrary manner against the wishes of the majority. His increased proclivity to use dictatorial methods instead of conforming to the principle of collective leadership was given as one of the reasons for his removal from power. If the future can be judged by the past, it can be expected that for an undetermined time after the 1964 reorganization of the party power-pyramid, the Presidium will exercise significant decision-making power. However, it is likely that one of the party leaders will gradually work himself into a position of more or less absolute power, and as this happens, the decision-making functions of the Presidium will decline progressively.

THE SECRETARIAT

The brief, modest description in the Statutes of the functions of the Secretariat belies the tremendous influence of this "subordinate" organ of the Party Central Committee. The Secretariat is officially empowered to "direct current work, chiefly in the selection of cadres and organization of check upon fulfillment" (Rule 39). After the 1952 reorganization of the central organs of the party, the Secretariat assumed the powers that had been discharged previously by the Orgburo and relinquished none of the tremendous power it had developed under Stalin's long tenure as Secretary-General.

The Secretariat was created in 1920 to discharge administrative functions for the Political and Organizational Bureaus of the Central Committee and to insure that the decisions of these organs and of the Central Committee were properly executed by subordinate organs. At that time it consisted of three full-time secretaries all of whom were members of the Central Committee. In 1922 Stalin, who was also a member of the Politburo and Orgburo, was appointed Secretary-General. His overlapping membership was intended to guarantee coordination of the decisions of the Politburo and Orgburo, which were superior to the Secretariat. The Secretariat was also intended to be strictly subordinate to the Central Committee and was to implement its decisions.

Under Stalin the Secretariat was transformed gradually from a subordinate body into the central apparatus of power within the party. Because the entire state and party apparatus came under his direction, he was able to misuse his great power to liquidate the "enemies of the people" and personal enemies within the central party apparatus. The personnel of all local and intermediate party organizations were selected, supervised, guided and removed or transferred to more important party or government positions by the Secretariat. Stalin was able to pack subordinate branches of the party apparatus with his supporters and through these to hand-pick a sufficent proportion of the delegates to the Party Congress to maintain effective control over the composition of the Central Committee. He used his position as Secretary-General with skill to establish absolute power for himself and to set a precedent for his successor. The opportunity which the leading officer of the party (formerly the Secretary-General, now the First Secretary) enjoys to place supporters in important governmental and party positions, especially on the Central Committee, explains how the Central Committee can "override" the Presidium, in the event of disagreement among members of the Presidium as during the 1957 struggle for succession. After Khrushchev's appointment as First Secretary in 1953, he was able, like Stalin, to eliminate personal rivals and to maintain an effective monopoly of power. However, because police power was limited after the fall of Beria, he lacked one of Stalin's most powerful weapons of control. In the case of both Khrushchev and Stalin the combination of an able man, the key position, and disunited opponents who feared one another enabled the "moderate" Secretary to remove both real and potential opposition. Once a supreme leader is established, the Central Committee, Presidium and all other governmental and party organs tend to become docile. However, Khrushchev's removal from his position as First Secretary and from his other positions of power suggests that even after one man attains supremacy, these organs have latent power which, under appropriate circumstances, may be exercised to alter radically the locus of power within the party.

During recent years the membership of the Secretariat has varied between five and ten. The Central Committee elected by the Twenty-Second Congress (1961) established a nine man Secretariat.[24] Members of the Secretariat are selected in the same manner as members of the Presidium: a slate of Secretaries is designated by the dominant party leader or leaders for formal election by the Central Committee. Secretaries are invariably high ranking party leaders who may simultaneously be members of the Presidium of the Central Committee, or important governmental officers such as the Chairman of the Presidium of the Supreme Soviet or the Chairman of the Council of Ministers of the U.S.S.R. The overlapping membership between the most important party and governmental organs makes it more convenient for party leaders to govern the U.S.S.R. through the duly elected governmental organs which are legally responsible for governmental functions.

Although the powers assigned to the Secretariat by the Statutes are modest, the Secretariat, in fact, assumes major responsibility for the total functioning of the party and the state. Among the functions which it discharges are: (1) the selection, training and appointment of the vast force of full-time party functionaries who manage the party apparatus; (2) direction of the party apparatus; (3) supervision and control over governmental organs, agencies and offices, and all other organizations, including trade unions, youth organizations, and cultural, scientific, and educational institutions and societies; (4) administration of public opinion media. These tasks are administered through a number of major departments (Figure 2) that function directly under the Secretariat. These departments assume responsibility for the supervision of propaganda and agitation; educational affairs; party, trade union and Komsomol affairs; the selection of cadres and personnel; cultural and scientific affairs; building, trade, transportation and communication, finance and planning organs; heavy industry; light industry; agriculture; armed forces political administration; relations with the Communist Parties of other states; and foreign affairs. Each department is headed by either the First Secretary himself or by one of the other Secretaries. Obviously, many of these departments function in areas which in other countries come almost exclusively under the jurisdiction of the state. The problem of coordination between party and state decisions is, however, almost non-existent because the leading positions in governmental organs are ordinarily held by high ranking party functionaries. The U.S.S.R. is governed by a small number of party leaders, and especially by the First Secretary and the other party leaders who are members of the Secretariat or the Presidium of the Central Committee of the C.P.S.U.

Since the Secretariat assumes responsibility for the efficient functioning of the party, and for the economy and the administration of the entire country, it is of crucial importance to the Secretariat that a trusted and competent staff be selected for party and governmental organs. Neither Soviet citizens in general nor even party members are considered sufficiently trustworthy and capable to choose, by democratic procedures, personnel to fill important governmental and party positions. Consequently the Secretariat frequently manipulates elections to insure that candidates acceptable to it will be elected. Moreover, no limitations are placed on the sphere of jurisdiction of the Secretariat and particularly of the First Secretary. Directives may be issued by the Secretariat with reference to any sphere of party, governmental, economic, scientific, cultural or personal activities. More than any other organ of the party, the Secretariat is responsible for the violation of the democratic principles of the Party Statutes.

THE CENTRAL INSPECTION COMMISSION

The Central Inspection Commission is elected by the Party Congress and has limited control powers over the Central Committee and its subordinate organs. This control, however, is formal rather than substantive, since the Party Statutes (Rule 37) limit the Commission's functions to checking on the promptness of the conduct of affairs in central bodies of the party and auditing the treasury and undertakings of the Central Committee of the C.P.S.U.

Intermediate Party Organizations

Each Union Republic, with the exception of the R.S.F.S.R., maintains a party organization similar in structure to that of the All-Union organization. As previously indicated, party affairs within the R.S.F.S.R. are managed by the Central Committee of the C.P.S.U. through its Bureau for the R.S.F.S.R., rather than by an independent republican party organization. In the Union Republics, the "highest" party body is the Republic Party

Congress which is supposed to be convened at least once every two years in most republics or at least once every four years in a few republics (Ukraine, Belorussia, Kazakhstan and Uzbekistan). The Congress can be convened more often under special circumstances. In most Union Republics, the Congress has met with a fair degree of regularity even during the Stalin era. However, like the All-Union Congress, the republican congresses have functioned primarily to provide automatic approval for the decisions of the party leaders. Each Congress elects an Inspection Committee and a Central Committee which is required to assemble at least once every four months. The Central Committee, in turn, selects a Presidium and a Secretariat, the key organs which control party affairs within the republic. The First Party Secretary, who is ordinarily a *de facto* appointee of the First Secretary of the C.P.S.U., occupies a position of considerable power and influence. Included among the members of the Secretariat and the Presidium are important officials such as the Chairman of the Supreme Soviet of the Union Republic, the Chairman and Vice-Chairmen of the Council of Ministers of the Union Republic, First Secretaries of important regional party organizations, and perhaps one or two chairmen of major economic administrations.

In November, 1962, at Khrushchev's insistence, the organization of the party at and below the Union Republic level was revamped in accordance with the production principle. Parallel party organizations with separate committees and Secretariats for each of industry and agriculture were established at all levels. The only formal coordinating link between the Industrial Party Organization and the Agricultural Party Organization in a given geographical area was provided by the Central Committee at the Union Republic level. Each Central Committee established a Bureau for Industry and a Bureau for Agriculture, and presumably members of the two Bureaus were expected to confer about and coordinate the activities of the lower level Industrial and Agricultural Committees. One of the first major decisions of the post-Khrushchev leadership was to disband the separate Industrial and Agricultural Party Committees and to re-establish party organizations which correspond with the major political-administrative divisions of the country.[25] With the abolition of the dual structure of the party, an organization essentially similar to that which existed prior to 1962 was reintroduced.

The structure of the party organizations at the intermediate levels corresponds to that of the Union Republic party organizations, but the terminology is different; the meeting of delegates is called a Conference and the permanent committee is shorn of the adjective "central." As a general rule, each Party Committee has a First Secretary and two assistant Secretaries who exert a considerable amount of influence within their sphere of jurisdiction, and approximately ten subordinate departments, the titles and functions of which vary from area to area, depending upon type and variety of industrial and agricultural projects within the area of supervision. All party organizations have ideological and organizational departments which are usually headed by a Secretary. While the dual structure of the party was still in existence, Party Committees in agricultural areas were staffed with a number of inspector-party organizers who worked directly with party organizations on state and collective farms and gave them help in meeting "their chief task, increasing the output of agricultural products."[26] Party Committees in industrial areas had a staff of instructors each of whom supervised the work of one or more subordinate organizations; the instructor was supposed to uncover and criticize inadequacies, to provide concrete remedial guidance, to keep the responsible Secretary informed of the activities, strengths and shortcomings of the lower party organization, and to identify local party activists with potential for leadership. It is likely that the inspector-party organizers and the instructors, or officials who perform similar functions under different titles, will be retained under the current organization.

Within the limits of the sphere of jurisdiction, the duties, rights and responsibilities of the Congress or Conference, the Committee and the Secretaries of the intermediate organizations correspond to those of their counterparts of the central party apparatus. In all their work they are to be guided by the Program and Statutes of the C.P.S.U. and are to organize execution of the directives of the Central Committee of the C.P.S.U. (Rule 41). Rule 42 of the Party Statutes lists as the chief duties of the republic, territory, province, region and district party organizations and their executive bodies:

> (a) political and organizational work among the masses and their mobilization for accomplishment of the tasks of communist construction, for all-round development of industrial and agricultural production and for the fulfillment and overfulfillment of state plans; concern for the steady rise in the living standard and cultural level of the working people;
> (b) organization of ideological work; propaganda of Marxism-Leninism; increasing the communist awareness of the working people; guidance of the local press, radio and television; supervision of the work of cultural enlightenment institutions;
> (c) guidance of the Soviets, trade unions, the Young Communist League, cooperative enterprises and other public organizations through the Party groups within them; the ever broader enlistment of the working people in the work of these organizations; development of the initiative and activeness of the masses as a necessary condition for the gradual transition from a socialist state system to communist public self-government. Party organizations do not supplant Soviet, trade union, cooperative and other public organizations of the working people and must not permit a merging of the functions of Party and other agencies or unnecessary parallelism in work;
> (d) selection and placement of executive cadres and the rearing of them in the spirit of communist ideology, honesty and truthfulness and a high sense of responsibility to the Party and the people for the work entrusted to them;
> (e) broad enlistment of Communists in the conduct of Party work as unsalaried workers, as a form of public activity;
> (f) organization of various institutions and enterprises of the Party within the bounds of their republic, territory, province, region, city or district and

guidance of their work; distribution of Party funds within their organizations; systematic reporting to the higher Party body and accountability to it for their work.

This rule demonstrates clearly the attempt of the party to maintain rigorous control over all aspects of social organization.

Although the operations of the C.P.S.U. are characterized by rigid centralized control, the nature of the all-inclusive control or "guidance" which the party attempts to impose upon all spheres of activity, the geographical expanse of the country, and the need to adapt general directives to fit local conditions, make it inevitable that lower level party officials must exercise a considerable amount of executive initiative. The election of committees and secretaries at all levels is, of course, subject to the sanction of higher party organizations, up to the Central Committee of the C.P.S.U.; any higher party organization may veto designations or remove lower level officials from their party responsibilities. Within his own sphere of jurisdiction, each party official has residual power, which increases from officials in the lower to the intermediate and higher levels of the party hierarchy. At all levels, party functionaries exercise considerable influence over the activities of the Soviets, youth organizations, trade unions, cultural organizations and economic units. Party functionaries are expected to assume active leadership in the resolution of economic problems, and to take steps to ensure that the economic plan is fulfilled and over-fulfilled. During recent years, attempts have been made to ensure that party officials who exercise supervisory control over industrial and agricultural units have had adequate training and experience in that particular branch of the economy. Since party functionaries assume partial responsibility for the selection of cadres for positions in all economic, social and cultural institutions, as well as for party positions, they have at their command a vast amount of patronage which substantially increases their local power. Partial control over the allocation of funds for public projects and, at the primary level, supervision of the allocation of housing to individuals also increases the power of local party officials.

The responsibilities of the party organizations for propaganda and agitation include the publication of orthodox party literature, the selection of editors for party newspapers and other publications, supervision of the political training of party and governmental officials and propagandists, the organization of lectures and other forms of ideological education for party members and the masses, and general control over all cultural and educational endeavors to ensure that ideological orthodoxy is maintained and strengthened. Party officials direct election campaigns so as to foment popular consensus in the party's leadership of the state, and participate directly in the selection of candidates for elective posts in both the party and state apparatus.

In all spheres of activity the chief duty of the party official is to carry out and enforce the directives and decrees of the central party leadership. For a number of obvious reasons, it is not easy for the party functionaries to fulfill the multitude of tasks to the complete satisfaction of their party superiors. A party secretary may be able to perform in an exemplary manner in several areas, but because of limitations due to his training, experience, personality or time, may perform at less than the expected standard of efficiency in some other areas. Since party control through the lower level party organizations and officials is designed to permeate all aspects of life in the U.S.S.R., the party official is expected to be highly proficient in many areas. On occasion, the party line with respect to certain problems changes so rapidly or so often that lower level party officials may not know what policy they are expected to enforce. Excellent plans for the enforcement of a defunct policy may have to be discarded at a moment's notice. Lower level party officials are used as convenient scapegoats to account for failures which would, without scapegoats, be embarrassing for the infallible leaders. The rate of turnover among party officials in the lower echelons of the party hierarchy tends to be very high, sometimes amounting to 50 percent during a one-year period. Those who survive over a period of years generally move upward to positions of greater power and prestige.

The Primary Party Organizations

The primary party organization is the lowest level in the party pyramid. As of January, 1965, there were 311,907 primary organizations.[27] Primary party organizations may be established in places of employment such as plants, factories, state farms, collective farms, units of the Soviet army and educational institutions, wherever there are no fewer than three party members. In employment units with more than 50 party members and candidate members, party organizations within the overall primary organization may be set up in shops, livestock brigades or departments with the authorization of the superior Party Committee. These organizations and primary organizations with fewer than 50 members may sub-divide by brigades or other production units into party groups. In large enterprises and institutions with more than 300 party members and candidate members, and in other organizations with more than 100 communists where special production conditions and geographical dispersion make it necessary, the primary organization may be subdivided into shop, sector or territorial units with the rights of primary organizations on the authorization of the higher level Party Committee. These subdivisions are designed to facilitate meetings and to intensify party activity.

The highest body of the primary organization is the party meeting which is held not less than once a month. The primary or shop party organization elects a bureau for a term of one year to conduct current work;

the number of its members is fixed by the party meeting. Organizations with fewer than 15 members elect a secretary and an assistant secretary instead of a bureau. As a rule, organizations with fewer than 150 members do not have a full-time paid secretary. Collective farm organizations with more than 50 members, and industrial organizations with more than 300 members may, with the approval of the superior Party Committee, elect a committee to serve as the executive organ of the organization.

The broad network of primary party organizations is the foundation of the party; they make it possible to exert party influence on all branches of the national economy, culture, state administrative organizations, and public organizations, without exception.[28] The very extensive duties and functions of the primary party organizations are described in detail in Article 58 of the Statutes:

The primary Party organization:
(a) admits new members to the C.P.S.U.;
(b) rears Communists in a spirit of devotion to the cause of the party, ideological conviction and communist ethics;
(c) organizes the study by Communists of Marxist-Leninist theory in close connection with the practice of communist construction and opposes any attempts at revisionist distortions of Marxism-Leninism and its dogmatic interpretation;
(d) concerns itself with enhancing the vanguard role of Communists in labor and in the socio-political and economic life of enterprises, collective farms, offices, educational institutions, etc.;
(e) acts as the organizer of the working people in carrying out routine tasks of communist construction; heads socialist competition for the fulfillment of state plans and pledges *of the working people;* mobilizes the masses for disclosing and making better use of the internal reserves of enterprises and collective farms and for widely introducing in production the achievements of science, technology, and the experience of leading workers; works for the strengthening of labor discipline and for a steady rise in labor productivity and an improvement of quality of output; shows concern for protecting and increasing public wealth at enterprises and state and collective farms;
(f) conducts mass agitation and propaganda work; rears the masses in the spirit of communism; helps the working people to develop skills in administering state and public affairs;
(g) on the basis of broad development of criticism and self-criticism, combats manifestations of bureaucracy, localism and violations of state discipline; thwarts attempts to deceive the state; takes measures against laxity, mismanagement and waste at enterprises, collective farms and institutions;
(h) assists the region, city and district Party committees in all their activity and accounts to them for its work.
The Party organization must see to it that every Communist observes in his own life and inculcates in the working people the moral principles set forth in the Program of the C.P.S.U., *in the moral code of the builder of communism.*

The work of the primary organization is directed by the secretary and the party bureau. Either the secretary himself or his delegated representative is responsible for the recruitment and training of agitators, the organization of political study circles, lectures and conferences, supervision of Komsomol units and the collection of party dues. The close contact of the primary organizations with the masses and their multiplicity of functions make them the chief instrument of party domination over Soviet society. The work of all managerial personnel in every enterprise, office, farm, school and state institution is supervised. Decisions or lack of decisions by managerial personnel may be criticized through opinions, recommendations and censures, reports of which are sent to the appropriate party organs. Errors and shortcomings of governmental officials are reported to the latter's administrative superiors as well as to the appropriate party organs. In 1959 the primary party units were authorized to establish special control commissions composed of party activists to check on the fulfillment of state orders and deliveries, the rational use of equipment, and the quality of output, and to propose measures to reduce costs and increase output. Subsequently, much of the work of these commissions has been taken over by local branches of the Party-State Control Committee.

The primary party organizations are charged with the task of guiding the masses in their everyday labor and activities toward the achievement of the party's goals of perfecting socialism and eventually establishing communism. To this end they conduct political orientation meetings and classes on Marxism-Leninism for the workers, propagandize the party program, publish shop and office newspapers, recruit and train new party members, direct socialist competitions and use other techniques to improve production norms, to stimulate labor efficiency and discipline, and to promote the social and cultural interests of the workers. They also function as the eyes and ears of the party at every level of social organization, and ferret out wrongdoers, grafters, parasites, incompetents and anti-social and criminal elements. The primary party organizations form the major link between the party elite and the masses.

As might be expected, the primary organizations do not perform all of these functions with maximum efficiency. The Soviet press is replete with complaints about the failure of the primary organizations to work with the masses, dullness of ideological indoctrination, poor organizational work within economic units, and misdemeanors of party members which pass unpunished by their organizations. One of the most frequent complaints is that the members of the primary party organizations attempt to cover up shortcomings and errors in their sphere of operation, whether or not they have responsibility for the errors, because of fear of censure and punishment.

The Party Members

Any citizen of the Soviet Union, who accepts the Party Program, takes an active part in communist construction, works in one of the party organizations, carries out party decisions and pays membership dues, may be a member of the C.P.S.U. (Rule 1). Admission is open to socially conscious and active workers, peasants and representatives of the intelligentsia, devoted to communism, who have attained the age of eighteen (Rule 4). Young persons up to twenty years of age inclusive may join the party only via the Y.C.L. This rule postpones but does not prohibit the application for party affiliation by youths who are not members of the Komsomol.

The admission procedure is designed to provide a thorough scrutiny of the political, moral, and occupational qualities of prospective members. The applicant must file a declaration of his desire to join the party, complete a questionnaire which covers his personal, educational and occupational history, and provide recommendations from three persons who have belonged to the party for at least three years and have known and worked with the applicant for at least one year. Y.C.L. members may substitute the recommendation of the Y.C.L. district or city committee for the recommendation of one party member. Persons who formerly belonged to other parties (before the 1917 revolution, or in another country prior to having become a citizen of the U.S.S.R.) may join the party in conformity with the regular procedure, but only if their admission is ratified by the province or territory committee or the Central Committee of a Union Republic Communist Party. Sponsors are held responsible for the objectivity of their description of the applicant's political, work and moral qualifications. Applications are thoroughly reviewed by non-staff party commissions of approximately fifteen members. According to a recent statement in *Partiinaya zhizn:*

". . . the members of these commissions and Party committee instructors study materials on admissions and visit collective and state farms, enterprises and institutions to hear the opinions of communists and non-Party people concerning comrades who have applied for Party membership. Before the question of admission is brought up in the bureau, there is extensive discussion with the applicant in the commission. One of the secretaries of the Party committee takes part in the talks. This practice gives the Party agency a chance to gain a fuller impression of the comrade who is entering the Party."[29]

Applications are then deliberated on an individual basis by the general meeting of the primary organization, and if approved, are referred to the district or city party committee for ratification.

The successful applicant must serve a probationary period as a party candidate for at least one year. During this time he must familiarize himself with the program, statutes, doctrine and activities of the party and demonstrate loyalty, diligence and other qualities deemed necessary for party membership. During the applicant's period of candidature, the primary organization is expected to guide his preparation through lectures and discussions on political topics, the "personal approach," meaningful assignments and "comradely guidance." Candidates pay the same fees as party members, and may participate in all the activities of the organization. However, they may not serve on executive committees or as delegates to conferences and their votes are of advisory value only. After one year the candidate is reevaluated. The primary party organization may decide that because of negative personal or other qualifications, the individual should be dropped as a potential party member, or that the period of preparation should be extended, or that the applicant is acceptable, in which case party membership is recommended. Again, the decision of the primary party committee requires ratification by the superior party committee.

The obligations of party members are impressive. According to Rule 2 of the Statutes, it is the duty of each party member:

(a) to fight for the creation of the material and technical base of communism, to set an example of the communist attitude toward labor, to raise labor productivity, to take the initiative in all that is new and progressive, to support and propagate advanced experience, to master technology, to improve his qualifications, to safeguard and increase public, socialist property—the foundation of the might and prosperity of the Soviet homeland;

(b) to carry out Party decisions firmly and undeviatingly, to explain the policy of the Party to the masses, to help strengthen and broaden the Party's ties with the people, to be considerate and attentive toward people, to respond promptly to the wants and needs of the working people;

(c) to take an active part in the political life of the country, in the management of state affairs and in economic and cultural construction, to set an example in the fulfillment of public duty, to help develop and strengthen communist social relations;

(d) to master Marxist-Leninist theory, to raise his ideological level and to contribute to the molding and rearing of the man of communist society. To combat *resolutely* any manifestations of bourgeois ideology, remnants of a private-property psychology, *religious prejudices* and other survivals of the past, to observe the *principles* of communist morality and to place public interests above personal ones;

(e) to be an active proponent of the ideas of socialist internationalism and Soviet patriotism among the masses of the working people, to combat survivals of nationalism and chauvinism, to contribute by word and deed to strengthening the friendship of peoples of the U.S.S.R. and the fraternal ties of the Soviet people with the peoples of the socialist countries and the proletarians and working people of all countries;

(f) *to strengthen* the ideological and organizational unity of the Party in every way, to safeguard the Party against the infiltration of persons unworthy of the lofty title of Communist, to be truthful and honest with the Party *and people,* to display vigilance, to preserve Party and state secrets;

(g) to develop criticism and self-criticism, to boldly disclose shortcomings and strive for their removal, to combat ostentation, conceit, complacency and localism, to rebuff firmly any attempts to suppress criticism, to resist any actions detrimental to the Party and the state and to report them to Party bodies, up to and including the Central Committee of the C.P.S.U.;

(h) to carry out unswervingly the Party line in the selection of cadres according to their political and work qualifications. To be uncompromising in all cases of violation of the Leninist principles of the selection and training of cadres;

(i) to observe Party and state discipline, which is equally binding on all Party members. The Party has a single discipline, one law for all Communists, regardless of their services or the positions they hold;

(j) *to help in every way to strengthen the defense might of the U.S.S.R., to wage a tireless struggle for peace and friendship among peoples.*

Party members, with the exception of the full-time paid party officials, are expected to perform these many and demanding duties without remuneration. On the contrary, individuals pay for the privilege of being members of the Communist Party of the Soviet Union. In 1961 membership dues comprised 67.8 percent of the party budget, income from publishing was 31.7 percent and other revenue .5 percent. An initiation fee in the amount of 2 percent of monthly earnings is assessed upon admission as a candidate member of the party, and thereafter candidates and members contribute from .5 to 3 percent of their monthly income as dues, with the percentage assessment increasing with the rate of pay. Failure to pay dues for three consecutive months may result in being dropped from the party. Needless to say, the majority of party members do not fully discharge their obligations to the party. Articles in the Soviet press indicate that many party members put self-interest before the interest of the party and the communist cause, fall far short of the party ideal in their work and personal habits, adopt a passive attitude toward party work, or have only limited knowledge of the party program and Marxist-Leninist ideology. Despite the careful selection procedure, and the subsequent guidance and training of successful applicants, reports that a party member has been arrested for criminal misdemeanors are not uncommon. In 1964 almost 31,000 persons were expelled from the party "for various actions incompatible with the title Communist."[30]

In exchange for the assumption of the exacting obligations, the party member is, according to Rule 3 of the Statutes, granted the following rights:

(a) to elect and be elected to Party bodies;

(b) to discuss freely questions of the Party's policies and practical activities at Party meetings, conferences and Congresses, at the meetings of Party committees and in the Party press; to introduce motions; openly to express and uphold his opinion until the organization has adopted a decision;

(c) to criticize any Communist, regardless of the position he holds, at Party meetings, conferences and Congresses and at plenary meetings of Party committees. Persons guilty of suppressing criticism or persecuting anyone for criticism must be held to strict Party responsibility, up to and including expulsion from the ranks of the C.P.S.U.;

(d) to participate in person at Party meetings and bureau and committee meetings at which his activity or conduct is discussed;

(e) to address questions, statements or proposals to Party bodies at any level up to and including the Central Committee of the C.P.S.U. and to demand an answer on the substance of his address.

If a clause, such as "under certain circumstances" were appended to each stated right, the Statutes would correspond more closely to reality. Examples of infringements of the right to elect and be elected to party bodies have already been described. Certainly, at least in the past, the right to criticize was violated in the extreme. In Khrushchev's report to the Twentieth Party Congress, Stalin was, among other things, accused of suppressing criticism and, accordingly, should have been expelled from the party. Khrushchev also stated that those who dared to complain about former police chief

Beria were shot. Under such circumstances, many party members, no doubt, found that preservation of life was more important than fulfillment of the rights of the Party Statutes. Leading party officials admit that at the local and intermediate levels of the party organization, party members are often afraid to criticize or reveal the shortcomings or even the illegal activities of party officials for fear of expulsion from the party or other reprisals.[31]

The party has never allowed indiscriminate admission to its ranks.[32] Admission standards have been rigidly maintained to protect the party from infiltration by opportunists, careerists, enemies of the people, anti-party elements, incompetents and luke-warm supporters. According to Khrushchev "If we were to say that anyone who wanted to could join our Communist Party we would probably have many tens of millions of members. But we say that we do not need this. To become a member of the Party one must not only understand communism but also be an active fighter. Not all of those who support the idea of the Communist Party are capable of this."[33] Even after full membership and positions of prestige within the party have been attained, the threat of expulsion is always real and iminent for those who fail to maintain the party's standards for loyalty and efficiency. Members or candidate members who fail to perform the duties set forth in the Statutes or commit other offenses may be warned, advised, reprimanded, demoted to candidate status for a period up to one year, or may be subjected to the "highest party penalty," expulsion from the party. Expulsion may be followed by other sanctions, such as dismissal from a job, transfer to an undesirable location, and sometimes by police sanctions; exile, deportation or imprisonment. Reasons and evidence to justify criminal prosecution are not difficult to find for former communists who have proved disloyal, unreliable, disreputable, negligent or incompetent. The turnover in party membership is fairly high; some members find the duties and obligations too exacting and take the easy way out by failing to pay membership dues. During 1964 almost 69,000 persons were expelled or dropped from the party for various reasons.[34]

The majority of Soviet citizens do not qualify for party membership, while many who qualify have little motivation to become party activists. Reluctance to join the party may be due to any one of several factors. Many Soviet citizens, like many citizens in other countries, have little interest in politics or are more preoccupied with personal than with political matters. No information is available to permit an estimate of the number of persons who refrain from joining the party for ideological reasons, but it is probable that there are many such people. A goodly number, no doubt, find the obligations too exacting or fear the consequences of expulsion. Membership in this elite group is fraught with risk to the family as well as to the individual.

Reasons for joining the party vary from person to person. Some may believe so thoroughly in the correctness of the ideology that they urgently desire to belong to the elite vanguard and to assist in building a communist utopia. Some join for opportunistic reasons. Others, including successful industrial captains and members of the armed forces may be reluctant to reject an invitation to join the party; pressures that can be applied are often convincing arguments in favor of assuming "social responsibilities" toward the working people. For the ambitious, party membership offers many potential rewards. Party membership is a prerequisite for most positions of leadership, power and responsibility. By rising within the ranks of the party, the member may eventually be able to penetrate the power elite. If, however, he recognizes that his political acumen and fortitude are inferior to his technical and managerial skills, he may prefer a bureaucratic career within the state administration, where the risks are somewhat less and the tenure prospects are better. Party membership offers competent and reliable persons a vehicle of rapid upward social mobility and a medium to attain high professional status.

Party Growth and Social Composition

In 1965 approximately 5 percent of the population of the U.S.S.R. were members of the Communist Party. At no time in the past, did party membership exceed this small percentage of the total population. Because of the difficult circumstances under which the party was established it had to have a conspiratorial character and a small but disciplined membership. Even after the Bolsheviks seized power, Lenin presented cogent arguments in favor of the elitist principles and his instruction that the chief thing is not an increase in membership but an increase in the quality of the party's ranks has been followed by his successors. The emphasis has always been on quality rather than quantity. Nevertheless, as indicated in Table 1, membership in the Communist Party of the Soviet Union has increased from a mere 23,600 conspirators in January, 1917 to almost 12 million party members and candidates in January, 1965. The post-Stalin leadership has attempted to strengthen its links with the masses by enlarging the size of the party and at the same time expanding its social base.

The party can increase or decrease membership with relative ease. The rate of increase has been accelerated considerably during the past several years. During the interval between the Twentieth Party Congress (1956), and the Twenty-Second Party Congress (1961), party membership increased by more than two and one-half million, of whom more than half came from the ranks of the Y.C.L.[35] Almost twice as many new members were accepted in 1960 (545,155) as in 1956 (283,211).[36] From October 1, 1961 to January 1, 1965, membership in the party increased by more than two million, with the average yearly increase exceeding 620,000. The party could, however, increase its size considerably more than it has.

Increased membership would add to the active support of the regime and, since elections are still manipulated, would not endanger the position of the party leadership. However, more full-time paid party officials would be required to check on the members. Moreover, because of the party's complete monopoly of power in the U.S.S.R., it can function without a numerically strong party membership.

Table 1

Membership in the C.P.S.U. for Selected Years*

January 1	Members	Candidates	Total
1917			
1918			23,600
1933	2,203,951	1,351,387	115,000
1938	1,405,879	514,123	3,655,338
1945	3,965,530	1,794,389	1,920,002
1952	6,013,259	868,886	5,760,369
1956	6,767,644	405,877	6,882,145
1959	7,622,356	616,775	7,173,521
1961 (Oct. 1)	8,872,516	843,489	8,239,131
1963	9,581,149	806,047	9,716,005
1965	10,811,443	946,726	10,387,196
			11,758,169

*Source: Merle Fainsod, *How Russia is Ruled* (Cambridge: Harvard University Press, 1953), p. 212; *Partiinaya zhizn*, No. 1, January, 1962, pp. 44-54; *Partiinaya zhizn*, No. 8, April, 1963, pp. 14-20; *Partiinaya zhizn*, No. 10, May, 1965, pp. 8-17.

Just as the party has increased party membership by liberalizing admission standards, it has used the purge or *chistka*, as an effective instrument for the removal of members. Purges occurred as early as 1921 when the first mass purification campaign against opportunists and class enemies who had infiltrated the party took place under Lenin's direction. Under Stalin the purge became an institutionalized form of terrorism through which he destroyed all potential opposition and consolidated his personal autocratic power over the party apparatus. From January 1, 1933 to January 1, 1938 party membership dropped by over 1,700,000 because of the purge, despite the addition of thousands of new members during this period. For many, expulsion from the party constituted only a minor portion of the punishment for the alleged wrong-doing. Recently released figures state that of the 1966 delegates to the Seventeenth Party Congress in 1934, 1,108 were killed, and of the 139 members of the Central Committee elected by the Seventeenth Congress, 98 were destroyed; thus, 56 percent of the delegates and 70 percent of the Central Committee were victims of the purge.[37]

Purges have been both beneficial and detrimental to the Soviet system. Their chief advantage is the preservation of the monopoly of power for the party by removing all real and potential opposition. Party unity is safeguarded, and the army, police and all other organizations are kept strictly subordinate to the party under the threat of the purge. However, the purge technique has several associated disadvantages. Cruelty and brutality seldom arouse admiration. Although the Soviet population is powerless, the party has probably lost the respect and active support of many citizens because of its terroristic methods. More important to the Soviet leadership is the disapproval of potential friends of the Soviet Union. Stalin's bloody purges antagonized millions of citizens in other countries, particularly in the Communist-ruled countries of Central Eastern Europe where his system of terror was brutally emulated. Realizing the detrimental effects of the bloody purges, the post-Stalin leadership posthumously exonerated many of the purged leaders, both in the U.S.S.R. and Central Eastern Europe, and after executing Beria and his collaborators, halted the bloody purges. Khrushchev's use of the purge was more humane. The members of the "anti-party" faction were publicly chastized and were removed from positions of power and responsibility but were not murdered. Although Khrushchev limited himself to the "guilt" purge, he too used the purge technique effectively to eliminate personal rivals and factionalism within the party. Khrushchev's successors appear to be following his lead.

Stalin's drastic purges in the mid-1930's weeded out more than half the membership of the party, including many of those in leading positions, and left the party in a weakened condition. However, during World War II membership trebled, because ideological standards were lowered, and persons who distinguished themselves in battle were gathered into the ranks of the party as patriotic examples. Heroism became the ideological value symbol of the Communist Party in its greatest struggle for survival. Following the war, those who failed to perfect their ideological preparation were dropped from the party and more rigorous admission standards were reinstituted. Khrushchev stated: "By getting rid of those casual people, the Party has become stronger and more solid."[38] During the late 1950's and early 1960's a party growth was again encouraged.

If the party members were the rulers of the Soviet Union, the social composition of the party would be of crucial importance. However, since all major decisions are made by the party leadership rather than the members, it is of little consequence if the percentage of party members from a particular group does not correspond exactly with the percentage of that group in the total population. The Communist Party does, however, seek to be "represented" at all social levels, in all production and organizational units, and in all segments of the population, so that it will be informed about activities, aspirations, and the general state of mind of the entire population. In the absence of democratic forms of expression, the party uses its members to communicate to the leadership the feelings and wishes of the population. More important, the membership is used as a network of agents to create social consensus in its policies and maintain effective control over mass expression and behavior. To achieve this omnipresence of the party within

Soviet society, all occupational groups, nationalities, geographic areas and social strata must be represented in the party.

The official recruitment policy of the C.P.S.U. toward selected occupational groups has varied from time to time. During the early post-revolutionary period, there was discrimination against the peasantry and especially against the intelligentsia educated under Tsarism, while the workers were favored. By the mid-1930's Stalin began a campaign to recruit increasing numbers of the technical intelligentsia. Immediately preceding World War II administrative employees were accorded favored treatment. Formal impediments to the recruitment of peasants were removed during the 1930's but by 1939 rural areas had only 20 percent of the membership although 68 percent of the total population resided in rural areas. The rural-urban discrepancy has decreased gradually, although farm workers are still less well represented than any other group. Currently, approximately one-third of the party members and approximately one-half of the total population reside in rural areas. Party membership of the Soviet intelligentsia has increased proportionately more than that of any other group. Since the party with its many responsibilities needs highly trained and competent people in key positions, it is not surprising that it has admitted large numbers of the intelligentsia to its ranks. However, during the late 1950's, Khrushchev initiated a campaign to accelerate the recruitment of collective farmers and blue collar workers. This policy has been continued by the present leadership.

Although the increased emphasis on the recruitment of workers and collective farmers has held in check, to a certain extent, the tendency for over-representation of the administrative, managerial and technical intelligentsia, this stratum continues to represent the predominant element in the party. Table 2 summarizes 1960 admission rates to the party and party membership by occupation at time of admission for the years 1961 and 1965. In 1961, and again in 1965, blue collar workers, including state farm workers, accounted for slightly over one-third of the party membership, collective farmers one-sixth, and managers, technical experts and personnel in science, education, public health, and the arts approximately one-third. The rate of admission of workers and collective farmers in 1960 was higher than for previous years, as reflected by percentage of membership in 1961, whereas the admission rate for the employee category, which included the intelligentsia, declined. However, from 1961 to 1965 the percentage membership of collective farmers decreased slightly while that of the intelligentsia increased slightly. Moreover, the figures for percentage of membership markedly underestimate the proportion of party members who could be described as members of the intelligentsia since social classification in party statistics is determined by occupation at time of entry into the party. With increased education and experience, and with the help of their party membership, a large proportion of the young people who are admitted as workers and collective farmers eventually become managers, administrators or technical experts. In addition to being numerically strong within the party, members of the intelligentsia fill most of the leading posts.

Table 2

Admission Rates and Membership by Occupational Status

Occupational Status	% of Members Admitted in 1960	% of Total Membership Jan. 1961	% of Total Membership Jan. 1965
Workers	43.1	35.0	37.3
Collective Farmers	21.7	17.3	16.5
Employees	34.3	47.7	46.2
Included among employees:			
Engineers, technicians, agronomists, economists, architects	23.5*	13.4	15.0
Heads of organizations, institutes and enterprises		4.8	3.6
Personnel in science, education, health, and the arts		10.3	10.8
Personnel in trade and public catering		2.3	2.7
Personnel in inspection, accounting and clerical work		5.6	5.0
Other employees		11.2	9.1

Source: The Party in Figures (1956-1961), *Partiinaya zhizn*, No. 1, January, 1962, pp. 44-54 (C.D.S.P., Vol. XIV, No. 3, pp. 3-6, 25); The C.P.S.U. in Figures (1961-1964), *Partiinaya zhizn*, No. 10, May, 1965, pp. 8-17. (C.D.S.P., Vol. XVII, No. 29, pp. 14-18)

*The 23.5% includes "engineers, technicians and other specialists." Admission figures are not available for the other categories of employees.

Table 3 presents the distribution of party membership by Union Republics and by ethnic groups, and for comparison purposes, includes the corresponding distribution of the total population. The party leaders have not committed the blunder of giving membership preference or of refusing to admit new members on the basis of ethnic or national origin, (although some observers, on the basis of rather inconclusive evidence, assert there has been a quota for Jews), and have, at the same time, attempted to secure balanced party representation in all Union Republics. Nevertheless, substantial disparities exist between Union Republics and between ethnic groups. The R.S.F.S.R. has a disproportionately high number of party members, while membership rates in all other republics, with the exception of the Georgian and Armenian S.S.R.'s are low in proportion to the total population. Similar trends are apparent with respect to party membership by ethnic groups: Russians, and to a lesser extent, Georgians and Armenians, are over-represented while Uzbeks, Moldavians and Lithuanians are particularly under-represented. One of the primary reasons for the disparities is the interest of the local population and the success of party indoctrination and recruitment. Since the mid-1950's emphasis has been placed on increasing party membership in the under-represented Union Republics and ethnic groups, and a trend toward decreased disparities is evident. Russian party members, however, because of their numerical preponderance, continue to play a dominant role in the C.P.S.U., and to occupy many of the leading positions in the party organizations of non-Russian areas.

Table 3

Distribution of Population and Party Membership
By Union Republics and By Ethnic Groups (1965)

Republic	% of Total Population	% of Party Membership	Ethnic Group	% of Total Population	% of Party Membership
R.S.F.S.R.	55.8	66.7	Russians	54.9	62.4
Ukraine	19.9	15.5	Ukrainians	18.0	15.4
Kazakhstan	4.6	3.8	Kazakhs	1.7	1.5
Uzbekistan	4.0	2.7	Uzbeks	2.9	1.7
Belorussia	3.8	2.7	Belorussians	3.8	3.3
Georgia	1.9	2.1	Georgians	1.3	1.7
Azerbaidzhan	1.8	1.7	Azerbaidzhani	1.4	1.2
Moldavia	1.4	.7	Moldavians	1.1	.3
Lithuania	1.3	.7	Lithuanians	1.1	.5
Kirghizia	1.0	.7	Kirghiz	.5	.3
Latvia	1.0	.8	Latvians	.7	.4
Tadzhikistan	1.0	.6	Tadzhik	.7	.4
Armenia	.9	.9	Armenians	1.4	1.6
Turkmenistan	.8	.5	Turkmens	.5	.3
Estonia	.6	.5	Estonians	.5	.3
			Other	9.5	8.8
U.S.S.R.	100.0	100.0			
			U.S.S.R.	100.0	100.0

Source: The Party in Figures (1961-1964), *Partiinaya zhizn,* No. 10, May, 1965, pp. 8-17. (C.D.S.P., Vol. XVII, No. 29, pp. 14-18)

Although women are granted complete equality with men, women constitute only about one-fifth (2,372,461 in 1965) of the total party membership. This represents a significant proportionate increase since the pre-World War II period. There has been no discrimination by the party against women, but membership by women in the party is less than that by men because women are late-comers to politics, and because many women conclude realistically that they cannot combine the discharge of party duties with homemaking and careers. The highest party positions are held by men but women are becoming increasingly important in Soviet politics. The Twentieth Party Congress elected a woman (Mme. Furtseva) to both the Presidium and the Secretariat of the Central Committee. The Twenty-Second Party Congress elected five women as full members and six women as candidate members of the Central Committee, and a female chairman of the Central Inspection Commission of the C.P.S.U. (N. A. Muravyeva).[39] Several women have important posts as regional first secretaries.

The party caters to a fairly youthful membership. By 1965 more than three-quarters of the party members had been raised under Soviet rule.[40] At that time 6 percent of the members had been with the party for more than 30 years, 51 percent for 10 to 30 years, 19 percent for 4 to 10 years, and 24 percent had membership of three years standing or less. Party officials point out that the combination of goodly numbers of experienced cadres and young people "make it possible for party organizations to adhere unswervingly to the Leninist principle of combining old and young cadres in placing party forces."[41] Despite the frequent purges which have removed whole factions of older leaders, the top echelon of the party elite are, on the average, considerably older than the majority of the party members.

Since the educational level of the entire population is improving, increasing numbers of party members are well educated. Table 4 presents the educational achievements of party members and candidates in 1961 and 1965. Party members are encouraged to improve their educational qualifications, since leadership roles in party work, and in the administration and the economy can be entrusted only to well-trained persons. Promising younger party members may be selected for additional training in administrative, organizational and propaganda methods in one of the party schools. A Higher Party School attached to the Central Committee provides advanced training for candidates for leading positions at the All-Union, republican, territorial or provincial levels. Only persons who have graduated from a higher educational institute, and are recommended strongly by a high level party committee, are eligible for admission. The Union Republics and some of the territories and provinces operate two and four year party schools for candidates with higher and secondary education respectively. Party schools at this level are designed to provide training for potential, intermediate level party officials. The party schools provide intensive training in a vast array of subjects including Marxism-Leninism, history of the party and the Soviet Union, the international working class and national-liberation movements, law, party and state administration, planning, trade, finance, accounting and technology relevant to major branches of industry and agriculture. The Academy of Social Sciences (formerly the Marx-Engels Institute) is also maintained by the Central Committee, under its Agitation and Propaganda Department, to provide intensive training in Marxism-Leninism and the social sciences for party specialists who are to be assigned to important positions as journalists, editors and research writers. Republican and intermediate party organizations offer a number of short intensive courses on various topics, including Marxism-Leninism, propaganda techniques, administration, technology and planning to enhance the efficiency of party functionaries at the city and district levels. Obviously, the party leadership attaches great importance to the training and qualifications of the current and potential party leaders.

Table 4
Formal Education of Party Members, and Candidates.

Educational Level	Percentage 1961	Percentage 1965
Higher education	13.7	15.0
Incomplete higher	2.9	2.6
Secondary	27.2	30.1
Partial secondary education	28.4	27.9
Elementary	27.8	24.4

Source: The C.P.S.U. in Figures (1961-1964), *Partiinaya zhizn,* No. 10, May, 1965, pp. 8-17. (C.D.S.P., Vol. XVII, No. 29, pp. 14-18)

The chief problem with which the party has to contend in regulating the composition of its membership is the establishment of a feasible balance between the well-educated technical, administrative and cultural intelligentsia, and the rank and file workers and collective farmers. To discharge effectively its responsibilities for governing the country, operating the complex economy, and controlling all social and cultural institutions, the party needs the services of the most competent members of the intelligentsia. On the other hand, worker and peasant members are important to the party in terms of maintaining close contact with the masses; blue collar workers serve as effective agents of manipulation and sources of information at the grass-roots level. Underemphasis on the recruitment of the intelligentsia would deprive the party of indispensable leadership material; underemphasis on recruitment of workers and collective farmers could result in the alienation of the party from the masses.

De-Stalinization

At the Twentieth Party Congress in February, 1956, Mikoyan and Khrushchev surprised both Soviet citizens and Western observers by condemning Stalin posthumously. Although for years non-Soviet authorities had referred to Stalin as a cruel dictator and had alleged that Soviet citizens lived in an oppressive police state, Soviet officials had vehemently denied the charges. Finally, three years after Stalin's death, top party leaders admitted that grave excesses had occurred during the Stalin era. Both the initial condemnation by Khrushchev and Mikoyan and official explanations of the development of the "cult of Stalin," which have appeared subsequently, place absolutely none of the blame for Stalin's excesses on the structure and functioning of the party. According to the *History of the Communist Party of the Soviet Union:*

"The cult of Stalin arose in definite, concrete historical conditions. Incredible difficulties attended the building of socialism. . . . The complicated international and domestic situation called for iron discipline, a high degree of vigilance and the strictest centralization of leadership. In conditions of bitter attacks by the imperialist states, Soviet society had to make certain temporary restrictions on democracy. . . . In those years Stalin held the post of Secretary General of the Central Committee of the Party. . . . He rendered great services. . . . Naturally, this earned him great prestige and popularity. However, as time went by all the successes achieved by the Soviet Union under the leadership of the Party began to be ascribed to him. The cult of his personality was gradually built up.

"The development of this cult was, to a very large extent, facilitated by certain negative personal qualities of Stalin. . . . The successes achieved by the Communist Party and the Soviet people, and the praises addressed to Stalin turned his head. Excessively overestimating his role and services, he came to believe that he was infallible and began to encourage people to extol him. His words began to be more at variance with his deeds. During the last years of his life, the cult of his personality caused particularly great damage to the leadership of the Party and the State.

"The errors and shortcomings it engendered impeded the progress of Soviet society, caused it great damage, and stood in the way of the creative initiative of the masses. But, contrary to the falsehoods spread by the enemies of Socialism, *they could not change the thoroughly democratic and genuinely popular character of the Soviet system. The policy pursued by the Party was a correct one, and it expressed the interests of the people.*" (Italics added)[42]

An official admission of the dictatorial methods used by Stalin, combined with the claim that the Soviet system was "thoroughly democratic" and the policy of the party "expressed the interests of the people," is typical of the propaganda which is directed at the Soviet people. Errors were indeed made, but according to party statements, these were the errors of individuals; the party itself was in no way responsible or guilty, and remained infallible, in spite of the errors of Stalin and his henchmen. Thus the Soviet people are told that even though the party allowed itself and the entire state to be completely dominated by a cruel dictator who ordered the imprisonment or execution of thousands of innocent people, "the policy pursued by the Party was a correct one," democratic principles remained in force, and the interests of the people were served.

Why was the open criticism ventured? Since Stalin was dead, his mistakes could have been conveniently forgotten or other scapegoats, such as Beria, could have been blamed. A definitive answer cannot, as yet, be given to this question because the party leaders divulge very little information about the process of decision-making within the inner sanctum of the party. It is almost certain that the de-Stalinization campaign was instigated by Khrushchev and that several of his most powerful colleagues, including Molotov, Voroshilov and Kaganovich, opposed his decision. A number of Khrushchev's remarks suggest that conflict over de-Stalinization was a causative factor in the 1957 leadership crisis, since, according to his statements, his adversaries vehemently opposed an exposé of the truth about the Stalin era because they themselves bore "personal responsibility for many mass repressions against Party, Soviet, economic, military and Y.C.L. cadres."[43]

Obviously, dissension over the Stalin myth issue was only one of the areas of disagreement among Stalin's successors. The collective leadership of the early post-Stalin period was apparently in sharp conflict over many issues, including who should hold the power, how the party should be run, what to do about the Stalin myth, and a number of important matters relating to foreign and domestic policy. Of these issues the crucial one was not de-Stalinization but who should wield the power, since the individual or faction which succeeded in dominating opponents in the power struggle would have a decisive voice in settling other issues. Although there has been some speculation that Khrushchev consciously decided to use the de-Stalinization issue as a convenient weapon through which he could divide and weaken opposition to his bid for supreme leadership of the party, it is more likely that he merely made after-the-fact use of a situation which had developed on a somewhat unplanned basis. At any rate, in the process of exposing Stalin's errors, he made every attempt to discredit his adversaries by linking them with the unsavory conditions of the Stalin era. Khrushchev's attempt to create the impression that he and his supporters were totally innocent with respect to the repression and cruelty of the Stalin era, while his opponents had co-responsibility for the miscarriage of justice, bordered on the ludicrous. He too had condoned inhumane decisions and had extolled Stalin's virtues. For example, after the second of the Great Purge trials which resulted in death and prison sentences for many outstanding Bolshevik leaders for crimes such as sabotage, treason and revisionism, Khrushchev had proclaimed:

> "Comrade workers . . . and all working people of our country. We are gathered here, on Red Square, to raise our proletarian voice in complete support of the sentence passed by the Military Collegium of the Supreme Court against the enemies of the people, the traitors of the Motherland, the betrayers of the worker's cause, the spies, the diversionists, agents of fascism, the vile, despicable Trotskyites. . . . These murderers aimed at the heart and brain of our party. They have lifted their villainous hands against Comrade Stalin. By lifting their hands against Comrade Stalin they lifted them against all the best that humanity possesses. For Stalin is hope; he is expectation; he is the beacon that guides all progressive mankind. Stalin is our banner! Stalin is our will! Stalin is our victory!"[44]

All members of the post-Stalin leadership, Khrushchev and his supporters included, had been Stalin's accomplices to a greater or a lesser extent, but accomplices nonetheless. The party principle of criticism and self-criticism, as it has been translated into practice, enabled Khrushchev, after he had consolidated his power, to censure his erstwhile colleagues for serving as henchmen to Stalin and for making use of Stalin's techniques to serve their own selfish purposes. However, according to Soviet custom, the supreme leader himself is immune from criticism. Thus Khrushchev's opponents were never given the opportunity to defend themselves in public against Khrushchev's accusations, which were undoubtedly fairly well deserved, or to issue counterattacks against Khrushchev, which, since he was far from guiltless, would have destroyed the guilt-free image which he attempted to establish. The subservience of all media of communication to the recognized party leader provided Khrushchev, during the period of his ascendancy, with complete protection. He could condemn Stalin, Stalinist tactics, and his own opponents for their cooperation with Stalin to his heart's content with no fear of reprisal. However, though he used the de-Stalinization campaign to great advantage to consolidate his own power, it is improbable that his primary initial motivation for launching the campaign was to discredit his opponents because the famous "Secret Speech," made before he consolidated his power, did not contain personal attacks on his colleagues and because, had he not been able to attain dominance, the discrediting game could have been a dangerous double-edged sword.

Undoubtedly there were many other reasons for initiating the de-Stalinization campaign, and it is entirely possible that a number of the party leaders, who were subsequently denounced by Khrushchev in the course of the campaign, may have initially supported the exposure of Stalin's errors. A genuine revulsion for Stalin's dictatorial methods and excesses may have contributed to the emphasis on collegiality which was apparent immediately following his death and to the willingness of many of the members of the party leadership to criticize the "cult of personality." Some, and perhaps most, of the high command may have believed sincerely that drastic remedial action was essential if the unhealthy situation created by Stalin's dictatorship was to be rectified. The major official reason which was given for the open criticism of Stalin was to prevent the reoccurrence of similar phenomena.[45] Khrushchev consistently maintained, though his actions may well have been at variance with his words, that leadership must be based on the collective principle and on the "correct" Marxist-Leninist policy with the active creative participation of millions of people. Apparently, the immediate post-Stalin leadership sensed considerable apathy among the masses who had been terrorized by Stalin. They may have hoped that by criticizing Stalin and inspiring in the masses the hope that a new era was beginning, they could arouse the people and encourage them to use their latent energy to assist in communist construction and the materialization of other party goals. Since success and progress in the Soviet Union influences enthusiasm for communism, both in the U.S.S.R. and in other countries, de-Stalinization may also have been intended to strengthen the international communist movement. The criticism of Stalin was also, according to official party statements, designed to consolidate the party, foster the creative development of Marxism-Leninism, and to extend "socialist democracy." Those leaders who supported the attack on the Stalin myth may have believed that the frank admission of Stalin's errors would exonerate his successors and strengthen the respect of people everywhere for the Soviet system of rule by one party. The rather faltering course of the de-Stalinization movement until Khrushchev achieved ascendancy in 1957 may have reflected fear on the part of some of the top leaders that if one man were to achieve supremacy, he might use the campaign to the extreme detriment of his rivals, just as Khrushchev did. Criticism of Stalin might also have been held in check initially by opposition from old-guard Bolsheviks, who sincerely believed in the need for strict centralization, doctrinal inflexibility and police methods of government.

Whether pressure for greater freedom of discussion was one of the causes or the result of the de-Stalinization campaign, or both, there has been, since the umbrella of Stalin's infallibility and the threat of his erratically tyrannical methods have been removed, a trend toward greater freedom of discussion within the Communist Party and, in fact, in Soviet society as a whole. During the past several years open, though controlled, debate has flourished on many issues of public policy, including matters such as educational policy, military strategy, economic organization and policy, and particularly freedom of aesthetic expression. Perhaps of greater importance is the fact that fallen party leaders have not been executed or jailed although, in most cases, the political line which they had been promoting was at variance with that of their successors. However, neither Khrushchev's rivals nor Khrushchev himself were given the opportunity to make a public statement of their positions, nor were the people allowed the opportunity to express support for their policies. Despite the evident relaxation, freedom of discussion is still drastically limited.

Although Khrushchev's decision to expose the myth of the Stalin era earned for him a considerable amount of personal popularity with the Soviet public which perhaps was one of his goals, it may be that his decision to launch the de-Stalinization campaign was the greatest single tactical blunder in his political career. The relaxation of tension which was a natural outgrowth of the criticism of Stalin's methods unleashed forces within the party and society as a whole which made it more difficult for Khrushchev, as the top party leader, to maintain the rigid type of control over society that had characterized Stalin's rule. The trend away from police methods of government which de-Stalinization required reduced considerably the impregnability of the top leader's position. Moreover, the attack on Stalin had negative international repercussions which Khrushchev must not have anticipated. Stalin had been the recognized leader of the international communist movement as well as of the C.P.S.U. Khrushchev angered the leaders of several other Communist Parties, particularly Mao Tse Tung of the Chinese Communist Party, by denouncing Stalin without consulting them, and indeed, without even warning them in advance. Khrushchev's almost impetuous denunciation of Stalin and his attempt to elevate himself to the leadership position of the world communist movement provided the Chinese leaders with a weapon to use in their own attempts to control the movement. If Stalin were no longer to be the idol, his replacement should be, according to the Chinese, not the upstart Khrushchev, but the seasoned leader, Mao Tse Tung. One of the factors which probably contributed to the decision to remove Khrushchev from power was the role which he had played in the development of the Sino-Soviet conflict and the fact that as long as he was the recognized leader of the C.P.S.U., he constituted an almost impenetrable barrier to the solution of the conflict.

Leaders of Communist Parties in the "socialist bloc" reacted to the de-Stalinization in a variety of ways: anger over not being informed that Khrushchev would admit to the world what they, the majority of whom had been unwilling puppets, had known all along; relief, because Khrushchev's criticism of Stalin suggested that the leader of the C.P.S.U. would no longer dare act in such a dictatorial way to the leaders of fraternal parties; trepidation, because of the possibility that the exposure would serve as an impetus for the eruption of the latent hostility which many of the people of East Central Europe felt for their communist overlords. The Hungarian uprising might not have occurred if it were not for the de-Stalinization campaign, and Soviet control over the countries of Central Eastern Europe might have remained as strong and inflexible as it was during the Stalin era. The decision to admit the errors of the Stalin period thus contributed substantially to a decrease in the strength and solidarity of the world communist movement. On the other hand, it may, during the intervening years, have strengthened the Communist Parties in a number of the Central Eastern European countries, since these parties are now operating more independently from Moscow and hence can be more responsive to their own people.

Khrushchev's open criticism of Stalin, and his admission that cruelty, injustice, repression and intolerance had prevailed during the time that Soviet propaganda had portrayed life in the Soviet Union as an emerging utopia, was in fact an announcement to the world that the Western criticisms and evaluations of life under communist rule had been much closer to the truth than the Soviet statements. Communism and the statements of communist leaders and propagandists were thus made a legitimate subject for ridicule within the communist bloc as well as in non-communist states, and the faith of many erstwhile devoted communists and communist sympathizers was severely shaken. Finally, by indulging in some of the very misdemeanors for which he criticized Stalin, Khrushchev paved the way for his own downfall.

Khrushchev's Dismissal

On October 18, 1964, the leading papers of the Soviet Union (*Pravda* and *Izvestia*) carried the following simple announcement:

"A plenary session of the Central Committee of the Communist Party of the Soviet Union was held on October 14.

"The plenary session of the Central Committee of the C.P.S.U. granted the request of Comrade N. S. Khrushchev that he be released from the duties of First Secretary of the Central Committee of the C.P.S.U., member of the Presidium of the Central Committee of the C.P.S.U. and Chairman of the U.S.S.R. Council of Ministers in view of his advanced age and deterioration in the state of his health.

"The plenary session . . . elected Comrade L. I. Brezhnev First Secretary of the Central Committee of the C.P.S.U."

A companion article announced that the members of the Presidium of the U.S.S.R. Supreme Soviet had acted unanimously to release Khrushchev from the duties of the Chairman of the U.S.S.R. Council of Ministers and to appoint A. N. Kosygin to fill the position. The announcements and the subsequent editorials and the articles about the new leaders included no word of praise for Khrushchev and no expression of regret over his retirement. On October 13, Khrushchev, as the supreme leader of the C.P.S.U. and virtual dictator of the Soviet Union, probably wielded more personal power than any other individual during the current era. By October 15, Khrushchev was stripped of his great power, retired, cast aside, denied the role of the respected elder statesman and almost certainly placed under close guard to prevent any attempt on his part to stage a comeback.

Although the official announcement stated that Khrushchev had retired, presumably voluntarily, because of advanced age and poor health, his successors apparently did not expect anyone to believe that he had withdrawn from the public scene voluntarily. There can be no doubt that he was removed from power, and it is probable that his dismissal was engineered through a palace *coup d'état*. Soviet officials have provided very little information about what actually happened, but it would appear that the events which surrounded his dismissal were more or less as follows. While Khrushchev was away from the Kremlin on his many good-will tours in other states, visiting enterprises and institutions in various parts of the Soviet Union, and finally, vacationing in Sochi, his trusted lieutenants in Moscow were making careful preparations to remove him from power. Khrushchev, who had over a considerable period of time manifested signs of grandiosity and faith in his own infallibility, was apparently totally oblivious to the strength and organized nature of the opposition to his policies and leadership. Only a few hours before his downfall, he promised the astronauts in space a glorious reception in Moscow. Had he had any premonition of the plot against him, his power as First Secretary of the C.P.S.U. would have permitted him to squelch it immediately. A hastily convened Central Committee, because the power structure in the U.S.S.R. gives its members no alternative, would have unanimously approved a decision by Khrushchev to dismiss, in disgrace, the leaders who had plotted against him. His opponents would have been labelled an "anti-party faction," and measures would have been taken to effect their complete defeat and to add to the grandeur of Khrushchev's position. But Khrushchev's opponents acted with consummate caution and skill. No hint of the palace revolution came to Khrushchev's attention until he was confronted with a virtual *fait accompli*. Dissenting members of the Secretariat and the Presidium of the Central Committee of the C.P.S.U. made their plans and recruited supporters from among their own members under a cloak of complete secrecy. During the final crucial meeting, members of the top leadership who had not been involved in organizing the plot had little choice but to acquiesce. Had Mikoyan, for example, who may have been almost as surprised as Khrushchev himself when confronted with the plot, chosen to offer a strong defense of Khrushchev, he would have been given no choice but to share Khrushchev's demotion. Whatever opposition there might have been among the top party leaders was eliminated effectively before Khrushchev was summoned to return to Moscow. He was allowed to argue his own case in the Central Committee, but his opponents knew that he would be unable to manipulate it to stage a comeback. Even if the majority of the members of the Central Committee were strongly pro-Khrushchev, and it may be assumed that many of the members did have considerable personal loyalty to Khrushchev, since they owed their rise within the ranks of the party to him, and that others genuinely supported many of his policy decisions, they realized that since Khrushchev no longer controlled the Secretariat and the Presidium, to oppose those who had succeeded in wresting his power from him would be to commit an act of political suicide. Despite the trend toward greater freedom of discussion which developed during the post-Stalin period, Khrushchev's speech to the Central Committee was never published, and to date, neither the rank-and-file party members nor Soviet citizens know what he said in his own defense. In the realm of decision-making, the failure to publish Khrushchev's speech, and to make public statements about the events which surrounded and led to his dismissal, is of little consequence. Even if Khrushchev had enjoyed overwhelming public support, rank-and-file party members and Soviet citizens in general would have had no channels through which they could express their support for him and his policies, and would have had no choice but to submit impotently to the decisions of the new leaders. The presentation of the issue to the Central Committee carried little risk for the new leaders because all avenues through which Khrushchev might have foiled their plans were blocked effectively. Unlike Stalin, Khrushchev did not have a strong police force under his personal command, and it may be assumed that potential support from military leaders had already been neutralized. The opportunity which Khrushchev was given to defend himself before the Central Committee may have been intended to convey the impression to those who did not believe the official announcement of his voluntary retirement that his dismissal was effected in conformity with the Party statutes and legal norms.

If the majority of the members of the Secretariat and Presidium of the Central Committee of the C.P.S.U. deemed it necessary to remove Khrushchev from power, why was it necessary to form a conspiracy and to remove him by means of *coup d'état?* The answer is simple. For all the verbal emphasis which the statutes of the C.P.S.U. and the constitution of the U.S.S.R. place on democracy, constitutionality and responsibility to the electorate, there is no formal provision for the removal of the top party leader once he has consolidated his position of power. The top party leader, the virtual dictator of the U.S.S.R., as Stalin and Khrushchev were, occupies an almost impregnable position of power. His power is such that he can remove and render harmless any less powerful leader or leaders who might in any way constitute a threat to his absolute dominance. There is no mechanism whereby the people, or even intermediate and high-level party leaders, can express their approval or disapproval of the top leader of the party in any manner which would affect his security in his position or his tenure as leader. The top party leader can be removed from his position only through death or perhaps a physical or mental disability which would make it impossible for him to hold and retain the reins of power, resignation or a *coup d'état*. Although Khrushchev was over 70 years of age when removed, his opponents were apparently unwilling to wait for death to relieve them of his leadership, and apparently had little faith that he would resign voluntarily, although he had hinted occasionally that he might. Therefore, they chose to form a conspiracy against him. A conspiracy, to be effective, must be planned and implemented in secret, and therefore is a potential, and at the same time, a highly risky weapon for a handful of persons among the top leadership only. Regardless of how the Soviet people felt about Khrushchev, they could have done nothing to hasten or to hinder his removal from power.

A most interesting question, of course, is why was Khrushchev removed from power. The most simple and reasonable answer seems to be that the party leaders who composed the anti-Khrushchev faction were not pleased with the decisions which Khrushchev imposed upon them, the party and the country, that they believed their decisions to be superior to those of Khrushchev and that they wanted to wield the power themselves. Each one, no doubt, had certain reservations about the wisdom and reliability of some or all of the others with whom he had allied himself against Khrushchev, and more than one may have harbored the hope that he would eventually inherit the power which the group was wresting from Khrushchev. Some of the conspirators may have had a sincere and unselfishly motivated desire to rescue the party and the country from what they deemed to be Khrushchev's inadequate and dangerous dictatorship.

The new Soviet leaders and their spokesmen in the press have been extremely cautious, almost tight-lipped, with respect to providing reasons for Khrushchev's dismissal. After the initial formal announcement which stated merely that he had resigned because of advanced age and poor health, Khrushchev's name has been conspicuously absent in the Soviet press. However, statements in an editorial which was relased shortly after his dismissal provided, in an impersonal manner, some of the official reasons for his removal. The editorial stated in part:

> "Experienced and influential leaders who know their jobs enjoy well-deserved authority among us. . . . But legitimate respect has nothing in common with excessive glorification and praising of a leader, when every word spoken by a person who stands at the 'summit' is passed off as a revelation and his acts and deeds are regarded as infallible. Such an approach can only revive the way of the period of the cult of the personality, and the party will not stand for it. . . . An atmosphere of genuine exactingness is inconceivable without the strict observance of the norms of inner-Party life and the principles of Soviet democracy—that is, everything that enables the masses to control and, when necessary, to correct the leader, whether he be the director of an enterprise . . . or a state or Party leader of the highest rank. . . . But life shows that not all comrades have completely overcome the practices, forms, and methods of work that evolved during the period of the cult. . . . It is precisely for this reason that the Party is so demanding in questions of observance of collective leadership, of Leninist norms of Party life in all sectors of the Party and state apparatus. Not a single communist, not a single Party collective has the right to ignore it when someone displays conceit, stops taking the opinions of his comrades into account, shows no concern for the development of criticism or for the creative rather than the merely formal discussion of questions at plenary sessions, assemblies and meetings. Even the most authoritative person cannot be permitted to escape the control of the guiding collective, the Party organization, or get the idea that he knows everything and can do everything, that he has no need for the knowledge and experience of his comrades. In this matter every collective must be completely implacable and persistent, must be able to check the high-handed person in time . . . we must expose the shortcomings in every collective and eliminate them, fight against bombastic phrases and braggadocio, over-hasty conclusions and hare-brained schemes that are divorced from reality."[46]

According to these statements, which contain the essence of the official condemnation, Khrushchev was removed because he put himself above the party. He did not operate in accordance with the principle of collective leadership, but instead imposed his decisions on the party and the state. In some cases, he was poorly qualified to make decisions without careful consultation with his colleagues; in other cases decisions were put into effect without adequate preparation. Numerous errors could have been avoided, and certain "hare-brained schemes" would not have been adopted had Khrushchev not strayed from the principle of collective leadership. Moreover, Khrushchev, though he roundly condemned Stalin for the cult of the personality, fostered his own cult, conveying the impression that he was virtually infallible, that all that he did was good and that major credit for all successes and advances should legitimately be accorded to him. The failures, of course, were due to the shortcomings of others. There is ample evidence to suggest that the charges against Khrushchev were well founded. His own speeches indicated that as his tenure and security in the position of the foremost leader of the C.P.S.U. increased, he became increasingly grandiose. He, himself, indicated that some of his programs and decisions did not meet with the approval of other high ranking leaders, and he appeared to take almost taunting pleasure in announcing that his decisions would be made operative despite their objections. One of the important areas of disagreement was over the reorganization of the party into agricultural and industrial sub-units which was pushed through by Khrushchev in November, 1962, and repealed by his successors in November, 1964.

Khrushchev's successors may eventually subject the majority of his errors to public scrutiny. However, it is unlikely that they will analyze and attempt to provide a solution for the underlying party problem which enabled Khrushchev to "get out of hand." The essence of the problem is that once a party leader is able to attain a position of dominance over his colleagues, the party has no technique, short of conspiracy, to remove him or to curb his power by constitutional means. The problems of limiting the power of the top party leader and of the orderly transfer of power from a leader who no longer meets with the approval of the majority to a new leader, who is selected by the party members or even by the power elite within the party, remain and are likely to remain, despite statements to the contrary in the Party Statutes.

Impact on the Individual and Society

A full discussion of the impact of the Communist Party on Soviet society and Soviet citizens would require volumes. The C.P.S.U., or more accurately the leadership of the C.P.S.U., governs the country through a state apparatus which is completely subservient to the party apparatus, determines foreign and domestic policy, manages the economy and educational institutions, establishes goals for Soviet society and guides, supervises and controls the activities and operations of every organization and institution in the U.S.S.R. The party is the dominant force which shapes the lives of Soviet citizens and determines the type of society in which they shall live.

The party declares that it "exists for the people and serves the people" and that it acts "for the people" and "in the name of the people." The people, however, have never been given the opportunity to delegate to the party the right to act for them and in their name. Without consulting them, the party decides what is best for the people. Because all spheres of Soviet society are so firmly controlled by the Communist Party, the people have no recourse but to cooperate with the party, to work toward the goals which the party has set for them, and to accept the favors and rewards which the party deems it appropriate for them to have. The efficient network of party observers which permeates Soviet society permits the party to know about and hence to punish those individuals who do not work diligently for the materialization of party goals. The development of organized opposition to the party rule is an absolute impossibility. The people are held in the iron grip of the dictatorship of the party leaders.

The dictatorship has on occasion resulted in complete disregard for the inviolable rights of human beings, mass repressions, cruelties and hardships. Basic democratic rights, even those guaranteed by the Party Statutes and the Constitution of the U.S.S.R., have been flagrantly violated. Errors of many kinds have been made. Millions of people have existed with the barest necessities of life. It is inevitable that strong, but impotent, resentment against the "dictatorship of the proletariat" has been experienced by millions of Soviet citizens.

However, the party has handled its relations with the people of the Soviet Union with considerable skill. The full strength of the most powerful propaganda machine in the world has been used to convince the Soviet people of the rightness and necessity of the actions of the party. The opponents of the Soviet way of life are portrayed as heinous enemies. The alternatives to the Soviet way of doing things are presented as being entirely unacceptable. Conflicting information from non-Soviet sources is drastically limited. Many Soviet citizens have no reasonable basis for comparison of their way of life with that of citizens of other countries. The party attempts to convince the people that all its actions are designed for their ultimate good, that their welfare is always the prime consideration. The comprehensive network of party organizations and members has been used as a technique to propagandize the party program, to "educate" the people to accept party standards, to inform the party about the activities of Soviet citizens and to provide the party with information about the needs, desires, aspirations and level of "social consciousness" of people in all walks of life. The party has made skillful use of this information. Consistently, throughout its rule, the party has let the people know that it recognizes many of their immediate needs and has made at least token efforts to satisfy some of them and to explain why continued hardships and deprivations have been necessary. Long range goals are always phrased in terms of what will be good for the people.

Although the party's control over the entire society is complete, it is advantageous for it to have the active support and cooperation of the majority of the population. Vigilance, a complicated systems of checks, and coercion have been used to control passive obstructionism. But much more important, in the long run, has been its technique of appealing to the needs of the people, and attempting to satisfy some of their most urgent desires. The Tsar, who believed himself to be divinely ordained, felt little need to play to the desires and aspirations of the people. The Soviet regime, though in most respects as autocratic as that of the Tsars, recognizes that the support of the people is crucial to the materialization of communist goals, and concurrently, recognizes the importance of making the people feel that satisfaction of their needs is the ultimate, though sometimes remote, goal of the party. The majority of the current population of the Soviet Union do, in fact, enjoy many advantages which were not available to their forefathers who lived in the Tsarist era. Their political rights, though minimal by Western standards, are more extensive than under Tsarism. More important in terms of Soviet morale in relation to the C.P.S.U. is what many citizens have gained in educational, economic and cultural opportunities. Though the general standard of living is much lower than in the United States, living conditions have been improving progressively. Most of the improvements, as for example in standards of living, are largely the result of improved technology and increased industrialization, and would have occurred, perhaps even in a larger measure, without the guidance of the party. The party, nevertheless, takes full credit for every improvement.

Communist ideology stresses the dignity of the common man. Many of the practices of the C.P.S.U. have violated this ideological tenet, as well as all other ideological principles. Mass imprisonments, the forced collectivization of agriculture, the transfer of whole segments of the population against their wishes to a new location, the extraction of confessions by torture, the official dissemination of obvious untruths and many other violations of human rights could hardly contribute to man's sense of dignity. Nevertheless, in other ways, the C.P.S.U. has made attempts to enhance the dignity of the common man, and thereby, to gain greater cooperation from him. The common man is told that it is for him that all the efforts are being made, and he is encouraged to play a significant, but highly controlled and supervised, part in materializing the goals which have been set for him. Opportunities to serve society within the framework determined by the party and hence to advance himself are plentiful. The party provides many outlets for the energy of the ambitious. Parentage, racial or national origin are no longer irrevocable fetters which bind the Soviet citizen to a permanent lowly status. Hardships in the present are countered by promises of a great and glorious future which each individual can help to materialize. The party attempts to mobilize all the energy of the people for the struggle to achieve what the party has deemed is good for them.

However, the party, for all its skill in playing on the needs and the aspirations of the people, has left the door open for widespread and deep seated cynicism. Overwhelming and pervasive as the propaganda machine of the party may be, the Soviet people must, and there is considerable evidence to support this hypothesis, be aware of the fallibility of the "infallible" party and the discrepancies between lofty theory and the actual practices of the party leadership. For example, the incongruity between the authoritarian, autocratic practices of the C.P.S.U. and the relatively democratic principles of the Party Statutes and the Constitution of the U.S.S.R. must be painfully apparent to millions of Soviet citizens. When and if deviations from democratic principles are admitted, the threat of capitalist encirclement, war-time emergency, the exigencies of the cold war or the need to handle other problems of immediate and vital consequences have been offered as excuses. Soviet leaders also argue that complete democracy can be achieved only in the stage of communism when all social and economic inequalities have been eradicated. These excuses, however, cannot constitute adequate justification for the outrageous violations of ideological and party principles. Is it reasonable to assume, for example, that the U.S.S.R. is able to react more effectively, from its point of view, to the exigencies of the cold war, if lower level party officials are selected by their party superiors rather than by rank and file party members? To Westerners, such an assumption seems utterly unjustified. To Soviet citizens, many of the discrepancies between theory and practice must be regarded as unnecessary and humiliating.

Party doctrine stresses that the party's goal is to serve the common man, that party officials are not to place themselves above the people, and that party members are to exemplify the moral characteristics of the "new Soviet man." How cynical Soviet citizens must feel when they must deal with arbitrary, high-handed party officials, drunk with their own sense of power, who sometimes use the authority of their positions to acquire an abundance of material goods not available to the ordinary citizens. Higher level party officials do, of course, attempt to curb such behavior in subordinates, but it does happen, according to official Soviet statements, with sufficient frequency to justify doubts among the populace about the careful selection procedure of the infallible party, and about the moral characteristics and the goals of the officials selected by the party to "guide" the construction of the new society.

Numerous other reasons for a cynical attitude toward the party exist. The party "guides" the economy, but the populace has been subjected to totally unnecessary deprivations with respect to the availability of consumer goods. Scarce materials are sometimes used for the production of unattractive low quality items, for which there is no demand, while there is marked underproduction of some almost essential items. Because of inadequacies in the system of distribution, people may have to stand in line for hours to purchase items which were readily available only a few days before. The C.P.S.U. has a penchant for reorganization. No sooner do the people get used to working in and dealing with a particular organizational form than the party decides that a radical reorganization is necessary. It is inconceivable that a large number of Soviet citizens do not think (to themselves) that if party leaders are so wise, and if they are guided in every decision by the "scientific" theory of Marxism-Leninism, surely they should be able to organize the internal affairs of Soviet society more efficiently and consistently.

One of the most powerful reasons for cynicism toward the party is the party's own treatment of its erstwhile leaders. While Stalin lived, his closest associates cooperated with him to propagate the myth that he was virtually infallible, almost a god. Accomplishments in every field were due to his leadership, his genius, his guidance. For a short time after his death, his god-like stature was maintained. But in 1956 the new party leaders announced that Stalin, far from being the perfect leader who had, as a good Soviet leader should, guided all his decisions and actions in accordance with Marxist-Leninist ideology, had in fact been an irascible, self-centered, cruel tyrant. Stalin, the leader, had committed grievous errors, but the party, and the party leaders who preempted party power after Stalin's death, had been infallible and guiltless throughout the Stalin era. Khrushchev's explanations of how Stalin had been able to attain dictatorial status must have left the Soviet people with serious questions about why the infallible party and the infallible party leaders who succeeded Stalin had permitted an unworthy person to gain control of the party and the Soviet Union, and why he had not been stripped of his power when his inadequacies became apparent.

The pattern of a "good" man turning into a "bad" man almost overnight, has since Stalin's denunciation, become commonplace. The Supreme Soviet, under the guidance of the party, always picks a "good" man to be Chairman of the Council of Ministers, but Stalin, Malenkov, Bulganin, and finally, Khrushchev all turned out to be "bad" men. Party leaders are always "good" men, but after periods of service during which they received considerable adulation, Molotov, Kaganovich, Saburov and Pervukhin also turned out to have been "bad" men. Most of the manifestations of malfunctioning in the Soviet system are blamed on lower level party and state officials who have proved to be unworthy incumbents of the high offices for which they have been so carefully selected.

From 1956 until October, 1964, the impression was conveyed that Nikita S. Khrushchev had always been "right." His exploits during the early years of the Soviet Union, and particularly his contributions to the Soviet victory in World War II, were acclaimed. But Khrushchev, the man who had been so right for so long suddenly turned out to have been so wrong that he was dismissed from all his positions of power and relegated to ignominious oblivion. When Stalin, the tyrant, died the Soviet people wept. When Khrushchev, who had eased the tyranny and introduced policies which made life a little more pleasant for most Soviet citizens, was dismissed, people within the U.S.S.R. gave no sign of grief, disappointment or sympathy. They merely went about their business as if no event of importance had happened. Why? Probably because in the last three decades they have been told too many different things about Stalin, Khrushchev, Malenkov, Molotov and other leaders, about China, and the West, particularly the United States, about what and who is "good" and what and who is "bad" to have very deep beliefs about any one or any thing. When Khrushchev was dismissed the Soviet people were supposed to believe that all setbacks and inconveniences which occurred during his period of leadership were the result of his "hare-brained" schemes, and this belief was supposed to strengthen their loyalty to the infallible regime. However, it seems likely that Khrushchev's dismissal increased not loyalty to the system but rather cynicism toward the party and its rule.

Addendum

The Twenty-Third Congress of the Communist Party of the Soviet Union which met in March, 1966, approved a number of changes in the Statutes of the C.P.S.U.[47] Several of the changes are intended to improve the qualitative composition of the party. Henceforth, persons up to the age of twenty-three may join the party only via the Y.C.L. Persons who recommend applicants for admission to the party must have been members of the party for at least five years. The rules pertaining to expulsion from the party have been strengthened somewhat, and the policy of transferring a member to the status of a candidate member as a party penalty has been abolished. The norms for the renewal and turnover of the composition of party bodies and Secretaries of party organizations have been deleted from the Statutes. The Statutes now merely state that the principles of systematic renewal and continuity of leadership must be observed, but party organizations are no longer required to ensure that the turnover rate attains a specified percentage.

In view of the fact that the C.P.S.U. Central Committee and its Presidium and Secretariat have typically handled most of the party affairs for the R.S.F.S.R., the Central Committee Bureau for the R.S.F.S.R. has been abolished. Thus, the U.S.S.R. and the R.S.F.S.R. will unequivocally share a party organization, whereas the other Union Republics will continue to have separate republican party organizations. Whereas previously the majority of Union Republics convened a Party Congress every two years, while a few convened a Congress every four years, the new Statutes specify that Congresses of the Communist Parties of all Union Republics are to be held at least once every four years.

The other major changes in the Statutes were primarily terminological. Henceforth, the Central Committee will elect a General Secretary, rather than a First Secretary of the C.P.S.U. Central Committee, and the title of the Presidium of the Central Committee has been changed to the Politburo of the Central Committee. Like the old Presidium, the new Politburo is to "guide the work of the Party between plenary sessions of the Central Committee."

The Politburo elected by the Twenty-Third Congress includes eleven members and eight candidate members (Members: L. I. Brezhnev; G. I. Voronov; A. P. Kirilenko; A. N. Kosygin; K. T. Mazurov; A. J. Pelse; N. V. Podgorny; D. S. Polyansky; M. A. Suslov; A. N. Shelepin; and P. Ye. Shelest. Candidate Members: V. V. Grishin; P. N. Demichev; D. A. Kunayev; P. M. Masherov; V. P. Mzhavanadze; Sh. R. Rashidov; D. F. Ustinov; and V. V. Shcherbitsky). Eleven persons were elected to the Secretariat (General Secretary L. I. Brezhnev and Secretaries Yu. V. Andropov; P. N. Demichev; I. V. Kapitonov; A. P. Kirilenko; F. D. Kulakov; B. N. Ponomarev; A. P. Rudakov; M. A. Suslov; D. F. Ustinov; and A. N. Shelepin). Many of the members of the new Politburo and Secretariat were also members of one or both of the leading organs of the party during Khrushchev's period of leadership. The Central Committee elected by the Twenty-Third Party Congress consisted of 195 members and 165 candidate members.

Reports to the Congress by Brezhnev, the General Secretary, and Kosygin, member of the Politburo and Chairman of the Council of Ministers, confirmed the general line taken by the party for the last several years.[48] In Brezhnev's review of the foreign policy activities of the C.P.S.U., he stressed the importance of cooperation and solidarity between socialist states and fraternal parties, and expressed the hope that relations with the Communist Party of China and the Albanian Party of Labor can be improved. He reviewed what he described as the "deepening of the contradictions of the capitalist system," roundly condemned the "aggressive policies of imperialism," and promised continued Soviet support for national-liberation movements, the Vietcong, the world communist movement, and international peace and security.

In his report on the internal situation, Brezhnev, as Soviet leaders have for decades, stressed the importance of the guiding role of the party; the need to adhere to party principles, such as collective leadership, and the combination of inner-party democracy with iron discipline; and the importance of constructive party guidance rather than petty tutelage. A considerable portion of his report was devoted to the "ideological-upbringing work of the party." Apart from a few scarcely veiled references to Khrushchev's inefficiency, the substance of Brezhnev's report differed little from the report which Khrushchev delivered to the Twenty-Second Party Congress. The report on the economy and the directives for the new Five Year Plan which were delivered at the Congress will be reviewed in the chapter on the economy.

REFERENCES

1 For additional information about the historical development of the C.P.S.U. see Leonard Schapiro, *The Communist Party of the Soviet Union,* (New York: Random House, 1959).

2 For excellent examples of the arbitrariness of the local authorities see George Kennan, *Siberia and the Exile System,* (New York: The Century Co., 1891).

3 For the history of the growth of conspiratorial groups and societies and the spread of revolutionary doctrines in Russia from 1825 to 1905 see Franco Venturi, *Roots of Revolution: A History of the Populist and Socialist Movements in the Nineteenth Century Russia,* (London: George Weidenfeld & Nicholson, Ltd., 1960).

4 Lenin, *Works, op. cit.,* Vol. 8, p. 96.

5 Cf. Harry and Bonaro Overstreet, *What We Must Know About Communism,* (New York: W. W. Norton and Co., 1958), pp. 103-15.

6 Lenin, *Works, op. cit.,* Vol. 4, p. 468.

7 Cf. Schapiro, *The Communist Party of the Soviet Union, op. cit.,* pp. 38, 45-6, 205-7.

8 V. I. Lenin, *Selected Works,* ed., J. Fineberg, (New York: International Publishers, 1938), Vol. 2, pp. 133, 139.

9 Lenin, *Works, op. cit.,* Vol. 31, p. 8.

10 N. S. Khrushchev, *Pravda,* Oct. 19, 1961.

11 F. Kozlov, *Pravda,* Oct. 29, 1961.

12 N. S. Khrushchev, *Pravda,* Oct. 29, 1961.

13 Lenin, *Works, op. cit.,* Vol. 5, p. 396.

14 Joseph Stalin, "Foundations of Leninism," *Problems of Leninism,* (Moscow: Foreign Languages Publishing House, 1954), p. 97.

15 V. N. Titov, "Report of the Credentials Commission of the Twenty-Second Party Congress," *Pravda,* Oct. 22, 1961, pp. 5-6.

16 *Ibid.*

17 Cf. *U.S.S.R. Illustrated Monthly,* Nov., 1961, No. 11, p. 3.

18 *Kommunist,* No. 13, Sept., 1961.

19 N. Mitkin, *Kommunist,* No. 13, Sept., 1961.

20 "Communique of the Plenary Session of the Central Committee of the Communist Party of the Soviet Union," *Pravda,* Nov. 17, 1964, p. 1. (C.D.S.P., Vol. XVI, No. 45, p. 3)

21 The Presidium elected in 1961 included the following full members: N. S. Khrushchev; F. R. Kozlov; G. J. Voronov (former Party Secretary in the Orenburg region who was appointed Chairman of the R.S.F.S.R. Council of Ministers in November, 1962); L. I. Brezhnev (Chairman of the Presidium of the Supreme Soviet until July, 1964, when he became Secretary of the C.P.S.U. Central Committee); A. I. Mikoyan (First Vice-Chairman of the Council of Ministers of the U.S.S.R. until July, 1964, when he became Chairman of the Supreme Soviet); A. N. Kosygin (First Deputy Chairman of the Council of Ministers of the U.S.S.R.); D. S. Polyansky (Chairman of the Council of Ministers of the R.S.F.S.R. until November, 1962, when he became Vice-Chairman of the Council of Ministers of the U.S.S.R.); N. V. Podgorny (First Secretary of the Ukrainian Communist Party); M. A. Suslov and O. V. Kuusinen (both Secretaries of the C.P.S.U.); M. Shvernik (Chairman of the Party Control Committee). The alternate or candidate members were: V. V. Grishin (Trade Union leader); K. T. Mazurov (First Secretary of the Belorussian Communist Party); V. P. Mzhavanadze (First Secretary of the Georgian Communist Party); S. R. Rashidov (First Secretary of the Uzbek Communist Party); V. V. Shcherbitsky (Chairman of the Council of Ministers of the Ukrainian S.S.R.).

In October, 1964, N. S. Khrushchev was removed from the Presidium and F. Kozlov was granted a leave for medical treatment. L. I. Brezhnev replaced N. S. Khrushchev as the First Secretary of the C.P.S.U., and A. N. Kosygin replaced N. S. Khrushchev as the Chairman of the Council of Ministers of the U.S.S.R. P. Ye. Shelest and A. N. Shelepin were elected as full members of the Presidium and P. N. Demichev was elected as a new candidate member. O. V. Kuusinen died in the summer of 1964.

In October, 1964, members of the Presidium included: L. I. Brezhnev; G. J. Voronov; A. I. Mikoyan; A. N. Kosygin; D. S. Polyansky; N. V. Podgorny; M. A. Suslov; M. Shvernik; A. N. Shelepin; P. Ye. Shelest. The alternate members were: V. V. Grishin; K. T. Mazurov; V. P. Mzhavanadze; S. R. Rashidov; V. V. Shcherbitsky; P. N. Demichev.

22 "Communique of the Plenary Session of the Central Committee of the Communist Party of the Soviet Union," *op. cit.*, p. 1.

23 N. M. Shvernik, *Pravda*, Oct. 26, 1961.

24 The Party Central Committee elected by the Twenty-Second Congress re-elected to the Secretariat the following members: N. S. Khrushchev, First Secretary of the Party Central Committee; F. R. Kozlov; M. A. Suslov; and O. V. Kuusinen. Newly elected secretaries were: P. N. Demichev and I. V. Spiridonov, regional party leaders of Moscow and Leningrad respectively; A. N. Shelepin, the former chief of the security police, L. F. Ilyichev and B. N. Ponomarev, department heads of the Central Committee in charge of domestic propaganda, and the party's international relations respectively. From 1961 until October, 1964, the most important change in the Secretariat was the appointment of L. I. Brezhnev in July, 1964. When Khrushchev was removed in October, 1964, Brezhnev became the First Secretary of the Central Committee. In November, 1964, Kozlov was relieved of his duties on the Secretariat because of poor health, and V. I. Polyakov, who had been appointed during the interim period was removed for unstated reasons. Members of the Secretariat, as of November, 1964, were: L. I. Brezhnev, M. A. Suslov, P. N. Demichev, I. V. Spiridonov, A. N. Shelepin, L. F. Ilyichev, and B. N. Ponomarev.

25 "Resolution of the Plenary Session of the C.P.S.U. Central Committee on Merging Industrial and Rural Province and Territory Party Organizations," *Pravda*, Nov. 17, 1964, p. 1.

26 N. S. Khrushchev, "The Development of the U.S.S.R. Economy and Party Guidance of the National Economy," *Pravda*, Nov. 20, 1962, pp. 1-8. (C.D.S.P., Vol. XIV, No. 46, pp. 3-8, 14)

27 "The C.P.S.U. in Figures (1961-1964)," *Partiinaya zhizn*, No. 10, May, 1965, pp. 8-17. (C.D.S.P., Vol. XVII, No. 29, pp. 14-18)

28 *Ibid.*

29 V. Zagorin, "Admissions to the Party Must Be Guided," *Partiinaya zhizn*, No. 8, April, 1963, pp. 14-20. (C.D.S.P., Vol. XV, No. 21, pp. 14-17)

30 "The C.P.S.U. in Figures (1961-1964)," *op. cit.*, pp. 8-17.

31 N. Antonov, "One Must Fight For a Man," *Pravda*, Aug. 17, 1963, p. 2.

32 Zagorin, "Admissions to the Party Must Be Guided," *op. cit.*, pp. 14-20.

33 N. S. Khrushchev, *Pravda*, Feb. 22, 1960.

34 *Partiinaya zhizn*, No. 10, May, 1965, pp. 8-17.

35 *Ibid.*, No. 1, Jan., 1962, pp. 44-54.

36 *Ibid.*

37 L. Shaumyan, "30th Anniversary of the Seventeenth Party Congress," *Pravda*, Feb. 7, 1964, p. 2.

38 Khrushchev, *Report of the Central Committee of the C.P.S.U. to the Twenty-Second Congress of the Communist Party of the Soviet Union, op. cit.*, p. 158.

39 Titov, "Report of the Credentials Commission of the Twenty-Second Party Congress," *op. cit.*, pp. 5-6.

40 *Partiinaya zhizn*, No. 10, May, 1965, pp. 8-17.

41 *Ibid.*, No. 1, Jan., 1962, pp. 44-54.

42 *History of the Communist Party of the Soviet Union*, (Moscow: Foreign Languages Publishing House, 1960), pp. 670-1.

43 N. S. Khrushchev, *Pravda*, Oct. 29, 1961.

44 *Ibid.*, Jan. 31, 1937.

45 *Ibid.*, Oct. 29, 1961.

46 "Exactingness Is an Important Feature of Party Guidance," *Partiinaya zhizn,* No. 20, Oct., 1964, pp. 3-7. (C.D.S.P., Vol XVI, No. 2, pp. 4-6)

47 "Resolution of the Twenty-Third Congress of the Communist Party of the Soviet Union on Partial Changes in the C.P.S.U. Statutes," *Pravda,* April 9, 1966, p. 4. There were 4,620 delegates with a deciding vote and 323 delegates with a consultative vote. The total membership of the C.P.S.U. in March, 1966, was 12,471,000, including the candidate members, organized in 320,000 primary party organizations.

48 L. I. Brezhnev, "Report of the C.P.S.U. Central Committee to the Twenty-Third Congress of the Communist Party of the Soviet Union," *Pravda,* March 30, 1966, pp. 2-9; A. N. Kosygin, "The Directives of the Twenty-Third C.P.S.U. Congress for the Development of the U.S.S.R. National Economy in 1966-1970," *Pravda,* April 6, 1966, pp. 2-7.

CHAPTER III

YOUTH ORGANIZATIONS

"We are the Party of the future and the future belongs to the youth. We are the Party of innovators, and innovators are always followed more willingly by youth. We are the Party of selfless struggle against time-worn decay, and youth is always the first to participate in a selfless struggle."

—V. I. Lenin.[1]

The history of youth organizations in the U.S.S.R. represents a persistent and strenuous attempt by the party to win the unswerving support of the maturing generations, to utilize youthful enthusiasm, energy and idealism for the materialization of communist goals and to mold the behavior, thoughts, goals and aspirations of young people to conform with and strengthen the Soviet system. Communist interest in the use of youth organizations anti-dates the existence of the Soviet state. As early as 1903 Lenin advocated that youth should be organized under the guidance of the Communist Party and in 1918 on Lenin's behest the All-Russian Communist League of Youth was established. To honor Lenin's memory the organization was renamed the Russian-Leninist Communist League of Youth in 1924 and the All-Union Leninist Communist League of Youth in 1926 (abbreviated as Y.C.L., Young Communist League, or Komsomol, derived from *Kommunisticheskii soiuz molodezhi*).[2]

The Soviet government, under the direction of the party, has since its inception paid extraordinary attention to the organization and indoctrination of youth. If society were to be restructured according to the Marxist-Leninist ideal, drastic social changes and revisions of the accepted modes of behavior would be required. The Bolshevik leaders realized that people reared under Tsarism could not be counted on as reliable, willing and effective builders of the new society because of conflicting goals, beliefs, morals and habits. The builders of the new communist society had to be energetic, self-sacrificing, idealistic and willing to break with the past. The party urgently needed people willing to work enthusiastically without even an adequate supply of the basic necessities of life, and the only rewards it could offer in exchange for the self-sacrifice was the glory of working toward an ideal, and the promise that the idealistic belief in the future was justified. It is not surprising that the party leaders have attempted to use young people as allies in their drive to restructure society.

104

What has been the history of the effort to organize and indoctrinate Soviet youth? What values do the Communist Party and the Soviet government seek to implant in youth? How does the party maintain control over the organizations? What are the activities of the youth organizations? How successful have the authorities been in achieving their goals with youth?

History of Youth Organizations

Early in the twentieth century there was an upsurge of radical activity among Russian youth, especially in centers of higher education. Many youth organizations which espoused radical social and political views were established in various centers, particularly Moscow and St. Petersburg, and enjoyed enthusiastic initiations but short careers. Often, the collapse of a youth organization was due to the establishment of a rival organization sponsored by young Bolsheviks or because of internal undermining by Bolsheviks on the instructions of the party. The Bolshevik Party was not willing to sanction the development of a popular youth movement under auspices other than its own.

Although fully aware of the indispensable role of youth in the achievement of their goals, the Bolsheviks had no youth auxiliary prior to the October Revolution. However, the party did have a large number of youthful members. The establishment of an official Bolshevik youth organization was delayed because of conflicting views about the form, purposes and responsibilities of such an organization, membership requirements, and the problem of inculcating discipline without destroying the initiative of youth. During the first year after it seized power the party, burdened with many urgent problems, limited its organizational activities with youth to the formation of youth units in regions where their control was assured, and to infiltrating and gaining control of established youth groups. In the fall of 1918, at the invitation of the Petrograd and Moscow youth groups which were firmly controlled by the party, an All-Russian Congress of Youth convened in Moscow. This meeting was subsequently referred to as the First Congress of the Komsomol.

At the First Congress, the basic organizational structure of the League and its relationship to the party was outlined. The All-Russian Congress was established as the highest authority of the League and a Central Committee was elected to conduct day to day activities between Congresses. It was unanimously decided that "the League, being—for the purpose of demonstrating the self-standingness of youth—a fully independent organization, is in its revolutionary work, in solidarity with the Russian Communist Party."[3] After the Eighth Party Congress (1919) a joint resolution was issued by the Central Committees of the party and the Komsomol to the effect that "the Central Committee of the RCLY (Komsomol) is directly subordinate to the Central Committee of the RCP (Party) . . . and

. . . local organizations of the RCLY work under the control of the local committees of the RCP."[4] Each local party organization was instructed to establish a Komsomol unit in its locale of operation if one had not already been established. Thus, shortly after it was established, the Y.C.L. accepted clear cut lines of party control, and party domination of the Komsomol was guaranteed. The role assigned to the Komsomol by the party was to serve as a source of trained reserves for the party, to organize and rear youth in a communist manner, to build communism and to defend the Soviet Republic.[5] The party-designated tasks were formally accepted at the second Y.C.L. Congress. Although there have been modifications of details, the general structure and purpose of the Y.C.L. have remained unchanged. The Communist League of Youth is an organization sponsored, dominated and controlled by the party; its major function is to assist in the materialization of goals specified by the party.

Fired with enthusiasm for the utopian program of the Communist Party, the small core of Russian youth who participated in the establishment of the Komsomol were devoted and self-sacrificing fighters for communism. Revolutionary zeal was at its highest pitch. As one Komsomol leader put it:

> "Perhaps the League will consciously order you to be the very man who lays down his dead body so that the others can advance over him, and you must do this for you are a member of a great class. This great whole must conquer, but we don't know who will perish. And if death is ordered by our Party and League, we must accept it in the interest of the common cause."[6]

During the Civil War almost all Komsomolites, including sixteen year old boys, were in the Red Army. After the Civil War, Komsomolites were asked to assist in the rebuilding of the ruined economy, to fight for the transformation of old Russia into a modern country, to introduce large scale industrialization, electrification and modern techniques, and to modify the backward agricultural methods. With concrete tasks assigned, and the promised reward of an imminent glorious future, for Lenin predicted in 1920 at the Third Y.C.L. Congress that in ten to twenty years a communist society would emerge,[7] young Komsomolites gave of themselves unstintingly. They fought in the Red Armies, participated in economic construction, were among the first underground workers in the Donbass mines, studied Marxism, propagandized the party program, indoctrinated other youth, argued for improved social conditions, organized agricultural communes, conducted anti-religious campaigns and strove for self-improvement according to the wishes of the party. All these things the most ardent young Komsomolites did willingly and gladly because they believed implicitly that their efforts and sacrifices would be rewarded by the materialization of the goals of the party.

The failure of a World Revolution abroad and the introduction of the New Economic Policy (NEP) in 1921 caused a precipitous decline in the enthusiasm and zeal of the members of the Young Communist League. Concrete tasks changed from heroic protection and uplifting of the motherland to more prosaic and less appealing duties such as waging a "conscious struggle" against alcoholism, tobacco and sexual licentiousness,[8] developing in youth "a spirit of competition," combatting political deviationism and developing vigilance against "bourgeois temptations."[9] Bukharin, in 1922, pointed out, ". . . there has come after the period of intense heroic struggle and with the shift to the New Economic Policy, a sort of demoralization, a sort of moral crisis among Communist youth and among youth in general."[10] Thousands of young people were unemployed. Working conditions were unenviable and living arrangements and standards of living were worse. Even more important, young people were affected by the retreat from the goal of communism. The NEP, which reintroduced private enterprise and other bourgeois capitalistic practices, especially in agriculture, was interpreted as a retreat from socialism, and hence a betrayal. Soviet youth questioned the value of their previous sacrifices and of struggling for goals which seemed to be receding from realization.

Disillusionment associated with the NEP resulted in a marked drop in Komsomol membership. However, as Komsomolites were given increased responsibility in education and indoctrination, especially with reference to younger children, enthusiasm and membership increased steadily. At the Fifth Komsomol Congress (1922), the Y.C.L. was instructed to form local groups called "Young Pioneers" for children aged ten to fourteen years. Komsomolites were to supervise the indoctrination of these children, and to inculcate in them class consciousness, esteem for creative labor, striving for knowledge and willingness to subordinate personal interests to those of society.[11] Komsomolites were thus given a responsible role in the molding of the "new man," since the Pioneer organization was to be to the Pioneer something like what the family used to be.[12] In 1926, the Y.C.L. was advised to establish the "Little Octobrist" organization for children below Pioneer age.[13] The important responsibilities delegated to the Y.C.L. with reference to the communist upbringing of young children probably acted as a positive motivating factor. Moreover, Komsomolites were rallied to fight against enemies of communism, such as the kulaks (rich farmers), religious organizations, rural capitalistic elements, bureaucrats, saboteurs, nationalists and deviationists, and for the establishment of such Bolshevik virtues as discipline, confidence, vigilance, "organizedness," solidarity, atheism and mastery of Leninism.[14] On the other hand, many Y.C.L. members must have reacted negatively to increased party control over the organization, rigid limitations on independent action by the Y.C.L., and the progressive decline of the practice of intra-organization democracy.

The announcement of the First Five Year Plan (1928) produced an outburst of zealous enthusiasm among Komsomolites. The fervor was upheld by Stalin's announcement at the Sixteenth Party Congress (1930) that the Soviet Union had entered the "period of socialism and was progressing toward a completely socialist society," and by the statement at the Ninth Komsomol Congress (1931) that in one or two more Five Year Plans "we shall live in a developed socialist society."[15] During this period, the Y.C.L. was again assigned numerous concrete tasks. They were urged to increase production by forming "initiative" or "shock" groups, to perform special production feats, to organize socialist competitions that would involve the masses, to increase production by encouraging inventions, improved methods, vigilance against waste and against saboteurs, to work to the utmost of their ability, to set a good example, etc.[16]

In 1929 the Y.C.L. Central Committee effected the first working mobilization of youth. Seven thousand young people were sent to build a tractor factory in Stalingrad, 66,000 to build new factories in the Urals and Siberia, 36,000 to work in the Donbass mines, 20,000 to work as lumberjacks and 2,000 to work in the gold fields.[17] During the First Five Year Plan approximately 350,000 Komsomolites worked on the Dnieper Dam, the Moscow bearing factory, the Turkestan-Siberia R.R., and other important projects. In 1932, 120,000 Komsomolites participated in the building of a new industrial center on the Amur River in the Far East, named Komsomol'sk on the Amur in their honor. Although the Soviet leadership considered participation in these projects to be a "university for youth," it was soon recognized that well educated specialists were indispensable. During the First and Second Five Year Plans thousands of Komsomolites, many of whom continued to work in industry, studied diligently at the newly established technical institutes, to prepare themselves to meet the demands of the economy for engineers, industrial managers and other specialists.

The Y.C.L. was asked to serve the party in agriculture by helping to force and speed up collectivization. Komsomolites were sent by the thousands to rural areas to participate in the collectivization, to serve as propagandists, to instruct peasants in the use of tractors and other farm machinery and to staff the new machine-tractor stations. Rural Komsomol members were urged to join the kolkhozy (collective farms) and by June, 1929, 15,000 had done so. This number does not seem high, in comparison to a total Komsomol membership of over 2 million by that time. It reflects, in part, the fact that rural residents, in general, resisted the program of the party more strongly than urban residents. Since there were relatively few party members in most of the agricultural areas, the Komsomolites occupied many of the most important positions. They served simultaneously as propagandists, organizers, specialists and watchdogs. Every ideological shortcoming, technical error, breach of discipline, and sign of waste or opposition was to be reported immediately to the party. The Komsomolites performed the task of revolutionary vigilance against enemies of the state, and at the same time, spread communist ideology among the masses, and combatted illiteracy, religious influence, waste and parasitism.

Concrete and challenging tasks, observable achievements, and renewed faith that socialist goals would be realized in the foreseeable future tended to sustain zeal for Komsomol activities during the late 1920's and 1930's. However, other factors tended to detract from the zeal of some of the Y.C.L. members. Some broke under the strain of overwork, and others were demoralized by the harsh realities of collectivization, famine in the villages, and the brutality of party-sponsored police agencies. For some the glory of the promised future was not sufficient to counteract the drab reality of insufficient food, inadequate housing, poor working conditions and the complete lack of luxuries in the present, and their enthusiasm waned. Stalin's announcement in 1936 that socialism had been attained might have been the signal for a joyous outburst by people who had struggled and sacrificed, if the socialism which he proclaimed had been other than a tawdry imitation of the promised utopia. Some of the people perhaps accepted the flaws in the operation of the system, and perceived Stalin's announcement as a sign that much had been accomplished and much more could and would be accomplished in the future. But many people, young and old alike, must have been disheartened because of the obvious difference between the pronouncements of their leaders and the actual, and none too pleasant, facts of the situation. The development of the Stalin cult also must have had a detrimental effect on the morale of at least some Komsomolites. As it became increasingly advisable for Komsomolites and all others in the U.S.S.R. to refer to Stalin as the "teacher," "the beloved leader," "the father," the "model for all Komsomolites," and the "genius" responsible for all progress in the U.S.S.R., at least some people must have evaluated Stalin and his contributions with some degree of accuracy. Those who perceived that, although Stalin's accomplishments were outstanding in many respects, he was by no means infallible, that he violated some of the most basic principles of Marxism-Leninism, that he was partially responsible for the Bloodly Purges of the 1930's which decimated the ranks of the Komsomol as well as of the party, must have reacted, at least inwardly, against the cult of the individual. Many Y.C.L. members and leaders must have had some doubts about the goals toward which they were striving, about the party leaders, and the party program, and about their own personal integrity as they mouthed the accepted phrases about the beloved Stalin.

The excessively long interval of thirteen years which elapsed between the Tenth Komsomol Congress (1936) and the Eleventh Komsomol Congress (1949), entirely contrary to Komsomol regulations, can be explained on the basis of political upheavals associated with the Bloody Purges, the war and emphasis on reconstruction after the war. A large number of events which affected the attitudes, enthusiasm and activities of Komsomol members, and the Soviet people in general, occurred during the interval. The Purge "removed" many of the most prominent Komsomolites and their positions were filled by trusted replacements. The regulations of the League with regard to replacements were totally disregarded; intra-organizational democracy declined to a new low point. The introduction of tuition fees for secondary and higher education during the war, and the establishment of Labor Reserve Schools disappointed and discouraged many young people who were not able to materialize their plans for a higher education. The goal of approaching communism was reiterated, and young people were asked to believe that they were building and would live in a communist society. However, there were few visible signs of progress toward the better future.

Defections during the early weeks of Soviet involvement in World War II have been interpreted as evidence for poor morale among the Soviet people as well as being due to inadequate military leadership and equipment. That low morale was a contributing factor is entirely possible; the Soviet regime had, after all, demanded much from the people and had given them few tangible rewards in return; the glories of the promised future would necessarily seem more remote with the involvement of the U.S.S.R. in a life and death struggle; initially, the Soviet armies were poorly equipped, and many of the most competent military leaders had been victims of the purge. It is perhaps not surprising that some Soviet citizens decided that Soviet defeat was inevitable, that life under Nazi rule would be no more intolerable than under Soviet rule, and that the most reasonable decision was to ally themselves willingly with the Germans. However, better leadership and equipment, in addition to the mass atrocities committed by the Nazis, soon stiffened the resistance of wavering citizens. Hatred for the Germans contributed to a strong surge of national feeling, and the Soviet people rallied strongly behind their government.

Soviet authorities state that Komsomolites made a brilliant showing in World War II. During the first few weeks, 260,000 Komsomolites went to the front, where they served as propagandists and as a buttress against defection as well as front line soldiers. On the Leningrad front ninety percent of the Komsomol members fought the foreign invaders. In the Stalingrad organization seventy-five percent of the members helped to defend the city. The first Soviet heroes during World War II were Komsomolites, airmen Stephen Zdorovcev, Peter Charitonov and Mikhail Zhukov. Over three and one half million Komsomolites were awarded orders and medals for fortitude and courage. Out of 11,000 heroes of the Soviet Union,

7,000 were affiliated with the Komsomol. On April 30, 1945, a Russian Komsomolite, Mikhail Egorov, and a young Georgian, Meliton Kantaria, raised the red banner of victory over the Reichstag. The Y.C.L. received the Order of Lenin for its services in World War II.[18]

As soon as the war was over the Komsomol was asked by the party to assist in the mammoth task of rebuilding the ruined country. Members worked at such tasks as reconstructing Stalingrad, the flooded mines in Donbass and destroyed dams. Brigades of Komsomolites worked on the Volga-Don Canal, raised electric power stations in Moscow, built a sky-scraper university in Lenin's Hills in Moscow, a sports stadium in Luzhniky and created another new city, Komsomol'sk on the Volga. The Y.C.L. was awarded a fourth Order of Lenin on its thirtieth anniversary in 1948. At the Eleventh Congress (1949) tasks assigned to or assumed by the League included education and indoctrination, economic activities, vigilance against enemies and military preparedness. Extraordinary stress was placed on indoctrination, perhaps to counteract the effects of wartime contacts with people in other European countries where the standards of living and the personal freedom of ordinary citizens amazed onlookers from the U.S.S.R.

From the Eleventh Komsomol Congress (1949) to the Twelfth Congress (1954) Komsomol membership doubled, reaching a new high of almost nineteen million, and including roughly one third of Soviet youth in the eligible age group.[19] There were no new major reasons for youth to be discontented with the regime, and several measures may have contributed to increased or sustained morale. Tuition fees were abolished shortly after the end of World War II, the number of educational institutions increased considerably, and generous stipends were granted to young people who demonstrated academic competency. New attention was being devoted to the production of consumer goods which had long been relegated to second place in relation to producer goods. Great improvements in living conditions were promised. Y.C.L. responsibilities in industry, agriculture, education, indoctrination and culture continued, and Komsomolites were assigned particularly challenging tasks in relation to the development of the virgin lands. For their efforts, Komsomolites were able to bask in elaborate praise from the party, such as "By heroic struggle and valorous work for the good of the motherland, the Y.C.L. has won the universal esteem and love of the Soviet people."[20] On the other hand, some Komsomolites must have questioned privately certain features of the system. For example, the revised statutes of the Y.C.L. which were adopted at the Twelfth Congress[21] stressed intra-organization democracy while, in fact, the relatively democratic principles in the old regulations had been violated frequently. When the mighty Stalin, to whom all including foremost party officials had openly expressed the deepest devotion, was being demoted from his pedestal, surely some Komsomolites questioned whether other "glorious" features of the regime might not also prove to be transitory, or not so valuable or good as they were being depicted. Some no doubt chafed under the necessity of accepting without question the ideology, program, policy and commands of the party leaders, resented the privations under which their system forced them to live, doubted the feasibility and even the value of the goals toward which they were forced to work, questioned the validity of the criticisms of the social orders of other countries, and hated the regime for the brutality and injustice which it practiced.

In the report of the Y.C.L. Central Committee to the Thirteenth Congress (1958) Shelepin stressed the enhanced role of the Y.C.L. in economic work, the need to improve ideological training, and Y.C.L. participation in all spheres of communist construction and in the International Youth Movement.[22] Khrushchev gave delegates to the Thirteenth Congress advance notice of the major educational reform which was introduced in December, 1958.[23] At the Fourteenth Congress (1962) Pavlov, the First Secretary of the Y.C.L. Central Committee, announced that directives to the League which stemmed from the decisions of the Twenty-Second Party Congress included: (1) Young people must apply all their energies to creating the material and technical base of communism and making maximum use of the reserves of industry and agriculture; (2) The rearing of the new man is the foundation of the ideological work of the Y.C.L.; (3) Strengthen ties between school and life more actively; (4) Strengthen friendship and cooperation with the youth of the world; (5) Every Y.C.L. is a militant and vital collective tightly linked with youth.[24] Khrushchev in his address to the delegates emphasized the need for every young person to see the interests of the people as his own highest interest and for all people to give their best to society, the importance of the development of new regions and of raising labor productivity so that the growing needs of all citizens might be met, and the need to strive actively to eliminate the parasitic and hooligan element in society.[25] Khrushchev advised Y.C.L. delegates that attacks from the old world will continue until the red banner of communism, the red banner of labor, is finally raised over the whole globe. He commented that the West understands that the strength of Soviet society lies in the moral and political unity of the people, and in the fact that the young generation have a great aim in life. Khrushchev also cautioned young people not to become conceited because of their accomplishments. Komsomol delegates were encouraged to believe that communism would be attained in the foreseeable future, and that much of the responsibility for achieving this goal was theirs.

The Little Octobrists

Fourteen and one half million children aged seven to nine are members of the Little Octobrist Organization which was established in 1926.[26] Five Octobrists form a link which is led by a senior Pioneer member. Five Octobrists links are united into a group led by a Komsomol member. Activities of the Little Octobrists include supervised play, and participation in socially useful labor such as clean up campaigns and collecting scrap metal. Emphasis is placed on scholastic excellence, political education and upbringing designed to inculcate the desired characteristics of the new Soviet man.

Membership in the Little Octobrists is not restricted. The organization is replete with symbolism designed to appeal to the very young. Few children can withstand the social pressure to join the Little Octobrists, since most of their peers are members, and many leisure-time activities are centered around the organization. Membership in a party-affiliated organization from a very early age constitutes a form of conditioning which inclines the rising generation favorably toward the party. The party seizes every opportunity to mold the thoughts and attitudes of the Soviet youth during their most impressionable years.

The Young Pioneers

The V. I. Lenin Children's Communist Organization of Young Pioneers works under the leadership of the C.P.S.U. and under the day-to-day supervision of the Y.C.L.[27] According to Pioneer regulations, Pioneer troops are formed in schools and children's homes where there are no less than three Pioneers (Rule III). The senior leader of a Pioneer troop is a Y.C.L. member assigned by the district or city Y.C.L. committee. Currently, the organization has a staff of 60,000 full-time group leaders.[28] Working with the senior leader is a troop council, consisting of three to fifteen persons elected by the troop, and a chairman elected by the council from among its members. Very small troops elect a troop chairman instead of a council. The Pioneer leader and troop council are expected to cooperate with teachers and principals to ensure that Pioneers study well, and are disciplined and active in labor and community work. They are expected to organize and conduct Pioneer gatherings, talks, competitions, exhibits of Pioneer work, trips and excursions, to draw Pioneers into various circles, games, sports and other mass activities, and to give assignments to detachments and individual Pioneers. At the same time, the council is expected to see that Pioneers are not overloaded with group, community and other assignments.[29]

Troops having at least twenty members may subdivide into detachments which, as a rule, include Pioneers in the same grade. Detachments are led by a Y.C.L. member who works in close contact with the classroom teacher, and under the supervision of the Senior Pioneer leader. A detachment may elect a small council or a chairman. Detachments with more than twenty members may subdivide into units, each of which elects a unit leader.[30] Pioneer troops within a district or city comprise the district or city organization of Young Pioneers. These organizations, in turn, form the region, province, territory or republic organizations which together comprise the V. I. Lenin Children's Communist Organization of Young Pioneers. Leadership of the Young Pioneer organizations at all levels is entrusted to the corresponding Y.C.L. committees which operate under the instructions of the corresponding party organizations (Rule IV).

School children from nine to fourteen years of age are eligible for membership. A detachment or troop decides by open vote whether a child who has indicated his desire to become a Pioneer is to be admitted.[31] Few if any children are excluded. The initiation ceremony is attended by all Pioneers of the school, their leaders, teachers and honored guests.[32] Pioneers march in quasi-military formation into an assembly hall decorated with pictures of Lenin and other Soviet symbols. The initiates, dressed in Pioneer uniform, the boys in a white shirt and dark trousers, the girls in a white blouse and dark skirt, are awarded a red kerchief, a Pioneer badge and a membership card. It is explained that the three corners of the kerchief symbolize the party, the Komsomol and the Pioneers, the pillars of the Soviet state. The badge is decorated with a red flag on which are the hammer and sickle, and a campfire of five logs burning with three flames. The five logs symbolize the continents, the three flames the Third International with its promise of future world revolution.[33] The Young Pioneer oath is recited: "I, a Young Pioneer of the Soviet Union, solemnly promise in the presence of my comrades to be faithful to Lenin's precepts and to defend firmly the cause of our Communist Party and the victory of communism. I promise to live and to study so as to become a worthy citizen of our Soviet homeland" (Rule I). To the call "Be ready to fight for the cause of the Communist Party," the Pioneer answers: "Always ready!" (Rule I).

It is the duty of the Young Pioneer to fulfill the Pioneer oath; to study diligently, to be disciplined in and out of school, to respect teachers and elders and to be polite; to be industrious, to respect the labor of others and to safeguard public property; to take part in community work; to help parents and adults; to be honest and truthful; to be a good comrade and to help those who are younger; and to participate in physical culture and sports (Rule II). Rights include participation in the discussions and work of the unit, detachment or troop, to be elected as a unit leader or council member, and to request a recommendation from a troop council for Y.C.L. membership (Rule II).

The preamble to the regulations states that the organization is

". . . to help the school and the teacher struggle for high scholastic progress and discipline and for the pupils deep and firm knowledge, to edu-

cate in school children a keen mind and curiosity, persistence and industrious-
ness and to instill in children a regard and love for manual labor, habits for
doing things for themselves and an ability to do any work within their
capacity . . . to concern itself with the health of children and the correct
organization of their leisure, to promote extensive enlistment of school children
in physical culture, study and shopwork circles, groups of young nature
lovers and amateur art groups, and to conduct mass games, excursions, and
trips."

In all these endeavors the age, interests and demands of the children are
to be taken into account.

Pioneer activities are designed to influence the moral, political, educational and physical development of children, to provide vocational guidance and experience, and to permit them to use their leisure time in interesting, meaningful and acceptable ways. Concrete examples from the life
of Soviet people, the school, and Pioneer activities are to be employed to
teach Young Pioneers about the correctness and virtues of the Communist
Party, the great socialist homeland, the successes of the Soviet people in
building communism, the degeneration of hostile imperialist countries, and
the value of subordinating their personal interests to those of the group.[34]
Many of the Pioneer activities are conducted through circles composed of
10-15 children. In any given year, a Pioneer may participate voluntarily in
two circles of his own choice. Through the circles, children can participate
in a wide variety of activities such as dancing, foreign languages, choral
singing, chemistry, photography, aviation, astronautics, painting, puppetry,
boating, nature study, music or driver training. When appropriate, there
may be circles on the same subject for different age groups. In every school
there is supposed to be a Pioneer Room which may be used for circle meetings as well as for formal meetings of the entire detachment or troop. In
more populated areas there are Pioneer Palaces or Pioneer Houses, staffed
with trained leaders and equipped with facilities such as dark rooms,
laboratories, libraries, auditoriums and musical instruments. However,
reports in the Soviet press indicate that many Pioneer Rooms are poorly
equipped, Pioneer Palaces are sometimes operated inefficiently, and the
leadership provided to circles is all too frequently of mediocre or inferior
quality.[35] Disinterest on the part of Pioneers is a common problem.

During the summer vacation three to four million children between
the ages of seven and fifteen spend a month at a Pioneer camp.[36] The
camps are designed to enhance "all-round development of the child's
abilities" and to provide "a healthful, interesting vacation."[37] At a camp,
children may participate in socially useful labor such as working in
orchards or farm plots, draining swamps, clearing land, planting trees,
prospecting for minerals, preparing athletic fields, or establishing their own
work shops, hot houses or apiaries. In addition, there may be meetings with
war or labor heroes, visits to historic sites, Young Pioneer friendship campfires, athletic contests and festivals. Parents are required to pay no more

than half the cost of the camp, and many children, such as those of widows, single mothers, and disabled war and labor veterans, are issued free passes.[38] An attempt is made to provide appropriate substitute activities for children not able to attend summer camps. Included are exploratory trips and tours, organized games and amusements, activities in Pioneer Palaces and Houses, and school recreation halls, and free daytime use of stadiums, swimming and boating areas, and parks under the jurisdiction of trade unions.[39]

The Pioneer training program is divided into three age groups, each one requiring specific skills and knowledge.[40] All Pioneers must during their membership learn to swim, ski and play some athletic game. Ten and eleven year old children must know the history of national holidays, construct some useful object for their school, plant a tree, and be able to do simple mending. They also take at least two all-day hiking trips. Twelve and thirteen year old Pioneers must be able to describe local places of historical interest and construct several household articles. On their three to four day hikes they learn to use a compass, pitch a tent and give first aid. Older Pioneers must be able to learn things on their own and to teach younger children. They learn to ride a motorcycle, drive a tractor and car, study photography and advanced sports and acquire practical knowledge of radio and electricity. By the age of fifteen every Pioneer must win his "Be Prepared for Labor and Defense" badge.

It would appear that the extra-curricular and leisure time activities of Soviet children are organized so carefully and with so much concern for individual interests that each Young Pioneer would be so constantly involved in meaningful, educational or socially useful tasks of interest to him that he would seldom, if ever, be bored or tempted to indulge in "petty bourgeois" un-Soviet-like behavior. However, in the realm of children's activities and in many other areas as well, the Soviet leaders would, no doubt, agree fully with the poet Robert Burns that "The best laid schemes of mice and men gang aft a-gley."[41] Although official criticism of the Young Pioneer organization has decreased during the last few years, many complaints and criticisms are still published. The decreased criticism may reflect genuine improvement or may merely indicate that party and Y.C.L. leaders are temporarily too involved in matters more urgently requiring their attention to attend to shortcomings of the Young Pioneer organization.

Frequently reiterated are statements about the shortcomings of the quality of Y.C.L. leadership which is provided for the Young Pioneers.[42] As a rule, Young Pioneer leaders are pupils about to graduate from secondary school, who regard this work as merely a stop gap. No educational institution especially trains leaders, and often the Young Pioneer leadership is entrusted to poorly prepared people, assigned on the basis of availability rather than quality. More than half the leaders work with their troop for less than a year and not infrequently, troops are left without leaders for months at a time. Because of inadequate leadership, Pioneer meetings are often dull and boring. The interests of the children, the differences in their ages, and appropriate motivating techniques are often neglected.[43] For example, the same talk may be given for Pioneers in the third and the seventh grades. Lengthy reports are given instead of lectures which are clear and understandable to the children. Pioneer meetings may be devoted to classroom subjects such as "The Noun" or "The Soils of the U.S.S.R." Some Pioneer leaders conduct current event instruction by lining up all the Pioneers from the third to the eighth grade, shouting "Attention" and reading a newspaper aloud.[44] Often the number of circles from which to choose is very limited, and circles are not always adequately led. In many units and detachments Pioneer meetings, parades, festivals, campfires and assemblies are held rarely. Too frequently, Pioneers are not allowed to exercise any initiative on their own.[45] Members of the troop and detachment councils are sometimes appointed by teachers and Pioneer leaders instead of being elected. New members may be admitted without consultation with Pioneer members. Young Pioneers may be excluded entirely from the leadership of detachments and troops, and all decisions may be made by adults. There is much unnecessary regimentation of Young Pioneer work, and meetings may be conducted according to prescribed outlines and prepared scripts.[46] Under such circumstances, children become bored with Pioneer activities and try to avoid them.

Soviet authorities concede that there are still some Young Pioneers who show lack of discipline and regard for socialist property, disdain for manual labor, an unwillingness to participate actively in socially useful labor, rudeness, selfishness and dishonesty.[47] Others err by adhering to religious beliefs and practices. The Pioneer leaders and Y.C.L. executive bodies are criticized for adopting a conciliatory attitude toward such misbehavior, contenting themselves usually with dull moral admonition, criticism of bad behavior and giving the guilty child a "goingover" at Pioneer meetings. It is argued that stronger and more positive approaches are required.

The fact that the Young Pioneer organizations are criticized is not indicative of gross failure. Criticism is used by the Soviet leadership to hasten the removal of shortcomings, to warn the population that the party is fully aware of and unwilling to tolerate shortcomings, and to demonstrate to the rest of the world that criticism of party controlled institutions is permissible in the U.S.S.R. If the Pioneer organizations were not making a substantial contribution to the realization of the goals of the leadership for Soviet society, they would have been abolished or drastically revised. Their structure and overall functioning have not been changed substantially since their inception. It is probable that the Young Pioneer organizations are performing their tasks in a relatively acceptable manner from the point of view of the Soviet leadership. However, since the "new Soviet man" is still in the process of development, and the majority of Pioneer leaders and members have not yet approached the Soviet ideal, errors and failures in the operation of the organization are to be expected.

The Young Communist League

MEMBERSHIP REQUIREMENTS

Membership in the Young Communist League is open to "leading young people devoted to the Soviet homeland" (Rule 4).[48] Admission requirements include recommendations by two Y.C.L. members of at least one year's standing, by one Y.C.L. member and a Pioneer Troop Council or by one member of the Communist Party. Y.C.L. membership is granted on an individual basis after a favorable decision by the primary Y.C.L. organization is confirmed by the bureau of the district or city Y.C.L. committee. Any person accepted into the ranks of the Y.C.L. between the ages of 14 and 26, acknowledging the Y.C.L. Statutes, working in one of its organizations, submitting to all decisions of the Y.C.L. and paying membership dues is considered a Y.C.L. member (Rule 1). Members who request permission to remain in the League after they attain the age of 26 may be allowed a two year extension by the primary organization. Members of an executive body of the Y.C.L. may retain membership after the upper age limit is reached (Rule 1). Typically, a large percentage of the leading officials of the League have been well over the upper age limit of 26. For example, of the 1,236 delegates to the Thirteenth Congress (1958) over half were 26 years of age or older, 13.4 percent were over 30, and 8.3 percent were over 32; only 32 percent had less than seven years service in the League.[49] League membership may be held concurrently with party membership. Sixty percent of the delegates to the Thirteenth Congress were members or candidate members of the Communist Party.[50]

Organization of the Y.C.L.

The organization of the Young Communist League parallels that of the Communist Party of the Soviet Union at all levels. The major subdivisions of the Y.C.L. in hierarchical order are the All-Union Y.C.L. organization, the Y.C.L. organizations of the Union Republics, the region, territory or provincial organizations, the city or district organizations, and the primary organizations. The internal structure of the Y.C.L. organization at each level also corresponds to that of the party. Each Y.C.L. organ in the pyramidical structure is controlled and supervised by the corresponding party organ, and by the superior Y.C.L. organ.

The All-Union Y.C.L. Organization

THE CONGRESS

The highest body of the All-Union Leninist Young Communist League is the Y.C.L. Congress which, according to the Statutes, is to be convened not less than once every four years. Since the 1954 revision of the Statutes, the Congress has been convened regularly. However, prior to 1954, when there was a statutory provision that the Congress should be convened at least once every three years, Congresses were held in 1931, 1936, 1949 and 1954.

The Statutes specify that the Congress is to elect the Y.C.L. Central Committee and Central Inspection Commission and to hear and approve their reports; and to determine the general line of Y.C.L. work and its current tasks. Like its counterpart, the Congress of the C.P.S.U., it is not a policy making body. The Y.C.L. Congress does little more than to provide rubber-stamp approval for the policy dictated by the party to the top echelon Komsomol leaders. For example, the published reports of the last several Congresses do not mention even one dissenting vote with reference to the agenda, reports or resolutions. All persons who are nominated for membership in the Central Committee and Central Inspection Commission are invariably elected. The election to leading positions of a high proportion of the delegates who are permitted to deliver reports to the Congress suggests that higher officials exert strong control over the choice of nominees. Despite reiteration of the need for criticism and self-criticism, during the last several Congresses criticism has been limited to safe topics, i.e., a particular Komsomol official has been lax in implementing the decisions of the party; the party or a higher Komsomol body should provide more guidance; work with children's theatres should be improved. Criticisms of the correctness of the basic ideology or the decisions of the party or Komsomol leaders are not permissible. Delegates have refrained from discussing violations of the Statutes of the League such as the failure to convene a Congress or to replenish membership of the Y.C.L. Central Committee from among the candidate members. There is no evidence that constructive proposals ever emanate from Congress delegates. Apparently the only acceptable spontaneous utterances from delegates, who have not been selected to give reports, are "prolonged stormy applause" when a high ranking party official gives an address, along with shouts of "Long live the Communist Party." The Congress does not play an active role in determining the policy of the League.

The complete conformity of the delegates, and their apparent subservience to the dictates of the high ranking party and Komsomol officials seems incongruous with descriptions of them as "our glorious Soviet youth," and "the flower of the young generation of our glorious country."[51]

However, in some respects Soviet and Western behavioral ideals vary substantially. The good Komsomolite is expected to accept without question the decisions of the party and of the Y.C.L. leaders. His duty is to implement decisions rather than to make or appraise them. Since the delegates include some of the most intelligent and highly educated representatives of Soviet youth, many must disagree with some of the decisions of the leaders, and must be aware of and concerned about the discrepancies between ideology and practice, and the violations of League principles. The positive rewards associated with conformity and submissiveness, combined with fear, must be essential ingredients of their passive acceptance. Of course, the number of delegates, which is typically around thirteen hundred, makes the Congress an unwieldly body for free discussion and effective policy determination.

CENTRAL COMMITTEE

The Y.C.L. Central Committee, elected by the Congress to direct the work of the Y.C.L. in intervals between the All-Union Congresses (Rules 20, 23), is also a large and somewhat unwieldly body. The Central Committee elected by the Thirteenth Congress included 120 members and 57 candidate members, almost 15 percent of the total number of delegates to the Congress.[52] In the event of loss of members by the Y.C.L. Central Committee, its membership is to be replenished from among the candidate members (Rule 20). However, not one of the 47 candidate members who were elected at the Eleventh Congress served as a full member at the opening of the Twelfth Congress, although many of the full members were not present.

According to the rules, the Y.C.L. Central Committee directs all the work of the Y.C.L. in the intervals between Congresses, represents the Y.C.L. in state institutions and organizations, names the editorial board of *Komsomolskaya pravda* and other Central Committee publications, and distributes and controls the manpower and resources of the Y.C.L. (Rule 23). The Central Committee is required to hold a plenary session not less than once every six months and to keep Y.C.L. organizations regularly informed about its work (Rules 21, 22). Because of its size, and for other reasons, the Central Committee is not substantially more powerful than the Congress as a policy making body.

CENTRAL COMMITTEE BUREAU AND THE SECRETARIAT

The real power of the organization is held by the Central Committee Bureau and the Secretariat which are elected by the Central Committee from among its members. The Bureau is empowered to direct all work of the Y.C.L. between plenary sessions of the Central Committee, and the Secretariat is empowered to direct current work of an organizational and executive nature (Rule 23). Membership in these bodies is typically small. After the Thirteenth Congress the Central Committee elected a Central Committee Bureau with 17 members and 7 candidate members, and a nine man Secretariat. Typically, members of the Bureau and the Secretariat are high ranking party members, frequently members of the Central Committee of the C.P.S.U. Bureau members and Secretaries, working in close contact with party leaders, determine policy and make decisions for the entire Y.C.L. organization. Delegates to the All-Union Y.C.L. Congress approve without discussion the reports and decisions made for them by these officials. Rather than being responsible to the Congress, the body which elects them, the Bureau members and the Secretaries are responsible to, supervised by, and take orders from the leaders of the C.P.S.U. Although the guiding principle of the organizational structure of the Y.C.L. is democratic centralism, it is difficult to perceive democratic features in the non-accountability of the executive, legislative and administrative organs of the organization to the membership. That the policy involves centralism is readily apparent.

THE CENTRAL INSPECTION AND THE CREDENTIALS COMMISSIONS

The Central Inspection Commission inspects the speed and correctness of the conduct of affairs in the central bodies of the Y.C.L., the treasury and budgetary expenditure and the organizational condition of the apparatus of the Y.C.L. Central Committee (Rule 25). Thus, the statutes provide for a body, elected by the Congress, which could serve to keep within statutory limits the activities of the Central Committee, its Bureau and the Secretariat. Although certain budgetary and other excesses may have been limited because of reports by the Central Inspection Commission, there is no evidence that it has ever made reports critical of the top echelon Komsomol officials. As is frequently the case in Soviet organizations, a commendable statutory provision for the control of the activities of high ranking officials by the rank and file does not, and in all probability is not intended to, function toward that end.

Pavlov, in his report to the Fourteenth Congress, asserted that inspection commissions at lower levels in the Y.C.L. tend to check only on the financial activities of Y.C.L. committees and on their action in response to letters. He recommended that they should also attend to the excessive formalism, endless talking and bureaucracy that sometimes occurs.[53] Reports of the Central Inspection Commission at the All-Union level indicate that the scope of its activities are similarly limited.[54] Adoption of Pavlov's suggestions would expand the functions of the Inspection Commissions, but a check on basic statutory violations would still not be permissible.

The Central Inspection Commission elected by the Twelfth and

Thirteenth Congresses had memberships of 31 and 37 respectively. Although the statutes do not prohibit overlap between the membership of the Central Committee and the Central Inspection Commission, overlap has, in fact, been avoided completely. Separation of the two bodies is, of course, appropriate since the Central Inspection Commission is supposed to check on the functioning of the Central Committee. The most generous interpretation of the *de facto* separation is that delegates to the Congress are aware of its necessity, and nominate members accordingly. However, the lack of overlap is probably due to the control of nominations and, hence, elections by top ranking Komsomol and party officials.

The Credentials Commission is required to establish that the elections of delegates to the Congresses are conducted in accordance with the requirements of the Y.C.L. Statutes, and to establish the validity of the credentials of all delegates. It compiles information about the age, education, occupation, length of Y.C.L. service, party membership, and national origin of the Congress delegates, and about the establishment of new Y.C.L. primary organizations and the admission of new members.[55] The reports of the Credentials Commission are typically descriptive rather than analytical. No violations in the election procedures are reported, although it is probable that violations, especially in the selection of nominees, are common.

Y.C.L. PUBLICATIONS AND FINANCES

The Y.C.L. is one of the biggest publishers in the country. Major publications are the *Komsomolskaya pravda* and *Pioneerskaya pravda,* the nationwide organs of the Y.C.L. and the Pioneers respectively. All told, approximately 200 Y.C.L. and Young Pioneer newspapers and magazines are published with a per-issue circulation of 22,500 copies.[56] The publishing house of the Y.C.L. Central Committee issues some 350 books and pamphlets yearly with an overall sale of more than 23,000,000 copies.[57] Earnings of Y.C.L. publishing houses constitute approximately 40 percent of the Y.C.L. budget. The remainder of the income comes from entrance and membership fees.[58] The chief item of expenditure is for republic Y.C.L. organizations.[59] Another expense is for training or refresher courses for executive personnel of the province, territory and republic Y.C.L. organizations. The Young Pioneer organization is financed primarily from the proceeds from the publication of 25 newspapers and 34 magazines for children. Additional funds are provided by the Ministry of Education to subsidize junior naturalist clubs, hobby centers and art circles.[60] Young Pioneer summer camps are supported mainly by the trade unions.

Intermediate Y.C.L. Organizations

At the republic, territory and province levels, the organization of the

Y.C.L. is essentially similar to that at the All-Union level. For each Union Republic the highest Y.C.L. body is the Congress; for each territory and province it is the Conference. Corresponding to the Central Committee of the Y.C.L. are the Union Republic Central Committee and the territory or province Y.C.L. Committee. These bodies are guided in their work by the decisions of the All-Union Congresses and the Y.C.L. Central Committee (Rule 26).

The Congress or Conference must be convened once every two years to hear and approve the reports of its executive committee and Inspection Commission, to discuss problems of Y.C.L. work in the republic, territory or province, and to elect the Inspection Commission, and delegates to the All-Union Y.C.L. Congress (Rule 27). Like the All-Union Congress, Congresses at these levels are not influential policy making organs.

The duties of the Union Republic Central Committee and the territory and province Committee are specified in greater detail than the duties of the All-Union Central Committee. The Committee

> ". . . represents the Y.C.L. in Soviet, trade union and other organizations, guides the work of lower-echelon organizations, organizes work on the communist upbringing of young people, mobilizes the forces of young people for carrying out the tasks of building communism posed by the C.P.S.U., ensures fulfillment of the decisions of the Y.C.L. Central Committee, the development of criticism and self-criticism and the training of Y.C.L. members in the spirit of an uncompromising attitude toward shortcomings, appoints the editorial boards of Y.C.L. organs which function under its control, distributes within the jurisdiction of its organization the manpower and resources of the Y.C.L., administers the province, territory or republic Y.C.L. funds and regularly informs the Y.C.L. Central Committee of its activities" (Rule 29).

Plenary sessions of the Committee must be held at least once every four months (Rule 30). As at the All-Union level, a Bureau and Secretaries are elected to handle current work. Secretaries must have been Y.C.L. members for at least three years and must be party members (Rule 28).

District and city Y.C.L. organizations operate under the supervision of a Union Republic, territory or province organization. Each of these organizations has a Conference which must be convened yearly, a committee which must hold a plenary session every three months, a bureau and secretaries. Secretaries must have been Y.C.L. members for not less than two years and must be members or candidate members of the C.P.S.U. However, for the first time in the Y.C.L. hierarchy, there is a statutory provision for exceptions to the requirement that secretaries be members or candidate members of the party (Rule 32). This concession may be a sign of the party's increased confidence that Soviet youth are satisfactorily subservient to party control. The duties of the city and district organizations are similar to those of higher level organizations except that the sphere of jurisdiction is more limited.

Criticisms by Komsomol leaders indicate that the intermediate Y.C.L. organizations do not always fulfill their obligations satisfactorily. For example, specific committees are taken to task for espousing great causes and ending with "nothing but pious wishes"; tolerating violations of the rules of socialist living; formalism, endless talk and bureaucracy; being indifferent to poor workers and loafers; concerning themselves primarily with the collection of information and statistical compilations, with a concomitant lack of knowledge of the actual state of local affairs; passing numerous decrees but failing to check on whether any of the decisions are being carried out; and, most terrible of all, for passing decrees on matters under the sole jurisdiction of the party.[61] Others are criticized because Y.C.L. membership has decreased, religious influence and outdated attitudes toward women have not been successfully combatted, and political and ideological education has not been adequate to combat hooliganism, drunkenness and other unacceptable behavior.[62]

On the other hand, official praise is published more frequently than criticism. Particularly common is praise for Y.C.L. participation in the construction of major national economic projects such as hydro-electric stations, metallurgical plants, refineries and apartment buildings.[63] Praise is also given for patriotic initiative in striving to complete important projects ahead of schedule; successes in corn and sugar beet raising; establishing youth lecture bureaus, consultation centers, and ideological commissions dealing with the party program, and clubs of revolutionary glory and international friendship clubs; sponsoring cultural circles, exhibits and performances; strengthening political education by establishing study circles to deal with topics such as "Communism—the Practical Task of Our Generation," "Principles of Communist Ethics" and "Two Worlds—Two Kinds of Youth"; and mass participation circles to study particular political events of major importance, party documents or the concrete tasks facing Y.C.L. organizations.[64] Examples of praise and criticism are informative with reference to the scope and variety of activities in which the Y.C.L. organizations are involved.

How well do the intermediate Y.C.L. organizations meet the requirements imposed by the party? The party appears to be relatively well satisfied with their performance. It is rare that a Committee or organization has to be reprimanded for attempting to usurp authority that has not been delegated to it by the party. Apparently, the lesson that initiative is permissible only with respect to carrying out the decisions of the party along party prescribed lines has been well learned. Also, the party has techniques, which are not specified in the statutes, to remove inefficient or otherwise objectionable Komsomol officials. That not all operations are carried out with maximum efficiency in all of the organizations all of the time is to be expected, as would be the case in any other country or under any other system. In the Soviet Union official praise is seldom given to subordinates unless it is fully warranted. The fact that many intermediate Y.C.L. organizations and committees are praised indicates that they are performing their party-imposed tasks well. The criticisms indicate that there is room for improvement, and that the party is not willing to tolerate inefficiency and poor work.

Primary Organizations of the Y.C.L.

At the foundation of the Y.C.L. are approximately 400,000 Y.C.L. primary organizations which include more than 21 million members.[65] Primary organizations are set up in any industrial, agricultural, military and educational institution where there are at least three Y.C.L. members (Rule 36). As a general rule, one primary organization encompasses all Y.C.L. members within a particular enterprise or institution. However, industrial enterprises or educational institutions with more than 100 members, and agricultural enterprises with more than 50 members may obtain permission from the district or city Y.C.L. committee to form primary organizations within departments, classes or brigades. Within primary organizations, Y.C.L. groups may be established in smaller units such as shops and shifts (Rule 37). The subdivision of excessively large primary organizations is probably designed to increase the involvement of each member in the goals and activities of the organization and to make it more difficult for individual members to shirk responsibility.

The primary Y.C.L. organization elects a Y.C.L. committee to conduct current work. An organization within a department, class or brigade elects a bureau with a tenure of one year. Organizations with a membership of less than 10 elect a secretary instead of a committee or bureau. As a rule, the committee and bureau members and secretaries are fully employed and perform their Y.C.L. duties on their own time and without pay. Very large primary Y.C.L. organizations may have full-time staff employees only upon the authorization of the Y.C.L. Central Committee (Rule 39).

As the foundation of the Y.C.L., the activities of primary organizations determine to a large extent the successes and failures of the organization as a whole. The Statutes describe the responsibilities of the primary organization as follows:

> "The primary Y.C.L. organization unites members of the Young Communist League, thoroughly develops the Young Communists' initiative and activity, draws them into active public work and directly links the Young Communist League with the broad masses of young people. The tasks of the primary Y.C.L. organization consist of:
> (a) Education of the rising generation in the spirit of communism, political education of Y.C.L. members and young people, helping young men and women to master knowledge, culture, science and technology, and mobili-

zation of all the forces of youth for practical accomplishment of the tasks of communist construction.

(b) Concern for improvement in the working and living conditions of young people and a rise in their living standards and cultural level, organization of interesting mass cultural projects and drawing of Y.C.L. members and young people into regular participation in physical culture and sports.

(c) Check-up on the fulfillment by every Y.C.L. member of the duties set forth in the Y.C.L. Statutes.

(d) Enlistment of new members in the Y.C.L. and their political education.

(e) Development of criticism and self-criticism and the training of Y.C.L. members in an uncompromising attitude toward shortcomings.

(f) Cooperation with the district Y.C.L. committee, city Y.C.L. committee or political department in all their work.

"Y.C.L. organizations must be genuine and active bearers of Party directives in every sphere of socialist construction, particularly where there are no primary Party organizations" (Rule 38).

What are the concrete activities of Y.C.L. primary organizations in relation to these tasks? Considerable emphasis is placed on political education. A fairly large proportion of the meetings may be devoted to discussions or lectures on various aspects of Marxism-Leninism, the practical tasks of building communism, new developments in the party program, etc. Apparently these activities do not always arouse and hold the interest of the members. Criticisms indicate that the weaknesses of the political education program are qualitative rather than quantitative. Excessive formalism, haranguing, stilted discussions, repetitiveness and lack of opportunity for free participation by the members are reported frequently as reasons for disinterest and poor attendance at meetings by Komsomolites. A former leading Y.C.L. official complained:

"Political education is conducted in the Y.C.L. in isolation from concrete tasks, and often without connection with life. In this work we are mainly occupied with cud chewing, with idle repetition from year to year of the same old general principles, naturally leaving young people unsatisfied. As a result of major shortcomings in political education, some members lose interest in the Y.C.L. and slip away from its influence."[66]

Urgent pleas by the Y.C.L. and party leaders are made for improvement in the ideological education at the primary level.[67] The First Secretary of the Y.C.L. Central Committee stated:

"We must use all the resources of ideological work to help the Party inculcate in young men and women a sense of pride in the great accomplishments of the Soviet homeland; we must convincingly show the advantages of the socialist system. We must smash every attempt by hostile ideology to penetrate into the circles of Soviet youth; we must expose to public censure those who in dark corners seek to spread ideas, views and ways that are alien to us. We must instill in young people ideological firmness, the ability to stand up for communist convictions. Our propaganda must help young men and women to orient themselves correctly in life and must magnify their strength for accomplishing the noblest of intentions and aspirations."[68]

To train young people in the spirit of Soviet patriotism, Y.C.L. organizations are instructed to

". . . explain to them better the great achievements and victories of our homeland in the economic, political and cultural spheres, and the advantages of the socialist system which liberated the energies of the people, gave the working people a genuine freedom and democracy, made them masters of their country and made it possible to transform our homeland rapidly and beyond recognition."[69]

The Central Committee advised the Y.C.L. organizations to give more help to young people in studying Marxism-Leninism, to explain to them the party teaching on classes and class struggle, social revolution, the dictatorship of the proletariat, the paths of transition from capitalism to socialism, the nationality question, proletarian internationalism, the party's role in the struggle for the victory of socialism, socialist democracy, etc.[70] To achieve more effective political education, the Central Committee directed the primary organizations to abandon stereotype in lecture work, to organize informative, lively talks, lectures and question and answer evenings, and to make more extensive use of such forms of agitation work as meetings, parades, agitation and cultural brigades, wall newspapers, broadcasts, etc.[71]

Many factors probably contribute to the lack of enthusiasm for ideological indoctrination.[72] Those who serve as educators may feel obligated to adhere closely to the most firmly established dogma since the party line may change without notice. Audiences have heard the established dogma over and over again from a variety of sources. Many young Soviet citizens may attempt to avoid meetings which they anticipate would be boring and educators expecting a bored audience may not exert themselves to present their old material in an interesting manner. Among Komsomolites, there are probably a number who disagree with the official ideology, or at least resent the fact that they are not allowed to question certain aspects of it. Many may have no strong feelings against the ideology, but may have a strong preference to use their time for pursuits of their own choice. Political education conducted through the medium of study circles might evoke somewhat more enthusiasm among the Komsomol members. Here, at least, participants may choose the area of emphasis, as for example, some less familiar facet of Marxism-Leninism or potential techniques for application of the Party Program in their own enterprise or shop. No doubt, like young people in other systems, Komsomolites experience more enthusiasm and genuine interest in ideology when they are permitted to assume an active role in its implementation, even if, as is the case in the U.S.S.R., participation in ideological development is completely denied to them.

In addition to attending to the political education of young people, the primary organizations are expected to manifest an interest in and to influence their academic, scientific, technological and cultural education. Academically proficient Komsomolites are expected to encourage and assist other young people in the acquisition of knowledge. Organizations recommend to the appropriate authorities that particularly talented or qualified young persons be accepted for additional training in higher educational institutions. Meetings or circles study new scientific or technological developments and consider their application in specific segments of the economy. The political implications of Soviet space accomplishments are discussed. Efforts are made to inform industrial and agricultural authorities and rank and file workers of new developments which might improve economic efficiency. In the cultural sphere, attention is devoted to increased interest and elevated taste for artistic, musical and literary works.

For these activities, all of which involve a certain amount of initiative, creativity and independent action on the part of the Komsomolites, considerable interest is evidenced and no doubt, some worthwhile goals are accomplished. However, as might be expected, some Y.C.L. groups carry their activities to objectionable extremes. For example, a goal of some primary organizations is to improve the personal grooming and dressing habits of young people. A *Komsomolskaya pravda* correspondent quotes a revealing letter from a Leningrad docent:

> "Here is what I saw in Sochi . . . Young Communist street patrols were literally hunting down young men wearing brightly colored shirts and young women wearing slacks. They ripped or slashed the shirts. The same fate befell the slacks. Black shirts also invited persecution on the grounds that 'Black-shirts' used to exist. The method of knocking someone's teeth in, is not in my opinion, the best educational method. To tear and ruin clothing, even though it may seem funny, is inappropriate and illegal, and to chop off a girl's hair(such incidents happened in Sochi) is sheer violence."[73]

"Music Patrols" have broken up orchestras that did not comply with the standards for good music set by the patrol.[74] "Artistic Patrols" smashed easels or destroyed paintings or drawings which did not meet with their approval. Naturally, such behavior on the part of Y.C.L. groups has not met with the universal approval of mature Soviet citizens. On the other hand, their vigilant behavior is condoned and even praised by some respected individuals. For example, a composer referred to the "Music Patrols" as "an expression of initiative of young people to beautify our everyday life."[75] He added, "To be neutral in politics these days is to be artistically barren, to write and create not knowing for what and for whom."

Why do Komsomol groups carry their "cultural uplifting" activities to objectionable extremes? No doubt some young people are genuinely concerned about improving the Soviet way of life. Y.C.L. organizations have been directed by the Central Committee to intensify ideological and educational work among young people in creative areas, to wage a sharp struggle against unhealthy sentiments and views which exist among some young creative workers, and to oppose works of literature and art which portray Soviet reality in a distorted fashion and thereby harm the cause of training young people.[76] At the Fourteenth Congress the task of serving as esthetic censors was clearly delegated to the Y.C.L. organizations. The Y.C.L. First Secretary stated:

> "Heavy crystal chandeliers, thick velvet draperies, ink stands depicting a boar hunt in all but life size—all this is quite out of keeping with Soviet peoples ideas of beauty and comfort. Who needs this tastelessness, this merchant-class swank! All these plush, gilt idols of the old mercantile esthetics must be laid to rest along with the sculptured roof cornices, spires and statues that have been expelled from Soviet architecture. The performers slobbering tearfully to guitar accompaniment about broken hearts, loneliness and seduced damsels give of an even mustier smell. . . . These are all goods from the same shelf, from that same putrid assortment of joys and sorrows of the petty-bourgeois world. . . . The Central Committee of the Young Communist League and the Y.C.L. organizations working together with the Composers' Union, should take serious pains to guard youth from this ersatz stuff; they should pay attention to the kind of music that is being heard on the dance floors, in the parks, on the variety stage and over the radio and exert an active influence on the repertoire of the amateur performing groups."[77]

The suggestion that the Y.C.L. should work with the Composers' Union was apparently not meant to limit Y.C.L. activity, since the Composers' Union would have no influence over interior decoration and certain other "bourgeois signs of decadence." Moreover, the First Secretary in no way censured primary Y.C.L. groups for excesses such as those described in the preceding examples. In view of the position taken by Komsomol officials, it may be assumed that many Y.C.L. members who participate in the patrol type activities believe that they are making a legitimate contribution toward the improvement of society by attempting to eradicate modes of expression and behavior which they deem undesirable.

Many Y.C.L. members who engage in patrol activities of the abusive type may be using these activities as an outlet for deepseated frustration with their role in the regime. In many spheres, their actions are closely circumscribed by the dictates of the party; expressions of antipathy or distaste for the system and way of life which has been imposed by the party are not permissible; they must carry out the orders of their political superiors even if they intensely disagree with them; they are powerless to change the system or to effect any change in the way of life except along party prescribed lines. Many of them may feel impotent, powerless and deeply frustrated by the limitations placed on them by the system. Although they are free to obtain some relief from frustration-induced tensions through constructive work in the economy, or through physical culture, academic, or other cultural or artistic pursuits, these outlets might not be sufficiently satisfying to some young people. Some turn to hooliganism, drunkenness and other anti-social activities. But such activities have the disadvantage of being socially condemned. Some of the patrol activities, which in many societies would be considered rank hooliganism, have, however, a certain amount of social sanction and respectability because they are directed toward socially acceptable goals. Thus, in a sense, the patrol activities permit the participants to be destructive and anti-social under the guise of being constructive, responsible citizens. At the same time, as a Soviet author points out, it permits them to play with power, which though it is small, is nevertheless flattering to their egos.[78]

Almost half of the report of the Y.C.L. First Secretary to the Fourteenth Congress (1962) was devoted to the theme: "Young people must apply all their energies to creating the material and technical base of communism and making maximum use of the reserves of industry and agriculture."[79] Pavlov stated:

> "The effort to achieve a steady rise in the productivity of labor has held a central place in the work of the Y.C.L. Completion of shift assignments in six hours, active participation in the modernization of equipment and in automation and mechanization, the effort to achieve smooth-running and efficient production and to turn out the finest products in the world, the mastering of allied vocations by young workers and the improvement of their skills—these have become a normal part of the activities of many Y.C.L. committees. . . . The Y.C.L. must help in the introduction everywhere of the most progressive production methods and important discoveries and must act more boldly against routine and stagnation. . . . Y.C.L. organizations are obliged to make a more vigorous effort to prevent a single machine, machine tool or assembly from standing idle for no good reason, to keep public property from being squandered. The nationwide Y.C.L. raids for uncovering and putting to use uninstalled and superfluous equipment have played an important part in cultivating in young people a thrifty, proprietary attitude to what belongs to the people. . . . Rural young communists should become enthusiasts for the adoption of intensive farming systems that make it possible to obtain maximum output per hectare of plowland. . . . The Y.C.L. must wage a more active struggle for careful and economical use of equipment in animal husbandry, too . . . etc."[80]

In addition to general economic directives, specific goals may be set for Y.C.L. participation in the economy. For example, among the concrete tasks specified by the Y.C.L. First Secretary at the Thirteenth Congress were within given periods of time: to fatten at least 40,000,000 pigs; to set up rabbit breeding sections on collective and state farms; to plant at least 500,000 hectares of communal orchards and vineyards and 200,000 hectares of shelter belts; to plant trees and shrubs along specified highways; and to collect at least 3,000,000 tons of scrap metal. The Y.C.L. was also directed to assume patronage over a number of industries or construction projects: first-line Y.C.L. construction projects included seven blast furnaces, three open hearth furnaces, nine coke batteries, several metallurgical plants and their mines, railroad electrification, oil and gas industry enterprises, chemical enterprises, etc. Y.C.L. organizations were directed to send detachments of young enthusiasts to these construction projects and to struggle for preschedule completion of them. In addition, it was proposed that "the Y.C.L. committees jointly with the economic councils, select at least 1,000,000 Y.C.L. members and young people, primarily from among those who have finished secondary schools, and send them as soon as possible, on a voluntary basis, to construction projects in the eastern and northern regions of the country and Kazakhstan."[81]

The concrete tasks are delegated by the All-Union Y.C.L. Central Committee to the Y.C.L. organizations lower in the echelon, which in turn delegate to each primary organization its specific responsibility in materializing the goals. Thus, a specific primary organization may be advised that in addition to raising the productivity of labor in its own locale of operation, it is responsible for fattening 10,000 pigs, mechanizing the milking of 5,000 cows, collecting 8 tons of scrap metal and selecting 10 young people to be sent "on a voluntary basis" to a particular construction project. Additional concrete tasks may, with the approval of the higher level Y.C.L. organizations, be assumed by a Y.C.L. organization at any level.

Economic tasks assigned to primary organizations may, depending on the circumstances, the organization and individual Y.C.L. members, be regarded as onerous duties, or as gratifying challenges. Reasons for lack of interest or resentment toward the assigned tasks include disillusionment with the regime, lack of time because of employment obligations, academic pursuits, and other Y.C.L. duties, unwillingness to sacrifice personal pleasure for the good of society, and low motivation, particularly on the part of farm youths who receive minimal compensation for their work on the collective farm, and must spend much of their off-duty time working on the private farm plot to obtain necessities. In some cases, tasks are assigned to primary organizations which do not have resources crucial to their fulfillment, i.e., a rural organization in an area which has a total of 300 cows might be instructed to mechanize the milking of 1000 cows. Frequently, assigned tasks and pledges are simply ignored or forgotten.

For many Y.C.L. members productive activities in economic spheres may contribute to the satisfaction of basic emotional needs, such as the need to strive actively toward a meaningful goal, and the need for achievement and recognition. Young people are fully encouraged to give of themselves for a meaningful cause, increased standards of living for all and a stronger homeland. As a rule, the results of their successful efforts are tangible and concrete. Successes are acclaimed by Komsomol and party officials. By challenging youth in the economic sphere, and permitting them to make significant contributions, Soviet officials are utilizing skillfully the energy and inventiveness of youth to achieve the economic goals of the Communist Party, and at the same time are partially gratifying some of their basic needs and thereby strengthening their allegiance to the system.

The effectiveness of the Y.C.L. in the economic sphere, in terms of motivation, increased productivity and allegiance to the Communist Party, depends to a large extent on the operation of the primary organizations. If the effectiveness of the primary organizations could be evaluated meaningfully in terms of Komsomol contributions to Soviet economic and military accomplishments, it could be concluded that, in the main, the primary organizations have usually fulfilled their tasks very well. At present millions of Komsomolites work in various branches of industry and on collective and state farms. There are in operation Komsomolite blast furnaces, open hearth furnaces, rolling mills, concrete plants, etc. Numerous items such as machinery and machine tools are stamped with the label "Komsomolec" (Komsomolite). When the party appealed to the Komsomol for help in cultivating virgin lands, more than 350,000 young people left their native cities, where life with their parents was easier, to help expand agricultural production. Pavlov reported to the Fourteenth Y.C.L. Congress that during the preceding 4 years 800,000 young patriots went to construction sites on Y.C.L. passes, more than 3,000,000 young men and women were working in construction sites in the Far North, Central Asia, the Baltic area and the Far East, and that the Y.C.L. had made significant contributions through the discovery and utilization of idle machines, the elimination of unproductive demurrage in transport operations, and the completion of crash projects.[82] Komsomolites have participated actively in Soviet space exploration. Each of the first four Soviet cosmonauts had been members of the Y.C.L.

These examples are indicative of excellent work on the part of the Y.C.L., and hence on the part of Y.C.L. primary organizations and individual members. However, not all organizations and members have been exemplary. Reports of shortcomings in Y.C.L. work are numerous in the Soviet press.[83] The most frequent complaint is that the Y.C.L. units make grandiose promises and pledges which are never translated into concrete action. Primary organizations are criticized for poor organizational work for the determination of potentials and techniques to eliminate shortcomings and for ignoring obvious approaches to increase productivity. The primary organization does not always support the excellent suggestions of an individual member and sometimes is lax about reprimanding and reorienting careless, lazy or slovenly workers. The rights of young workers may be emphasized more strongly than their duties and responsibilities. Y.C.L. units do not always attempt to ensure that workers are assigned to positions in accordance with their qualifications. Often, the best Y.C.L. cadres are not selected to go on Y.C.L. passes to participate in difficult projects in remote areas. The Secretary of a City Party Committee complained that some Komsomolites when confronted with difficulties in remote areas take a defeatist attitude about what they can do to improve conditions, and instead merely criticize others for the backward state of affairs. He added:

". . . not all Y.C.L. workers are ideal themselves. Six young people from Minsk failed to settle down in their new environment and already have found themselves in the dock. They have been tried for hooliganism. More than 100 'settlers' frightened by the difficulties have deserted. . . . A Y.C.L. assignment is not an award, not a certificate of merit for services rendered, but merely an obligation to win this merit in the future."[84]

Apparently some young people on Y.C.L. assignments have felt entitled to living arrangements and other accommodations superior to those of the local people.

In part the shortcomings of Y.C.L. groups in the economic sphere may be attributed to failures in the ideological education of young people, and to the fact that the "new Soviet man" is far from being a materialized reality, even among the younger generation. But other factors are also involved. The Y.C.L. primary organizations and members operate in an imperfect environment. Some of the best intentions of Y.C.L. groups may be thwarted by disinterested, inefficient or hostile economic administrators, the organizational structure within the economy, red tape, bureaucracy and a number of other factors. Repeated rejection of good ideas tends to decrease their frequency. Moreover, young people in the Soviet Union are overburdened with a multitude of responsibilities and duties in educational, cultural and political areas as well as in the economy. Some primary committees receive so many letters, directives and forms from their superior committees that little time is available for constructive leadership within the local organization. Finally, as would be expected in any society, some Y.C.L. members, and committee members as well, are lazy, inefficient, or dull.

Another duty of the primary organizations was stated explicitly at the Fourteenth Y.C.L. Congress:

> "The Y.C.L. committees are called upon to give constant attention to creating normal working and living conditions and facilities for study and leisure for young workers and collective farmers, . . . and to uphold the interests of youth boldly and with determination. All this is highly important for eliminating the turnover in cadres and anchoring young people at enterprises and construction sites. The Y.C.L. must give every measure of encouragement and support to those young men and women who are eager to become cadre workers, and conversely, it must wage a struggle against drifters of all kinds, against people who like to make their living the easy way."[85]

Approved activities include establishing and beautifying parks and recreation areas, forming hobby clubs and study groups and arranging appropriate meeting places, working with the trade unions to ensure the observance of laws on adolescent labor, assisting in the construction of dormitories, and purchasing equipment for the use of young people from funds raised by drives to collect scrap metal, medicinal herbs or by other means. Primary responsibility for physical culture and sports has been delegated to the trade unions and the Y.C.L.[86] Primary organizations are expected to build and supervise playgrounds and hikers' hostels, to encourage young men and women to train as athletes and as athletic instructors and judges, to sponsor sports festivals and competitions, and above all, to be active sportsmen themselves. Some organizations are highly praised for their work in these areas while others are roundly chastized.

During recent years considerable attention has been devoted to the problem of hooligans, parasites, drunkards, drifters and other anti-social elements in Soviet society.[87] Y.C.L. organizations have been instructed to

> ". . . proclaim relentless and determined war against all kinds of 'zoot-suiters', aristocrats and other parasites and hoodlums. All of them must be forced to work, and to work honestly as befits Soviet people. The Y.C.L. organizations should not stand aloof in embarrassment from young men and women who do bad things. It is our duty to do everything to re-educate and win to our side even those who go wrong, to make real Soviet people of them. . . ."[88]

Criticisms suggest that frequently Y.C.L. committees and members fail to intervene when Y.C.L. members and other young people engage in socially deviant behavior. Complaints such as the following are common: When a couple of tipsy hoodlums begin to raise a rumpus at a Y.C.L. club, members call the militia instead of handling the situation themselves; when a Y.C.L. member or other young person begins to drink heavily, to absent himself from work, or behave in other undesirable ways, the Y.C.L. organization and its members fail to inquire into causes and to institute rehabilitation measures; because Y.C.L. leaders show poor concern for leisure activities, some young people seek to entertain themselves with drinking bouts and hoodlum activities; many dormitories are dirty, uncomfortable and overcrowded with married and single people often sharing the same room; some dormitories have no radio loudspeakers, Red Corners or washstands, but the Y.C.L. organizations fail to report negligent executives to party or Soviet authorities.[89] Although some Y.C.L. organizations are undoubtedly lax, it is probable that many organizations perform their duties in these areas in a relatively satisfactory manner. The party does not look kindly on Soviet citizens who perform their assigned duties inefficiently.

If primary organizations were to perform all assigned duties with maximum efficiency, and to use their own initiative to assume new responsibilities as required by the local situation, in line with the directives and policy established by party and Y.C.L. officials, members of Y.C.L. committees and indeed, all Y.C.L. members would be required to work full time for the Y.C.L. However, almost all Y.C.L. work at the primary level is performed on an unpaid basis by persons who are engaged in full-time work in the economy or in educational institutions. Many of the Y.C.L. members may have little time, energy or creativity to spare for the multitude of Y.C.L. duties they are expected to assume. It is not surprising that few primary organizations earn the unqualified praise of their superiors.

Duties of Y.C.L. Members

In addition to his duties within the Y.C.L. organization, each Y.C.L. member has individual responsibilities. Y.C.L. obligations include:

(a) persistently to assimilate knowledge, culture, science and technology, relating every step of his studies, training and education to participation in building communism; to be an active fighter for the fulfillment of the policies of the Communist Party; to strengthen the ranks of the Y.C.L. in every way. . . ,

(b) to work constantly at increasing his awareness, to study the fundamentals of Marxism-Leninism and to explain the policies of the Communist Party to the broad masses of young people,

(c) to set an example of work and study. . . ; in all ways to safeguard and strengthen public, socialist property as the sacred and inviolable basis of the Soviet system,

(d) boldly to develop self-criticism and criticism from below, to expose and seek to eliminate shortcomings in work and to report to leading Y.C.L. bodies . . . irrespective of the persons involved,

(e) to be honest and truthful, to observe the rules of socialist community life, to combat vestiges of capitalism in the minds of young people, to combat drunkenness, hoodlumism, religious beliefs and uncomradely attitudes toward women,

(f) strictly to observe Y.C.L. discipline . . . to take an active part in the work of the Y.C.L. organization and to carry out the assignments of the organization promptly and precisely. . . ,

(g) to keep military and state secrets and to display political vigilance. . . ,

(h) to study the military arts, to be selflessly devoted to the great socialist homeland and to be ready to give for it all his strength and, if need be, his life (Rule 2).

A mandatory requirement for all members of the Komsomol is to master Marxism-Leninism. About four million Y.C.L. members participate in study circles devoted to Marxist-Leninist ideology, and the structure, function and responsibilities of the Communist Party. Over half of the approximately 230,000 study circle instructors are party members and all are experienced propagandists. Many Komsomolites who are not members of study circles engage in self-study programs to master the teachings of Marx, Engels, Lenin and the speeches of contemporary Soviet leaders. All Soviet youth are given a thorough political indoctrination, but Komsomol members receive additional indoctrination, training and experience in carrying out the party goals. Hundreds of thousands of Komsomolites propagandize the party program and act as agitators in situations where older party members would be less effective. The Komsomol is a reservoir of party members and also provides additional millions of non-party Bolsheviks, that is, non-party members who subscribe to and support the party program. Party members observe Komsomolites for a number of years and attempt to determine whether a firm belief in Marxism-Leninism was the reason for joining the youth organization. Those who joined for careerist purposes can usually be discovered and excluded from party membership.

The superordinate goal of the Komsomol is to develop staunch defenders and builders of socialism and eventually of communism. Y.C.L. members are trained in Soviet patriotism in contradistinction to what the Soviet writers refer to as bourgeois nationalism. The youth are expected to develop and use their individual talents for the benefit of the entire Soviet society rather than for their own advantage, since communist ideology holds that what is good for society is good for the individual. Komsomol members are advised that they are citizens of the most progressive country in the world, and that the U.S.S.R., under the guidance of the Communist Party, has provided a model for all People's Democracies and will become an example for all less fortunate countries. It is stressed that the achievement of communism requires that Y.C.L. members must have self-enforced discipline, must achieve a single will, and must perform faithfully all tasks imposed by the party and the government. Every member of the youth organization is to develop strength, courage, initiative, and to become an educated, diligent, accurate worker with a high sense of responsibility, a true servant of the people. All good qualities are to be strengthened and channelled into socially useful work while undesirable qualities such as vanity, conceit, laziness and overconfidence are to be curtailed. Each student Komsomolite is required to study diligently to master his chosen field, and at the same time to strive for the superiority of the collective (the whole class) rather than to work selfishly toward his own personal superiority and self-aggrandizement. Physical culture is stressed because good physical condition is required for the building and the defense of the Soviet motherland. Komsomolite members in the armed forces supplement the work of special political instructors by propagandizing the party program. Self-sacrifice for the common cause is demanded of Komsomolites who must be willing to perform any task assigned by the party or the government.

The conflicting demands of initiative and discipline with unconditional subordination of all Komsomol members to the leading bodies of the organization have led to numerous conflicts and purges of Komsomol officials. The difficulties of Y.C.L. leaders resemble those of party leaders. Only highly disciplined persons who are willing and able to fulfill the demanding task of following the party program, rules and directives exactly may become leaders. Yet initiative is a necessary prerequisite to fulfill the party requirements. Komsomolites are trained to act as leaders for Young Pioneer groups and as counselors in their summer camps, and are expected to serve as examples to the younger group as the foremost fighters for communism. They thus become accustomed to leading as well as to being led.

Although the Y.C.L. is predominantly a political organization the members also receive training and experience in natural sciences, especially in summer camps, and in hobbies, athletic, cultural and recreational activities. The demands which Soviet society places on its youth, however, far outnumber the pleasant leisure time activities. Many young people have responded enthusiastically to the challenge and the demands, but complaints in the Komsomol newspaper indicate that among the Y.C.L. members there are a few scoundrels, hoodlums, drunkards, shirkers, parasites and persons who would prefer an easier life. On the other hand, conditioning for decades, examples, environmental factors, ideology, idealism and prestige have contributed to the raising of generations of Komsomolites who in the main have been dedicated Soviet citizens and diligent builders of communism. Judged objectively, their record would seem to be impressive.

The Rights of Y.C.L. Members

In exchange for the weighty obligations which the Y.C.L. member must assume, he is granted the statutory right to take part in discussion of all problems of the work of the Y.C.L., in Y.C.L. meetings and in the Y.C.L. press; to elect and be elected to Y.C.L. bodies; to criticize any Y.C.L. functionary and any Y.C.L. body at Y.C.L. meetings; to insist on personal participation in all cases involving his activities or behavior; to address any questions, complaints, or statements to any committee of the Y.C.L. right up to the Y.C.L. Central Committee. Y.C.L. bodies must give attentive and careful consideration to the complaints and statements of Y.C.L. members and promptly take the necessary action in regard to them (Rule 3). These formal rights are violated very frequently.

Internal Y.C.L. Democracy

The Y.C.L. is described by Soviet authorities as a democratic organization. However, its mode of operation tends to be highly undemocratic. The Y.C.L. admits its complete subservience to the party in its own Statutes, which state:

> "The Young Communist League is linked to the Communist Party of the Soviet Union and is its reserve and aide. Under the guidance of the Communist Party, the Young Communist League trains young people in Soviet patriotism. . . . The Y.C.L. is strong by reason of its ideological conviction and devotion to the Party cause. . . . The Y.C.L. has the duty of helping the Communist Party of the Soviet Union to carry out its main tasks. . . . The Y.C.L. is the aide of the Communist Party in all state and economic work. . . . The Y.C.L. requires all its members to fight persistently and untiringly to carry out all the decisions of the Communist Party and the Soviet government. . . . The Y.C.L. does all its work under the direct guidance of the Communist Party of the Soviet Union. The Y.C.L. Central Committee . . . is directly subordinate to the Party Central Committee. The work of local Y.C.L. organizations is guided and supervised by the republic, territory, province, city and district Party organizations concerned."

In event of a difference of opinion between a Y.C.L. and a party committee, the decision of the party committee must be adopted by the Y.C.L.

As if party supervision of Y.C.L. activities at all levels were not a sufficiently pervasive form of control, all key positions in the youth organization must be held by tested members of the C.P.S.U. Only district, city and primary Y.C.L. units may elect non-party members as secretaries of Y.C.L. committees and then only in "individual cases." The combination of party supervision of Y.C.L. activities and party members in all the major Y.C.L. posts has effectively blocked the possibility that Komsomol units might use the "broad initiative" which has been granted to them to engage in activities which have not been approved by the party. Although the Statutes state that "all Y.C.L. members are assured the unrestricted right to challenge candidates and to criticize them" (Rule 15), for the past thirty-odd years this right has been seldom, if ever, used, partly because candidates for elected positions are approved, if not selected, by the superior party unit. If the Y.C.L. were a democratic organization, in which the candidates for election were proposed by a peer group, it is improbable that all nominated candidates would be accepted without challenge and elected unanimously. Moreover, the party, with complete disregard for Y.C.L. regulations, has not hesitated to install or to remove Komsomol officials arbitrarily. All-Union Y.C.L. Congresses have not been convened in accordance with the regulations when the party considered it politically inexpedient. With such pervasive party control and intervention, it would be impossible for the Y.C.L. to operate as a democratic organization.

Democratic centralism is advanced as the "guiding principle of the organizational structure of the Y.C.L." Since the Y.C.L. and the party adhere to identical definitions and practices of democratic centralism, a discussion of the practice of democratic centralism within the Y.C.L. would be repetitious. It is sufficient to reiterate that the emphasis in practice is on centralism rather than democracy. Likewise, the Y.C.L. Statutes grant to the members "democratic" rights which correspond to the rights of party members within the party organization, i.e., the free and businesslike discussion of all questions of the work of the Y.C.L. organization, and the rights of criticism and self-criticism (Rule 14). The party and higher level Y.C.L. organizations may permit the primary organizations to discuss freely non-policy matters such as the selection of a day for a scrap metal drive, designation of an editor for the wall newspaper and measures to strengthen political indoctrination or to increase labor productivity within the economic unit. At committee meetings issues under the exclusive jurisdiction of the organization may also be explored and discussed freely. Elected officials, who at the lower levels of the organization are not necessarily respected party members, may occasionally be evaluated critically by the members. However, higher level Komsomol officials who are party members of some stature, must not be criticized frankly by rank and file Komsomolites or lower level officials. Only safe or innocuous criticism is permitted; for example, members might deplore that greater effort had not been exerted to implement some aspect of the party program. Self-criticism, likewise, tends to center around shortcomings in carrying out the party program, e.g. "Y.C.L. organizations are still doing a poor job of enlisting young people in concrete activities and are still organizing their recreation unsatisfactorily. We are still timid and backward in introducing new and interesting developments in Y.C.L. work."[90] In point of fact, few meaningful or caustic criticisms are directed upward in the Y.C.L. organization, but there is nothing to impede the flow of criticism in the opposite direction. Internal democracy as described in the Y.C.L. Statutes is not materialized in practice.

Impact on the Individual and Society

Youth organizations are one of the major techniques which the Soviet regime uses in its attempt to transform society to correspond to the goals of the party leadership. The activities of the youth organizations, as an aide to the party, are centered around five major tasks: (1) the indoctrination and control of youth; (2) propagandization and implementation of the party program; (3) the involvement of young people in economic tasks designated by the party; (4) the development of staunch defenders and builders of socialism and eventually of communism; (5) the molding of the "new Soviet man."

All Soviet youth, and indeed, all Soviet citizens, are subjected to an unending stream of propaganda; academic subjects are taught from a Marxist-Leninist point of view; literature and art must portray "Soviet reality"; the interpretation of scientific findings must support dialectical materialism; every lecture, article in the press, and radio and television program must conform to the demand to indoctrinate the public. Since it would be virtually impossible to live in the Soviet Union without being overwhelmingly exposed to Soviet propaganda, why has the party deemed it expedient to use the youth organizations to expand and intensify the indoctrination? One reason is that the Soviet approach to the individual, society and the state differs so radically from that which has traditionally prevailed in the territory of the U.S.S.R. and in other areas of the world, that the party still finds it necessary, even after almost five decades of intensive indoctrination, to use every available technique to combat "the relics of the past." The youth organizations, which include almost all the children in Little Octobrist and Pioneer age groups and approximately one third of the young people in the Y.C.L. age group, are an effective channel which only leaders with a great lack of political and social astuteness would have overlooked. The party also recognizes the vast difference between being an active propagandist and a passive recipient of information and ideas. Y.C.L. members not only receive political indoctrination;

they are required to explain to others the ideological basis of the Soviet system and the party program. By serving as active propagandists they supplement indoctrination from other sources, and, perhaps more important, may themselves develop stronger convictions and enthusiasm for Marxist-Leninist ideology.

Through the youth organizations, the party maintains almost complete control over Soviet youth in a manner which is, in the main, reasonably acceptable to the young people themselves. Without a rigid system of control, the most likely potential source of opposition to the regime or to certain aspects of the party program would be from young Soviet citizens or youth groups. Because of the careful supervision, the indoctrination and the channeling of the energy and enthusiasm of youth into activities designed to assist in the achievement of party goals and to strengthen the allegiance of youth to the party, Soviet youth are an unlikely source of actions or even ideas directed toward social change other than those changes sponsored by the party. Thus, the youth organizations serve to neutralize what might otherwise be a potential source of an anti-party movement. The party has ample forces at its command to learn about and to squelch potential opposition, but for obvious reasons, it prefers to prevent opposition rather than to deal with it. The party control techniques are so inclusive and pervasive that even without the controlling influence of the youth organizations, Soviet youth would be unable to affect any substantial social change that was not instigated by the party, or even to express freely ideas opposed to those of the party. Many Soviet youth may, of course, be deeply frustrated because they are denied the opportunity to act upon or even discuss radical ideas. Young people in the Soviet Union who would dare to oppose the party or any aspect of the party program would be given ample reason to regret their rashness; staunch followers and supporters of the party may be rewarded in personally meaningful ways. The party has structured its youth program around the goal of rearing active supporters rather than impotent opponents, and rather than being a source of radical social ideas, as youth in so many systems are, the majority of the members of Soviet youth organizations are active supporters of the Soviet regime. Thus, the youth organizations have contributed substantially to the stability of the social and political system by virtue of their lack of opposition as well as through their positive support. The party could have achieved an equivalent control over youth through other techniques, but through the youth organizations, control is maintained in a socially acceptable manner, and numerous valuable by-products accrue to the party.

One of these by-products is propagandization and implementation of party policy. All Y.C.L. members must study, understand, accept and strive for the materialization of the party program. They are allowed to believe that their contributions are of great importance. The party leaders have utilized very effectively the technique of generating enthusiasm for their program by having most of the group members assume responsibilities, commensurate with their capabilities, for its development. In 1946 the author observed an incident which illustrated the personal involvement of a Soviet youth, when he overheard an interchange between a group of Czechs and a young Soviet soldier, a Komsomolite, who had been wounded in World War II. In reply to a question about how he liked Czechoslovakia the soldier made favorable comments. When asked whether people in the Soviet Union dressed as well, lived as comfortably and had as many luxuries as the Czechs, he answered quite frankly that the Soviet people did not live as well as the Czechs. But then he added "If we had concentrated on light industry and luxuries as you did to the detriment of the development of our heavy industry, we would not have been able to defeat the Nazi invaders. We would have been enslaved and you would not have been here at all." The conversation was ended. This incident also illustrates why the entire population of the U.S.S.R. is being indoctrinated constantly. In order to transform the under-developed Tsarist Russia into an industrial power, extreme sacrifices were and still are expected from the Soviet people. The Soviet people know that even now the standard of living in Western countries is higher than in the U.S.S.R. The Soviet leadership had to provide reasons for the poverty along with hope for a better future. Recent improvements in living conditions have eased the tasks of the leaders in this respect and the promise of significant improvements in the future serves as a powerful incentive. Political indoctrination, which includes the promise of a bright future, has been used as a substitute for high standards of living.

The fact that in the U.S.S.R. all youth are given a political education or indoctrination does not distinguish Soviet society from other societies. In all societies youth are indoctrinated with the prevailing ideologies. The differences are in the intensity of the indoctrination and the requirement in the U.S.S.R. that all people must subscribe to the one official ideology. The Soviet leadership realizes that the indoctrination must be thorough because Soviet ideology is at variance with ideologies which have been accepted for a millennium, because of the demands which Soviet ideology places on the individual and because no deviation from the official ideology can be permitted. In non-communist countries, young people are subjected to a variety of ideological influences, and there is no requirement that all young people must be taught or must believe exactly the same ideology; variations within the overall ideological framework are permitted and sometimes even encouraged. Likewise, young people in non-communist countries may join various organizations with distinct and sometimes conflicting goals and purposes. Soviet youth may join only the official youth organizations, and are not, at least with party sanction, subjected to any ideology in addition to or at variance with the official version of Marxism-Leninism. The indoctrinational programs of the youth organizations, the school, and subsequently, the job, the trade union, the military service and all cultural and public communication media are designed to instill and bolster belief in the superiority of Soviet ideology. The goals served by youth organizations in the U.S.S.R. and in other countries differ. Because of the complete exclusion of other ideologies, the absence of ideological variations between indoctrinational agencies, and the intensity of the indoctrination program, Soviet youth organizations serve as more efficient tools for indoctrination than youth organizations in other social systems. The youth organizations have played a major role in molding the thoughts, goals, values and aspirations of the current generation to conform with the demands of the party.

Soviet youth organizations are frequently criticized, by non-communist authors, for their high degree of regimentation. Life in the U.S.S.R. is most certainly highly regimented. However, the regimentation is a natural outgrowth of the Soviet ideology; to achieve communism, youth has to be raised in the spirit of collectivism, and hence, a certain amount of regimentation is inevitable. The Soviet world out-look makes it appropriate for the youth organizations to educate their members to work to the best of their ability for society rather than for themselves. The "new Soviet man" is supposed to be a collectivist in both work and leisure. The Soviet citizen is conditioned to say "ours," and to describe nothing as "mine" with the exception of personal property. The talented person is expected to share his talent, and to contribute more than the less talented person who will be cared for by society if necessary. Currently, the more talented and efficient person still receives higher remuneration, but the eventual goal is to have each person contribute to society according to his ability and to receive from society according to his need. There can be no doubt but that some Soviet citizens strongly resent regimentation and that many are more highly motivated to work for their own benefit than for the benefit of society. However, there are also apparently many Komsomolites and party members who work diligently for the good of society with no desire for personal reward.

Komsomol involvement in economic tasks has served two major purposes for the party. First, productivity of labor has been increased because of socialist competitions organized by the Y.C.L., Y.C.L. vigilance in reporting errors, shortcomings and waste, and Y.C.L. participation in major economic tasks such as the cultivation of the virgin lands. Second, through their work in the economy, young Komsomolites are able to make concrete and measurable contributions to the fulfillment of goals which they have been taught to hold sacred. Actual progress in the economic sphere supports the belief that party promises in other spheres will eventually be fulfilled, and in general, serves as a powerful reinforcer. Komsomolites and other young people tend to esteem the party more highly because it has given them important economic tasks, combined with high praise for their accomplishments, and token, but highly meaningful, improvements in their current standards of living.

Komsomolites are supposed to be trained and in turn to train other young people to be staunch builders and defenders of socialism and eventually of communism. It is the sacred duty of all Y.C.L. members to strengthen socialism and to prepare for communism in every conceivable way. Komsomolites must maintain physical fitness and develop appropriate skills so that they will be prepared to defend their country; all tasks delegated to them by the party must be performed with efficiency and enthusiasm; they must actively combat all that is un-Soviet or anti-Soviet such as foreign influence, ideological deviation, religion, laziness, wastefulness and unacceptable ways of dressing and behaving. Perhaps even more important to the party than the numerous duties performed by Y.C.L. members, is that young people should develop and maintain an unsullied belief that the promises of the party will materialize, and that the party goals and the means for realizing the goals are both realistic and irreproachable. The Y.C.L. is expected to instill in its members and other young people an unshakeable belief in the rightness of the party, its program and in the certainty that the party will lead them eventually to communism.

The youth organizations are charged with the task of assisting in the development of the "new Soviet man," a man who at a given level of social development will fit into the contemporary society and concurrently strive to effect the changes necessary to produce a higher level of social development. The exemplary behavior of Y.C.L. members is expected to influence parents, teachers, older co-workers and other young people who are not members of the Komsomol. The party uses the youth organizations as a channel through which to establish new norms of social conduct to fit the goals of the party for society at a given time. Emulation and the transfer of positive effect are preferred methods for effecting social changes. However, when individual members of society do not conform with the party approved standards of conduct, youth organizations are to participate in effecting the desired change. They are expected to take action themselves, or to report to the appropriate party or state authorities all instances in which individuals or groups do not conform with the mores of Soviet society. Thus, by serving as the eyes and ears and sometimes the hands of the party, as well as by striving to be exemplary citizens themselves, members of the youth organizations constitute a powerful force in effecting party designated social changes.

The youth organizations serve to resolve social conflict and contradictions between the "old" and the "new" in Soviet society. In the U.S.S.R. there are still strong and unwanted vestiges of the past. Religious influence has not been eradicated. Although the constitution guarantees that there shall be no discrimination on the basis of sex, some social groups attempt to keep women in a traditional subservient role. Individualism has not been replaced entirely by the spirit of collectivism. Some individuals and groups resist the introduction of new techniques in the economy. The family unit in some instances is a particularly potent bearer of the traditional, a force resistant to the new Soviet way of doing things. Soviet youth organizations are standard bearers for anything new which is introduced by the party, and opponents of anything old which is condemned by the party. Youth groups are, of course, not permitted to instigate new ideas or approaches independently, but are encouraged to adopt as their own all party sponsored innovations. When the forces of tradition such as those conveyed by the family and the church, and the forces representing the new, such as those conveyed by the youth organizations, converge on the young Soviet person, forces representing the new have powerful advantages on their side. Adolescents have a strong need to be similar to their peers. In western society many young people are thrown into a serious conflict because of differences between parental and peer group standards. In the U.S.S.R., parents and other traditional forces in society have, in most cases, to fight with blunted weapons. With few exceptions, youth organizations attempt to impose on young people the standards approved and sponsored by the party. When the standards of parents or other social groups are in opposition to those of the youth organization, a variety of social forces including education, political indoctrination, and anti-religious propaganda, are brought to bear against the "old." Thus, the peer group in the form of the youth organizations almost always wins in a struggle against the forces of traditionalism. Soviet youth may be less troubled by conflict between the "young" and the "old," or the "new" and the "old," than youth in other societies where the forces of the "old" usually have "right" on their side. In Soviet society the forces of the "new" have "right" on their side since what is to be new is determined by the party. On the other hand, some Soviet youth may be deeply frustrated because they are denied the right to serve as instigators of new ideas.

What rewards accrue to individual members of the youth organizations? Why do Soviet youth join the Komsomol? One advantage of Y.C.L. membership is that it increases the probability of admission to the party. Some Soviet citizens express either a genuine or simulated keen desire for party membership. Gherman Titov, a Soviet cosmonaut, stated in his autobiography, 'My greatest honor was the decision of the Central Committee of the Communist Party to take me into its ranks. . . . I was very much moved and proud of that recommendation . . . when I . . . read the Central Committee decision to admit me to the Party, my hands dropped with surprise and emotion. I had not expected that, nor even dreamt of it."[91] Although statements such as Titov's are probably made and published primarily for propaganda purposes, party membership is, in fact, a reward since it may open the door to the best careers. From the Thirteenth to the Fourteenth Y.C.L. Congress (1958-1962) 1,269,000 Komsomolites were accepted as members of the Communist Party.[92] However, the majority of Komsomolites do not become party members, and persons who are not Y.C.L. members may be brought to the attention of the party because of outstanding performance in any area of endeavor. Thus, although the prospect of party membership may influence some young people to join the Komsomol, it is not, in itself, a sufficient explanation for the assumption of the weighty tasks of the Y.C.L. by so many young people.

On the contrary, membership in the Komsomol itself has many appealing features. Young people are assigned major tasks which are meaningful to them. They are given a cause to fight for, a purpose in life, and this cause is fully supported by the major source of authority in the society, the party. Rather than fighting against, they are encouraged to fight for and with those that control the power. Y.C.L. members are accorded a certain amount of stature and dignity by the party and the state; the organization is asked to perform important services, and for its efforts is praised publicly. Many young people may derive sincere enjoyment from serving their country. Moreover, membership in the organization serves as a prestige symbol for the individual. The Soviet regime has utilized fully the idealism of youth. Many young people have a sincere faith in the future of communism, and are motivated to contribute to its establishment.

Another important reason for Soviet youth to join the Komsomol is that all competing organizations such as the Boy Scouts and church groups have been abolished. If a young person does not join the Y.C.L. he cannot affiliate with any other group composed exclusively of young people. Many of the recreational, cultural and athletic events of interest to young people are organized or sponsored by the Y.C.L. Acceptance in the in-group, in this case an in-group sponsored by the party, requires Y.C.L. membership. The out-group, the non-Komsomolites, are denied the privilege of organizing. Thus many young people might join the organization for personal or social reasons.

Since there are so many reasons for a young person in the Soviet Union to join the Y.C.L., why does the Komsomol incorporate only about one third of the eligible age group? Not all Soviet youth meet the requirements for membership in the Komsomol. Some young people may refrain from joining because of the influence of their parents, because they want to avoid the additional indoctrination or would be bored by it, or because they do not agree with the goals of the party and the Y.C.L. However, it is likely that the majority of non-members have not joined for reasons entirely acceptable to the regime. Many young people are so fully occupied with educational pursuits and work in the economy that they would be unable to participate effectively in Komsomol activities. Their position *vis a vis* the regime is more secure if they do not join than if they join but perform their Y.C.L. functions in an unsatisfactory manner. By focusing diligently on educational and economic matters, they too serve society in a manner sanctioned by the party. Lack of affiliation with the youth organization does not necessarily reflect passive opposition to the regime.

The Soviet authorities have encountered many obstacles which have interfered with or impeded materialization of their goals for youth. The social and economic structure within which the party has had to conduct its work with youth has been far from ideal from the Soviet point of view. Early in the history of the regime, the party had many opponents including parents, educators and the clergy who strongly influenced young people. Old habits, attitudes, beliefs and ways of doing things are not easily modified; even now, many people try to transmit religious beliefs and traditional attitudes to their children. The "new Soviet man" has not emerged. Young people are influenced by the individualism, self-aggrandizement, selfishness, drunkenness, deceit and cruelty, which is manifested by so many mature Soviet citizens. Moreover, Soviet society has not been able to offer youth many tangible rewards for the sacrifices they have been required to make. Promises have been plentiful, but it is only recently that some of the promises have shown signs of materialization, as for example, the increased availability of consumer goods.

Probably no individual in the U.S.S.R. fulfills all his Y.C.L. obligations completely, and some Y.C.L. members fall far short of the expected norms. The Soviet press cites examples of laziness, drunkenness, hooliganism, timidity, boastfulness, greed, lack of initiative, egocentrism and irresponsibility, among Komsomol members. Some young people in the U.S.S.R. manifest envy for what they imagine to be the American way of life—the life of rich people, with luxurious homes and fabulous wardrobes (luxury items are very expensive in the U.S.S.R.), cars (which only a few Soviet citizens can afford), privacy, gaiety and leisure. Such young people arouse the ire of the party.

Of more importance to the regime than isolated examples of misbehavior are the underlying causes of the misbehavior, some of which are an outgrowth of the party's own policy. Although the majority of Soviet youth may be active or at least passive supporters of the party program, scattered evidence suggests that a goodly number of young Soviet citizens are restive, albeit impotently restive, under the restrictive control of the party. Reasons for the restiveness are not hard to find. Young people, like all other Soviet citizens, must be completely subservient to the party. Personal strivings and personal goals must be absolutely secondary to the goals of the party for society. The vast discrepancies between the ideological pronouncements of the party leaders and the stark reality cannot but breed a certain amount of cynicism. The promised glorious future which seems to be continuously receding into the more distant future may have acquired the quality of a tarnished dream which can no longer stir the imagination as it did during the early years of the regime. The oft reiterated party and Komsomol appeals, which may be based on lofty but seldom practiced principles, are often reacted to with apathy and boredom. Some Soviet youth apparently react adversely to the many restrictions and limitations which their regimented society imposes upon them. Some of the cases of anti-social behavior are almost certainly expressions of frustration with respect to the rigidly prescribed limits within which the young people can express themselves.

Though the party and its program does not meet with the complete approval of all Soviet youth, the young people who are experiencing malcontent pose no threat to the stability of the regime. Some of the discontented people would probably not be contented under any other social system either. Apparently the majority of those who are expressing their dissatisfaction in an anti-social manner are not persons who are endowed with leadership qualities. At any rate the party would not allow the development of an organized faction which opposed the regime, or for that matter, any organized faction which was not sponsored by the party. Not all Soviet youth behave completely in accord with the party dictates, but on the whole, the party, with the help of the youth organizations, has achieved rather remarkable success with respect to its goals for youth.

REFERENCES

1 V. I. Lenin, quoted in *The U.S.S.R.—As It Is,* (Moscow: State Publishing House of Political Literature, 1959), p. 92.

2 For a comprehensive history of Soviet youth organizations see Ralph Talcott Fisher, Jr., *Pattern for Soviet Youth,* (New York: Columbia University Press, 1959).

3 "The First All-Russian Congress of the RCLY, Oct. 29-Nov. 4, 1918," 3rd ed., Moscow-Leningrad, *Molodaia gvardiia,* 1926, p. 98.

4 "The Second All-Russian Congress of the RCLY, Oct. 5-8, 1919," stenographic account, 3rd ed., Moscow-Leningrad, *Molodaia gvardiia,* 1926, pp. 45-6.

5 *Ibid.,* p. 13.

6 "The Third All-Russian Congress of the Communist League of Youth, Oct. 2-10, 1920," stenographic account, Moscow-Leningrad, *Molodaia gvardiia,* 1926, p. 31.

7 *Ibid.,* pp. 21-2.

8 "The Fifth All-Russian Congress of the RCLY, Oct. 11-19, 1922," stenographic account, Moscow-Leningrad, *Molodaia gvardiia,* 1927, pp. 113-4.

9 "The Fourth Congress of the RCLY, Sept. 21-8, 1921," stenographic account, Moscow-Leningrad, *Molodaia gvardiia,* 1925, p. 29.

10 "The Fifth Congress," *op. cit.,* p. 114.

11 *Ibid.,* pp. 344-8.

12 "The Seventh Congress of the All-Union Leninist Communist League of Youth, March 11-22, 1926," stenographic account, Moscow-Leningrad, *Molodaia gvardiia,* 1926, pp. 469-72.

13 *Ibid.,* pp. 43-5.

14 "The Eighth All-Union Congress of the ALCLY, May 5-16, 1928," stenographic account, Moscow, *Molodaia gvardiia,* 1928, pp. 18-26, 443-4.

15 "The Ninth All-Union Congress of the ALCLY," stenographic account, Moscow, *Molodaia gvardiia,* 1931, p. 61.

16 "The Eighth Congress," *op. cit.,* pp. 43, 576.

17 *The U.S.S.R.—As It Is, op. cit.,* p. 94.

18 *Ibid.,* p. 96.

19 A. N. Shelepin, "Report of the Y.C.L. Committee to the Twelfth Congress," *Komsomolskaya pravda,* March 20, 1954, pp. 2-4.

20 "To the Twelfth Congress of the All-Union Leninist Young Communist League (Party's Message to the Congress)," *Komsomolskaya pravda,* March 20, 1954, p. 1.

21 "Statutes of the All-Union Leninist Young Communist League Adopted by the Twelfth Y.C.L. Congress," March 25, 1954, *Komsomolskaya pravda,* March 30, 1954, p. 2.

22 A. N. Shelepin, "Report of the Y.C.L. Central Committee to Thirteenth Congress," *Komsomolskaya pravda,* April 16, 1958, pp. 2-5.

23 N. S. Khrushchev, "Train Active and Conscious Builders of Communist Society," *Pravda,* April 19, 1958, pp. 1-3.

24 S. P. Pavlov, "Report of the Y.C.L. Central Committee and the Young Communist League's Task Stemming from the Decisions of the Twenty-Second Party Congress," *Pravda,* April 17, 1962, pp 2-7.

25 N. S. Khrushchev, "Young Builders of Communism, Carry High the Banner of Lenin," *Pravda,* April 21, 1962, pp. 1-2.

26 "On the Red Kerchiefs Shines the Light of Communism," *Komsomolskaya pravda,* Feb. 6, 1963, pp. 1, 3.

27 "Regulations of the V. I. Lenin Children's Communist Organization of Young Pioneers," *Komsomolskaya pravda,* April 10, 1954, p. 2.

28 Yuri Iziumov, "Youth Pioneer Organization in the U.S.S.R.," unpublished speech provided by the Soviet Embassy, Washington, D.C.

29. *Ibid.*

30 *Ibid*

31 *Ibid.*

32 Cf. Merle Fainsod, "The Komsomols—A Study of Youth Under Dictatorship," *American Political Science Review,* Vol. XLV, No. 1, March, 1951, pp. 18-40. The description of the initiation ceremony is based on Professor Fainsod's article and *The Regulations of the Young Pioneers Organization.*

33 Cf. Fainsod, "The Komsomols," *op. cit.,* pp. 18-40.

34 Z. P. Tumanova, "On the Work of the V. I. Lenin Young Pioneers Organization," *Komsomolskaya pravda,* March 24, 1954, p. 2.

35 S. Soloveichik, "The Palace Is not Merely for Show," *Komsomolskaya pravda,* Dec. 29, 1963, p. 2.

36 "Young Pioneer Camp Time Is Drawing Near," *Sovetskaya Rossia,* April 12, 1958, p. 4.

37 *Ibid.*

38 *Ibid.*

39 *Ibid.*

40 Iziumov, "Young Pioneer Organization," *op. cit.*

41 Robert Burns, "To a Mouse," in *Selected Poems,* (New York: Thomas Y. Crowell and Co., 1892), pp. 104-6.

42 Pavlov, "Report of the Y.C.L. Central Committee," *op cit.,* pp. 2-7.

43 Tumanova, "On the Work of the Young Pioneers," *op. cit.,* p. 2.

44 Cf. Tumanova, *Ibid.*

45 "On the Red Kerchiefs Shines the Light of Communism," *op. cit.*, pp. 1, 3.

46 Cf. Tumanova, "On the Work of the Young Pioneers," *op. cit.*, p. 2.

47 "Resolution of the Twelfth Congress of Young Communist League on Work of the V. I. Lenin Young Pioneers Organization," *Komsomolskaya pravda*, March 24, 1954, p. 1.

48 "Statutes of the All-Union Leninist Young Communist League," *op. cit.*

49 V. Ye. Semichastny, "Report of the Credentials Commission of the Thirteenth Y.C.L. Congress," *Komsomolskaya pravda*, April 17, 1958, p. 2.

50 *Ibid.*

51 Khrushchev, "Young Builders of Communism," *op. cit.*, pp. 1-2.

52 Cf. "Y.C.L. Central Committee Elected by Thirteenth Congress," *Komsomolskaya pravda*, April 19, 1958, p. 6.

53 Pavlov, "Report of the Y.C.L. Central Committee," *op. cit.*, pp. 2-7.

54 Cf. V. I. Khazarov, "Report of the Central Inspection Commission," *Komsomolskaya pravda*, March 20, 1954, p. 5.

55 Cf. Semichastny, "Report of the Credentials Commission of the Thirteenth Congress," *op. cit.*, p. 2.

56 Pavlov, "Report of the Y.C.L. Central Committee," *op. cit.*, pp. 2-7.

57 *Ibid.*

58 Khazarov, "Report of the Central Inspection Commission," *op. cit.*, p. 5.

59 *Ibid.*

60 Iziumov, "Young Pioneer Organization in the U.S.S.R.," *op. cit.*

61 Cf. Pavlov, "Report of the Y.C.L. Central Committee," *op. cit.*, pp. 2-7, and Shelepin, "Report of the Y.C.L. Central Committee to Thirteenth Congress," *op. cit.*, pp. 2-5.

62 Cf. S. Pkhakadze, "Concern about Communist Upbringing of Young People," *Zarya Vostoka*, March 5, 1957, p. 3.

63 Shelepin, "Report of the Y.C.L. Central Committee to Thirteenth Congress," *op. cit.*, pp. 2-5.

64 Cf. Pavlov, "Report of the Y.C.L. Central Committee," *op. cit.*, pp. 2-7.

65 "The Youth of the Country Is With the Leninist Party," *Pravda*, June 30, 1963, p. 2.

66 A. N. Shelepin, "On Activities and Problems of Soviet Youth," *Pravda*, Feb. 28, 1956, p. 8. (C.D.S.P., Vol. VIII, No. 12, pp. 6-8)

67 Cf. *Ibid.*; and "Decree of the Plenary Session of the Y.C.L. Central Committee on Improving Ideological and Upbringing Work of Y.C.L. Organizations Among Y.C.L. Members and Young People," *Komsomolskaya pravda*, Feb. 28, 1957, p. 15 (C.D.S.P. Vol. IX, No. 10, pp. 16-8); and Pavlov, "Report of the Y.C.L. Central Committee," *op. cit.*, pp. 2-7.

68 Pavlov, "Report of the Y.C.L. Central Committee," *op. cit.*, pp. 2-7.

69 "Decree of the Plenary Session of the Y.C.L. Central Committee," *op. cit.*, p. 1.

70 *Ibid.*

71 *Ibid.*

72 Cf. Fainsod, *How Russia Is Ruled, op. cit.*, pp. 283-306.

73 N. Kolesnikova, "Patrol in Knee Pants—Concerning a Southern City, Maturity of Views and the Young Communists Battle for Good Taste," *Komsomolskaya pravda*, Dec. 13, 1960, p. 2.

74 Cf. Yury Milyutin, "Concerning the Roots of 'Lilies of the Valley,' 'The Lipsi' and Good Jazz," *Komsomolskaya pravda*, Sept. 23, 1962, p. 4.

75 *Ibid.*

76 "Decree of the Plenary Session of the Y.C.L. Central Committee," *op. cit.*, p. 1.

77 Pavlov, "Report of the Y.C.L. Central Committee," *op. cit.*, pp. 2-7.

78 Kolesnikova, "Patrol in Knee Pants," *op. cit.*, p. 2.

79 Pavlov, "Report of the Y.C.L. Central Committee, *op. cit.*, pp. 2-7.

80 *Ibid.*

81 Shelepin, "Report of the Y.C.L. Central Committee to Thirteenth Congress, *op. cit.*, pp. 2-5.

82 Pavlov, "Report of the Y.C.L. Central Committee," *op. cit.*, pp. 2-7.

83 Cf. *Ibid.;* and Shelepin, "Report of the Y.C.L. Central Committee to Thirteenth Congress, *op. cit.,* pp. 2-5.

84 A. Mokrinsky, Secretary of the Khabarovsk City Committee, *Komsomolskaya pravda,* Jan. 13, 1957, p. 1.

85 Pavlov, "Report of the Y.C.L. Central Committee," *op. cit.,* pp. 2-7.

86 *Ibid.*

87 Khrushchev, "Young Builders of Communism," *op. cit.,* pp. 1-2; and Shelepin, "Report of the Y.C.L. Central Committee to the Twelfth Congress," *op. cit.,* pp. 2-4.

88 Shelepin, *Ibid.*

89 Cf. A. Sukontsev and I. Shatunovsky, "Uninhibited Hoodlums and Timid Activists," *Komsomolskaya pravda,* April 3, 1954, p. 3; and A. Belkin, "Why Were the Young Communists Silent," *Komsomolskaya pravda,* May 8, 1954, p. 5.

90 Shelepin, "On Activities and Problems of Soviet Youth," *op. cit.,* p. 8.

91 Gherman Titov, "First Man to Spend a Day in Space," *The Soviet Cosmonaut's Autobiography as told to Pavel Barashev and Yuri Dokuchayev,* (New York: Crosscurrents Press, 1962), p. 108.

92 Pavlov, "Report of the Y.C.L. Central Committee," *op. cit.,* pp. 2-7.

Chapter IV

SOVIET FEDERALISM

The Multi-National State

The Soviet Constitution describes the U.S.S.R. as a "federal state formed on the basis of a voluntary union of equal . . . Republics . . . ." Soviet federalism was developed as a technique to unite under Soviet rule the multi-national population which had lived under Tsarist control. Although citizens of the U.S.S.R. are often referred to as Russians, only slightly more than one-half of the population of the U.S.S.R. belong to the Russian nationality. The remainder of the inhabitants of the U.S.S.R. represent well over one hundred different nationalities with distinct languages and dialects. Table 1, which summarizes national and linguistic affiliation on the basis of 1959 census figures, indicates the magnitude of the ethnic and linguistic diversity. No other political entity, except perhaps the British Empire at its zenith, has incorporated such ethnic, linguistic and cultural diversity. Although Lenin would have preferred to establish a unitary state, the multi-national composition of the population, in combination with other features inherited from the Tsarist regime, made it expedient for him to compromise by establishing a system of power which was federal in form, but unitary in substance.

The Soviet Heritage from Tsarist Imperialism

The Tsarist empire, in addition to being multi-national, was heterogeneous in religion. More than one-half the Tsar's subjects subscribed to the Russian Orthodox faith, but there were large numbers of Muslims, Roman Catholics and Jews, as well as a few Protestants. The level of cultural advancement varied markedly among different ethnic groups. The three major Slavic groups—the Great Russians, the Ukrainians (called Little Russians during the Tsarist era), and the Belorussians (White Russians), who constituted seventy-five percent of the population, had different but closely related languages and similar cultures. Traditionally, most of the Slavs had belonged to the Orthodox Church, but following a Uniate movement inspired by the Poles, many Ukrainians and some other Slavs recognized the authority of the Pope. The cultural and political traditions and the languages of the Armenians, Georgians, Letts, Lithuanians,

Table 1

National and Linguistic Affiliation in the U.S.S.R.*

Nationality	Number (in 1,000's)	Linguistic Affiliation** (Percentage)	Nationality	Number (in 1,000's)	Linguistic Affiliation** (Percentage)
Total for U.S.S.R.	208,827†	94.3	Greek	310	41.5
Russian	114,588	99.8	Buryat	253	94.9
Ukrainian	36,981	87.6	Yakut	236	97.5
Belorussian	7,829	84.1	Kabardian	204	97.9
Uzbek	6,004	98.4	Kara-Kalpak	173	95.0
Tatar	4,969	92.1	Karelian	167	71.3
Kazakh	3,581	98.4	Hungarian	155	97.2
Azerbaidzhanian	2,929	97.6	Gypsy	132	59.3
Armenian	2,787	89.9	People of the North including:		
Georgian	2,650	98.6	Nenet	25	85.7
Lithuanian	2,326	97.8	Evenki	24	53.9
Jewish	2,268	20.8	Khant	19	77.0
Moldavian	2,214	95.2	Chukchi	12	93.9
German	1,619	75.0	Other	48	75.4
Chuvash	1,470	90.8	Gagauz	124	94.0
Latvian	1,400	95.1	Rumanian	106	83.3
Tadzhik	1,397	98.1	Kalmyk	106	91.0
Polish	1,380	45.5	Ingush	106	97.9
Mordvinian	1,285	78.1	Tuvinian	100	99.1
Turkmenian	1,004	98.9	Uigur	95	85.0
Bashkir	983	61.7	Finnish	93	59.5
Kirgiz	974	98.7	Karachai	81	73.9
Estonian	969	95.1	Adighe	80	96.7
Peoples of Dagestan including:			Abkha	74	95.5
Avar	268	97.1	Kurd	59	89.9
Lezghian	223	92.7	Khakass	57	86.0
Darghin	158	98.6	Altais	45	88.6
Kumyk	135	98.0	Balkar	42	97.0
Lak	64	95.8	Turk	35	82.2
Nogai	41	84.3	Cherkess	30	86.6
Tabasaran	35	99.2	Chinese	26	69.3
Other	21	99.3	Czech	25	49.0
Udmurt	623	89.1	Aissor	22	64.3
Mari	504	95.1	Dungan	21	94.8
Komi and Komi-Permyak	431	86.7	Iranian	21	44.7
			Abaza	20	94.8
			Vep	16	46.1
Chechen	418	98.8	Shor	15	83.7
Ossetian	410	89.7	Slovak	14.7	61.2
Bulgarian	324	79.3	Tate	11	70.8
Korean	314	79.3	Other	64.2	62.5

*Source: *Pravda,* February 4, 1960. The nationalities and native languages of the population were recorded in the census on the basis of the personal statements of the persons being counted. The nationality of children was recorded as stated by the parents.

**The percentage of members of a given nationality who considered the language of that nationality to be their native language.

†By January, 1966, the total population increased to approximately 232 million; hence in most cases the figures for the component nationalities are somewhat deflated.

Estonians and other ethnic groups were very different from their Russian overlords. Some of the subjugated ethnic groups, such as the Protestant Finns and the Roman Catholic Poles, were more culturally advanced in certain respects than the Russians. Among the more advanced non-Russian segments of the population, aspirations for national independence tended to be strong. The Asian peoples within the empire had, in the main, very backward cultures. Although few of the Asian peoples aspired to national independence, they clung to their own languages and customs and to the Muslim religion.

The Tsarist regime which had managed through military force and annexation to accumulate a huge empire and to unify it politically, had also to contend with its multi-national character. During the late nineteenth and early twentieth centuries, the Tsarist government adopted a policy designed to effect the total cultural and religious assimilation of the non-Russian groups into the dominant culture. The Orthodox faith and the Russian language were to be imposed by persuasion or persecution. All non-Orthodox churches were subjected to discriminatory practices, but the Roman Catholic Church was held in the greatest disfavor because its recognition of a foreigner as a religious leader was considered to be a particularly disunifying force within the empire. The native languages of almost one-half of the population were to be replaced by Russian; for example, in Poland, Russian was made the official language in courts, on railroads and even in universities.

The empire was dominated politically, economically and socially by a tiny minority of Russian aristocrats and upper middle-class who formed the elite. Great Russians constituted most of the bureaucracy in all national regions. The masses of people were subjugated by an absolutistic bureaucracy which recognized few, if any, restraints upon its arbitrary powers in dealing with the non-privileged classes and nationalities. Russification stirred up strong resentments against the Tsar and his government and against Great Russians in general. The minority nationalities clung to their languages, cultures and religions with zeal and determination, despite the discrimination and political pressures to which they were subjected by the officials. Instead of acting as a unifier, as it was intended, the shortsighted policy of Russification resulted in heightened national consciousness, increased hostility against the state and the Russian overlords, and eventually in separatist revolutionary movements aimed at secession from the empire. Moreover, national and anti-Russian sentiment tended to unite all classes against the common Great Russian enemy and thus served to obliterate class antagonisms within minority groups.

Marxist-Leninist Theory and Practice on State Structure and National Self-Determination

The Russian Bolshevik Party faced a serious dilemma with reference to state structure and national self-determination. As a revolutionary party dedicated to the overthrow of the Tsarist regime and the establishment in Russia of a dictatorship of the proletariat, it was expedient for the Bolsheviks to take advantage of the widespread anti-Russian sentiments which prevailed among the minority nationalities of the empire to win allies and adherents to its revolutionary goal. Thus it was expedient to use the principle of national self-determination as an ideological slogan to weaken and overthrow the Tsarist state. But, in agreement with the stand taken by Marx and Engels, the Bolsheviks believed that for the dictatorship of the proletariat a unitary centralized state was greatly superior to a federal union and to a confederation. In essence, the Bolsheviks recognized that the intensification of nationalistic sentiments would be advantageous to them prior to the seizure of power, but that after the establishment of the proletarian dictatorship, the existence of nationalistic sentiments would impede the formation of a unitary centralized state. Because of their conflicting goals, the position taken by the Bolshevik leaders varied from time to time.

Marx wrote relatively little about the problem of nationalities since for him class, rather than national antagonisms, constituted the basis for human progress. He argued that nationalism and patriotism are inflicted by the capitalists on the masses who then become ready tools for imperialistic wars. His goal was internationalism. He urged proletarians of all countries to unite and to replace national consciousness by class consciousness. Although he stated that the workers would be better off in a large unitary state than in a small national state, he did not advocate national oppression and definitely rejected the notion of superior and inferior races. For the dictatorship of the proletariat, Marx and Engels favored a unitary, indivisible republic organized in terms of democratic centralism. They argued that such a proletarian state would permit extensive self-government, limit bureaucratic centralism and command from above, remove various barriers to economic and social progress, and contribute to the development of class consciousness and the workers' movement. However, Marx and Engels conceded that in certain concrete historical situations, the establishment of a federal state might constitute progress, e.g., as a transition from monarchy to a centralized republic or as a technique to solve nationality problems.[1]

Fundamentally, Lenin and other members of the pre-revolutionary party leadership agreed fully with Marx and Engels that a unitary proletarian state operated on the basis of democratic centralism would be vastly superior to a federal system. Moreover, they predicted that in the stage of the "bourgeois-democratic" revolution, the nationality problem in the territories of the Russian Empire would be solved by the overthrow of Tsarism and a declaration guaranteeing civil and hence national equality; i.e., the nationality problem would be solved in a unitary state. In 1903, Lenin wrote that the function of the proletariat is to unify the broadest masses of all nationalities in the fight for a democratic republic and for socialism. He stated explicitly that it is not the purpose of the proletariat to advocate federalism and national autonomy, since these would necessarily lead to demands for autonomous national states.[2] The preservation of the centralism which had been established by the Tsarist government was advocated, since federalism and autonomy would weaken the workers' movement and its class struggle.[3] Federalism was opposed for both economic and political reasons. The proletariat was to defend large states against medieval particularism and to support the economic unification of large territories which would in turn facilitate the struggle against the bourgeoisie. Lenin conceived a centralized state as a giant step forward toward the future socialist unity of the entire world.[4] Nevertheless, largely because he believed that local nationalism would contribute to the disintegration of Tsarist authority and hasten the proletarian revolution in Russia, Lenin insisted at the 1903 Congress that the principle of national self-determination be adopted as an ideological slogan.

Opposition to the principle of national self-determination was strong among the Polish and Russian Marxists. Rosa Luxemburg, Bukharin and Piatakov spearheaded the anti-national line with the argument that the growth of national independence movements would split the unity of the proletariat and turn the proletariat of each nationality into an appendage of its bourgeoisie. They favored the growth of a united proletarian movement which would combat national particularism, and argued that national secessions would be a setback for the socialist cause.

Although it was Lenin who advocated that the Bolsheviks include the right to national secession as a major principle in their revolutionary program, he was fundamentally opposed to secession and strongly favored a unified state in preference to national independence or even federalism. In his 1913 analysis he advocated *territorial* autonomy and democratic local self-government, but flatly rejected *national* autonomy which would require special institutions guaranteeing freedom of national development. He wrote:

> "Autonomy is our plan of construction of a democratic state. Secession is not our plan at all. We do not agitate for secession; we are against it. However, we are for the *right* to secede because the Great Russian nationalism made co-operation among nations so ugly that sometimes free secession may even strengthen the union among nations. . . . The right of self-determination is an *exception* to our general principle of centralism. This exception is absolutely necessary in view of Great Russian arch-reactionary nationalism. . . ."[5]

Thus Lenin's advocacy of the principle of national self-determination, in spite of his belief in the superiority of a centralized unitary state, was based on his realization that proletarian internationalism could not be imposed by the Russian proletariat upon the non-Russian masses by compulsion. Recognition by the Russian proletariat of the cultural equality of the minority nationalities of the empire was considered a prerequisite to winning their trust and friendship. He regarded nationalism as the normal reaction of subject nationalities to imperialism. By recognizing the national aspirations of the non-Russian peoples of the empire, he hoped to disarm the anti-Russian sentiments of the minority nationalities of all social classes and to encourage the growth of proletarian solidarity among the non-Russians and the Russian proletariat. Support of nationalistic aspirations was an illustration of the Bolshevik technique of "retreating one step to advance two steps." By giving partial sanction to nationalistic aspirations, the Bolsheviks hoped to hasten the advent of the proletarian revolution and by strengthening proletarian solidarity, to pave the way for the establishment of a united proletarian state.

Advocacy of the right for national self-determination did not prevent the Bolsheviks from building a unitary proletarian party. Although some of his colleagues suggested that the party should be organized along federal lines, Lenin maintained that a confederation of proletarian parties organized on a nationality basis was incompatible with proletarian internationalism. Since the party constituted the core of the future socialist society, a highly centralized party structure was deemed essential. Through the united proletarian party the masses were to be united, organized and educated in accordance with the ideals of proletarian internationalism. The united party organization was to transcend national divisions and to work among the masses to inculcate internationalist values. Federal party structure would, Lenin believed, have bred national estrangement and isolation between the autonomous units of the proletarian vanguard. Tactically, a centralized party would be able to act in a more concerted fashion to promote the revolutionary overthrow of the Tsarist state, to transform the empire into a socialist state, and eventually to draw all nations into a federation of socialist states. Moreover, the united proletarian party would help to counteract the disunifying forces associated with national particularism.

After the "bourgeois democratic" revolution in March, 1917, Lenin's position with respect to federalism was modified substantially. Tsarism had been overthrown, but the nationality problem remained unsolved. The Provisional Government had neither the time nor a method to cope with it. He asserted, in agreement with Marx and Engels, that under certain circumstances such as the existence of a major nationality problem, a federal system may not only be convenient, but actually indispensable to gain the support of the various nationalities for the communist cause. After the Bolsheviks seized political power, Lenin had to deal concretely with the problem of national particularism. He was torn between a desire to extend the area of Bolshevik power and the expediency of recognizing the national secessionist drives of many of the non-Russian territories of the former empire. His solution was a compromise. In November, 1917, under the signature of both Lenin and Stalin, the new Soviet government issued a "Declaration of the Rights of the Peoples of Russia" which guaranteed the equality and sovereignty of the people of Russia; the abolition of all national and national-religious privileges and restrictions; the free development of all national minorities and ethnic groups; and the right of the various peoples to full self-determination, even to the point of secession and the formation of independent states.[6] The right of self-determination was given to the proletarians only because it was believed that the upper and middle class wanted national self-determination and political separation while the working class did not. When some of the minority groups of the former Tsarist empire attempted to secede after the Bolshevik Revolution, Stalin clarified the Bolshevik stand on self-determination. He stated:

> "All this points to the necessity of interpreting the principle of self-determination as a right not of the bourgeoisie, but of the working masses of the given nation. The principle of self-determinism must be an instrument in the struggle for socialism and must be subordinated to the principles of socialism."[7]

When put to the test, the party chose to interpret the right to self-determination as the right to unite as well as to secede; if the bourgeoisie of a particular state were to instigate secession moves, the Russian proletariat, in the form of the Red Army, were obligated to assist the proletariat of the sister state to exercise the right of self-determination. The party, of course, retained the right to interpret the interests of the proletariat and, whenever expedient, held that the interests of the proletariat were best served by fraternal cooperation and political union with the proletariat of the Russian state.

On Lenin's recommendation the Third All-Russian Congress of Soviets in January, 1918, voted to replace the unity of the former Tsarist state by a federal "voluntary union" based on equality of nations. In practice, those territories which could be subjugated by the Red Army were prevented from seceding while regions which came under the effective power of nationalist forces were recognized as independent states. Various explanations were developed to justify these apparently paradoxical policies. Although the right of any nationality to secede was recognized formally, the Bolsheviks maintained that the proletariat of any national group must be given military aid to seize power and to exercise its right to unite its people with the Russian proletariat. The principle of national self-determination was subordinate to the principle of the class struggle of the proletariat. Thus the interests of the proletariat of any nation, as interpreted by the party, took precedence over national strivings to establish an independent state. The international proletariat was obligated to assist its national units in the consolidation of socialism. The Bolsheviks attempted to aid their party confreres in Finland, Poland and the Baltic region, but the power of the nationalists and their foreign allies proved too strong. The Bolsheviks recognized these secessionist states and hoped that they would thereby encourage the proletarians in these states to improve their class consciousness and forge an international movement to overthrow the rule of their bourgeois nationalist elite. Though in theory the Bolsheviks strongly favored a united proletarian state, the exigencies of the situation forced them to accept a form of federal union and to recognize the principle of national self-determinism when no other alternative presented itself.

The Political Basis for Soviet Federalism

In 1918 the new Bolshevik state was designated as the Russian Soviet Federated Socialist Republic (R.S.F.S.R.), and was described as "a federation of Soviet republics founded on the principle of a free union of the peoples of Russia." The Bolshevik struggle to reclaim Tsarist patrimony was complicated by its own bitter struggle for survival against widespread insurrection, counter-revolution and allied intervention. By 1921, Soviet power was more or less firmly established in the Ukraine, Belorussia, Georgia, Armenia and Azerbaidzhan; in each of these states intervention by the Red Army had been the decisive factor which had ensured Bolshevik control. Since these more advanced non-Russian areas had adequate native communist cadres, they were allowed to establish Soviet Socialist Republics (S.S.R.'s) which were nominally independent and equal to the R.S.F.S.R. Governmental authority was thus decentralized, in theory, by means of an alliance between these nominally independent states and the R.S.F.S.R. However, unitary control on behalf of the R.S.F.S.R. was imposed by the Communist Party and the Red Army.

The Red Army was the chief instrument through which the Bolsheviks reclaimed the Tsarist empire. However, factors in addition to the strength of the Red Army bolstered the Bolshevik cause. In most areas the anti-Bolsheviks were supported by foreign interventionist armies; the Bolsheviks made skillful appeals designed to direct native patriotic sentiments against the "foreign invaders." Many native leaders who did not sympathize with the Bolshevik program deemed it, nevertheless, more acceptable than the reactionary policies espoused by the leaders of the Whites (opponents of the Bolsheviks). In addition, the Bolshevik promises and slogans had genuine appeal value for many of the peasants and members of the oppressed national minorities who harbored the hope that the

Bolsheviks would serve as true liberators. On the other hand, opposition to Bolshevik control was very strong in some areas and among some segments of the population, particularly the Tsarist elite and propertied classes. Even some of the native communist leaders constituted a source of opposition primarily because of a well-founded fear of Russian hegemony.

After the conclusion of major military operations in 1921, the Bolsheviks controlled most of the former empire with the exception of Finland and the Baltic states, and held most of the subject nationalities in the grip of their military power just as their imperialist predecessors had. The supreme governing organs of the R.S.F.S.R. were the Central Executive Committee of the All-Russian Congress of Soviets, which exercised legislative powers, and the Council of Commissars which directed the administration of public policies through a number of centralized administrations (commissariats) and a hierarchy of local Soviets with their executive committees. The nominally independent Soviet Socialist Republics established governmental organs which corresponded to and were subservient to the R.S.F.S.R. organs. Although in some regions power was nominally vested in autonomous-type states controlled by the unitary Communist Party which was supported by the Red Army, in many regions the Russian Bolsheviks exercised nominal as well as real power. The obvious continuity of Russian rule caused tension between the party and the local population, which tended to revert to its traditional elite groups in opposition to the Bolsheviks. The Bolsheviks recognized that to realize their political goals, it was essential to remove this source of hostility and to win the support of the workers and the peasants for the ideals of socialism. Since the active participation of the masses was essential for economic as well as for political reasons, the Bolsheviks attempted to recruit reliable local cadres in sufficient numbers to exercise local power through the Communist Party in the name of the people. Insofar as possible, the Bolsheviks used local communist cadres rather than Russian administrators to impose Soviet socialism on the masses of subject peoples.

In 1921, Lenin, in the name of the Central Committee of the Russian Communist Party, directed the communist leaders of the Georgian, Armenian and Azerbaidzhan Soviet Socialist Republics to form a federation. This measure was strongly opposed, particularly in Georgia, where Menshevik influence was strong. Georgian resistance to the federation was spearheaded not by the Mensheviks, however, but by a group of Georgian communists, led by Mdivani. An attempt by the Georgians to secede and establish an independent national state free from all Russian Bolshevik control was crushed by force and the insubordinate local communists were purged. Georgia, Armenia and Azerbaidzhan united to form the Transcaucasian Soviet Federated Socialist Republic in 1922.

Late in 1922 the Congress of Soviets of each of the Ukraine, Belorussian and Transcaucasian S.S.R.'s, acting on instructions from the party, passed resolutions urging the formation of a union state. In 1924 the major step in the formal federalization of state power was taken when the nominally independent Ukrainian S.S.R., Belorussian S.S.R. and the Transcaucasian S.F.S.R. united in a federal union with the R.S.F.S.R. to form the Union of Soviet Socialist Republics (U.S.S.R.). At its inception, the U.S.S.R. incorporated most of its present territory. Soviet borders were, of course, expanded as a result of World War II, and the annexation of the Baltic states in 1940. New Soviet Socialist Republics were carved out of the vast territory which was originally included in the R.S.F.S.R. In 1925 the Turkmen and Uzbek S.S.R.'s were added to the Union, and in 1929 the Tadzhik Autonomous Soviet Socialist Republic (A.S.S.R.) was granted Union Republic status. In 1936 the Transcaucasian S.F.S.R. was dissolved and Georgian, Armenian and Azerbaidzhan S.S.R.'s were re-established, and two new Union Republics, the Kazakh S.S.R. and the Kirgiz S.S.R., were admitted to the Union. The Karelian and Moldavian A.S.S.R.'s were enlarged and elevated to Union Republic status in 1940, and Estonia, Lithuania and Latvia were incorporated as new territories of the U.S.S.R., each with Union Republic status. In 1956 when the Karelo-Finnish S.S.R. was transformed into the Karelian Autonomous Republic within the R.S. F.S.R., the number of Union Republics was reduced to fifteen.[8] On joining the U.S.S.R., each of the Union Republics retained the right of self-determination unto secession. However, although both the 1924 and 1936 Constitutions of the U.S.S.R. give formal recognition to this right, no legal provision has ever been made for its use.

Autonomous Republics (A.S.S.R.'s) without the right of secession were formed to allow for the cultural autonomy of large and compact national minorities within a Union Republic. Autonomous Regions and National Areas were formed to serve the same purpose for numerically smaller national minorities. The number of each of these has varied from time to time. At present the U.S.S.R. is composed of fifteen Union Republics, nineteen Autonomous Republics, nine Autonomous Regions and ten National Areas. The degree of autonomy decreases and the amount of guidance and tutelage increases from Union Republic status to National Area status. Population, geographic location, cultural development, political reliability and the number of communist cadres are factors which have entered into the determination of whether a nationality group was to enjoy first, second, third or fourth status.

Stalin specified the criteria for legal status as Union Republics as follows: First, only those nationalities who were located along the external periphery of the U.S.S.R. could theoretically secede, and therefore, claim the privilege of becoming Union Republics. Second, the nationality which gives its name to the republic must constitute a more or less compact majority within the republic. Finally, in order to maintain its position as an independent state, the population of a Union Republic should be at least one million.[9] None of these criteria have been adhered to completely. Most important, at no time has the party leadership had the slightest intention of permitting any Union Republic to secede. Even as he expounded on the need for a Union Republic to be in a position to exercise the right to secede, Stalin added: "Of course, none of our Republics would actually raise the question of seceding from the U.S.S.R.!"[10] Any republican leader who ever hinted at the possibility of such an intention has been declared an "enemy of the people." The party has made much of the right to secede as a technique to reduce national antagonisms, but has been fundamentally opposed to secession, and has effectively prohibited even the slightest gesture in the direction of secession. In most cases the nationality which gives the name to the republic constitutes a majority within the republic. However, in some republics the original ethnic majority has been outnumbered by another national group because of massive population movements associated with industrialization.[11] With the exception of the Karelo-Finns, who number less than 300,000, but were elevated to Union Republic status from 1940 to 1956 in order to pressure the Finnish Republic into a neutralist foreign policy, the population of all Union Republics exceeds one million. A number of nationalities, including the Tatars, Germans, Jews, Chuvash, Poles and Mordvinians, have the requisite numerical size to constitute Union Republics, but have been denied this privilege because of geographic dispersion, location or for political reasons.

Soviet jurists describe the principles of their "socialist federation," which they maintain differs markedly from a "bourgeois federation," as follows: (1) The socialist federation was introduced as a technique to solve the problem of nationalities, and to strengthen friendship and co-operation among nations. The party pays constant attention to the interests of all Soviet nations, and acts for the removal of conflicts and mistrust among nations and nationality groups. (2) The federation is based on the dictatorship of the proletariat, which functions under the guidance of the Communist party. Soviet power is the organizational and political expression of the power of the workers' class and all working people. (3) The socialist federation is based on the principles of voluntary union and complete equality of all members of the federation. (This principle, incidentally, is designated as a constitutional principle because it is included in the constitution as a basic law of the Soviet state. Apparently, this means that the federal union is voluntary because the constitution describes it as voluntary!) (4) The socialist federation differs from Western federations because it is based on a national-territorial principle, that is, it is a union of territories differing by national composition of the population. (5) The organizational legal principle of the socialist federation is democratic centralism, which guarantees unity in all basic problems and development of initiative and independence according to local conditions, peculiarities, and needs.[12]

According to Soviet jurists, the U.S.S.R. is a union of sovereign national Soviet republics. After the October revolution, independent republics were created in accordance with the principle of self-determination and independent state existence. The U.S.S.R. was legally created by a treaty between the four contracting parties, the R.S.F.S.R., Ukrainian S.S.R., Belorussian S.S.R. and the Transcaucasian S.F.S.R., all independent states. The Union Republics are described as the legal founders of the U.S.S.R., and the creation of the U.S.S.R. is presented as an expression of the sovereignty of each Union Republic, which stems from its right for self-determination. Soviet jurists affirm that the sovereignty of the Union Republics is original rather than derived, since each Union Republic retained its sovereignty, although in some areas sovereign rights were delegated voluntarily to the U.S.S.R. and its organs.[13] After the formation of the Union, the U.S.S.R. likewise became sovereign through the extensive rights which were delegated to the Union organs by the Union Republics. It is claimed that in the "higher" form of socialist federation, "the sovereignty of the Union as a whole and the Union Republics as members of the U.S.S.R. is mutually supplementary and constitutes a harmonious unity."[14]

Soviet jurists provide a unique, and in some respects, highly misleading explanation and description of Soviet sovereignty. They assert that an important characteristic of the socialist state is that sovereignty belongs in reality, not just nominally, to the Soviet people, who exercise it via their socialist state and particularly through the representative organs of state power. Because an exploiter's class does not exist, the sovereignty of the people allegedly forms an identity with the Soviet state, and the Soviet people, *under the leadership of the Communist Party,* exercise state authority. In addition to being the bearers of political and state sovereignty, the Soviet people are described as the bearers of sovereignty in the economic and territorial spheres, since all land, Soviet territory, natural resources and the basic means of production "belong" to the people. The sovereignty of the Soviet people in any sphere is, of course, a complete myth. Another unique characteristic attributed to Soviet sovereignty is its nationality basis and the identity between the sovereignty of the Soviet state and national sovereignty which rests on the right of self-determination. State sovereignty allegedly belongs to both the U.S.S.R. and to the Union Republics; the creation of the U.S.S.R. is described as an act which proves the original sovereignty of the Union Republics. The "proof" of the original sovereignty is obviously meaningless; the leaders of the Union Republics, who were puppets of the Russian Communist Party, were directed by the party to form a union; the Red Army stood by to ensure acquiescence; the people were not consulted. The jurists state that the U.S.S.R. cannot deprive the Union Republics of their sovereignty, and the Union Republics cannot, while they are members of the Union, claim rights that belong to the Union organs; only the U.S.S.R. organs can make changes in the constitution regulating the competence of the U.S.S.R. and the Union Republics. The Soviet jurists conclude that "the sovereignty of the Union and the Union Republics are in dialectical unity and supplement one another."[15]

The Union Republics are described by Soviet jurists as sovereign because they have all the necessary prerequisites for state sovereignty. First, each Union Republic exercises state power independently with the exception of those spheres that come under the exclusive jurisdiction of the U.S.S.R. Second, each Union Republic approves and enforces its own constitution. In fact, the constitution of a Union Republic must be approved by the U.S.S.R. and must conform to the constitution of the U.S.S.R.[16] Minor variations between the constitutions of Union Republics are permitted to take local peculiarities into consideration. Third, each Union Republic has the right freely to secede from the U.S.S.R.[17] This right is not only considered to be proof of the voluntary character of the Union, and the material guarantee of the sovereignty of the Union Republics, but it is also supposed to distinguish between socialist and "bourgeois" federations. Stalin pointed out that although no Union Republic would want to secede, the legal right to do so demonstrates fundamentally new relationships among the nations of the Soviet multi-national state.[18] Fourth, the territory of a Union Republic cannot be changed without its consent.[19] Fifth, each Union Republic has its own state citizenship and right to grant citizenship to foreigners. U.S.S.R. citizenship is automatically conferred on citizens of a Union Republic. Sixth, since 1944, Union Republics have had the right to enter into direct relations with foreign states and to exchange diplomatic and consular representatives with them.[20] In practice, this right is no more meaningful than the right to secede, with the exception that two Union Republics are members of the United Nations at the behest of and to serve the purposes of the U.S.S.R. The U.S.S.R. constitution states that each Union Republic has its own republican military formation.[21] This pronouncement is even more misleading than the articles which give the Union Republics the *right* to secede and the *right* to enter into direct relations with foreign states; no Union Republic has its own military formation. Finally, the legal status of the Union Republics as sovereign socialist states is guaranteed by the U.S.S.R., which gives military, economic and political protection to them, and supports their independence in harmony with democratic centralism. Soviet jurists base their theory of sovereignty on the written constitution, in spite of the fact that practice and even intent have differed significantly from the formal constitutional principles.

In reality, the Union Republics of the U.S.S.R. are permitted to exercise very few of their constitutionally guaranteed sovereign rights.

The union of the Autonomous Republics with the R.S.F.S.R. or other Union Republics is described as a socialist federation based on Soviet autonomy, a form lower than the federation of sovereign republics. This federal form has been used particularly for the unification of small nationalities with the Russian nation. Although the Azerbaidzhanian, Georgian, Uzbek and Tadzhik S.S.R.'s have Autonomous Republics or Autonomous Regions within their borders, these four republics are usually described as unitary states while the R.S.F.S.R. is described as a federal republic. Some Soviet jurists maintain that all of these states are based on federal unions of a special kind.[22] Typically, an Autonomous Republic has been established when a national minority forms a relatively large, compact majority in a limited area within the Union Republic. Soviet jurists point out that the federation of Autonomous Republics with Union Republics differs from the federation between sovereign Union Republics in several important respects.[23] First, in a federation based on autonomy, no new state is created as a result of the unification of a majority nation with minority nationalities. The creation or abolition of an Autonomous Republic or territory does not have any constitutive importance from the point of view of the given Union Republic, i.e., the Autonomous Republics did not create the R.S.F.S.R., while the Union Republics did create the U.S.S.R. via unification. Each Autonomous Republic within the R.S.F.S.R. is, according to its constitution, part of the R.S.F.S.R.[24] Second, in comparison to the Union Republics, the Autonomous Republics lack some important characteristics of state sovereignty such as the independent exercise of state power and the right to secede. They have, however, certain restricted characteristics of state sovereignty, i.e., they approve their own constitutions, subject to the approval of the Supreme Soviet of the Union Republic of which they are a component part; they have territorial supremacy in that in theory, but not necessarily in practice, their territory cannot be changed without their approval; and they have their state citizenship. The final peculiarity of a federation based on autonomy is that the national autonomies do not cover the whole territory of any Union Republic, and that not all citizens of the Union Republic are simultaneously citizens of an autonomous unit.

The Bolshevik leaders selected the federal structure for the new state for several reasons. Initially, the federalization of power strengthened central authority over those non-Russian areas which established nominal independence after the October Revolution. As with the American federal experiment, the basic motivation was to strengthen the political bonds between the new republics by means of an institutional unification of power. Federalism was selected in preference to a unitary state organization primarily because of the multi-national structure of the population. National animosities toward the Russians were so strong in certain regions that if a socialist culture were to evolve, it would have to be under the leadership of the native communist cadres. The appeal of socialism to much of the population could be fostered best through their national aspirations. According to Lenin's analysis of imperialism, the masses of Asia were crucial to the complete victory of socialism, and therefore, it behooved the Communist Party to champion the national interests of the Asian peoples within the Soviet state. The attainment of national self-government by Asian national groups within a socialist system of economic development was expected to serve as a powerful incentive to other subjugated national groups. By creating a socialist federation of national republics with the external trappings of self-government, the Communist Party hoped to attract the masses of Asia and to hasten their revolution against Western imperialism. Soviet federalism was to become the banner of liberation for the oppressed peoples of Asia who, according to Lenin, would contribute greatly to the collapse of international capitalism and the world triumph of socialism.

The Soviet claim that the Union Republics are sovereign states within the socialist federation is debatable. Those constitutional rights most directly bearing on the sovereignty of the Union Republics and most different from the rights of the component units of non-Soviet federations, i.e., to secede, to maintain military organizations, and to enter into direct foreign relations, are not to be exercised, and in reality, are little more than paper rights. In fact, because of the centralized Communist Party with its strict discipline and central control over the economy, trade unions, youth organizations, education, the police force and the procuracy, the label, unitary, fits the Soviet federation more accurately than it fits many states which consider themselves to be unitary.

CULTURAL ASPECTS OF SOVIET FEDERALISM

Joseph Stalin, the son of a Georgian father and an Ossetian mother, served along with Lenin as one of the chief architects of Soviet federalism and its nationality policy. As Commissar of Nationalities in the first Bolshevik government, and later as supreme leader of international communism, he forged a policy designed to reconcile the unitary interests of the communist movement with the diversities of national folkways. His slogan, "national in form, socialist in content," was descriptive of this policy: diversification of national groups in language and culture was permissible, provided that the socialist way of life prevailed in political and economic spheres. Stalin did not expect nationalism to disappear immediately with the advent of socialism. He realized that national sentiment was deeply rooted in the folkways of the peoples and that they could not be rudely torn away from their language, customs and group culture without causing irreparable damage to the unity of the Soviet state and to the communist movement. National characteristics required constructive handling by the proletarian state during, and after, the initial phase of socialist construction. He predicted that not until the beginning of the transition from socialism to communism would nationalities begin to wither away concurrently with the beginning of a process of assimilation of the diverse peoples of the Soviet Union into a single nationality.

Although a unilingual and unitary state would have been preferred, Stalin advocated cultural autonomy for definite territorial units. On his advice, the Soviet leaders decreed that all national groups were to be treated with absolute equality, both with reference to rights and obligations. All cultures and all languages were to be put on an equal basis. The Tsarist policy of banning the use of the non-Russian languages in the schools, courts, press and administrative offices was reversed. Backward ethnic groups who had never developed a written language were aided by cultural anthropologists and philologists to express themselves in a literate manner through their own language. The most neglected and suppressed groups benefited most from the statewide attempts to stamp out illiteracy and the emphasis on educational opportunity. Native music, dancing, theatre, literature and art forms were encouraged, and the expression of national consciousness in these activities was not prohibited. The permissive attitude toward cultural autonomy was, of course, designed to serve the aims of the party. Both Lenin and Stalin hoped that official sanction for national languages and cultures would satisfy national pride, eliminate strivings for national independence and concurrently pave the way for internationalism. It was expected that people who were given greatly increased freedom in matters deeply important to them would be more enthusiastic about the entire Soviet system.

Although cultural diversification has been permitted and national cultural values have been for the most part respected and even encouraged, the Soviet leaders have not changed their ultimate goals: the national cultures must be proletarian and socialist in content. No expressions of bourgeois nationalism or national deviationism by the nationality groups are tolerated. Local communist cadres and the governing elites in the non-Russian regions of the Soviet Union are expected to develop the proletarian consciousness of the masses and to infuse them with socialist values. All national groups must support the Soviet system, accept the communist political ideology and develop the socialist way of life. When socialist content clashes with national aspirations, religious convictions or long-established customs, the socialist content has priority in all cases and under all circumstances. On occasion, restrictions have been placed on the activities of segments or members of certain national groups, such as Tatars who have clung to religious practices in conflict with Soviet mores, or Jewish groups who have engaged in Zionist activities. In most cases, such restrictions cannot be described fairly as manifestations of racial or ethnic discrimination. Rather the restrictions represent attempts on the part of the regime to eradicate all forces which interfere with or impede progress toward the goals of socialism and communism. From the point of view of the regime, the national origin of the individuals or groups involved is probably irrelevant. What is relevant to the regime is that certain individuals or groups, regardless of their national origin, cling to customs, traditions and goals at variance with party-imposed values.

The policy of socialist assimilation is directed toward the ultimate goal of internationalism. During the intermediate period the policy of assimilation involves a rigorous attempt to convert members of all nationalities into Soviet citizens, who via socialism are to attain communism. One facet of the policy of developing a Soviet patriotism, distinct from both national and international patriotism, is to give all nationalities a sense of common inheritance. Public attention has been directed to the great poets, writers, artists and composers of the minor nationality groups as well as to those of the numerically more significant Russians. Their works have been translated into many languages and displayed or performed in all regions of the Union. Conversely, historically great men who were strongly nationalistic to the detriment of unity are repudiated or ignored. The practice is to eliminate or minimize those factors which might weaken the solidarity of the peoples of the U.S.S.R. and to introduce and maximize unifying forces.

Although the Soviet leaders would prefer to have Russian as a universal language, they realize that its forcible introduction would be detrimental to the achievement of long-range goals. However, without a policy of forcible Russification, the Soviet leaders are succeeding far more deftly than the Tsars in diffusing the Russian language and culture among the heterogeneous national groups. The decree that each native language would be the official medium in its region has made it necessary for many Russians residing in non-Russian areas to learn the local language. In compensation, Russian, which is taught in numerous non-Russian schools, has become the second language throughout most non-Russian areas of the Soviet Union, and thereby the common medium of expression between the different nationalities. In the 1959 Census, 124,600,000 persons indicated that Russian was their native language; of these, 10,200,000 belonged to non-Russian national groups. Millions of Russians reside in non-Russian Union Republics, all of which have a very heterogeneous national and linguistic composition. Table 2 presents the distribution of the national groups in the Ukrainian and Kazakh Republics. The Ukrainian Republic is fairly representative in that it derives its name from the majority national group. Well over seven million Russians live in the Ukraine. In the

Kazakh Republic, the Kazakhs, with only 29.6 percent of the population, constitute a minority. Because of economic expansion, there has been a great influx of other nationalities, particularly Russian, who with 43.1 percent of the population greatly outnumber the Kazakhs. Necessity and circumstances seem to be combining to make Russian a common linguistic tool. However, by legalizing and defending the primacy of the local language among each non-Russian nationality group, resentment toward the Russian language has been effectively nullified. The Russian language, itself, is being modified and enriched by the absorption into its vocabulary of many words and expressions from the non-Russian languages.

Table 2

Distribution of National Groups in the Ukraine and Kazakh Republics*

National Group	Ukrainian Republic		Kazakh Republic	
	Number (in 1,000's)	% of Total	Number (in 1,000's)	% of Total
TOTAL	41,869	100	9,310	100
Ukrainian	31,852	76.1	762	8.2
Kazakh	—	—	2,755	29.6
Russian	7,400	17.7	4,014	43.1
Jewish	840	2.0	—	—
Polish	363	0.9	53	0.6
Belorussian	291	0.7	108	1.2
Moldavian	239	0.6	—	—
Bulgarian	219	0.5	—	—
Hungarian	149	0.4	—	—
Greek	104	0.2	—	—
Rumanian	101	0.2	—	—
Tatar	—	—	192	2.1
Uzbek	—	—	137	1.5
Korean	—	—	74	0.8
Uigur	—	—	60	0.6
Dungan	—	—	10	0.1

*Source: Pravda, February 4, 1960.

Assimilation of cultures is being effected, not by the one-way integration of non-Russians into the majority culture, but by the gradual synthesis and fusion of the customs, folkways and characteristics which are vibrant and meaningful contributions to the communist program. Stalin realized that to be effective with reference to the goals of the party, the policy of national diversification had to be combined with strong unifying forces. Assurance that socialist assimilation would take place among the minority nationalities as well as among the Russians was provided by the centralization of the party, the trade unions, the Procuracy, the police and military forces, and by the centralized institutions of the socialist economy.

ECONOMIC FOUNDATIONS OF SOVIET FEDERALISM

Economic planning has fostered national integration among the people of the U.S.S.R. in three major ways. First, it has resulted in the transfer of millions of people from one region to another. Western Siberia, the central Asian regions and the Far East, because of extensive economic development, have received a particularly large influx of population. This, of course, has resulted in increased intermingling of all nationalities, an important factor in removing nationality barriers. Since the Great Russians are more numerous than the other nationalities, the increased intermingling should result in the gradual Russification of the Soviet people, even if this goal is not being fostered deliberately by the party. Secondly, economic planning has increased the interdependence of the national regions. Planned industrialization has made the Union Republics less self-sufficient economically than before. If they were to be permitted to secede from the Union, most of the Union Republics would have to reorganize their economies so drastically that great hardship would result. Finally, although economic planning has already brought personal suffering to many, vastly more have benefited from it in terms of higher living standards. The vast majority of the Soviet people attribute to socialism their improved economic and social status relative to that of their parents and grandparents under Tsarism.

Because of centralized economic planning by the Communist Party and the All-Union government, the economically underdeveloped regions of the Soviet Union have been industrialized and urbanized to the point where they are no longer economic colonies of Russia. Their populations have been raised economically and socially to levels which approach those of the Russians. Economic and social integration of the Russian and non-Russian peoples of the U.S.S.R. is being accomplished with a minimum of ethnic discrimination. The resultant equalization of status and living standards among the various nationalities of the U.S.S.R. has done much to reduce national resentments and to develop a unitary loyalty on the part of the diverse peoples of the country to the Soviet state and the Communist Party.

Federal Representation of the Nationalities

All Soviet nationalities are given direct or indirect representation in the major legislative, executive and administrative organs of state power in the central government: the Supreme Soviet of the U.S.S.R., the Presidium of the Supreme Soviet of the U.S.S.R., and the Council of Ministers of the U.S.S.R. The Soviet of Nationalities, one of the chambers of the Supreme Soviet, is designed explicitly to give appropriate representation to national groups. The Constitution fixes representation in the Soviet of Nationalities at twenty-five deputies for each Union Republic, eleven deputies for each Autonomous Republic, five deputies for each Autonomous Region, and one deputy for each National Area.* Table 3, which presents the national affiliation of deputies elected to the two chambers of the Supreme Soviet in 1958, indicates that the various national groups are also represented in the Soviet of the Union, which is elected on a population rather than a national basis. There is no legal requirement that the deputies of the Soviet of Nationalities be of the nationality of the major group within the territory which they represent. If this were true, the Russians would be entitled to only twenty-five seats. Although the party apparently wants to have all, or at least most, nationalities represented in the Soviet of Nationalities, it has not applied a proportional rule in the allocation of seats or in the selection of deputies. Many of the lesser nationalities enjoy substantial representation in the Soviet of Nationalities relative to their numbers in the total population, while the Russians and Ukrainians with almost three-quarters of the total population have less than one-third of the seats. Representation of the smaller national groups in the Soviet of Nationalities counteracts the preponderance of Russian and Ukrainian deputies in the Soviet of the Union.

Table 3
National Affiliation of Supreme Soviet Deputies**

Nationality	% of Total Population	Soviet of Nationalities		Soviet of the Union	
		Number	%	Number	%
Russian	54.9	147	23.0	421	57.0
Ukrainian	18.0	39	6.1	153	20.7
Belorussian	3.8	26	4.1	29	3.9
Uzbek	2.9	29	4.5	19	2.6
Kazakh	1.7	20	3.1	15	2.0
Georgian	1.3	36	5.6	9	1.2
Azerbaidzhanian	1.4	32	5.0	11	1.5
Lithuanian	1.1	20	3.1	9	1.2
Moldavian	1.1	16	2.5	4	.5
Latvian	.7	22	3.4	5	.7
Tadzhik	.7	22	3.4	6	.8
Armenian	1.4	29	4.5	7	.9
Turkmen	.5	20	3.1	5	.7
Estonian	.5	22	3.4	4	.5
Kirgizian	.5	15	2.3	4	.5
Others	9.5	145	22.7	37	5.0
TOTAL	100.0	640	100.0	738	100.0

**Source: *The U.S.S.R.—As It Is,* (Moscow: State Publishing House of Political Literature, 1959), pp. 64-65.

The nationalities of the U.S.S.R. are represented indirectly by the Chairmen of the fifteen Presidia of the Union Republic Supreme Soviets,

*In 1966 representational norms were changed to thirty-two deputies for each Union Republic.

who hold the rank, *ex officio,* of Vice-Chairmen of the Presidium of the Supreme Soviet of the U.S.S.R. However, the Vice-Chairmen are seldom able to participate in the deliberations of the Presidium, since they are not often present in Moscow, and their membership is largely symbolic. Much the same is true of the membership *ex officio,* which the Chairmen of the Union Republic Councils of Ministers possess on the U.S.S.R. Council of Ministers. In theory, at least, the Union Republics, and the major nationality groups of the U.S.S.R., are given representation on the higher state organs which are nominally responsible for the issuance of most legislation and the principal administrative decisions of the federal government.

If the formal organs of state power in the U.S.S.R. exercised effective authority as provided in the Constitution, instead of merely nominal deliberating functions to formalize the decisions made by the supreme party organs, the representatives of the Union Republics within the federal government might acquire greater significance. Then the federalist character of the Soviet regime might be expressed by a clash between the Russian and non-Russian interests. It is perhaps indicative of the caution of the party that of the 640 members of the Council of Nationalities over 75 percent are party members, while all the members of the Presidium and Council of Ministers at the All-Union level are high-ranking party members. Coordination between the party's will and the formal acts of the government is achieved by having the same persons in the decision-making positions within both the party and the government. The largely symbolic value of Union Republic representation in the federal organs of government of the U.S.S.R. serves to affirm the constitutional principle of equality among the major nationalities and the federative character of their "voluntary union." It camouflages the reality of Russian hegemony over the party and the government of the U.S.S.R. which results naturally from their numerical preponderance and makes associations between Russians and non-Russians more palatable to the latter. However, despite the dominant role of the Russians, since Lenin's death, only one Russian, Malenkov, has held the top party position and then, only for a brief period. The party and, hence, the U.S.S.R. has otherwise been led by non-Russians; Stalin, Khrushchev and Brezhnev.

Federalism does not operate even in theory in the decision-making organs of the Communist Party. A leading official at the Fourteenth Party Congress (1925) declared: "Our party . . . is a centralized party. All the national Parties which exist among us—the Ukrainian, Transcaucasian, Central Asian—all exist with the legal right of regional or provincial committees; the Party remains centralized, a unity from top to bottom."[25] The Leninist principle of democratic centralist organization bases membership upon strict ideological conformism and absolute discipline and loyalty to the decisions of the higher party organs. The central, intermediate, and local apparatus of the Communist Party, staffed by professional party functionaries who are trained and appointed from the center, rules the party organizations with iron-clad authority. This party elite, in turn, is responsible for the nomination of reliable bureaucratic officials at each level of administration which is nominally operative under an elected Soviet, also a carefully recruited institution which is manipulated by the party. The result of this is that responsible officials of the Union Republic and subordinate units of administration are members of a unitary structure of power. Irrespective of their national origins, they are first communists, and second, loyal servants of the Soviet state.

If the various nationality groups were permitted real autonomy in the exercise of their constitutional powers, instead of being shackled by the overriding powers of the central government and the unitary party machine, and if the locus of decision-making power at the central level really operated as the Constitution prescribes, instead of being subordinated to the party leadership, federalism might acquire some significance in the Soviet Union. However, since the entire territory of the U.S.S.R. is governed by the centralized apparatus of the Communist Party, nationality representation within the elective organs of government is meaningful only in terms of public morale. The people can be told that a deputy from Moldavia has an equal voice in the government as one from the R.S.F.S.R., which might be the truth, since the vote of neither significantly affects public policies. The Communist Party of the Soviet Union is using particularistic national sentiment to the advantage rather than to the detriment of party goals, and is allowing the nationalities equal opportunity to become socialist and internationalist.

Federal Division of Powers

Governing powers under the U.S.S.R. Constitution are federally divided between the All-Union government and the fifteen Union Republican governments. The scope of the legislative, executive, administrative and judicial powers which the Constitution (Article 14) vests by enumeration in the central government is extraordinary for a federal state. The U.S.S.R. organs have responsibility for: (1) foreign affairs, including conduct of foreign relations; questions of war and peace; national defense and security; and foreign trade; (2) the overall administration of the economy, including formulation and supervision of economic plans; administration of banks, industrial, agricultural and trade enterprises under All-Union jurisdiction; general guidance of industry and construction under Union-Republican jurisdiction; administration of transport and communication of All-Union importance; the use of land and natural resources; and labor legislation; (3) finance, including approval of the state budget; determination of taxes and allocation of revenues to Union Republican and local budgets; direction of monetary and credit systems; contracting and granting of loans; (4) constituent powers, including admission of new republics, and the formation of new Autonomous Republics and Autonomous Regions; confirmation of alterations of boundaries between Union Republics; (5) legal matters, including enforcement of the fundamental laws; citizenship and the rights of foreigners; formulation of principles concerning the judicial system, judicial procedure and criminal and civil codes; (6) culture and social welfare, including education; public health; insurance; marriage and family affairs; (7) miscellaneous matters such as organization of a uniform system of national economic statistics, and acts of amnesty.

The only enumerated power which a Union Republic may exercise, in addition to the formal rights to secede, to have its own constitution and military formation, and to approve territorial changes, concerns "the solution of problems pertaining to the administrative-territorial structure of the regions and territories of the Union Republic" (Article 28). Even this right must be exercised within the limitations fixed by U.S.S.R. legislation concerning the defense of constitutional forms of government. The central government, acting through its Presidium of the Supreme Soviet, retains the exclusive right to interpret the exercise of this power. In compensation for the limited number of enumerated powers, the Union Republics are left with all residual powers not expressly delegated to the central government. However, since the authority of the central government embraces education, public health and welfare, and judicial and economic matters which, in most nations, are under the jurisdiction of governmental units at the provincial, state or local level, the Union Republics can exercise initiative within only very circumscribed spheres.

Certain spheres of activities come under the joint jurisdiction of the U.S.S.R. and the Union Republics. For example, the U.S.S.R. Supreme Soviet determines only the global budget for each Union Republic, while the detailed budget laws are approved by the individual republics.[26] The Union Republics direct the "preparation and fulfillment" of the budgets of the lower governing units and establish state and local tax assessments "in conformity with U.S.S.R. legislation." During the post-Stalin era, the Union Republics were allowed increased responsibility for the preparation of state plans for the development of the national economy, the administration of industries and construction, and the supervision of factories and other economic establishments within their borders. The Union Republics also build roads and administer local transport and communications. Joint jurisdiction has been expanded to legislation concerning the organization of courts and court procedure and approval of civil and criminal codes. However, the Union retained the right to determine basic principles and to issue general directives, which the Union Republics must abide by in working out specific laws and orders. Joint jurisdiction is purportedly practiced to combine centralized leadership with considerable independence and initiative on the part of the Union Republics in carrying out decisions of the central government. Soviet authorities claim that centralized leadership and local initiative supplement one another and that animosity between the central and republican governments is nonexistent. Certainly, no animosity could be expressed by the Union Republican leaders, since it would not be tolerated by their superiors. In essence, joint jurisdiction amounts primarily to the fact that the governments of the Union Republics serve as subordinate territorial-administrative units which administer policies determined by the C.P.S.U. and affirmed or given legal status by the organs of the central government. The Union Republics are able to exercise limited initiative in determining how best to implement policies established by the central organs, but their role in determining the policies is inconsequential.

Although there is no implied power clause in the U.S.S.R. Constitution, there is no states'-rights tradition limiting the power of the All-Union government in the interpretation of its powers. According to the so-called "competence of competence" of the U.S.S.R., its Supreme Soviet may amend its Constitution to broaden or narrow its jurisdiction and thus to broaden or narrow the jurisdiction of the Union Republics. Since the Union Republics have no material sphere of competence which is exclusively theirs, the central government may legislate in any field. According to the principle of the priority of the All-Union laws, the U.S.S.R. may issue legislation or other normative acts binding over the entire territory of the Union. In the event of a divergence between the law of a Union Republic and a law of the U.S.S.R., the law of the U.S.S.R. prevails.[27] During the past several years the powers of the Union Republics have been extended gradually on the initiative of the central government, which has, of course, retained the right to restrict or withdraw power as it sees fit.

The constitutions and all constitutional legislation of the Union Republics must conform with provisions which are prescribed in the U.S.S.R. Constitution. The judge of such conformity is the central government. As previously indicated, the rights guaranteed to the Union Republics by the U.S.S.R. Constitution lack substance. The All-Union Constitution guarantees that each Union Republic must consent before its territory is altered. The only example of the dissolution of a Union Republic was in 1956 when the Karelo-Finnish S.S.R. was reduced in status to an Autonomous Republic by an act of the Presidium of the U.S.S.R. Supreme Soviet. No mention was made of whether the authorities of that Republic had been consulted. However, whether they were consulted or not, and what the wishes of the population were, is inconsequential. Decisions made at the higher level are binding. No legislation has provided for the exercise of the right to secede. Apparently, the right to secede must be authorized by the Communist Party of the Soviet Union and consented to by the Supreme Soviet; under the existing circumstances there is no possibility for Union Republic leaders to petition for such permission without fear of punishment. Other major rights such as to enter into direct foreign relations and to maintain separate military defense forces either cannot be exercised, or are exercised only when it fits the purpose of the Communist Party of the U.S.S.R. In fact, the jurisdiction of the Union Republics is more limited than the jurisdiction of the states within the United States, despite the Soviet claim to the contrary and the Soviet emphasis on the independence, autonomy and sovereignty of the component republics of the U.S.S.R.

In the event a Union Republic should violate the provisions of law through the improper exercise of its powers, its acts would be null and void, since U.S.S.R. laws take precedence over Union Republic laws. The Presidium of the U.S.S.R. Supreme Soviet has the power to nullify Union Republic legislation. The titular membership of fifteen Union Republic Presidium chairmen on the Presidium of the Supreme Soviet of the U.S.S.R. has not provided any real check on the latter organ, since it is empowered to act without the participation of the Union Republic representatives. The Union Republics have no legal recourse against interference by the central government in their functions. The Supreme Court is not empowered to implead the central government or to inquire into the "constitutionality" of its legislative and executive decisions. Like the Presidium and Council of Ministers, it too is an emanation of the Supreme Soviet, and its competence is limited to enforcement of federal laws and decrees in accordance with the interpretations laid down by the Presidium.

The Union Republic executives (Councils of Ministers) are subordinated to the U.S.S.R. Council of Ministers, just as their legislative organs are subordinate to the All-Union legislature. The Council of Ministers of the U.S.S.R. may suspend decisions and orders of the Councils of Ministers of the Union Republics and of the regional Economic Councils, to which management of the industrial sector has been delegated. Actual annulment of suspended decrees and orders is performed by the Presidium of the U.S.S.R. Supreme Soviet. Decisions and orders of the Council of Ministers of the U.S.S.R. are binding upon all Union Republic organs of government. Again, the judge of the propriety and/or legality of such acts is vested in the Presidium of the U.S.S.R. Supreme Soviet.

The consequence of this wholesale subordination of Union Republic organs to the U.S.S.R. Presidium and Council of Ministers is to reduce the Union Republic governments to the status of regional sub-divisions of the central government. The relationship is not unlike that which exists between the central authorities and the locally constituted authorities of a unitary state. Even so important a function as constitutional revision is vested exclusively in the Supreme Soviet of the U.S.S.R., although here the Union Republics have the theoretical, but not the actual, right to exercise a veto through their elected delegates to the Soviet of Nationalities. The Soviet of Nationalities is the only potentially "federal" institution in the U.S.S.R., since it might employ its legislative and constitutive powers to obstruct the unitary organs of the U.S.S.R. from imposing central authority upon the Union Republics and their territorial sub-divisions. However, the Presidium of the U.S.S.R. Supreme Soviet is empowered to dissolve the Supreme Soviet in the event of a disagreement between the two houses, to conduct a direct popular referendum, and to exercise legislative authority itself. Moreover, deputies to the Soviet of Nationalities are too well-trained in subordination to the dictates of the party leadership to assert themselves in opposition to policies recommended by the party. Thus the Soviet of Nationalities could not effectively curb the exercise of power by the central government over the Union Republics.

In practice, constitutional conflicts between central and republican governments are precluded by the political monopolization of leadership at all levels of government by the highly centralized Communist Party. The central leadership of the party is in command of the central government, while its carefully picked subordinates in the Union Republics are equally in command of the Union Republic governments. Should a "constitutional conflict" between the U.S.S.R. and the Union Republics ever occur, the central leadership of the Communist Party would be able to remove from office the governing personnel at the Union Republic level without difficulty. Only a revolution within the party itself could sustain any effort by the Union Republics to "federalize" power within the U.S.S.R.

Impact on the Individual and Society

Soviet federalism has been developed within the context of Stalin's nationality policy and resembles its basic characteristic: it is federal in form and unitary in content. The obvious reason for this is that federalism was designed to serve as a transitional form of state organization until a unitary socialist consciousness had evolved. Federalism in the U.S.S.R. has served as an organizational device to spread the communist value system, develop a new patriotism to the Soviet state and build a socialist economy.

The goal of the Soviet nationality policy and federalism was not to create viable national cultures or truly autonomous Union Republics, but to integrate, assimilate and unify the multi-national society into a proletarian socialist culture. The Communist Party of the U.S.S.R., confronted with the difficult task of governing and unifying a multi-national state, introduced a bold and imaginative policy toward nationalities. This policy has not been an unqualified success since, for example, nationalist aspirations have not completely disappeared.[28] Like all other Soviet policies, the nationality policy has been modified from time to time to serve the needs of the party. The goals of the party have been given priority over promises to national groups. However, in spite of some violations of the official policy to the non-Russian peoples in the Soviet Union, the communist approach represents a significant improvement over pre-revolutionary practice.

Although designed to strengthen unity and to serve the purposes of the party, linguistic and cultural autonomy have been meaningful concessions to the national groups. These, along with the leveling-up process in living standards, educational opportunities and party directed civic participation among the people of the U.S.S.R., have greatly abated national jealousy and tensions. While the process of assimilation is far from complete, the federal approach to the administration of public policies through national communist cadres and the recognition of national cultural autonomy within a centralized socialist structure of power has won over hundreds of people to the Communist Party and the Soviet state. Loyalty to the Soviet Union has gradually supervened particularist identifications among most of the peoples of the U.S.S.R. However, despite Soviet claims to the contrary, it is unlikely that nationalistic aspirations have been eliminated; if Soviet power were loosened, several national groups might strive to assert their independence. On the other hand, the relatively small proportion of defection and collaboration with the Germans which occurred during World War II, and the genuine pride expressed by Soviet citizens of all nationalities with respect to Soviet accomplishments lend credence to the view that a Soviet people has emerged. The change in Soviet terminology from "the peoples of the Soviet Union" to "the Soviet people" might well be justified.

REFERENCES

1 Cf. Marx in a letter to Kugelmann, Nov. 29, 1869.
2 Lenin, *Works, op. cit.,* Vol. 6, p. 328.
3 *Ibid.*
4 V. I. Lenin, *Works,* (Prague: SNPL, 1957), Vol. 20, p. 39.
5 *Ibid.,* Vol. 19, pp. 499-500.
6 "Declaration of the Rights of the Peoples of Russia," *Izvestia,* Nov. 16, 1917. Quoted in James H. Meisel and Edward S. Kozera (editors), *The Soviet System,* (Ann Arbor, Mich.: George Wahr Publishing Co., 1953), pp. 25-6.
7 J. Stalin, "Report on the National Question," *Sochineniya,* Vol. 4, pp. 31-2.
8 The names of the present Union Republics, with their populations according to the 1959 census figures, and population estimates for 1964 in brackets are as follows: Russian S.F.S.R., 117,534,000 (124,777,000); Ukrainian S.S.R., 41,869,000 (44,636,-000); Belorussian S.S.R., 8,055,000 (8,454,000); Armenian S.S.R., 1,763,000 (2,072,-000); Georgian S.S.R., 4,044,000 (4,410,000); Azerbaidzhan S.S.R., 3,698,000 (4,-381,000); Uzbek S.S.R., 8,106,000 (9,714,000); Tadzhik S.S.R., 1,980,000 (2,341,-

000); Kazakh S.S.R., 9,310,000 (11,568,000); Kirgiz S.S.R., 2,066,000 (2,488,000); Moldavian S.S.R., 2,885,000 (3,245,000); Lithuanian S.S.R., 2,711,000 (2,895,000); Latvian S.S.R., 2,093,000 (2,210,000); Estonian S.S.R., 1,197,000 (1,259,000). From January, 1959, to January, 1966, the total population of the U.S.S.R. increased from 208,807,000 to approximately 232,000,000; therefore the above figures for the populations of the Union Republics are somewhat deflated. The annual increase in population is about 3½ million.

9 Stalin, *Problems of Leninism, op. cit.,* p. 705.

10 *Ibid.*

11 *Pravda,* Feb. 4, 1960.

12 Cf. Sovětské státní právo (Soviet State Law), (Prague: Orbis, 1960), pp. 155-6.

13 *Ibid.,* pp. 157-8.

14 *Ibid.*

15 *Ibid.,* p. 172.

16 Constitution of the U.S.S.R., Article 16, and Constitution of the R.S.F.S.R., Article 19. Since the constitutions of all Union Republics have similarities, further references will be made only to the Constitution of the R.S.F.S.R.

17 Constitution of the U.S.S.R., Article 17, Constitution of the R.S.F.S.R., Article 15.

18 Stalin, *Problems of Leninism, op. cit.,* p. 704.

19 Constitution of the U.S.S.R., Article 18, and Constitution of the R.S.F.S.R., Article 16.

20 Constitution of the U.S.S.R., Article 18a, and Constitution of the R.S.F.S.R., Article 16a.

21 Constitution of the U.S.S.R., Article 18b, and Constitution of the R.S.F.S.R., Article 16b.

22 E.g., I. D. Levin in Voprosy sovietskogo gosudarstva i prava (Problems of the Soviet State and Law), Moscow: Gosiuridizdat, 1957.

23 (Soviet State Law), *op. cit.,* pp. 160-3.

24 Constitution of the R.S.F.S.R., Article 13 (1937).

25 Fourteenth Congress of the All-Union Communist Party (b), (Moscow-Leningrad, 1926), pp. 881-2.

26 The Law on budgetary rights of the U.S.S.R. and Union Republics was approved by the U.S.S.R. Supreme Soviet on Oct. 30, 1959. (See Vedomosti Verkhovnogo Sovieta S.S.S.R. Article 4, No. 221, 1959.)

27 Constitution of the U.S.S.R., Articles 19 and 20.

28 For another evaluation of the Soviet nationality policy see Alex Inkeles, "Soviet National Policy in Perspective," in Samuel Hendel (ed.), *The Soviet Crucible,* (New York: D. Van Nostrand, 1963), pp. 341-56.

Chapter V

MARXIST-LENINIST THEORY OF DEMOCRACY AND SOVIET ELECTORAL PRACTICES

Marxist-Leninist Theory of Democracy

It is appropriate to preface a discussion of the theory and practice of democracy in the U.S.S.R. by two statements: (1) It is exceedingly difficult to achieve a consensus on the meaning of concepts such as democracy and freedom, and (2) Soviet and Western definitions of democracy and freedom differ in fundamental respects. Evaluation of the Soviet theory and practice of democracy requires explicit realization that Soviet leaders do not subscribe to and do not aspire to operate on the basis of Western definitions, just as Western leaders do not subscribe to Soviet definitions of democracy and freedom. The basic value system adopted by the Marxists-Leninists, though similar in some respects to that subscribed to by most of the Western world, is in other respects very different. Both Western and Soviet officials are aware of the existence of the different value systems, albeit both deny the validity of values other than their own. However, both Western and Soviet officials tend to overlook the fact that different value systems must almost necessarily give rise to different practices with respect to democratic processes and individual freedoms. Soviet spokesmen seem to be unwilling to concede that the most legitimate evaluation of the practices of democratic rights and freedoms in the U.S.A. is with reference to the value system subscribed to by the majority of American citizens. Westerners, likewise, tend to evaluate Soviet institutions and governmental and social processes in terms of the Western rather than the Soviet value system. Each side seems to be saying "you are bad because you don't want what we say everyone should want, and besides that, your various governmental, social and economic practices cannot possibly achieve for you what we think you ought to have." Neither side seems to be willing to evaluate the practices of the other in terms of the other's goals. The net result is that just as people in the Soviet Union tend to misperceive the operation of the political, social and economic systems in the West, Westerners likewise tend to misperceive the Soviet system. As an eminent American social scientist commented, ". . . there *is* a mirror image in Soviet and American perceptions of each other and . . . this image represents serious distortions by *both* parties of the realities on either side. . . ."[1]

Despite numerous undemocratic practices in the U.S.S.R. and the belief in the West that Marxists-Leninists are the enemies of democracy, Marxist-Leninist ideology is not anti-democratic. Lenin, though he insisted on the absolute authority of the Party's Central Committee, was "fiercely committed to democracy and individual liberty."[2] Marxist-Leninist writers consistently stand fully in favor of democratic theory and democratic practices. The democracy and liberties to which the Marxists-Leninists aspire are not, however, identical with those held sacred by most Westerners. A major source of contention between Soviet and Western spokesmen is not whether democracy and liberty are "good" or "bad" or should be practiced. All agree that democracy and liberty are "good" and should be practiced. The disagreement concerns what constitutes democracy and freedom, and how democracy and freedom, according to the different interpretations, can be best achieved.

A full discussion of the various meanings of democracy and liberty, and of practices which conform to the many interpretations of these concepts is beyond the scope of this book. Nor is it the purpose of this book to compare critically democratic concepts and practices in the U.S.S.R. and the Western world. Rather it is relevant to present Marxist-Leninist interpretations of democracy and freedom and to describe Soviet practices which derive from or are related to the ideology.

Among the many differences between the Soviet and Western interpretations of freedom and democracy, perhaps one of the most basic differences revolves around the concept of economic freedom. In the Western world the freedom of an individual to own productive property and to earn a profit from such ownership is held to be a constitutional, if not an inalienable, right which is vital for the maintenance of individual freedom and essential for the economic well-being of the nation. Marxists, on the other hand, consider private ownership of the means of production to be harmful to society and to the majority of the members of society, since they believe that private ownership is the primary mechanism for "exploitation of man by man." Private ownership of the means of production, according to the Marxists, results in gross economic, and hence political, social and educational, inequalities and allows for those who have economic power to control, dominate and subjugate the masses who are dependent on the capitalists for the opportunity to earn a livelihood. In a capitalist state, the Marxists assert, the masses are denied "freedom from wage slavery, poverty, social inequality, insecurity. . ." and hence their guaranteed political and legal rights and freedoms are virtually meaningless. Marxists maintain that a minimum prerequisite for political equality is equality of opportunity in the economic and social spheres. They define freedom, not in terms of free enterprise and the right to accumulate property, but in terms of freedom from unemployment, the guaranteed right to work, freedom from class privileges or restrictions based on social or racial origin, freedom of opportunity to obtain an education commensurate with one's ability, freedom from worry about medical bills and maintenance in old age, and so forth. Without these freedoms, the Marxists say, there can be no equality and hence no democracy in the political sphere because even if universal suffrage is practiced, those who have freedom in the economic and social spheres, by virtue of their economic power, are able to control the votes of the socially and economically underprivileged masses. Marxists maintain that the types of freedom which they hold to be most important can be guaranteed only if the means of production are publicly owned and individuals are not allowed to accumulate wealth which would enable them to exploit other individuals economically and, hence, produce social and political inequalities. Thus in the Western world, private ownership of the means of production is considered an essential component of individual freedom, and the manifestation of, if not a prerequisite for, the operation of democratic processes. Marxists, on the other hand, believe that private ownership of the means of production restricts the individual freedom of the masses and greatly impedes the operation of democratic processes. The basic differences in the interpretation of the meaning of freedom, and the approaches through which freedom can be maximally attained, account largely for the differences in interpretation of democracy and the implementation of democratic practices in the Soviet Union and the Western world.

Marxists-Leninists on the Evolution of Democracy

According to the Marxists-Leninists, democracy evolves from lower to higher forms. Very low in the Marxist-Leninist hierarchy is what they refer to as the "bourgeois democracy" practiced in capitalist countries; a better, but far from perfect, form of democracy develops under the dictatorship of the proletariat; as the need for the dictatorship of the proletariat disappears, a new and higher form of "socialist democracy" evolves which is to pave the way for the eventual perfection of democracy under communism. The Marxists-Leninists concede that "bourgeois democracy" is superior to an absolute monarchy or an oligarchy in that it provides more favorable conditions for social progress. However, they argue, because it allows and even fosters and protects gross economic inequalities, it cannot engender full and consistent democracy for the broad masses of the working people. The bourgeois state is described as a coercive instrument used by the exploiting class, the capitalists, to oppress all other classes. Marxists maintain that gross economic inequalities and economic exploitation of man by man preclude the practice of true democracy in spite of democratic forms such as universal suffrage, parliamentary methods and declarations of equality and freedom before the law.

Rather than being an instrument to express the will of the majority of the toilers and to assure its realization, universal suffrage in a democratic republic is described as a technique of bourgeois domination. In Marx's words, universal suffrage allows the masses "once every few years, to decide which particular representative of the oppressing class should be in parliament to represent and to oppress them."[3] Elections in capitalist states, the Marxists assert, are manipulated by the capitalists, who are able to control or influence all other classes—the workers, farmers, employees, small businessmen and professional groups—to determine who will be elected and to control the elected representatives through economic power and economic threat. Marxists argue that in a classless society, or a society composed of non-antagonistic classes, one political party is sufficient to represent the interests of all the people. In capitalist states, they say, where there are several classes with sharply antagonistic economic interests, there is a need for several political parties, each of which represents a particular class, as is common in many European countries, or for two parties with smaller differences in combination with many pressure groups, as in the United States. However, the Marxists assert, the existence of more than one political party does not, in practice, serve the needs of the various classes because the bourgeoisie, with the concentration of power and wealth, can insure that its interests will be served by the elected representatives. The bourgeoisie, according to the Marxists, either selects its own candidates or supports candidates selected by other groups who are willing to cooperate. Since election campaigns are very expensive, the power of money is decisive in determining who will be elected. The Marxists argue that the formal political affiliation of the elected candidate is inconsequential, since almost all candidates are either selected or supported by the bourgeoisie. Khrushchev said of the two major parties in the United States:

> ". . . both represent the interests of the exploiting class. Therefore, at election time there is bickering between various candidates representing the monopolists, the factory and plant owners—that is, the class whose domination the Soviet people ended back in 1917. The chief difference between the Republican and Democratic Parties in the U. S. A. is the fact that the Republican Party's emblem is an elephant and the Democratic Party's, a donkey. You can imagine how limited a choice confronts the American voter."[4]

Once elected, the Marxists say, the candidate is supposed to vote for the interest of his bourgeois supporters; if he does not, he will not be reelected. Engels wrote that in a democratic republic "wealth wields its power indirectly, but all the more effectively" by means of "direct corruption of officials" or "the alliance of the government with the stock exchange."[5] Lenin described the democratic republic as "the best possible shell for capitalism . . . it establishes its power so securely, so firmly, that no change, either of persons or institutions, or practices in the bourgeois republic can shake it."[6]

Bourgeois democratic systems, Soviet writers argue, are democratic in relation to the exploiting capitalist class, but undemocratic in relation to the exploited masses. Democracy, freedom and equality in a capitalist society, they say, means merely "democracy—for the rich, freedom—for the rich, equality—for the rich."[7] Formal equality in the eyes of the law is virtually meaningless, a Soviet spokesman stated:

> ". . . while man's actual status is determined solely by his wealth. As Anatole France pointed out, the millionaire and the pauper are equally free to sleep under the arches of the Seine bridge—but the former prefers to live in his mansion, while the latter does not have any choice. Society can give its members genuine freedom only if it can first and foremost guarantee their material welfare and economic independence. . . . The most extensive and lavishly proclaimed freedom is worthless unless it has a material basis. Under such 'freedom,' man has only two alternatives—to fall into line, or starve."[8]

Soviet authorities claim that in a capitalist state a democratic facade is used to disguise the class rule of capital; that true rule by the people is impossible under capitalism because capitalism is based on and perpetuates gross economic inequalities, which preclude the existence of social and political equality.

Proletarian democracy, which develops under the dictatorship of the proletariat, is described by Marxists as infinitely more democratic than "bourgeois democracy." They maintain that democracy and dictatorship are not mutually exclusive because a system may be dictatorial in relation to certain classes and democratic in relation to other classes. Whereas "bourgeois democracy" is described as democratic in relation to the capitalist class, and dictatorial in relation to the masses, proletarian democracy is described as democratic in relation to the masses of working people and dictatorial in relation to the former exploiters and all potential counter-revolutionary elements. "The dictatorship of the proletariat," Lenin wrote, "inevitably brings with it not only changes in the forms and institutions of democracy, generally speaking, but precisely those changes that lead to an unprecedented extension of the actual utilization of democracy by those oppressed by capitalism, by the toiling classes."[9] One of the chief tasks of the dictatorship of the proletariat, according to Soviet authorities, is to extend democracy and freedom within the limitations of the reality situation and to pave the way for eventual profound extensions of both democracy and freedom. A number of objective reasons purportedly limit freedom and democratic practices during the initial phase of the proletarian dictatorship; the power of the former exploiting class must be broken, and this requires that the former oppressors must themselves be oppressed; in order to provide the economic basis for a free and democratic society, as defined by the Marxists, private ownership of the means of production must be abolished, and public ownership established; class barriers must be broken down; the remnants of class privilege or class repression must be eliminated; the people must be trained to accept and operate effectively within the new Soviet concepts of freedom and democracy. Some of these changes require that the rights and freedoms of certain groups, particularly the members of the former privileged classes, be drastically restricted, while the rights and freedoms of other groups, particularly members of the working class, be gradually, or in some respects, abruptly increased.

Thus, during the period of the dictatorship of the proletariat, according to Soviet spokesmen, the foundations are laid for the type of democracy and freedom toward which Marxists aspire. Private ownership of the means of production is abolished and, accordingly, the economic basis of exploitation of man by man is removed. The removal of the basis for economic privilege, along with other measures, paves the way for social, cultural and, hence, political equality. Gradually class antagonisms are eliminated and society moves toward a classless state. The eradication of class conflict makes it reasonable for one political party to represent and reflect the political interests of all members of society. These changes, however, all take time; the former privileged classes strive to maintain their power and special prerogatives, and constitute a force opposed to change; decades are required to eradicate the remnants of social and cultural inequalities; formerly oppressed, underprivileged people are not immediately ready to assume the responsibilities of self-government and administration of the economy and cultural institutions. If the masses of inexperienced people were allowed to assume too much responsibility, without adequate preparation in terms of experience as well as in terms of the development of appropriate organizational forms, the result would be chaos. Consequently, during the period of the dictatorship of the proletariat, the Marxists believe that it is necessary for the party, as the vanguard of the working class, the political organization which expresses the interests of all the working people, to maintain a firm hold on the reins of power and to use this power to shape society and its members in such a way that eventually a more nearly perfect form of democracy can be practiced, and a higher level of freedom can be enjoyed by all.

Socialist democracy is described by Soviet authorities as "a new, higher historical type of democracy of the people which grew out of the proletarian democracy of the period of transition from capitalism to socialism."[10] This is the form of democracy which is purportedly practiced in the U.S.S.R. at present. Socialist democracy is allegedly different from the form of democracy practiced during the period of the dictatorship of the proletariat in that some of the goals which were pursued during that period have now, according to Soviet authorities, been achieved. It is claimed that as a result of the economic and social changes of the transition period, a new class structure has been formed; the exploiting classes—capitalists, landlords and kulaks—have been abolished, and Soviet society has become a society of working people—workers, peasants and intelligentsia, whose interests are non-antagonistic; social and political privileges and restrictions have been abolished, including practices such as preferential rates of representation for workers and poor peasants and the disenfranchisement of certain social groups which were introduced during the period of the dictatorship of the proletariat to protect the gains of the working people. All classes and strata are alleged to be equal in their relation to political power, the state and the means of production, and in their rights and duties. Although social distinctions have not been totally eradicated, it is argued that the distinctions which remain are between people with equal rights who are engaged in different branches of the economy, such as workers on collective farms and workers in state factories; these distinctions are not based on relations of domination and subordination, are non-antagonistic and decrease as society develops.

One of the stated tasks of the period of socialist democracy is the gradual obliteration of all class distinctions. Party leaders point out that prestige and fame have ceased to be the monopoly of any particular social group and are accorded to persons regardless of social origin for excellence in any sphere of work; higher education is not the special privilege of any specific groups, and there are no fixed boundaries between classes or strata; members of the peasantry may become workers and vice versa and manual workers may become members of the intelligentsia. According to a Soviet statement:

> "Full equality, the gradual effacement of distinctions between classes, and social justice are characteristic features of class relations under socialism, which help to consolidate the unity of society . . . socialism replaces the age-old struggle of classes by their solidarity and unity arising from the community of aims, ideology and ethics. The abolition of the exploiting classes and the socialist transformation of all the petty bourgeois classes lay the foundation for the moral and political unity of society."[11]

Soviet authors assert that during the period of socialist democracy, the function of the state changes radically; most important, the state ceases to function as an instrument of class suppression. However, socialist society needs state organization for several reasons. First, the state serves as a suitable form of public leadership in the economy, social relations and cultural development. Second, even under socialism, there are inequalities in the satisfaction of the needs of the people, as well as manifestations of private-ownership psychology; machinery is required to regulate the measures of labor and consumption, to protect public and personal property and to prohibit anti-social actions. Finally, since socialism has not triumphed on a world-wide basis, the state is necessary for the protection of society against external enemies and from spies, saboteurs and other enemies of socialism within the society. Moreover, under socialism the functions of the state are greatly enhanced in certain spheres, including the organization of social production and the direction of the economy; communist education and the development of a socialist culture; safeguarding socialist property; protection of the rights and interests of citizens, of their personal property and of public order; and defending the country against outside attack. Since the function of the state is somewhat different under socialism than it is during the period of transition from capitalism to socialism, its methods are also different. The most significant change, according to Soviet spokesmen, is that administrative compulsory measures can be increasingly replaced by methods of persuasion of the people.

Soviet authorities place great emphasis on the extension of the social and political rights of the working people under socialism. As indicated previously, they argue that only if the masses of people are given the freedom from economic exploitation, which can be attained solely through abolition of the private ownership of the means of production, can class and social distinctions be abolished, and only if people have equal rights in the economic and social spheres can political equality be meaningful. They assert that under socialism the provision of the indispensable material basis transforms formal rights and freedoms into actual rights and freedoms. Genuine political equality is purportedly ensured by the actual equality of the people in relation to the means of production, and hence their equal right to participate "as real masters" in making decisions which affect all society. It is asserted that only socialism creates such a unity of interests of all sections of society that political problems can be settled in a democratic way without class coercion. Party leaders hasten to add that the unlimited freedom of the individual is not a goal of socialist democracy, since the establishment of private enterprises, anti-social acts, fascist propaganda, racial discrimination, the writing of books that might corrupt youth and all other activities which are harmful to other people or to society must be prohibited. They describe socialist democracy as a *directed* rather than an unlimited democracy, a democracy directed by the party and the state in the interest of the further development of socialism and the building of communism. The development of genuine socialist democracy, they say, requires constant attention on the part of society, the party and the state including a struggle against "erroneous views," administrative-bureaucratic tendencies and disbelief in the intelligence and power of the people.

The party attaches great importance to the development of socialist democracy as a fundamental prerequisite for the normal and rapid development of society. "Broad democracy," Soviet writers say, "enables each member to feel a fully fledged master of society and stimulates the creative initiative of the masses, without which socialism cannot advance a single step."[12] The political rights and freedoms which party spokesmen emphasize include the principle of electivity, removability and accountability of all persons holding office and the principle of electivity and accountability of all state organs; public organizations of the working people exercise increasing control over the activities of executive bodies; millions of Soviet citizens participate directly in administering the affairs of the society, either as elected representatives of the people or as activists; and the Komsomol, trade unions and other public organizations exert considerable influence on the machinery of the state. In short, the people are described as the controlling force in Soviet society. Marxists emphasize that social and economic rights of the working people are an integral part of democracy. The right to work, rest and leisure, to education, material maintenance in old age and illness are considered to be the basis of genuine freedom and happiness. Without these, political rights are held to be empty formalities. Under socialism, they say, "Democracy is vested with a new meaning and is extended to all segments of the society. Socialist democracy is not a mere formal proclamation of rights because special emphasis is placed on the provision of the possibilities for the exercise of these rights."[13]

Soviet leaders gamely admit that socialist democracy has not yet been perfected largely because the people themselves have not yet progressed fully toward the establishment of the type of society that would permit its fullest exercise. However, at the same time, they point out that "Soviet democracy is not marking time, but is constantly developing. . . . "[14] Manifestations of the development of democracy in which they take particular pride include economic and social measures, political rights, and particularly the increased role of the public in the administration of justice, the economy and cultural institutions.

The development and perfection of socialist democracy is described as a stepping stone on the way to the emergence of the "highest and most perfect form of democracy" which is to be practiced under communism. A Soviet official described the process as follows:

"Conditions for the gradual withering away of the state and the transition to communist self-government by the people are being created in the process of the full-scale construction of communism. The management of the affairs of society will pass from official organs of state power into the hands of society as a whole. That will lead to the disappearance of a special category of people engaged exclusively in government. Every citizen will help run the affairs of society. There will no longer be any need of coercion by the state, since all human actions and activities will be governed by a high sense of civic duty, by public opinion and communist morals. This process is already taking place: many functions that used to be the prerogative of state organs have been transferred to social bodies. The maintenance of public order, the safeguarding of citizens' rights and interests, supervision of cultural and medical services and of sports and physical culture—in all these fields the part played by voluntary bodies is becoming decisive. A corresponding steady reduction in the size of the state apparatus is taking place."[15]

The Party Program states:

> "All-round extension and perfection of socialist democracy, active participation of all citizens in the administration of the state, in the management of economic and cultural development, improvement of government apparatus, and increased control over its activity by the people constitute the main direction in which socialist statehood develops in the period of building communism."[16]

Soviet leaders state that as their society approaches communism, more and more of the functions now performed by governmental bodies will be transferred to public organizations. This will allow the state to concentrate on basic problems such as economic development and the coordination of all aspects of social development. Moreover, decisions arrived at collectively by the people will take into account local conditions and interests, and the people will "carry out more willingly, consciously and with greater readiness decisions which have been drawn up with their participation, with their knowledge and with consideration for their interests and proposals."[17] An eventual goal is for the people to administer all the affairs of society and for the state to become superfluous. According to Lenin, the state can "wither away" only when

> ". . . people gradually *become accustomed* to observing the elementary rules of social intercourse that have been known for centuries and repeated for thousands of years in copy book maxims, when they become accustomed to observing them without force, without compulsion, without subordination, *without the special apparatus* for compulsion which is called the state."[18]

In the future, Soviet spokesmen say,

> ". . . there will be no general need for compulsion against any part of society, since all citizens, without any administrative regulation will discharge their duty in productive work and in the defense of the country, and observe the standards and rules of the socialist community."[19]

Thus the Marxist ideal for society involves very definite notions about freedom and democracy. The ideal society, according to the Marxists, is one in which social classes have been totally eliminated; all people are to be treated equally with respect to opportunity, satisfaction of needs and obligations to society. The interests of society and of all members of society are to be in harmony, and each individual, by working for the welfare of society as a whole, is at the same time to be enhancing his own personal well-being. All members of society are to be free from economic exploitation, and the material needs of all are to be satisfied adequately and equitably; they are to be free from social privileges and restrictions and free to serve society to the best of their ability. The ideal society, as conceived by the Marxists, is to be highly democratic in that all people are to be equally free in the sense described above; all people are to be equal in terms of actual as well as formal rights and obligations; all people are to have equal political rights; the role of the formal state apparatus is to become increasingly less important, and responsibility for the administration of most public affairs is to be transferred to the people who will govern themselves through their public organizations; the absence of social and economic privileges is to rule out the possibility that one or a few individuals can, by virtue of the power that derives from special privileges, dominate the conduct of public affairs; because the interests of all members of society will be in harmony, basic conflict cannot arise in the administration of public affairs; the people will be in agreement about the goals which should be pursued, and differences of opinion which may arise about suitable techniques for the achievement of agreed-upon goals can be resolved by democratic consensus; the identity of interests will eliminate the need for compulsion. In short, in the ideal Marxist society, a high level of democracy will be practiced because all members of society will gladly work for the welfare of society as a whole; all will have equal rights, privileges and obligations; and all will participate fully and equally in the administration of the affairs of society.

This, then, is the Marxist ideal. What about Soviet reality? Perhaps the most harshly discrepant note is that in spite of the constantly reiterated claim that Marxist ideology and Soviet practice are highly democratic, the Soviet people have never been given the opportunity to even express an opinion about the acceptability of the ideal toward which they are expected to strive. Marxist-Leninist democratic theory does not include the concept that the people should be able to select the goals for society. The ideal, outlined by Karl Marx and Friedrich Engels and adapted somewhat by leaders of the C.P.S.U., has been imposed upon the Soviet people. One of the tasks of the party is to mold the consciousness of the people so that they will accept and strive for the ideal which has been selected for them and which they are not free to reject. The system is essentially paternalistic and authoritarian in that the people have had absolutely no voice in the crucial decision about what constitutes an ideal society. Flattering statements by the party leaders about "faith in the power and intelligence of the common people" are belied by "the party knows best" policy with reference to the most basic problems.

Given that democratic procedures were totally excluded in the selection of the ideal toward which Soviet society is striving, and that Soviet concepts of democracy and freedom, as selected by the party leaders for the Soviet people, are radically different from the concepts of democracy and freedom subscribed to by most Western peoples, what is the relationship between Soviet practice and the Soviet ideal? Is the Soviet Union "totally undemocratic," as some Western authorities claim, or does practice represent an approach to the Soviet ideal, as Soviet spokesman maintain? Since Soviet concepts of freedom and democracy are extremely inclusive, it would be impossible to provide in one chapter sufficient information on which to base answers to this question. Initially, information will be presented about the Soviet electoral system and the organization of the government of the U.S.S.R. An examination of the economic, judicial and educational systems, and of individual rights, privileges and obligations in subsequent chapters will provide additional information on which to base decisions about freedom and democracy in the U.S.S.R. At this point, only one preliminary generalization will be made: the substance of Soviet democracy and freedom is not as real as Soviet leaders claim, nor is it as non-existent, particularly when evaluated in terms of the Soviet value system, as anti-Soviet writers claim.

Elections and Self-Government Under Tsarism

The reaction of the people of the U.S.S.R. to Soviet electoral practices and representative organs is more comprehensible if the limited opportunities for participation in self-government during the Tsarist era are taken into consideration. The Tsar and his advisors, with the aid of a highly centralized bureaucracy, took pains to limit popular participation in the exercise of governmental responsibilities.. Individual rights and liberties were highly restricted. The population of Tsarist Russia was permitted only token participation in representative government in three institutions— the village assembly, county and provincial councils *(zemstva)* and city councils, and after 1906, the Imperial Duma.

The village assembly, an institution with a long history, which was given increased responsibilities following the abolition of serfdom in 1861, gave the peasants some experience in self-administration. Elders and judges were selected by direct election. Though closely supervised, the assembly was permitted to handle local problems such as the distribution of land, inheritance disputes and small legal matters. However, in 1889 the Tsarist government restricted the jurisdiction of the village assembly by appointing Land Captains, officials from the local nobility, who were given autocratic power to supervise the peasants. Village communes *(mir)* were officially abolished in 1906 when the government decided to create a new class of independent farmers; however, many of the communes were not actually dissolved until 1917.

Following the abolition of serfdom, and with it the administrative authority of the estate owner over his serfs or "souls," local governing bodies, called *zemstva*,[20] were established in the counties and provinces. Three classes of citizens—members of village communities, private landowners and townspeople—elected electors or commissioners, who in turn elected delegates to the *zemstvo*. An indirect system of voting by *curia* allowed the large landowners to dominate the assembly. Each county *zemstvo* consisted of an elected assembly, presided over by the marshal of the county nobility, and an executive board chosen by the delegates from among their own members. The county *zemstvo* elected representatives to the provincial *zemstvo* which also elected its own executive board.

The *zemstva* were responsible for the administration of local affairs including public health, roads, education, veterinary service, improvement in farming methods, poor relief, prisons, etc. However, there were many limitations on the freedom of action and effectiveness of the *zemstva*. The imperial government restricted the taxing authority of the *zemstva* and required them to use as much as three-quarters of their limited finances to meet obligations imposed by the imperial government so that relatively little money was left for health, education and other local projects. After 1866 the publicity of *zemstvo* debates was restricted and controlled by the local governors and in 1890 the electoral laws were modified so that the majority of seats in almost all *zemstva* assemblies were held by the nobility. The number of peasant representatives diminished accordingly. In addition, instead of choosing their own representatives, the peasants were permitted only to elect candidates from whom the local officials chose *zemstvo* delegates. The *zemstvo,* thus, represented the nobility more effectively than it did any other class.

Self-government in the cities followed a similar pattern. In 1870 cities were permitted to set up governmental machinery similar to the rural *zemstva*. City councils were controlled by the relatively few large taxpayers, since the few citizens who paid one-third of the city taxes elected one-third of the delegates; those who paid the second third of the taxes also elected one-third of the delegates; and the very numerous small taxpayers elected the final third of the delegates. The city council was designed to perform the same kind of functions as the *zemstvo* and had inflicted upon it the same kind of restrictions and interference.

Although the franchise favored the wealthy few, both the *zemstva* and the city councils attracted some of the most enlightened and public-spirited men in the country. In spite of supervision, interference and inadequate finances, these bodies performed some commendable services in education, public health, agriculture, etc. Some training in self-government and public administration was acquired by the delegates and the employees of the *zemstva* and city councils. Citizens, in general, became more interested in, and familiar with, the advantages and responsibilities of self-government. However, since these local governing bodies were critical of the central government, the latter took steps to increase its control over them. Thus, instead of having expanding powers as they gained in experience, their powers were curtailed, and they tended to become increasingly less representative of all classes in the population. The Tsar and his autocratic advisors would not readily relinquish their power. The *zemstva* and city councils were permitted to exercise only very limited powers of self-government.

After the Revolution of 1905, the Tsar agreed reluctantly to the formation of a national representative legislative assembly called the Imperial Duma. Concurrently, freedom of speech and assembly were promised along with democratic franchise and the principle that no law could be made without the consent of the Duma. Delegates to the Duma were selected on the basis of indirect voting. For the first Duma, suffrage was fairly broad; however, persons under twenty-five, women, students, soldiers, sailors and many specifically enumerated individuals or groups were disfranchised. Most urban dwellers who paid real estate or business taxes, or rented property had the right to vote for electors who then chose delegates to the Duma. In cities, electors were chosen by two categories or *curiae,* the high taxpayers and "the others." In rural areas, the categories of voters were the large landowners, the small landowners, and the peasants. The rural population was given higher representation because the Imperial government assumed it would be more conservative than the urban population.

Before the first Duma met, the power promised to it was sharply curtailed by the Tsar. A second legislative chamber, the State Council, was created with powers equal to that of the Duma. Half the members of this upper house were appointed by the Tsar and the other half were elected by the nobility, clergy, provincial *zemstva,* universities and other institutions. The Tsar also issued "Fundamental Laws" which decreed that to become law, a bill must be approved by both houses and signed by the Tsar who retained an absolute veto. The Tsar announced that he would retain control over foreign affairs, appointments, censorship, police, armed forces, significant budgetary items and even over convening and dismissing the Duma. Ministers were to be responsible to the Tsar who appointed them, rather than to the Duma. The Tsar also retained the power to govern by decree when the Duma was not in session. The "Fundamental Laws" stated that supreme autocratic power belongs to the Tsar and that obedience to the Emperor was "ordained by God Himself."

When the first Duma convened in the Spring of 1906, the delegates attempted to introduce universal suffrage, direct elections, amnesty for political prisoners, dissolution of the State Council and ministerial responsibility. The Duma was, however, almost totally powerless and was dissolved by the Tsar after it had been in session for little more than two months of its five-year term. Measures were taken to have the second Duma more subservient to the imperial autocrat. For example, legal technicalities were used to rob thousands of their vote and "undersirable" candidates were eliminated. Nevertheless, the second Duma attempted, with complete lack of success, to introduce liberal reform measures. It was dissolved after being in session for only one hundred days.

The Tsar, dissatisfied with the composition of the first two Dumas, violated his own Fundamental Laws by tampering with electoral regulation. Membership in the Duma was reduced by eighty, with the peoples of Eastern Siberia, the Caucasus and Poland having their representation cut by two-thirds and the nationalities of Central Asia being completely disfranchised. Only 15 percent of the population retained the right to vote. The indirect election was a two-stage affair for the great landowners and a four-stage affair for peasants. The *curiae,* or voting categories, were structured to provide the large landowners with a 500-to-1 advantage over workers. The number of electors, who in turn chose the Duma delegates, was manipulated to provide the few landed gentry with over half the votes, while the peasants, urban-dwelling property owners and workers had approximately 20, 25, and 2 percent of the votes respectively. The large landowners were assured at least half of the seats in the Duma, and actually controlled almost all of the seats since in the final selective stage, all *curiae* voted together and the nobility with over half the votes was able to select delegates for the other *curiae* as well as for its own.

Although the third and fourth Dumas had social compositions which satisfied the Tsar, even these conservative bodies occasionally voted against his programs. The Tsar's countermeasure to opposition was to recess the Duma for three days and to issue his order as an "emergency decree." When the Duma convened, it would be presented with the *fait accompli.* In spite of its limited power, the Duma was not a completely useless institution. Throughout its history most of its members worked cautiously and conscientiously for improved government. The population respected it and considered it a permanent institution. It helped to systematize the opinions of at least the educated members of society, and it protested vigorously against the corruption and inefficiency involved in Russia's war effort. And finally, it did provide a relatively small number of people with limited experience in the practice of self-government.

The regulations and restrictions surrounding the Dumas, especially the third and fourth, have been described as the most ingenious and involved ever devised to defeat the purposes of democracy.[21] The electoral system combined class and territorial-district representation. Tsarist elections were indirect, inequitable in favor of the large landowners and manipulated. They were not designed to elect a body which would practice self-government. Rather, the elections were intended to serve as token appeasement to the demands of certain groups within the population and at the same time to elect a "representative" body which would in no way interfere with the autocratic power of the ruling minority. Tsarist elections and the treatment of the three institutions which under Tsarism were granted limited self-governing privileges demonstrate the difficulty that the Russian people had in acquiring and holding democratic rights.

Early Soviet Electoral Practices

After the Bolsheviks seized power, they recognized the need for an electoral system which would superficially comply with the democratic ideology of Marxism-Leninism and, at the same time, would insure the dominance of the communist minority. They found in the Tsarist electoral procedures, which were skillfully designed to weight the votes of the numerically small friendly classes and to exclude or limit the participation of radical or non-subservient groups, an excellent prototype to achieve their own goals. Elections during the initital period of the Soviet regime resembled Tsarist elections in that they were largely indirect, manipulated from above, biased in favor of friendly classes and were not universal. As during the Tsarist era, Soviet elections were intended to reflect democratic concessions which were more token than actual, since in neither case were the "representative" assemblies permitted to exercise political power to any meaningful extent.

No provision for the electoral rights of citizens was made in the first Constitution of the U.S.S.R. (1924), primarily because no All-Union official was elected by direct vote. Prior to the introduction of the 1936 Constitution, direct elections were practiced only for the selection of members of the Soviets of rural and urban settlements. The local Soviets elected delegates to the district congress, which in turn elected delegates to the provincial congress. The procedure of electing delegates to the next congress in the hierarchy proceeded through the Union Republic Congress to the Union Congress of Soviets, the major federal institution which was purportedly representative of the people. Since popular elections were for local organs of state power only, it was reasonable that the electoral procedures should be embodied in the Constitutions of the Union Republics rather than in the Constitution of the U.S.S.R. Although the Constitutions of the different Union Republics agreed rather closely on electoral provisions, since all were modelled on the 1918 Constitution of the R.S.F.S.R., local variations between and within republics in electoral practices were common. The Tsarist tradition is evident in the combination of direct and indirect elections, and the hierarchy of Soviets and congresses. The indirect elections of delegates to the intermediate and higher Soviets made it possible for the communist minority in the local Soviets to utilize their superior organization to secure party control over the higher Soviets. Moreover, the system of indirect elections provided the Communist Party, which was fully cognizant of its lack of popular support, with ample opportunity for manipulation from the top, and greatly facilitated the tasks of the party with the intermediate and higher Soviets. During the formative decades of the new Soviet state (1917-1936), the people could not be trusted to elect "good" representatives above the level of the local Soviets. However, direct elections at the local level did constitute a meaningful concession to the masses of the people.

Representation in the Soviets was weighted in favor of the urban proletarians, who constituted a minority of the population, in comparison to the peasants. For example, one delegate to the Union Congress of Soviets represented 25,000 voting workers or 125,000 rural inhabitants. Workers received double representation in the higher Soviets, since urban Soviets were permitted to elect delegates directly to all levels of congresses as well as to participate in the indirect election of delegates through the hierarchy of congresses. Rural Soviets had the right to direct election of delegates to the district congress only. By biasing the franchise in favor of the workers, the communists were able to guarantee their hegemony within the higher Soviets to the disadvantage of the various socialist parties which derived their strength from the peasants. Even after competitive parties had been dissolved, weighted representation for the workers continued to be practiced, partly because the Communist Party had to devote its attention to more urgent matters than revising electoral practices, partly in order to eliminate the possibility that non-party elements in the higher Soviets might be strong enough to attempt to turn the representative system of the proletarian state into a tool of counter-revolution, and partly because the communists deemed it more practical from the point of view of control to favor the workers for membership in the higher Soviets.

All adult (18 years and over) members of the working class in both rural and urban areas had the right to vote and be elected unless deprived of the franchise by law. Voting privileges were denied to all class enemies of the proletariat: those who hired labor for the purpose of extracting profit, engaged in trade or lived on unearned income; and former landowners, capitalists, members of religious orders, officials of the Tsarist regime, members of the Tsarist police force, etc. It was considered both politically unwise and incompatible with Lenin's theory on the workers' state to allow former exploiters and oppressors equal rights and liberties with the proletariat and its peasant allies. However, Soviet ideology was so international that foreign proletarians who resided in Soviet territory were enfranchised and could be elected to the Soviets.

Electoral Commissions were given responsibility for the preparation of registration lists, notification of voters and for conducting electoral assemblies. Because the Electoral Commissions exercised very considerable influence over the selection of deputies, their composition was carefully regulated from the top down. The Republic Central Election Commission was formed by the Central Executive Committee of the republic. At each of the lower administrative units in the hierarchy (province, territory, district, city and local Soviet), the Electoral Commission was established by the Executive Committee of the corresponding Soviet, but the President of the

Commission was appointed by the immediately superior Executive Committee on the nomination of the superior Election Commission. The numerical size of the Election Commission decreased from the upper to the lower levels of the administrative hierarchy. The composition of the Commission at each level was regulated by law and was designed to represent the various sections of the population. For example, the Provincial Election Commission consisted of a president, nominated by the Central Electoral Commission and approved by the Presidium of the Republic Central Executive Committee, and ten members approved by the Provincial Executive Committee. The ten members included two representatives of the Provincial Executive Committee, two representatives of peasant mutual-aid societies, and one representative from each of the trade union council, the Komsomol, the Communist Party, the city Soviets, the national minorities and the Red Army.[22] The representative character of the Electoral Commissions has been offered by Soviet authorities as an example of the "profound democracy" of their electoral practices.

The higher Electoral Commissions ensured that elections were conducted in the interests of proletarian democracy, and supervised and provided lower Electoral Commissions with necessary information and instructions. Local Electoral Commissions were required to: establish, verify and publish lists of those deprived of electoral rights, and examine complaints; mail an official notice of the election to each person entitled to vote; lay out precincts; organize electoral assemblies; delegate members to act as presiding officers for each electoral assembly; inform the Executive Committee of the responsible Soviet and the supervising Electoral Commission of the results of the election.[23]

The decisive phase in the election procedure was the nomination of candidates. The procedure involved a series of pre-election meetings at which various groups proposed and discussed candidates. The meetings were carefully watched and supervised by both the party and the local officials. Formal nomination was not made until the day of the election at the electoral assembly, but the preparation for the nomination was so carefully supervised and controlled that after the system had been in operation for a few years, it was customary for the party cell, the trade union and other local organizations to propose identical lists of candidates whose number corresponded to the number of vacancies to be filled. During the pre-election campaign, candidates unacceptable to the party were eliminated, and candidates acceptable to the party and strongly supported by the populace were given the backing of the party. The pre-election eliminations permitted an impressive demonstration of solidarity between the party and the populace on the actual day of voting. In fact, it was rare for the people to have any choice between candidates on election day. The decisive problem was the selection of the correct candidates for nomination and, hence, election.

Voters were convened at designated centers on election day where they voted by open show of hands. Those who opposed the party-approved candidates ran the risk of being persecuted or of being discriminated against by the authorities. However, in spite of the predetermined outcome of the election, this ancient method of "direct democracy" did result in the development of considerable interest in the electoral process, and party cells found it expedient to support locally strong candidates.

Current Soviet Electoral Practices

On Stalin's initiative, the Seventh Congress of Soviets of the U.S.S.R. (February, 1935) adopted a resolution to amend the existing constitution and electoral system by "democratizing the electoral system . . . replacing not entirely equal suffrage by equal suffrage, indirect elections by direct elections, and the open ballot by the secret ballot."[24] As leader of the party, Stalin was dissatisfied with the increasing "bureaucratism" of the state administration. He apparently hoped that by arming the people with electoral freedom to reject candidates who did not enjoy popular approval, the local party apparatus throughout the U.S.S.R. might locate better candidates who knew how to exercise control, through the Soviets, over the administrative apparatus and to check such vices as "careerism" and bureaucratism. He asserted that: "Universal, equal, direct and secret suffrage in the U.S.S.R. will be a whip in the hands of the population against the organs of government which work badly."[25] Although the changes were definitely in the direction of democratizing the franchise and electoral practices, the Communist Party had no intention of introducing electoral contests or of sharing its political power with other groups. The modifications in the electoral law were designed to increase the nominal participation of the masses in the selection of deputies to representative organs and to increase the probability that the selected deputies would be of a calibre acceptable to the party and the people.

The 1936 Constitution of the U.S.S.R. (formerly referred to frequently as the Stalin Constitution because it was prepared by the Central Committee of the C.P.S.U. under Stalin's direction) marked the formal transition from "proletarian democracy" to "socialist democracy." The Soviet leadership declared then that the class of entrepreneurs had been eliminated, and that the population of the U.S.S.R. consisted of two friendly classes, the workers and the peasants. The new Soviet intelligentsia, recruited from the peasants and workers and employed by the state, was not considered to be a separate class. Disfranchisement and unequal voting privileges were deemed neither necessary nor expedient under the new "socialist constitution" because the class consciousness of the peasants had increased considerably, and no exploiting class remained.

The electoral norms of the Soviet Union are contained in Articles 134-142 of the U.S.S.R. Constitution and the Electoral Law of January, 1950. The constitutions of the Union Republics were changed to conform with the law of the U.S.S.R. All citizens of the U.S.S.R. who have reached the age of eighteen, irrespective of race or nationality, sex, religion, education, domicile, social origin, property status or past activities, have the right to vote in the election of deputies with the exception of persons who have legally been certified as insane or convicted of a major crime. All deputies, from the primary level of the local Soviet to the highest organ of state power, the Supreme Soviet of the U.S.S.R., are chosen on the basis of direct elections. Indirect elections have been completely abolished. Equal suffrage has replaced weighted representation in favor of the workers. Separate rooms or curtained voting booths to permit voting in secret must be provided in each precinct. Soviet authorities have taken all necessary measures, both constitutional and practical, to ensure that the suffrage is indeed universal, equal and direct, and that facilities are provided for voting in secret.

Electoral Commissions, similar in composition and hierarchical structure to those formed prior to the 1936 Constitution, are established several weeks prior to the election.[26] Whereas under the former system, the Electoral Commission was responsible for the establishment of lists of the disfranchised and for conducting the electoral assemblies at which both nominating and voting occurred, the formal duties of the Electoral Commission now include registering nominees, preparing ballots, conducting the polls, counting the results and providing mandates for the elected deputies. The most important function of the Electoral Commission, selection of the one person who will be listed as the official candidate if a number of candidates are proposed, is not prescribed by law.

Registration of voters is handled by the executive committees of the local Soviets and by the unit commanders of all military forces. Electoral lists are posted at least thirty days before the election so that a citizen may have recourse to the executive committee and the People's Court if his name is not included on the election rolls. Voters who move after the compilation of the voting lists, or who will be traveling or otherwise absent from their residence on election day, may secure a voting certificate which may be presented to the polling authorities in any precinct on election day. Few, if any, Soviet citizens are denied the right to cast a ballot.

Districts for representation are established by the executive committee of the Soviet for which the deputies are to be elected, i.e., by the Presidium of the Supreme Soviet of the U.S.S.R. for the election of its deputies and by the executive committee of the provincial Soviet for its deputies. Election precincts are established by the decree of the executive committee of the locality not later than forty-five days prior to the election. Precincts must include at least fifty, but not more than three thousand, registered voters.

To be eligible as a candidate for election to the Supreme Soviet of the U.S.S.R. or a Union Republic Supreme Soviet, citizens must have attained the age of twenty-three or twenty-one years, respectively. Otherwise, any person who has the right to vote also has the right to be elected. Candidates need not meet a residency requirement. One individual may, during a single election campaign, be nominated by several districts as candidate for Soviets at different levels in the hierarchy, but no individual can be the candidate of more than one district for membership in a Soviet at a given level, i.e., the candidate of one district for membership in the local Soviet and the Supreme Soviet of the U.S.S.R. could be nominated by a second district for membership in the provincial Soviet, but not for a local Soviet or the Supreme Soviet, since he is already the candidate of the first district for Soviets at these levels.

The nomination of candidates continues to be the crucial phase of the election. The Constitution states: "The right to nominate candidates is secured to public organizations and societies of working people: Communist Party organizations, trade unions, cooperatives, youth organizations and cultural societies" (Article 141). Since various organizations are empowered to make nominations, it would seem plausible that, on occasion, more than one candidate would be nominated for a given office. Indeed, constitutional provisions definitely take the possibility of multiple candidates into account, since the law provides that every properly nominated candidate who officially accepts nomination must be registered by the Electoral Commission and that all duly registered candidates must be included on the ballot.[27] Violations of these regulations are subject only to administrative and not court review, since the Executive Committee of the Soviet has the right to protest any nomination within two days after registration, and the refusal of an Electoral Commission to register a candidate may be appealed to the next Electoral Commission in the hierarchy, whose decision is final.[28]

Soviet ballots have so consistently listed only one candidate for each office that the value of the constitutional provisions has been justifiably questioned by non-Soviet authors. This somewhat euphemistic rebuttal appears in *Soviet State Law:*

"As for the bourgeois propagandists' allegation that the Soviet electoral system permits only one candidate in each constituency, it is the result of either ignorance or deliberate slander. The Soviet law provides for election of one deputy from each constituency, but does not restrict the rights of organizations and societies to nominate any number of candidates they desire. It goes without saying that this right cannot be interpreted as meaning that these organizations and societies have a duty to nominate not one, but two or more candidates in each constituency."[29]

The fact remains that Soviet ballots are printed with only one name per office. The following explanation of why the ballot lists only one candidate is typical of the official propaganda:

> "All Soviet people have common interests and the same goal—the building of a new society. There are no classes with conflicting interests in the U.S.S.R. Industrial workers, collective farmers, and intellectuals work together to achieve this goal. The Communist Party which guides the entire life of the country, all its economic and cultural affairs, enjoys the supreme confidence of the people.
>
> "Since the interests of the people and the Communist Party are one and the same, and since there are no antagonistic groups or classes, there is no reason for several candidates to appear on the ballot. At nominating meetings, where all possible candidates are discussed and voted on, both Communists and non-Party people agree on the one they consider best suited as their representative."[30]

How is this facade of unanimity achieved? What is the procedure for selecting the one official candidate for each office?

At the initiation of the election campaign, large numbers of nominating meetings are held by enterprises, kolkhozy, factory shifts, etc., and by party, trade union and Komsomol organizations. Various candidates are proposed and evaluated. During initial meetings, the party is able to delineate among potential candidates those who have considerable support from the electorate, and members of the nominating meetings learn which potential candidates are acceptable to and would be supported by the party. Individuals who do not meet both criteria are eliminated. The party prefers nominations to be made by general meetings of voters rather than by organizations such as the party or the trade union, as this heightens the illusion of public control. In conformity with the Soviet emphasis on collectivism, nominations must be made by groups rather than by individuals. Each organizational unit selects a candidate acceptable to the members of the group and to the party. Frequently several groups or organizations select the same candidates either because of genuine widespread support or because of the coordinating activities of the party. In this case, the same slate of candidates may be submitted by several groups.

However, it may happen that different groups or organizations support different candidates. In this event, representatives of the various nominating groups convene to select from the proposed candidates the one candidate whose name will be officially submitted to the Electoral Commission. Occasionally, pre-nomination agreement is not reached, and more than one nomination for each office may be submitted to the Electoral Commission. However, even then, only one name is listed on the ballot. The final choice of the official candidate may be made in one of several ways, none of which are provided for in the Constitution. An article in *Soviet Russia Today* described one method of achieving unanimity at this stage.

"The practice is for the district election committee to call delegated meetings to sift the nominations from the local organizations and to arrive at placement of candidates on the ballot. The law does not restrict the number of candidates that can be put on the ballot for a given office but the practice in the last two elections showed that in an overwhelming majority of the cases the district election committees, in cooperation with representatives of the nominating meetings, unanimously chose a most favored candidate to be placed on the ballot without opposition."[31]

In some cases the final selection is made by the Electoral Commission, the Executive Committee of the Soviet to which the deputy is to be elected, and local party leaders. If these groups are not able to reach agreement, a decision is made by the higher level Electoral Commission or party organization. The pride which Soviet officials take in the representative character of the composition of the Electoral Commissions is understandable when one considers that if pre-nomination agreement is not reached, the Electoral Commission, under the direction of the party, makes the final selection of candidates for nomination and, hence, election. Although the people are, indeed, allowed to participate in the selection of candidates for election, their voice is not decisive. No attempt is made to apply democratic principles of equal, direct and secret suffrage during this all-important phase of the election procedure, and by no stretch of the imagination can it be assumed that all members of the electorate are equally influential in the choice of potential candidates, even within the preliminary meetings in which potential candidates are selected. The Soviet nominating procedure is relatively efficient in relation to its intended purpose, that is, the selection of well-qualified and acceptable candidates for election to public office. The procedure, though not entirely lacking in democratic elements, is, however, not nearly as democratic as Soviet authorities suggest, since the electorate serves merely in an advisory rather than decision-making capacity and because, inevitably, some segments of the electorate are able to wield more influence than others.

Soviet citizens are frequently subjected to the slogan "we must send our best sons and daughters to the Soviets." To be selected as an official candidate is considered an honor and a reward. The voters and officials of each electoral district are charged with the responsibility of selecting one candidate for each office who will strengthen the ties between the party and the electorate. It is felt that rivalry among candidates would invite the growth of factionalism which might endanger party unity or pit non-party groups against the party, thus alienating the party from the people. The nominee need not be a member of the party as long as he recognizes the role of the party in Soviet society as the elite vanguard of the people and submits to its guidance. Such persons are referred to as "non-party Bolsheviks." Since a major purpose of Soviet elections is to elicit popular consensus in the party, it is essential that the candidates are acceptable to the voters. If a non-party nominee demonstrates greater popularity than a party member, he may be selected as the candidate, if his political reliability is satisfactory. Such persons are eventually invited to join the party. The nominating procedure serves as a method of distinguishing grass-roots leaders among the masses and presenting them for recognition by the party. It provides millions of people with the opportunity to participate nominally in the selection of deputies to governmental organs, and in general, helps to strengthen the ties of the Communist Party with the masses.

The nomination of candidates is followed by an elaborate election campaign conducted by trade unions, youth, professional and other mass organizations as well as by the party. The need for an election campaign might be questioned when the principle of one candidate for one office excludes competition. The party uses the election campaign as a convenient opportunity to intensify political indoctrination and to focus favorable attention on its accomplishments in the solution of domestic and international problems. This is intended to convince the Soviet people that the party is a blessing and that they are, indeed, fortunate to be governed by so capable a leadership. Millions of party members and candidates, aided by youth groups, mass organizations and other volunteers are enlisted as agitators to build up popular enthusiasm for the party and its candidates. Pre-election literature in the form of millions of pamphlets is distributed and all media of communication are used in the campaign. The population is reminded of differences between Tsarist Russia and the U.S.S.R. in fields such as economy, education, medicine and science; the opportunities for self-government under the Tsarist and Soviet systems are contrasted. The masses are challenged to increase standards of production as an indication of their appreciation of the Soviet system. An attempt is made to contact every voter. While the pre-election campaign does act as an impediment to a boycott, or even laxness on the part of the electorate, its major purpose is to inspire the Soviet people with appreciation and with a sense of awe in the monolithic unity and massive power of the Communist Party and its subsidiaries. Rather justifiably, the state meets the entire expense of the pre-election campaign.

More than citizens of any other country, Soviet citizens exercise their right to vote. In many precincts and elections districts, voting turnout is complete and official statistics reveal that less than 2 percent of all eligible voters are remiss. Election procedures make it difficult for a voter to neglect this civic responsibility. His registration as a voter is accomplished for him by the Soviet. Elections are always held on Sunday, a legal holiday, usually in a highly festive atmosphere with music, flags and pictures of party leaders. Precincts are small so that getting to the polls does not constitute a problem, and provisions are made for shut-ins, hospitalized persons, merchant seamen, etc., to cast their votes. Polls remain open from

6 a.m. to 10 p.m., even if all registered voters in the precinct cast their vote early in the day, so that no person with a voting certificate could be inadvertently robbed of his franchise. Social pressures are carefully organized to stimulate individual participation, and the propaganda line is cleverly designed to motivate the voter's interest. The psychological pressure to conform is extremely high. If moral suasion and social pressures fail to prompt the Soviet citizen, the uncomfortable fear of being singled out by party vigilantes as a non-spirited citizen invariably motivates even the most retrograde, and these would seem to constitute a small minority, to make a show of interest in the election. The slogan: "He who is not with us is against us" encourages citizens not only to vote, but to vote "right."

After the usual procedure of checking the individual's identification against the registration list, the voter is given a separate ballot and envelope corresponding to each vacancy for which the voting is being held. The instructions to the voter indicate that he should vote for only one candidate and that he should cross out the names of candidates whom he does not want, leaving only the name of the one for whom he is voting. In practice there is always only one name on the ballot. Although the voter may indicate by crossing out the name that he does not wish to vote for the candidate, he does not have the right to vote for an alternative candidate. The meaning of a vote is clear. An affirmative vote is an indication of approval of the regime and the officially sponsored candidate. A scratched ballot can be interpreted as disapproval of the regime, or, at the very least, as disapproval of the candidate who has been approved by representatives of the regime. Available evidence indicates that the secret polling booths required by law are always available, but seldom used. In answer to a question about why people are not required to use a closed polling booth, a Soviet spokesman replied rather vaguely that:

> "In many cases candidates are personally known to voters. Therefore, when the voters come to the polling place, they already know for whom they are going to vote and consequently have no intention of striking a nominee's name off or writing in some other name on the ballot. That is why they do not step into the booth but merely drop the ballot in the box. However, many voters do go with their ballots into the closed booths before voting. This is entirely up to the voter."[32]

Since an affirmative vote can be cast without marking the ballot, some Soviet citizens may refrain from using the polling booths to make it clear their vote is affirmative. By using the polling booth, a citizen may run the danger of being considered one of those few who cast a dissenting ballot if any dissenting votes are registered in that precinct.

Few dissenting ballots are cast; usually approximately 98 percent of the voters indicate their approval of the selected candidates. However, the electorate could prevent the election of a candidate if at least one-half of the voting citizens crossed out the name of the candidate, or if a majority of the registered voters in the district failed to cast ballots. Thus the absence of alternative candidates does not absolutely limit the outcome of the election. On occasion the Soviet press has reported the electoral defeat of certain candidates. In this event the Electoral Commission is required to proceed within two weeks with a new election. The degree of popular support gives the party some indication as to whether the electorate is pleased or dissatisfied with the locally selected candidates. The information, however, is not necessarily highly valid, since many voters feel obliged to vote affirmatively.

Verification of all voting tabulations are made by the district Electoral Commission and again by the higher Electoral Commission. The results are officially proclaimed by the district Electoral Commission. Interference with the right of Soviet citizens to cast their ballots freely is punishable by as much as two years of imprisonment, and election frauds by officials are punishable by as much as three years of imprisonment.

Although great care is taken by the party organizations and the Electoral Commissions to ensure that only politically reliable and competent candidates are nominated and that no nominee is allowed to be registered who might cast discredit upon the party or the Soviet, Soviet election norms provide for popular recall of elected representatives for reasons of incompetence, violations of socialist morality or legal offenses. Recall procedures may be initiated on notification by the Procuracy or at the request of any organization which has the right to nominate. The organization sponsoring the recall motion must inform the deputy of its complaints and the deputy has the right to justify his actions. The Soviet of which the deputy is a member examines the relevant information, and if it determines that the proposal for recall is justified, the appropriate Electoral Commission is empowered to conduct a recall election. A deputy is considered recalled if a majority of the electorate in the district support the recall motion. Further control is exercised by all Soviets over newly-elected representatives through a Credentials Commission which may recommend that the Soviet refuse to seat the deputy; refusal to seat or recall requires that a new election be held within two months to fill the vacancy.

Impact on the Individual and Society

Soviet elections serve a multitude of purposes. However, unlike the elections in most countries, they are not intended to determine which political party shall govern the country. The role of the Communist Party and its program are not issues in Soviet elections in a direct sense, but rather the election serves as an instrument by which the masses are permitted to corroborate and assist the party in its responsible task of selecting competent and honest representatives who will be able to collaborate effectively with the party in materializing the party program with maximum speed and in furthering the ideals of the Marxist-Leninist ideology. Communists would never admit that there is any conflict between the party and the masses in the Soviet Union. If there are faults with the Soviet administration, these are blamed on individual failures within the bureaucracies of the party and the state. The party is as interested as the people in eliminating these incompetents from their responsible positions and replacing them with more capable officials. Soviet elections are a technique through which the party is helped by the electorate to improve the efficiency of the operation of the entire society by staffing the Soviets with the most competent citizens. The advantages of selecting competent, responsible citizens for public positions accrue to the entire society.

To the non-Soviet world the Soviet system seems to lack some of the most essential ingredients of democracy: the right to organize political parties which oppose certain of the policies of the political party which currently controls the governmental apparatus; the right to choose from among independently nominated candidates the officials who will be responsible for a certain period of time, for enacting and executing the laws of the state; and the right to criticize the policies and practices of the government. Soviet elections, likewise, appear to be rigged and fraudulent because of the controlled manner of nominating candidates and the plebiscitory form of the electoral consultation. Communists, on the other hand, though they recognize that it does not always function perfectly, consider the system as a whole to be eminently equitable and democratic. Communists do not question the vanguard conception of their party; they accept as a basic value the legitimacy of the communist hegemony over the state; they believe that the party reflects the interests of all the people in the state and, therefore, there is no need for a diversity of political parties. Soviet spokesmen argue that their method of selecting candidates for election embodies democratic practices, since the masses of people are permitted to participate actively in this most crucial phase of the election, rather than being allowed to choose on election day between two perhaps equally unacceptable candidates who have been chosen by others, as they say happens in capitalist states.

Although the party's hegemony over Soviet society is something over which the Soviet people have no control whatsoever, its status as the real sovereign becomes legitimate only through the expression of the consensus of the people in its leadership.[33] The elections provide the people with the opportunity to express consensus, but the opportunity to express lack of consensus is almost non-existent. The only way in which mass discontent against the regime can be manifested in the U.S.S.R. is by mass absenteeism from the polls or rejection of the candidates. Such a form of civil boycott has never occurred, and since many inherent hazards would be associated with it, it is most unlikely in the future. On the other hand, the active interest which Soviet citizens take in elections would seem to indicate that the majority of them interpret their role in the same manner as the party does. It is reasonable that they should concur with the interpretation of the party in view of their lack of experience with electoral systems in which a choice is permitted, the effective indoctrination to which they are subjected, and the fact that it is to their advantage, as well as the party's, to select competent candidates.

Soviet elections are intended to develop civic consciousness and political consensus among the people toward the Communist Party and the Soviet state. The pre-election campaigns provide the party with an excellent opportunity to conduct active and meaningful political indoctrination of the masses. As a participant in the mass nominations of candidates, albeit mainly in an advisory capacity, the Soviet voter is allowed to feel that he shares responsibility with the elite groups in the selection of candidates. As a member of the electorate which ratifies the party's choice of candidates for representative public offices, he is given a voice in the election of the formal governing organs of the state. The Soviet electorate is permitted in this way to feel that it really selects and elects its own public representatives and that through these it participates in the exercise of public power. Identification of the masses with the party and the Soviet state is thus fostered by the appearance of democracy, while the substance of the leadership remains elitist.

Almost every adult citizen participates in the Soviet elections in one or more ways. Millions of people participate in the nomination of candidates; the number of agitators involved in the pre-election campaign has been estimated at over fifteen million; approximately ten million people are required to staff the election boards. About one hundred and forty million electors cast votes, over 98 percent of the registered voters, and all but an infinitesimal proportion of these formally endorse the regime by voting in favor of the official candidate. The very act of endorsement, even though a free choice is not involved, may instill in some citizens a sense of responsibility for and identification with the regime. Although the millions of people who participate in Soviet elections do not exert effective control over the governmental machinery, many of them may feel that they are being given an opportunity to participate actively in the affairs of state. Some Soviet citizens, of course, may consider the entire election procedure to be nothing more than an empty farce, or may resent deeply the fact that the highly lauded electoral policy essentially denies the Soviet voter the right to make a choice when he casts his ballot. However, because of the skillful use of propaganda and indoctrination, it is likely that such people constitute a small minority, and it is certain that they, regardless of their number, do not constitute effective opposition to the regime.

Currently over 1,800,000 persons serve as deputies to Soviets at the various levels.[34] A large and required turnover allows for the election of approximately one million new deputies every few years. It is customary in the Soviet Union to reward civic-minded citizens and Heroes of Socialist Labor by nominating and electing them to one of the Soviets. The manipulation of elections makes it possible to provide a highly cherished reward system for the masses. The incentive to become a member of a Soviet has probably encouraged many citizens to improve their labor performance records, and to raise the level of their social and moral conduct to attract favorable attention to themselves. Participation of thousands of deputies in the affairs of the Soviets has fostered among the masses the illusion that they are self-governing, and it is probable that their respect and liking for the party which has granted such political privileges has been consequently strengthened.

An officially endorsed defense of mass elections in the U.S.S.R. is the view that they serve to educate and train the people in tasks of democratic self-government. According to party propagandists, the present transition phase of democratization of power is to form a bridge between the earlier regime of party dictatorship and the eventual workers' democracy. During the transition phase the party considers it necessary to train millions of persons to assume administrative responsibilities as members of the Soviets and their committees, whose tasks are to supervise and control the acts of the bureaucratic functionaries; eventually, these people's committees, operating under the supervision of the party, are expected to assume active administration from the professional bureaucracy. By allowing limited popular participation in a controlled electoral process, the Soviet leadership satisfies an ideological demand of communist dogma. It also strengthens the moral status of the Soviet Union among foreign communists and their sympathizers, and facilitates the tasks of the communist parties in Western democratic countries. Finally, the apparent enthusiasm and active voters' response to communist leadership provides some tangible evidence, regardless of the validity, that the Soviet regime enjoys considerable, if not overwhelming, consensus from its population, which may build up the legitimacy of the Soviet Union among non-communists in the Western world.

The Soviet electoral system is formally far more democratic than it was during the Tsarist era and during the early years of the Soviet regime. Many Soviet citizens may perceive the right to direct, equal and universal suffrage as a meaningful improvement. But just as the Tsarist regime manipulated elections to support the hegemony of the ruling minority, so the Soviet regime manipulates elections by different techniques to support the hegemony of the Communist Party. Soviet elections are lacking in that freedom of choice of both candidates and alternative policies which, to Western traditions and values, underlie a political democracy. But it is not justifiable to judge the meaning of Soviet elections to citizens of the

U.S.S.R. in terms of the Western set of values. Both the traditions and the political goals of citizens of Western societies are vastly different from those of Soviet citizens. Soviet elections may be regarded by the people of the U.S.S.R. as involving significant democratic concessions. Nevertheless, the essence of democracy is lacking because the Soviet people have been denied a choice of goals.

REFERENCES

1 Urie Bronfenbrenner, "The Mirror Image in Soviet-American Relations: A Social Psychologist's Report," *The Journal of Social Issues,* Vol. 17, No. 3, 1961.

2 Arthur E. Adams, "Democratic Ferment Behind the Curtain," in Harry G. Shaffer (ed.), *The Soviet System in Theory and Practice,* (New York: Appleton-Century-Crofts, 1965), pp. 330-33.

3 V. I. Lenin, *The State and Revolution,* quoted in Emile Burns (ed.), *A Handbook of Marxism,* (New York: International Publishers, 1935), p. 744.

4 N. S. Khrushchev, *Pravda,* March 17, 1962, p. 1. (C.D.S.P., Vol. XIV, No. 12, p. 4)

5 Lenin, quoted in Burns, *A Handbook of Marxism, op. cit.,* p. 731.

6 *Ibid.*

7 *Fundamentals of Marxism-Leninism, op. cit.,* p. 549.

8 V. Denisov, *Communism Stands for Freedom.* Reprinted in Shaffer, *The Soviet System in Theory and Practice, op. cit.,* pp. 356-70.

9 Lenin, *Works, op. cit.,* Vol. 28, p. 442.

10 *Fundamentals of Marxism-Leninism, op. cit.,* p. 728.

11 *Ibid.,* pp. 733-4.

12 *Ibid.,* p. 739.

13 *Ibid.,* p. 729.

14 Denisov, *Communism Stands for Freedom, op. cit.,* pp. 366-7.

15 *Ibid.,* p. 367.

16 "The Program of the Communist Party of the Soviet Union," *op. cit.,* p. 92.

17 *Fundamentals of Marxism-Leninism, op. cit.,* p. 838.

18 Lenin, *Works, op. cit.,* Vol. 25, p. 434.

19 *Fundamentals of Marxism-Leninism, op. cit.,* p. 840.

20 zemstvo (singular), zemstva (plural)

21 Samuel N. Harper and Ronald Thompson, *The Government of the Soviet Union,* (New York: D. Van Nostrand Co., Inc., 1949), p. 8.

22 Cf. George Barr Carson, *Electoral Practices in the U.S.S.R.,* (New York: Frederick A. Praeger, Inc., 1955), p. 29.

23 *Ibid.,* pp. 33-4.

24 J. Stalin, *Leninism: Selected Writings,* (New York: International Publishers, Co., Inc., 1942), p. 379.

25 From *Izvestia,* March 5, 1936, as reproduced in James Meisel and Edward Kozera, *Materials for Study of the Soviet System, op. cit.,* p. 223.

26 The time for the establishment of the Electoral Commission varies with its level. Higher level Commissions must be established earlier than the subordinate Commissions.

27 Articles 84 and 87, Statute on Local Elections, Adopted by the Presidium of the Supreme Soviet of the R.S.F.S.R., Oct. 8, 1947.

28 Article 85, R.S.F.S.R. Statute on Local Elections.

29 A. Denisov and M. Kirichenko, *Soviet State Law,* (Moscow: Foreign Languages Publishing House, 1960), p. 362.

30 Mikhail Strepukhov, "How Is the U.S.S.R. Supreme Soviet Elected?" *U.S.S.R., Soviet Life Today,* March, 1962, p. 10.

31 Theodore Bayer, "Your questions answered," *Soviet Russia Today*, April, 1950, p. 24, as reproduced in Carson, *Electoral Practices in the U.S.S.R.*, *op. cit.*, pp. 62-3.

32 Queries from Readers, *U.S.S.R.*, *Soviet Life Today*, Feb., 1963, p. 49.

33 Cf. Howard R. Swearer, "Popular Participation," in Howard R. Swearer and Richard P. Longaker (editors), *Contemporary Communism*, (Belmont, Cal.: Wadsworth, 1963), pp. 82-6.

34 Denisov, *Communism Stands for Freedom*, *op. cit.*, p. 363.

CHAPTER VI

THE LEGISLATIVE, EXECUTIVE AND ADMINISTRATIVE
ORGANS OF THE U.S.S.R.

Real Power and Formal Authority

The Constitution of the U.S.S.R. provides for legislative, executive and administrative state organs which are formed either on the basis of direct elections by the people or appointment by the elected representatives of the people. However, under the monolithic power structure of Soviet society, all significant decision-making powers are monopolized by the Communist Party, which is the source of all authority for the exercise by the formal organs of the government of their legally delegated functions.[1] The leading role of the Communist Party in the activity of Soviet state organs is justified by Soviet theorists on the grounds that the party is dedicated to the struggle for the interests, welfare and happiness of the people; the party applies the "scientifically founded" tenets of Marxism-Leninism for the betterment of the people; the party enjoys the undivided support of the Soviet people who regard it as their fighting vanguard. The claim that the party enjoys the undivided support of the Soviet people is, of course, an unsubstantiated hypothesis which the party leaders have been unwilling to test by legitimate methods.

Soviet authorities claim that without the guiding and organizing force of the Communist Party and its Central Committee, efficient and well-coordinated work by the state organs would be impossible. They stress consistently that the leading role of the C.P.S.U. does not mean that the party supplants the state organs. At the Eighth Party Congress it was resolved that: "The functions of the Party collectives should in no way be confused with the functions of state organs as represented by the Soviets. . . . The Party must put its decisions into practice through the Soviet organs, *within the bounds of the Soviet Constitution*. The Party seeks to direct the activity of the Soviets, but not supplant them."[2]

On the other hand, since the party assumes full responsibility for all the affairs of the U.S.S.R., Soviet authors make straightforward statements about the dominant role played by the party in the operation of the organs of the state. A text on *Soviet State Law* indicates:

210

"The Communist Party forms the leading core of all state organs. . . . The congresses and conferences of the Communist Party and the plenary sessions of the Central Committee of the Communist Party regularly discuss questions relating to the organization and activity of the Soviet state organs. . . . The Communist Party not only plays a decisive role in the preparation and adoption of decisions by the Soviet state organs, but systematically controls the fulfillment of these decisions. . . . Its guidance of the state organs is expressed first of all in the fact that it promotes the best Party members to key positions and through them carries out its political line in all state organs. It keeps check on the work of the state organs, lays bare the mistakes and shortcomings in their activity and thus strengthens and improves the state apparatus. Finally, every state organ is guided by the directives of the Party when planning its work."[3]

The leading role of the party in the activity of the organs of the Soviet state is guaranteed by the fact that every important decision of a state organ is based on the directives of the party and party organs. Lenin considered the flexible unification of party institutions with state institutions to be a source of unusual strength in the politics of the Soviet government and the only guarantee of successful work by state organs.

According to contemporary communist sources, the leading task of the party in the work of the organs of state is based on democratic principles and is an absolute condition for success in their work.[4] The reality of these "democratic principles" is highly questionable. The C.P.S.U. does not consist of elected representatives of the Soviet people, nor have the Soviet people ever been given the opportunity to give it the mandate to lead, guide, or supervise them or their governing organs. They have no right to transfer political power from the C.P.S.U. to an alternative political party. The Constitution of the U.S.S.R., which is considered to be the fundamental law of the Soviet Union, mentions the Communist Party only in the Chapter which deals with the fundamental rights and duties of citizens, and then, as it were, almost tangentially: Article 141 indicates that along with other organizations the Communist Party has the right to nominate candidates for public elections; Article 126 guarantees citizens the right to unite in public organizations, and after listing several organizations, indicates that "the most active and politically-conscious citizens in the ranks of the working class, working peasants and working intelligentsia voluntarily unite in the Communist Party of the Soviet Union, which is the vanguard of the working people in their struggle to build communist society and is the leading core of all organizations, both state and public." The right of the C.P.S.U. to direct, guide and supervise the work of state organs was preempted by the party; its dominant position was acquired by force, rather than by a mandate from the people.

In reality, the people of the U.S.S.R. are governed by the party leaders, rather than by the organs of state power, in spite of the constitutional provisions and the Soviet theory of democracy, described in the preceding chapter. A primary purpose of the state organs is to provide the

Party Organs   State Organs

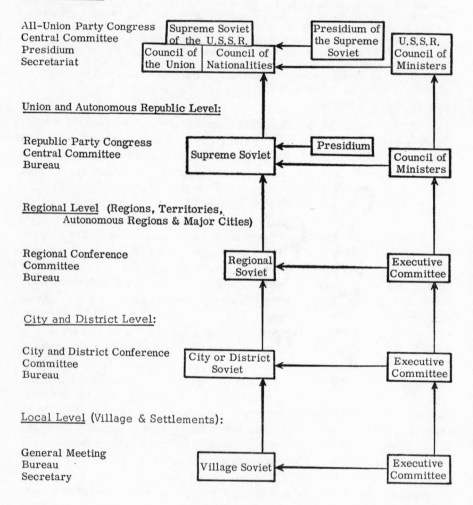

All Union Level:

All-Union Party Congress
Central Committee
Presidium
Secretariat

Union and Autonomous Republic Level:

Republic Party Congress
Central Committee
Bureau

Regional Level (Regions, Territories, Autonomous Regions & Major Cities)

Regional Conference
Committee
Bureau

City and District Level:

City and District Conference
Committee
Bureau

Local Level (Village & Settlements):

General Meeting
Bureau
Secretary

Figure 1. Outline of the governmental structure of the U.S.S.R. with corresponding party organs at each level.

Arrows denote direction of formal responsibility from subordinate to superior organs. Each Presidium, Council of Ministers and Executive Committee is theoretically responsible to the Soviet which created it and to the corresponding organ at the next level in the hierarchy. All elected organs are responsible, in theory, to the electorate. State organs at each level are supervised by the corresponding party organs.

legal instruments through which the party legitimates its power. The state organs constitute the formal structure of institutionalized power through which the party exercises real power over Soviet society. Through the representative Soviets the party enlists popular participation among a wider stratum than the party membership in the vital task of materializing the directives of the party and eliciting public approval and consensus for party-conceived policies and programs. Since the party assumes the role of mere guide to the state, the onus of public resentment can always be deflected onto the bureaucratic mignons of the state administration.

The state organs also assist the party in developing a system of controls over the administrative bureaucracy which is responsible for implementation of party decisions. The state organs thus form a juncture between real power, which proceeds from the top echelon of the party in a downward direction, and the nominal authority, which theoretically proceeds upwards from the people through their elected representatives.

Party control over state organs is facilitated by the fact that the hierarchy of state organs parallels the organization of the Communist Party. Figure 1 outlines the structure of Soviet governmental organs, and indicates the corresponding party organization. The top party leaders control all subordinate party organizations and the central government of the U.S.S.R. Intermediate and local units of the governmental structure are supervised by the superior organs of the government and by the party unit at the corresponding level. Thus, at each level the organs of the government are dominated by the party which is, in turn, dominated by the party leaders. Although the Constitution specifies that governing authority is the prerogative of the people, in actuality, governing authority is exercised by the leaders of the C.P.S.U. who are neither elected by, nor responsible to, the people.

Central Government Organs

THE SUPREME SOVIET OF THE U.S.S.R.

The three major organs of the central government are the Supreme Soviet of the U.S.S.R., the Presidium of the Supreme Soviet of the U.S.S.R., and the Council of Ministers of the U.S.S.R. The Supreme Soviet is described as the "highest organ of state power," and according to constitutional law, it is assigned exclusive exercise of the legislative power of the U.S.S.R. (Articles 30 and 32). The Supreme Soviet consists of two chambers, the Soviet (Council) of the Union and the Soviet (Council) of Nationalities, each of which is elected normally for a term of four years. The Soviet of the Union, which is elected on the basis of one deputy for every 300,000 of the population (Article 34), is purported to represent the "common interests of all the working people" in the Soviet Union.[5] The Soviet of Nationalities, which is elected on the basis of thirty-two deputies from each Union Republic, eleven from each Autonomous Republic, five from each Autonomous Area, and one from each National Area,* reflects the federative principle, and is alleged to represent the "particular, specific interests" of the numerous nationalities of the U.S.S.R.[6] Until 1966 each Union Republic elected only twenty-five deputies to the Soviet of Nationalities. Since the number of deputies to the Soviet of the Union increased as a function of population growth while representation in the Soviet of Nationalities remained constant, a marked discrepancy developed in the number of deputies elected to the two chambers. In 1962 the Soviet of Nationalities had 652 deputies while the Soviet of the Union had 791. Of these, seven deputies in each chamber were elected by the armed forces. With the change in the norms of representation, an approximately equal number of deputies will be elected to each chamber in the forthcoming elections, 767 to the Soviet of the Union and 750 to the Soviet of Nationalities.[7]

Soviet authorities stress that the two chambers are equal in rights and functions and that the deputies to both are representatives of workers, peasants and intellectuals. One chamber is not considered to be higher than the other, nor is one chamber intended to serve as a check on the other. The deputies of neither chamber have special privileges or restrictions. The two chambers are elected simultaneously, under the same suffrage qualifications, convene simultaneously, serve for the same period, and have equal rights and powers to initiate legislation (Articles 37 and 38). A law is adopted if passed by both chambers by a simple majority vote in each (Article 39). Such legislation is published, following certification by the Chairman and Secretary of the Presidium of the Supreme Soviet in the language of each Union Republic (Article 40). Elaborate, but unnecessary, provisions for the reconciliation of differences between the two chambers are outlined in the Constitution. Initially, a conciliation commission formed by the chambers on a parity basis is to attempt to resolve the differences. If it fails, the question is to be reconsidered by the chambers. Finally, if no compromise or agreement is reached, the Presidium of the Supreme Soviet can dissolve the Supreme Soviet and order new elections. However, since both chambers have always unanimously approved party-sponsored policies and legislation, there has never been a need for conciliation, nor is it likely that the need will arise.

COMPOSITION

Soviet authorities devote considerable effort to demonstrate that all strata of Soviet society are represented in the Supreme Soviet. The class

---

*"Decree of the Presidium of the U.S.S.R. Supreme Soviet, On Change of Norm for Representation from Union Republics in the Soviet of Nationalities," *Pravda,* March 20, 1966, p. 1.

composition of the highest popular assembly is presented as evidence of its truly representative character. Table 1 describes the class, occupation, education, age, party and nationality attributes of deputies elected to the Supreme Soviet in 1962. Since Soviet classification, in terms of class composition, is based predominantly on social origin rather than current occupational status, many of the deputies who are categorized as workers or peasants might more appropriately be considered as members of the intelligentsia. The percentage of deputies who are actually employed currently as workers and peasants is probably much smaller than Soviet figures indicate, as many of them are engaged in administrative, executive or high-level technical work as farm or factory managers, engineers, economic supervisors, technical specialists or scientists. Despite Soviet emphasis on the preponderance of worker and peasant deputies, membership seems to be highly biased in favor of the political, economic and educated elite. Over three quarters of the deputies are members or candidate members of the party, although less than 5 percent of the population of the U.S.S.R. belongs to the party. Almost one fifth of the Supreme Soviet membership goes to full-time governmental officials, including members of the Executive Committees of the intermediate and lower Soviets, employees of the Soviets, and ranking officials of major state economic organizations. Full-time party, Y.C.L. and trade union officials, many of whom carry the rank of First Secretary in one of the intermediate or local party or Y.C.L. organizations, also constitute almost one fifth of the membership. Many of the most prominent party leaders are Supreme Soviet deputies, and in fact, electoral districts compete for the honor of being represented by one of the top party leaders. Of the sixty-three deputies affiliated with military units, the only two with ranks as low as major were Cosmonauts Titov and Gagarin. Membership to the highest legislative assembly is to a considerable extent reserved as a reward for deserving citizens; more than three-quarters of the deputies are ordinarily Heroes of the Soviet Union, Heroes of Socialist Labor or recipients of other orders and medals. The Party Program stipulates that at least one third of the deputies should be replaced at each election in order to improve the work of the Soviets and to allow new millions of builders of communism to pass through the school of state administration. Accordingly, in 1962 approximately 70 percent of the deputies were newly elected and the reward of Supreme Soviet membership was distributed on a wider basis. Whether the deputies are drawn chiefly from the upper echelons of society, as the facts seem to indicate, or from the workers and peasants, as Soviet sources claim, is of no great importance with reference to the Supreme Soviet's functioning as a legislative assembly. Regardless of the source and composition of its membership, it is the subservient tool of the Communist Party.

Table 1
Composition of the Supreme Soviet (1962)*

| | Percentage of Total | |
Description	Soviet of the Union	Soviet of Nationalities
Newly elected deputies	67.5	72.5
Began adult life as peasant or worker	51.5	52.9
Directly engaged in production	45.4	44.0
Currently workers	25.1	21.5
Currently collective farmers	22.4	22.2
Governmental officials	13.5	24.4
Party, Y.C.L., and trade union officials	21.2	16.7
Educators, artists, scientists, etc.	10.0	11.2
Military officers	4.9	3.8
Party members or candidates	76.4	75.2
Non-party people	23.6	24.8
Women	27.2	26.8
Under 30 years of age	13.7	15.5
Over 50 years of age	28.2	26.1
Higher or incomplete higher education	53.2	52.1
Complete or partial secondary education	37.7	35.6
No secondary education	9.1	12.3
Recipients of orders and medals of the U.S.S.R.	78.8	72.4
Number of Nationalities Represented	37	55

*Source: "Report by Deputy M. S. Sinitsa, Chairman of the Credentials Committee of the Council of Nationalities," *Pravda,* April 25, 1962, p. 3; and "Report by Deputy L. N. Yefremov, Chairman of the Credentials Committee of the Council of the Union," *Pravda,* April 25, 1962, p. 3.

THE STATUS OF DEPUTIES

Since the Supreme Soviet ordinarily meets only briefly twice a year to listen to reports and ratify decisions made by other organs, the deputies are not considered to be parliamentarians or professional lawmakers. Soviet authorities state that deputies who work full time, either directly in industry, agriculture, education or science, or as administrative officials in a governmental organ are in an excellent position to know the wishes, needs and criticisms of the electorate. The deputy is required to participate in the work of the Supreme Soviet and its commissions, to ascertain that the laws which he approves are enforced in his constituency, and to report to the electorate on his work and on the work of the Supreme Soviet. A conscientious deputy tends to be overworked. Between sessions, in spite of his full-time employment, he is expected to visit factories, collective farms and various institutions, to inform the people of the activities of the Supreme Soviet, and to help them with their problems. All questions posed by his electorate must be answered either orally or by mail.

Although the deputy is described by Soviet leaders as the servant of the people whom he represents in the Supreme Soviet, he functions primarily as the servant of the regime. Because of the plebiscitory nature of the uncontested elections, the people do not have an adequate opportunity to give the deputy their mandate. Since he works with or visits the people, he may have a reasonably accurate picture of their desires and grievances. However, unless the deputy is a member of the party leadership, he has little opportunity to make direct use of this knowledge to influence the legislative course of events, since his main participation in the work of the Supreme Soviet is to ratify decisions which have already been made by the party leaders. The decisions of the party leaders are, of course, influenced by the information which they receive from deputies and other sources concerning the views and wishes of the people. On the other hand, the deputy does serve as the emissary of the regime among the electorate. He explains and justifies the resolutions of the party which have been legalized by Supreme Soviet approval. By virtue of his office, he is in an excellent position to build up consensus for the party program and policies and to exhort the people to work diligently for the materialization of party-conceived goals. Moreover, each deputy serves the regime by providing irrevocable evidence to the people that their representatives are permitted to participate in the work of the Supreme Soviet which is, however nominally, responsible for the making of laws, and that the interest of the central government in the people is sufficiently great that the deputy is required to maintain close contact with them.

The deputy enjoys immunity from arrest and prosecution for acts and activities which are connected with the performance of his duties as a deputy, and he cannot be held to legal responsibility without the consent of the Supreme Soviet or its Presidium. Like other rights in the U.S.S.R., the deputies' right to immunity has not always been respected; during the Stalin era, deputies were removed, imprisoned and even executed, without the approval of the Supreme Soviet, and sometimes without trial. As reimbursement for the expense of carrying out his duties, each deputy receives a monthly allowance, plus a daily allowance during the sessions of the Supreme Soviet. He is granted free rail and water transportation within the U.S.S.R. and, since 1958, free air transportation to sessions of the Supreme Soviet and to electoral districts.[8]

SESSIONS

Sessions of the Supreme Soviet of the U.S.S.R. are convened by the Presidium of the Supreme Soviet regularly twice a year, while extraordinary sessions may be convoked by the Presidium on its own initiative or at the request of any Union Republic (Article 46). During World War II the Supreme Soviet met irregularly, and the election scheduled for December, 1941, was postponed until after hostilities ceased. From 1946 until 1953 the Supreme Soviet met annually, and since 1953, it has been convoked regularly twice a year. As a general rule, the Supreme Soviet meets for only four to ten days per session. The two chambers frequently meet jointly to hear reports from the party leaders and leading members of the Council of Ministers. The first business for each chamber of a newly elected Supreme Soviet is to elect a Chairman and four Vice-Chairmen. The initial meetings, which are held separately, are opened by senior deputies. The Chairman and Vice-Chairmen thereafter preside at the meetings of the chambers and have charge of the conduct of business and proceedings. Joint meetings are presided over alternately by the Chairman of the Soviet of the Union and the Chairman of the Soviet of Nationalities.

A considerable amount of preparatory work for Supreme Soviet sessions is performed by a Council of Elders attached to each chamber and composed of deputies who have previously served in the Supreme Soviet. Representatives from all regions, territories and republics are included. Since the Council of Elders is an internal organ of its chamber, rather than an official organ of the state, it is not prescribed by the Constitution. The Council of Elders may propose or review the lists of candidates for the commissions and other organs of the chamber, determine that various republics, territories and regions are justly represented, suggest procedural rules and recommend items to be included on the agenda and their order of presentation.

The activities of the newly elected Supreme Soviet which met in April, 1962, are typical for Supreme Soviet sessions, and indicate that the highest popular assembly in the U.S.S.R. is not a deliberative body.[9] The Soviet of the Union elected unanimously and without discussion the Chairman and the four Vice-Chairmen who were nominated by a representative of the Council of Elders. A deputy speaking for the Council of Elders recommended the following agenda: election of standing commissions; ratification of the decrees of the Presidium; selection of a new Presidium; report on negotiations in Geneva; formation of the U.S.S.R. Council of Ministers; selection of the U.S.S.R. Supreme Court; working on the draft of the new U.S.S.R. Constitution. After the agenda was approved unanimously with no discussion, deputies speaking on behalf of the Council of Elders or for groups of deputies from designated regions nominated slates of candidates to serve on Credentials, Legislative, Budget and Foreign Affairs Commissions. All candidates were approved without discussion. Thus, in one short meeting, the Soviet of the Union approved its agenda and selected 119 officials. In a separate meeting of the same duration, the Soviet of Nationalities approved an identical agenda, and elected an Economic Commission, in addition to standing commissions corresponding to those elected by the Soviet of the Union. Obviously, the agenda and the lists of candidates are prepared carefully in advance; deputies are selected for the honor of making the formal proposals; and automatic ratification is a foregone conclusion.

Procedural rules remain fairly constant from session to session. Typically, meetings are held from 10 a.m. until 2 p.m. or from 4 p.m. until 8 p.m. The order of reports to be included on the agenda is approved by the Chairman. Any group of fifty or more deputies has the right to nominate its own co-reporter. Reporters are allowed one hour for a report and thirty minutes for conclusions. Co-reporters are allowed a total of forty-five minutes. Deputies are allowed twenty minutes for the first speech and five minutes for the second speech.[10] Schedules for separate and joint meetings of the two chambers are established by mutual agreement.

Detailed examination of the activities of a Supreme Soviet session indicates clearly that it serves more effectively as an institution in which party policy is announced and ratified than as an independent legislative organ. The activities of the December, 1964 session may be taken as typical. At 10 a.m. on December 9, separate sessions of the Council of the Union and the Council of Nationalities opened in the Kremlin Theater and the Great Kremlin Palace, respectively. Since this was not the initial meeting of a newly elected Supreme Soviet, it was not necessary to establish standing commissions which are elected for the entire term of the Supreme Soviet. Each chamber heard a brief report from its Credential Commission, recommending recognition of the credentials of the few deputies who had been elected since the previous session. The agenda, unanimously approved by both chambers, included: ratification of the October 15, 1964 decrees of the Presidium of the Supreme Soviet of the U.S.S.R., which relieved Khrushchev of his duties as Chairman of the Council of Ministers and gave the position to Kosygin; the state economic plan for 1965; the state budget for 1965; the chairman of the Constitutional Commission; the vice-chairman of the Constitutional Commission; the vice-chairman of the Presidium of the U.S.S.R. Supreme Soviet from the Tadzhik Republic; and confirmation of decrees of the Presidium.[11] A joint meeting of the two chambers opened at 11 a.m. in the Great Kremlin Palace. Since the separate meetings lasted less than one hour, the deputies obviously had no time to debate the proposed agenda or to suggest modifications. However, the agenda had been, no doubt, debated previously in the commissions. The deputies, like members of a theatre audience, sat in block formation facing the stage, or presidium, where the chairmen and vice-chairmen of the two houses were seated. Members of the Central Committee of the Communist Party were treated to "stormy, prolonged applause" as they proceeded to seat themselves at the presidium. Deputy A. N. Kosygin, Chairman of the U.S.S.R. Council of Ministers, and Deputy V. F. Garbuzov, U.S.S.R. Minister of Finance, delivered lengthy reports on the state plan for the development of the national economy[12] and on the state budget,[13] respectively. Both of these deputies indicated that they were speaking for the U.S.S.R. Council of Ministers in presenting detailed plans for "consideration" or "consideration and approval" by the Supreme Soviet. Discussion of the reports began in separate meetings of the two chambers at 4 p.m. Each chamber heard a report from the chairman of its Budget Commission, and the Council of Nationalities heard an additional report from its Economic Commission.[14] The reports were devoted chiefly to an elaboration, expansion or confirmation of the report initiated by the U.S.S.R. Council of Ministers. Some of the reasons for failure of plan fulfillment and certain recommendations for improvement were also discussed. The commissions in both chambers moved that the state budget prepared by the Council of Ministers be approved, subject to minor changes. The discussion of the plan and the budget, conducted separately by the two chambers, extended over three days—an evening session of each chamber on December 9, morning and evening sessions on December 10, and a morning session on December 11. The discussion consisted entirely of formal reports from deputies, who were, in the main, high-ranking officials such as the Russian Republic Minister of Construction and the Vice-Chairman for the U.S.S.R. State Committee for Construction Affairs. The probability of being selected to make a speech apparently increases with the importance of the political and governmental status of the deputy. Speeches by deputies centered around a few fixed themes: the need to introduce measures to ensure the fulfillment of the directives of the C.P.S.U.; the accomplishments or needs of the particular economic unit or territorial region with which the deputy is affiliated; shortcomings caused by certain state agencies; problems arising from the excessive centralization of guidance, the multiplicity of agencies, and parallelism in the activities of state organs; recommendations to eradicate shortcomings and to enhance progress toward communist construction; the need for more houses, hospitals, schools, etc. There was no place on the agenda for the free exchange of opinion, or for spontaneous discussion. Representatives of the Council of Ministers, the Chairmen of Commissions of Supreme Soviet chambers, and a few pre-selected deputies reported to and informed the rank and file deputies whose chief function it was to listen and to learn, rather than to deliberate and affect policy.

The entire session of the Supreme Soviet followed a similar pattern. The Secretary of the Presidium of the Supreme Soviet informed the deputies of the decrees which had been issued by the Presidium during the interval since the last session of the Supreme Soviet.[15] The deputies were asked by the Presidium to "adopt the laws and resolutions, the drafts of which have been submitted for your consideration." Although the decisions of the Presidium involved the removal of Khrushchev and the appointment of Kosygin, major revisions in the organization and personnel of the U.S.S.R. Council of Ministers, minor constitutional amendments, a one-year reduction in the required period of training in certain schools, and changes in the border between two Union Republics, the motion for ratification was voted on without detailed consideration by the elected representatives of the Soviet people. Khrushchev was removed as Chairman of the Constitutional Commission, and on instructions from the Central Committee of the party, Brezhnev was elected to this position.[16] In their concluding remarks, Kosygin and Garbuzov indicated that the national economic plan and the budget for 1965 had received unanimous approval and that the constructive recommendations made by deputies in their reports would be considered carefully by the Council of Ministers.

Reports published in the Soviet press suggest that during the entire proceedings of the Supreme Soviet, no deputy raised a dissenting voice about any aspect of Soviet internal or foreign policy. Certain administrators, Economic Councils and by implication, Khrushchev, were criticized, but the criticism was for inefficiency in implementing the decisions of the party. Deputies may question the adequacy of certain techniques or administrative organs for the achievement of certain goals, but they are neither expected nor permitted to question the correctness of the policy outlined by the party. They are given ample opportunity to approve, but have neither the opportunity nor the right to disapprove the decisions of the party leadership. They may, however, bring matters to the attention of the party leadership who, in turn, make use of the information provided by the deputies in establishing policy.

SUPREME SOVIET COMMISSIONS

To expedite work, each chamber of the Supreme Soviet elects four standing commissions: a Credentials Commission with twenty-one members; a Commission on Legislation with thirty-one members; a Budgetary Commission with thirty-nine members; and a Commission on Foreign Affairs with twenty-three members. In addition, the Soviet of Nationalities has had since 1957 an Economic Commission composed of a chairman and thirty members, two from each republic. These commissions are elected from among the deputies at the first session of a newly elected Supreme Soviet for the whole term of its office. Provisional or temporary commissions may be established to deal with specific problems, such as health, education, investigation and audit. As a rule, the temporary commissions are established by the Supreme Soviet as a whole, rather than by the individual chambers. Because of the short duration of the Supreme Soviet meetings, it is deemed necessary that all questions and problems which will be dealt with during the Supreme Soviet session should be studied, prepared and evaluated in advance by the commissions. Commissions meet at least once every three months, or more often if necessary, to hear and to evaluate reports and proposals from various agencies and particularly from branches of the U.S.S.R. Council of Ministers, such as the U.S.S.R. Council of the National Economy, and the U.S.S.R. Ministry of Finance. Members of the commissions are freed from their basic employment for the duration of the meeting of the commission. Each commission is responsible to the Soviet which established it and, between sessions of the Supreme Soviet, to the chairman of the establishing Soviet. Within a commission, all questions are decided by a simple majority vote if two thirds of the members are present to constitute a quorum. A member who does not condone the majority decision may present a minority report during the Supreme Soviet session.

Commissions are entitled to introduce legislative proposals as well as to consider and evaluate the legislative proposals of the Presidium of the Supreme Soviet, the Council of Ministers of the U.S.S.R., and of other organs which have legislative initiative. Commissions do not, however, have administrative prerogatives. They have the right to demand relevant materials from ministries, institutions and officials, but are not empowered to issue acts containing compulsory regulations. Recently the party authorized an expansion of the functions of the commissions to include systematic control over the activities of ministries and other administrative units and promotion of execution of decisions adopted by the Supreme Soviet. Apparently, the party wants the commissions, as organs of a popularly elected assembly, to play a critical watch-dog role and thereby to foster implementation of party programs, and at the same time, to enhance the impression of government and control by the people.

The Legislative Commissions are charged with preparing and considering draft laws to be introduced for the approval of the Supreme Soviet, except for those draft laws which come under the jurisdiction of another standing commission. The commissions may prepare proposals for laws either on their own initiative or at the request of the chambers. Examples of draft laws which have been prepared and submitted to the Supreme Soviet by the Legislative Commissions are a law on the extension of the legislative rights of the Union Republics and a Statute of the Supreme Court of the U.S.S.R. With the consent of the chairman of the respective chamber, the commissions may make proposals to the Council of Ministers concerning the necessity of elaborating certain draft laws. Proposals for legislative measures such as the reorganization of education, the pension plan, and the basic principles of criminal laws may be published in newspapers in order to invite comments and suggestions from rank-and-file Soviet citizens. The participation of the broad masses in the preparation of legislative proposals in this manner is described by Soviet authors as an example of the broad democratic basis of the Soviet system.

The Budget Commissions and the Economic Commission of the Soviet of Nationalities submit conclusions on draft laws relating to the state budget and report their findings concerning the execution of the budget and on the work of executive agencies concerned with budgetary affairs. They have the right to initiate draft laws on financial and budgetary questions for consideration by the Supreme Soviet. Typically, the report of a Budget Commission to its respective chamber incorporates a recommendation that the state budget as presented by the Council of Ministers be modified in certain definite and relatively minor respects, a considerable amount of statistical information about the growth of certain branches of the economy, of labor productivity, state expenditures on housing or education, etc., and some very sharp criticism about the work of specified state organs, along with concrete suggestions for improvement. The Budgetary Commissions, like the other standing commissions, perform a valuable service to the regime in that they, as organs established by the elected representatives of the people, launch criticisms against bureaucracy and administrative inefficiency. For example, the Chairman of the Budget Commission of the Soviet of the Union reported:

> "Examination of the report materials shows that a number of Union Republics have difficulty implementing their budgets during the course of the year. This stems from the fact that the U.S.S.R. Ministry of Finance pays insufficient attention to questions of further improving the forms and methods of the interrelation between Union-republic and Union budgets . . . nor can we consider expedient the existing practice whereby, when republics turn out additional consumer goods, all the revenue from the turnover tax accrues to the Union budget. The Budget Committee proposes . . . channeling up to 50% of the turnover tax received from above-plan output . . . into the budget of the Union Republic concerned . . . . It is impossible to tolerate the fact that in many cases the heads of chemical plants and combines do not take the needs of trade organizations and light-industry enterprises into account but continue to produce . . . products in obsolete assortments that do not meet the consumers' requirements . . . . Unfortunately . . . the U.S.S.R. State Planning Committee, the U.S.S.R. Council of the National Economy [and other government agencies], are paying considerably less attention to the matter of reconstruction than to new construction."[17]

The Economic Commission was established in the Council of Nationalities to have among the highest organs of the U.S.S.R. a commission designed to take into account the specific requirements of the various nationality groups, to assist in the economic and social-cultural development of the republics in harmony with their economic, national and other peculiarities, and at the same time, to provide additional tangible evidence that the Communist Party and the Union government are interested in the needs of the individual nations of the Soviet Union. The commission is required to evaluate national economic plans for the Soviet of Nationalities and the Supreme Soviet as a whole, and to make recommendations concerning appropriate measures with reference to economic development, health, culture and housing in the Union Republics and their cities and villages. A report on one aspect of the work of this commission illustrates the activities of Supreme Soviet commissions:

"In 1960-1961 the Committee of the Economy of the Council of Nationalities made a thorough investigation with the participation of many deputies and volunteers from among scientists and personnel of ministries, planning agencies, and the administrative agencies of the Union Republics, of the degree to which the development of electrification in the Union Republics corresponded to the undertakings of the Seven-Year Plan. Serious shortcomings in the planning of electrification and, in particular, a reduction in the generation of electric power in certain republics were discovered. On the recommendation of the Committee of the Economy the higher and central agencies of state administration of the U.S.S.R. and the Union Republics eliminated these shortcomings. Data accumulated by the Committee of the Economy revealed that development of public utilities and other urban services was lagging behind the rates at which housing and cultural and household services were progressing. The standing committees consult with each other and discuss jointly many problems of an economic nature, particularly those related to the budget. Moreover, they involve a large group of active citizens."[18]

The Commissions on Foreign Affairs are authorized to submit to their chambers and to the Presidium of the Supreme Soviet their recommendations and conclusions concerning the conduct of foreign affairs, including questions on the ratification or annulment of international treaties. These commissions may initiate legislation or recommend modification of legislation introduced by other organs on questions of foreign policy.

The commissions provide one of the most effective opportunities for deputies to engage actively in deliberations of state policy, since the major debates over matters which are presented to the Supreme Soviet occur in the commissions. In addition to their regular meetings the commissions usually convene several weeks prior to a session of the Supreme Soviet to prepare their reports and conclusions. Members of the commissions are specialists on matters dealt with by the commission, whereas most of the deputies are not specialists in the given area and are too busy with their other duties to increase substantially their competency in the fields of finance, economics, legislation or foreign affairs. A commission has the right to examine documents, discuss proposals with individual ministers, and to confer with outside specialists in economics, education, industry and other areas. Interested deputies who are not members of a commission may request permission to participate in the work of the commission with a consultative vote.

The commissions do not make substantial use of their prerogative to propose new legislation and to submit counterproposals to legislation introduced by other organs. There is no evidence that a Supreme Soviet commission has ever recommended against or harshly criticized legislation proposed by the Presidium of the Supreme Soviet or the Council of Ministers with the sanction of the Communist Party. Like other tools of the regime, the commissions function primarily to determine techniques for the more efficient implementation of policies formulated by the party leadership and to legitimize the dictatorship of the party through sponsorship of party decisions by an organ of the elected representatives of the people. The fact that the commissions do actually make some recommendations and do criticize certain agencies for inefficiency in implementing directives is interpreted by Soviet writers as a manifestation of democracy in practice. However, since the commissions can exercise the right to criticize neither the basic philosophy of the Soviet approach nor the major policy decisions of the Communist Party, the exercise of democracy through the commissions is distinctly limited.

POWERS OF THE SUPREME SOVIET

The Constitution empowers the Supreme Soviet to exercise all rights vested in the U.S.S.R. insofar as they do not come within the jurisdiction of other organs that are accountable to it, that is, the Presidium of the Supreme Soviet or the Council of Ministers and the Ministries of the U.S.S.R. (Article 31). Soviet theorists point out that legislation is the main, but not the sole function, of the Supreme Soviet. As the highest organ of state power, the Supreme Soviet creates a number of state organs which are nominally responsible to it. During the first session of a newly elected Supreme Soviet, the two chambers in joint sitting elect the Presidium of the Supreme Soviet, appoint the Council of Ministers of the U.S.S.R., and elect the Supreme Court of the U.S.S.R. (Articles 48, 56, and 105). At seven-year intervals the Procurator-General of the U.S.S.R. is appointed (Article 114). According to the Constitution, each of these organs is under the supervision and control of the Supreme Soviet, and is required to report on its activities to the Supreme Soviet or, in the interval between sessions, to the Presidium of the Supreme Soviet. The Supreme Soviet has the constitutional right to recall any or all members of these organs and to change their composition as it deems necessary. In fact, the participation of Supreme Soviet deputies in either the selection or the dismissal of members of these organs is minimal. Obviously, little time can be devoted to deliberations concerning the most highly qualified candidates during the one brief joint meeting of the Supreme Soviet devoted to selection of members of these organs. Moreover, the Constitution limits the Supreme Soviet's choice of candidates for some of these organs; for example, the chairmen of the Presidia of the Supreme Soviets of the Union Republics are made vice-chairmen of the Presidium of the Supreme Soviet, and the chairmen of the Supreme Courts of the Union Republics are members of the U.S.S.R. Supreme Court by virtue of their offices. In these cases, the actions of the Supreme Soviet constitute appointment or ratification rather than election. It is likely that lists containing the exact number of members for each organ are approved in advance by the Presidium of the Central Committee of the Communist Party, and are presented to the Supreme Soviet deputies for automatic approval. After the approval of a report on the activities of the Council of Ministers by its chairman, the chairman of the Presidium of the Supreme Soviet or a pre-selected deputy, on the explicit recommendation of the Central Committee of the Communist Party, moves that the incumbent chairman of the Council of Ministers be reappointed or nominates a new chairman. As always, the motion is approved unanimously. The new chairman is responsible for the formation of a new Council, all members of which must be approved by the Supreme Soviet. In fact, new members of the Council of Ministers are ordinarily appointed and old members are released by decree of the Presidium of the Supreme Soviet on the recommendation of the Chairman of the Council of Ministers. The Supreme Soviet merely adds dignity to the procedure by supplying automatic ratification, sometimes long after the event. In many respects the Supreme Soviet, rather than being the supervisor, is the instrument of its own Presidium and of the Council of Ministers, both of which are tools of the Communist Party.

The leading role of the Supreme Soviet is constitutionally confirmed by the provision that the Constitution of the U.S.S.R. can be amended only by decision of the Supreme Soviet, adopted by a majority of not less than two thirds of the votes in each of its chambers. In spite of this provision, almost all of the constitutional amendments have been made by decree of the Presidium of the Supreme Soviet, and have been presented to the Supreme Soviet for ratification only after the changes have been put into effect. For example, in December, 1962, the Secretary of the Presidium of the Supreme Soviet reported to the Supreme Soviet:

> "In accordance with the resolution adopted on November 23, 1962, by the plenary session of the Party Central Committee, the Presidium of the U.S.S.R. Supreme Soviet on November 24, 1962, issued a number of decrees on the formation and reorganization of the U.S.S.R. agencies of state administration."[19]

Presidium decrees to which he referred included the formation of major new agencies such as the U.S.S.R. Council of the National Economy and the Party-State Control Committee, along with several other agencies of lesser importance, the renaming and reorganization of several agencies, the transformation of several ministries and committees from All-Union organs into Union-Republican organs, and the abolition of several other governmental organs. Since the Constitution lists explicitly the composition of the Council of Ministers and enumerates the All-Union and Union-Republican ministries (Articles 70, 77, and 78), the decrees of the Presidium constituted either a violation or an amendment of the Constitution. To rectify this formal discrepancy, the Presidium presented the Supreme Soviet with a draft law for the amendment of the Constitution at the same time as it announced the decrees which had *de facto* amended it. The Supreme Soviet's role as the "highest organ of state power in the

U.S.S.R." was further degraded by the fact that the organizational changes which necessitated a revision of the Constitution were initiated by the Presidium on the basis of a resolution adopted by the Central Committee of the Communist Party. The party, a non-state organ, also joined with the Presidium and the Council of Ministers to establish a Party-State Control Committee to replace the State Control Commission, a state organ, the abolition of which the party had ordered. These major organizational changes were initiated only two weeks prior to a scheduled session of the Supreme Soviet, and some of the changes were made only three days before the Supreme Soviet convened. The actions of the party and the Presidium of the Supreme Soviet immediately prior to the December, 1962, meetings of the Supreme Soviet typify long-standing common practice in the U.S.S.R., and confirm the thesis that the Supreme Soviet functions as a ratifying, rather than a policy-making, organ.

Although according to the Constitution the Supreme Soviet has exclusive power of legislation, laws changing the basic norms of society or at variance with the Constitution have frequently been issued by organs which do not have the constitutional right to make laws. For example, in the 1940's the Presidium violated or amended the Constitution by issuing decrees which increased the legal work day and modified the constitutional requirements for Supreme Soviet deputies. Many decrees issued by the Council of Ministers constitute the establishment of laws, for example, the definition of crimes against socialist property with the stipulation of associated penalties. Decrees are frequently issued jointly by the Council of Ministers and the Central Committee of the Communist Party, and often these decrees have been enforced for months before presentation to the Supreme Soviet for ratification.

Despite the number of decree-issuing organs and agencies in the U.S.S.R., Soviet jurists maintain that legislative power is the exclusive prerogative of the Supreme Soviet. To support this myth, the acts or decisions of the various decree-issuing organs are given different labels: laws or statutes are issued by the Supreme Soviet; decrees or edicts, by the Presidium; decisions, orders, decrees or ordinances, by the Council of Ministers; and resolutions, or more appropriately, orders, by the C.P.S.U. Although the Communist Party does not have the constitutional right to issue orders or to establish law in the U.S.S.R., an order by the C.P.S.U. is binding on all Soviet state organs. Soviet jurists consider laws established by the Supreme Soviet to be of a higher order than the decrees, edicts, orders and decisions issued by the state organs created by the Supreme Soviet. In theory, the Presidium merely interprets statutes and laws established by the Supreme Soviet, while the Council of Ministers does not create new laws, but merely "issues decisions and orders on the basis and in pursuance of the laws in operation" (Article 66). However, the acts of the Presidium and Council of Ministers are more frequently based on orders or resolutions of the C.P.S.U. than on the laws or statutes established by the Supreme Soviet, are much more numerous, and in general, much more precise. Moreover, the legalistic distinction between the acts of the Supreme Soviet and the acts of the organs created by it is inconsequential from the point of view of their binding force. The people of the Soviet Union are equally obligated to abide by the laws, decrees, decisions and orders issued by all the higher state organs, and this obligation is supported by court action.

Even those laws which are approved directly by the Supreme Soviet are seldom initiated within the Supreme Soviet. Theoretically, legislative initiative is granted to both chambers of the Supreme Soviet, the Presidium of the Supreme Soviet, the Council of Ministers of the U.S.S.R., the commissions of both chambers, a collective of Supreme Soviet deputies (usually about fifty), the Supreme Court of the U.S.S.R., and the Procurator-General of the U.S.S.R. In practice, most of the legislation approved by the Supreme Soviet is introduced by the Presidium or the Council of Ministers.

Soviet spokesmen uphold the legislative importance of the Supreme Soviet by stressing the fact that major legislative proposals such as Five and Seven Year Plans, the state budget, economic reorganizations, etc., are presented to it for approval, albeit sometimes after the proposal has been put into effect. However, the time devoted in the Supreme Soviet to the discussion of a major item of legislation rarely exceeds a few hours, if indeed the proposal is discussed at all, and approval is invariably granted with total or almost total unanimity. Reasons for the lack of dissenting votes are worth considering. Most important, no legislation is proposed in the Supreme Soviet unless it has the official sanction of the party. The majority of deputies are party members or candidates, and all are supporters of the party program. Since the bill has received the prior approval of the party, the deputies do not construe their duty to involve deciding whether or not the bill should pass; rather, as members of a "working body," their duty is to consider the application of the bill in their places of work. Differences of opinion may arise over how to make the bill more workable, but not over whether the bill should be passed. Such differences can be resolved without difficulty. Major proposals are, of course, carefully evaluated and debated by the leaders of the Communist Party prior to presentation of the proposal to governmental organs for formal approval. Considerable debate may also occur during the discussion of the bill in the Supreme Soviet commissions. Daily newspapers cover the meetings of the Supreme Soviet and report on the unanimity, but pay less attention to the debates which occur in the commissions.[20] The unanimous decisions, which are criticized and questioned in the West, are highly prized in the U.S.S.R.

because, like the elections, such decisions are interpreted as a manifestation of support for the party program.

Although theoretically the Supreme Soviet is the sole legislating organ in the governmental machinery of the U.S.S.R., it may be concluded that it operates primarily to provide formal ratification for legislation proposed by the party through the Council of Ministers or the Presidium of the Supreme Soviet. The Supreme Soviet does, however, serve the Soviet regime well in a number of non-legislative capacities. Most important, it has symbolic importance in that it supports the myth, propagated by Soviet leaders for the indoctrination of the Soviet citizens and people in other countries, that the laws of the U.S.S.R. are made by the elected representatives of the people. It permits a large number of Soviet citizens to engage nominally in the high affairs of state, and during the process, to develop enthusiasm for the program and accomplishments of the regime, which they are expected to convey to their constituents. Although by no means the only, or even the most frequently used, platform for the announcement of national policy, major policy changes are often announced by the party leaders at Supreme Soviet sessions. Since approval by the Supreme Soviet is guaranteed in advance, there is considerable propaganda value attached to making certain announcements, particularly those which might be viewed unfavorably by many of the people, to the representative assembly. Finally, it provides the formality of approval of governmental policy by the elected representatives of the people.

THE PRESIDIUM OF THE SUPREME SOVIET OF THE U.S.S.R.

The Presidium of the Supreme Soviet of the U.S.S.R., which is described as "the highest permanently functioning organ of state power in the U.S.S.R.,"[21] is like a miniature Supreme Soviet in continuous session. According to the Constitution, the competence of the Presidium is in most respects identical with that of the Supreme Soviet, with the major exceptions that it is fully accountable to the Supreme Soviet and that its actions and decisions require Supreme Soviet ratification. The smaller governmental organ is deemed necessary for several reasons. First, the Supreme Soviet with its large membership (currently 1,443 deputies) is too cumbersome a body for adequate handling of legislative details. Secondly, since the Supreme Soviet ordinarily convenes only twice a year, some of its authority must be delegated so that its duties can be performed while it is not in session. Finally, it permits the party leaders to act speedily and directly to give legal force to their policy decisions. This is facilitated by the fact that Presidium members are full-time political leaders who maintain close contact with the party leadership, while the rank-and-file deputies are engaged in full-time jobs in addition to their political work.

The Presidium is elected at a joint meeting of the two chambers at the initial session of a newly elected Supreme Soviet and retains its powers until a subsequent newly elected Supreme Soviet forms a new Presidium. All members of the Presidium, including a chairman, fifteen vice-chairmen, a secretary, and sixteen members, are chosen from among Supreme Soviet deputies. As a concession to federalism, the Constitution stipulates that each Union Republic must be represented on the Presidium by a vice-chairman, usually the chairman of the Presidium of the Supreme Soviet of the Union Republic. Soviet jurists state that this practice ensures that the representatives of the Union Republics will be of equal stature.[22] In general, there is an attempt to make the Presidium representative of various sub-divisions in the entire population, and members may be selected to represent various nationalities, the armed forces, trade unions, youth organizations, women and other special interest groups. In addition to representational considerations, demonstrated competency is a prerequisite for selection because of the magnitude and importance of the functions assigned to the Presidium. All members of the Presidium are party members, and several may be outstanding party leaders, including members of the Presidium of the Central Committee of the Communist Party. It is, of course, these party leaders who wield the power of the Presidium. Superior officers of the Supreme Soviet, such as the chairmen of the chambers, and members of the Council of Ministers may not be selected as members of the Presidium since, in theory, the Presidium is responsible to the Supreme Soviet and supervises the activities of the Council of Ministers.

The Presidium of the Supreme Soviet is often called the collegiate or "Collective President" of the U.S.S.R. Its chairman acts as the titular head of state, and in foreign countries is commonly referred to as the President of the U.S.S.R. Technically, the chairman is the equal rather than the superior of the other Presidium members. Soviet sources stress that his authority derives solely from his Presidium membership, that he acts only in the name of the Presidium and that all decisions are those of the collective. Until recently it was appropriate to point out that although all of the men who served as chairman of the Presidium enjoyed popular respect, none of them seem to have exerted particularly great influence on the affairs of the party or the state. The first chairman, Kalinin (1919-1946), had been a worker and a show peasant of the revolution. When Kalinin died, the position was given to Shvernik (1946-1953), a trade union leader, who was replaced by Voroshilov (1953-1960), a former metal worker and soldier. When Khrushchev publicly exposed Voroshilov as a member of the "anti-party" faction, he magnanimously suggested that Voroshilov be treated with leniency in view of the value of his past services to the state and the party. In 1960, at the age of seventy-nine, Voroshilov asked to be relieved of his duties as Chairman of the Presidium because of "health" reasons. On Khrushchev's nomination, the Supreme Soviet elected Leonid Brezhnev to succeed Voroshilov. During the period of his chairmanship, Brezhnev's power within the party apparently increased markedly. At any rate, in July, 1964, again on Khrushchev's recommendation, Brezhnev was awarded the position of Secretary of the Central Committee of the C.P.S.U., and Mikoyan, a party stalwart of long standing, was appointed Chairman of the Presidium. By October, 1964, Brezhnev, the former Chairman of the Presidium, in alliance with other powerful party leaders, effected Khrushchev's dismissal and attained for himself the top position in the party and hence, the top position in the U.S.S.R. In December, 1965, N. Podgorny replaced Mikoyan as Chairman of the Presidium; Mikoyan retained his membership in the Presidium.

Although all major decisions of the Presidium may be made by the collective, the chairman, nevertheless, enjoys a unique position. He receives foreign envoys and delegates, represents the Soviet Union in national affairs, awards medals, orders, and honorary titles in the name of the Presidium, and is conspicuous at major state affairs. He presides at meetings of the Presidium, co-signs, with the Secretary of the Presidium, all its official acts, including laws and decrees approved by the Supreme Soviet, decrees of the Presidium and its directives to the various organs of the U.S.S.R. The duties of the chairman may be delegated to a vice-chairman, but the duties of the vice-chairmen, as the chairmen of the Presidia of the Supreme Soviets of the Union Republics, may prevent them from participating actively in all the affairs of the Presidium of the Supreme Soviet of the U.S.S.R. A minimum operating quorum is ensured by the chairman, secretary and a number of the members who are stationed permanently in Moscow. The secretary of the Presidium is responsible for current work and supervises the administrative units, such as the economic, foreign affairs and judicial sections, which are established by the Presidium.

COMPETENCE OF THE PRESIDIUM

As the highest permanently functioning organ of state power, the Presidium of the Supreme Soviet has extensive rights and duties which are enumerated in Article 49 of the Constitution. It convenes the Supreme Soviet and co-ordinates the activities of the two chambers, but does not conduct the sessions. It is not empowered to veto Supreme Soviet decisions and can dissolve the Supreme Soviet only in the event of disagreement between the two chambers. At the expiration of the term of office of the Supreme Soviet, the Presidium orders new elections. It may, however, postpone elections because of a state of emergency, and thereby, prolong the Supreme Soviet term. The Presidium establishes the Central Election Commission, forms electoral districts for elections to the Soviet of Nationalities and the Soviet of the Union, and prescribes certain of the forms to be followed in an election campaign.

The Presidium, rather than the Supreme Court of the U.S.S.R., has the right to interpret the laws of the U.S.S.R. Soviet jurists assert that since the laws are established by the Supreme Soviet, the Presidium, as the organ and aide of the Supreme Soviet, is especially well-equipped to interpret the laws. The Presidium may interpret a law on its own initiative or at the request of the Supreme Court or the Procurator-General. Theoretically, the right of the Presidium to interpret laws is supposed to ensure that all laws, including the Constitutions of the Union Republics, are in conformity with the Constitution of the U.S.S.R. and that the laws are applied with uniformity throughout the territories of the U.S.S.R. Actually, although referred to by Soviet authorities as the "guardian of the Constitution," the Presidium often issues decrees which are at variance with constitutional stipulations or with laws previously approved by the Supreme Soviet. The constitutionality of a Presidium decree has never been questioned, nor is this likely to happen, since the Presidium, as the judge of the constitutionality of all decrees, orders and laws, is itself not subject to constitutional check, except by the Supreme Soviet. All activities of the Presidium are, of course, carefully supervised by the party leadership.

According to the Constitution, the Presidium is theoretically higher than the Council of Ministers, since the Presidium has the right to annul decisions and orders of the Council of Ministers if they do not conform to the law, and during the intervals between Supreme Soviet sessions, to appoint and release ministers of the U.S.S.R. on the recommendation of the chairman of the Council of Ministers, subject to subsequent approval by the Supreme Soviet. However, the Presidium does not exercise significant supervisory powers over the Council of Ministers largely because both organs are subservient to the party leadership and both contain a number of high-ranking party leaders. Ordinarily the Council of Ministers contains more powerful party leaders than the Presidium. No measure of any importance introduced by the Council of Ministers has ever been overruled by the Presidium, and the only orders of the Council of Ministers which have been annulled have been those which have become defunct because of organizational or other changes. Although the formality of appointing and releasing ministers is handled by the Presidium, decisions about who should be appointed and released are made by the party.

As the collegiate head of the state, the Presidium performs a number of important executive functions. In addition to appointing and releasing Ministers of the U.S.S.R., it appoints and removes the high command of the Armed Forces, selects and recalls Soviet diplomats and receives diplomatic representatives of foreign states. Its formal jurisdiction in military and foreign affairs is extensive. It has the right to proclaim martial law, to order general or partial mobilization, to ratify or denounce international treaties and may even declare war under certain circumstances. Orders, medals and titles of honor, which are used extensively by the U.S.S.R. for motivational and political purposes, are instituted and awarded by the Presidium. The Presidium, like the chief executive of other nations, also exercises the right of pardon. It has the right to grant Soviet citizenship to foreigners and to withdraw citizenship status from "persons not worthy of being Soviet citizens." Between Supreme Soviet sessions it may sanction the arrest or prosecution of a Supreme Soviet deputy.

Of all the prerogatives granted to the Presidium, the most important is the right to issue decrees, and thus to function as one of the major sources of law in the U.S.S.R. Because of the brief and infrequent meetings of the Supreme Soviet, and for other reasons, much of the legislative business of the country is handled by the Presidium and the Council of Ministers. Many of the decrees of the Presidium, such as decrees establishing electoral districts, awarding orders and titles of honor, and appointing plenipotentiary representatives to foreign countries, do not contain new legal norms. A large number of decrees do, however, establish new legal norms, e.g., the creation of new criminal offenses; amendment of the law on criminal liability for state crimes; modification of civil law; adjustment of the system of benefits for persons who work in remote regions; and modification of the law on state pensions. Presidium decrees involving the establishment or abolition of governmental agencies, as discussed previously, constitute amendments or, if viewed less leniently, violations of the Constitution.

Soviet jurists write at length and somewhat vaguely about the similarity and differences between the jurisdiction and powers of the Supreme Soviet and its Presidium. The laws of the Supreme Soviet and the decrees of the Presidium are purportedly similar in that both are acts of higher organs of state power and because of the uniformity of problems which are handled by the two organs. Areas under the jurisdiction of both, but in which the Presidium has typically assumed the dominant role, include ratification of international treaties, questions concerning marriage, the family and property relations, and some defense questions. The Presidium has assumed the power to annul a law if it is outdated, contradictory to a new law, or if required by the practice of state activity.[23] The claim by Soviet jurists that Supreme Soviet laws "have greater judicial force" than Presidium decrees[24] is, as was pointed out previously, meaningless from a practical point of view, since laws and decrees are equally binding for all state organs and Soviet citizens. The other major difference between laws and decrees is that Presidium decrees which involve modification of legal norms or major governmental reorganizations are subject to approval by the Supreme Soviet. However, this also is merely a formal distinction, since the decrees of the Presidium are binding and operative as soon as they are issued, and Supreme Soviet ratification is invariably given.

In many respects the Presidium dominates the Supreme Soviet, despite the fact that the Presidium is legally accountable to the Supreme Soviet, which elects and may remove its members. The domination of the Supreme Soviet by its Presidium is analogous to the domination of the Party Congress by the Party Presidium. In spite of constitutional and statutory provisions to the contrary, the typical Soviet practice is for a popular assembly to be *de facto* accountable to and the instrument of its executive committee, rather than the reverse. The Supreme Soviet, for example, has never been known to censure the Presidium for any of its activities, and has consistently provided automatic ratification for all Presidium decrees.

The Presidium of the Supreme Soviet of the U.S.S.R. fulfills three functions: legislative, executive and judicial. As a legislative organ, it exercises legislative initiative within the Supreme Soviet and issues decrees which have binding force even before Supreme Soviet ratification. In its executive function, it receives diplomats, confers titles, and more important, appoints officials. As a judicial organ, it interprets the laws of the U.S.S.R. Since the Presidium is a small and carefully selected body, which works under the direct supervision and control of the party leaders, it serves effectively as an organ of the state which is able to translate party decisions and policies into state action with a minimum of delay.

THE COUNCIL OF MINISTERS OF THE U.S.S.R.

The third major governmental organ of the Soviet Union is the Council of Ministers or Government of the U.S.S.R., which is described by the Constitution as the "highest executive and administrative organ" of the state. The Council of Ministers is appointed at a joint meeting of the two chambers of the Supreme Soviet and is responsible and accountable to the Supreme Soviet or, in the interval between sessions, to the Presidium of the Supreme Soviet (Articles 56, 64, and 65). Although the Supreme Soviet appoints the members of the Council of Ministers, it exercises no control over their selection. The general practice is for the chairman of the Council of Ministers to surrender his powers formally to a newly elected Supreme Soviet, which in turn compliments the chairman on the work of the Council, and commissions him to submit proposals for a new government. The chairman submits a list of candidates which has received the prior approval of the party leadership, and the list is automatically ratified by the Supreme Soviet.[25] Occasionally the procedure has varied when the party has decided that the incumbent chairman is to be replaced. The term of office of the Council of Ministers coincides with that of the Supreme Soviet, but frequently both the composition and structure of the Council of Ministers changes substantially during the four-year term.

Figure 2 summarizes the organization of the U.S.S.R. Council of

Ministers and lists the All-Union and Union-Republic Ministries, and the major state councils and committees which constituted the chief organizational units of the Council of Ministers (as of the summer of 1965) after extensive revisions were introduced in 1962 and 1963. The Council of Ministers consists of the chairman of the Council; the first vice-chairmen and the vice-chairmen (the number is not fixed by law); the head (minister or chairman) of each of the major organizational units of the Council of Ministers; the deputy chairmen of a few of the major councils or committees, such as Supreme Council of the National Economy and the State Planning Committee; and ex officio, the chairmen of the Council of Ministers of the Union Republics. Membership in the U.S.S.R. Council of Ministers has fluctuated because of frequent changes in the number and organization of subordinate administrative units. Reorganizations have been introduced in an attempt to increase efficiency, for political reasons, and to cope with the expansion of state functions. In recent years membership has varied around sixty. The Council of Ministers has almost always been larger than the corresponding executive and administrative organs in other countries.

The chairman of the Council of Ministers, invariably either the recognized leader of the party or an important party official, is frequently referred to as the Premier or the Prime Minister of the U.S.S.R. The chairman is appointed to an unfixed term of office by the Supreme Soviet and is responsible to the Supreme Soviet for all actions of the Council. Constitutionally, he may be removed from office only by the Supreme Soviet. In fact, the chairman of the Council of Ministers is selected by the Presidium of the Central Committee of the Communist Party on the recommendation of the First Secretary. When the First Secretary himself is chairman of the Council of Ministers, as Stalin (1941-1953) and Khrushchev (March, 1958-October, 1964) were, the position is an extremely powerful one, and nothing short of the type of conspiracy that was used against Khrushchev can force the incumbent from office. The decision to remove Khrushchev from the top government post was made by the Presidium of the Central Committee and confirmed by the Central Committee. The Supreme Soviet, which is legally responsible for the selection and dismissal of the chairman of the Council of Ministers, merely ratified the decision which had been made by the party leaders. Persons other than the three "supreme party leaders" (Lenin, Stalin and Khrushchev) who have held the position (Rykov, 1924-1930; Molotov, 1930-1941; Malenkov, 1953-1955; Bulganin, 1955-1958) were eventually removed either because the supreme party leader suspected their loyalty or because he had decided to assume the position himself. Kosygin, who was awarded the position after Khrushchev's dismissal, is regarded as an extremely powerful man and a potential candidate for supreme party leadership. However, it is conceivable that he

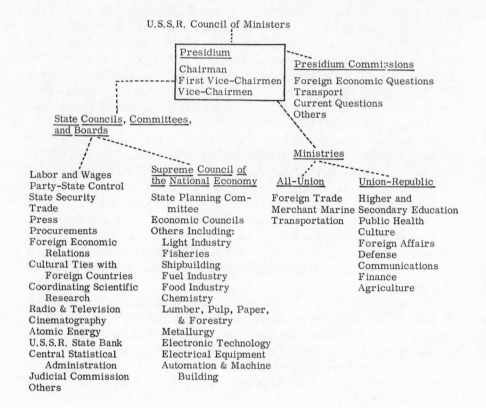

U.S.S.R. Council of Ministers

Presidium

Chairman
First Vice-Chairmen
Vice-Chairmen

Presidium Commissions

Foreign Economic Questions
Transport
Current Questions
Others

State Councils, Committees,
and Boards

Ministries

Labor and Wages	Supreme Council of the National Economy	All-Union	Union-Republic
Party-State Control	State Planning Com-	Foreign Trade	Higher and
State Security	mittee	Merchant Marine	Secondary Education
Trade	Economic Councils	Transportation	Public Health
Press	Others Including:		Culture
Procurements	Light Industry		Foreign Affairs
Foreign Economic	Fisheries		Defense
Relations	Shipbuilding		Communications
Cultural Ties with	Fuel Industry		Finance
Foreign Countries	Food Industry		Agriculture
Coordinating Scientific	Chemistry		
Research	Lumber, Pulp, Paper,		
Radio & Television	& Forestry		
Cinematography	Metallurgy		
Atomic Energy	Electronic Technology		
U.S.S.R. State Bank	Electrical Equipment		
Central Statistical	Automation & Machine		
Administration	Building		
Judicial Commission			
Others			

Agricultural Committee

Ministry of Agriculture
State Procurement
Farm Machinery Association
Others

Figure 2.   Organization of the Council of Ministers of the U.S.S.R.

Sources: "Resolution of the U.S.S.R. Supreme Soviet: On Formation of the U.S.S.R. Government, the U.S.S.R. Council of Ministers," *Pravda*, April 26, 1962, pp. 1-2; "Report by Deputy M.P. Georgadze, Secretary of the Presidium of the U.S.S.R. Supreme Soviet: On Ratification of Decrees of the Presidium of the U.S.S.R. Supreme Soviet," *Pravda*, Dec. 14, 1962, p. 6; "Report by Deputy M.P. Georgadze, Secretary of the Presidium of the U.S.S.R. Supreme Soviet: On Ratification of Decrees of the Presidium of the U.S.S.R. Supreme Soviet," *Pravda*, Dec. 20, 1963, p. 3.

may be removed by the First Secretary (currently Brezhnev), who may want to consolidate his power by assuming the position himself or by awarding it to a trusted lieutenant who would not constitute a threat to his own dominant position.

The chairman of the Council of Ministers presides at important meetings of the Council, signs its ordinances, advises the Presidium of the Supreme Soviet about the appointment and dismissal of ministers and committee chairmen, exercises the right to suspend the orders of ministers, and in general, guides the work of the Council. He maintains extremely close contact with the Secretariat and Presidium of the Central Committee of the Communist Party, and uses the Council of Ministers as an effective tool for the implementation by the state of the decisions made by the governing organs of the party. The chairman, together with the first vice-chairmen and sometimes the vice-chairmen, form a policy-making group referred to as the "inner cabinet" or Presidium of the Council of Ministers. The vice-chairmen are invariably high-ranking party officials, some of whom may concurrently be members or candidate members of the party Presidium. Party officials who have served as vice-chairmen of the Council of Ministers include Malenkov, Beria, Molotov, Bulganin, Kaganovich, Pervukhin, Saburov, Kosygin and Mikoyan. First vice-chairmen are seldom burdened with administrative responsibility for the direction of a ministry or committee. Instead, as members of the "inner cabinet," they assist the chairman by supervising and coordinating the work of the numerous administrative agencies of the central government and by planning and formulating top-level policy for the government. A close liaison is maintained by members of the inner cabinet. Meetings of the entire Council, presided over by the chairman or a vice-chairman, are ordinarily held several times a month. Meetings of the full Council are used by members of the inner cabinet to inform the ministers of high policy, to criticize them for shortcomings, to hear and discuss problems confronting them, to coordinate their activities, and to correct ministerial decisions and actions. *Ad hoc* inter-ministerial committees are established to study controversial issues and to report on them to the Council.

Ministers and others of equivalent rank hold office at the pleasure of the chairman of the Council, although formal appointment and removal is vested in the Presidium of the Supreme Soviet or the Supreme Soviet itself. Ministers need not be Supreme Soviet deputies, and rather than being influential party leaders, are usually highly competent administrators, technicians or experts, who have demonstrated complete loyalty to the party and have impressed the party leaders favorably. Some of the most efficient and reliable members of the Council are eventually selected for membership in the Central Committee of the Communist Party, and a few may be elevated to the inner circle of power, if the party leaders are ex-

tremely well-pleased with their work. On the other hand, persons of ministerial rank operate under the constant threat of the personal disgrace and
professional ruin that usually follows in the wake of any error, whether it be
administrative, technical, or political. The turnover has been considerable.
It is not unusual for persons who have held ministerial rank, or even the
rank of chairman or vice-chairman of the Council of Ministers, to be
assigned to relatively insignificant posts in undesirable places.[26]

The similarities and differences between Soviet ministers and their
American and British counterparts is of interest. Soviet ministers, like the
Secretaries in the United States government, need not be selected from
among elected representatives of the people. Rather they are selected by
the chief executive from people of known competence and demonstrated
loyalty. British cabinet ministers are almost always selected from the House
of Commons, although in rare cases, a member of the House of Lords,
which is not a popularly elected assembly, may be invited to join the government. Soviet ministers are experts in the areas which they administer,
while their British and American counterparts frequently are not. Soviet
ministers, however, in spite of their expertness, are much less free to initiate
policy than the British or American non-experts. The tenure of a British
minister or an American Secretary, in general, depends upon the tenure of
his political party, while the tenure of a Soviet minister depends on approval by, rather than the tenure of, his party. The Supreme Soviet plays
no part in enhancing or diminishing the role or prestige of a minister, as
can be done by the British House of Commons or the American Congress.

Ministries of the U.S.S.R. are of two types, All-Union or Union-
Republican. Successive reorganizations since 1957, designed to effect decentralization, have reduced the number of All-Union Ministries to three—
Foreign Trade, Transportation and Merchant Marine. The All-Union
Ministries involve a high degree of centralized control; each ministry directs the branch of state administration entrusted to it throughout the
territory of the U.S.S.R., either directly or through bodies appointed by it;
all decisions are made at the center and are transmitted as orders to subordinate agencies. Union-Republican Ministries allow for a certain amount
of decision-making at the Union Republic level, since each Union-Republican Ministry directs the branch of state administration entrusted to it
through corresponding ministries in the Union Republics. Administrative
subdivisions of the ministry, which are located in a particular Union Republic, are supervised by the corresponding Union-Republican Ministry
of the Union Republic. In general, Union-Republican status is reserved
for ministries which are responsible for matters in which local peculiarities
should be considered, or for which a high degree of uniformity among
Union Republics is not absolutely essential to the economic or political welfare of the U.S.S.R. Included among the Union-Republican Ministries

after the 1963 reorganization were Higher and Secondary Education, Public Health, Culture, Foreign Affairs, Defense, Communications, Finance and Agriculture. Although the Union-Republican Ministries do allow for a certain amount of local autonomy, the counterpart ministries at the Union Republic level are fully responsible to the Council of Ministers of the U.S.S.R., as well as to the Council of Ministers and the legislative organs of the Union Republic. This is an example of the combination of horizontal and vertical responsibility which is commonly practiced in the U.S.S.R.; administrative organs are responsible, vertically, to the superior organs in the hierarchy, and horizontally, to the popularly elected local Soviets. In the event of a difference of opinion between the central and republican authorities, the republican authorities are required to implement the orders of their superiors at the center. Thus, for example, the Council of Ministers of the U.S.S.R. may annul any order of the Council of Ministers of a Union Republic or of any of its ministries.

Each ministry is headed by a minister who is the "sole director" and is held personally responsible to the Council of Ministers and the Supreme Soviet for all the decisions and activities of his ministry. Although the minister, unless he is a party leader, may have little influence in the determination of major overall policy, he is, nevertheless, an important and powerful administrator within his own sphere of jurisdiction. His main task is to implement the policy decisions of his political superiors, but in doing so, he must necessarily exercise some discretion in the operation of his own ministry. Despite the fact that his activities are subjected to numerous extra-legal and legal controls, such as party supervision and intervention, and the right of the Council of Ministers to annul his orders, his administrative power is extensive and he bears responsibility for numerous important decisions. In addition, he advises, makes suggestions and submits proposals to his political superiors.

Since the coordination and direction of the activities of a ministry is an excessively complex task, the minister necessarily delegates some of his responsibility to subordinates. Each ministry is divided into a number of chief administrations or subdivisions, including administrative units such as Personnel, Planning and Supply, and production or territorial units which vary from ministry to ministry. The principle of "one-man" management prevails at all lower levels. The chief or director of each subdivision is held solely responsible for his sphere of jurisdiction and must report directly to his administrative superior. In contradistinction to the principle of unitary command is the principle of collegial management, which is equally popular in the U.S.S.R. Each minister is provided with a collegium of deputy ministers and other advisors who are appointed by the Council of Ministers. The collegium of the Ministry of Culture, for example, includes deputy ministers, Ministers of Culture from the Union Republics, playwrights, editors, directors of theatres and art publishing houses and artists.[27] The minister is expected to confer with his collegium with reference to a variety of problems associated with the operation of the ministry, such as the fulfillment of plans, the selection of personnel, techniques to improve efficiency, organizational changes, etc. Also attached to each ministry is a technical council to advise the minister on technical matters, a chief inspection office to check on the implementation of administrative decisions, and an advisory council composed of representatives from enterprises directed by the ministry and from local organizations. The function of the advisory councils is to keep the minister and his departmental heads cognizant of local conditions and new developments and to permit them to utilize more fully the practical experience of persons directly involved in the work supervised by the ministry. Although none of these advisory bodies are elected or appointed by elected organs, their function is merely to advise, not to decide. Only the minister, himself, has the legal authority to issue directives for the operation of the ministry. If his directives are not condoned by his superiors, he is held personally responsible.

THE COMPETENCE OF THE COUNCIL OF MINISTERS

Article 69 of the Constitution empowers the Council of Ministers to coordinate and direct the work of the Supreme Council of the National Economy, the All-Union and Union-Republic Ministries, state committees and all institutions subordinate to them; to supervise the entire economy, including the preparation of the national-economic plan and the state budget; to adopt measures for the maintenance of public order; to exercise general guidance in the sphere of relations with foreign states; to set military draft quotas and to direct the general organization of the Armed Forces; to form state committees and, when necessary, special committees and central administrations under the Council of Ministers of the U.S.S.R., for economic and cultural affairs and defense. Thus its jurisdiction encompasses regulation of the entire economy, national defense, internal security, foreign affairs, education and culture. No aspect of life within the U.S.S.R. is unaffected by the decisions and actions of the Council of Ministers and its subordinate organs. Soviet authors openly declare that all actions and decisions of the Government of the U.S.S.R. are directly controlled and supervised by the Communist Party. For example, a text on *Soviet State Law* asserts: "Throughout the entire history of the Soviet socialist state, the Soviet Government has based its activity on the directives of the Communist Party—of its congresses, conferences and central committee."[28] Since the powers of the Council of Ministers are great, it constitutes an extremely effective tool for the implementation of party policy by a legally constituted organ of the state.

The Council of Ministers of the U.S.S.R. exercises general guidance and control over all branches of economy and culture throughout the territory of the U.S.S.R. Direct or indirect control over the entire administrative apparatus is exerted through the many institutions under its jurisdiction, including the State Committees and Commissions, the All-Union and the Union-Republican Ministries, the Supreme Council of the National Economy, the Economic Councils and the Council of Ministers of the Union Republics. Much of the work of the Council of Ministers is associated with the organization and activity of subordinate administrative organs. It establishes, abolishes and determines the structure and functions of committees, commissions, ministries, bureaus and industrial administrations. Its power to appoint officials is one of its important methods of control. In addition to selecting candidates for appointment by the Supreme Soviet or its Presidium as ministers or chairmen of State Committees, the Council of Ministers directly appoints deputy ministers, the collegial organs of the ministries, and the heads of all institutions under its jurisdiction. It supervises the work of all ministries and State Committees, evaluates their reports and approves or suspends decisions and orders issued by a minister, a committee chairman, the Council of Ministers of a Union Republic or by an Economic Council.

Constitutional control over the economic plan and the budget is nominally vested in the Supreme Soviet as the "exclusive legislative organ." In practice, major financial and economic policies are determined by the party. The Council of Ministers, which is given direct responsibility for the administration of the plan, also supervises the preparation of the economic plan and the state budget. Under the supervision of the Council, the State Planning Committee formulates the overall national economic plan; and the Union Republics, Economic Councils, ministries and subordinate organs formulate plans for specific segments of the economy. Practical control over the state budget, including both sources of revenue and expenditures, is exerted by the Council which determines the rates of taxation and other assessment rates; allocates revenue for the budget of each Union Republic and its subdivisions and for the various segments of the economy, such as agriculture, industry, national defense, education and health; regulates credit relations; and establishes wage rates, prices and social insurance benefits. Prior to being submitted to the Supreme Soviet for approval, the budget and economic plan are studied by commissions of the Supreme Soviet. It is probable that the minor changes which are recommended by the commissions are submitted to the Council of Ministers before the commissions report to the Supreme Soviet. The Supreme Soviet invariably approves the economic plan and budget as prepared by the Council of Ministers, subject to the minor revisions recommended by the commissions. Thus the Council of Ministers, under the direction of the party leaders, formulates the plan, assumes responsibility for its administration and regulates all phases of the economy.

Because the Council of Ministers is responsible for the maintenance of public order, for the protection of the interests of the state and for safeguarding the rights of citizens, it has substantial authority over the police force and also over many of the regulations the police are required to enforce. The Council has, by decree, defined what constitutes a crime against socialist property and established the associated penalty and has issued decrees pertaining to tardiness, absenteeism, petty theft, defacement of socialist property, sabotage, inefficiency, poor management and defective commodities. It has the right to take action to disclose and eliminate shortcomings in the work of the state apparatus, including illegal acts committed by individual officials. Although the activities of the police agencies are supervised by the Council, the relationship of the Secret Police to the Council or to any other agency with the exception of the higher echelons of the Communist Party, has typically been nebulous.

The Council of Ministers' involvement in foreign affairs exceeds that of the Presidium of the Supreme Soviet to which the Constitution assigns treaty-making rights. The Council prepares most of the treaties for ratification by the Presidium, and on its own, confirms many treaties and agreements which do not require ratification. It operates embassies and consulates and may order acts of reprisal, withdraw recognition or sever relations with other states. It supervises almost all trade, economic and cultural relations with foreign states. The committees on Foreign Economic Problems and Cultural Ties with Foreign Countries and all agencies related to national defense, including the Ministry of Defense, State Committee on Defense, and the Atomic Energy Committee, are under the jurisdiction of the Council. In addition, it controls the annual draft quota, the organization, training and equipment of the military forces and the appointment of high-ranking military officers.

All state committees, commissions and central agencies which deal with economic, cultural and defense questions are under the jurisdiction of the Council of Ministers. The establishment of a major committee, such as the Supreme Council of the National Economy, is based on a directive from the party, a subsequent recommendation by the Council of Ministers, a decree by the Presidium, and finally, ratification by the Supreme Soviet. The heads of major committees are members of the Council of Ministers with ministerial rights, and their appointments require confirmation by the Supreme Soviet. Fairly frequently a committee or commission is created to carry on some aspect of the work of a ministry which has been abolished. For example, when the U.S.S.R. Ministry of Justice was abolished in 1956, a Legal Commission was established to codify and systematize legislation. In 1959 the All-Union Ministries of Air Force Industry, Defense Industry and Radio Technical Industry were transformed into state committees for Air Force Technique, Defense Technique and Radio Electronics when the organizations and enterprises which they had guided were transferred to Economic Councils. Occasionally a state committee is transformed into a ministry; for example, the Ministry for Higher and Secondary Special Education was created out of the State Committee for Higher Education, and the Ministry of Culture replaced the State Committee for Art. The chief difference between ministries and state committees is that the former directly guide and supervise subordinate organizations and enterprises, while the latter work out overall plans, directives and technical improvements, but do not directly supervise any branch of the economy. The organizational structure of a committee is consequently less complex than that of a ministry. Although the major committees are considered to be relatively permanent, and can be abolished or transformed only by action of the Supreme Soviet or its Presidium, such action is taken frequently and the list of state committees and commissions of the U.S.S.R. Council of Ministers varies greatly from time to time. Less important committees and commissions may be established or abolished directly by the Council of Ministers which also nominates their leading people, none of whom have ministerial status. Included among such committees are temporary fact-finding agencies, and other committees with short-range goals, subordinate administrative agencies, and collegial committees established to serve a single purpose, such as to select the winners of the Lenin prizes for excellence in scientific and artistic works.

The Council of Ministers functions as a major legislative organ of the U.S.S.R. In principle, the legislative-type actions of the Council of Ministers are supposed merely to amplify laws which have been ratified by the Supreme Soviet, since the Council is empowered by the Constitution to issue "decisions and orders on the basis and in pursuance of laws in operation" (Article 66). Moreover, the Constitution stipulates that decrees of the Council of Ministers may be annulled by the Supreme Soviet or its Presidium (Article 49). In practice, the Council of Ministers does not restrict its decree-issuing authority to amplification or implementation of existing statutes, nor is there an effective check on the legality of the decrees issued by the Council of Ministers. There are several reasons for this. First, because the Council of Ministers assumes overall responsibility for the administration of the country, it is inevitable that a large number of administrative and policy decisions are required concerning matters not specifically covered by the formal laws. Second, the leading members of the Council are simultaneously leading members of the party, and all major decisions of the Council have either been made by or approved by the party. The probability is infinitesimal that the Supreme Soviet would challenge a party-approved decision of the Council, even if the decision were at variance with existing legislation. Moreover, particularly important decisions of national scope are announced jointly by the Council of Ministers and the Central Committee of the C.P.S.U.[29] It is these major decrees, co-sponsored by the C.P.S.U., which are most likely to violate the constitutional norms. However, since the party is "above the government," its formal endorsement of a decree or decision is interpreted as signifying mandatory adoption. Third, the Supreme Court of the U.S.S.R. has not been empowered to engage in judicial review of legislation or to serve as a check against the violation of the Constitution by the executive and legislative branches of the government. A Soviet source states: "The decrees and dispositions of the Council of Ministers are not subject to oversight in respect to their legality by any organ except superior organs of state authority. Acts of the government are obligatory for unconditional application by all, including the courts."[30] Thus checks on the legality of the decrees of the Council of Ministers are for all practical purposes nonexistent. As previously indicated, most of the statutes which are presented to the Supreme Soviet for consideration and adoption are initiated and formulated by the Council of Ministers. The rationale for this practice is that the ministries, in their executive-administrative capacities, are cognizant of problems requiring legislative action, and because of their specialized knowledge, are well-equipped to draft detailed legislation. The Council of Ministers' widely used legislative initiative, combined with its almost unlimited power to issue decrees, both with regard to subject matter and laws in operation, indicates that it, not the Supreme Soviet, is, *de facto,* the major legislative organ of state machinery in the U.S.S.R. Consequently, the Council of Ministers may be described as the leading executive-administrative, legislative, and managerial tool of the state and of the Communist Party.

Soviet Administrative Machinery and Practice

PRINCIPLES OF ADMINISTRATION

Soviet writers state that the organizational structure of Soviet administration is guided by the principles of democratic centralism, production-territorial organization and dual responsibility. The essence of democratic centralism, as previously indicated, is the "absolutely binding character of decisions of higher bodies on lower bodies." At the apex of the pyramidical structure of Soviet administration is the inner bureau of the U.S.S.R. Council of Ministers, composed of important party officials and sometimes headed by the supreme party leader himself. At the next level are the ministries and state committees, each headed by a Council member who is responsible to the Council. Subordinate to the minister or committee chairman are the heads of the departments into which the ministries and committees are subdivided. Also subordinate to the U.S.S.R. Council of Ministers are the Councils of Ministers of the Union Republics. The Councils of Ministers of the Union Republics supervise the Economic Councils, the Council of Ministers of the Autonomous Republics and the territorial, regional and district administrative units, which in turn supervise the administration of the local urban and rural units. According to the principle of dual responsibility or dual subordination, each administrative unit is responsible horizontally to the popular assembly which ostensibly created it, and vertically, to the corresponding organ at the next level in the hierarchy. Thus the Council of Ministers of a Union Republic is responsible to the Supreme Soviet of the Union Republic and to the Council of Ministers of the U.S.S.R.; a republican Party-State Control Committee is responsible to the Union-Republic Council of Ministers and to the U.S.S.R. Party-State Control Committee.

The "production-territorial" principle specifies that within a particular geographic area, all enterprises engaged in a given line of production are coordinated within one administrative hierarchy. A decentralization movement, initiated in 1957, transformed several All-Union Ministries into Union-Republican Ministries, and established economic regions, with Economic Councils as the superior administrative units within each region. Each Economic Council is subdivided into a number of chief administrations or production branches which may be further subdivided into combines which direct the manufacture of goods from a single raw material and trusts which coordinate the work of several related enterprises. Factory directors are responsible either to the director of a trust or combine or to the head of a chief administration of an Economic Council. The decentralizing reorganization was designed to increase the autonomy of local administrative organs, abbreviate the hierarchial chain of command, speed up decision-making and bring administrative officers into closer contact with field conditions. Nevertheless, the organization of Soviet administration remains highly centralized, and the locus of control remains at the center.

The centralist character of Soviet administration is obvious; its democratic character is not. The chief justification for characterizing Soviet administration as democratic is the constitutional stipulation that administrative-executive organs are strictly accountable to the elected assemblies, i.e., the Council of Ministers of the U.S.S.R. to the Supreme Soviet of the U.S.S.R. As previously indicated, the form may be democratic, but the practice is not. Although at the very lowest level of governmental activity, the local Soviet, the popular assembly may occasionally take its executive committee to task for overstepping its authority or for introducing unpopular measures, at the higher levels, where the executive organs are directed by powerful party officials, popular assemblies invariably provide rubber stamp approval. The domination of the Supreme Soviet by the Council of Ministers is characteristic of the relationship between the elected assemblies and the appointed executive organs at all levels in the hierarchy.

The use of the term "democratic" with reference to Soviet administration is justifiable only if democracy is interpreted as the clever utilization by the regime of "mass participation" to facilitate the achievement of goals established by the party and the central administrators. Citizens are encouraged to strive diligently to increase productivity by improving work methods, by submitting suggestions for technical or organizational improvements and by reporting shortcomings, errors and illegal activities to superior authorities. Groups of *aktivs* are organized for the express purpose of improving labor productivity and administrative efficiency, and administrators are expected to confer with representatives of the *aktiv* before introducing major changes. Public organizations, such as the Komsomol and the trade union, are encouraged to serve in an advisory capacity to administrators and to take active measures to materialize the goals of the regime. As previously indicated, advisory bodies, composed of experts actively engaged in practical work, are formed to advise ministers, department heads and other important administrators. Thus while orders and directives flow from higher to lower organs in the administrative hierarchy, information is submitted by the lower to the higher organs. This information is indispensable for the smooth functioning of the complex administrative apparatus. Insofar as possible, top echelon administrators use local initiative and local information to foster achievement of centrally designated goals. However, each administrator is held solely responsible for all aspects of the conduct of agencies or enterprises under his administration. Soviet administration is thus highly centralized, but is democratic chiefly in the sense that the masses are encouraged to participate actively in materializing policies formulated by the party leadership and propagated by the central organs of state power.

SELECTION OF PUBLIC ADMINISTRATORS

Soviet administrative personnel constitute a vast, expanding and cumbersome bureaucracy; it is estimated that approximately fifteen million administrative, managerial and technical officials fall into the category of public employees. This figure, of course, excludes all persons engaged directly in production, since almost all employed persons in the U.S.S.R. are state employees with the exception of collective farmers and persons employed by the party, trade union and youth organizations. The excessively large bureaucracy reflects attempts by the party and the state to maintain firm control over all instruments of power: economic, military, ideological and political. The chief function of many of the bureaucrats is to supervise, inspect and report on the work of other bureaucrats. The diversion of skilled personnel from production to supervisory or inspection roles has constituted a recurrent theme in the Soviet literature on self-criticism.

The State Commission on Civil Service, under the joint guidance of the Council of Ministers and the Central Committee, works to improve administrative management throughout the state apparatus. The regime has consistently attended to the training, selection and placement of public employees, since their function in the smooth attainment of party goals is fully recognized. The Commission on Civil Service establishes standard job classifications for government employees, places limits on the number of officials who may be employed by a particular agency, and recommends procedures related to salary scales, organizational structure and the utilization of personnel. It may, in cooperation with the inspection unit of the Ministry of Finance, inspect governmental agencies with the goal of detecting waste and duplication of functions and may recommend reduction of overstaffed units or organizational modifications.

Soviet authorities admit frankly that the party controls the selection of ranking governmental officials and important members of the administrative bureaucracy. Prior to 1948, the chief function of the Cadres Administration of the Central Committee was to select and recommend party members for party and governmental positions. This function is currently performed by production-branch sections of the Central Committee. State employees need not be party members, but appointees must be politically reliable and astute, since the highest duty of state employees is the execution of party directives, and according to Soviet writers, only those well-versed in Marxism-Leninism are able to foresee, predict, and hence, direct efficiently. Competitive examinations are used only occasionally in the selection of civil servants. High-ranking officials are selected directly by the Council of Ministers or by a responsible minister; the Communist Party, of course, exercises decisive guidance and control over such appointments. Each ministry has a "cadres section" that keeps rosters of information about present and potential officials, the need for new officials and the availability of candidates. This information is available to the minister or department head who has legal responsibility for the selection and appointment of subordinate administrative and technical officials. Most ministries and branches of industry are affiliated with institutes of higher education which train candidates according to established specifications. Thus a large proportion of administrative employees are recruited directly from the training institutions. Graduates are referred to the appropriate government agency for placement and are usually required to remain on the assigned job for a minimum of three years. Since quotas for admission to the training institutions are established on the basis of the projected needs of the ministry or agency, the supply of newly trained specialists corresponds closely to the number of positions available. Bureaucrats who are trained in institutions which are not affiliated with a particular ministry or agency have no assurance of future employment in public administration.

Administrative positions are eagerly sought by Soviet citizens, in spite of extremely high work standards and the serious consequences of errors or misjudgment, which may include demotion, financial penalties and even deprivation of freedom. Members of the administrative hierarchy, in general, earn higher salaries, receive a disproportionately high number of bonuses and awards and are accorded higher social status than persons of corresponding training and competence in non-administrative positions. Efficient administration is indispensable for the smooth functioning of the regime and for the materialization of party goals, and the party rewards those who make commendable contributions in the administrative sphere.

ADMINISTRATIVE CONTROLS

The Soviet regime cannot dispense with its bureaucracy, and at the same time, the cumbersome and overswollen administrative apparatus has constituted a constant source of dissatisfaction for the party and state leaders. Attempts to develop techniques to control the bureaucracy, to add to its efficiency, to force it to maintain strict accountability to the party leadership, and to organize it to facilitate smooth materialization of the party goals have, ironically, typically added to its unwieldiness.

Regardless of the explicitness of directions issued by the party and superior administrative officers, all exigencies cannot be anticipated, and all administrators, from a U.S.S.R. minister to a factory director, are required, on occasion, to make independent decisions. The Soviet totalitarian regime, therefore, requires numerous controls to ensure that decisions conform with party policy and the overall state plan and to curb opportunities for administrators to use their positions for personal aggrandizement. A complex system of administrative control techniques has been developed incorporating the activities of the party, the state machinery, the Party-State Control Committee, the legal apparatus, the planning agencies, the Ministry of Finance and other administrative units, the administrators themselves and the masses of the people and their public and social organizations.

Of all forms of control over the administrative apparatus, that exerted by the party is, of course, the most important. The party establishes the goals which state administrators are expected to achieve and has assumed the right to interfere or issue directives in any phase of state administration. Stalin, in a statement which has retained its essential validity throughout the years, pointed out:

> ". . . not a single important political or organizational question is decided by our Soviet and other mass organizations without guiding directives from the party. *In this sense* it could be said that the dictatorship of the proletariat is, *in essence,* the 'dictatorship' of its vanguard, the 'dictatorship' of its party, as the main guiding force of the proletariat."[31]

Since the organization of the state apparatus corresponds to that of the party, a party organization is on hand to inspect, advise, report, and when necessary, to control at each level of state administration. Officials at any level of the state apparatus can be appointed or removed on the recommendation of the party, and all mass organizations which serve in an advisory capacity to state administrative officials, or which "inspect" the work of state organs, are dominated by party members. Soviet state officials have no choice but to submit to party interference and adhere to party directives. Soviet officials would be foolhardy to question the legality or justifiability of party intervention.

The centralized nature of the Soviet administrative apparatus, in conjunction with the practice of vertical responsibility, enables higher level governmental organs to exert significant control over subordinate organs. All decisions of higher level organs are absolutely binding on all subordinate organs. The Council of Ministers of the U.S.S.R. can, for example, annul the orders of individual ministers or of the Council of Ministers of a Union Republic, and can recommend the dismissal of individual ministers or officials at any level. Lower level executive organs have similar rights with respect to the agencies and officials which they supervise. State officials at all levels watch their subordinates zealously because the errors and illegal acts of subordinates reflect unfavorably on their superiors. Although the Supreme Soviet and its Presidium have not used the constitutional right to question the legality of decisions made by the Council and by individual ministers, the existence of the right may tend to limit the extravagance of administrative action. At the lower levels in the administrative hierarchy, a popular assembly has, in fact, occasionally annulled the decisions of its executive committee.

The Party-State Control Committee (transformed into the People's Control Committee with unchanged functions in December, 1965),[32] which operates under the direct guidance of the Party Central Committee and the U.S.S.R. Council of Ministers, has extensive control powers.[33] Established in 1962, the Party-State Control Committee is a Union-Republican agency, with units at each level of the administrative hierarchy, and in all enterprises. At all levels of its operation, a definite attempt is made to involve "the broad masses of Communists and all working people" in the activities of the committee.[34] At the local level, groups formed from representatives delegated by the party, trade union, Y.C.L. and collective farmer organizations are established to assist the committee with its work in shops, brigades, educational institutions, collective farms and housing units.

The Party-State Control Committees are required to:

". . . render assistance to the Party and state in implementing the Party Program, in organizing systematic checkups on the actual execution of Party and government directives, in further improving the guidance of communist construction, in the struggle for the all-round upsurge of the socialist economy, in the observance of Party and state discipline and socialist legality . . . and to put a decisive end to violations of Party and state discipline, to manifestations of localism, a narrowly departmental attitude to matters, hoodwinking, report padding, mismanagement and extravagances; they must wage a ruthless fight against bureaucratism and red tape, bribe-taking, speculation, abuse of office, and any encroachment on socialist property."[35]

In addition to checking on the execution of party and government directives throughout the administrative hierarchy from the ministries to the enterprises, sub-units of the Committee supervise the fulfillment of economic plans, disclose internal reserves and unused potentials, and make recommendations for the most expedient use of money and materials. Officials of governmental and economic organizations are required to eliminate disclosed violations and shortcomings without delay. The Party-State Control Committees have the right to rescind orders that are illegal or harmful to the interests of the state; to impose fines on responsible officials who cause material damage to the state or to cooperative and public institutions; to call guilty persons to account, impose disciplinary penalties, demote officials or remove them from their posts; and to submit materials on abuses and other criminal actions to the Procurator's office.[36] In short, "the Party-State Control Committees and the entire huge army of their activists must so order their work that bureaucrats, red-tape artists, parasites, bribe-takers, thieves, speculators, and hoodwinkers will feel the inevitability of punishment and will tremble before the great power of the Soviet public."[37] Many an able and honest Soviet administrator may tremble, not before the "great power of the Soviet public," but before the "great power of the bureaucrats" who have a mandate from the party and the state to check into the legality, economic feasibility and appropriateness of his every action.

Legal controls over Soviet administration are provided by the Procuracy, the courts and the system of state arbitration. The Procurator General is vested with supervisory power over the execution of laws by all ministries, subordinate institutions, public servants and citizens of the U.S.S.R. (Article 113). In practice, the Procuracy has paid little attention to the legality of the actions of higher level state organs and officials, but has occasionally challenged the legality of ordinances issued by local Soviets, and has rather frequently initiated criminal action against local governmental officials for illegal activities. Recently there have been recurrent reports of arrests of state officials on charges of embezzlement as manifested by ostentatious homes and expenditures far out of line with known legal earnings. Thus the Procuracy serves to limit the abuses of local administrators, but has little impact on the activities of higher level state officials.

Soviet administrators are surrounded by a framework of legal restrictions incorporated into the criminal codes. Violations which are punishable by imprisonment include bribery, pilfering state or public property, padding state reports, the release of industrial goods of inferior quality, mismanagement of a governmental or public office based on a careless or dishonest attitude, willful entry into an unprofitable business venture, repeated failure to honor commitments for inter-regional or inter-republican deliveries and negligence in the use or maintenance of farm machinery.[38] The death penalty may be applied for repeated bribe-taking and for pilfering state or public property in "especially large amounts," according to a 1961 decree of the Presidium of the Supreme Soviet. Administrative fines may be imposed on directors, chief engineers and other responsible officials for inefficiency, such as tardiness in meeting contract obligations and poor utilization of resources.

Gosarbitrazh, a system of state arbitration for settling disputes between government enterprises, is established under the Chief Arbitrator who is responsible to the Council of Ministers of the U.S.S.R. Gosarbitrazh functions as a commercial court with reference to disputes between economic agencies subordinate to different ministries or Economic Councils concerning the execution of a contract, delayed deliveries, refusals to accept delivery, complaints about the quality of goods, price disputes and other property disputes.[39] Gosarbitrazh may rule to invalidate a contract, assess responsibility for violations, order that certain amendments be made by a designated time and submit information about illegal acts to the Procuracy.

The central government exercises extensive supervisory and investigatory control over administrative and economic units through the State Planning Committee, the Ministry of Finance, the State Bank and allied agencies. The State Planning Committee, which is organized on the model of a Union-Republican ministry, but has a higher degree of centralized control than is usually associated with such ministries, oversees the preparation of the economic plan and the fulfillment of quotas. On the basis of guidelines and policies established by the party leadership, the central planning agencies coordinate the preliminary economic plans submitted by the republics, ministries and their subordinate units, including the Economic Councils, intermediate Soviets and enterprises. Each branch of administration, and ultimately through channels, each enterprise, is assigned a definite set of tasks which are to be fulfilled within a specified time interval. Success in fulfilling or overfulfilling the assigned tasks may be followed by promotion in the administrative hierarchy, prestige and financial rewards. Failure may result in demotion, disciplinary action or even legal sanctions. Soviet administrators and bureaucrats have shown considerable skill in creating the impression of extraordinary efficiency. Frequently used techniques include drafting plans which can be fulfilled and even overfulfilled with no particular effort, underestimating material resources at their disposal, deliberately overestimating raw material requirements, producing goods of inferior quality, etc. To counteract such activities, the central planning agencies and other state organs have developed numerous control techniques, including internal checks, such as independent reports from units within the agency, and field inspection to evaluate progress and detect evasions. Inspectors have the right to arrive at an enterprise or government department unannounced and to examine records, materials and other data without limitation. The budget prepared by the U.S.S.R. Ministry of Finance allocates funds to each level of government and indicates how these funds are to be used. The Ministry of Finance requires periodic reports of all financial operations and operates its own complex system of controls to ascertain that its directives are being implemented. It has its own inspection-control apparatus which has free access to all financial records of all enterprises and government agencies. Violations of budgetary regulations are reported to the Procuracy for criminal prosecution. Enterprises applying for short- or long-term credit must provide the State Bank with detailed financial information. Any indication of divergence from the plan may result in the denial of credit, which may in turn be followed by failure of the enterprise to fulfill the plan and the consequent disgrace of the administrator.

Internal controls within the enterprise or government department are also important. Since each administrative official is responsible for all actions and decisions of his subordinates, careful supervision and control of their activities is essential for his own protection. At the same time sections within enterprises, such as the accounting section, are for self-protection, constantly on the alert for violations by the chief administrators or other officials. Moreover, labor discipline is strictly enforced; absenteeism or tardiness without acceptable reasons is penalized, and each employee is required to carry a "labor book" which provides an official record of past employment, reasons for transfer, reprimands, awards, etc. Positive controls such as promotions, awards, bonuses and prestige are also used liberally to help the regime achieve its goals.

Police organs, particularly the Committee of State Security (KGB), operate in nearly every enterprise and government department. They are constantly on the alert for violations such as disloyalty, disclosure of government secrets, destruction of socialist property, sabotage, financial or other deviations from the plan, mismanagement, or any other type of action which would constitute a violation of state discipline or an impediment to the materialization of goals established by the party. Other organizations and groups which provide additional important checks on the activities of administrative officials include the trade union, Komsomol, professional organizations, commissions assigned to the Soviets and particularly the *aktivs,* all of which are expected to strive for the implementation of the goals of the regime, to submit proposals to increase output, to uncover shortcomings and to expose administrative laxity. All citizens are encouraged to participate in self-criticism and in "criticism from below." The constant danger of exposure by subordinates no doubt reduces the number of violations by officials and supervisors. Criticism from below is sometimes used as an expedient rationale for removing administrative officials for political reasons, as well as for inefficiency or other evidences of unsatisfactory administration. The Soviet press is used by the regime as a major instrument of control. By propagandizing, explaining, justifying and focusing attention on the directives and goals of the party, it serves as a powerful tool of indoctrination. In addition, letters from "ordinary citizens" who complain about mismanagement, misappropriation of funds and maladministration are published frequently. Although some of these letters may be genuine and voluntary expressions of disapproval, the majority of the letters are probably instigated by the party as a device to inform the public that the party is cognizant of all misdemeanors, to keep administrators on the alert and to justify the removal of officials. The published letters, whether party-sponsored or spontaneous, are never critical of the policy outlined by the party leaders; criticism is confined exclusively to dissatisfaction with techniques, approaches and officials responsible for translating the policy into reality. Obviously, each administrator is under constant surveillance by representatives of the state and the party. The fact that some administrators dare to violate state discipline, in spite of the constant surveillance, is evidence of strong conflicting pressures. The fact that some administrators are successful in perpetuating violations over a period of time is evidence that the complex system of control incorporates elements of weakness, perhaps because of its very complexity.

Leading party and governmental officials frequently complain about the unsatisfactory implementation of directives, faulty products, misappropriation of funds, excessive and unnecessary paper work, unreliable officials and overstaffed administrative units. It is difficult to judge how the efficiency of the Soviet administrative apparatus compares with that of other countries because state control and ownership greatly increases the size and the complexity of the administrative structure. Complaints similar to those expressed by Soviet spokesmen could be made, at least occasionally, about the administration of most countries. However, there is ample evidence that the complex system of checks and controls which is used in the U.S.S.R. falls far short of meeting its objective. Although the regime has attempted to establish single, well-defined lines of administrative command to attain both flexibility and well-defined responsibility, its reluctance to trust the administrative officials has led to the introduction of such a complicated system of controls and countercontrols that the lines of responsibility are blurred and flexibility is necessarily restricted except at the highest levels. Each enterprise and agency is subjected to supervision, control, inspection and spying from such a multitude of external and internal officials that, in spite of the attempts to establish definite lines of administrative command, administrators may have difficulty determining to whom they are responsible and exactly what their responsibilities are. Moreover, the restrictive nature of some of the controls may contribute to inefficiency by limiting the initiative of all but the highest administrators and by influencing officials to use non-productive, and sometimes illegal, techniques to mask unsatisfactory conditions which could be rectified if analyzed openly. The expenditures involved in financing the control and inspection agencies, the overswollen bureaucracy, the use of non-productive techniques and the inhibition of local initiative must cost the regime millions of rubles per year.

The regime is not prepared to dispense with the bureaucracy or with the checks and controls over the bureaucracy. The very structure of the totalitarian system requires that those entrusted with its administration be under constant surveillance themselves. A system of controls and checks, especially by the party, is essential for the survival of the Soviet system. However, the efficiency of the Soviet bureaucracy could probably be increased substantially if the number of checks and controls were curtailed considerably. Simplification and coordination of the control agencies could eliminate some of the sources of confusion and inertia, and at the same time, retain necessary control techniques. In the fifth decade of Soviet rule, thousands of able administrators are available to the government. Full utilization of their talent requires that they be accorded greater confidence and trust. Experimental maneuvers designed to increase efficiency have been common; for example, the economic "decentralization" policy introduced in 1957 was an attempt to improve efficiency by relaxing some of the rigid control from the center, and Khrushchev's relaxation of Stalin's system of terror was intended, in part, to evoke initiative and to encourage all sections of the nation to participate in managing national and economic affairs. On the whole, the Soviet administrative system has, in spite of its expensiveness and complexity, served the regime well. On the credit side, from the Soviet point of view, administrators and workers alike have been kept subservient to the party, productivity has increased very substantially, standards of living have improved markedly, and the U.S.S.R. has emerged as one of the two greatest world powers.

Union and Autonomous Republics

As previously indicated, the U.S.S.R. is a federal union of fifteen Union Republics, some of which contain Autonomous Republics. The federal constitution states that each Union Republic may exercise state authority independently, except in those spheres of jurisdiction assigned specifically to the U.S.S.R. The high degree of centralized control maintained by both the party and the central organs of the state limits very considerably the constitutionally guaranteed sovereignty of the Union Republics. Each Union and Autonomous Republic has its own constitution which must conform to the Constitution of the U.S.S.R. The major governmental organs of each republic are a Supreme Soviet, a Presidium of the Supreme Soviet, and a Council of Ministers, all of which are very similar to the corresponding organs of the federal government.

The essential structural difference between the Supreme Soviet of the U.S.S.R. and the Supreme Soviets of the Union and Autonomous Republics is that the former is bicameral, while the latter are unicameral. Soviet authorities[40] state that even multinational Union Republics, such as the R.S.F.S.R., have no need for two chambers in the Supreme Soviet, since the specific interests of all nationalities are represented in the Soviet of Nationalities of the Supreme Soviet of the U.S.S.R. In the multinational states (R.S.F.S.R., and the Azerbaidzhanian, Georgian, and Ukrainian S.S.R.'s), each Autonomous Republic is represented by a vice-chairman of the Presidium of the Supreme Soviet of the Union Republic. Each republic establishes the rate of representation and the numerical composition of its own Supreme Soviet. Supreme Soviets vary in size from more than eight hundred deputies in the R.S.F.S.R. to less than two hundred deputies in the Estonian S.S.R. Rates of representation in the Union Republics vary from one deputy per 150,000 of the population in the R.S.F.S.R. to one deputy per 5,000 of the population in the Kirghiz, Tadzhik, Armenian and Turkmen S.S.R.'s. Representation in the Autonomous Republics vary within the range of one deputy per 4,000 to 20,000 of the population. The Supreme Soviets of the Union and Autonomous Republics, like the Supreme Soviet of the U.S.S.R., are elected for a four-year term, convene regularly twice a year, may be convened for an extraordinary session under certain circumstances, require a simple majority for the approval of legislation, and elect Credential, Foreign Affairs, Budgetary and Legislative Commissions. Most Supreme Soviets elect commissions for industry and transport, agriculture, public education and culture, public health and social security, and other matters. The standing commissions have the legal, if not the actual, right to oversee or check into the activities of all organs of administration within the republic which are subordinate to the Supreme Soviet.

The Supreme Soviet of a Union or Autonomous Republic, as the "highest organ of state power" within the republic, has powers which correspond to those of the U.S.S.R. Supreme Soviet, except that the sphere of jurisdiction is more limited. Each Supreme Soviet is entitled to elect its own Presidium; to adopt and amend its own constitution, subject to the approval of the superior Supreme Soviet; to approve the state economic plan and budget, and to determine state and local taxes and fees in harmony with All-Union legislation; to form economic administrative areas; to exercise the right of amnesty and pardon; and to form the republican Council of Ministers and elect the republican Supreme Court. Union Republics also have certain nominal rights with respect to secession from the U.S.S.R., the organization of military formations and participation in foreign Affairs. Union Republic organs supervise the activities of the Autonomous Republic organs, confirm the constitutions of the Autonomous Republics, define the boundaries of their territories, and suspend decisions and orders which are illegal or ill-advised. Supreme Soviets at both levels can amend or annul orders of subordinate local governments. Although the jurisdiction of the Supreme Soviets of the Union and Autonomous Republics has been extended gradually in recent years, they still do not function as decisive policy-making organs. Their brief sessions are used to confirm earlier decrees of their Presidia and to listen to reports from officials of the party and the Council of Ministers on topics such as the state economic plan and budget, budgets for the local governments, road construction, educational reform and forestry conservations. Like the national Supreme Soviet, the Supreme Soviets of the republics serve primarily as simple ratifying instruments for plans and policies of the C.P.S.U. and the national governmental leadership. Decisions made by the republican party leaders and the Council of Ministers with respect to internal matters are also submitted to the Supreme Soviets of the republics for automatic ratification.

Decisions which the republican governments are entitled to make are made primarily by the Presidium of the Supreme Soviet and by the republican Council of Ministers. The structure of the republican Council of Ministers resembles that of the national Council. Each Council is composed of a Chairman, vice chairmen, ministers, and the chairmen of state committees, such as the Council of the National Economy, the State Planning Committee, and the Party-State Control Committee. Usually the Chairman of the Council of Ministers recommends that the chairmen of the Economic Councils be included in the Council of Ministers with ministerial rank. Each Council is guided and directed by an "inner bureau" composed of the Chairman, vice-chairmen, and selected leading members of the Council. The Council is appointed by the Supreme Soviet on the recommendation of the Chairman of the Council, who is selected by the party. It is, in theory, accountable to the Supreme Soviet and its Presidium.

Ministries of the Union and Autonomous Republics are of two types: Union-Republican Ministries and Republican Ministries. All republics have Union-Republican Ministries to correspond to the Union-Republican Ministries of the national government (Higher and Secondary Education, Public Health, Culture, Foreign Affairs, Defense, Communications, Finance and Agriculture). These ministries are simultaneously responsible to the Council of Ministers of the given republic and to the corresponding ministry at the national level. Within the republic they direct the branches of state administration entrusted to them, with the exception of a limited number of undertakings which are directed unilaterally by the corresponding U.S.S.R. Ministry. Republican Ministries exist only in the Union and Autonomous Republics and do not have corresponding organs in the central government. These ministries direct branches of state administration within the republic under the supervision of the Council of Ministers. Republican Ministries in Autonomous Republics are also subordinate to the corresponding ministry in the Union Republic. The system of Republican Ministries varies between republics on the basis of economic, geographical, geological and other factors. Most republics have a Republican Ministry for Automobile Transport and Highways, Municipal Economy, Defense of Public Order, Local Industry, Trade, Education, Social Security and Construction. Some republics have ministries for Irrigation, Inland Water Transportation or Oil Industry. Almost all state committees and boards which are established by the central government have counterpart units in the republics. Thus each republic has a Council for the National Economy, a State Planning Committee, a State Procurement Committee, a Party-State Control Committee and Committees for Food Industry, Fisheries, Metallurgy, etc. Each of these committees is responsible to the corresponding committee in the national government as well as to the Council of Ministers of the republic.

The rights and duties of the Council of Ministers of a republic parallel those of the U.S.S.R. with the additional stipulation that all decisions of the Council of a republic must be in harmony with the laws and decrees of the U.S.S.R. Supreme Soviet, Presidium and Council of Ministers. The Council of the republic is constitutionally entitled to: coordinate and direct the work of the ministries and other institutions under its jurisdiction; coordinate and supervise the work of representatives of All-Union Ministries; adopt measures to implement the national economic plan and the state and local budgets; adopt measures to maintain public order; direct and supervise the work of the Council of Ministers of Autonomous Republics and the Executive Committees of subordinate Soviets; give guidance regarding the relations of the republic with foreign states within the framework of the general rules specified by the U.S.S.R.; direct the organization of military formations of the republic; and establish special committees for economic and cultural affairs. Almost all of these functions are materialized, except that no Union Republic has its own military formation, and the relations of Union Republics with foreign states are determined almost exclusively by the party which acts through the central government.

Since 1954 there has been a marked trend toward extending the jurisdiction of the Union Republics in governmental, economic and cultural spheres. Beginning in 1954 the judicial powers of the Union Republics were extended to include organization of the courts and legislation over a number of important matters, including civil, criminal and labor laws. In 1955 the governments of the Union Republics were granted considerably increased jurisdiction over planning, investment, budgeting, organization of wages and guidance of agriculture and other branches of the national economy. Several All-Union Ministries were transformed into Union-Republican Ministries and a number of industries and enterprises were transferred from All-Union to Union-Republic jurisdiction in 1956. Included in this transfer were the food, meat and milk, fish, pulp and paper, and textile industries; materials for construction; automobile transportation; riverboats; and health. The Union Republics were also authorized to transfer raw materials, buildings, equipment and transportation facilities from one ministry or organization of the republic to another. In 1957 the Union Republics were given jurisdiction over all questions concerned with approval of specifications, technological conditions, standards and retail prices for foodstuffs and industrial consumer goods produced for retail by enterprises supervised by Union-Republican Ministries. One of the most significant transfers of jurisdiction to the Union Republics occurred in May, 1957, when the U.S.S.R. was divided into economic regions, each of which is headed by an Economic Council which is directly subordinate to the government of the appropriate Union Republic. Direction of the Economic Councils by the U.S.S.R. Council of Ministers is exclusively through the Council of Ministers of the Union Republics. The Economic Councils supervise all economic organs and enterprises within their jurisdiction, including much of the heavy industry which was previously guided centrally by All-Union Ministries; they prepare current and long-term plans for the development of the economy of the economic region in conformity with the economic plan for the state as a whole. Additional, less dramatic, transfers of jurisdiction have occurred during the intervening years. In 1965 leading officials of some of the Union Republics recommended that the Union Republics be allowed to make major budgetary adjustments within the period of a plan, including the transfer of large sums of money from one organizational unit to another. Currently the governments of the republics supervise all local governments, and are responsible for planning and administering most of the industry and agriculture within their boundaries. The republics also have a significant measure of authority over primary and intermediate education, social security, health, housing, road construction and maintenance, transportation, local communications and a number of cultural activities and organizations.

Despite the authority and rather broad functions of the republican organs, the republics are required to operate within the legislative, budgetary, planning and political framework imposed upon them by the central government, and are absolutely obliged to adhere to the policies and instructions of the central and republican organs of the party. The republican governments do, however, possess a significant and increasing degree of administrative authority, although they are not entitled to make policy decisions of consequence. Even the party leaders do not claim that the powers of the republican governments were extended because of a genuine desire to increase their independence and thereby, to materialize some of the democratic rights which are given such a prominent place in communist ideology. The primary reason for the extensive reorganization and transfer of jurisdiction was to improve production efficiency. By reducing some of the links in the administrative chain, it was possible to decrease delays in securing approval for necessary modifications, to take into account national and local differences and to utilize local initiative and local resources more efficiently. Control by the party has, however, in no way been diminished. Party directives are equally binding whether issued to the government of the U.S.S.R. or the government of a Union Republic. Under Khrushchev's leadership the leading role of the party remained unchanged, but opportunities for the use of local initiative and experimentation were increased. Although Soviet theorists assert that the decentralization of jurisdiction represents a marked increase in practice of self-government, what has actually happened is that Union and Autonomous Republics have been granted significantly more administrative authority without concurrent increases in the crucial ingredients of self-government.

Local Organs of State Power

LOCAL SOVIETS

The Constitution provides that Soviets of Working People's Deputies, elected for a term of two years, shall be the organs of state power in the Territories, Regions, Autonomous Regions, Areas, Districts, cities and rural localities (Articles 94 and 95). These Soviets direct the work of the organs of administration subordinate to them, ensure the maintenance of public order, the observance of the laws and the protection of the rights of citizens, direct local, economic and cultural affairs and draw up the local budgets (Article 97). Local Soviets are empowered to adopt decisions and issue orders within the limits of the powers vested in them by the laws of the U.S.S.R. and of the Union Republics (Article 98). The executive and administrative organ of a local Soviet is the Executive Committee elected by it, consisting of a chairman, vice-chairmen, a secretary and members, except in the case of very small localities where executive and administrative functions are performed by the chairman, vice-chairman and secretary (Articles 99 and 100). The executive organ of a local Soviet is directly accountable both to the Soviet which elected it and to the executive organ of the superior Soviet (Article 101).

Since the system of local Soviets has been created in harmony with the administrative-territorial division of the Union Republic, there are some differences between Union Republics. The R.S.F.S.R., the largest Union Republic both in territory and population, has all types of administrative-territorial units and hence all types of Soviets: Territorial, Regional, Autonomous Regions, National Areas, Districts, City and Village Soviets. Some of the small republics have only District, City and Village Soviets. The mutual subordination and superiority of individual Soviets depends on the size and population of the territory and also on political, national or economic factors. For example, nationality factors may be the prime consideration in determining whether the Soviet of an Autonomous Region will be subordinated to the Soviet of the territory of which it is a component unit or to the Supreme Soviet of the Autonomous or Union Republic. Because of their economic importance the Soviets of major cities, such as Moscow, Leningrad, Kiev and Sevastopol are subordinated to a Territorial or Regional Soviet or even directly to the Supreme Soviet of the Union Republic. District Soviets are created within some large cities to improve the administration of the local communal economy, or because of other concrete political or economic factors; the structure and competence of these District Soviets within a city correspond more closely to the Soviets of smaller cities than to the District Soviets of rural territories. Apart from deviations such as these, the most common hierarchical arrangement of the local Soviets is as follows: the highest Soviets within the system of local Soviets are the Territorial and Regional Soviets and the City Soviets which are directly subordinate to the Supreme Soviet of the Union Republic. At the next level are the District Soviets and the City Soviets which are subordinate to Regional or Territorial Soviets. At the lowest level are City, Village and Settlement Soviets subordinate to the District Soviets.

The Union and Autonomous Republics approve the Regulations Governing Elections to Local Soviets which establish the numerical composition of the local Soviets. In 1959 the following norms were established: Village and Settlement Soviets from 20 to 50 deputies (instead of the previous 15-35); District Soviets from 40 to 80 deputies (previously 35-60); City and City District Soviets at least 50 (previously 35); Soviets of National Areas from 40 to 80 deputies (previously 35-60); and Territorial and Regional Soviets from 100 to 300 (previously at least 70). Election districts and representational norms are established within this general framework, e.g., one deputy may be elected to Territorial Soviets for every 11,-000-15,000 citizens; to District Soviets for every 1,000 citizens (but not to exceed 80 deputies), etc. In 1963 more than 1,958,000 deputies were elected to the local Soviets.

Territorial Soviets are established only in the largest Union Republics (the R.S.F.S.R., and the Ukrainian, Belorussian, Uzbek, Kazakh, Kirghiz, Tadzhik and Turkman S.S.R.'s). Regional Soviets exist only in the R.S.F.S.R. The Territorial (Regional) Soviets administer territories which in area, population and economic output may be superior to many Western and Central European countries. Since it would be impossible to provide detailed guidance and supervision from one territorial center, the activity of the Territorial (Regional) Soviets has the character of overall guidance. The transfer of enterprises and organizations from All-Union to republican supervision was followed by a transfer from republican to local supervision, and within the local Soviets from Territorial to District and City supervision. Generally, the Territorial Soviet supervises all but the most important enterprises and establishments indirectly through subordinate District and City Soviets.

The May, 1957, decentralizing reorganization placed most industrial and construction enterprises under the jurisdiction of either a Union Republic or a local Soviet. The majority of enterprises subordinated to a Union Republic were placed under the supervision of an Economic Council. Since the Economic Council and the Soviet (particularly at the Territorial or Regional level) supervise enterprises within the same territorial unit, some mutual working relationships have been established. For example, the planning agencies of the Soviet and the Economic Council cooperate in preparing economic plans. Leading workers of the Economic Council participate in the meetings of a Territorial (Regional) Soviet and deputies and members of the Executive Committee of the Soviet participate in the work of the technical-economic units of the Economic Council. The Council of Ministers of the Union Republic or the Economic Council, itself, may authorize deputies of the Soviet to participate in the supervision of enterprises subordinate to the Economic Council. This supervision may include socio-cultural services, the protection of public order, the observance of laws, and the rights of workers and employees, but does not extend to basic production activity. Representatives of the local Soviet have the right to report shortcomings to either the Economic Council or the Council of Ministers of the Union Republic, which may use disciplinary or other techniques to remedy the situation. Previously it was necessary to report infractions directly to the ministries in Moscow, but this was deemed unsatisfactory for a number of reasons.

Territorial (Regional) and City Soviets which are subordinated directly to the Supreme Soviet of a Union Republic generally guide the activity of Soviets subordinate to them, especially the District Soviets and the District Soviets within cities. In general, Territorial (Regional) Soviets assume responsibility for somewhat broader problems than City Soviets, since in addition to providing guidance for industry, construction, business and cultural establishments, they also have organs for the guidance of agriculture, which City Soviets do not have. Soviets of Autonomous Regions and National Areas have approximately the same competence as Regional or District Soviets, in addition to some special rights stemming from the national character of their population.

City Soviets may be, according to their importance, subordinated to the highest Soviet of a Union or Autonomous Republic or the Soviet of a Territory, Region, District, Autonomous Region or National Area. As a rule, only cities with more than 100,000 inhabitants may be subdivided into District Soviets. The jurisdiction of a City District Soviet varies somewhat from one city to another. In general, City Soviets direct city transportation, water supply, sewerage, electricity and other enterprises and organizations of importance to the entire city and supervise educational, medical and cultural institutions. City District Soviets may exercise more specific supervision over these enterprises, and in addition, supervise other institutions which are entirely within their borders. Recently, the jurisdiction of the City and City District Soviets has been expanded in the spheres of education, health, social security and culture.

District Soviets serve as the major governmental administrative unit in areas which are primarily rural. Currently districts are being enlarged in an attempt to simplify the administrative machinery on an All-Union basis. District Soviets supervise the Soviets of small cities, villages and settlements, provide direct guidance for local industry and socio-cultural affairs within the district, and perform important functions with reference to the supervision of agriculture. Direct guidance of the kolkhozes (collective farms) was transferred to the District and Village Soviets and their organs when the Machine and Tractor Stations (MTS) were abolished in 1958. To implement the work of the District Soviet as the basic link of guidance over kolkhoz agriculture, two new organs were created under the Executive Committee of the District Soviet: the District Agricultural Inspection Commission and the Production-Technical Council. These organs are dually subordinated to the District Soviet and its Executive Committee, and to the Territorial (Regional) Agricultural Administration, or to the Ministry of Agriculture in republics not subdivided into Territories and Regions.

The District Agricultural Inspection Commission is led by a deputy chairman of the Executive Committee of the District Soviet. Its members are agricultural specialists, including agronomists, botanists, zoologists and accountants. Among its functions are: propaganda; the introduction of the most advanced agricultural techniques; the organization of seed selection, insemination and veterinary services; land conservation; supervision of the control of pests and diseases; and guidance in accounting methods. It has the right to inspect kolkhozes, sovkhozes (state farms), Repair Technical Stations (R.T.S.), and Maintenance and Service Stations (M.S.S.), and may submit proposals for the removal of shortcomings to the leaders of these organs and to the Executive Committee of the District Soviet. Although the Agricultural Inspection Commission relies heavily on organizational mass work and recommendations, its directives with regard to agro-techniques, zoo-techniques and seeds are obligatory for all kolkhozes and sovkhozes.

The Production-Technical Council prepares current and perspective plans for the development of agriculture in the District, and is supposed to foster adoption of advanced agricultural techniques. Yearly planned tasks are fixed for the kolkhozes according to the needs of the state, and on the basis of the general directive, each kolkhoz works out its own plan taking into account local conditions. This plan is then studied by the District Soviet and its Executive Committee, and if it does not correspond with the obligations of the kolkhoz to the state, it is returned for revision. Membership in the Production Technical Council is numerically large, often from sixty to one hundred members, including the leader of the District Agricultural Inspection Commission, chairmen of kolkhozes, agricultural specialists and even rank-and-file workers. The Production-Technical Council does not have administrative authority, but its proposals with respect to planning and technical improvements may be enforced by the District Soviet and the Agricultural Inspection Commission.

Village Soviets and Soviets of Settlements, along with those City Soviets that are subordinated to District Soviets, are the lowest link in the system of local Soviets. Village Soviets may be known as Soviets of stanitsas, hamlets, kishlaks, auls, etc. Because they are the most numerous and the closest to the people, the Village Soviets constitute a vital part of state administration in the U.S.S.R. Since 1954 there has been a trend toward the enlargement of the Village Soviet. Previously, a single kolkhoz, sovkhoz or consumer cooperative may have been supervised by and required to report to several Soviets. Unnecessary apparatus and other shortcomings were reduced by the enlargement of the Village Soviets. Previous to this change, the administrative organ of the Village Soviet was the chairman, his deputy and the secretary. Currently most Village Soviets form an Executive Committee. The authority of Village Soviets has been expanded with their enlargement. Village Soviets are entitled to: assist in the preparation of kolkhoz production plans and submit opinions to the Executive Committee of the District Soviet; supervise the fulfillment of regulations by the agricultural artel and rescind the decisions of the artel if these do not conform with law (such action must be reported immediately to the District Executive Committee); approve the leading officials of village schools, health institutions and cultural establishments; approve plans for the construction of socio-cultural establishments; supervise the work of the District Plenipotentiary of Militia on their territory; approve the local budget, and if revenues exceed expenditures, rule on the use of the excess funds. The Executive Committee of the Village Soviet is required, on occasion, to call a meeting of the entire population of the village to discuss problems important to the village as a whole, as well as problems of district, regional or even state importance.

A Settlement Soviet is established in workers' settlements or health centers where the majority of the population is engaged in industrial, socio-cultural or medical work rather than in agriculture. The activity of the Settlement Soviet corresponds more closely to that of a City Soviet than to a Village Soviet. Thus, for example, the Settlement Soviet may deal with relatively large funds for the construction of apartment houses. In Village Soviets this does not happen because the majority of dwelling places are owned by the kolkhozes or by private individuals. Moreover, the state taxes and fees which are handled by the Settlement Soviet compare to those of a City Soviet rather than to the Village Soviet.

SESSIONS

Meetings or sessions of the local Soviets correspond to Supreme Soviet sessions at higher levels of state structure. Meetings, to be attended by all deputies, must be called by the Executive Committee of the Soviet a specified number of times per year. In most Union Republics, Territorial (Regional) Soviets must meet at least four times per year; City Soviets, City District Soviets, District Soviets and Village Soviets, at least six times per year; and City Soviets in cities with district divisions, at least four times per year. Extraordinary meetings may be called on the initiative of the Executive Committee, the Executive Committee of a superior Soviet, or on the request of one third of the deputies of the given Soviet. Certain topics or problems which are under the exclusive jurisdiction of the Soviet, and, therefore, cannot be dealt with by its Executive Committee, must be brought before the entire Soviet in a general meeting. Included among these are: approval of the local budget and economic plan; verification of the mandate of deputies; election of the executive organs of the Soviet; creation of standing commissions; the establishment of a new department under the Executive Committee, and approval of its leaders; election of courts within the jurisdiction of the Soviet; and annulment or modifications of the decisions of a lower Soviet.

Soviet authorities[41] refer to the sessions of the local Soviets as a profound expression of truly democratic methods, since wide sections of the public are encouraged to participate actively in preparation for the sessions and in the work of the local Soviets. The expression of criticism and self-criticism permitted by this participation is described as an effective technique to counteract red tape and the conceit sometimes found among state officials. The Executive Committee, standing commissions and deputies most involved in the specific economic or cultural problems under consideration assume primary responsibility for the preparation for the meeting, but heads of institutions, kolkhoz chairmen or even workers and peasants may be permitted to participate. The Executive Committee is required to inform all deputies, and in the case of Village Soviets, sometimes all inhabitants of the village, of the date, place and program of the meeting a specified number of days (usually five or ten) ahead of time. Deputies of higher Soviets may participate in the meetings of lower Soviets in an advisory capacity. Representatives of state offices, enterprises, cooperatives, social organizations, military units, workers and members of a kolkhoz may be invited to participate or, on their own initiative, may obtain permission to do so. All persons who attend may participate in the discussion, but in order to maintain the working character of the Soviet, the chairman recognizes a deputy in preference to a non-deputy. Only deputies have the right to vote. Recently local Soviets have been encouraged to vary their meeting place with reference to the major topic to be discussed at the meeting, e.g., to meet at a kolkhoz to discuss agricultural production or at a hospital to discuss health problems. This innovation is designed to improve the practical, as well as the theoretical, correctness of decisions, to give the electorate a better chance to acquaint itself with the activities of the Soviet and to improve the supervision of the Soviet by the electorate.

Criticisms of the functionings of the local Soviets appear frequently in the press.[42] Often mentioned is a tendency for the Soviet to delegate to its Executive Committee prerogatives which should be exercised by the representative organ itself; apparently, many important problems involving the work of economic, cultural and other agencies which should be resolved at sessions of the Soviets are considered only by Executive Committees. Often Soviets give only superficial consideration to major problems and hence, subordinate administrative agencies are given only very general and vague guidelines. In translating these general guidelines into concrete operation, minor administrative officials sometimes introduce major policy changes concerning matters that should be decided by the representative organs. The failure of Executive Committees to convene sessions at the proper time is a common complaint. Also, the preparation for meetings is frequently inadequate, and the deputies and population are not always familiarized with proposed decisions. The proposals of deputies are sometimes totally disregarded. Many local Soviets fail to comply with the provisions for extensive public participation, and bureaucratic methods have by no means been eradicated. Soviet authorities also point out that interference by higher administrative agencies, including superior Soviets, ministries and departments, has a detrimental effect on the work of local Soviets.

STANDING COMMISSIONS

Corresponding to the standing commissions of a Supreme Soviet are the standing commissions of a local Soviet. As a rule, local Soviets establish commissions to deal with local industry, municipal economy and services; road building and communications; agriculture and agricultural procurements; public health, education, culture and recreation; budgetary and financial questions; and trade. Whether commissions to cover all of these spheres of activity are formed, and whether others are added, depends on the size of the Soviet and other local conditions. The commissions, which serve primarily as consultant specialists to the Soviet, are not vested with administrative power. If they were given administrative rights, they would duplicate the functions of departments of the Executive Committee which deal with the same sphere of activity. Instead, the commissions exercise general supervision over the work of the corresponding departments of the Executive Committee; draw conclusions on questions to be considered by the local Soviet or submit questions to the Soviet or the Executive Committee on their own initiative; assist in verifying the execution of the decisions of the Soviet; ascertain the needs and requirements of the population, etc. Their main task is to ensure the successful fulfillment of the economic plans, to raise cultural and material standards, to organize effective control by the local Soviets over the work of bodies subordinate to them and to consolidate the ties of local organs of state power with the population.

The commissions are empowered to confer with, or receive consultation from, representatives of various organizations and experts in different branches of the administration, to request necessary information and documents from local organizations and institutions, and to demand explanations from responsible individuals concerning causes for the non-execution of decisions passed by the Soviet. With the approval of the Soviet or its Executive Committee, the recommendations of a commission may be enforced. In most republics the Executive Committee is required to consider the proposals of a standing commission within a specified time interval. Members of a standing commission are usually deputies, but some republics allow experts who are not members of the Soviet to be elected to a commission. In most republics a member of a commission cannot simultaneously be a member of the Executive Committee of the Soviet, and a deputy who heads a department of the Executive Committee may be a member of only those commissions which are not connected with the work of the department which he leads. These restrictions have been introduced because one of the functions of the commissions, as organs of the Soviet, is to supervise the activities of the Executive Committee and its departments. Standing commissions are not subject to dual subordination. They are organs only of the Soviet which elected them and are not subordinate to the Executive Committee of the Soviet or to the commission of the same name in a higher Soviet. However, close cooperation between the commissions of Soviets of different levels is encouraged.

The nature of the work of a standing commission varies with local conditions and other factors, including the initiative and energy of its members. A Commission for Public Education, for example, is expected to help enforce universal compulsory education, to assist in the organization of educational work, to suggest measures to improve education, including the provision of educational aides, to supervise the provision and maintenance of school buildings and equipment, and to take measures to expand the number of schools and children's establishments. A Commission for Local Industry is expected to render general assistance to local industry, including measures to ensure the fulfillment of plans, utilization of unused resources, reduction of production costs, increased quantity and quality of output, and the most parsimonious use of materials and equipment. It should also help to organize socialist competitions, conduct political, educational and cultural work at factories and introduce measures to improve the conditions of workers. Reports in the Soviet press indicate that some commissions perform their duties in an exemplary manner, but others seldom meet and pay only the most perfunctory attention to their assignments.

The Party Program envisages a gradual transfer to standing commissions of an increasing number of matters now within the competence of the departments and administrations of the Executive Committee. To effect this transition, Soviet experts are recommending a number of changes in the legal status of the commissions.[43] First, it is recommended that the commissions be given the right to adopt decisions of an obligatory nature on certain fundamental questions. Second, the chairman of a commission should, by virtue of his position, be a member of the Executive Committee. Third, the regulation which prohibits heads of departments from being members of the corresponding commission should be repealed. There is some evidence that the commissions, which now include more than three quarters of the deputies of the local Soviets, are expanding their activity in the field of government administration. For example, a number of local Soviets have established commissions to supervise corrective labor establishments. These commissions have the right to recommend reduced terms of imprisonment.

THE EXECUTIVE AND ADMINISTRATIVE ORGANS OF LOCAL SOVIETS

The executive and administrative organs of local Soviets—or the local organs of state administration—are the Executive Committees and their departments and administrations. The Executive Committee of the local Soviet is elected for a two-year term at the first session of a newly elected Soviet. Membership in an Executive Committee varies with the level of the Soviet, the number of deputies and relevant local conditions. As a general rule, the chairman is a local party functionary, and most of the members are full-time, paid officials of the local government, many of whom serve as heads or administrators of the departments and administrations which are responsible to the Executive Committee. An Executive Committee is directly responsible to the Soviet which elected it and also to the Executive Committee of the superior Soviet. Overall guidance is provided by the Council of Ministers of the Union Republic.

The Executive Committee of a local Soviet exercises guidance over all cultural, political and economic activities within its territories on the basis of decisions approved by the respective Soviet and higher state organs. According to the Regulations Governing Local Soviets, the Executive Committee also guarantees that, within its territory, all constitutional norms and all other legal decisions are adhered to by all organs and citizens; guides the activity of subordinate branches, administrations and enterprises, as well as the work of lower Soviets and their Executive Committees; organizes audiences of citizens and deals with their complaints and requests; calls and prepares the meetings of the Soviet; prepares for elections; and assists deputies and standing commissions in their organizational mass work.

The Executive Committee assumes responsibility for the preparation of the local annual and quarterly plans for economic and cultural development in conformity with the economic plans of the U.S.S.R., the Union Republic and higher Soviets. It is expected to introduce measures to ensure the fulfillment or overfulfillment of the plans. As a result of the decentralizing reorganization, the local organs of state administration exercise direct control over a number of local industrial, as well as agricultural, establishments. The Executive Committee of the local Soviet is empowered to direct the building and utilization of new houses, schools and other public buildings, the organization of public services, the building of roads, etc. It also administers libraries, museums, theaters and other cultural and educational establishments, directs schools and other children's establishments and organizes festivals and amateur performances. One of its most important duties, of course, is to organize and conduct mass political work to educate the people in the spirit of communism.

The Executive Committee is entitled, within the limits of the power vested in it, to adopt decisions and issue orders which are binding within the territory of the local Soviet. It may issue so-called binding decisions (an unfortunate choice of terms, since all normative acts of local Soviets and their Executive Committees are binding), the violators of which are subject to administrative punishment including a fine, not to exceed one hundred rubles, or corrective labor, not to exceed one month. Because binding decisions pertain to exceptional cases, such as natural catastrophies, epidemics or fishing in waters of local importance, their validity is automatically terminated after a specified interval, usually two years.

Departments and administrations of the local Soviet are established under the supervision of the Executive Committee to direct particular branches of state activity. The Constitution of each Union and Autonomous Republic establishes the system of departments and administrations to be established at each Soviet level. Therefore, there are slight variations between republics, and even within republics, on the basis of specific economic and political features. In the R.S.F.S.R. departments for public health, municipal services, public education, social security, finance and a general department and administrations for motor transport and highways, internal affairs, culture, local and fuel industry, building materials industry, trade and agriculture are established by the Executive Committees of Territorial and Regional Soviets. Additional departments or administrations may be established with the permission of the R.S.F.S.R. Council of Ministers. A Planning Commission and a Personnel Sector function under the chairman of the Executive Committee. In addition, branches of the All-Union committees are established by the Territorial and Regional Soviets. The administrative structure at the District Soviet level is somewhat simpler. In addition to the Personnel Sector, Planning Commission, Agricultural Inspection Commission and Production and Technical Council, the following departments are established: motor transport and highways, public education, culture, militia, public health, social security, trade and finance. With the permission of the superior Soviet, administrations may be established for local industry, commerce, communal economy or to take into account specific local peculiarities. City Soviets usually include departments for health, culture, public education, social security, commerce, finance, administration, militia and a plant commission. Village Soviets have no departments or administrations. Village administrators, selected from the working people for three-month periods, assist the Executive Committee.

The departments and administrations of the Executive Committee are subordinate to the Executive Committee, the local Soviet and to the corresponding department or administration of the superior Soviet. The heads of the departments and administrations are supposed to be nominated by the local Soviet. In the intervals between sessions of the local Soviet, changes in personnel may be made by the Executive Committee, subject to subsequent confirmation by the Soviet. Appointment to the most important positions may require confirmation by the relevant minister. The heads of departments and administrations need not be deputies of the Soviet, since these officials are not involved in overall policy formation. Soviet authorities complain that, too frequently, Soviets give purely formal approval to members of the Executive Committees and department chiefs without giving adequate consideration to the qualifications of the candidates.[44]

The powers exercised by each department or administration within its branch of state activity are extensive. For example, the administration for local and fuel industry exercises technical control and guidance over all organizations subordinate to it; submits to the Executive Committee plans for quality and quantity of output, finances and capital construction; makes assignments regarding production and construction and attempts to ensure the fulfillment of production plans. The administration is expected to promote local initiative, to introduce advanced methods of production, to improve the organization of labor and wages, to upgrade the technical skills of the workers and to promote overall productivity and efficiency. A general department which operates under the Executive Committee takes care of matters that do not fall directly under the jurisdiction of any other department or administration, organizes audiences for citizens and arranges that appropriate action be taken with respect to complaints and requests.

The local Soviets are encouraged to draw the broad masses of the people into public activity. Street and block committees, parents' committees in the schools and other groups are formed to give local organs of state power practical assistance in carrying out their political, economic and cultural tasks. A street committee, which usually has five to seven members, is elected for one to two years by open public vote by the residents of the street. Its composition must be approved by the Executive Committee under the direction of which it operates. Such committees have no administrative rights. They assist the local Soviet in a variety of ways, such as participating in public beautification campaigns, caring for parks, and reporting shortcomings or introducing improvements in children's establishments. In the Ukraine alone 2,625,000 volunteers are said to be involved in the activities of the local Soviets. In some Districts in the Kazakh S.S.R., the departments of education, public health, road building, trade and urban services have been turned over to the public; volunteer organizations, in cooperation with the standing commissions of the local Soviets, reportedly supervise the corresponding branches of the administration.[45]

Local Soviets are considered to be "schools of state administration for millions of workers and peasants,"[46] and one of the most effective devices for engaging the masses in the service of the party and the state. Certainly, when heads are counted, mass participation is impressive, since millions of people serve as deputies or as members of committees attached to the local Soviets. Thus the leadership is able to point to evidence in support of the claim that the regime is popularly based. To many Soviet citizens participation in state affairs, however nominal, may be a source of pride and satisfaction and may serve to heighten their allegiance to the party which in reality governs them. On the other hand, although the party does not permit the masses or their elected representatives to make decisions of importance, it gains substantially from their activities, since their participation greatly facilitates realization of the party program.

Although a broad range of functions has been delegated to the local Soviets, their independence is very much more restricted than Soviet sources indicate. Either the local party organization or a superior Soviet may rescind or modify the decisions of a lower Soviet. To facilitate this, local party leaders invariably hold important positions in the Soviets. Moreover, local Soviets lack financial autonomy, since budgetary matters are largely controlled by the central authorities. However, since the party leadership and the central government cannot assume responsibility for every contingency, a limited amount of autonomy must necessarily be awarded to the local Soviets.

Official criticism of the activities of local Soviets run the gamut of infringements, laxness and violations: elections and meetings are not always scheduled in accordance with regulations; the public is not encouraged to participate in the affairs of the Soviet, and is not informed of its activities; the economic and cultural functions of the Soviet are performed poorly; Soviet sessions are stereotyped rituals, dominated by the Executive Committee; illegal alliances are formed between members of the Executive Committee and officials of the local party organization or plant managers to cover up shortcomings; and so forth. Nevertheless, the local Soviets serve the regime reasonably well in three extremely important ways. First, they are convenient tools to implement the economic and cultural policy of the party in local areas, industries and enterprises; second, they encourage utilization of local initiative along lines established by the party and the central government; third, the local Soviets provide an opportunity for millions of citizens to participate in governmental activities and consequently to admire and support the party that provides such rights.

Addendum: Changes in the Council of Ministers of the U.S.S.R. and the Union Republics

It has been stated previously that Soviet leaders have a penchant for reorganization. During the interval between the completion of this chapter and its publication, a major reorganization of the Council of Ministers of the U.S.S.R. with corresponding changes in the Councils of Ministers of the Union Republics has been initiated. These changes, which were first announced by Kosygin in an address to the Plenary Session of the Central Committee of the C.P.S.U. in September, 1965,[47] are, at time of writing, still in the process of being introduced. Kosygin announced that in order to improve the management of industry, the branch form of industrial management would be substituted for an organization based on the territorial-production principle. Accordingly, a large number of industrial ministries have been established, many industrial committees have been transformed into industrial ministries, committees have been added and deleted, and in some cases, the lines of responsibility within the Council of Ministers have been changed.

Included among the changes are: (1) The establishment of the following All-Union Ministries: Heavy, Power and Transport Machine Building; Machine and Tool Industry; Machine Building for Construction, Road Building and Civil Engineering; Tractor and Farm Machine Building; Motor Vehicle Industry; Chemical and Petroleum Machine Building; Electrical Equipment Industry; Instrument Making, Means of Automation and Control Systems; Machine Building for Light Industry and the Food Industry and Household Appliances; and General Machine Building. Kosygin stated that the machine building industries are being brought under All-Union control because of need for uniform technical guidance, the standardization of designs and the unification of parts and units of the machines within the branch as a whole. (2) State committees have been transformed into All-Union Ministries for Gas Industry; Transport Construction; Aviation Industry; Defense Industry; Radio Industry; Shipbuilding Industry; Electronics Industry; and Medium Machine Building. (3) Newly formed Union-Republican Ministries include: Ferrous Metallurgy; Non-Ferrous Metallurgy; Coal Industry; Chemical Industry; Petroleum Extracting Industry; Petroleum-Refining and Petrochemical Industry; Lumber, Pulp-and-Paper and Wood-Processing Industry; Building Materials Industry; Light Industry; Food Industry; and Meat and Dairy Industry. (4) Formerly operative state committees have been transformed into Union-Republican Ministries for: the Fish Industry; Geology; Installation and Special Construction Work; Trade; Irrigated Farming and Water Resources. (5) A major new organ called the U.S.S.R. Council of Ministers' State Committee for Material and Technical Supply has been established. This committee is responsible for the organization of material and technical supplies. (6) A number of organs are to be abolished including the U.S.S.R. Supreme Council of the National Economy, the U.S.S.R. Council of the National Economy, state committees for the branches of industry, the Councils of the National Economy of the Union Republics, and Committees for Co-ordinating Scientific Research. Also to be abolished are the Economic Councils of the economic regions, but these Councils are to continue their responsibilities until all industries are placed under ministerial control. (7) The Party-State Control Committee has been transformed into People's Control Committee.[48] (8) The Union Republics have reorganized their committees and Ministries to correspond with those established at the All-Union level. In addition, each Union Republic has established a number of Republican Ministries, in most cases by transforming state committees into Ministries. Newly established Republican Ministries in the R.S.F.S.R. include: Grain Products and Mixed Fodder Industry; Fuel Industry; Local Industry; and Everyday Services to the Population.

After the 1965 reorganization, members of the U.S.S.R. Council of Ministers include: the chairman, first vice-chairmen, and vice-chairmen; the chairmen of the Councils of Ministers of the Union Republics; the U.S.S.R. Ministers; and the chairmen of major U.S.S.R. committees and boards such as for State Planning, Construction, Material and Technical Supply, People's Control, Labor and Wages, Science and Technology, Vocational-Technical Education, Procurement, Foreign Economic Relations, State Security, the State Farm Machinery Association, the State Bank, and the Central Statistical Administration.[49] Since the major purpose of the reorganization was to improve industrial planning and management, its implications will be discussed in the chapter on economy rather than at this point.

Impact on the Individual and Society

The provisions of the Constitution of the U.S.S.R. and other legal documents which describe Soviet governmental practices suggest that the Soviet people enjoy opportunities for self-government equal to the opportunities available in the most advanced democratic countries. The involvement, and it might be said, the typically enthusiastic involvement of millions of Soviet citizens in one aspect or another of governmental activities, heightens the illusion that Soviet people enjoy a significant measure of self-government. However, the actual involvement of Soviet citizens in the development of governmental policy is extremely minimal. Although they go through the forms and motions of governing themselves, Soviet citizens are ruled by the Communist Party of the Soviet Union. Governmental organs at all levels are tools of the leaders of the C.P.S.U., who make all crucial policy decisions. The elected organs of the people are, according to the Constitution, entitled to establish the law of the land, but the decisions which these elected organs make are exactly the decisions which they are instructed to make by the party leaders. The party leaders who make the decisions are not elected by the people, responsible to the people, cannot be removed from power by the people, and the people have never been given the opportunity to assign policy-making powers to them. Since the decision-making power is withheld from the elected representatives of the people, there can be no significant measure of self-government.

Although the Soviet people and their elected representatives are denied the right to select and establish major policies, they are permitted and encouraged to participate actively in the administration of the policies which have been imposed upon them by the party leaders. Governmental organs are convenient instruments through which party policy decisions are given legal sanction and translated into action. In a sense, the governmental organs serve primarily as administrative agencies for the party; the party decides what is to be done, the popular assemblies approve the decisions of the party leaders, and the executive and administrative organs of the government implement the decisions. Hundreds of thousands of Soviet citizens "participate in governmental activities" as deputies to the Soviets, officials of the governmental agencies and volunteer assistants. Their participation, however, almost exclusively involves implementing directives which have originated with the party leaders. No popular assembly, not even the Supreme Soviet of the U.S.S.R., could dare to vote against the policy decisions of the Presidium of the Central Committee.

From the Western point of view, it may seem outrageous that the foreign and domestic policy of a huge and populous nation like the U.S.S.R. should be made almost exclusively by a handful of top party leaders who are not, by any stretch of the imagination, elected representatives of the people. From the point of view of most Soviet citizens, the situation may not appear to be so intolerable. In the first place, the party leaders are, in terms of their own long-range goals, committed to serve the interests of the people of the U.S.S.R. They need the support of the people; they would be in serious trouble if they made decisions which would be basically and irrevocably detrimental to the welfare of the people, not because the people would be in a position to rid themselves of party domination, but because economic productivity would decrease and progress toward the ultimate communist utopia peopled by the "new Soviet man" would be impeded. Consequently, the party leaders must take into account the needs and aspirations of the people, about which they are reasonably well-informed, when they make the policy decisions. In many cases the decisions which the party leaders make may not differ appreciably from those which the elected representatives of the people would make, themselves, were they accorded decision-making authority. When the party leaders make decisions which do not correspond to the immediate desires and aspirations of the people (and it should be noted that popular assemblies in democratic nations also find it expedient on occasion to approve an unpopular measure, such as a tax increase), explanations and propaganda are used with skill in an attempt to convince the people that the decision was made to serve their own ultimate good. Moreover, potentially unpopular decisions are almost always introduced through the Supreme Soviet of the U.S.S.R., or if the decision pertains to a local matter, through one of the lower Soviets, to convey the impression that the decision was made, or at least approved, by the elected representatives of the people. Second, although the popular assemblies do not make the important policy decisions, members of the assemblies and officials of organs and agencies subordinate to the popular assemblies, do provide much of the information on which the decisions are based. Party leaders must necessarily pay attention to the findings and recommendations of the standing commissions of the Soviets, to informal reports from deputies who are in close contact with the people and to officials of governmental agencies who are responsible for administering the policy established by the party. If they did not make use of such information, as well as information which seeps up through the party channels, they would run the risk of making an excessive number of ill-advised decisions. Third, the party has found it expedient to grant increasing amounts of administrative authority to the organs of state power, and particularly in the last decade, to the local organs. State and governmental officials at all levels command a considerable amount of administrative authority and, within the guidelines established by the party, are able to make decisions which affect their fellow citizens in fairly important ways. The majority of Soviet citizens probably either accept or are more or less resigned to the fact that they will have to live out their days in a party-dominated society in which private enterprise is barred. The majority of these people probably accept what appears to be inevitable and concern themselves relatively little about techniques to change the overall structure of society, except along party-directed lines. Rather, it is likely that they are concerned with matters of more immediate and practical relevance, such as the location of a proposed highway or hospital, the extension of school facilities, so that their children will not have to attend school in the evening shift and provision for more adequate housing or recreational facilities. Since matters of this nature are, at least in part, under the jurisdiction of the local Soviets, the people may feel that through their elected representatives, they are indeed entitled to engage in self-governing activities. The rather extensive participation of the public in the activities of the local Soviets heightens this impression. Thus the Soviet people may not feel that they are deprived of their self-governing rights, and may in fact feel, as at least one American author observed, that party decisions reflect the interests of the people, and that the people are permitted to participate in meaningful ways in the affairs of the government and the state.[50]

The actual participation of Soviet citizens in governmental affairs amounts chiefly to consultation, administration and implementation of policies which have been determined by the party. The Soviet people may believe, as they are told by their leaders, that they have self-governing rights which greatly exceed the rights of the masses of the people in Western nations. They may, for a variety of reasons, including indoctrination and the value which they place on the participation which they are allowed in the affairs of state, have developed a *sense* of being self-governing which greatly exceeds their actual self-governing prerogatives. However, regardless of how the people feel or what the leaders claim, there can be no negation of the fact that the party leaders have preempted the crucial decision-making power. Rather than being self-governing, the Soviet people are governed by the leaders of the Communist Party.

REFERENCES

1 Cf. Milovan Djilas, *The New Class,* (New York: Frederick A. Praeger, 1957), pp. 70-102.

2 "Resolutions and Decisions of the C.P.S.U. (Eighth Congress), Part 1, (Prague: SNPL, 1954), p. 386.

3 A. Denisov and M. Kirichenko, *Soviet State Law,* (Moscow: Foreign Languages Publishing House, 1960), pp. 205-6.

4 *(Soviet State Law), op. cit.,* p. 241.

5 Stalin, *Problems of Leninism, op. cit.,* p. 707.

6 *Ibid.*

7 M. P. Georgadze, "What Is New in Elections," *Pravda,* March 25, 1966, p. 2.

8 *Vedomosti Verkhovnogo Sovieta S.S.R.,* No. 15, July 24, 1958.

9 Cf. "Communique on Sessions of the U.S.S.R. Supreme Soviet," *Izvestia,* April 24, 1962, pp. 1-2.

10 Cf. Denisov and Kirichenko, *Soviet State Law, op. cit.,* pp. 229-30.

11 "Yesterday in the Kremlin," *Pravda,* Dec. 10, 1964, p. 1.

12 A. N. Kosygin, "On the State Plan for the Development of the U.S.S.R. National Economy in 1965," *Pravda,* Dec. 10, 1964, pp. 1-4.

13 V. F. Garbuzov, "On the U.S.S.R. State Budget for 1965 and on the Fulfillment of the U.S.S.R. State Budget for 1963," *Pravda,* Dec. 10, 1964, pp. 4-5.

14 I. S. Senin, "On the State Plan for Development of U.S.S.R. National Economy in 1965, on U.S.S.R. State Budget for 1965 and on Fulfillment of the U.S.S.R. State Budget for 1963," *Pravda,* Dec. 10, 1964, p. 6; M. A. Yasnov, "On State Plan for Development of U.S.S.R. National Economy in 1965, on U.S.S.R. State Budget for 1965 and on Fulfillment of U.S.S.R. State Budget for 1963," *Pravda,* Dec. 10, 1964, pp. 6-7; and O. I. Ivashchenko, "On State Plan for Development of U.S.S.R. National Economy in 1965, on U.S.S.R. State Budget for 1965, and on the Fulfillment of U.S.S.R. State Budget for 1963," *Pravda,* Dec. 10, 1964, p. 7.

15 M. P. Georgadze, "On Ratification of Decrees of Presidium of U.S.S.R. Supreme Soviet," *Pravda,* Dec. 12, 1964, p. 2.

16 "Yesterday in the Kremlin," *Pravda,* Dec. 12, 1964, p. 1.

17 I. S. Senin, "Chairman of the Budget Committee of the Council of the Union," *Pravda,* Dec. 11, 1964, p. 2. (C.D.S.P., Vol. XVI, No. 51, pp. 3-4)

18 A. E. Lunev, "The Further Development of Democracy in Soviet State Administration," *Sovetskoe gosudarstvo i pravo,* 1962, No. 7. (Soviet Law and Government, Winter, 1962, pp. 33-40)

19 M. P. Georgadze, "On Ratification of Decrees of Presidium of the U.S.S.R. Supreme Soviet," *op. cit.,* p. 6.

20 The activities of the commissions are reported in *Vedomosti Verkhovnogo Sovieta S.S.R.*

21 V. Karpinsky, *How the Soviet Union Is Governed,* (Moscow: Foreign Languages Publishing House, 1950), p. 51.

22 *(Soviet State Law), op. cit.,* p. 193.

23 Cf. Denisov and Kirichenko, *Soviet State Law, op. cit.,* p. 239.

24 *Ibid.*

25 V. Karpinsky, *The Social and State Structure of the U.S.S.R.,* (Moscow: Foreign Languages Publishing House, 1949), pp. 87-8, provides a description of the formation of the Soviet Government which makes absolutely clear the purely appointive function of the Supreme Soviet. "The government of the Soviet Union was formed in the following manner," he wrote. "The head of the outgoing government, Comrade J. V. Stalin, submitted a written statement to the chairman of the joint session of the cham-

bers declaring that the government surrendered its powers to the Supreme Soviet. The Supreme Soviet accepted the statement of the government and unanimously commissioned Comrade Stalin to submit proposals for a new government. At the next joint sitting of the chambers, the chairman announced the composition of the new government, as proposed by Comrade Stalin. After statements by deputies, the chairman declared that there was no objection to any of the proposed candidates and that none of the deputies insisted on a roll-call vote. The composition of the Council of Ministers as proposed by Comrade Stalin was then voted on as a whole and unanimously adopted amidst loud applause passing into an ovation in honor of Comrade Stalin who was elected chairman of the Council of Ministers of the U.S.S.R. and Minister of its Armed Forces."

26 After having been chairman of the Council of Ministers for eleven years and then Foreign Minister for over fifteen years, Molotov served briefly as chairman of the Committee of State Control before he was assigned as Soviet Ambassador to Outer Mongolia. Eventually he was expelled from the party and retired from public life. Shepilov took a teaching position when he was removed as Foreign Minister in 1957, while Malenkov and Bulganin were given minor technical posts. Bulganin has since retired.

27 "In the U.S.S.R. Ministry of Culture," *Sovetskaya kultura,* May 21, 1963, p. 2.

28 Denisov and Kirichenko, *Soviet State Law, op. cit.,* p. 257.

29 "State System of the U.S.S.R.," *U.S.S.R. Soviet Life Today,* Nov., 1962, p. 31.

30 A. A. Askerov, N. D. Durmanov, M. P. Kareva, V. K. Kotok, I. D. Levin, I. P. Trainin, *Soviet State Law,* (Moscow: State Publisher of Judicial Literature, 1948), pp. 295-6.

31 Joseph Stalin, "Concerning Questions of Leninism," *Works,* (Moscow: Foreign Languages Publishing House, 1954), Vol. 8, p. 39.

32 "On Ratification of Decrees of the U.S.S.R. Supreme Soviet," *Pravda,* Dec. 10, 1965, p. 2.

33 For a detailed description of the organizational structure and functions of the Party-State Control committee of the Party Central Committee and the U.S.S.R. Council of Ministers see "In the Party Central Committee and the U.S.S.R. Council of Ministers," *Pravda,* Jan. 18, 1963, p. 2.

34 *Ibid.*

35 *Ibid.*

36 *Ibid.*

37 *Ibid.*

38 "Criminal Code of the R.S.F.S.R.," *Pravda,* May 25, 1961; *Pravda,* Dec. 30, 1961.

39 Cf. Vladimir Gsovski, *Government, Law and Courts in the Soviet Union and Eastern Europe,* (London: Steven and Sons, Ltd., 1959), Vol. 1, pp. 586-7.

40 Denisov and Kirichenko, *Soviet State Law, op. cit.,* p. 242.

41 *Ibid.,* p. 283.

42 E.g., cf. Iu. A. Tikhomirov, "Representative Organs of Government and the Development of Government Administration During the Period of Building Communism," *Sovetskoe gosudarstvo i pravo,* No. 2, ("Soviet State Law and Government," Fall, 1962, pp. 12-22).

43 *Ibid.*

44 *Ibid.*

45 "Some Problems of Party Organizational Work Under Contemporary Conditions," (Moscow: VPsh and AON Publishers, 1961), pp. 241-2.

46 Karpinsky, *How the Soviet Union Is Governed, op. cit.,* p. 71.

47 A. N. Kosygin, "On Improving the Management of Industry, Perfecting Planning and Strengthening Economic Incentives in Industrial Production," *Pravda,* Sept. 28, 1965, pp. 1-4.

48 "On Ratification of Decrees of the Presidium," *op. cit.,* p. 2.

49 "Law of the U.S.S.R. on Introducing Changes in and Additions to Article 70 of the U.S.S.R. Constitution," *Pravda,* Dec. 10, 1965, p. 2.

50 Konrad B. Krauskopf, "Russia, a Land of the Free?", in Harry G. Shaffer, (ed.), *The Soviet System in Theory and Practice, op. cit.,* pp. 337-42.

Chapter VII

SOVIET ADMINISTRATION OF JUSTICE

Soviet law is one of the important means of implementing the policy of the Communist Party and the Soviet state.[1]

Historical and Ideological Factors

The official Soviet attitude toward rule by law has been subject to frequent and extensive revisions throughout the years. The revisions, innovations and sudden theoretical reversals have been, however, manifestations of a coherent unifying trend: law in the Soviet Union is an instrument of the party. Every major change has been instigated by the party as a technique to help it achieve its goals for Soviet society. Theories and practices which have been officially sanctioned in one decade have been condemned as highly erroneous in a subsequent decade; and the proponents of such theories and practices have been demoted from the status of leading jurists to "enemies of the people." Yet, all these theorists adhered to the principle that the major task of Soviet law is to implement the policy established by the party. For example, in 1921, P. I. Stuchka wrote, "Law is a system (or order) of social relationships which correspond to the interests of the dominant class and is safeguarded by the organized forces of that class."[2] Since the Communist Party appropriated the right to express the interests of the dominant class, law *ipso facto* had to be molded to serve the party. In 1935, Vyshinsky, the leading jurist during the Stalin era, wrote: "There might be a collision and discrepancies between the formal commands of law and those of the proletarian revolution. These collisions must be solved by the subordination of the formal commands of law to those of Party policy,"[3] and in 1962 Gorkin stated, "The principal task of Soviet justice is to facilitate in every possible way the attainment of the single goal of all Soviet people—the construction of a Communist society."[4] The conditions of society and the specific tasks assigned to law and to the legal and extra-legal apparatus have changed but the superordinate task has remained the same: Soviet law is a tool to be used to implement the policies of the Communist Party.

The early Bolsheviks were somewhat handicapped in their attempts to develop a coherent theoretical and practical approach to legality and the administration of justice by the impracticality of the theoretical heritage bequeathed by Marx and Engels. The position taken by Marx and Engels on the role of law in society may be summarized briefly as follows. Law is an instrument of bourgeois injustice, a technique by which the ruling class keeps toilers in subjugation. As a reflection of the material conditions of society, law protects the interests of the propertied classes and excludes the interests of the propertiless masses. Law is politics, an instrument of state power, to enforce the dominance of the ruling class. Justice is a meaningless formal concept which masks the harsh inequalities existing between social classes. The state itself developed primarily as a means of protecting the interests of the dominant class. Eventually the proletariat will rise up against its oppressors, seize state power, introduce public ownership of the means of production, eradicate the vestiges of capitalism and a classless society will emerge. When class antagonisms have been eliminated, the coercive instruments which the ruling classes have used to maintain their position of power will be superfluous. Neither the state nor law will be necessary since both are merely instruments for maintaining property relations that will no longer exist. Thus, instead of providing a guideline for the development of a legal system during the period of transition from capitalism to socialism and communism, Marx and Engels merely repudiated law as a tool of bourgeois injustice and predicted that a state administered legal order would be unnecessary in a classless society.

By the mere act of seizing power the Bolsheviks by no means eliminated class antagonisms, crime, conflict between individuals and many other forms of behavior in social intercourse which are, in all societies regulated by a code of rules which is administered chiefly by organs of the state. Hence the need for a system of law continued. However, the early Bolshevik leaders, as faithful Marxists, had to proclaim that the Tsarist system of law was an unwanted vestige of the bourgeois past. They had, however, neither the time, experience, nor theoretical guidelines for the development of systematic substitute techniques to regulate society in areas for which regulation was indispensable, at least during the transition period. During the initial phases of the Soviet regime, the legal system was extremely chaotic, because of the complexity of the problems, the inexperience of the administrators, and particularly because of the conflict between the Marxist dictum and the realities of the situation. Throughout the decades of Soviet rule, there appears to have been a trend toward increased awareness of the need for a rational, stable legal system but every modification in theory or practice, whether it has been the adoption of a practice common in capitalist countries, or a "socialist innovation," has necessarily been interpreted as a manifestation of socialist legality derived from the teachings of Marx, Engels or Lenin. The entire history of the Soviet legal system is a series of attempts to compromise between the demands of

Marxist-Leninist theory and the realities of the social and economic situation as viewed by the party leaders in terms of their goals for society. Since the party policy has been revised extensively from time to time, Soviet jurists have faced an extremely difficult task, and it is small wonder that the leading jurists of one period have been the scapegoats of the next.

Lenin, a lawyer by training, accepted the classical Marxist conception of the state and law as instruments of coercion and class domination. Although he accepted the Marxist doctrine of the "withering away" of the state, he deemed it necessary to establish a new proletarian state apparatus to crush the bourgeoisie. He maintained that when all forms of capitalism and bourgeois exploitation were eradicated, there would be no need for the state, state imposed coercive techniques or for a system of law since, he said, the fundamental purpose served by the state and by all laws and rules was to enable the ruling class to maintain dominance over the exploited masses.[5] Lenin may have truly believed that in a society in which exploitation was eliminated, coercive measures would be unnecessary and administration could be of things rather than of persons. But the society in which he served as supreme leader was not free from exploitation, and he soon realized that in addition to the indispensable exploitation of the former exploiters, extreme coercive measures would be required to unify the proletariat and to make the masses an effective tool of the Communist Party, and that without a coherent system of regulations to govern social intercourse, chaos was inevitable.

Immediately following the Bolshevik revolution an attempt was made to replace the traditional or "bourgeois" political and legal institutions by a proletarian state operating through what Lenin referred to as a system of "accounting and control." A network of "People's Courts" were established to replace the former court system.[6] Tsarist laws were to be applied by the courts only insofar as those laws were not superseded by revolutionary law and were not in conflict with "revolutionary legal conscience." Measures directed at the abolition of pre-revolutionary practices and institutions included decrees on the nationalization of industry, banks and foreign trade, general compulsory labor, distribution of commodities through ration cards, appropriation of farm surpluses, restrictions on private ownership, inheritance and private trade. A year after the Bolshevik revolution a decree forbade any reference whatsoever to Tsarist laws. Initially, anyone who enjoyed civil rights could practice law but subsequently salaried legal representatives were appointed by the local government and clients paid fees to the state. Actually, during the early years of the Soviet state, the courts were relatively inactive. The entire society was in such a chaotic state that civil litigation was limited, and most criminal cases were handled by Cheka and special revolutionary tribunals.

Cheka, the all-Russian Extraordinary Commission, was established in

December, 1917, to organize the struggle against counterrevolution and sabotage.[7] Concurrently a network of revolutionary tribunals was established to investigate or try offenses of special significance to the security of the state, i.e., counterrevolutionary moves, sabotage and destruction of socialist property. Revolutionary tribunals were instructed to fix penalties in accordance with "the circumstances of the case and the dictates of the revolutionary conscience." Initially, the activities of the Cheka were of a relatively mild nature and most of the acts of violence against the bourgeoisie were committed by undisciplined mobs rather than by state organs. However, the strength of the opposition to the Soviet regime, and many counterrevolutionary crimes including sabotage and assassinations induced the Cheka to introduce extremely stern measures, starting in February, 1918. Local Soviets were ordered by the Cheka to "seek out, arrest and shoot immediately" all persons connected with anti-Bolshevik organizations, enemy agents and spies, counterrevolutionaries, speculators and buyers and sellers of arms to the counterrevolutionary bourgeoisie when such individuals were "caught red-handed in the act."[8] As the system of terror gained momentum, the need to catch an indivdual in a counterrevolutionary-type act was no longer mandatory. A leading official of the Cheka announced:

> We are no longer waging war against separate individuals, we are exterminating the bourgeoisie as a class. Do not seek in the dossier of the accused for proofs as to whether or not he opposed the Soviet government by word or deed. The first question that should be put is to what class he belongs, of what extraction, what education and profession. These questions should decide the fate of the accused. Herein lies the meaning and the essence of the Red Terror.[9]

Tens of thousands of people, including members of the former nobility, the bourgeoisie, White Guards, peasants, the clergy and deserters from the Red Army were executed without trial, and many more were sent to forced labor camps. "Revolutionary expediency" was the guiding principle. Any person whose actions or origins could be construed as endangering the gains of the revolution was subjected to summary punishment. Execution without the due process of law was used as indiscriminately by the Whites as by the Reds.

The initial period of the Soviet regime was characterized by its lack of law, civil rights and legal forms. With the abolition of the exploiting classes, asocial behavior was expected to disappear. In the interim period, a major task of the proletariat was to develop effective techniques to eradicate exploiters and the vestiges of capitalist ideology and behavior. The 1919 Principles of Criminal Law, stated:

> . . . the proletariat ought to work out rules for repressing its class enemies, ought to create a method of struggle with its enemies and to learn to dominate them. . . . Criminal law . . . has as its task the struggle against the breakers of the new conditions of common life in the transitional period of the dictator-

ship of the proletariat. Only with the final smashing of the opposing overthrown bourgeoisie and the intermediate classes and with the realization of
the communist social order will the proletariat destroy the state as an organization of coercion and laws as the function of the state.[10]

By 1921, the Bolshevik leaders recognized that if their regime was to
survive, drastic revisions in policies, particularly in the economic sphere,
would be required. The New Economic policy (NEP), a "strategic retreat," reintroduced some of the features of capitalism, including a certain
amount of private enterprise. Simultaneously, a revision of the legal system
was required for a number of reasons: the NEP required the restoration of
some features of capitalist law; the chaos resulting from the relative lawlessness of the early period was a source of concern; some Bolshevik leaders,
alarmed by the growing power and autonomy of the Cheka, wanted to
institute measures to curtail its activities. In a relatively short time a Civil
Code, a Criminal Code, a Code of Civil Procedures, a Code of Criminal
Procedures, and a Judiciary Act were enacted to provide a legal structure
which, on paper, incorporated most of the common European practices.
Law was tolerated because the advance toward socialism had been impeded
temporarily, and because it still served a useful purpose as an oppressive
instrument of state policy.

A hierarchy of courts was established. Trials and appeal procedures
followed the West-European pattern. An innovation was the introduction
of people's assessors, lay citizens, to serve as trial judges along with the
regular judge. The Civil Code incorporated matters traditionally covered
in the codes of capitalist countries, i.e., property, mortgages, inheritance,
contracts, legal transactions and ownership. It also introduced "socialist"
features, which indicated that law was intended to serve the interests of
the state, and that the guarantee of private rights was subordinate to the
socio-economic needs of the state. The qualifying clauses considerably reduced the legal value of the private rights specified in other sections of the
code. Moreover, the code indicated that a major reason for granting private rights to citizens was for the "purpose of developing the productive
forces of the country."[11]

The first Criminal Code (1922) described the purposes of Soviet
criminal law as providing "legal protection of the State of toilers from
crimes and socially dangerous acts."[12] In the subsequent code (1926) the
terms crime and punishment were deleted completely in favor of the terms
"socially dangerous acts" and "measures of social defense." The Soviet
Criminal Code (of both 1922 and 1926) included the usual provisions
about complicity, intent, self-defense, insanity, etc. and set maximum and
minimum penalties for various crimes. Special attention was given to
crimes against the state and the administrative order. The most reprehensible feature of the code was the doctrine of analogy which indicated that

if a "socially dangerous act is not directly specified by the code, the basis and limits of punishment for it shall be determined by applying the sections of the code which specify crimes of the kind closely resembling the act."[13] The doctrine of analogy provided the party with an extremely convenient political tool: if it served the purpose of the state or the party to imprison or otherwise punish an individual, it was relatively easy to find some act which could be shown to resemble a legally prohibited act, and coercive measures could be applied with an appropriate show of legality. Machinery also existed to deal with such individuals on an extra-legal basis. Moreover, the principle of "revolutionary legal consciousness," which continued to permeate the entire legal system, could be applied as a weapon of discrimination against any person who constituted a potential danger to the revolutionary cause.

During the NEP, as indeed during the entire Soviet regime, Soviet authorities interpreted law as a political weapon and instrument of party policy. In 1923 a leading jurist wrote: "We look at the court as a class institution, as an organ of government power, and we erected it as an organ completely under the control of the vanguard of the working class. Our judge is, above all, a politician, a worker in the political field."[14] Throughout the years this interpretation has changed very little. In 1952 another leading Soviet jurist wrote:

> The Soviet science of criminal law openly declares that the interpretation of criminal laws is essentially a political interpretation. The only correct and truly scholarly interpretation of criminal law is the interpretation which is permeated by Communist partisanship. The smallest departure from this principle results in a sliding-down to the position of bourgeois objectivity, and leads to the hideous violation of socialist legality.[15]

Soviet theorists on occasion have had some difficulty reconciling the theme that Soviet law is a positive political weapon with the Marxist dictum that law is a capitalistic vestige. Thus Pashukanis, a leading legal theorist until 1936, argued that ". . . ethics, law and State are the forms of a bourgeois society. If the proletariat is forced to use them, it does not mean that there is a possibility of the further development of these forms by way of filling them with the socialist content."[16] Subsequently, and especially around 1936, Soviet theorists were required to renounce the notion that all forms of law were unwanted but perhaps necessary vestiges of capitalism and emphasis was placed on development of a new and higher form of socialist law. In his recantation Pashukanis stated that "all talk about the withering-away of law under socialism is just opportunistic nonsense."[17]

The Bolshevik leaders, frightened by the almost unlimited powers which had been preempted by the Cheka, abolished it in 1922 and transferred its functions to the State Political Administration (GPU). Along with other tasks, the GPU was charged with responsibility for suppression of counterrevolutionary outbreaks and sabotage. Although the GPU had authority to undertake searches, seizures and arrests, certain procedural restraints were imposed upon it. Most important was the stipulation that most criminal cases, including those involving counterrevolutionary crimes, were to be judged by the courts. However, when it fitted the purposes of the regime, the GPU (the OGPU after the establishment of the U.S.S.R. in 1924) was used as a terroristic weapon. The legal and procedural restraints were designed to prevent the OGPU from becoming an independent entity in society but not to restrict the party's arbitrary use of the police as an instrument of terror.

In 1928 the NEP gave way to a policy of total planning. The chief political tasks of the period were to eliminate class distinctions and exploitation, to rid the society of all vestiges of capitalism and to transform the working population into active and conscious builders of a classless society. It was believed that with the arrival of socialism, social conflict would be eliminated, legal codes would be unnecessary and law would "wither away." Law as an instrument of a dominant class was to be replaced by the plan, which as a rational rather than a coercive instrument, was to regulate all relationships within society. Private property, private rights and exploitation were to be eliminated; crime was to become increasingly rare; and conflict of interests disputes were to be settled on the basis of social-economic expediency. Thus attacks on law as a carry over from capitalism were renewed—an attempt to create a stable permanent system of proletarian law was considered both useless and dangerous, particularly since it was argued that the legal superstructure in the bourgeois-capitalist society represented formal protection for the capitalist entrepreneurs. Formal law was subordinate to the law of the revolution; "provisional extraordinary measures" were considered permissible, particularly with reference to forced collectivization; Soviet jurists stressed the importance of "revolutionary expediency" and of "maximum elasticity" and flexibility in legal procedures. Since it was stipulated that law was subordinate to the policies and class interests of the Soviet state, it was accepted that laws and the administration of justice were to serve political goals. In anticipation of the ultimate withering away of law, several law schools were closed and courses on "economic-administrative law" were substituted for courses on civil law. The Civil Code was retained apologetically because it was recognized that "capitalist relations" and "bourgeois psychology" had not been totally eliminated.

With the decline of law, control by the party, police and administrative organs was strengthened. Particularly important was the increased strength of the OGPU. Nepmen or private traders, the old intelligentsia and kulaks were the prime objects of oppression. Hundreds of thousands who ostensibly opposed the Soviet regime were executed or sent to forced labor camps. Show trials were staged to justify the harsh measures instituted against such a large proportion of the population. Control by the OGPU was enhanced by its jurisdiction over the vast network of forced labor camps and by the introduction of an obligatory passport system in 1932. In 1934 the powers of the OGPU were transferred to the People's Commissariat of Internal Affairs, or NKVD, which was made responsible for state security, all police, guards and internal security officers, penal institutions, fire departments and a number of other matters. Certain paper limitations were placed on the power of the secret police. For example, the NKVD was authorized to "issue orders regarding administrative deportation, exile, imprisonment in corrective labor camps for a term not exceeding five years."[18] Nevertheless, during the period of the Great Purge, the arbitrary power of the secret police reached previously unattained heights. The NKVD served as one of Stalin's major weapons to consolidate his own power within the party and the power of the party over the entire Soviet society.

In the mid 1930's a new party line emphasized the importance of law, the need to restore law as a respectable institution, and the need for stability in law and other aspects of Soviet society. The signal for the changed attitude toward law was given by Stalin who stated: "It is time that we put an end to a situation in which not one but a number of bodies legislate. Such a situation runs counter to the principle that laws should be stable. And we need stability of laws now more than ever."[19] A stable system of law was required to coordinate the complex economic structure, and for propaganda purposes it was expedient to affirm that the structure of Soviet power was based on law rather than revolutionary expediency. The 1936 Constitution, which was designed to make the entire structure of the Soviet government appear legally based and free from arbitrary rule, was upheld as a symbol of stability, legality and respectability.

The new emphasis on the desirability of a firm and stable legal structure required substantial modifications of the theoretical positions of Soviet jurists. Whereas it had previously been asserted that law attains its developmental peak under capitalism and must necessarily wither away under socialism, in the late 1930's Vyshinsky had to argue that "history demonstrates that under socialism, on the contrary, law is raised to the highest level of development."[20] Soviet law had to be described as entirely of socialist and Soviet origin and jurists were required to demonstrate that the new Soviet approach to law was derived from the pronouncements of Marx, Lenin and particularly Stalin. Stalin stated that jurists who had espoused the withering away of the state and law by degrees had demonstrated inadequate understanding of dialectical materialism which teaches that great social changes occur as the result of contradictions, rather than by direct transition from one phase to another: strengthening of both the state and law had to precede their ultimate withering away. The negative and nihilistic approach to law had to be abandoned in favor of the positive position that law is a form of social control which contributes to the transition to communism. Programs were introduced to inculcate among the masses a new respect for law, the legal profession gained prestige and new law schools were opened. "Bourgeois" institutions such as money, property, criminal sanctions, family, law and the state, instead of "withering away" were accorded a new "socialist" basis. "Revolutionary legality" was redefined as the strict observance of laws which had been established by the revolution. Statutory limitations were placed on the application of the doctrine of analogy and personal guilt was again considered an essential element of crime.

Nevertheless, it was admitted frankly that "suppression and the use of force" were still essential.[21] Even while talk about the restoration of law movement was at its height, the purges which were effected by the NKVD under Stalin's direction gained momentum. Socialist legality, in the strict sense of the term, was adhered to only when it fitted the purposes of the regime, or more specifically, the supreme party leader. Law continued to be completely subservient to the party and the party remained entirely above the law. A Soviet theorist stated that law was the "expression of the ideology of Soviet society. The meaning of law must therefore be explained by reference to the most important works and documents expressing Soviet ideology—the works of Lenin and Stalin and the programs, decisions and resolutions of the All-Union Communist Party."[22] Legal precedents and principles remained secondary to the changing dictates of the party. Law was necessary for the maintenance of order and to stabilize relations within society, but the party and its tool, the government, were above the law. Citizens had no recourse against the arbitrary decisions of the government or the party, which on the one hand upheld the need for a stable system of law, and on the other hand openly violated the legal principles which they themselves introduced. For example, the 1936 Constitution made discrimination on the basis of nationality punishable by law, but during the war entire national groups, not just individuals who had demonstrated disloyalty, were dispersed or removed far from their original habitat. The Great Purge, in which thousands of persons were executed or exiled without the due process of law, indicated that rule by law was a convenient fiction, and that politics remained above the law.

During the Stalin era, Soviet law was described as vastly superior to bourgeois law and as a positive force in the construction of communist society. Law was purported to defend the property of the socialist state, to assist in the struggle against capitalist encirclement, to discipline those who violated the norms of society, and to educate citizens in Soviet morality and the principles of communism. The use of "suppression and force" side by side with the due process of law was justified on the grounds that dangers from without and within threatened the stability of the social order. Jurists were not allowed to protest against or even to indicate that they were aware of the extensive violations of the established legal order. Legal writers were required to pay homage to the party line which stated that the Soviet legal system was superior to that of the West, and that law was a political weapon.

After the Twentieth Party Congress and particularly after the Twenty-Second Party Congress the party line, with respect to the legal order, underwent drastic revision, and jurists were free to criticize the legal practices and philosophy of the preceding period. Their criticisms confirm what the West had long known—that the restoration of law movement from the early 1930's until Stalin's death had not included the application of legal principles in matters of political importance. Innumerable gross violations of socialist legality have been revealed by Soviet authorities. The errors and atrocities which were committed during the Stalin era are not, however, attributed to any weakness in Marxist-Leninist ideology, but as would be expected, are considered to be among the harmful consequences of the cult of the personality. Stalin, Beria and Vyshinsky are accorded primary responsibility for the violations. The personality cult, it is argued,

> . . . helped to create an atmosphere of scorn for the law. The norms of laws were often violated unceremoniously. The guarantees of individual rights were not observed and that lead to arbitrariness, to condemnation of innocent people. Stalin often spoke of strict observance of laws and the need to strengthen legality, but in fact allowed the most intolerable flouting of laws. This could not but undermine faith in law and did nothing to teach citizens to abide by the norms of law and fulfill the obligations they entailed. This reduced the sphere of the Party's influence on the masses through Soviet legality, through Soviet law.[23]

Vyshinsky's theories, which until Stalin's death were officially sanctioned, are depicted by contemporary jurists as "anti-scientific and false"; his theories incorporated a distorted interpretation of the essence and tasks of the proletarian dictatorship, Soviet law and socialist legality, and an incorrect, non-Marxist understanding of dialectical and historical materialism.[24] One of his most serious errors was his emphasis on the coercive nature of the task of the proletarian state during the period of the proletarian dictatorship. According to contemporary critics:

> Suppression, coercion and violence and consequently, repression in all its forms, were what permeated all of Vyshinsky's concepts. . . . This entirely excluded the socialist state's vast organizational, cultural and educational work to insure the application of norms of Soviet law and ignored . . . the wholly voluntary and fully conscious application of the norms of law by the majority of the population, inasmuch as they expressed the peoples' will and interest. State coercion, of course, had a definite place in law with respect to people who violate the norms of law. But socialist law cannot be reduced solely to coercion. Implementation of the norms of Soviet socialist law, which ex-

presses the will of the monolithic Soviet nation, is made possible primarily by vast ideological, economic and educational work, by highly conscious and voluntary adherence to its norms by the citizens themselves.[25]

Additional criticisms of Vyshinsky reflect the corruptness of the entire legal system during the Stalin era. Vyshinsky is criticized for: (1) openly advocating that criminal proceedings against citizens should be intensified; (2) providing theoretical justification for forced confessions by attaching the power of conviction to the admission of guilt; (3) increasing the possibility of criminal action against innocent persons through his emphasis on complicity; (4) increasing the number of unjustified convictions by advising the courts to pass verdicts on the basis of maximum probability rather than on the basis of absolute truth; (5) holding the defendant responsible for proving the correctness of the assertions which he made in his own defense; (6) justifying the superiority of expediency over legality by upholding the rule of analogy and by advising judges to be guided "not so much by the provisions and instructions of law as by their legal consciousness."[26] Thus Soviet authorities in the post-Stalin era admit freely that during the period which followed Stalin's demand for "stability of law," miscarriages of justice were distressingly numerous despite the official restoration of law movement and the claim that under socialism a new and higher form of legality had emerged. Marxism-Leninism and contemporary Soviet leaders, rather than being held in any way responsible for the abuses of justice in the preceding period, have emerged as the champions of a true and higher form of justice which is to replace the arbitrariness and lawlessness which preceded it. During the period following the Twentieth Party Congress a new restoration of law movement was launched officially. The harmful and erroneous theories that developed during the cult of the personality are to be completely eradicated and "a bold and creative treatment of the new problems posed by life, by the practice of building communism"[27] is to be developed.

The Party Program states that the immediate task of Soviet justice is to secure strict observance of socialist legality, to eradicate all violations of law and order and consistently to implement the sacred demand: "The duty of the Soviet people is to uphold legality and law and order, display intolerance for abuses and combat them." The overall goal is the gradual elimination of crime and all causes of it. Measures for the attainment of this goal include "maximum strengthening of socialist legality and law and order in the country, improvement of legislation and thorough protection of the rights of Soviet citizens."[28] The new socialist legality allegedly involves "strict observance of the norms of law by all legal institutions, officials and citizens."[29]

The Soviet critique of the administration of justice during the Stalin era highlights some of the most flagrant abuses. Miscarriages of justice,

Constitution of the U.S.S.R.[32] Although the specific features of laws and court procedures may vary from republic to republic in accordance with local conditions, the basic principles of criminal, civil and process law are regulated by All-Union legislation. Since the laws established by the U.S.S.R. are in force in every Union Republic (Article 19), supervision by the federal Supreme Court has the obvious advantage of enforcing uniform court procedures.

THE PEOPLE'S COURTS

The People's Courts are established to correspond to a territorial district, city or city zone. Prior to 1958, the district of a People's Court was based on population factors, and within one administrative district there were sometimes several People's Courts, each presided over by one judge who was responsible for all agenda, civil as well as criminal. A consolidation reduced the number of People's Courts by one half, and is intended to encourage specialization, the exchange of experiences and standard court practices and to strengthen the association between the court and the party, Soviet and other organizations.[33]

The People's Courts are exclusively courts of original jurisdiction. They deal with the majority of civil cases including property disputes between individuals and enterprises, alimony, inheritance and labor relation problems. Criminal cases entrusted to the People's Courts include theft, tax evasion, violation of the electoral law, failure to meet state obligations and embezzlement. Crimes with important political implications, such as counterrevolutionary acts or theft of socialist property, and crimes that carry the death penalty or imprisonment for more than ten years are not within the jurisdiction of the People's Courts.

Judges for the People's Court are elected for a five year term by the electorate of the area of the court's jurisdiction on the basis of direct, universal, equal suffrage by secret ballot. The number of judges elected to serve in a given People's Court varies with the population of the area under the court's jurisdiction. Some large districts and cities elect fifteen or more judges whereas others may elect only one.[34] Any eligible citizen who has reached the age of 25 may be elected. Legal education is not an official prerequisite for candidature for judgeship. By 1959, over half of the people's judges had university level legal training, and most of the others had some legal training in secondary school, but a considerable number had no formal legal training whatsoever.[35]

The People's Court, like all Soviet courts, is collegial. Courts to which a number of judges are elected are headed by a chairman who gives organizational direction to the work of the court.[36] The bench is composed of one judge and two "people's assessors." People's assessors are elected for a period of two years from among citizens eligible to vote and who have attained the age of 25. Election is by public meetings of working people at their places of work or residences. The system of direct election is designed to permit the electorate to choose from among people who are well known to them, the best, the most active and the most conscientious to dispense justice. Again, legal training is not a prerequisite although lately short courses have been conducted to increase the legal knowledge of the assessors. The election period for assessors was reduced from three years to two years in 1958 to permit a larger number of citizens to participate actively in the administration of justice. From fifty to seventy-five people's assessors are elected in each court district; almost one half million assessors are elected every other year.[37] Assessors are empanelled to serve in the court for not more than two weeks per year. While on duty, the assessor has the rights and duties of a judge. The judge and the two assessors who constitute a trial bench are expected to decide all questions, both of law and fact, jointly by majority vote. However, because of the superior legal training and experience of the judge, the assessors frequently defer to his opinions and decisions.[38] Judges have been criticized for imposing their decisions on the assessors.[39] People's assessors retain their regular salaries or wages while serving in court or receive recompense from the state in an amount fixed by law. Should an assessor be called upon to assume the role of judge, he is paid the same salary as the judge for the two week period. Since the 1958 court reorganization, it has been customary to replace a temporarily absent judge by another judge from another district. Only in exceptional cases, or in remote districts, does an assessor replace the judge in court.[40] Formerly the practice was common.

Soviet sources stress the importance of the people's assessors as direct representatives of the people in the administration of justice. A Soviet professor stated:

> Since the people's assessors come from the people and have their confidence, they are able to introduce the wisdom of the people, experience gained in life, into the work of the court, and are also able to delve deeply and understandingly into the bewildering complexity of human relations, into the circumstances attending any criminal or civil case.[41]

The use of people's assessors is said to correspond to the requirement that the working masses are supposed to conduct the affairs of state. The electorate has the right to withdraw its mandate or to recall any judge or people's assessor who has failed to carry out his duties or to conduct himself in an acceptable manner. Judges are obligated to report to the electorate regularly about the work and activities of the People's Court. These reports are expected to improve the conscientiousness of Soviet citizens, to inform them about and to encourage them to adhere to the laws and rules of the socialist way of life, and to propagandize Soviet law among the population. Moreover, the reports allow for grass root evaluation of judicial activities which is informative for the higher authorities.

INTERMEDIATE COURTS

Intermediate courts are established to correspond to the administrative territorial division of the Union and Autonomous Republics. Thus, in the R.S.F.S.R. intermediate courts are established within each territory, region, Autonomous Republic, national region, national area and certain cities. In some of the smaller Union Republics, which are not subdivided into territories and provinces, only the Supreme Court of the Union Republic is above the People's Court. Each intermediate court has a collegial bench consisting of a president, several vice-presidents, ordinary judges and people's assessors. All members of the bench are elected by the corresponding Soviet of Working People's Deputies, which has the right to recall both judges and people's assessors.

The intermediate courts assume original jurisdiction over all civil cases which are beyond the jurisdiction of the People's Courts and over more important criminal cases such as counterrevolutionary crimes, theft of socialist property, and crimes against state administration. Civil cases handled by these courts include divorces and major disputes between enterprises and state and public institutions. The intermediate courts supervise the work of, and hear appeals from, the People's Courts, have the right to assume jurisdiction over a case which could be tried by a lower court, and to remand cases to a lower court. Cases of original jurisdiction are heard by a judge and two assessors; appeals are heard by three judges. Judges are assigned to criminal or civil panels which specialize in trying particular types of cases. Each intermediate court is required to report on its activities either directly to the Soviet which elected it or to the Executive Committee of the Soviet. The reports are supposed to be educational; included may be information about the results of the court's efforts to deal with violations of law such as embezzlement of kolkhoz property and inefficient handling of cattle or machinery, and its work designed to protect the rights and interests of citizens and enterprises, and to strengthen work discipline.

The Supreme Court of the Union Republic is the highest judicial organ in the republic. Its collegial bench, which is elected by the Supreme Soviet of the Union Republic for a five year term, corresponds to that of the intermediate courts. It has original jurisdiction over all civil and criminal cases of extreme importance, including crimes committed by ranking republican officials, cases of great political significance, and cases initiated by the Procurator or the Presidium of the Supreme Soviet of the Republic. All lower and intermediate courts within the republic are supervised by the Supreme Court, which can reverse verdicts, hear appeals and remove cases from lower courts to assume jurisdiction itself. The independence and stature of the Supreme Courts of the Union Republics was increased considerably by the abolition of the All-Union Ministry of Justice and by the Statute on the Supreme Court of the U.S.S.R. (1957) which provided that all cases, both criminal and civil, must be tried and decided definitively by the courts of the Union Republics. Prior to 1957 the Supreme Court of the U.S.S.R. had the right to demand the record of any case from any court after the case had been closed, and to review cases which had not been reviewed by a higher judicial organ of the Union Republic.[42] Currently, the U.S.S.R. Supreme Court may intervene only if it appears that the Supreme Court of a Union Republic has pronounced a decision, judgement or sentence which contradicts All-Union legislation or violates the interests of other Union Republics. Thus, all cases except those which are under the jurisdiction of Military Tribunals are heard by the judicial organs of the Union Republics.

MILITARY COURTS

Military Tribunals are permanently established military courts which operate under the direct supervision of the U.S.S.R. Supreme Court. Judges are elected for a period of five years by the Supreme Soviet of the U.S.S.R. from persons on active military duty who have attained the age of 25. People's assessors are elected for a two year term by public vote at a meeting of the military unit from among persons on active military duty. Military commanders have neither the right to appoint nor review the Military Tribunals.

The military courts deal with all violations of law and criminal acts by military personnel or members of the police force committed while on active duty; all acts of espionage; and in territories under martial law, all crimes, regardless of the offender, committed against public order and the security of the state.[43] Until 1958, the jurisdiction of military courts over cases involving civilians was considerably more extensive than it is at present; for example, if an illegal act was committed by several people, one of whom could be tried by a military court, the military court assumed jurisdiction over all of the accused.

Lower military courts function only as courts of the first instance. Higher military courts function as courts of the first and second instance, and supervise the activities of the lower courts. The military courts have a record of dealing with important political and military crimes in a very summary manner which afforded little protection to the defendant. The right of appeal is generally less liberal than in civil courts, but sentences may be reviewed by higher tribunals.

THE SUPREME COURT OF THE U.S.S.R.

The Supreme Court of the U.S.S.R., the highest judicial organ of the nation, has a bench of twenty people's assessors and thirty-one professional judges; sixteen are elected by the Supreme Soviet and the other fifteen are the chairmen of the Supreme Courts of the Union Republics. The inclusion of the chairmen of the Supreme Courts of the Union Republics is intended to foster a more standard application of socialist legality throughout the U.S.S.R., to allow for consideration of national peculiarities in formulation of directives, and to permit an exchange of views. Membership in the Supreme Court was reduced appreciably (78 judges and 35 assessors in 1951; 68 judges and 25 assessors in 1957) following a 1957 Statute, which transferred many of the functions of the Supreme Court of the U.S.S.R. to the Supreme Courts of the Union Republics. The court's term of office is five years.

Supreme Court judges are divided into collegia specialized in military, civil or criminal cases. The Military Collegium hears appeals and protests against sentences pronounced by Military Tribunals. The protest may be made by the chairman or vice-chairman of the U.S.S.R. Supreme Court, the Procurator-General of the U.S.S.R. or his deputy, the Chief Military Procurator, or the chairman of the Military Collegium. Civil and criminal collegia review decisions by the Supreme Court of a Union Republic protested by the chairman or vice-chairman of the U.S.S.R. Supreme Court or the Procurator-General of the U.S.S.R. or his deputy if the decisions contradict All-Union legislation or violate the interests of other republics. Individuals may bring a case to the U.S.S.R. Supreme Court only through a successful petition to the U.S.S.R. Procurator-General or the chairman of the Supreme Court of the U.S.S.R. or their deputies. If none of these officers recommend review, the individual has no recourse, and the decision of the Supreme Court of the Union Republic is final. When the U.S.S.R. Supreme Court functions as an appellate court, the bench consists of three professional judges. The Supreme Court of the U.S.S.R. assumes original jurisdiction over civil or criminal cases of exceptional military, political, or legal significance as, for example, when a very high ranking government official is involved. Cases of the first instance are heard by one judge and two people's assessors. Decisions are final, subject only to *ex officio* review by a Supreme Court plenary session.

Plenary sessions of the Supreme Court must be held not less than four times a year.[44] At least two thirds of all members and the Procurator-General of the U.S.S.R. must be in attendance; people's assessors do not participate in plenary sessions. Decisions are adopted by simple majority vote. The plenary session hears protests against the decisions of the collegia of the U.S.S.R. Supreme Court and the Supreme Courts of the Union Republics, proposes or discusses draft legislation concerning judicial matters, and may, if the occasion were to arise, settle disputes between the judicial bodies of the Union Republics. The most important function of the

U.S.S.R. Supreme Court plenary session is to issue general principles and directives aimed at guiding the work of lower courts. For example, the lower courts have been ordered to raise the quality of court hearings in cases of crimes by minors; to observe strictly legal norms regarding the right of the accused to defense; to enforce the law vigorously with respect to those who make attempts on the life, health and dignity of the militia and people's volunteers; to distinguish between first offenders and dangerous recidivists; to improve their work with respect to prevention, determination of the causes and punishment for pilfering of state and public property; to pay more attention to the complaints of citizens; and to hold more court hearings in the institution or organization where the crime was committed. The Supreme Court of the U.S.S.R. does not have the right to evaluate the constitutionality of laws or decrees issued by the Supreme Soviet or its Presidium or by the Council of Ministers. Soviet leaders have rejected the concept of separation of powers and the courts cannot act as a check against violation of the Constitution by the legislative and executive branches of government. The party, which controls all branches of the government, could not tolerate a judicial system that would interfere with its activities.

INDEPENDENCE OF JUDGES

Soviet writers emphasize that the Soviet Constitution (Article 112) and the Fundamentals of Legislation on the Judicial System proclaim the independence of judges and their subordination to the law alone. The principle of the independence of judges is said to derive directly from the stipulation by Marx that "The judge has no other superiors except the law. But the judge is obliged to interpret the law when applying it to a particular case, in the way that he *comprehends* it upon conscientious consideration."[45] It is claimed that all sentences and decisions of the courts are based on the law to which the judges are subject and the convictions by which they are guided; judges alone are held responsible for the legality and validity of court decisions; no executive or administrative organ or official of the state may bring pressure to bear on the court or demand a decision that contravenes the law.[46]

A number of procedures purported to guarantee the independence of judges are incorporated into Soviet judicial codes. The chairman of the court is required to be the last person to vote in order to avoid influencing the assessors. At meetings of the court, no non-judge or assessor with the exception of a court servant or court secretary may be present. Judges can be recalled only by those who elected them or following prosecution for a criminal act. The arrest and criminal prosecution of a judge requires the approval of the supervising Supreme Soviet or its Presidium. Judges are required to report on the activities of the court to their electorate which has the right to demand that particular cases be dealt with by the court, but must not under any circumstance request that a judge arrive at a particular concrete decision in a given case. Evaluation by the electorate of the activities of the court is to be based only on cases which have been closed. Supervision of the judge by the public is presented as a manifestation of the "profound democracy" of the Soviet judicial system. However, in practice, much of the supervision is provided by state and party organs rather than by the masses of the people, and the guarantees of judicial independence are not always upheld.

The right to nominate candidates for judgeship is secured by the party, Komsomol, and other organizations totally subservient to the party. Almost all Soviet judges are members of the C.P.S.U. The active role of the party in selecting suitable candidates is accepted as a fact of life. An official of the Central Committee of the C.P.S.U. wrote:

> The political and ideological tempering of the personnel of courts, prosecution and militia is a most important task before Party organizations. It is difficult to assure strict observance of legality, and to achieve success in the elimination of crime, if the personnel to whom this most important matter has been entrusted are not morally stable, totally devoted and *politically mature*. [italics added][47]

Even the recall procedure is controlled primarily by the party and state officials subservient to the party. For example, a disciplinary bench associated with each court may recommend that the competent Law Committee, Council of Ministers or Executive Committee initiate the recall of a judge.[48] It is very likely that recall measures, and even expressions of dissatisfaction with the general conduct of the court's work require the approval of the party.

Since judges and assessors are elected and can be recalled by "the people," the court must necessarily take into account what "the people" want, which in turn is dictated by the party. Direct interference by party organizations in the work of the court has constituted a basis for concern. A party official complained:

> Thus far not every local Party organization has succeeded in giving capable leadership to the activity of the procurator's office, militia and courts. Certain Party committees allow incorrect interference in the decisions of specific court cases, and not infrequently provide protection for Party members who have committed criminal acts. This is wholly impermissible. This undermines the principle of the independence of the courts and their subordination solely to the law. . . . It deprives the judicial and prosecuting agencies of independence and instills irresponsibility in them, disorganizes judges and procurators, and impels them to adopt illegal decisions.[49]

The preceding quotation exemplifies one of the dilemmas which confronts the Soviet system. Judicial independence may be desired as an abstract value and for practical purposes, such as to encourage stability in social interactions and respect for law among the masses and to permit the regime to describe its judicial process to the world as fair and objective. On the other hand, the party is totally unwilling to relinquish its control over the judicial system. The general result is that Soviet courts probably do enjoy a considerable measure of independence in deciding ordinary criminal and civil cases, whereas cases involving political crimes or the security of the state not infrequently invite direct guidance from the party. No court, and no judge in the U.S.S.R. can be apolitical. A Soviet judge must, like all other officials, be a "builder of communism"; hence his independence cannot lead to disagreement with governmental policy directed by the Communist Party, though he may be relatively independent of local interests which conflict with the law. A Soviet professor described the dependence of the judge on the policy of the party and the government as follows:

> The independence of Soviet judges should not be construed in the sense of their independence from the socialist State. The court is an agency of the Soviet Socialist State. The court may not serve any other cause but the cause of building up a socialist society, may not carry on any other policy but the policy of the Communist Party and the Soviet Government, may not carry out any will but the will of the Soviet people.[50]

Although it can be concluded that judges are by no means independent of party control, the contemporary concern about the independence of judges may represent a liberalizing trend. Early Bolshevik jurists rejected *in toto* the concept of impartiality and independence of judges; in 1923, Krylenko wrote: "Our judge is above all a politician, a worker in the political field. . . . No court was ever above class interests. . . . The court . . . remains . . . a weapon for the safeguarding of the interests of the ruling class."[51] Vyshinsky, who emphasized even more definitely the subservience of the court to the party, wrote: "The general Party line . . . forms the basis of the work of the Soviet court. . . . The Party establishes the general principles of judicial policy, supervises their proper fulfillment, and controls the judicial policy."[52] He added that the doctrine of independence of judges "acquires, under the conditions of proletarian dictatorship, a counterrevolutionary character."[53] The current position on independence of judges, while fully affirming the subservience of the judicial system to the party, at least makes explicit the value of freeing judges from the dictates of the local party organizations as well as from personal and local influences.

COMRADES' COURTS AND VOLUNTEER GROUPS

Decisions made at the Twenty-First Party Congress paved the way for an upsurge in the participation of Comrades' Courts, public order squads and other social organizations in the enforcement of social order. Comrades' Courts were first established during the period of War Communism as a device to increase labor discipline and to deal with minor offenses and disputes of little general significance. By the late thirties the activities of the Comrades' Courts had become quite unimportant, because of the monopolization of public authority by the central government and the severely repressive measures which stifled social initiative. In 1959, a campaign for "the expansion of the role of the public in the administration of justice" was launched when Khrushchev declared:

> Problems of security in our social order, and enforcement of the rules of socialist co-existence should, to an ever increasing degree, become the business of social organizations. . . . Socialist society forms such voluntary agencies of enforcement of the social order as people's militia, comradely courts and similar institutions. They will discharge in a new manner . . . social functions. . . .[54]

A 1959 law in Comrades' Courts states:

> The main task of the comradely courts is to prevent violations of the law and all actions which harm society, education of the people by means of crime prevention and social influence, creation of an atmosphere of intolerance for anti-social behavior of any kind. Comradely courts are clad in the confidence of the collective and express its will . . . duties include educating Soviet citizens in the spirit of communist attitude toward work, socialist property, observance of the rules of socialist co-existence, promoting within the Soviet people the spirit of collectivism, comradely help, respect for dignity and honor of the citizens.[55]

A related law holds the entire society responsible for the maintenance of law and order.[56] Each Soviet citizen is held responsible for abiding by the law and for acting as a law enforcement officer by demanding that others likewise conform to the rules of the socialist legal order. In conformity with this requirement, squads, variously known as the people's militia, people's detachments or public order squads are formed to work on a part-time, unpaid basis to protect public order, prevent various types of law breaking and "bring unrestrained hooligans and rowdies to their senses."[57] Such detachments are supposed to be detailed in apartment buildings, enterprises, public places, recreational areas and streets.

Comrades' Courts may be set up in factories, apartment houses, collective farms and other organizations. Members are elected for a two year period by open ballot at a general meeting. Members of the court select their own chairman, vice-chairman and secretary. The court meets irregularly as the occasion demands. Meetings, presided over by the chairman, and two members of the court appointed by him, are held after working hours. Among matters over which it may take jurisdiction are tardiness or absence from work without valid reason; delaying production because of carelessness; minor property disputes; shirking socially useful work and leading a parasitical life; insults, beatings, drunkenness, bad language; failure to fulfill the duties of bringing up children; violations of apartment regulations; illicit home distillation for personal consumption; petty profiteering; and petty misappropriation of state or public property.[58] Cases are heard in public. Procedural guarantees applied in regular court cases, such as the rights of the defendant to be informed of the charges in advance, to bring in witnesses and to be assisted by defense counsel are waived. The defendant or the injured party may, however, challenge the presiding officer or members of the court if he can show they have a personal interest in the outcome of the case. The case is discussed by the members of the meeting and a decision made by majority vote is pronounced publicly. The court has the right to impose admonitions, reprimands, fines up to fifteen rubles and small amounts of damages in cases of personal injuries. The offender may also be placed under the supervision of his immediate collective for a specific period. There is no right of appeal against the decision. The effectiveness of the court action is supposed to lie primarily in its educational value and in the shame felt by the offender. However, the court is also empowered to apply "corrective measures" including a recommendation to the People's Court that a tenant be evicted from his apartment or to the head of the enterprise that a worker be dismissed, transferred from a position which involves the upbringing of adolescents or the handling of valuable goods, or assigned to physical labor with a reduction in pay for a maximum of fifteen days.

Under the anti-parasite laws, a Comrades' Court may recommend that a person who leads a "parasitic mode of life," i.e. does not work, takes a job only for the sake of appearances or derives income through non-labor means, be sentenced for two to five years exile with compulsory labor at a specified location.[59] This sentence has to be confirmed by the Executive Committee of the local Soviet. In spite of the severity of the sentence, the accused is not protected by the normal rules of evidence and proof. He has neither the right to defense nor the right to appeal. The People's Court handles parasite cases which involve violence or the threat of violence to exhort a means of support from others, but even here the procedural guarantees of the 1958 Fundamentals of Justice need not be applied. The only procedural protection under the anti-parasite laws is the requirement that the trade union, residential collective, procuracy or some other organization or official must issue a warning of the dangers of pursuing the parasitical behavior sufficiently in advance to allow ample time for rectification. Apparently, the warning is not always issued. Reports in the Soviet press indicate that, in at least a few cases, gross miscarriages of justice have occurred through misapplication of the anti-parasite laws.

The extent of public participation in the administration of justice can be gauged partially by the existence of almost 200,000 comrades' courts which deal with approximately four million minor cases per year.[60] Public measures are applied to every fifth violator, and it is reported that more than 99 percent of those taken into custody or warned, go on to do honest work and do not commit second offenses.[61] Five and one-half million

strict observance of the laws. In this way the public can be more concretely impressed with the heinousness of breaking the regime's commandments than it would by hearing a stereotyped lecture on the desideration of law-abidingness."75

There can be no doubt that such measures have an effect on the legal consciousness of the masses.

According to the Soviet evaluation, the Procuracy has been fulfilling its designated functions of supervising the enactment and execution of legal orders and serving as an "eye" for the central government and the party in a relatively satisfactory manner. However, Soviet sources admit that there is room for improvement. One problem is that errors are made by members of the Procuracy because of their lack of knowledge of the law and legal procedures and sometimes, because of negligence or indifference. Such problems are compounded by the fact that orders from above are sometimes conflicting, unclear or even at variance with the laws. During the post-Stalin era attempts have been made to improve the personal, educational and experiential qualifications of Procurators. The Statute on Procuracy Supervision provides that Procurators and investigators must have higher legal education and that Procurators and senior investigators must have at least one year of experience as a lower level investigator, unless the Procurator-General of the U.S.S.R. approves the appointment of persons without these qualifications. Another problem is that satisfactory organizational forms have not been worked out for the delineation of duties within the Procuracy. In a post-Stalin reorganization the Procuracy was divided into specialized departments, with jurisdiction over general supervision, criminal trials, civil trials, pre-trial investigations, education, places of detention, etc.76 Although the consensus is that the reorganization has enhanced efficiency, recurrent criticism suggests that the demarcation of authority in some cases is not sufficiently precise, and in other cases, as for example between the pre-trial investigation department and the criminal trial department, the division of responsibility results in inefficiency.

The Constitution of the U.S.S.R. specifies that the organs of the Procurator's office perform their functions *independently of any local organs whatsoever*. Despite occasional reports of bribe taking, corruption, collusion and attempts by local party organizations and officials to influence the activities of the Procuracy,77 the bulk of the evidence suggests that, in general, the Procuracy operates with considerable integrity and independence from local pressures. However, the Procuracy, like all other branches of the governmental apparatus is completely subservient to the Communist Party. Although the Procurator-General is nominally responsible only to the Supreme Soviet of the U.S.S.R. and its Presidium, Vyshinsky's statement that the Procuracy is "indissolubly associated with the directing organs of the Communist Party"78 is still valid. The independence and impartiality of the

Procuracy is curtailed chiefly by the party leaders. For example, the party may issue instructions to the Procuracy concerning violations which are to be considered "particularly heinous," areas to be stressed in educational programs, and even to find an appropriate violation to justify legal action against an official who has been selected by the party as a scapegoat or an example. Because the needs of the party are served by a relatively stable system of law enforcement, most of the laws are enforced most of the time in a reasonably impartial manner by the Procuracy. The party, however, which is the guiding force in the establishment of laws, has reserved for itself the right to determine which laws shall be enforced at a given time with reference to specific individuals.

Ministries of Justice and Judicial Committees

In 1936 an All-Union Ministry (Commissariat) of Justice was established to supervise the activities of the republican Ministries of Justice, which in turn supervised judicial practice within the republic. The All-Union Ministry was also instructed to codify existing laws and to assist in the drafting of legislative bills. The All-Union Ministry was abolished in 1956 "to remove excessive centralization in the administration of justice."[79] Supervision of judicial agencies was transferred to the Ministries of Justice of the Union Republics which were again categorized as republican ministries. Concurrently, a new Judicial Committee was attached to the Council of Ministers of the U.S.S.R.; its duties include "codifying and systematizing Soviet legislation, drafting government instructions and considering in a preliminary way, legislative bills . . . and government resolutions on matters of uniform standards and procedures."[80] Although the abolition of the All-Union Ministry of Justice may have effected decentralization in some minor respects, the Soviet government retained the more significant forms of centralized control over justice. For example, the Supreme Court of the U.S.S.R. is charged with the supervision of the judicial activities of all the judicial organs of the U.S.S.R. and has the right to review *ex officio* cases decided by the Supreme Courts of the Union Republics and to issue directives to the lower courts. The highly centralized Procuracy, which operates completely under the supervision of the central government and organs of the party, serves to counteract even more powerfully the transfer of control of the administration of justice from the All-Union to the republican governments.

In the early 1960's the majority of the Union Republics transformed their Ministries of Justice into Juridicial or Law Committees in order to eliminate parallelism in the guidance of courts, and to "reduce and perfect the administrative-managerial apparatus." [81] The Juridicial or Law Committee, subordinate to the republican Council of Ministers, is responsible for codification and systematization of legislation, preparation of draft legislation on assignment, and guidance of lawyers' collegia and agencies for the registry of writs of citizenship. Unlike the Ministry of Justice, it does not exercise guidance or control over the courts which operate under the supervision of the Supreme Court.

Soviet Lawyers

Soviet lawyers may be divided into two categories, the *jurisconsult,* a salaried employee who serves as legal advisor to the director of an enterprise, and the *advocate,* a member of a collegium of lawyers who engages in law practice for private clients on a fee basis. The jurisconsult interprets laws and regulations defining the rights and duties of the enterprise, represents the enterprise in arbitration proceedings, assists in the preparation of contracts, makes decisions regarding workers' rights with respect to overtime, schedules, and pay rates and brings charges against defenders on behalf of the enterprise. The jurisconsult's role in the administration of justice and the political importance of his activities is not great, since enforcement of the policy of the regime, labor discipline, high productivity, etc. is the responsibility of the director of the enterprise and the local party organs. Therefore, persons with legal training whose political reliability does not qualify them for membership in a legal collegium may be hired as jurisconsults.

The right to practice law in the Soviet Union is restricted to members of a lawyers' collegium.[82] The basic educational requirement for membership is graduation from a higher law school, combined with at least two years legal experience which may be acquired by serving as a judge, procurator or investigator. Under exceptional circumstances the Executive Committee of an intermediate or higher Soviet may approve the admission of an advocate who does not meet all qualifications. Political reliability is an important prerequisite. In most Union Republics lawyers are organized into republican, regional and district collegia. The latter are responsible for establishing consultation offices or legal bureaus in local areas. The governing bodies of a lawyers' collegium consist of a general meeting of the members (or in a large organization, a conference), a presidium and an auditing commission. The general meeting, or conference, convenes at least once a year to elect the presidium and auditing commission and to give general guidance to the presidium. The presidium, which exercises general supervisory control within the collegium, sets up legal consultation offices and guides and inspects their work; admits and expels members; assigns advocates to consultation offices; appoints and removes heads of consultation offices with the approval of the Executive Committee of the respective Soviet; approves budgets and dispenses funds; reports on the work of the collegium to the appropriate governmental body; takes measures to improve the ideological, political and legal competence of advocates; organizes the participation of advocates in the public dissemination of Soviet laws; studies the causes of crime and submits proposals to state and public organizations.[83]

The staff composition and location of legal consultation offices are established by the presidium of the lawyers' collegium with the concurrence of the Executive Committee of the respective Soviet. Each consultation office is headed by a director who assigns work among the advocates with due regard for their qualifications, work load and requests by clients; sets fees, keeps records and distributes payments to the member attorneys; and in general, supervises the work done by advocates.[84] An advocate's work is paid for from funds received by the consultation office from citizens, enterprises, organizations and collective farms for legal aid.[85]

Advocates are liable to disciplinary action for violation of regulations, a negligent and unconscientious attitude toward the discharge of their duties and other acts that degrade the calling of a lawyer, including acceptance of monetary remuneration other than for legal consultation.[86] The most severe disciplinary measure, expulsion from the collegium, which in effect prohibits the individual from practicing law, may be invoked by the presidium of the collegium or by the responsible state organ. Soviet authorities point out that governmental intervention has decreased as the collegia have become organizationally stronger and more careful in their selection of candidates for the bar.[87] The most important aspects of the organization and activity of the bar, such as the selection and training of personnel, verification of the legality of decisions made by its agencies of self-government, and procedures for payment of legal aid, are carried out under the general supervision of government agencies, usually the Juridicial or Law Committee of the Council of Ministers.[88] The extent of governmental control is variable. For example, in the Kazakh S.S.R. the Law Committee has the prerogative to dissolve the presidium of a legal collegium which does not provide adequate leadership and to set dates for new elections. Soviet authors have criticized this regulation as an undemocratic infringement on the rights of the collegium since "the presidium of the college of attorneys is the elected agency of a public organization, and the dissolution of such a body prior to the execution of its term is something within the competence only of the organization which chose it."[89] These spokesmen recommended that dissolution by administrative fiat be replaced by presentation of reasons for dissolution to the membership at an extraordinary general meeting. This example is presented to illustrate that in some instances Soviet citizens are permitted to voice public criticism of governmental regulations.

Regulations governing the legal collegia emphasize that, in all its activities, the bar must promote: (1) protection of the rights and legal interests of citizens, enterprises, institutions and organizations; (2) observance and reinforcement of socialist legality; and (3) administration of justice.[90] Although the regulations vary slightly from one republic to another, all incorporate standard functions of the bar such as provision of defense counsel and representation of the interests of injured parties, civil plaintiffs and civil respondents in criminal cases; legal representation in criminal cases; preparation of legal documents; providing legal advice; rendering legal assistance to enterprises, institutions, organizations and collective farms; and mass education with respect to Soviet law.[91] Additional functions are specified in certain republics; for example, several republics (Estonia, Kazakhstan, Tadzhikistan and Uzbekistan) attempt to provide more effective protection of the rights of citizens before administrative agencies by allowing for legal representation in administrative cases, such as the settlement of pensions and administrative eviction.[92]

A number of recently introduced regulations are intended to allow the Soviet advocate to perform his functions with somewhat greater freedom and, at the same time, to serve his client better. During the Stalin era the defense counsel was permitted to participate only in the court proceedings, but since 1958 the defense counsel may participate in the case from the moment the accused is notified of the completion of the preliminary investigation, and in cases of minors, from the moment of presentation of the indictment.[93] However, the defense counsel may be present during the interrogation of the accused only with the sanction of the investigator.[94] One Soviet publication stated that the Union Republics have incorporated regulations "to the effect that defense is carried out not only before the court but in the preliminary investigations,"[95] but more recent articles mention specifically that defense counsel is permitted *after* the completion of the preliminary investigation. The reference to participation during the preliminary investigation may be an over-generalization based on the special provisions for defense accorded to minors. Even provision for the participation of the defense counsel following the completion of the preliminary investigation is not as inclusive as might be expected on the basis of the formal statutes. In practice, the militia agencies investigate approximately half of all crimes, including those for which the law provides quite severe penalties.[96] If the crime is investigated by the militia, rather than by agencies of the Procuracy, the defense counsel is not permitted to participate in the case until it is heard in court.[97] The limited rights of the defense counsel in cases investigated by the militia are described by Soviet jurists as an unnecessary limitation of the rights of the participants which should be rectified by new legislation.[98]

In all republics the advocate has some immunity from the duty to testify against his client. According to R.S.F.S.R. regulations, "A lawyer must not divulge information imparted to him by a client in connection with the rendering of legal aid in a given case. A lawyer may not be examined as a witness on the circumstances of a case that has become known to him in connection with the discharge of his duties as a defense lawyer in the case."[99]

Soviet authors stress the advantage of this guarantee to the citizen but argue that the present regulations are inadequate since the immunity clause refers only to a given case and does not prohibit the divulgence of information derived from legal aid in general.

A Soviet lawyer is prohibited from accepting cases in which his personal or economic interests might be in conflict with the interests of the client. In line with this regulation, attorneys are not permitted to hold other positions, except as teachers or in research. Because some advocates in the past have abandoned clients whose prospects for a favorable judgment were slight, almost all of the republics have incorporated the requirement that a lawyer may not give up the defense of an accused person after having accepted the case. The lawyer is obligated to avail himself of all means and methods stipulated by law for the defense of the rights and legitimate interests of his clients. However, the regulations are explicit that the defense counsel must assist in the administration of justice. Thus, he is bound to serve simultaneously as the defender of his client and as the defender of socialist morality. A Soviet author commented that the lawyer cannot "confine his task merely to the interests of his client, 'as such', as an individual, isolated person, but must think first of all of the interests of the people, the interests of the state."[100] Herein lies one of the most difficult problems which confront the Soviet advocate. He must concurrently defend his client and serve as an agent of public policy. In most civil and non-political criminal cases this may not constitute a problem, but in cases involving political crimes, a strong defense could be interpreted as opposition to the state. During the Stalin era, the defense attorney in a political case ordinarily did little more than to point out extenuating circumstances and recommend clemency. Despite recent liberalizing trends, the role of the defense counsel in political cases is still seriously circumscribed. The legal interests of the client must be defended "from the point of view of the interests of the state."[101]

A Soviet author, arguing against violations of the truism "a defender must defend" reported a case to the contrary. A defendant, accused of stealing gold, denied his guilt, only to have his own defense counsel insist that he was in fact guilty. Gross violations of the court procedure were not protested. An appeal against the death sentence had to be initiated by the convicted man, since the defense counsel refused to take action. The higher court found evidence in the case record indicating that the defendant, though he may have been connected with the thieves, could not have been directly involved in the actual robbery. The author asserted that the division of functions between the defense counsel and the prosecutor must be maintained in order to protect society from criminal elements and, at the same time, to ensure that the innocent are not convicted; both are necessary to defend the interests "of the people, of the state, of man."[102] As previously

indicated, the Procurator may come to the defense of an otherwise unde-
fended person.

Within the past two decades, standards of legal practice have been
raised appreciably. The overall educational level of advocates has been
raised and stricter regulations have reduced the incidence of infringements
such as demanding extra fees to guarantee a more vigorous defense, and
the initiation of unwarranted lawsuits. Although government control over
an ostensibly free profession has concomitant disadvantages, the hierarchical
supervisory structure somewhat limits the danger that a Soviet citizen will
be treated unjustly simply because of the unethical or inefficient practices of
his lawyer. At the same time, the regulation that the lawyer must defend
socialist morality somewhat reduces the likelihood that a guilty, but powerful, defendant will be acquitted because of the efforts of a skillful and well-
paid lawyer. Recently incorporated regulations, such as at least limited
secrecy of client-lawyer communications, are indicative of a progressive
trend. But the major problem in legal practice in the U.S.S.R. remains
unsolved. Soviet lawyers, like judges and members of the Procuracy, must
above all else promote the interests of the party and the state. In the event
of a conflict between legal ethics and political obligations, politics must be
given priority over law.

Fundamentals of Soviet Criminal Legislation

Soviet criminal legislation is summarized in a series of laws which were
approved by the Supreme Court of the U.S.S.R. in December, 1958.[103] The
most important law enacted at that time was the Fundamentals of Criminal
Legislation for the U.S.S.R. and the Union Republics. According to the
new laws criminal legislation in the U.S.S.R. is designed "to protect the
Soviet social and state system, socialist property, the person and the rights
of citizens and socialist law and order *in toto* from criminal acts"; protection is extended to "the person and the political, labor, property and other
rights of a citizen."[104] The formal statement of the protection of the rights
and even the property of individual citizens constitutes an improvement
over the previous code.

The new code reintroduced the concepts of crime and punishment.
Crime is still defined as a "socially dangerous act," but the term punishment has replaced "measures of social defense." The purpose of punishment currently includes retaliation as well as the prevention of crime and
the reform, reeducation and rehabilitation of offenders.[105] The penalties for
certain crimes have been decreased and the maximum term of imprisonment has been reduced from twenty-five to fifteen years, but penalties for
particularly grave crimes against the state and against the person have
increased in harshness. Capital punishment had been abolished by the
Presidium of the Supreme Soviet in 1947 but was reintroduced in 1950 for

high treason, espionage, wrecking and sabotage. The 1958 code reaffirmed the ideal of the complete abolition of the death penalty, but extended the number of crimes punishable by death to include banditry, terroristic acts against representatives of foreign states and premeditated murder under aggravating circumstances. In 1962 rape, bribe taking by public officials and attempts on the life of a policeman or a citizen volunteer charged with maintaining public order were added to the crimes subject to capital punishment.[106] A law of 1933 had stated that persons over the age of twelve were subject to any kind of punishment specified by law, but present regulations state that the death penalty may not be passed on persons under the age of eighteen when the crime was committed nor may it be applied against a woman who was pregnant when the crime was committed, or when the sentence is passed or is to be carried out.

The maximum term of deprivation of liberty, fifteen years, may be imposed on dangerous habitual criminals and for exceptionally grave crimes; otherwise the sentence is not to exceed ten years. Deprivation of liberty sentences may be served in a prison, a corrective labor colony or a labor colony for juveniles. A prison sentence is considered to be a more severe form of punishment than assignment to a corrective labor colony; dangerous recidivists may be required to serve the entire sentence in a prison; prisoners who behave well may have the second half of a prison sentence commuted to detention in a labor colony; persons who "wilfully transgress against the regime" of the corrective labor colony may, on court order, have up to three years of imprisonment substituted for detention in a labor colony. Since, according to the 1926 code, a sentence in a corrective labor camp constituted a more severe form of punishment than a sentence in a prison, it may be concluded that conditions in the corrective labor colonies are greatly superior to those which previously obtained in the corrective labor camps. In 1960 an official of the Supreme Court of the U.S.S.R. stated: "As a general rule the sentence of deprivation of liberty must be served in a corrective labor colony at the place where the guilty person is convicted. This ensures the convicted persons speedy return to honest labor activity by influences brought to bear on him by members of his family, public organizations from his former place of work, etc."[107] A request for conditional release or the substitution of a milder measure of punishment for persons who have "proved their reform by their exemplary behavior and an honest attitude toward work" may be initiated by the administration of the detention institution and must be acted on by a court.[108] Juveniles, ordinary offenders and perpetrators of grave crimes may be released conditionally after one third, one half or two thirds respectively of the sentence has been served; habitual criminals are not eligible for the substitution of a milder penalty.

Soviet citizens may be exiled or banished for a period not to exceed five years for a variety of misdemeanors including anti-Soviet agitation and propaganda, violation of the equality of rights of nations and races, and for leading a "parasitic mode of life." Usually, exiles are sentenced to obligatory resettlement and compulsory labor in a specified location. During recent years, thousands of parasites have been subjected to this form of punishment. Critics within the U.S.S.R. point out that insufficient attention has been devoted to the reform of the exiled parasites. The militia in the region of deportation, who are responsible for the general supervision of the exiles, complain that they get little help from the directors of enterprises, Y.C.L. organizations and local residents.[109] Although enlistment in work at the place of deportation is compulsory, many managers refuse to employ parasites because they have production quotas to fulfill and do not want to be burdened with "workers who need nursemaids and watchmen."[110] Exiles who are willing to work may not be accepted. Often exiles are settled together in a single building and are given jobs together in a single brigade or in a brigade with seasonal workers. Rather than working with "strong" workers, they have only the example of others just like themselves.[111] In many cases parasites are left to their own devices and according to a Soviet author ". . . here is the result: one who has gone astray is banished to be reformed by labor, and he finds himself in a seventh heaven! He is not forced to work and gets money and packages from relatives."[112] Persons who avoid work in areas of deportation may be sentenced by a court to corrective labor with 10 percent deduction in pay and, if corrective labor is evaded, to a period of deprivation of freedom. Apparently many of the exiles have been subjected to the more severe form of punishment largely because of the poor preparation of the areas of deportation for dealing with the parasites. One of the chief functions of the anti-parasite law seems to have been to relieve large urban areas of "undesirables" by more or less dumping them on remote communities which do not know what to do with them. Currently attempts are underway to use and retrain the exiles more efficiently.

A variety of other penalties, some of which are more or less unique to the U.S.S.R., are also used. A convicted person may be sentenced for periods up to one year of corrective labor without deprivation of liberty, usually at his place of work or in the vicinity of his residence. Deductions of up to 20 percent of his earnings are made for the benefit of the state and reeducational measures are to be applied by the collective. Persons sentenced to long prison terms or to death may have part or all of their personal belongings confiscated by the state. Provision is made for the exclusion of articles essential to the convicted person and others dependent upon him. Since the late 1950's many state officials who enriched themselves in the form of elaborate dachas and other personal belongings at the expense of the state have had their property confiscated. As a supplementary penalty for crimes associated with particular positions or activities, an individual may be deprived of the right to hold that position or engage in that activity for a specified period. Imprisonment in lieu of a fine or a fine in lieu of imprisonment is not permitted. The amount of a court imposed fine must be determined by the gravity of the offense and the property status of the guilty person. Extensive use is made of public censure which involves a reprimand addressed to the offender in public by the court; the press may be used to give the reprimand additional publicity. Any person convicted of a grave crime is deprived of orders, medals and titles of honor. A penalty which was listed in earlier codes but is no longer used is the declaration of the guilty person as an enemy of the people with deprivation of citizenship and banishment from the U.S.S.R. forever or for a definite period. A Soviet authority lists as an essential difference between the new and earlier codes the "complete rejection of deprivation of liberty with detention in corrective labor camps."[113] Most Western authorities react with skepticism to the claim that the notorious labor camps of the Stalin era have been eliminated completely, although it is conceded that conditions in the camps may have improved considerably.

A few examples of the measures of punishment associated with specific crimes provide concrete illustrations of Soviet law in practice. High treason, espionage, terrorism and wrecking are punishable by seven to fifteen years deprivation of liberty with confiscation of property or by death and confiscation of property. Sabotage and terroristic acts, not involving murder, against the representatives of a foreign state are punishable by eight to fifteen years deprivation of liberty with confiscation of property. The sentence for unlawful travel abroad or unlawful entry into the U.S.S.R. is one to three years. In some cases, the statutory provision for punishment varies with the consequences of the act; for example, the loss of documents containing state secrets is normally punished by deprivation of liberty for one to three years, but if the loss entails serious consequences, the sentence is from three to eight years. For some crimes the court may select between a corrective labor or deprivation of liberty sentence. Generally, the deprivation of liberty period is longer than the corrective labor period; for example, failure to report crimes against the state is punishable by deprivation of liberty for one to three years or by corrective labor for six months to one year.

Soviet authorities stress that one of the progressive features of their criminal legislation is the principle of strict individuality in passing sentence, depending on the concrete circumstances of the case, the gravity of the crime and the character of the guilty person.[114] To be taken into consideration are: extenuating circumstances such as youthfulness, sincere remorse, self-denunciation and difficult personal and family problems; aggravating circumstances such as a previous criminal record, the serious consequences of the crime, personal greed, unusual cruelty and the incitement of minors to participate in the crime. A statute of limitations prohibits the court from imposing a more severe penalty than is provided by law, but the court may establish a punishment below the minimum laid down by law, or apply a more lenient type of punishment when it considers such mitigation necessary with regard to the extraordinary circumstances of the case and the personality of the offender (Section 37). The court may also impose a conditional sentence if it concludes that no useful purpose would be achieved by having the offender serve the imposed sentence. The reeducation and reform of probationers may be entrusted to public organizations or collectives, especially if the organization or collective petition that the offender should be given a conditional sentence. In 1959 the Supreme Court of the U.S.S.R. instructed the lower courts to de-emphasize criminal punishment and to rely, in so far as is reasonable, on reeducation and rehabilitative measures.[115]

Soviet authorities regard the involvement of the entire collective in the reform and reeducation of the probationer as a highly progressive feature of their criminal legislation and report that only slightly more than one percent of probationers assigned to work collectives for rehabilitation have committed second offenses.[116] If these figures are reliable they would reflect a rather remarkable accomplishment. Among the many Western scholars who have been highly skeptical about the reasonableness of the Soviet approach to probationers is a Professor of Criminal Law who commented: "That this task is a difficult one which can only be properly performed under the guidance of specialized social workers is recognized nearly everywhere in the world."[117] Soviet authorities question the validity of the assumption that trained social workers are necessarily able to rehabilitate first offenders more efficiently than members of a community acting in unison. They point out that a trained probation officer may be able to help the offender to understand the motives and circumstances associated with the original crime and even to develop more constructive approaches to meet his needs, but, without help from the community, neither the probation officer nor the offender may be able to eradicate or otherwise deal with the environmental factors which initially played a role in predisposing the individual to crime. In the U.S.S.R. members of the community are expected to assume responsibility for probationers and potential offenders and to initiate remedial action with respect to poor living and working conditions, rejection by potential employers, negative influences, etc.; constructive guidance is to be provided at all times, not just through periodic contacts with one responsible individual. The effectiveness of preventive and rehabilitation measures reflect on the prestige of the entire collective. Critics within the U.S.S.R. report that when the community takes its responsibilities seriously the results have been excellent but that too many communities have been negligent and probationers have not been supervised adequately.

In line with the criminal codes of most countries, the Soviet criminal code includes sections on non-imputability, necessary defense and extreme necessity. Mentally ill or mentally deficient persons who commit socially dangerous acts are not held criminally responsible although the court may order coercive measures of a medical character. Acts which would ordinarily be considered crimes, if committed in necessary defense or extreme necessity, such as to protect or avert a danger threatening the Soviet state, or to protect oneself or other citizens, are not treated as crimes. However, persons who commit a crime when drunk are not freed from criminal responsibility. Provision is made for the deduction of the period spent in custody, while awaiting trial, from the length of the sentence. Regulations governing limitation of criminal responsibility by lapse of time between the criminal act and the initiation of criminal proceedings are established, with the period of limitation increasing with the increased severity of the penalty associated with the crime. A sentence cannot be executed if it has not been executed within a specific time period following its final pronouncement. Again, the period of limitation increases with the increased severity of the sentence, varying from a minimum of three years to a maximum of fifteen years. A death sentence affected by the period of limitation statute may be commuted into deprivation of liberty. A person who has committed a crime may be relieved of criminal responsibility if, when his case is heard in court, the offense has lost its socially dangerous character, or the offender, because of his subsequent irreproachable conduct, can no longer be considered socially dangerous.

The most fundamental and important change introduced by the 1958 legislation is the re-introduction of the *nulla poena* rule which states that persons may be held criminally responsible only for committing acts which are *forbidden by law* (Article 3). This statement provides a formal rejection of the principle of analogy, which in the previous code had instructed the court to impose penalties for socially dangerous acts not directly provided for in criminal legislation by analogy with those articles of the criminal codes dealing with crimes most similar to the acts in question in their nature and significance. Moreover, the new code (Article 6) rules that whether an act is criminal and punishable is determined by the law which was in force at the time of its commission; a law which makes an action punishable or increases the penalty has no retroactive force. Thus, Soviet citizens can no longer legally be held criminally responsible for acts which were not defined as crimes at the time of their commission. Another significant improvement is the rejection of the principle, contained in the earlier code, that permitted the court to impose penalties such as banishment and exile on persons who had not committed a definite crime but were declared "a danger to society" on the basis of their connection with criminal circles or foreign elements. In practice, innocent relatives of persons who committed crimes against the state, left the U.S.S.R. illegally or otherwise broke the state imposed mores were subjected to punishment under this principle. Soviet authorities maintain that the *nulla poena* rule and the statement that criminal punishment can be inflicted only by order of a court (Article 3) merely formalize what has been the established practice for several years.[118] They add that since the Special Board of the Ministry of Internal Affairs was abolished in September, 1953 all forms of criminal penalties have been imposed only by the appropriate courts at public trials.[119] Strict enforcement of these regulations would constitute a major improvement in the administration of justice in the U.S.S.R.

Criminal Court Procedure

The 1958 code lists the tasks of Soviet criminal procedure as:

". . . the speedy and full detection of crime, the exposure of the guilty and the guarantee of the correct application of the law so that every person who commits a crime shall suffer just punishment and not one innocent person shall be prosecuted or punished. Criminal court procedures must facilitate the strengthening of socialist legality, the prevention and eradication of crime and the education of citizens in the spirit of the unconditional fulfillment of Soviet laws and respect for the rules of the socialist way of life" (Article 2).

Contemporary Soviet jurists stress the need for investigating officials and courts to seek out and divulge exonerating as well as incriminating facts to ensure that no innocent person is convicted.[120] This emphasis ties in with the repudiation of court practices in the Stalin era when, it is now freely admitted, many completely innocent persons were convicted for grave offenses. Also lauded as a progressive innovation is the assignment of responsibility to the courts for preventing and eradicating crime.

Criminal cases are usually initiated by the Procuracy or the militia. The law states that no person may be arrested except by order of the court or with the sanction of the Procurator (Article 6). A subsequent article (Article 32) specifies that agencies of inquiry and investigation may arrest a suspected criminal but stipulates that the Procurator must be informed within 24 hours of the grounds and motives for the arrest. The Procurator must confirm the arrest or release the individual within 48 hours. During the Stalin era the rule that arrests require the sanction of the Procurator or a court was violated frequently, especially by the secret police, and even as late as 1958 Soviet jurists argued for the need to enforce this rule.[121] However, available evidence indicates that the procedural guarantees are being applied with increasing consistency.

The most important phase of investigation for criminal and, particularly, political cases occurs prior to the trial in the preliminary investigation or inquiry. According to the Fundamentals of Criminal Court Procedure, the preliminary investigation in criminal cases is conducted by investigators of the Procurator's office and for particularly severe crimes against the state (e.g. espionage, high treason, terrorism, anti-Soviet propaganda and agitation) by investigators of agencies of state security as well. Preliminary investigation is obligatory for serious crimes; less severe crimes, which might nevertheless carry quite severe penalties, are subjected to a less formal investigation called an inquiry, which is conducted by the militia. Inquiry is also used as an urgent measure of investigation to confirm that a crime has been committed and to identify suspects; the inquiry may involve search, seizure, taking evidence, detention and interrogation of suspected persons, and interrogation of the victim and witnesses. If the case is relatively uncomplicated, the material derived from the inquiry serves as grounds for the examination of the case in court.

The preliminary investigation is alleged to be an impartial hearing, conducted by a non-judgemental investigator, in which evidence provided by the defendant and his witnesses carries equal weight with that provided by the militia and the Procurator. However, even if the investigator is impartial, the defendant may be placed at a disadvantage, since only minors and persons suffering from physical and mental deficiencies may be assisted by defense counsel during this phase of the investigation, and his access to exonerating evidence may be limited by the fact that he may be held in custody. A suspect can be held in custody for a period not to exceed ten days before he is charged with the crime. After a formal charge has been made, he can ordinarily be held in custody during the investigation for a period not to exceed two months. In complicated cases the period of detention during the preliminary investigation can be extended to six months by an intermediate Procurator, or to nine months by the Procurator-General of the U.S.S.R. In lieu of preventive custody the accused may be released on the basis of a signed undertaking not to leave the place, or on personal surety or surety given by a public organization. Organs of investigation and inquiry require authorization from the Procurator to institute a search, to enter the home of a citizen, or to detain and seize correspondence. However, in urgent cases, the search may be made without authorization with the stipulation that the Procurator is informed within twenty-four hours. Before a search begins, the person must be asked to submit voluntarily the articles in question, and the search must be made in the presence of disinterested witnesses. A deputy chairman of the Supreme Court of the R.S.F.S.R. stated categorically that evidence obtained by illegal searches or seizure of correspondence is not admitted as evidence by the court.[122]

The results of the preliminary investigation or the inquiry are summarized and submitted to the Procurator, who may use the record to issue an indictment if he concludes that it provides sufficient evidence that a crime has been committed, and that the accused was involved in the commission of the crime. All records are sent to the court, which again evaluates the dossier to ascertain whether there are sufficient grounds for examination of the case in court, whether the case has been fully and correctly evaluated and whether there have been infringements of statutory rules. Without evaluating the question of factual guilt, the judge may agree that there are sufficient grounds to commit the accused for trial. If the judge disagrees with the conclusions of the indictment, the case is discussed collectively at an administrative session of the court. There, the decision might be to quash the case because of insufficient grounds for trial; to return the case for further investigation, if the preliminary investigation was inadequate, or if there are grounds for charging the accused with a graver crime, or for charging other persons; or to submit the case for trial. If the court accepts the case for trial, it may strike out specific points of the indictment or bring the charge under a less severe provision of criminal law.

Despite the fact that Soviet authorities stress the magnitude of the rights granted to the accused, there would appear to be serious limitations to his rights, at least prior to the hearing of the case in court. The regulations state that:

> "The accused has the right to: know what he is accused of and to make statements in respect to the charge against him; to submit evidence; to file petitions; to acquaint himself with the material of the preliminary investigation on its termination and with all material connected with the case; to retain counsel; to participate in the trial at a court of the first instance; to challenge the composition of the court; to appeal against the actions and decisions of the interrogating officer, the Procurator or the court. The accused has the right to the last word" (Article 21).

Practice varies considerably from what might be expected on the basis of the formal regulations. As previously indicated, defense counsel ordinarily does not participate in the case until the completion of the preliminary investigation, although statements made by the accused during the preliminary investigation are admissible as evidence in court. Moreover, if the case has been subjected to inquiry rather than to preliminary investigation, the defense counsel is not permitted to participate until the case is heard in court.[123] At least some Soviet jurists consider the restriction on the use of defense counsel prior to the actual trial to be a "limitation of rights,"[124] but other jurists merely comment that there is "no necessity for the participation of the advocate before the case is tried" because of the "simplicity of the cases subject only to inquiry."[125] Highly emphasized is the right of the accused to examine the materials of the preliminary investigation and all materials connected with the case. However, since a copy of the indictment may be given to him only three days before the case is heard in court,[126] he may have little time to prepare an adequate defense, either with or without the assistance of defense counsel.

Reports in the Soviet press indicate that the guaranteed rights of the

accused are sometimes violated. However, such reports are of a condemnatory nature, and it appears that, in the main, the regime attempts to adhere
to the statutory provisions. Khrushchev and his successors harshly criticized
the brutal infringements on human rights and dignity which were ad-
mittedly prevalent during the Stalin era: fabrication of evidence, physical
torture, police brutality, forced confessions, predetermined guilt and a general disregard for all procedural guarantees. Under Stalin, an arrest for a
political crime was tantamount to conviction. Rather than serving its stated
purpose of sorting out evidence, the preliminary investigation served only
to compile evidence of guilt, fabricated or otherwise, often including a
forced confession. The trial was not used to determine whether the accused
was guilty, since the decision concerning his guilt was made prior to his
arrest; rather, it was used to remove personal rivals of a party leader, to
warn would-be deviationists, to inform the public that the party was fully
aware of the activities of citizens, to pin the responsibility for economic
failure on a few officials and sometimes to punish those actually guilty of
espionage, treason or other crimes. Although the trial of Beria in 1953 and
Bagirov and his associates[127] in 1956 involved procedural violations strik-
ingly similar to the Stalin methods, available evidence suggests that, in general, the rights of the accused are honored to a greater degree and more
consistently than in the past decades.

According to the regulations all cases are publicly examined by the
court. A hearing may take place *in camera* only when necessary to protect
a state secret, or on order of the court in cases of persons under sixteen
years of age, in cases of sex crimes and to prevent the publication of in-
timate information about the lives of the participants. This list of exceptions provides legal sanction for secret trials in cases involving political
crimes. The ruling that the sentence must be pronounced publicly, even
for cases heard *in camera,* does nothing to ensure that procedural guarantees will be followed as conscientiously in secret political trials as in public
trials.

The trial court of the first instance is required to "examine any evidence in the case, interrogate the accused, the injured parties, the witnesses,
hear the conclusions of experts, inspect the exhibits, read out the minutes
and other documents" (Article 37). All participants, including the Procurator, accused, defense counsel and injured party enjoy the same rights
with regard to the submission and examination of evidence, and the filing
of petitions (Article 38). The participation of the accused is mandatory,
but "exceptional cases" may be heard in the absence of the accused (Article
39). Beria's trial constituted such an exceptional case. Although the Procurator's role is analogous to that of a public prosecutor, he is obligated to
withdraw the charge if he concludes that it is not supported by the facts
established by the trial. The court may permit representatives of public

organizations to participate in the hearing of a criminal case, either as public accusors or as public counsel for the defense (Article 41). In hearing the case, the court is limited to the case of the accused and the charge which has been placed against him. The charge may be altered by the court only if it does not worsen the position of the accused or infringe on his right to defense (Article 42). Once a case has begun, it cannot be interrupted except for allotted rest periods. The judgment of the court, whether condemnatory or acquitting, must be in accord with the law and must be based exclusively on the evidence heard during the trial (Article 43).

Judicial proceedings are conducted in the language of the Union Republic, Autonomous Republic or Autonomous Region. Persons who do not know the language of the court have the guaranteed right to acquaint themselves with the material of the case through an interpreter, and to use their own language in court.[128] The court session, particularly if the case is heard by a People's Court, is surprisingly informal and is designed to be educational. Approximately twenty-five percent of the criminal cases are tried at enterprises, institutions and farms rather than in regular courtrooms so that workers and employees may be instructed in the nature and consequences of the crime.[129] Ordinarily, there are speeches glorifying the regime or expressing extreme distaste for the crime under consideration; the propaganda value of these speeches is greater than their role in insuring justice. The Soviet judge, Procurator and even the defense counsel are responsible for the legal education of the masses; representatives of public organizations may also use the courtroom as an opportunity to demonstrate publicly the correctness of their thinking.[130]

A convicted person, his defense counsel and the victim of a crime have the right to appeal against the sentence of a court. The Procurator is bound to protest any illegal or unfounded sentence (Article 44). A court of the second instance checks on the legality of the sentence and the grounds for it on the basis of the material of the case and the newly submitted material. The appeal court may leave the sentence unchanged; annul the sentence and order a new investigation or trial; annul the sentence and quash the case; or change the sentence. Sentences may be reduced by applying a law on a less serious crime. If the court of appeal concludes that a harsher sentence or a law on a graver crime should be applied, a new trial is ordered in a court of original jurisdiction. The verdict of a Supreme Court is not subject to appeal or protest. Re-examination of a court sentence that is already in force is permitted only if requested by the Procurator or the chairman of the Supreme Court of the Union Republic or the U.S.S.R.

Principles of Civil Law

The dramatic aspects of Soviet criminal law during the preceding decades have diverted attention from Soviet civil law. However, Soviet sources state that at least 85 percent of all court cases are civil cases. The content and purpose of Soviet civil legislation is summarized in the prologue to the 1961 Principles of Civil Legislation.

> "Soviet civil legislation is a major means of further strengthening legality in the sphere of property relations and protecting the rights of socialist organizations and citizens. Soviet civil legislation is called upon actively to foster the accomplishment of the tasks of communist construction. It fosters the strengthening of the socialist system of economy, socialist property, and the development of its forms into uniform communist property; the strengthening of the plan and contract discipline and cost accounting; the prompt and proper fulfillment of deliveries; a steady improvement in the quality of output; the fulfillment of capital construction plans and increased effectiveness of capital investments; the implementation of state purchases of agricultural products; the development of Soviet trade; the protection of the material and cultural interests of citizens and the correct combination of these interests with those of society as a whole; and the development of creative initiative in science, technology, literature and the arts."[131]

A major portion of the code is designed to ensure the smooth functioning of the economy (contracts, deliveries, credit relations, etc.), but a number of clauses are designed to protect the civil rights of individuals. New procedural guarantees against unauthorized eviction and the illegal requisitioning of excess space in living quarters were probably highly welcomed by Soviet citizens. Stricter measures against the use of personal property, particularly in the form of housing, for the derivation of unearned income were introduced. For the first time, Soviet citizens and organizations have the right to demand by court action the refutation of false information defaming their honor and dignity. Court action is now required to establish lack of legal capacity because of feeble mindedness or mental illness (Article 9). The major clause on individual rights states:

> "Citizens may, in accordance with the law have property for personal ownership and the right to use housing and other property, inherit and bequeath property, choose their occupation and place of residence, have author's rights to works of science, literature and art, discoveries, inventions and rationalization proposals, and also have other property and personal nonproperty rights."

A word of caution in the exercise of these rights is inserted in Article 5 which states: "Civil rights are protected by law, with the exception of cases in which they are exercised in conflict with the purpose of these rights in socialist society in the period of building communism."

Differences between the Soviet Civil Code and corresponding codes in Western societies derive primarily from the public ownership of the means of production and state employment of the majority of the population. Within the framework of the Soviet social system, the civil guarantees accorded to its citizens are roughly the equivalent of those of other societies. Civil procedures generally follow the same pattern outlined for criminal procedures. A few unique features of Soviet civil procedures are worthy of mention. Concerted attempts are made to involve the public in civil cases; court hearings are often held in enterprises and institutions; public representatives may be appointed to participate in the hearing; the court may inform an enterprise that a case involving one of its employees is pending and may request that the collective attempt to resolve the difficulties out of court.[132] A third party may initiate action to have the conflicting rights of two other parties adjudicated; thus, a trade union may institute a suit against an employer on behalf of a member without the member's authorization. If the two parties to a civil court action decide to settle out of court, or the plaintiff decides to cancel his suit, the court may on its own discretion proceed with the action. The court may also decide to litigate issues related to, but not specified in the original suit, to grant the plaintiff awards in excess of what he sought, or to reverse the plea and grant the defendant unsolicited remedy against the plaintiff. If properly applied, such innovations could contribute to a more adequate administration of justice. There are few complaints in the Soviet press about the maladministration of the civil code. The interests of the regime as well as the individual are served by the stability resulting from uniform enforcement of the established civil law.

The Secret Police

No discussion of Soviet justice would be complete without reference to the activities of the security agencies which have paralleled the ordinary judicial apparatus. Ever since the Bolsheviks seized power, security agencies under various labels (CHEKA, GPU, OGPU, NKVD, MGB, KGV and MVD) have had broad powers, which were frequently overstepped, to ferret out "enemies of the people." The current state security organizations are the Committee on State Security (KGB) and the Ministry for Safeguarding Public Order which replaced the Ministry of Internal Affairs (MVD) in 1962.

Less is written in the Soviet press about the security agencies than about any other public organization. However, the broad range of their functions is at least partially indicated by the titles of the administrations into which they are divided. The overall function of the KGB is the prevention and detection of counterrevolution, espionage, treason and other political crimes. Its State Construction Trust and Economic Administration divisions are responsible for preventing and detecting offenses against state property in industrial enterprises, agriculture and transportation. The Border Troops and Political Administration of Border Troops police the frontier. The Foreign Administration and Administration for Counter-Intelligence supervise espionage agents and other Soviet personnel stationed abroad. The Secret Political Administration maintains surveillance over all Soviet citizens, keeps record of all potential suspects, arrests offenders and maintains numerous agents provocateur. Other divisions of the KGB are the Chief Administration of Prisons which maintains places of detention, the Administration of Special Sections which investigates the political reliability of its own personnel, the personnel of the Ministry for Safeguarding Public Order and of members of the armed forces.

The official reason for changing the name of the Ministry of Internal Affairs to the Ministry for Safeguarding Public Order was to allow for the name to reflect more accurately the function of the Ministry.[133] It is presumed that the divisions within the newly named Ministry correspond to those of its predecessor. One of the most important of these administrations is the Militia, or the regular police force. The Administrations of Economy, Internal Troops and Convoy Troops perform security functions in the economy, defense installations and police transit points. The Corrective Labor Colonies and Places of Detention Administrations have jurisdiction over the construction projects that are manned by persons sentenced to corrective labor and over local prisons and other places of detention. Local Air Defense, Fire Protection, Geodesy and Cartography and State Archives are also under the jurisdiction of this Ministry.

The Ministry for Safeguarding Public Order and the Committee on State Security are Union-Republican organs which are formally responsible to both the U.S.S.R. and republican Council of Ministers. Local branches are responsible to the republican organs of the Ministry or Committee and to the Executive Committee of the local Soviet. According to law, the activities of the secret police are also subject to some regulation from the Procuracy and the courts. Certain categories of cases must be transferred from the secret police to the jurisdiction of the court. The law states clearly that crime may be punished only in accordance with the sentence of a court. However, the history of the administration of justice in the U.S.S.R. demonstrates with unmistakable clarity that formal legal and constitutional provisions do not always accurately reflect practice.

From the beginning of the Bolshevik rule and definitely until the 1950's, the activities of the secret police have been one of the features of the Soviet regime most worthy of condemnation. Antagonists of the Soviet system have pointed correctly to the lawlessness and to the inhumane and terroristic methods used by the secret police to suppress all opposition to the regime, either real, potential or imagined, as a manifestation of the internal weaknesses of the Soviet system, and of the meaninglessness of the constitutional guarantees provided for its citizens. The tactics of the secret police, probably more than any other unworthy feature of the Soviet system, have influenced opinion in other nations against communism and the

U.S.S.R. In fact, knowledge about the methods of terror used by the Soviet secret police has led many citizens in other countries to equate communism with brutality and suppression and to exclude from consideration some of the more acceptable tenets of communism and the actual accomplishments of the Soviet regime.

Terroristic methods, administered chiefly but not exclusively by the secret police, have been one of the major techniques used by the regime to solidify and perpetuate its absolute control over all elements within the society. In many cases the actions of the secret police have had legal sanction in that the established laws granted them the right to arrest "socially dangerous elements" or on the "suspicion of espionage," even when no crime had been committed, and to mete out severe punishment. Completely innocent persons, including hostages, have been victimized. Former tsarist officials, people of bourgeois origin, kulaks, former members of non-Bolshevik parties and strongly nationalistic minorities have been particularly oppressed, but no category of citizens, including persons who considered themselves to be loyal Bolsheviks, has been exempted from surveillance and oppression. Punishments have included deprivation of political rights, imprisonment without trial, banishment to a distant region, deprivation of liberty in a prison or corrective labor camp, confiscation of property and execution. The secret police played a leading role in the Red Terror, the Great Purge, all lesser purges, and in forcibly eliminating opposition to the regime by eradicating dissenters and terrorizing the population into submission.

The methods of the secret police have been diabolically skillful for the inculcation of a widespread reaction of terror and docile subservience to the regime. Secret agents, massive demonstrations of power, midnight arrests with the complete disappearance of the victims, dossiers containing secret information on millions of citizens and officials, secret trials, forced confessions which usually incriminated innocent colleagues and associates, agents provocateur, rumors about the horrors of the forced labor camps, and numerous other techniques were used to intimidate, terrify and control citizens who had no reasonable basis for predicting if and when the seemingly omnipotent police would accuse them of having committed a poorly defined but "heinous crime" against the regime.

Since Khrushchev's denunciation of Stalin, Soviet leaders have admitted freely and condemned harshly the excesses of the past. Detailed accounts of the illegal arrests, methods of torture, and conditions in forced labor camps have been published in the Soviet press.[134] Now, we are given to understand, things are different. A 1962 Soviet article states: "Nothing in the state security agencies today bears the slightest resemblance to what they were like during the time of the cult of the individual. . . . There are no people in the Committee today who had a hand during the days of the

cult in the punishment of Soviet people innocent of any crime."[135] When
asked to describe his work, an investigator is reported to have said:

> "It is our business to deal with imperialist intelligence agents and with
> persons who commit especially dangerous crimes against the state, such as
> high treason, subversion and sabotage, as well as with violations of the rules
> on currency transactions, smuggling and the divulgence of state secrets."[136]

He commented that there probably had not been a case of sabotage since
the late 1920's, and that the treason cases involve war criminals who helped
the Germans to kill Soviet citizens. Much emphasis was put on countering
foreign intelligence activities, currency speculation and embezzlement of
state property. And he added,

> "There is another side of our activities . . . the restoration of the
> good names of people who were defamed during the period of the cult of
> the individual. This is a very big and politically important task. . . . Soviet
> legality is strictly observed in all our work. In recent years there has not been
> a single instance in the Committee of violation of legality, not a single instance
> of unwarranted arrest or the bringing of criminal proceedings against innocent
> persons."[137]

Soviet spokesmen insist that "socialist legality" requires complete and un-
deviating adherence to the established laws; that arbitrariness, lawlessness
and cruelty are no longer sanctioned; and that Soviet laws are designed
to ensure that not one guilty person will be unpunished and not one innocent person will be punished by the courts which are the exclusive agents
for meting out punishment.

Since Soviet authorities have typically maintained close surveillance
over information about the operation of the security agencies, a complete
and accurate assessment of the current situation is not possible. It seems
safe to conclude that the excesses of the secret police, though not necessarily eliminated, have been curbed substantially. An initial move in this
direction was made in September, 1953 with the abolition of the Special
Board of the Ministry of Internal Affairs which had the authority to sentence "socially dangerous" persons to "camps for correctional labor" for
five years, as well as to impose other severe punishments. It has been specu-
lated in the West that when the Special Board was abolished, its rights
may have been transferred to another section of the security agencies.[138]
However, the deputy chairman of the Supreme Court of the U.S.S.R.
stated categorically that since the Special Board was abolished all forms of
criminal penalties have been imposed only by the appropriate courts at
public trials.[139] The security agencies are still actively engaged in the preliminary investigations of important political crimes.[140] Party leaders claim
that forced labor camps have been completely abolished, and in spite of
the fact that many Western observers are skeptical, tangential evidence suggests that the number of inmates of such camps has been reduced con-

siderably, and that a "corrective labor" penalty is less onerous than in past years.

In comparison to Stalin, Khrushchev and his successors have placed more emphasis on positive techniques of control and less emphasis on negative techniques. It is possible, that because the demands made on Soviet citizens are decreasing while the rewards are increasing, their support for the regime might be more genuine, and therefore the need for terror tactics might be decreasing. If popular support for the regime grows, the number of arrests for political crimes and the need for intimidation and terrorism should decline accordingly. The partial relaxation of control by the secret police might be the result of increased popular support for the regime and at the same time, a bid for strengthening the ties between the people and their rulers. The post-Stalin leadership has operated on the principle that a pot of honey is sometimes more effective than a fist of iron. Nevertheless, there is evidence that the fist of iron would be used without hesitation should expediency require it. The trials of Beria and his associates involved summary techniques of justice highly reminiscent of the Stalin era. Though the power of the secret police may be substantially limited for the time being, it should be considered not as power which has been abolished, but rather as power held in abeyance to be called forth for use by the party leaders when it serves their purposes to use it.

Impact on the Individual and Society

The post-Stalin relaxation in the use of terror and the major judicial reforms enacted in 1958 are among the most important of the many changes which have occurred in the U.S.S.R. in recent years. The legal codes have obvious limitations; persons responsible for administering justice do not always adhere to the letter of the law; and in all probability terror-istic methods have not been completely rejected. Nevertheless, the overall improvement is so great that Soviet citizens may well be able to breathe more freely.

Evidence for increased respect for the legal rights of Soviet citizens is provided by several improvements in the legal codes, such as: (1) a statement of the *nulla poena* rule and the repeal of the rule of analogy; (2) only a court is entitled to rule on the guilt of a defendant, and to inflict punishment on him; (3) the provision of a statute of limitations; (4) the accused has the right to know the charges against him and to present a defense; (5) minors and physically and mentally handicapped persons have the right to defense counsel during the preliminary investigation; (6) the judge is subject to challenge; (7) the age of criminal responsibility is raised from fourteen to sixteen for most crimes; (8) the maximum term of imprisonment is reduced to fifteen years; (9) the severity of punishment for crimes against the person (e.g. murder and rape), as well as for certain crimes against the state, have been increased; (10) suspended sentences are applied more frequently for first offenders and minor offenses; (11) requirements for parole are less stringent and a criminal's record may be cleared within a shorter period of time. Soviet jurists claim that many of the improvements listed above had been common practice for years, and that the 1958 legislative action was important chiefly in that it provided formal approval for generally accepted practices. In many respects this is an unjustified claim; even now some of the improvements are not consistently enforced. However, the formal enactment clarifies the work of judicial personnel and benefits persons accused of criminal activity since the formal laws are at least potentially enforceable.

Soviet jurists, as well as their Western counterparts, are aware that the 1958 enactments leave much to be desired. For example, no legal statute in the U.S.S.R. proclaims the presumption of innocence until guilt is proven. Some Soviet jurists claim that the presumption exists in practice but the Supreme Soviet in 1958 did not accept the recommendation of many eminent jurists that the principle be formalized. In civil and ordinary criminal cases, the accused may, indeed, be presumed innocent until proven guilty. In the majority of political cases, particularly if the crime is a serious one, an arrest may still be tantamount to a conviction, and the defendant may be presumed guilty prior to his trial and ultimate conviction. Most Soviet jurists do, however, argue that it is the responsibility of the state to prove the guilt of the defendant rather than the responsibility of the defendant to prove his innocence. Soviet legal statutes do not provide for a writ of *habeas corpus.* Ordinarily, an accused person may be imprisoned up to two months and with the permission of the Procurator-General up to nine months while the preliminary investigation is being conducted. Although higher authorities or the party may intervene against unfair or dilatory practices, if it suits their purposes, a private individual has no techniques to force the authorities to bring the accused to court for a legal decision.

Most Soviet legal articles, extremely cluttered by propaganda statements, convey the impression that the defendant's unlimited rights to defense counsel is a manifestation of the concern of the regime for the protection of the rights of the individual. However, as pointed out previously, unless the accused is a minor or is physically or mentally incapacitated, defense counsel is not permitted to participate in the case until the completion of the preliminary investigation. In some cases the interval between the completion of the preliminary investigation and the trial is only three days. If a police inquiry is substituted for a preliminary investigation, the initial participation of the defense counsel is in the trial itself. Thus, in some cases the statutory right of the accused to avail himself of the services of a defense lawyer is relatively meaningless. A few Soviet jurists have stated boldly that the distinction between preliminary investigations and inquiries with respect to the participation of the defense counsel amounts to a serious limitation of the rights of some defendants and have argued that defense counsel should be available from the beginning of the investigation to the end of the trial.

Although not all of the statutory changes are as excellent as Soviet authorities claim, certain improvements which are not formally reflected in the statutes do seem to have been instituted, or are in the process of being accepted as general practice. One of these is the changed role of the confession. During the Stalin era, admission of guilt by the accused was accorded the power of conviction. This proposition justified the extraction of confessions by any method, including physical torture, and the threat of reprisals against families. Contemporary Soviet jurists consistently maintain that confession of guilt is evidence which, like all other evidence, is subject to the most careful checking and evaluation.[141] The downgrading of the power of a confession should do much to eradicate some of the most baneful practices which were common during the preliminary investigations and to strengthen the application of the principle that it is the duty of the court to establish the truth, and to base its judgments on established facts, rather than merely the "maximum probability of facts." However, Soviet jurists point out with regret that there are still some judges who accept a confession at face value and base decisions on it without verifying its objective reliability by comparing it with other evidence.[142]

Soviet legal authorities admit freely, and deplore the fact, that laws are not always consistently and fairly applied by the law enforcement authorities and the courts. A U.S.S.R. Supreme Court plenary session concluded:

> "In recent years the court agencies have improved the quality of their work somewhat, but individual courts still permit serious violations of the laws in hearing cases and the complaints of working people. Instances of unjustified convictions of citizens, and also the vindication of individuals committing crimes, instances of improper definitions of crimes, of measures of punishment inconsistent with the nature of the act and the personality of the culprit, of infringements of the defendant's right to defense and of violations of the schedule for hearing cases established by law are taking place in court practice."[143]

Particularly under attack is the failure to apply consistently the principle of combining severe measures of punishment for dangerous criminals with measures of social influence for less dangerous offenders. The chairman of the U.S.S.R. Supreme Court stated: "Completely unjustified extremes are engaged in—from the issue of sentences of deprivation of freedom for all crimes including those presenting little danger, to a literal and indulgent attitude toward dangerous criminals."[144] He complained that dangerous habitual offenders are sometimes given suspended sentences, and turned over for reeducation by the public, often completely without arrangements to ensure that rehabilitation measures will be attempted. On the other hand, some courts never give suspended sentences, even when the personality of the individual and the attitude of the personnel at his place of work are such that a second offense is unlikely. A Soviet jurist concerned with the same problem reported that a seventh grade pupil was sentenced to two years deprivation of freedom for attempting to steal a pair of children's shoes; at the same time, a "dangerous recidivist" who had been tried five times received a three month sentence for his latest theft.[145] Although the general consensus of Soviet opinion seems to be that such errors and discrepancies are typically due to misinterpretations of the intent of the law, there are suggestions that special leniency is granted occasionally to high ranking offenders, who demand and receive special consideration on the basis of their position or party membership.[146]

An extremely common complaint is that some judges and officials of the Procuracy are ignorant of both the procedural and substantive aspects of the law. The chairman of the U.S.S.R. Supreme Court commented that despite the requirement of the party and the law that procedural norms must be adhered to unswervingly ". . . one does encounter in the courts cases of erroneous classification of crimes and cases of violation of procedural norms. Errors are committed in the determination of punishments."[147] He concluded that in most cases these violations are based on "a shallow knowledge of legal requirements and an inability to apply the legal norms correctly in the examination of specific cases" rather than on "evil intent." In view of the numerous complaints about such violations, it would appear that the rights of a large number of Soviet citizens have been placed in jeopardy, and if the violations are indeed based on ignorance, extremely strong corrective measures are urgently required.

Less frequent, but nevertheless important, are complaints such as the following: the nature of the crime which has been committed is not always clearly specified; improper evidence is sometimes admitted and used in establishing a verdict; court records are poorly kept; party and state officials sometimes misuse their power and prestige to intervene in the judicial process and to influence a decision; the defendant is not always fully informed of his rights, and sometimes his rights are denied; superior courts do not always provide adequate supervision over the activities of the lower courts; law enforcement officials do not adequately fulfill their duty with respect to educating the public, and eliciting the full participation of the people in the rehabilitation of criminals and the elimination of crime.

The very fact that errors are admitted and that criticisms and suggestions for improvement are permitted constitutes a considerable improvement. However, it should not be concluded that Soviet jurists are by any means free to express unbiased opinions on all aspects of Soviet justice or to say all that ought to be said. Whereas it may be legitimate to place considerable faith in the criticisms which Soviet authors make about the administration of justice, their positive statements should be evaluated cautiously. For example, in 1961 three high ranking Soviet jurists wrote that consistent adherence in criminal procedures to the principle of objective truth *"was always characteristic of Soviet criminal procedure."*[148] Since the gross violations of the Stalin era are freely admitted these authors knew for sure that consistent adherence to the objective truth has not always been characteristic of the Soviet criminal procedure. Yet, they and many other authors make laudatory statements which they themselves must know to be erroneous, and which if accepted uncritically would lead to a biased and overly favorable evaluation of the Soviet system. Administration of justice in the Soviet Union has undoubtedly improved considerably during the past several years, but many more improvements will be required, particularly in the sphere of application, before it reaches the level of excellence which Soviet spokesmen claim was attained shortly after, if not before, the 1958 judicial legislation.

The Soviet Union, like all other states, needs the stability resulting from certain rules of conduct that are enforced. The party leaders are fully cognizant of the need for stability, for fair play between individuals and for the protection of society against anti-social behavior. A reliable system of law enforcement is essential for the effective operation of the government and the economy. Dire consequences in terms of economic and social disruption would follow if habitually a significant number of innocent persons were punished and guilty persons were allowed to enjoy the fruits of their wrongdoing. Stalin's terroristic methods demonstrated rather conclusively that the regime, itself, would gain little and lose much through the operation of a patently arbitrary and discriminatory judicial system. Punishment of the honest, conscientious, law abiding citizen along with the criminal and malingerer would, in addition to hindering economic progress, prevent the emergence of the "new Soviet man." In the period of full communism, crime and asocial behavior are to be "completely unknown." Whether or not this ideal is capable of ultimate realization, respect for law and legal norms is a basic prerequisite for its realization. Soviet leaders realize that fair and equitable administration of justice is required to engender the necessary respect for law, and to encourage the populace to give its enthusiastic support to the party program. Consequently, the regime stands to gain substantially by improving the administration of justice.

Any Soviet citizen who has had personal contact with the agencies responsible for administering justice might have reason to be disillusioned, because the legal codes are not always adhered to strictly. However, because the regime currently emphasizes protection of the rights of the individual, the ordinary citizen has much less reason than previously to fear that his rights will be trampled into the dust, and that at any moment he will be subjected to arbitrary accusation and punishment. Reduction in tension from the relaxation of fear, though the fear may justifiably not be completely eliminated, should upgrade the individual's personal happiness, creative energy and respect for the regime. Concurrently, it may be expected that fear-produced tension between individuals should also diminish, with the decreased likelihood that unjust accusations will be upheld, that innocent victims of oppression will be forced to implicate other innocent people, and that persons will be arrested and punished as "socially dangerous elements" or because they are related to or in some way connected with persons accused of wrongdoing. On the other hand, misapplication of the anti-parasite laws and the rights of the comrades' courts might serve to increase tension within groups.

The responsibility which the regime places on individuals and groups to prevent crime and to reeducate offenders may be simultaneously flattering and onerous. Although it may be interpreted as a manifestation of the trust and respect of the regime for the common man, it places on individuals and groups a responsibility which is difficult to fulfill acceptably. Since, in general, the responsibility is assigned to the group, preventive and reeducative measures are the responsibility of everyone and no one. A private individual may be reluctant to intervene in the affairs of another, or to draw the attention of the group to another person's behavior for fear of appearing to be a troublemaker. Consequently, the guidance which the regime expects the group to exert on its members may not always occur. On the other hand, the right of individuals and groups to criticize and to attempt to modify the behavior of associates and group members is sometimes carried to the extreme of unjustified harassment. Until the "new Soviet man" emerges, the "social control technique" cannot attain the desired level of effectiveness. Certainly this technique, though sometimes serving its desired purpose, perhaps even very efficiently, is fraught with problems.

One of the goals of the party is the ultimate total elimination of crime.[149] Soviet authorities state that "the socialist relations of production, . . . the noble principles of communist morality, the level of culture and education of the people, and their entire way of life create a real possibility for the complete elimination of such phenomena."[150] According to Soviet theorists the major prerequisites for the elimination of crime are the transformation of objective social and economic conditions which give rise to anti-social phenomena. Under advanced socialism and especially under full communism, they say, life will proceed so smoothly and needs will be met so adequately and equitably that the conditions which predispose an individual toward crime will be non-existent. Soviet authorities are forced to admit that, at present, they have made little progress toward the lofty goal of the complete elimination of all crime; the U.S.S.R. has its own fair share of thieves, hooligans, murderers, bribe takers and cheats. The fact that crime still exists under socialism despite changed social and economic conditions is explained in a variety of ways. Most important is the claim that for centuries "systems based on exploitation have inculcated and cultivated the spirit of individualism and money grubbing, the psychology of private property, moral callousness and many other base qualities" and these values and attitudes are transmitted from generation to generation even under socialism.[151] Added to the force of tradition is the claim that "imperialist propaganda" employs every possible device "to revive and support backward customs, habits and prejudices in the minds of Soviet people."[152] It is also admitted that during the period of transition to communism not all internal conditions which predispose an individual toward crime have been eliminated; for example, negligent or over indulgent parents, improper upbringing by the collective, irresponsible officials and poorly administered regulations are sometimes mentioned, but even these weaknesses tend to be blamed on tradition and bourgeois influence. There is little apparent recognition of the possible influence of factors such as arbitrary regulations, inadequate housing and recreational facilities and low standards of living, and no recognition whatsoever of the possibility that the Soviet system itself may, through oppressive regimentation, stifling of creativity in certain areas and in other ways, introduce new factors which contribute to the incidence of criminal behavior.

The Soviet program for the elimination of crime centers around (1) further strengthening of supervision by the agencies of state power over strict observance of the norms of Soviet laws and their execution; (2) comradely condemnation of anti-social acts, which is gradually to become the chief means of uprooting manifestations of bourgeois views, habits and customs; and (3) counterposing the harmful influence of bourgeois propaganda by using the totality of means available to act upon the consciousness of man: to employ to the fullest every economic and political lever, in private life and the life of society, and in law, to overcome the harmful vestiges of the past.[153]

Though it is unlikely that the Soviet citizen will ever live in a crime-free society, the Soviet citizen does live in a society in which the general system of dealing with crimes and administering justice is considerably more stable, consistent, reliable and equitable than in previous decades. For law-abiding citizens it is probable that peace of mind, and faith in and respect for the regime have increased, as injustices and deficiencies in the system of administering justice have decreased. However, many Soviet citizens might recall the verbal and even constitutional emphasis on the restoration of law which characterized the mid-1930's. Until after Stalin's death, the myth was officially maintained that the constitutional provisions and legal norms were strictly enforced and that rule by law prevailed, despite the fact that bloody purges and other forms of lawlessness were used or sanctioned by the party leader, and were not protested by those members of present party leadership who were in positions of power at that time. The principle task of Soviet justice is now, as it was during the early decades, to facilitate the attainment of goals set by the leadership of the Communist Party. Although the contemporary party leadership may believe that the goals of communism will be achieved more rapidly if justice in the true sense of the word prevails, the Soviet citizen has no guarantee that this belief will persist, or that exceptions to the rule will not be made. Law remains subservient to the party.

REFERENCES

1 P. S. Romashkin, "Problems of the Development of the State and Law in the Draft Program of the C.P.S.U." *Sovetskoe gosudarstvo i pravo,* 1961, No. 10. (Soviet Law and Government, Vol. I, No. 1, pp. 3-12)

2 P. I. Stuchka, "The Revolutionary Part Played by Law and the State—A General Doctrine of Law," reprinted in Hugh W. Babb. (trans.), and John W. Hazard, *Soviet Legal Philosophy,* (Cambridge, Mass.: Harvard University Press, 1951), p. 20.

3 A. Ia. Vyshinskii and V. S. Undrevich, *Course in Criminal Procedure,* Vol. I, *The Judiciary,* (2nd ed.), 1936, p. 36, quoted in Vladimir Gsovski and Kazimierz Grzybowski, (eds.), *Government, Law and Courts in the Soviet Union,* Vol. I, (New York: Frederick A. Praeger, 1959), p. 44.

4 A. F. Gorkin, "The Tasks Facing Soviet Justice Under Present Conditions," *Sovetskoe gosudarstvo i pravo,* 1962, No. 8. (Soviet Law and Government, Vol I, No. 3, pp. 3-11)

5 V. I. Lenin, "The State," A lecture delivered in Sverdlov University, July 11, 1919, reprinted in Babb, *Soviet Legal Philosophy, op. cit.,* pp. 1-15.

6 "Decree on People's Courts," Dec. 7, 1917, reprinted in James H. Meisel and Edward S. Kozera, *Materials for the Study of the Soviet System,* (Ann Arbor, Mich.: The George Wahr Publishing Co., 1953), pp. 28-30.

7 "Establishment of the Extraordinary Commission to Fight Counterrevolution," Dec. 20, 1917, reprinted in Meisel and Kozera, *Materials for the Study of the Soviet System, op. cit.,* pp. 35-6.

8 *Krasnaia gazeta,* Feb. 28, 1928.

9 Quoted in "Information on Russia," Senate Document 50, 67th Cong., 1st sess., Washington, D.C., 1921, p. 64.

10 "Collection of Laws and Orders of the R.S.F.S.R.," 1919, No. 66, Article 590.

11 Section 4, Civil Code, R.S.F.S.R. Laws, Jan. 1, 1923.

12 Section 1, Criminal Code, R.S.F.S.R. Laws, May 24, 1922.

13 Criminal Code of the U.S.S.R., 1922.

14 Quoted in Berman, *Justice in Russia, op. cit.,* p. 28.

15 Z. M. Chkhikvadze, "Soviet Criminal Law, General Part, 1952," quoted in Gsovski and Grzybowski, *Government, Law and Courts in the Soviet Union,* Vol. II, *op. cit.,* p. 937.

16 E. Pashukanis, "General Theory of Law and Marxism," (3rd ed.), 1927, quoted in Gsovski and Grzybowski, *Government, Law and Courts in the Soviet Union,* Vol. II, *op. cit.,* p. 49.

17 E. Pashukanis, Gosudarstvo i pravo pri sotsializme (State and Law under Socialism), *Sovetskoe gosudarstvo i pravo,* 1936, No. 3, p. 7, quoted in Gsovski and Grzybowski, *Government, Law and Courts in the Soviet Union,* Vol. II, *op. cit.,* p. 50.

18 *Izvestia*, July 11, 1934, p. 1.

19 Stalin, "On the Draft Constitution of the U.S.S.R.," *Problems of Leninism*, *op. cit.*, p. 564.

20 A. Ia. Vyshinskii, "Principal Tasks of the Science of Soviet Socialist Law," *Sovetskoe gosudarstvo i pravo*, 1938, No. 4.

21 *Ibid.*

22 *Fundamentals of Soviet State and Law*, (Moscow: Academy of Sciences of the U.S.S.R., Institute of Law, 1947), p. 63.

23 "For Complete Elimination of the Harmful Consequences of the Personality Cult in Soviet Jurisprudence," *Sovetskoe gosudarstvo i pravo*, 1962, No. 4, pp. 3-16. (Soviet Law and Government, Summer, 1962, pp. 24-32)

24 *Ibid.*

25 *Ibid.*

26 *Ibid.*

27 *Ibid.*

28 *Ibid.*

29 *Ibid.*

30 Denisov and Kirichenko, *Soviet State Law, op. cit.*, p. 301.

31 Oldrich Prusa and Collective, *Sovetské státní právo* (Soviet State Law), (Praha:Orbis, 1962), p. 362.

32 *Fundamentals of Soviet Criminal Legislation, the Judicial System and Criminal Court Procedure*, (Moscow: Foreign Languages Publishing House, 1960), p. 53.

33 M. S. Strogovich, Iu. A. Kalenov and A. A. Gertsenzon. "The New Laws on the Judicial System, the Criminal Code, and the Code of Criminal Procedure of the Russian Federation," *Sovetskoe gosudarstvo i pravo*, 1961, No. 1. (Soviet Law and Government, Vol. I, No. 1, 1962, pp. 32-42)

34 *Ibid.*

35 D. S. Karev, "Further Improvement of the Soviet Legal System," *Sovetskoe gosudarstvo i pravo*, 1959, No. 2.

36 *Ibid.*

37 Gorkin, "The Tasks Facing Soviet Justice Under Present Conditions," *op. cit.*

38 Cf. John N. Hazard, *The Soviet System of Government*, (Chicago: University of Chicago Press, 1957), p. 160; Boris A. Konstantinovsky, *Soviet Law in Action*, (Cambridge, Mass.: Harvard University Press, 1953), pp. 9-10, 15; and for an interesting commentary by Soviet citizens on the role of the assessor, see Ye. Rozanova and N. Shtanko, "Three People on the Judge's Bench," *Izvestia*, August 30, 1960, p. 3.

39 O. Chaikovskaya, "Feeling, Intelligence and the Law," *Izvestia*, Sept. 21, 1963, p. 4. (C.D.S.P., Vol. XV, No. 38, pp. 28-9)

40 Strogovich, Kalenov and Gertsenzon, "The New Laws of the Judicial System," *op. cit.*, p. 34.

41 K. P. Gorshenin, "The New Soviet Law on the Judicial System," in *Fundamentals of Soviet Criminal Legislation, op. cit.*, pp. 55-6.

42 Denisov and Kirichenko, *Soviet State Law, op. cit.*, p. 306.

43 "Statute on Military Tribunals," *Izvestia*, Dec. 26, 1958, p. 5.

44 For reports on Plenary session of the Supreme Court of the U.S.S.R., see *Pravda*, March 24, 1963, p. 4; *Pravda*, July 10, 1963, p. 4; *Izvestia*, Oct. 31, 1963, p. 3.

45 Quoted in Denisov and Kirichenko, *Soviet State Law, op. cit.*, p. 310.

46 Cf. Gorshenin, "The New Soviet Law on the Judicial System," *op. cit.*, p. 56.

47 N. Mironov, "Strengthening Socialist Legality and Law and Order," *Partiinaya zhizn*, 1962, No. 5. (Soviet Law and Government, Vol. I, No. 1, 1962, pp. 42-8)

48 "Edict of July 15, 1948: Statute Concerning the Disciplinary Responsibility of Judges," *Vedomosti*, 1948, No. 31; cf. Gorshenin, "The New Soviet Law on the Judicial System," *op. cit.*, p. 60.

49 Mironov, "Strengthening Socialist Legality and Law and Order," *op. cit.*, p. 47.

50 D. S. Karev, "Organization of Courts and Government Attorneys in the U.S.S.R.," quoted in Gsovski and Grzybowski, *Government, Law and Courts in the Soviet Union*, Vol. II, *op. cit.*, p. 521.

51 N. V. Krylenko, "Judiciary of the R.S.F.S.R.," quoted in Gsovski and Grzybowski, *Government, Law and Courts in the Soviet Union*, Vol. II, *op. cit.*, p. 516.

52 Vyshinskii and Undrevich, *Course in Criminal Procedure, op. cit.*, pp. 23-4.

53 *Ibid.*, p. 18.

54 N. S. Khrushchev, *Pravda*, Jan. 29, 1959.

55 "Model Act of Comradely Courts," *Izvestia*, Oct. 24, 1959, p. 2.

56 "Law on Increasing the Role of the Public in Combatting Violations of Soviet Laws and the Rules of Socialist Society," *Izvestia*, Oct. 23, 1959, p. 2.

57 Mironov, "Strengthening Socialist Legality and Law and Order," *op. cit.*, p. 44.

58 "On Introducing Additions and Amendments to the Statute on Comrades' Courts, " *Vedomosti Verkhovnovo Soveta RSFSR*, No. 43, Oct. 31, 1963, pp. 843-6.

59 For reports of comrade court action in which parasites are exiled for five year periods, see I. Zenin, "The Sponger," *Trud*, March 19, 1963, p. 4; and V. Golovachev and K. Raspevin, "Before the Court of the Public," *Pravda*, May 31, 1963, p. 4.

60 Cf. Gorkin, "The Tasks Facing Soviet Justice Under Present Conditions," *op. cit.*, p. 5; and N. Mironov, "Main Thing Is Prevention and Upbringing Work," *Izvestia*, June 2, 1963, pp. 2-4.

61 Mironov, "Main Thing Is Prevention and Upbringing Work," *op. cit.*, pp. 2-4.

62 *Ibid.*

63 Mironov, "Strengthening Socialist Legality and Law and Order," *op. cit.*, p. 44.

64 Gorkin, "The Tasks Facing Soviet Justice Under Present Conditions," *op. cit.*, p. 8.

65 Mironov, "Strengthening Socialist Legality and Law and Order," *op. cit.*, p. 44.

66 V. Privalsky and A. Spektorov, "Just and Comradely," *Izvestia*, June 1, 1963, p. 4. (C.D.S.P., Vol. XV, No. 22, pp. 28-9)

67 "Statute on Procuracy Supervision in the U.S.S.R.," *Vedomosti*, No. 9, May, 1955. (C.D.S.P., Vol. VII, No. 23, pp. 3-5)

68 *Ibid.*

69 S. G. Berzovskaya, *Supervision of Public Prosecution in Soviet State Administration*, (Moscow: State Publishing House of Judicial Literature, 1954), p. 36.

70 O. Chaikovskaya, "The Prosecutor Defends," *Izvestia*, July 17, 1963, p. 4. (C.D.S.P., Vol. XV, No. 29, pp. 31-2)

71 "Plenary Session of the U.S.S.R. Supreme Court," *Izvestia*, Oct. 31, 1963, p. 3.

72 "Conference on General Supervision," *Sotsialisticheskaya zakonnost*, 1961, No. 2, p. 67.

73 V. G. Lebedinskii, Sovetskaya prokuratura i ee deyatelnost v oblasti obshchego nadzora (Soviet Procuracy and its Activity in the Field of General Supervision). (Moscow: Gosudarstvennoe yuridicheskoe izdatelstvo, 1954), pp. 105-6.

74 D. Panasyuk, "Continually Improve the Forms and Methods of the Direction of Public Prosecution," *Sotsialisticheskaya zakonnost*, 1960, No. 6, pp. 20-2.

75 Glenn C. Morgan, *Soviet Administrative Legality*, (Stanford, Cal.: Stanford University Press, 1962), pp. 187-8.

76 "Bulletin of U.S.S.R. Supreme Soviet," No. 8, April 20, 1956.

77 "Are All Equal Before the Law," *Partiinaya zhizn*, No. 2, Jan., 1963, pp. 50-2, (C.D.S.P., Vol. XV, No. 7, pp. 10-11); "To Be Shot for Bribe Taking," *Kommunist Tadzhikistana*, Feb. 14, 1963, p. 3. (C.D.S.P., Vol. XV, No. 10, pp. 34-5)

78 Andrei Ia. Vyshinsky, *The Law of the Soviet State*, (New York: The Macmillan Co., 1948), p. 528.

79 "Edict of the Presidium of the Supreme Soviet of the U.S.S.R.," June 3, 1956.

80 *Ibid.*

81 "On Abolishing the Russian Republic Ministry of Justice and Forming a Juridicial Commission of the Russian Republic Council of Ministers," *Vedomosti Verkhovnovo Soveta RSFSR*, No. 15, April 18, 1963, p. 410. (C.D.S.P., Vol. XV, No. 18, p. 33)

82 "Statutes of the Bar," *Vedomosti Verkhovnovo Soveta RSFSR*, No. 29, July, 1962, pp. 457-64. (C.D.S.P., Vol. XIV, No. 41, pp. 5-7)

83 *Ibid.*, Article 19.

84 *Ibid.*, Article 25.

85 *Ibid.*, Article 35.
86 *Ibid.*, Article 40.
87 K. F. Gutsenko, "New Legislation in the Union Republics With Respect to the Legal Profession," *Sovetskoe gosudarstvo i pravo,* 1962, No. 3. (Soviet Law and Government, Fall, 1962, pp. 57-64)
88 *Ibid.*
89 *Ibid.*
90 *Ibid.*
91 *Ibid.*
92 *Ibid.*
93 Yu. V. Solopanov and S. V. Murashov, "The Soviet Militia as an Agency for Safeguarding Public Order," *Sovetskoe gosudarstvo i pravo,* No. 12, Dec., 1962, pp. 111-119. (C.D.S.P., Vol. XV, No. 7, pp. 7-11)
94 "Fundamentals of Criminal Court Procedure for the U.S.S.R. and Union Republics," Article 23.
95 Gutsenko, "New Legislation in the Union Republics With Respect to the Legal Profession," *op. cit.*, pp. 57-64.
96 Solopanov and Murashov, "The Soviet Militia as an Agency for Safeguarding Public Order," *op. cit.*, pp. 111-19.
97 *Ibid.*
98 *Ibid.*
99 "Statutes of the Bar," *op. cit.*, Article 33.
100 P. Kudryavtsev, *Literaturnaya Gazeta,* June 8, 1951.
101 A. M. Levin, P. A. Ognev and V. L. Rossel, *The Lawyer in the Soviet Court,* (Moscow: State Publishing House of Judicial Literature, 1960), p. 717.
102 O. Chaikovskaya, "The Lawyers," *Izvestia,* March 22, 1963, p. 4. (C.D.S.P., Vol. XV, No. 12, pp. 27-8)
103 *Fundamentals of Soviet Criminal Legislation, the Judicial System and Criminal Court Procedure,* (Moscow: Foreign Languages Publishing House, 1960).
104 "Fundamentals of Criminal Legislation for the U.S.S.R. and the Union Republics," Articles 1 and 7.
105 *Ibid.*, Article 20.
106 "On Introducing Changes and Additions in Articles 22 and 44 of the Principles of Criminal Legislation," *Vedomosti Verkhovnovo Soveta SSR,* No. 14, April 6, 1962, pp. 408-9. (C.D.S.P., Vol. XIV, No. 14, p. 18)
107 Smirnov, "Soviet Criminal Legislation," *op. cit.*, pp. 28-39.
108 *Ibid.*
109 A. Khodanov, "Seventh Heaven of the Parasite," *Komsomolskaya pravda,* August 29, 1962, p. 4.
110 *Ibid.*
111 V. Titov, "A Field Report on the Parasites," *Krokodil,* No. 2, Jan., 1962, pp. 6-7. (C.D.S.P., Vol. XIV, No. 9, pp. 14-15)
112 Khodanov, "Seventh Heaven of the Parasite," *op. cit.*, p. 4.
113 Smirnov, "Soviet Criminal Legislation," *op. cit.*, pp. 28-39.
114 *Ibid.*
115 "Decree No. 3 of the Plenum of the U.S.S.R. Supreme Court, June 19, 1959, on Application of Measures of Criminal Punishment by the Courts," *Sotsialisticheskaya zakonnost,* No. 9, Sept., 1959, pp. 13-15. (C.D.S.P., Vol. XI, No. 41, pp. 14-16)
116 Gorkin, "The Tasks Facing Soviet Justice Under Present Conditions," *op. cit.*, p. 7.
117 J. M. Van Bemmelen, in Z. Szirmai, (ed.), *The Federal Criminal Law of the Soviet Union,* (Leyden: A. W. Sythoff, 1959), p. 23.
118 Smirnov, "Soviet Criminal Legislation," *op. cit.*, pp. 28-39.
119 *Ibid.*
120 Anashkin and Minkovsky, "Basic Principles of Soviet Legislation on Criminal Court Procedure," in *Fundamentals of Soviet Criminal Legislation, the Judicial System and Criminal Court Procedure, op. cit.*, pp. 87-103.
121 "Bulletin of the Supreme Court of the U.S.S.R.," No. 4, 1958, pp. 1-20.

122 Anashkin and Minkovsky, "Basic Principles of Soviet Legislation on Criminal Court Procedure," *op. cit.,* p. 94.
123 Solopanov and Murashov, "The Soviet Militia as an Agency for Safeguarding Public Order," *op. cit.,* pp. 111-19.
124 *Ibid.*
125 Anashkin and Minkovsky, "Basic Principles of Soviet Legislation on Criminal Court Procedure," *op. cit.,* p. 96.
126 *Ibid.*
127 *Bakinskii Rabochii,* May 27, 1956.
128 Constitution of the U.S.S.R., Article 110.
129 Gorkin, "The Tasks Facing Soviet Justice Under Present Conditions," *op. cit.,* p. 7.
130 I. Perlov, "The Public Accuses and Defends," *Izvestia,* March 12, 1960, p. 2. (C.D.S.P., Vol. XII, No. 11, pp. 15-16)
131 "Principles of Civil Legislation of the U.S.S.R. and the Union Republics," *Izvestia,* Dec. 10, 1961, pp. 3-6. (C.D.S.P., Vol. XIV, No. 4, pp. 3-13, 20)
132 "Survey of the Work of the Court Agencies of the Republics on Enlisting the Public in the Hearing of Civil Cases," *Byulleten Verkhovnovo suda RSFSR,* No. 1, 1965, pp. 3-7. (C.D.S.P., Vol. XVII, No. 8, pp. 14-18)
133 Solopanov and Murashov, "The Soviet Militia as an Agency for Safeguarding Public Order," *op. cit.,* pp. 111-19.
134 A. V. Gorbatov, "Years and Wars," *Novy Mir,* No. 4, 1964, pp. 99-138. This is a moving autobiography by an army officer who was imprisoned for 30 months in the late 1930's.
135 A. Yevseyev and Vl. Nakarykov, "In the Name of Truth and Justice—Today We Play Host to Some State Security Committee Investigators," *Nedelya,* August 26-Sept. 1, 1962, pp. 4-5. (C.D.S.P., Vol. XIV, No. 35, pp. 12-14)
136 *Ibid.,* p. 12.
137 *Ibid.*
138 Gsovski, *Government, Law and Courts in the Soviet Union and Eastern Europe,* Vol. I, *op. cit.,* pp. 577-9.
139 Smirnov, "Soviet Criminal Legislation," *op. cit.,* p. 29.
140 "On Granting Agencies for Safeguarding Public Order the Right to Conduct the Preliminary Investigation," *Vedomosti Verkhovnovo Soveta SSR,* No. 16, April 17, 1963, p. 335.
141 "For the Complete Elimination of the Harmful Consequences of the Personality Cult," *Sovetskoe gosudarstvo i pravo,* 1962, No. 4. (Soviet Law and Government, Summer, 1962, pp. 24-32)
142 Gorkin, "The Tasks Facing Soviet Justice Under Present Conditions," *op. cit.,* p. 8.
143 "Strictly Observe the Laws," Plenary Session of the U.S.S.R. Supreme Court, *Pravda,* March 24, 1963, p. 4. (C.D.S.P., Vol. XV, No. 12, p. 29)
144 Gorkin, "The Tasks Facing Soviet Justice Under Present Conditions," *op. cit.,* p. 7.
145 Mironov, "Main Thing Is Prevention and Upbringing Work," *op. cit.,* pp. 2-4.
146 Mironov, "Strengthening Socialist Legality and Law and Order," *op. cit.,* p. 44; and Yu. Yakushev, "Law Is Written for All," *Pravda,* March 7, 1963, p. 2.
147 Gorkin, "The Tasks Facing Soviet Justice Under Present Conditions," *op. cit.,* p. 8.
148 Strogovich, Kalenov and Gertsenzon, "The New Laws on the Judicial System, the Criminal Code, and the Code of Criminal Procedure of the Russian Federation," *op. cit.*
149 Mironov, "Strengthening Socialist Legality and Law and Order," *op. cit.,* p. 42.
150 *Ibid.*
151 *Ibid.*
152 *Ibid.*
153 *Ibid.,* p. 43.

CHAPTER VIII

THE PLANNED ECONOMY

In Marxist-Leninist theory and Soviet practice, politics and economics are so inextricably interwoven that an adequate understanding of
government and politics in the U.S.S.R. would be impossible without a
detailed examination of economic goals, techniques and administration.
Marxist-Leninist political-economic theory could be summarized very
briefly as follows: mankind should strive toward the establishment of a
classless society in which all people enjoy abundance and live in harmony.
All major social changes and political revolutions are based on economic
factors. Mankind is divided into social classes on the basis of ownership or
non-ownership of the means of production. Those who own the means of
production exploit the propertiless masses and this economic exploitation
constitutes the major source of human misery. Class struggle between the
exploiter and the exploited is the major historical mechanism for the
modification of social organizations. The elimination of exploitation requires that all means of production be transferred from private to public
ownership. The wealthy capitalists, who have protected themselves well in
a variety of ways, including the establishment of a powerful state apparatus,
do not willingly relinquish their positions of power and wealth. Therefore,
the necessary changes in economic and social relations can be introduced
only if the formerly exploited class acquires political power and uses this
power to eliminate the basis of exploitation—private ownership of the
means of production. A political revolution is thus indispensable if major
economic changes are to be effected. Class struggle, based on economic inequality and injustice, is the force which precipitates the political revolution. Therefore, in this phase of social transformation, economic inequality
is the motivating force and acquisition of political power by the formerly
exploited class is the goal. In Marxist terms "politics has precedence over
economics" because techniques for the elimination of exploitation of man
by man and of class differences can be introduced only if political power is
acquired by the working class.[1] However, after the working class has attained firm control of the political power structure, "economics rather than
politics acquires prime importance," since a major economic transforma-

343

tion is required for the attainment of important political goals.[2] Political considerations, therefore, must determine major economic decisions.

The primary task of the Bolshevik Party in the early twentieth century was the acquisition of political power. Economic dissatisfaction and promises for economic gain were used by the party to achieve the political support necessary for a revolutionary upheaval. After the acquisition of political power in 1917 and the relative stabilization of power in the early 1920's, the Soviet leaders concentrated on the attainment of political goals through economic transformation and development. Nationalization of the means of production and the establishment of a rapidly expanding economy were intended, in theory, to eliminate economic exploitation and, with it, the economic basis for classes and class struggle, and to pave the way for economic abundance for all in a classless, harmonious society. Soviet leaders claim that exploitation of man by man has been eliminated with the abolition of private ownership of the means of production (they vehemently deny the not entirely unjustified accusation, that for exploitation of man by man they have substituted exploitation of man by the state). The state, with its planning and control techniques, moved in to fill the gap left by the virtual elimination of the spontaneous interaction of demand and supply.

In the U.S.S.R. political and economic goals are so interrelated that most of the governmental and political apparatus is designed to deal primarily with economic matters and all major decisions about economic goals and policies are made by political leaders. Economic decision-making rests on a political base; decisions about annual and long-term plans, the allocation of resources, the production level for major commodities, the choice of investments and price setting involve political considerations, as much if not more than, economic considerations. Soviet political leaders concern themselves with all kinds of economic details such as crop rotation, production scheduling, and the internal organization of enterprises, which are usually not attended to by Western political leaders. Currently, Soviet leaders consider economics to be their chief weapon for the attainment of three major political goals: the establishment of full communism in the U.S.S.R.; the adoption of the Soviet social system by many other nations; and successful military, political and economic competition with the most powerful nation in the world, the U.S.A. The chief function of many of the political and governmental organs is to determine economic policy designed to foster attainment of these goals and to organize, direct and control the entire economy.

Natural Resources

The direction of the development of the Soviet economy is, of course, intimately linked with the geography, climate and natural resources of the state. The U.S.S.R., the world's largest state, covers 8,648,000 square miles, one-sixth of the inhabited surface of the world. Soviet territory extends about 2700 miles from north to south and about 7000 miles from east to west. Sunrise over Vladivostok coincides with sunset over Moscow. Over one-half of Europe and one-third of Asia fall within the Soviet borders. Its coasts are washed by the Pacific, Arctic and Atlantic Oceans and by twelve seas, providing approximately 28,000 miles of coastline, mainly on the Pacific and Arctic Oceans, and the Baltic, Caspian and Black Seas. Its population of 232,000,000 (January 1, 1966) is outnumbered only by China and India.

Natural conditions within the U.S.S.R. vary greatly from one area to another. All climates except tropical are represented. Reindeer are raised in the frozen northland while tea, citrus fruits and cotton are produced in the subtropical south. The average temperature for January is -58°F in Verkhoyansk and 32°F in Tashkent.[3] The very sparsely populated northern tundra, which comprises approximately 10 percent of the total land area, is almost permanently frozen, and produces little other than fish and valuable furs. South of the tundra is a vast forested region, which contains approximately one-fifth of the world's timber resources, and covers approximately one-third of the land surface of the U.S.S.R. In the central region is the steppe, a relatively level treeless plain that includes the major agricultural area, only 834,000 square miles, of which 100,000 square miles were added by irrigation, swamp drainage and the recent cultivation of virgin land. About one-half (400,000 square miles) of this area has extremely rich black soil which is ideal for crop growing. South of the black soil strip is a less fertile brown soil strip, and in the far south are semi-desert and desert regions where, with irrigation, cotton, rice and other crops can be grown.

Over much of the U.S.S.R., climatic and soil conditions are far from ideal for farming, and only about 10 percent of the total area is, at present, suitable for intensive cultivation. Stony, sandy, clay-like or excessively acid soils, which can be cultivated, but are not well suited for farming, are characteristic of approximately half of the land surface. In the northern, and even in much of the central area, the very short frost-free season either prohibits crop growing or periodically ruins crops. Inadequate or barely adequate rainfall is typical in large areas, particularly in the south, where strong winds deplete the available moisture. Despite irrigation, dry farming techniques, water conservation programs and early maturing grains, drought, crop failure and early frost are constant dangers which frequently lower agricultural output. American agronomists have concluded that "Russia has never been, is not now, and probably never can become a really great and dependable producer of food grains. . . ."[4]

The Soviet Union is one of the richest countries in the world in natural resources. Soviet sources claim that it has the world's largest deposits of coal, peat, oil, iron ore, manganese, copper, lead, zinc, aluminum, nickel, tungsten, mercury, sulphur, potassium and phosphate salts. It has an abundance of natural gas, precious metals, asbestos, raw materials for the manufacture of cement, other metals, and radioactive ores for the production of atomic energy. The availability within the Soviet borders of almost all raw materials required by industry, an abundance of water power for conversion into hydroelectric energy, an excellent supply of fuel and vast forest reserves have contributed greatly to the ability of the U.S. S.R. to industrialize so rapidly. Soviet leaders claim that the U.S.S.R. has all the natural resources and climatic conditions necessary for it to become one of the world's most important industrial and agricultural powers.

Constitutional Provisions

The formal structure of the Soviet economy is outlined in Articles 4-7 of the Soviet Constitution. The Soviet Union is described as a "socialist state of workers and peasants" in which private ownership of the instruments of production has been replaced by socialist ownership. Socialist property is divided into state property and the property of collective farms and cooperative societies. State property includes the land, its mineral wealth, waters, forests, mills, mines, rail, water and air transport, communications, state farms, municipal enterprises, and most of the dwelling houses in cities and industrial areas. The socialist property of collective farms and cooperative enterprises includes common buildings, implements, livestock and products. Every collective farm household, in addition to its basic income from the common, collective farm enterprise, has for its own personal use a small plot of land, and as its personal property, a subsidiary husbandry on the plot, a house, livestock, poultry and minor agricultural implements. The law also permits a small private economy of individual peasants and handicraftsmen who may not hire labor other than members of their own family. The few private entrepreneurs are of negligible importance. Almost all Soviet workers are employed within the socialist economy, since the means of production are almost exclusively under socialist ownership.

State or public property, Soviet authors say, comes into being as the result of nationalization of large scale industry, transport, banking, and agricultural estates and particularly as a result of rapid economic development within the state sector. The socialist form of collective and cooperative property is said to begin with the simple pooling of the means of production owned by the peasants and is augmented by the joint labor of the peasants combined with technical assistance from the state.[5] (No mention is made of forcible collectivization and augmentation by the confiscated property of the dispossessed *kulaks*.) Public or state property is described as "the most perfect form since it represents the highest level of socialized production"; collective property is "a less mature form of socialist ownership since the means of production and the finished product belong to an individual collective body and not to the whole of society."[6] However, the form of collective property is not "immutable" and as a result of the amalgamation of collective farms, the establishment of enterprises jointly operated by a number of collectives, and the use of advanced technology, the collectives are gradually approaching state enterprises in their "form of organization and the character of labor."[7] The two forms of socialist property are described as identical in that "both exclude exploitation of man by man and presuppose collective labor performed in the public interest" and both offer "wide scope for the steady growth of socialist production and the raising of the living standard of the working people."[8]

Under socialism, labor and the means of production are purportedly related in such a way that

> ". . . those taking part in the production process collectively own the instruments of labor which they employ. This totally excludes the possibility of the means of production being converted by one part of society into a means of exploitation of the other part of society. Since they jointly own social property and jointly participate in the social production process, all people are equal and their relations are based on the principles of comradely cooperation and mutual assistance."[9]

In addition to "eliminating exploitation and paving the way for comradely cooperation," socialist ownership of the means of production purportedly creates a solid base for organizing, managing and planning the economy.[10]

One of the important attributes of the socialist economy, from the Soviet point of view, is that "the volume of social production and its structure, the distribution of labor and the means of production among the various branches of the national economy, commodity prices and wage rates . . . no longer come into existence spontaneously. They are planned by society itself."[11] Soviet sources are absolutely explicit about the locus of the control of the economy: "in saying that under socialism people consciously direct their own social development, one has in mind that they do this through the Party and the state, whose function it is *to lead and organize* the socialist economy."[12] Thus, as in the field of Soviet democracy, the economy and planning are theoretically in the hands of society itself, but direction is provided by the party and state officials during the period of training society to assume control. Parenthetically, the exceeding complexity of the operation of the planned economy of the U.S.S.R. makes it doubtful that the masses could assume effective control, even in the unlikely event that the party and party-dominated state organs relinquished control.

The goals of Soviet economic development have always been political and social as well as economic. Lenin defined the purpose of socialist production as "the planned organization of the socialist production process to

ensure the well-being and all-around development of all members of society."[13] The Constitution states: "The economic life of the U.S.S.R. is
determined and directed by the state-national economic plan, with the aim
of increasing public wealth, of steadily raising the material and cultural
standards of the working people, of consolidating the independence of the
U.S.S.R. and strengthening its defensive capacity" (Article 11). Soviet
theoreticians assert, in agreement with Lenin, that under socialism "the
surplus product does not go to the propertied class, but to all the people
and to them alone";[14] since the means of production belong to the working
people, "it is obvious that they cannot exploit themselves."[15] It is held to
be self-evident that the workers should strive constantly to increase the
production of material wealth since the whole social product can be used
"only for the satisfaction—direct or indirect—of the needs of the working
people."[16]

Historical Background

When the Bolsheviks gained control of Russia, they inherited a backward, ruined and exhausted country. By 1917, Tsarist Russia, with 16 percent of the world's territory and 8 percent of the world's population, contributed only about 2.6 percent of the world's industrial production. Agriculture, the leading branch of the economy despite backward methods and
low yields, represented 58 percent of the value of total production,[17] 67.5
percent of the value of exports,[18] and employed 75 percent of the working
force. Living standards and per capita production were well below the
norm for Europe. The average life expectancy was about 32 years.

Industrialization was financed by foreign loans, predominantly French,
British, German, American and Belgian. By 1914 Western powers owned
approximately 40 percent of the basic capital of major Russian banks and
industry; Russia owed foreign investors 5.9 billion gold rubles.[19] Heavy industry, which represented less than one-third of the value of industrial
production, concentrated on the production of weapons, ships, locomotives,
fuel, extraction of ores, and simple machines and agricultural tools. Most
machinery and even many simple tools were imported. Industry was located exclusively in the European cities and the vast potential of the country was greatly under-utilized. Labor productivity in industry was approximately one-ninth of American and one-fifth of British and German productivity. Industry suffered from fluctuations, crises and depressions.

The weak Russian economy was shattered by World War I. With 15
million men in the armed forces, there was a dearth of experienced workers.
Economic as well as political anarchy prevailed. Organizational forms and
transportation broke down, production materials were not available, and
many basic branches of industry were inoperative. War deliveries and
requisitions together with an absolute lack of manpower caused a catas-

trophic situation in agriculture, which became almost exclusively self-consuming. Production of consumer goods was very limited and distribution facilities were completely inadequate. The starving, poorly equipped armies suffered a series of severe military defeats, but Western powers encouraged the Russians to continue in the war by providing large loans. The foreign debt was more than doubled (an additional 7.68 billion rubles),[20] and inflation added to the economic chaos. The Provisional Government, established after the 1917 March revolution, fulfilled its treaty obligations to the Western powers. By November, 1917, when the Bolsheviks seized control, Russia was in a state of military, economic and social disaster.

The Bolshevik leaders were painfully aware of the military and economic weakness of the territory that they controlled. They realized that the peasantry constituted an uncertain ally that was prepared to feed the workers only if supplied with manufactured goods. It was obvious that their hope for victory in the struggle between capitalism and socialism lay in the economic sphere, even more than in ideology. But their handicaps, including a chaotic economy and low labor productivity, were equally obvious. Rapid industrialization, which the Bolshevik leaders believed required nationalization of the existent means of production, and the rapid accumulation of producer goods, appeared to be an absolute necessity. Foreign loans, the source of producer goods typically used by backward countries in the process of industrializing, were neither available nor acceptable. Capitalist entrepreneurs and governments were not willing to risk their funds with an unstable revolutionary government that advocated the overthrow of capitalism. Moreover, the Bolshevik leaders feared that indebtedness to antagonistic foreigners would compromise their independence. Consequently, the capital required for the reconstruction and industrialization of the new socialist state had to be derived from internal sources, namely, by the sacrifices of the Soviet people. Before long, the Soviet leaders concluded that economic planning was a practical necessity as well as a theoretical recommendation.

The period from October, 1917 to the summer of 1918 is sometimes referred to as the period of workers' control and land reform. In rapid succession, banks, land, foreign trade, major industries, railroads, domestic trade and finally almost all enterprises were nationalized.[21] A Supreme Council of the National Economy was established in December, 1917, to provide centralized coordination of the economy. A decree of November 14, 1917 gave workers the right to supervise management, to examine accounts, and to determine minimum production quotas; managers retained the right to issue directives. This decree was an attempt to benefit from the administrative and technical skills of the old managerial personnel, and, simultaneously, to keep politically unreliable managers under the surveillance of the workers. However, in many instances, the workers interfered with the decisions of management, and even converted factories to the production of consumer goods for their own use. Although normal market relations were expected to prevail, unstable currency, shortages of materials, disorganized transportation and poor management forced productivity to a new low and increased the economic chaos.

The period of War Communism (1918-1921), during which a civil war raged, was characterized by the attempt of the state to control and direct virtually the entire non-agricultural economy. Industry was almost totally nationalized. The workers' councils, which had proved highly disruptive, were brought under the control of the trade unions. Enterprise directors of "bourgeois origin," some of whom engaged in sabotage, were objects of suspicion. The lack of experienced and trusted economic administrators necessitated detailed state direction and control. However, the Supreme Economic Council which exercised the control was highly inexperienced and often operated on the basis of faulty information. Enterprises were issued production orders in exact physical terms, but more often than not, the materials necessary for production were not available. Transportation facilities were totally inadequate and large regions were practically isolated. Many factories were completely idle. Money was supposed to be withering away and was not used in wholesale and inter-enterprise transactions; even wages were paid in kind, if possible. Industrial and agricultural production dropped to approximately one-seventh and one-half, respectively, of the prewar level. Shortages of food and consumer goods, brutal requisitioning techniques and inefficient management contributed to the discontent of the populace. Unknown numbers died of starvation. Dissatisfaction with the regime was expressed by the workers through poor work habits, tardiness, absenteeism, strikes and even armed uprisings. The peasants, too, used armed uprisings, as well as more passive techniques such as producing only for their own use. The imminent collapse of the Soviet government appeared to be inevitable.

This reasonable prediction did not materialize chiefly because of the genius of Lenin. In 1921 the New Economic Policy (N.E.P.), which authorized a certain amount of free enterprise, was introduced by Lenin as a drastic remedial measure. The government retained its control over large industry, transportation, credit and banking, foreign trade and some of the domestic trade. Many small enterprises were leased to cooperatives and private individuals, including former owners. The normal use of money was reintroduced and even state enterprises operated on a profit principle. Private trade was legalized, retail merchants became numerous and many small manufacturing units were established. Compulsory deliveries from the peasants to the state were reduced considerably and peasants were allowed to sell their surplus produce in the open market. Industrial and agricultural production approached the prewar level.

However, the existence of a capitalist segment within the economy ran counter to the communist ideology. Moreover, the state was unable to procure sufficient grain to feed the Red Army and the expanding industrial working force, and to maintain the necessary balance between industrial and agricultural production and prices. Moving toward total socialization, the state gradually eliminated private entrepreneurs and traders by taxing their profits, and by restricting the availability of raw materials and the use of transportation facilities, and, at the same time, expanded state production and trade facilities. The socialization of agriculture was accomplished by forced collectivization and the liquidation of the kulaks in 1929 and the early 1930's. With the collectivization of agriculture, the Soviet state achieved almost complete control over the economy. The scene was set for full-scale economic planning.

In March, 1920, the GOELRO (State Commission for Electrification) was established as the first formal central planning agency. It drew up a perspective plan to reconstruct the national economy through electrification. This long term economic plan was intended to mobilize and inspire the Soviet people. Goals to be achieved during a ten to fifteen year period included the construction of thirty electric power stations, marked increases in the output of coal, iron, steel and other important commodities, and the approximate doubling of industrial output. Rather than being a carefully balanced plan based on detailed knowledge of the real situation, the GOELRO figures were heavily weighted with wishful thinking.

In 1921 the State Planning Commission or *Gosplan* was established to prepare a unified economic plan for the country, together with techniques to ensure its realization. Initially, the small staff of Gosplan (about 40 experts) limited itself to fact finding, coordinating the work of the planning organs of the commissariats and to studying the variables involved in the development of a comprehensive plan. Beginning in 1925, control figures, which purportedly reflected available resources, were published annually to establish goals for the major branches of the economy. In 1927 the Supreme Economic Council and the Gosplan were directed by the party to prepare a five year plan for the development of the Soviet economy. The first Five Year Plan went into effect on October 1, 1928. The overall plan, supposedly based on the "method of balances" in which goals reflected available resources, was subdivided into annual and even quarterly plans. Assignments were made by the central authorities through subordinate agencies, such as industrial commissariats and trusts, to the various enterprises whose duty it was to fulfill the assigned portion of the plan. Theoretically, counter-suggestions were to be sent through channels from the lower levels of the hierarchy to the central planning agencies. Usually, the plan for an enterprise was so late in arriving that the enterprise manager had to make predictions about his potential assignment and to operate without the plan for a period of weeks or even months.

The first Five Year Plan was designed to foster rapid industrialization which in turn would increase defense potential and provide the basis for the socialist reconstruction of transportation and agriculture (collectiviza-tion and mechanization). Because of the shortage of native technical and engineering personnel, many Western experts were hired. The completion of the plan was officially announced in December, 1932, only four and one-quarter years after its initiation. More than 1500 modern industrial enterprises were created including huge aluminum and tractor factories, smelting industries, and the Dnieper dam; transportation facilities were strengthened by the construction of the Turkestan-Siberian railway and the Moscow-Donets canal for the transportation of coal; collectivization, often ruthlessly implemented, reached the 60 percent level, instead of the planned 25 percent level, by 1932. Although substantial progress was made, not all goals were achieved; the production of consumer goods, grain, coal and numerous other items fell far below the figures established by the plan. Nevertheless, overall industrial production was approximately doubled, and an intensive plan of capital investment and increased socialization in all major economic spheres was accomplished.

The second Five Year Plan (1933-1937) was reported fulfilled in slightly over four years. Again some items such as steel were overfulfilled while items such as petroleum and particularly consumer goods were under-fulfilled. A large number of new industrial enterprises were established and the Moscow-Volga and White Sea-Baltic canals were built. Soviet sources indicate that capital investment was doubled in comparison to the first Five Year Plan and that industrial production in 1937 was six times higher than in 1913.[22] Western experts point out that Soviet statistics exaggerate the growth of production, because comparisons between different years are based on monetary prices, and extensive inflation magnifies differences be-tween the monetary values of production in comparison to the actual num-bers of physical units produced.

The third Five Year Plan was originally intended to cover the years 1938-1942. Because of the threat of war, increased defense potential was emphasized. Prior to the Nazi invasion, approximately 3000 new enter-prises were put into operation, and by 1940 it was claimed that industrial production was eight and one-half times greater than in 1913.[23] Heavy in-dustry production, machine building and electric energy output purportedly increased fifteen, thirty-five and twenty-five fold respectively. Immediately after the invasion, a short term "mobilization economic plan" was adopted and was followed by successive "war economic plans." Emphasis was placed on the construction of defensive weapons and on metallurgy. Approximate-ly 1,360 important industrial plants were removed to the eastern provinces and 3,500 new plants were constructed. The transfer of plants and the industrialization of the eastern part of the U.S.S.R. proved to be of utmost importance for the Soviet war effort. Soviet territory occupied by the Germans and their allies in 1941 included 33 percent of the entire Soviet industry, 47 percent of agriculture, and 50 percent of all cattle, and 88 million inhabitants.[24] The monetary value of the material damage suffered by the U.S.S.R. is estimated at 3,000 billion rubles. Either destroyed or heavily damaged were 1,710 cities, 70,000 villages, 31,850 industrial enterprises, 98,000 collective farms, 1,876 state farms, and 2,890 Machine Tractor Stations.[25] Machinery that was not destroyed was taken to Germany. The Nazis also appropriated a significant proportion of Soviet livestock, including seventeen million cattle, seven million horses and tens of millions of sheep and pigs.[26] Indirect losses caused by the disruption to the economy and the one-sided technical development of industry are difficult to estimate. And, of course, the most tragic loss was in terms of the millions of military and civilian war casualties.

The fourth Five Year Plan (1946-1950) concentrated on the reconstruction and development of the economy. The speedy post-war reconstruction without foreign aid constituted a very significant accomplishment. Cities, villages, collective farms and transportation were restored. Most of the industry transferred to the east remained there, and over 6,000 large scale industrial plants were established or rebuilt. Planned quotas for certain forms of industrial expansion and for many crucial industrial raw materials, including electric power, coal and petroleum, were overfulfilled. However, the planned production of many types of consumer goods and food was not achieved, and standards of living remained abysmally low.

The fifth Five Year Plan (1951-1955) emphasized the resumption of peaceful economic development. By 1955 the U.S.S.R. claimed that industrial production had increased 3.2 times over the 1940 level and 25 times over the 1913 level.[27] Comparable progress was not reported for agriculture; by 1950 gross farm output was reported as slightly more than double that of 1913. However, absolute production of meat, lard, and wool was below the 1913 level, there was less milk per capita than in 1913, and production of potatoes, vegetables and fruit was grossly insufficient. The sixth Five Year Plan (1955-1960) was discontinued in September, 1957, probably because of economic over-extension, heavy expenditures on space and military programs, and increased economic assistance to Eastern Europe. Short-term plans and directives were substituted until 1959, when the first Seven Year Plan was launched. In the meantime a major organizational change was introduced. In May, 1957, the principal of territorial administration was substituted for administration by industrial units. Most industrial ministries were abolished and the operative guidance of industry and construction was entrusted to Economic Councils (Sovnarkhozy) which were established in each of the 105 newly created economic regions. Since Soviet industry included more than 200,000 industrial plants and over 100,000 construction sites, administration from the center had become increasingly cumbersome. The Economic Councils, which administered a smaller number of enterprises in a smaller territory, were intended to achieve more efficient administration, increased local initiative, better utilization of productive capacity, and more efficient adjustments in the execution of the national plan. In 1963 the 105 economic regions were compressed into 47, primarily because coordination between the relatively small administrative units had not always been effective.

The first Seven Year Plan (1959-1965), adopted by the Twenty-First Party Congress in February, 1959, encompassed the goals established for previous plans: to expand all branches of industry, based on the priority of heavy industry, to increase the economic potential of the country and to raise the standard of living. Among the ambitious goals of the plan were increases, by 1965, in total industrial production, production of producer goods, and in production of consumer goods of 80, 85 and 62 percent respectively in comparison to 1959 production figures, and an investment of 1,940 to 1,970 billion rubles in the economy, almost as much as the total investment in the economy for all preceding years of Soviet power. Planned expenditures in billions of rubles for some of the major segments of the economy were as follows: oil and gas industries (170); building and building material industries (110); railways (110); chemical industry (100); power stations (125); iron and steel industry (100); light and food industries (80); agriculture (500, including 150 from the state); housing and public buildings (375).[28] Expenditures for space exploration and defense were not listed in the target figures. Despite the extensive financial allotment to the construction of housing, heavy industry retained its marked priority over the production of consumer goods; moreover, as the planned period progressed, funds for housing were cut back markedly.

The political aim of the Seven Year Plan was to create the material and technical base for communism and to enable the Soviet Union to equal and surpass in the shortest possible time the most developed capitalist countries, especially the United States, in per capita production. Accomplishment of these goals, Soviet leaders said, would require marked increases in capital investment and labor productivity, improved planning methods, proper utilization of the economic laws of socialism, and the elimination of extreme centralization of planning and administration. By 1970, according to Khrushchev, the Soviet Union is to lead the world in both absolute industrial production and in production per capita. This prediction was heralded in the U.S.S.R. as the coming historical victory of communism over capitalism through peaceful competition in the economic sphere. As is often the case in the U.S.S.R., goals and accomplishments have been rather widely separated.

The degree of economic planning, planning techniques, organizational forms, and successes or failures associated with economic plans have varied greatly throughout the years. Initially, Soviet planners had at their disposal a huge country with rich resources and a large population, composed primarily of peasants and unskilled laborers, many of whom were illiterate and hostile to the new regime. There was a marked shortage of qualified workers, technicians and engineers; resources were widely separated; transportation facilities were woefully inadequate; the necessary capital for expansion and development was not available; and the planners themselves were very inexperienced. On the other hand, the planners had some advantages: nationalization enabled them to plan for and, hopefully, to coordinate all branches of the economy; and unified economic leadership and control was provided by the party. In spite of the odds against the success of economic planning, numerous planning blunders, unenlightened party interference in the operation of the economy, and immeasurable suffering on the part of the people of the U.S.S.R., in two short decades of relative normality, 1930-1940 and 1950-1960, the country was transformed into a leading industrial power. The price for the rapid transformation was high. The overworked, underfed masses had to fight in the Red Army and to work on new and demanding jobs under the most difficult conditions. They were denied all luxuries and conveniences of modern living and frequently had barely enough essential food and clothing. Thousands starved to death during periods of famine. When the material situation began to improve slightly, all resources and energy had to be devoted to fighting a bloody war and, subsequently, to recovery from it.

By 1945 the U.S.S.R. had a staff of planners who, although far from omnipotent, had more experience than planners in any other country; a new Soviet intelligentsia had developed, and skilled technicians and professional people were available. In order to repair the war damage and to further develop the economy, the people continued to live at subsistence levels. Currently the economy of the U.S.S.R. is expanding rapidly. The people have tolerated the excessive deprivations partly because they had no choice, and partly because they were promised great improvements in the future. During the 1950's the promises finally began to materialize, and although standards of living in the U.S.S.R. are much lower than in the United States, the party leadership has promised the Soviet people that by 1970-1972 they will enjoy the highest standard of living in the world. It is almost certain that the Soviet leadership will not be able to honor these promises in such a short time. However, the promises of greatly improved standards of living are apparently made in all seriousness.

Planning and Industrial Organization

CENTRAL ORGANS

Economic planning in the U.S.S.R. has been directed toward two objectives, one political and the other economic. The first objective is to control the economy as a means of increasing political power and insuring political loyalty. Second, planning is used as an instrument of economic growth with the goal of increasing productivity and economic capabilities and "the ever more complete satisfaction of the rising material and spiritual needs of the people."[29] The party leaders contribute the political aspects and the overall objectives, while the economic aspect is said to be based on "plans worked out directly by the collectives of enterprises and construction projects, economic councils, ministries and departments."[30] Actually, the Central Committee of the C.P.S.U. maps out both the principal economic and political tasks of the plans, and control figures and directives for national economic development are approved by the Central Committee before they are submitted to the Soviet government.[31]

The institutional framework within which Soviet economic planning and industrial organs operate is exceedingly complex. Because of recurrent difficulties in the efficient planning and management of the economy, organizational changes have been frequent. The major industrial management and economic planning organs, as of the summer of 1965, are indicated in Figure 1.

THE SUPREME COUNCIL OF THE NATIONAL ECONOMY

The Supreme Council of the National Economy was established in March, 1963 as the "supreme state agency for guiding industry and construction."[32] It is directly subordinate to the Council of Ministers of the U.S.S.R., and its chairman, who along with other leading economic officials, is appointed by the Supreme Soviet, is concurrently First Vice-Chairman of the U.S.S.R. Council of Ministers, an indication of the extraordinary importance of this council. The basic tasks of the Supreme Council of the National Economy are to:

> "Guide (through the appropriate agencies) the work of all branches of industry and construction, and also to coordinate the work of planning and economic agencies in this field; ensure fulfillment of plan targets by industrial enterprises and construction organizations, the rational, efficient use of capital investments and material, labor and financial resources, the . . . growth of labor productivity, reduction of production costs and improvements in the quality of output; work out and implement measures for developing industrial production, and also resolve current questions that arise in the course of fulfilling state plans."[33]

The Supreme Council thus serves as the general supervisor of the entire economy. Its decisions are binding on all subordinate state and economic agencies.[34]

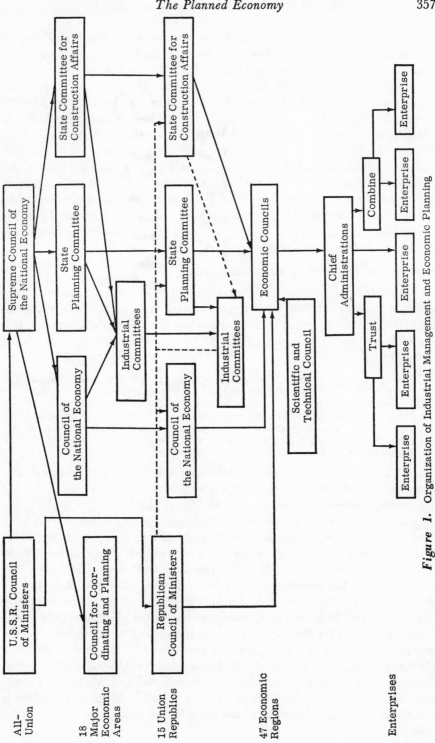

Figure 1. Organization of Industrial Management and Economic Planning

Directly subordinate to the Supreme Council of the National Economy are the three major Union-Republican economic organs: the U.S.S.R. State Planning Committee (Gosplan); the U.S.S.R. Council of the National Economy; and the U.S.S.R. State Committee for Construction Affairs. Also subordinate to it are the U.S.S.R. State Production Committees (Gas Industry, Medium Machine Building, Power and Electrification); U.S.S.R. State Committees (Co-ordinating Scientific Research, Aviation Technology, Defense Technology, Atomic Energy, etc.); the All-Union Farm Machinery Association; the U.S.S.R. State Construction Bank; and the State Commission for Reserves of Useful Minerals. The chairmen of these agencies, and sometimes representatives from Economic Councils and enterprises, participate in meetings of the Supreme Council of the National Economy to provide it with crucial information and to allow for maximum co-ordination between the various agencies.[35]

THE U.S.S.R. STATE PLANNING COMMITTEE

The U.S.S.R. State Planning Committee (Gosplan), with its subordinate branches at the Union Republic level, was reorganized in November, 1962, following severe criticism from the party leaders. Currently, it is the major economic planning organ of the central government. Its duties include:

> ". . . working out—in conformity with the Program of the Communist Party of the U.S.S.R. and Party and government directives—the state plans for the development of the national economy of the country on the basis of the plans of the Union Republics; . . . ensuring continuity in planning and consistency in plan targets; and . . . continuing to improve planning on the basis of the economic laws of socialism and scientific generalization of the experience of communist construction in the U.S.S.R."[36]

The Committee itself decided that its major task "is to make a comprehensive study of the integrated, completely finished plans submitted by the Union Republics and to compile the All-Union plan."[37]

Attached to the U.S.S.R. State Planning Committee are several State Branch Committees (Machine Building, Electrical Equipment, Light Industry, Food Industry, and others). These committees, which have jurisdiction over the leading scientific research and design institutes, are responsible for the introduction of new equipment and technology in production and for the level of technological development in the respective industry.[38] The State Branch Committees review the plans presented by the Union Republics for the development of the respective industrial branches and for scientific research for the entire country. Also attached to the State Planning Committee are the State Committee for Central Asian Cotton Growing and the State Committee for Vocational and Technical Education; the correct allocation of human resources and educational facilities is one of the important functions of the planning organs.

Meetings of the U.S.S.R. State Planning Committee are attended by ranking officials from state and party agencies, including members of the C.P.S.U. Central Committee, the chairman of the U.S.S.R. Council of the National Economy, and representatives from the U.S.S.R. Supreme Council of the National Economy, the Union Republic State Planning Committees, the Economic Councils, the U.S.S.R. State Committee for Construction Affairs, Industrial and Production State Committees, research and design organizations, the U.S.S.R. Academy of Sciences, etc.[39] The staff of Gosplan has been reduced considerably, but it is probably still divided into a number of functional departments such as finance, investment, labor and wages, prices and costs, and economic departments which study general economic problems and work out the summary sections of the plans for branches of industry and for republics.[40]

THE U.S.S.R. COUNCIL OF THE NATIONAL ECONOMY

The basic task of this agency is to put the economic plans into effect. It is granted managerial functions to enable it to make necessary adjustments in the allocation of resources between branches of the economy. Only questions that go beyond the bounds of the approved plan and budget need be submitted to the U.S.S.R. Council of Ministers for decision. Its creation in November, 1962, was an attempt to improve coordination, to reduce the delays involved in the settlement of concrete problems, to eliminate the necessity for innumerable conferences, and in general to increase economic efficiency.[41] The Council is responsible for ensuring the "unconditional fulfillment of assignments, laying the necessary groundwork, distributing orders for technological equipment and supplies sufficiently in advance, eradicating bottlenecks, etc."[42] Within the Council, administrations or departments have been created for agriculture, transportation and the most important branches of industry, along with chief administrations for inter-republic supplies of a number of major products, and for supplying equipment for the most important construction branches in a number of industries.[43] The Council of the National Economy carries out its functions through the Union Republic Council of Ministers, the Economic Councils, and the Ministries and agencies of the U.S.S.R.[44]

THE U.S.S.R. STATE COMMITTEE FOR CONSTRUCTION AFFAIRS

The third major central organ subordinate to the Supreme Council of the National Economy, the U.S.S.R. State Committee for Construction Affairs, provides centralized direction for all forms of major construction in the U.S.S.R. The Committee for Construction Affairs

". . . directs the organization of construction, the development of the construction industry and the mechanization of building jobs; works out draft long-term plans for the over-all mechanization and introduction of new technology in construction and also economical standard designs; checks the designs and estimates of major construction projects; approves and issues norms and technical specifications for construction designing . . . ; directs standardization of building components and research work in construction."[45]

After the 1962 reorganization, capital construction was removed from the jurisdiction of the Economic Councils and placed under the supervision of the Committee for Construction Affairs, whose approval is required for all new construction projects.[46] A number of reasons were given for the reorganization, including unnecessary construction; concurrent involvement in a large number of construction projects, few of which were completed and operational within the specified time; unwise selection of construction sites with the wide dispersion of units which, from an economic point of view, should have been in close proximity; overly numerous and unsatisfactory construction designs; and the poor quality of building materials and construction work. The State Committee for Construction Affairs was charged with the elimination of such shortcomings. It disallowed many proposed construction projects and used the funds which were released to complete projects which were underway; in conjunction with the U.S.S.R. State Planning Committee, measures were introduced to establish a unified technical policy in construction; chief administrations were created to deal with special forms of construction such as grain elevators, farm buildings and irrigation projects.[47] Recurrent criticisms in the Soviet press suggest that there is still much room for improvement in the organization of construction.

Directly subordinate to the State Committee for Construction Affairs are State Committees for: Transport Construction; Installation and Special Construction Work; Construction in the Central Asian Economic Region; the Building Materials Industry; Civil Construction and Architecture; Road Construction; and Communal Machine Building. An important new subordinate organization is the U.S.S.R. Chief State Construction Inspection Administration which is charged with exercising control over the quality of construction and installation work, structures and parts, and the observance of norms, regulations and standards. It has the right to halt construction and installation work that does not conform with required standards.[48] The work of the State Committee for Construction Affairs is supposed to be coordinated closely with that of the U.S.S.R. State Planning Committee, the U.S.S.R. Council of the National Economy, the corresponding organs in the Union Republics and the Economic Councils.[49]

The industrial state committees also play an important role in the economic planning and administration. Each committee submits to its superior organ plans for the development of its branch of industry, the introduction of new technology, capital construction, the output of products, and the concentration and specialization of industrial production.[50] The state committees differ from their predecessors, the industrial ministries, in that the ministries managed directly the enterprises in the respective branches, while the task of the committees is to work out the general line of economic and technical development for the industrial complex, to ensure the requisite technical advances, and to see that the necessary factors are incorporated into the state plan.[51] They do not have the right to issue orders to the Economic Councils.

INTERMEDIATE ORGANS: MAJOR ECONOMIC AREAS

Below the central organs are three major discrete, but somewhat over-lapping, levels of economic planning and industrial organization: eighteen "large economic areas" each headed by a Council for Coordination and Planning; fifteen Union Republics, with organs corresponding to those at the central level; and forty-seven economic regions, each headed by an Economic Council. The large economic areas (17 in 1961, increased to 18 in 1963) were established with the goal of providing a "more successful solution of economic problems arising within the limits of the separate economic regions."[52] It was pointed out that although planning by Union Republics is "still a highly important component part of planning in the national economy . . . the borders of the republics do not always coincide exactly with the present day economic borders" and that, because of limited size, localism, and a number of other factors, "many important problems in the national economy simply cannot be handled on the level of economic administrative regions . . . and local Soviets."[53] It was concluded that "the compilation of plans, especially long-range ones, for the development and distribution of production by major economic areas is the most effective means for carrying out the rational territorial division of labor and implementing the struggle against all types of localist tendencies."[54] Current or potential integration of economic development constituted the criterion for the establishment of the boundaries of the major economic areas. The R.S.F.S.R. is subdivided into ten areas and the Ukrainian S.S.R. into three; the Kazakh and Belorussian S.S.R.'s each constitute one area; the Latvian, Lithuanian and Estonian S.S.R.'s are grouped together in one area, as are the Azerbaidzhanian, Georgian and Armenian S.S.R.'s and the Uzbek, Tadzhik, Turkmenian and Kirgiz S.S.R.'s; the Moldavian S.S.R. has not been included in the composition of the major economic areas.[55]

Councils for Coordination and Planning are established in all areas except in Kazakhstan and Belorussia where the republican Gosplan and Council of the National Economy are responsible for coordination and planning. In the R.S.F.S.R. and the Ukraine these Councils are subordinate to the republican State Planning Committee while the Councils of the Trans-caucasus, Central Asian and Baltic major economic areas are subordinate to the U.S.S.R. State Planning Committee. These Councils are literally for coordination and planning and have only very limited executive functions. However, their membership composition indicates that the party considers their functions to be of great importance. Among the members of each Council are: high ranking party officials, chairmen of Councils of Ministers, Soviet Executive Committees, Planning Committees and Economic Councils, many (214 for the R.S.F.S.R. major regions) directors, chief engineers and designers from major enterprises and a number (74 in the R.S.F.S.R. regions) of scientists and other specialists.[56] The chairmen of the U.S.S.R. Council of the National Economy and Gosplan are also expected to participate. However, most of these officials are engaged in the work of the Councils on an intermittent basis, and the major work is conducted by a staff of from twenty to forty.[57] The Councils are expected to coordinate and plan the work of the Economic Councils within their boundaries, to study the basic problems of the integrated and effective development of the economy, and to work out proposals for presentation to the Councils of the National Economy and the Gosplans, both at the republican and All-Union levels.[58] Soviet economists predict that planning for major economic areas as distinct economic complexes will raise the level of overall planning, mobilize new reserves, minimize unnecessary wastage, control localism, and in general, foster economic development.[59]

REPUBLICAN ORGANS

The organizational structure at the Union Republic level corresponds to that of the U.S.S.R. Each republic has a State Planning Committee (republican Gosplan), a Council for the National Economy (some republics use the simpler title of Economic Council), and a State Committee for Construction Affairs, each of which is responsible to the Council of Ministers of the republic as well as to the corresponding organ of the central government. Republics also have State Committees such as for Power and Electrification, and for Geology; most republics have some industrial committees or ministries which have no counterpart at the All-Union level, such as a Chief Grain Products Administration and a Ministry of Water Resources. The importance of the republics in the economic sphere has increased substantially since 1955 and especially after the 1957 economic reorganization which placed the Economic Councils under their jurisdiction. In 1962 Khrushchev stated:

> "In order to carry to a logical conclusion the responsibility of the republics both for guidance of the national economy and planning, it is necessary to assign to the republics, to their planning commissions and economic councils, the drafting of plans and their realization. The local officials are better acquainted with the economic possibilities and natural resources of the republics, the reserves of manpower, and so on."[60]

The post-Khrushchev leadership has emphasized the need to increase the responsibility of republican organs for economic management and planning.

Most enterprises within the republic are under the jurisdiction of the republican organs and the Economic Councils which are responsible to the republican government. Republican authorities exercise considerable initiative in drafting the economic plan for the republic, in allocating materials and financial resources, and in control of retail trade. Although fundamental decisions pertaining to overall goals, output plans, patterns of investment, rate of expansion of the various economic branches, distribution and utilization of the national income, degree of improvement of the workers' standard of living, allocation of many basic materials, and other major policy matters are still the responsibility of the central organs, the republican organs have considerable influence on the decision-making process at the center, and a significant degree of autonomy in implementing plans approved by the central authorities.

ECONOMIC REGIONS

The next major level of planning and industrial organization is the economic region or *sovnarkhoz*. In 1957 the U.S.S.R. was divided into 105 economic regions each headed by a regional Economic Council, subordinate to the appropriate republican government. Planning and industrial management on a production basis was replaced by the territorial principle. The reorganization was considered necessary for a number of reasons. The industrial ministries, most of which were subsequently transformed into state committees with reduced powers, had been predominantly interested in reaching and surpassing their own targets, and there had been a wasteful lack of cooperation between enterprises under the jurisdiction of different ministries, along with a considerable duplication of facilities. Useful by-products were often discarded because the enterprise producing them and the enterprise potentially able to use them fell under the jurisdiction of different ministries. Local officials did not have the authority to reallocate raw materials between factories on the basis of economic expediency. Because of the lack of coordinated regional plans, materials which could have been acquired from neighboring enterprises were sometimes transported for hundreds of miles.

The establishment of 105 Economic Councils rectified some of these weaknesses, but new problems arose. In general, the boundaries of the economic regions were established to coincide with the administrative-territorial structure of Soviets rather than on the basis of relevant economic or geographic factors. In some cases, mutually interdependent, neighboring enterprises were placed in different regions, and thereafter, the administrative structure made it expedient for them to deal exclusively with enterprises within their own region. Planning efficiency was not optimal because the local planning officials did not have an overview of the entire economy.

Moreover, there was a trend toward autarky because each Economic Council was primarily interested in fulfilling plans in its own area. As early as 1958 Soviet economists were criticizing the excessive number and illogical borders of the economic regions.

In 1963 the 105 regions were compressed into 47 new economic regions.[61] The newly created Economic Councils constitute a very important link in Soviet economic planning and industrial organization. Soviet authorities state that:

> "The creation of large economic regions will make it possible to take fuller advantage of the ties that have been formed between industrial centers, to focus attention on the chief and basic questions of the development of industry, transportation and construction, and to maneuver material, technical and human resources more advantageously."[62]

The borders of the new regions were established on the basis of economic factors: for example, mines were assigned to the same region as ore processing plants and major textile industries were united into one region. For administrative reasons the borders of the republics were considered in establishing the new regions. Thus the Azerbaidzhan, Moldavian, Latvian, Armenian, Estonian, Belorussian and Georgian S.S.R.'s each constitute an economic region. The Kazakhstanian, Ukrainian and Russian republics are each subdivided into a number of regions; the latter reduced its economic regions from sixty-seven to twenty-four. The Lithuanian region includes a province of the R.S.F.S.R. because of similar specializations. Originally, the Uzbek, Kirghiz, Tadzhik and Turkmenian S.S.R.'s were combined to form a Central Asian region, identical with the larger economic area. However, in December, 1964, a decree of the Presidium of the U.S.S.R. Supreme Soviet "recognized the expiration" of the February, 1963 decree "On Forming the Central Asian Region."[63] The announcement did not indicate whether or not each of the component republics in the Central Asian region will be treated as a separate economic region. During the early 1960's, the Central Asian republics were subjected to special supervision from the central government, perhaps because of rather strong localistic tendencies in economic practices, or perhaps, as the Soviet leaders suggested, because these four republics have similar types of economies, all of which have been "lagging."

The Economic Council established in each economic administrative region constitutes the basic organizational form of industrial management and planning by the state. Each Economic Council is nominated by the republican government(s) and is responsible to it (them). Supervision is provided by the republican Council of Ministers, Council of the National Economy, and Gosplan. Typically, the chain of command is from the central government through the republican government to the Economic Council and, finally, to the enterprises within the region. The Economic

Councils supervise almost all industrial enterprises within the territory of their jurisdiction, except for construction projects which were assigned to the U.S.S.R. State Committee for Construction Affairs in 1962. At the same time, the Economic Councils were made responsible for most of the local industrial enterprises which had been supervised by the local Soviets.[64]

The internal organization of the Economic Councils varies from one to another, depending on local conditions. All of them have several functional divisions for matters such as technology, planning, labor and wages, finance, supplies and disposals, accounting and personnel. Each Council has a production administration for each major type of industry within its region, e.g. for heavy industry, light industry, machine building and textiles. The production administrations have jurisdiction over the plan assignments and budgetary arrangements of subordinate enterprises, and supervise the work of the enterprises on an operational and day-to-day basis.[65]

Attached to each Economic Council is an expert advisory board called the Technical Economic Council which renders assistance in planning and especially in solving major technological and economic problems. These boards consist of eminent scientists and specialists, front-rank workers, and leaders of party, governmental, economic, trade union, Komsomol and other organizations. They deal with "economic and technological problems of industry and construction, improvement of production or organization, the efficiency of production processes, stimulation of inventions, coordination and specialization of production, the organization of labor and wages, and also problems of rational production ties."[66]

The main tasks of the Economic Councils are "to improve the organization of production and planning at industrial enterprises . . . and to ensure a high rate of development of the productive forces, to utilize rationally and thriftily the material, labor and financial resources and all the natural wealth of the given economic area."[67] On the basis of plans prepared by the enterprises, the Economic Councils

". . . draw up summary plans which cover production, capital construction, the development and introduction of new technology, research and experimental designing work, repairs, coordinated deliveries of goods, shipments of goods by rail, water and motor transport, labor productivity and production costs, and also supplies of materials and equipment for all enterprises under their jurisdiction."[68]

Although the plans prepared by the Economic Councils on the basis of enterprise plans might be substantially modified at the republican level, either on the initiative of the republican organs or on instruction from the central organs, their role in providing information on which the national plans are based is important. Once the plan has been established, the chief function of the Economic Council is to supervise its fulfillment. Superior organs issue binding directives, but the Economic Council has a certain amount of latitude in determining how the directives will be fulfilled. For example, it controls an "investment reserve" amounting to 5 percent of the region's investment funds, which it may use to expand production, or to increase the labor force or wage fund as it sees fit, provided that planned commitments to key sectors are fulfilled;[69] it may modify planned investments within specific limits; materials may be reallocated between enterprises; quarterly production plans may be amended as long as annual production plans are not reduced; within prescribed limits, the composition of production may be altered; it disposes of obsolete or unnecessary equipment; and it negotiates with other Economic Councils with respect to matters of mutual concern, such as transportation and supplies.[70] Because of the problem of localist tendencies, priority must be given to contracts with enterprises in other regions, and penalties are imposed for violation of this regulation.[71] A percentage of overplan profits is retained by the Economic Council to be used for capital investment, housing construction, awards, bonuses, and in other ways which it determines. In November, 1963, the C.P.S.U. Central Committee recommended the preparation of a new statute on Economic Councils which would give them more extensive powers, and greater autonomy in deciding economic questions and in making use of reserves for increasing industrial output.[72] The new statute has not appeared, but during 1964 and 1965 there has been a trend toward increased responsibility and autonomy for the Economic Councils.

INDIVIDUAL ENTERPRISES

Individual enterprises constitute the main link in the Soviet economy. Their task, as described by a Soviet authority, is

". . . to fulfill the plan for all targets, to meet assignments with regard to volume of work, to fulfill all obligations under contracts, to put out goods of high quality and constantly improve that quality, to raise the quality of construction work, to build by the specified dates industrial premises, houses, cultural and other service establishments, . . . to increase labor productivity, to tighten up cost accounting, to ensure the maintenance and proper use of the fixed assets and circulating funds, to cut production and construction costs, and to raise profitability."[73]

Each enterprise is headed by a director who is appointed (and dismissed) by the superior Economic Council, subject to party approval. Most enterprises have a number of functional departments (planning, personnel, finance and accounting, etc.) and a number of production departments and workshops, each headed by a chief or foreman. The director, subject to the supervision of his superiors, theoretically, has full administrative control over the enterprise. Technically, he has the right to reorganize the enterprise to increase efficiency; to adapt the plan within certain limits when supply or other factors have changed in an unplanned way; to hire and dismiss personnel; to enforce labor discipline; and within the limits of his allotted wage fund, to set wage rates and award bonuses. His orders are binding on all subordinates.

The extent of the director's seemingly great control is, however, severely limited.[74] He has to adhere to the economic plan and his prestige depends upon its fulfillment and over-fulfillment, as measured by specific indices. He has little jurisdiction over what is to be produced, and although his control over the quantity and quality of products has been expanded somewhat, he is held responsible for non-judicious decisions. The director has relatively little control over the number of workers, their pay scale and hours of work, the prices he can charge, to whom he must sell and from whom he must buy, *ad infinitum*. An article by an enterprise director, published late in 1964, summarizes some of the restrictions under which directors must operate, and at the same time, illustrates some of the persistent problems in the planning and management of the Soviet economy. The director complained:

". . . frequently the most persistent efforts of advanced enterprises encounter insurmountable barriers and innumerable hinderances. Their chief source is the host of directive regulations, the restrictions on the rights and independence of the enterprises, the absence of genuine material self-interest in the results of the work.

"Gross violations of the established procedures occur in the mutual relations among enterprises. Despite contract obligations, materials, parts and finished goods are supplied late and are, moreover, often of bad quality. The enterprises receive their annual plans and their allocated supplies late. The decision of even the most urgent questions often drags on for months.

"The existing practice of production planning fetters the initiative of the enterprises' collective. The plant cannot draw up its annual plan independently, with regard for its possibilities. Although the next year's plan is, formally, agreed upon in August or September, the draft is generally torn up by the beginning of the plan year.

"The plan for labor productivity, wage fund, production costs, profits and administrative and management expenditures is handed to the plant each year without consulting the plant at all. No one even wants to look at the factory's calculations. As a result, enterprise managers have to conduct 'litigation' with the economic council all year long.

"The enterprise director is deprived of the right of establishing the composition of the staff . . . even within the wage-fund budget he cannot use personnel wisely. The director is given no leeway in setting the salaries of specialists.

"The director and the collective are now restricted in their power to spend the deductions from above-plan profits or above-plan reduction in production costs. The enterprise lacks the right to maneuver in expending the fund for new technology. What is more, the economic council often takes this part of the enterprise fund for its own needs without the knowledge of the plant.

"The expenditure of the wage fund, down to the last kopek, is dictated from above. The economic council withdraws any saving in the wage fund achieved in the enterprise. . . .

"The director does not have the right to write off defective equipment and materials. . . . He is not given the power to redistribute funds or material resources among quarters of the year or to shift them from one sector to another. He is forbidden to sell unused materials not needed by the plant. Without permission of the economic council he cannot give a school, kindergarten or nursery the most trivial supplies or insignificant equipment or tools."[75]

Innumerable other factors tend to limit the independence and efficiency of the director and the enterprise for which he bears responsibility. All financial transactions between enterprises and all short-term credit must be handled by the State Bank, which has the right to investigate the functionings of the enterprise and to refuse credit; many directors have complained about the refusal of credit when the shortage of funds within the enterprise was due to the delinquency of another enterprise. The activities of the director are subject to a complex system of controls: the party, the Procuracy, the secret police, the Party-State Control Committee, special inspectors from the Ministry of Finance, the central and republican Councils of National Economy and Gosplans, trade unions and even subordinates are on the alert for irregularities, improper use of machinery and materials, and the manufacture of goods of inferior quality. Many directors complain that they are required to attend so many meetings and to complete so many official forms that they have practically no time to devote to the crucial problems of production. Much additional time is wasted by both the director and the production units when semi-legal trades must be made between enterprises to make adjustments for the faulty allocations of supplies, i.e. one textile factory which received tons of dye, but only in one color, had to stop production temporarily, but was eventually able to negotiate trades with other factories which had been over-supplied with different colors of dye. Another major problem, which will be discussed in greater detail subsequently, is that of running an economically sound enterprise and, at the same time, meeting the various indices of plan fulfillment which do not always reflect economic efficiency.

During the early 1960's there was a great deal of talk in Soviet official circles about the need to make maximum use of local initiative by reducing the amount of "petty tutelage" over the enterprise and its director. The post-Khrushchev leadership has also expressed concern about this problem. Kosygin stated:

> "The improvement of economic management and planning requires the expansion of the economic independence of enterprises and a rise in their responsibility for the choice of the most economical ways of fulfilling the assignments of the state plan, together with the extension of the rights of enterprise directors, shop superintendents and foremen. The elimination of various kinds of petty tutelage over enterprises will open a broad road for the development of the initiative of the collectives of enterprises and collective farms in bringing about a further upsurge of the country's economy."[76]

One concrete step to increase the independence of enterprises was taken early in 1965 when the U.S.S.R. Council of the National Economy, acting on a decision adopted by the U.S.S.R. Supreme Soviet, announced that a substantial number of light industry enterprises would be allowed to establish direct ties with the stores that sell their products to the population.[77] The enterprises shifting to work under direct contracts are to be allowed to establish their own annual and quarterly plans for output volume, labor, production costs and other economic indices in accordance with orders from wholesale and retail trade organizations and stores.[78] These plans, however, will require the approval of the Economic Council. When production, sale and profit plans are fulfilled or over-fulfilled, the enterprise will be entitled to extra funds on a percentage basis. These funds can be used for bonuses, to introduce new technology or to improve the housing or cultural facilities of the workers. Thus, the members of the collective are to reap some of the rewards of increased economic efficiency. The new scheme also reflects concern for consumer demand; trade organizations may, in accordance with popular demand, make changes in their orders with respect to the style, type and color of goods until specified dates before the beginning of the quarter during which the goods are to be delivered. Enterprises which violate the established delivery schedule will be subject to disciplinary fines.[79] Soviet officials conclude that ". . . the transition of light industry enterprises to the new system for the planning and sale of output assumes, on the one hand, the material interest of factories and their workers in producing consumer goods of high quality and, on the other hand, control by the ruble over the results of production activity."[80]

Preliminary reports from enterprises which have already been switched to the direct contract policy have been enthusiastic. Widespread adoption of this policy, if its effectiveness is not ruined by new bureaucratic forms and restrictions, could conceivably eliminate or reduce some of the limitations under which Soviet enterprises operate and which have impaired the functioning of the entire economy. The direct contract policy should enable enterprises to operate on the basis of more realistic plans, allow production to reflect consumer demand more adequately, increase flexibility, eliminate a number of non-economical practices and give the director and workers a meaningful incentive, in terms of a monetary reward which reflects economic efficiency, to increase the effectiveness of the entire operation. This policy has, of course, been introduced on a more or less experimental basis in only some of the factories involved in the production of consumer goods. Even its widespread adoption would not constitute a panacea for all the problems inherent in the operation of the planned economy in the U.S.S.R.

Economic Planning

The national economic plan is the central coordinating mechanism through which the Communist Party and the Soviet government attempt to regulate the entire economy. The plan prescribes the tasks to be accomplished during a specified time interval, including the physical volume of production for major commodities, increases in capital accumulation, labor productivity goals and growth of the total national income. It specifies the portion of the national income to be assigned to consumption and investment, allocates major resources toward the accomplishment of prescribed goals, regulates wages, prices and taxes, and governs the composition and volume of domestic and foreign trade. The process of planning, the number of factors which must be considered in the preparation of the plan, and the frequent changes in the organization and methodological propositions provided by Soviet economists, present an incredibly complex picture. It is beyond the scope of this book to present the entire picture in all its complexity; only the most salient features will be emphasized.

Soviet authorities point out that the preparation of an economic plan, whether long-term or annual, requires a thorough analysis of the existing resources, including the material, financial, technical and labor potentialities, and the realized level of production. The planners must take into consideration the relationship between various branches of production, the number of employees, the technical and cultural level and output of the workers, wages, the cost of production, the total working capital, profits and reserves, the utilization of existing resources and recent achievements in science and technology. Much of this information is provided "from the bottom up" in the form of reports and preliminary plans submitted by enterprises through their supervising organs, and summarized successively by production administrations, Economic Councils, republican Gosplans and, finally, by the central planning organs. Concurrently, the needs of the national economy during the specified period are analyzed. The economic-political tasks established by the party and approved by the government constitute the major expression of needs.

An important task of the planning agencies is to couple resources and needs in order to determine the economic proportions that will be required during the period of the plan's action. The projected balance is expressed initially as control figures which indicate major investment targets and aggregate output targets for a number of the most important commodity groups. For example, the Seven Year Plan for 1959-1965 provided targets for industrial goods such as pig iron, steel, iron ore, coal, oil, gas, electrical power, lathes, motor cars and lorries, cement, fabrics, footwear, sugar and a number of agricultural products.[81] In addition, targets were set for the growth of basic economic indices, including national income, gross industrial output, gross farm output, transportation, number of factory and office workers, productivity of labor, retail trade, capital investment in industry, agriculture, housing and cultural facilities and real income of the population.[82] The preliminary control figures issued by the central planning agencies serve as guidelines to lower economic units in the preparation of their plans.

Soviet authorities stress that the transmission of information from "the bottom up" and directives from the "top down," with concurrent modifications based on mutual interrelationships, is a necessary and integral component of economic planning. The planning operation may be summarized as follows: the party leadership makes the major economic policy decisions on the basis of party goals for economic development and the information about available resources which has been supplied by the central economic organs. The central planning organs translate the policy decisions into concrete economic terms or preliminary directives. Guided by these directives, the lower planning organs work out concrete plans which are modified, summarized and transmitted through channels to the higher planning organs which, on the basis of more detailed information about the overall situation, may revise both the directives to, and the plans of, the lower planning organs. Preliminary directives and plans may be exchanged several times during the course of the year before the establishment of the final plan which purportedly achieves a maximum balance between the potential and the needs of the economy. Needless to say, the final plan is never entirely satisfactory; invariably in the course of the plan's operation all kinds of imbalances have emerged—improper allocation of resources, plans for related segments of the economy are not coordinated, temporal schedules are violated or are established without due regard for reality, unforeseen problems in some industrial branches have a detrimental effect on other branches, etc. Planning, administrative and production units are kept busy modifying the plan, removing bottlenecks, reallocating resources and making all kinds of adjustments to enable the economy to continue to function smoothly in spite of planning errors and oversights.

Economic planning is carried out in two major stages—perspective and current plans. The perspective, or long-range, plans cover a period of several years, usually five but sometimes seven, ten or fifteen and, in addition to their economic purpose, are intended to serve as morale-maintaining devices. Lenin wrote, "It is necessary to inspire the masses of workers and staunch peasants with a great program which extends for ten to twenty years."[83] Knowledge of long-range goals is supposed to be "a powerful factor which strengthens the revolutionary initiative of the masses of workers, peasants, and working intelligentsia."[84] From an economic point of view, the long-range plans provide the necessary temporal interval to put into operation large economic projects such as power plants and canals, to introduce major technological changes, to change proportions within the national economy and to train specialists. Perspective plans are not operational in the sense that they do not directly indicate what is to be accomplished by any specific enterprise. Actually, regardless of the efficiency of planning methodology, the foresight of the planners, and the exactness of the information with which they are supplied, all of which Soviet authorities recognize leave much to be desired, it would be impossible to plan with complete precision for even two or three years in advance. Any number of unexpected intervening factors could necessitate modifications in the plan: delays in construction work; the discovery of new sources of raw materials; a change in emphasis because of technological developments; adverse climatic conditions; uneven rates of growth among some sectors of the economy; unplanned changes in foreign trade relations; or a modification of long-term goals because of changes in the international situation.

Current plans are used to materialize the goals specified by the perspective plan, and to permit the planners to deal with present economic problems within the framework of long-range goals. Because the details of economic policy must be modified from time to time, as either the actual situation or the goals specified by the party leadership change, the short-range plans are considered necessary to provide the required flexibility and to remove disproportions which develop. The annual plans, subdivided into quarterly and monthly plans, are the operational expression of the economic policy outlined in the perspective plan. Current plans are concrete and detailed; the production and supply arrangements for each enterprise are specified.

The first draft of the current plan for a given enterprise is prepared by the enterprise itself on the basis of the centrally prepared control figures, technical norms and the production experience of the enterprise. The initial plan, as described by a Soviet economist, consists of seven major sections: (1) the *production plan* fixes the type and quantity of output; the production schedule by days, months and quarters; gross and saleable output; forms of production coordination and ties with other enterprises; the use of productive capacity, and other indices of technical and economic performance; (2) the *technical plan* outlines organizational measures for the modernization of equipment; improvement of production technology; and measures for improving the assortment and quality of output; (3) the *plan for labor and wages* includes targets for the number of workers, growth of labor productivity and the wage fund; (4) the *plan for production costs* sets assignments for the reduction of production costs; (5) the *material-supply plan* indicates the requirements for raw materials, fuel, electric power and new equipment and the sources for meeting these requirements; (6) the *capital construction plan* specifies construction work to be done at the enterprise, dates for commissioning new units, requirements in labor and building materials and targets for the reduction of construction costs; (7) the *financial plan* lists the funds needed for production, construction, wages, organizational and technical improvements, and repair and maintenance of fixed assets; anticipated income from the sale of goods; and financial relations between the enterprise and budgetary agencies (taxes, other payments, credits, etc.).[85] One of the crucial balances of the enterprise plan is the input-output ratio. As a general rule, approved input norms and required output norms for specific commodities are established by regions on the basis of the performance of average and better than average enterprises.

Materials are allocated in a variety of ways. Materials most crucial for the development of the national economy are controlled by the central authorities, and are allocated in planned quantities to the republics for further allocation. Central control of crucial supplies, which exist in scarce quantities, is intended to ensure that priorities established by the center are observed and that supplies produced in one republic will be available for use in other republics as needed. The republican Council for the National Economy allocates the centrally controlled supplies to the Economic Councils in line with their planned needs, which in turn allocate them to the enterprises. During recent years, increasing numbers of raw materials have been placed under the direct jurisdiction of the republic Councils of the National Economy. Relatively abundant raw materials are allocated directly to the Economic Councils, from which the enterprises may buy as much as they need. Locally available materials such as gravel and sand may be procured by the enterprise directly. A crucial task of the higher planning organs is to allocate key raw materials most efficiently and to obtain the proper balance between production and supply plans. Frequently, the required balance is not established—the supplies allocated to enterprises may be inadequate in relation to production plans or may be excessive in relation to productive capacity or the supply of supplementary materials. In general, materials allocated by the central and republican authorities require allocation certificates for the initiation of supply contracts. Recently the system of allocating supplies has been criticized harshly. In 1964 one Soviet expert stated:

"... in the sphere of material and technical supply we continue to have in essence a kind of 'rationing system.' Material and technical-supply goods are issued on the basis of allocation authorizations ... that have been allocated in advance to each enterprise in detail for all items. ... The cumbersome system of advance applications for the allocations, followed by repeated re-examinations of the allocations and, further the requirement of allocation authorization papers before the ... goods are released to the consumers—all this leads inevitably to disorders of metabolism in our economic organism. The allocation authorizations, like ration cards anywhere, are always traded in not for the particular amount of goods really needed at the given time and given place, but for the full quantity of goods assigned in the allocations. The result is that material valuables not needed at a given moment accumulate in some units, ... while acute shortages of these goods are felt in other units." [86]

Increased control by the Economic Councils over the allocation of supplies was intended to facilitate the removal of disproportions but, evidently, the supply allocation problem is far from solved.

The availability of the key supply items is a determining factor in the modification of plans presented by lower organs to higher organs. Early in the sequence of planning, information about approximate limits on the supply of a large number of key input materials is transmitted from the central organs, through the republican organs to the Economic Councils, which use the information to adjust the proposed plans of the enterprises. In an attempt to obtain adequate supplies and an output plan which can be fulfilled or over-fulfilled with relative ease, enterprises frequently over-estimate supply needs and underestimate reserves and production capacity.[87] The Economic Council is expected to reduce the slack in the plans of the individual enterprises, but since its motives are similar to those of the enterprise, the summary plan which it submits to the republican organs may incorporate inflated supply requests and under-capacity production plans. Thus at each level in the planning hierarchy, subordinate organs bargain with superior organs for a plentiful supply of input materials and for output targets which are not excessively high. The process of negotiation between levels, which is conducted with the full awareness of all involved, helps to eliminate some of the imbalances and the unrealistic features of the overall plan.

The smooth operation of all branches of the economy requires the establishment of a workable temporal sequence for the various phases of planning. Actually, dates have been set on paper for the completion of each phase of planning by each planning organ.[88] For example, before the end of May, the central agencies are to provide the republican agencies with the preliminary estimates of supply allocations and output quotas, and the republican agencies are to submit independent estimates for supply needs and potential outputs. By December 1 the entire planning process is to be completed, and by December 15 orders are to be issued for the delivery of goods for the first six months of the next year. In practice, the sequences are violated frequently.[89] The supply plan is often not completed before the end of the year, and sometimes enterprises do not receive final plans until March or even later. When the plan is not prepared on schedule, enterprises are ordinarily issued supplies on the basis of the supply plan for the preceding year; lack of an approved plan does not mean that an enterprise must cease functioning temporarily.

Soviet authorities emphasize that coordination of the plan estimates at the Economic Council, republican and central levels requires the preparation of a whole series of balances:

> "The synthesizing of plans and the preparation of summary plans in a region or republic and especially in the central planning bodies do not consist of mechanical addition of plans received from below. It is a process of all-round analysis and coordination from the standpoint of the state, effected with the aid of a whole system of balances: material, money and labor and the balance of the national economy of the Soviet Union. Thus the balance method of planning and the method of synthesis of plans are inseparably interconnected."[90]

One Soviet writer described the importance of the material balance in planning as follows:

"By means of the material balances, the material needs of the national economy are determined, means for increasing the material resources of the economy are uncovered and the necessary proportionality in the growth of individual branches of the national economy, in accordance with the demands of the law of the planned proportional development of the national economy, is established."[91]

The material balance, computed separately by the central planning organs for each key commodity, is essentially a coordinated summary of supply and demand. The supply side of the ledger includes currently available stocks, anticipated production and imports; the demand or distribution side of the ledger includes categories such as production needs by republics, and for construction, export, and increases in permanent, republican and Economic Council reserves. The summary sheet is based on detailed figures prepared by enterprises, Economic Councils, republics and State Committees, which indicate planned output by producing units, and planned needs by enterprises, industries, economic regions, construction agencies, etc. The export and import figures are supplied by the Ministry of Foreign Trade. The state reserve is a permanent reserve for use only in the event of a national catastrophe. Republican and Economic Council reserves may be used to eliminate disproportions resulting from inadequate planning, failure of supply units to uphold contracts and above-plan production. In the initial stages of planning, the preliminary material balance sheets are used for the establishment of the preliminary control figures; in the final stages, they are used as a basis for establishing the required balance. Typically, initial estimates indicate that demand is far in excess of supply. Measures taken to balance supply and demand include attempts to increase production through more efficient utilization of available capacity or by establishing new producing units (the latter is more often incorporated into the perspective plan), along with concurrent measures to reduce demand without lowering planned output. Measures to decrease demand include emphasis on the more efficient utilization of the material along with the use of substitute materials. Directives to increase the supply and decrease the demand are sent down through channels and information about increased supply and decreased demand is returned to the higher planning agencies. If these adjustments do not effect the required balance, the commodity is allocated to republics, Economic Councils and enterprises in amounts lower than requested; key sectors of the economy may receive amounts of the scarce commodity corresponding to original requests, while sectors of secondary importance receive considerably reduced allocations.

The eventual establishment of a material balance for one commodity may produce further imbalances with respect to other commodities. For example, if producers of the scarce commodity are required to increase their production, their supply needs for other commodities will be increased; the use of substitute materials increases the demand for them and for commodities which go into their production. All too often, according to Soviet officials and economists, the required balance between commodities is not achieved. Khrushchev deplored the lack of coordination between different groups of planners, within the same agency, who are responsible for establishing the material balance for different commodities. By way of illustration he reported that within the same planning agency, one group, aware of the large number of automobiles which were inoperative because of lack of tires, planned an increase in tire production; another group, acting independently, drafted plans to increase the output of automobiles. The result was that the entire increase in tire production was required to equip the new vehicles; transportation facilities could have been increased at a lower cost if more tires and fewer new vehicles had been produced. He complained that in the planning agencies,

> ". . . everyone sticks to his own knitting. One deals with motor vehicles but tires are of no concern. . . . Another takes care of tires but does not interest himself in other matters. And few think about linking everything into one complex, seeing to it that full harmony, so to say, is achieved in developing the economy, that everything develops in the necessary proportions. . . . The plans for production and capital construction are often poorly integrated with plans for material and technical supply. To make ends meet, artificially low norms are set for expenditure of raw materials and supplies, or resources scheduled for use in the first quarter, say, include materials and equipment from enterprises that actually will not begin operation until the third or fourth quarter."[92]

A Soviet economist reported:

> "One of the shortcomings of the existing planning system is the unilateral character of obligations. Our enterprises constantly receive certain plan goals from above . . . but the superior agency, as a rule, is in no way responsible to the subordinate enterprise for discrepancies in the plan. Plans for output, plans for labor, plans for financing, credits and material and technical supply often do not agree with one another. The reason for this is that the individual elements in the economy are planned separately. The present planning mechanism is so constructed that each line and column of the plan has its own master, but integration of the plan has not been organizationally provided for. Changes in one plan indicator are by no means always accompanied by the appropriate changes in the other indicators."[93]

The recent reorganizations of the management and planning agencies are intended to reduce some of the many shortcomings which have contributed to economic inefficiency.

The general procedure used to establish the material balance is also used to establish a labor balance, which is designed to ensure that the needs of the economy for workers will be optimally met. Incorporated into the balance sheets are the needs of different branches of the economy for different types of specialized workers, the currently available working force categorized by specialization, location, etc., the number of persons enrolled in educational institutions and recruitment potentials. Techniques to reduce discrepancies between demand and supply are introduced; members of the labor reserve and graduating specialists with three-year commitments are assigned to locations or industries with labor shortages; and enrollment quotas in training institutes and wage scales are manipulated. The overall goal is the most "rational utilization of labor resources," which "assumes, first and foremost, the establishment of such proportions in the distribution of manpower throughout the national economy as will yield optimum production results from a minimum input of labor."[94]

One of the major principles which is supposed to guide the preparation of the plan is the law of planned proportional development. Proportionality demands the utilization of all material, financial and labor resources and their distribution in optimal proportions, so that a harmony may be established between the production of goods and the needs of the national economy. Proportional development requires that a complex balance be established among all branches of the economy, and in the distribution of material resources, labor, capital investments, housing, consumer goods, transportation, *ad infinitum*. Proportionality, however, does not demand equality of development, since the prescribed objectives and optimal utilization of resources might require that certain branches of the economy develop more rapidly than others; for example, the production of capital goods has always been given priority over the production of consumer goods. This is known as the principle of the major link. The 1959-1965 plan singled out the oil, gas, power, iron, steel, non-ferrous metals and chemical industries as major links in the development of industry.[95] The key branches are given priority with respect to allocation of material resources, labor and capital investments. The principle of the major link requires that the situation be thoroughly analyzed to determine which sphere of production is, at a given time, of greatest importance for the fulfillment of given political and economic tasks.[96]

Soviet economists point out that plans must be both complex and realistic. The requirement for complexity results from the mutual relationships and causality of economic processes. Plans for individual economic branches and territories must be coordinated; for example, plan fulfillment in one branch of industry depends upon plan fulfillment in a number of other branches since reliable supply sources are indispensable. Reality requires that the plan be an effective tool for utilizing objectively existing economic potentialities in accordance with the goals expressed in the economic plan. In addition to establishing excellent coordination or balance between all economic units, the plan should avoid both minimalism and maximalism. It is well known, for example, that lower planning units often underestimate output capacity in order to obtain a plan that can be fulfilled with no "strain," and that superior planning organs sometimes allocate minimal supplies to the productive units. Minimalism leads to the non-utilization of all potentialities, the demobilization of workers and, consequently, to a reduction in production and consumption. Maximalism, on the other hand, has led to the tendency to build large industrial enterprises and power stations regardless of need and economic feasibility. For example, a fruit cannery was constructed in a non-fruit growing region and a chinaware plant was established thousands of kilometers from the nearest source of raw materials.[97] Unrealistic maximalism, of course, results in wasted materials and labor, disproportions and retarded economic development.[98] A realistic plan is supposed to uncover unused reserves and to "mobilize the working people to make optimal use of production potentialities in order to reach the highest degree of productivity of labor."[99] Needless to say, Soviet planners have not even approached their goal of maximum planning efficiency.

INDICES OF PLAN FULFILLMENT

One of the most persistent problems, which has plagued Soviet planners and has impaired economic efficiency, is the lack of adequate indices to express planned goals and to evaluate plan fulfillment.[100] In a planned economy the need for appropriate "success indicators" on which bonuses and other rewards for economic efficiency depend is of crucial importance to ensure maximum utilization of resources and the fulfillment of economic tasks. The primary material incentives which are used to encourage enterprises to increase production efficiency are bonuses and the enterprise fund, money which the enterprise is allowed to retain and use to reward outstanding workers, to improve housing and cultural facilities, and in other ways for the benefit of the personnel. Soviet officials admit, with regret, that not all of the factors on which bonuses and the enterprise fund depend reflect economic efficiency adequately. Fulfillment of the output plan is a basic prerequisite for the award of funds for use by the enterprise. However, the amount of the award depends on fulfillment and overfulfillment of the profit and cost reduction plans, subject to fulfillment of the plans for labor productivity, delivery and the introduction of new technology.[101] It will be shown subsequently that profit and cost reduction may constitute highly inaccurate measures of economic efficiency for a number of reasons, including the fact that prices in the U.S.S.R. do not necessarily reflect cost. Soviet authorities are justly concerned because they have not, as yet, developed a system of economic indices which will encourage all enterprises to operate with optimal efficiency and will ensure that the most productive and efficient enterprises receive the largest material rewards.

Throughout the years a variety of indices have been used to evaluate economic success: quantity of output in physical or financial terms; plan fulfillment and overfulfillment in terms of physical units such as tons or meters, or financial units such as saleable produce or value added; increases in labor productivity; ratios between capital expenditure and gross output; reduction in cost per unit of commodity, etc. No matter what index or combination of indices has been used, uneconomical distortions have developed in practice.

Soviet planners and economists have been devoting a great deal of attention to the problem of the establishment of indices which will express economic tasks adequately and, at the same time, allow for the evaluation and reward of economic efficiency. The problem is far from solved. Two eminent economists described some of the difficulties as follows:

> "The existing system of economic incentives is linked only with the degree of fulfillment of plans and does not account in a proper way for the utilization by enterprises of available reserves for the growth of production and improvement of qualitative indices. This leads to enterprises losing interest in increasing plan targets. Often factory directors spend a great deal of time and energy in obtaining reduced assignments, the fulfillment of which does not require special efforts in mobilizing hidden resources, in finding ways for increasing output with less outlays of labor, materials and monetary resources. The explanation for this lies in the fact that such economic incentives as profit, the enterprise fund and bonuses are not used sufficiently. The extent of encouragement does not correspond to the actual achievements of production, the strain of plan targets and measures promoting the growth of production and a rise in its effectiveness. The prevailing bonus system for the fulfillment and overfulfillment of the plan assignments encourages the factory director to strive for reduced production plans, which results in an inadequate use of the internal production resources of enterprises, and frequently even to their concealment. . . .
>
> "The main principle of the system of material stimulation of production is to combine the interests of the entire work collective and each worker of the enterprise with the interests of socialist society as a whole. Implementation of this principle requires, first, the selection of economically sound criteria which entitle people to material rewards and make the size of rewards dependent upon the results achieved in work; second, it requires the determination of the sources of the rewards, the amounts of which are coordinated with the enterprise's results, expressed in concrete indices of achieved economic effectiveness; and third, it requires that the amount of the rewards should depend not only on the extent of the plan fulfillment, but also on the degree of strain of plan obligations undertaken by an enterprise."[102]

Primarily because of their convenience, indices based on the volume of output have remained the "cardinal indices, determining all other plan indices."[103] Khrushchev, discussing the inadequacies of the popular quantitative success indicators, commented:

> "The existing indices of fulfillment of production plans give an insufficiently accurate characterization of the work of enterprises. . . . We calculate cement production in tons, although everyone knows there are different grades of cement and accordingly the production cost of a ton of cement varies. . . . The output of plants manufacturing reinforced concrete items . . . is measured in cubic meters without regard for the fact that the items differ and require different expenditures of labor to manufacture them. . . . Hence it is obvious

that quantitative indices alone, without regard for the variety of the items, do not provide a correct picture of an enterprise's work. Often a plant that has fulfilled the plan in tons by overfulfilling the assignment for less labor consuming but heavier products receives a bonus, while another plant which is engaged in making products that consume more labor but weigh less and which underfulfills the plan in tons, is deprived of a bonus."[104]

Soviet sources report numerous examples of distortions and undesirable production activities which derive from the choice of success indicators. The measure in which the quantitative indices are expressed determines the form of the distortion. As Khrushchev pointed out, when output is measured by weight, heavy items are likely to be overproduced with a consequent neglect of smaller, but nevertheless, important ones. If the plan is expressed in numbers (e.g. thousands of units), an excessive number of small items are produced. If road construction plans are expressed in kilometers, the length of the road is increased at the expense of width, quality and safe shoulders. A railroad branch consistently fulfilled or overfulfilled its quota for tonnage transported by keeping all unused tank cars full with water from a pipeline; and truck pools accumulated the ton-kilometers required by the plan by sending a number of trucks on unnecessary long runs.[105] State and collective farms that had low yields due to adverse weather conditions obtained seed and forage grain on loan from the state and after transporting the grain to the farms, redelivered it to the procurement station to meet the planned quota and consequently, had to obtain additional grain from the state.[106] Occasionally, indices which are highly unrelated to economic productivity are used; for example, when geological surveying units received plans in linear meters of drilling, surveyors were forced to undertake work that they knew to be useless in order to fulfill the plan. Surveyors who had discovered important mineral reserves but had not drilled the planned number of meters would be classified as "backward."

These particular forms of uneconomical activities are avoided through the use of other forms of quantitative indices, each of which, however, tends to encourage other distortions. For example, if gross value of output is used as a major success indicator, enterprises tend to avoid the production of inexpensive, but necessary, items such as small tools, spare parts, and cheap clothing, and to initiate, but not necessarily complete, large scale, and perhaps uneconomical, production or construction projects. An index based on saleable product minus material costs provides an unreliable estimate of production efficiency because of the manner in which prices are established. A labor productivity index encourages excessive capital expenditure for labor-saving machinery so that the output of a stable labor force can be increased. On the other hand, a success indicator based on the ratio of output to fixed equipment leads some enterprises to over-expand the labor force. Value added as an indicator overcomes several of the problems associated with other indicators but discourages economically sound co-operation between enterprises since each wants to be credited with the major portion of the value which is added to the basic raw materials. The currently popular reduction of production costs index discourages waste and the over-use of expensive materials but has a detrimental effect on the quality and assortment of products.[107] Indices based on the introduction of new technology and the fulfillment of deliveries are important for the efficient operation of the economy, but neither is sufficiently inclusive to serve as a major success indicator.

Since the time at which specific tasks are accomplished is of crucial importance for the accomplishment of subsequent tasks, rewards for plan fulfillment must necessarily be related to a temporal index. Hence tasks are assigned by years, quarters, and months and sometimes even days. This too results in an uneconomical practice referred to as "storming," a period of frenzied activity during the last few days of the planned period, followed by a relatively slack period. An extreme example of inefficiency resulting from an overly-literal interpretation of the temporal index of plan fulfillment appeared in *Izvestia:*

> "Once when I was driving along the Kharkov-Rostov road, I stopped at a petrol pump to fill up the tank. Several cars were waiting in front of me. It seemed that the petrol station was not selling any petrol. On the office door was the sign 'NO SALE OF PETROL TO-DAY'. I was surprised by this notice. No sale? What were the cars on the road to do—wait till tomorrow? I went in as though there were nothing unusual and asked to have my car filled up.
>
> "'Can't you read?' A man with a bristling little moustache looked up at me with surprise: 'It's written in black and white, No Sale To-day'.
>
> "'Haven't you got any petrol, then?'
>
> "'There's any amount of petrol. Baku is functioning properly, I'm glad to say.'
>
> "'Then why don't you fill up my car?'
>
> "'We've fulfilled our plan for to-day.'
>
> "'. . . How on earth', I exclaimed, 'can you expect a daily planned quota of petrol sales, if you can't plan the number of passing vehicles?'
>
> "'What d'you mean?' My interlocutor rose menacingly from his table: 'Are you opposed to State Planning, then?'"[108]

Although this example is atypical in its extremity, it illustrates two important weaknesses in the operation of the Soviet economy. First, some individuals gear their activities exclusively around the specified indices of plan fulfillment regardless of the intent of the directives: their goal is not to operate their sector with maximum efficiency, but rather, to appear efficient on the statistical records which are submitted to higher authorities. Second, none of the primary indices of plan fulfillment adequately stress satisfaction of demand or use-value. Thus, durability is not adequately evaluated, although a relatively small increase in production costs can usually substantially increase durability and hence, the use-value of a product.[109] Inadequate emphasis on use-value is particularly evident with respect to consumer goods and services where demand, though not totally without effect, is certainly not a prime regulator of supply. Soviet officials and citizens lament that clothing is deficient in quality and style, that children's clothing and shoes are not produced in an adequate number of sizes, and that some consumer goods which are not in demand are over-produced, while other goods which the consumers want are underproduced[110] The 1965 experiment in direct contract relations between producing units and trade organizations represents an attempt to link the production of consumer goods more closely with demand.

One chief source of weakness in the Soviet economy is that enterprises are rewarded for adhering to instructions. The evaluation of how well an enterprise has adhered to instructions is based on success indicators which are far from perfect measuring instruments, either in terms of accuracy or inclusiveness. The superior planning agencies literally cannot, and in fact, do not want to provide instructions regulating every minute detail since the value of local initiative is recognized and emphasized. However, the enterprise director and his subordinates, in their own self-interest, and also in the interest of the workers whose material rewards are affected by the performance rating given to the enterprise, are justifiably concerned with making a good showing on the major success indicators. Actual top level economic efficiency, consumer satisfaction, high quality of products and other important factors are sometimes forced into a secondary role.

Added to these problems is the fact that "there are serious shortcomings in the accumulation and spending of income left at the disposal of enterprises, which have a negative effect on the whole system of material stimulation."[111] Bonuses and the enterprise fund are intended to encourage the personnel of the enterprise to accept increased plan assignments and, in general, to maximize economic efficiency. However, as indicated above, the choice of success indicators plays a major role in determining the activities of the enterprise. The enterprise fund, which is ordinarily restricted to $5\frac{1}{2}$ percent of the wage fund,[112] is formed primarily from deductions (approximately 80 percent, according to one Soviet authority[113]) from above-plan profits. This makes the fund an unstable quantity which, because prices are not tied directly to costs, varies from enterprise to enterprise independently of actual efficiency. An enterprise which produces goods for which prices are set well above costs is likely to have a much more substantial enterprise fund than one which produces goods priced close to the cost of production. Enterprises which produce an assortment of goods tend, of course, to weigh the production mix in favor of the over-priced items. Since mastering the production of new items increases expenses, lowers profitability during the first year and, consequently, reduces the enterprise fund, enterprises tend to continue to manufacture outmoded goods.[114] Plants which have been provided with the most modern equipment tend to earn a higher rate of profit and hence, have more substantial enterprise funds than outmoded plants. The complaint is also made that in many enterprises which produce low profit goods, the enterprise fund is so small that it is of little interest to anyone.[115] Another weakness of the material incentive system is that whether or not a worker or group of workers receives an earned bonus depends upon the solvency of the wage fund. Thus, "shops which have fulfilled their plans in terms of indices, entitling them to a bonus, and which have a saving on the wage fund, were left without bonuses in a number of cases because the wage fund for the entire enterprise was over-spent."[116] One economist presented figures to show that in some enterprises it is all but impossible to obtain bonuses, while at other enterprises bonuses are virtually guaranteed. He pointed out that in either case the role of material incentive as a means for actively contributing to the growth of labor productivity is reduced.[117] Soviet authorities seem to agree that the enterprise fund does not generally serve its intended purpose, and comments by Kosygin and other Soviet leaders suggest that a major revision of the system of providing material rewards to enterprises and workers is contemplated.

Profit, as a regulator of the Soviet economy, has in the past played a secondary and inconsistent role for a variety of reasons. From a theoretical point of view, profit as a motivating force has been condemned as a vestige of capitalism. From a practical point of view, profit has had limited value as an economic criterion because of the wide discrepancies between profit and actual economic efficiency, due to factors such as prices which are not tied directly to production costs, the judicious location of industries, and differential state subsidies. Thus, for example, the profitability of mining enterprises in the non-ferrous metal industry varies from —70 percent to +150 percent.[118] An equally important consideration has been the problem of allocation of resources and the channeling of investments; the development of the economy in the required proportions for the accomplishment of designated goals could not be achieved, it has been maintained, if investment were governed by rate of profit.[119] Such a procedure might, for example, have resulted in the more rapid development of the consumer goods segment of the economy in comparison to producer goods segment. On the other hand, a number of serious problems, including some of those mentioned above, have developed because the profit motive has been underemphasized. Industrial enterprises operating on the basis of a planned loss (approximately 20 percent according to one estimate) may not be motivated to reduce the loss, since that would result in a decrease in the state subsidy. Material incentives, even for enterprises operating at a profit, are not sufficiently firmly grounded in maximum utilization of resources to serve as a strong incentive toward increased efficiency. Moreover, failure to calculate the comparative economic effectiveness of various courses of action has had a number of undesirable effects: enterprises have been poorly located in relation to raw material resources; the least expensive of two interchangeable products has not been selected for production; investments have been made in low-efficiency enterprises, etc.

During the early 1960's, a distinction between the role of profit, within the individual enterprise and in the national economy as a whole was stressed, and the respectability of profit as a basis for decision-making at the enterprise level re-emerged. Khrushchev, in a discussion of economic indices and success indicators, summarized the official position on profit as follows:

> "In this connection the question of profit as an index of the quality of work of an enterprise arises. Some economists overlook the fact that profit in the socialist economy has two aspects. If we take our socialist economic system as a whole, profit as an economic category does not have the same social import as marks profit in the conditions of capitalist society. In capitalist production profit is the aim of production, the basic incentive to its development. In the socialist economic system the chief purpose is to satisfy the needs of society. Our industry produces goods not to obtain profit, but because society needs these goods.
> "But the individual enterprise is a different matter. In this case the question of profit carries great significance as an economic index of the effectiveness of its work. How the enterprise functions—at a loss or at a profit; eating up public funds or increasing them—is of tremendous importance. Without calculating profit it is impossible to determine the level at which the enterprise is functioning and what contribution it is making to the public fund."[120]

Statements by Kosygin indicate that the new Soviet leaders are in essential agreement with Khrushchev's analysis.[121]

Discussions of the potential advantages and disadvantages of profit as an index of efficiency, an incentive and an "automatic self-regulator" of the economy have dominated Soviet economic journals since 1962. The debate has centered around proposals by Liberman and a number of other economists. Liberman's basic proposition is that the activities of the enterprises should be guided primarily by the profit motive and that the enterprises' financial rewards should be determined by earned profit calculated as a percentage of production funds.[122] To make this feasible he recommended that obligatory assignments be carried only as far as the Economic Councils which should assign to enterprises only the volume and assortment of commodities to be produced and their delivery dates. The enterprises should, within the limits of the overall assignment, be free to elaborate their own plans, including the establishment of indices for wage payments, labor productivity, manpower, reduction of production costs, accumulations, investment in new machinery and the negotiation of contracts with other enterprises. The Economic Councils would check, evaluate and improve on the plans submitted by the enterprises but would not have the right to alter the scales of profitability on which incentive payments would be based. Central authorities would maintain control over the general direction of economic development and the pattern of enterprise behavior through control over prices, rules governing the use of the incentive fund, and incentive scales. Incentive scales would depend on the overall profitability of various branches and groups of enterprises having approximately the same natural and technical conditions and would be established as standards for long-range activity. The danger that enterprises would start to make only profitable items would be counteracted by depriving the enterprise of all incentive payments if the required assortment of goods were violated; new products would be encouraged by a scale of supplements to, and reductions from, incentive payments; a number of other control techniques would also be introduced. Liberman pointed out that a major prerequisite for the adoption of his plan would be an overhaul of the system of pricing goods to bring prices and costs of production more closely in line. He argued that adoption of his proposals would "guarantee conscientiousness toward state interests and a stake in the maximum efficiency of production on the part of the enterprises themselves," encourage enterprises to maximize productivity and to decrease production costs, improve low-level planning, and relieve higher organs from "petty tutelage over enterprises and from costly efforts to influence production through administrative measures rather than economic ones."

The majority of the scholars who have written articles about Liberman's proposals grant that the role of profit as a regulator of the activity of enterprises should be increased.[123] However, almost all of the discussants have suggested modifications or expressed reservations. Commonly expressed reservations are that the assignment of priority to profit as an "automatically functioning mechanism" is "incompatible with the system of state controlled, planned management of the national economy"; emphasis on profit involves the risk that the state would not be able to enforce its own priorities; centralized planning of essentials to the economy would be weakened; a marked deterioration of capital construction with a scattering of resources would be inevitable, etc. There is general agreement among the discussants that a prerequisite for the rational utilization of profit as an index of economic effectiveness, whether in a major or a minor role, is the adjustment of prices to reflect necessary costs. Price revisions are, in fact, currently in progress.[124] The extraordinary amount of attention which has been devoted to the Liberman proposals, in combination with the Khrushchev and Kosygin statements legitimatizing profit as a guiding incentive for the operation of enterprises, suggests that a major revision in the role of profit in Soviet economic operations is in the offing.

Examples of the difficulties encountered within the Soviet economic system in planning, in evaluating plan fulfillment and in the use of material incentives to encourage maximum economic efficiency could be multiplied tenfold. Enough has been said to demonstrate that the problems are complex, the plan is not always a rational, integrated document, and it is not always implemented in accordance with the intentions of the planners. Two major additional points should be emphasized. First, Soviet authorities are well aware of the weakness and rough spots within their economic system and are devoting major attention to the development of techniques designed to eliminate the shortcomings. Kosygin, for example, has pointed out the need for experiments by individual Economic Councils and enterprises to evaluate the effectiveness of different organizational forms and indices.[125] According to prominent economists:

> "Perfection of the system of state plan indices requires that the goals set by the plan be expressed with the least number of indices, the greatest degree of generalization, and maximum clarity and intelligibility, and that the results of the work of the enterprises be assessed with great reliability. Solution of this problem will enhance the stimulating significance of plan indices, and contribute to a lessening of the number of planning indices and an increase in the effectiveness of material incentives."[126]

The importance attached to the solution of the general problem of relating material incentives to *de facto* efficiency is indicated by the large number of articles which criticize current operational practices and propose remedial action. A related problem which is receiving increased attention is how to combine the planned centralized management of the national economy with local initiative and independence at the enterprise level. Major policy changes designed to eliminate non-economical practices, to reward enterprises and individuals for actual economic efficiency and to increase the independence of local enterprises, without a concurrent reduction in overall control from the center, can be expected.

A second and even more important point to be stressed is that in spite of all its shortcomings, the Soviet economic system functions with a remarkable degree of efficiency. Overall productivity has increased rapidly. Most of the factories have the necessary materials most of the time. In general, the quality of producer goods is high and the quality and quantity of consumer goods, though still leaving much to be desired, have been improving steadily. Useless, defective and poor quality goods constitute a relatively small proportion of the total output. Many factors which are not specified in the economic plan tend to counteract the shortcomings which were discussed previously, and to foster economic efficiency.

Since the prestige of party and economic officials is intimately linked with the efficient and rational operation of the economic sector with which they are associated, it behooves them to make decisions in accordance with the overall intent of the plan and overall economic goals for society, rather than on the basis of narrow personal interests. All major economic decisions at all levels are checked by party officials; a few party officials may insist on the fulfillment of illogical formal requirements, but the majority of them are, in their own self interest perhaps, on the alert for techniques to improve actual economic efficiency. Economic officials and enterprise directors are expected to exercise their decision-making powers, however great or small, in the interests of productivity. For example, the fact that supplies are not immediately available through regular channels could provide a legitimate excuse for a break in production or non-fulfillment of the planned quota; however, the enterprise director who exerts effort and ingenuity to obtain the necessary supplies through unplanned channels is rewarded better, either in terms of money or prestige, than the one who accepts passively the limitations of the formal plan. Any director who would dare to produce only one size of shoes or only one thickness of wire so that he could easily overfulfill the plan for volume of output, cost reduction and labor productivity would be reprimanded severely or removed from his position in disgrace. Official wrath is directed against individuals and enterprises whose activities do not measure up to the required standards. Khrushchev's public denunciation of a specific factory which produced defective television sets is typical. He thundered, "The factory director . . . should burn with shame! An end must be put to such disgraces, comrades! People who only babble about how our goods should be the best in the world but themselves turn out shoddy goods should not be allowed, as they say, within cannonshot of the management of enterprises!"[127] In 1965 a number of officials responsible for the production of low quality goods were subjected to heavy fines and salary reductions.[128] Many officials have been reprimanded publicly for discarding byproducts, failure to introduce new technology, initiating unnecessary construction and for a number of other reasons.

The emphasis in the Soviet press on the negative aspects of the operation of their economy should not be interpreted as irrefutable evidence of economic chaos. Problems and errors are publicized to inform the populace that abuses and inefficiency will not be tolerated and to encourage the kind of behavior which is desired. Routinely efficient behavior is commonplace and does not require or warrant publicity. In fact public discussion of economic problems may indicate that the leaders of the party and government are so well pleased with the operation of their economy that they can afford to let the world know that it is not functioning perfectly.

FINANCIAL ASPECTS OF THE ECONOMIC PLAN

The U.S.S.R. Ministry of Finance assumes major responsibility for the preparation of the annual budget on the basis of overall national economic policies formulated by the leaders of the party. The Ministry of Finance collaborates closely with the U.S.S.R. Council for the National Economy and the U.S.S.R. State Planning Committee, since the budget

Table 1

Sources of Revenue and State Expenditure[1]
(In Billions of Rubles)

Item	1940 Amt.	1940 %	1950 Amt.	1950 %	1958 Amt.	1958 %	1963 + Amt.	1963 + %	1965 + Amt.	1965 + %
Total revenue	18.0	100	42.3	100	67.2	100	87.6	100	99.6	100
Turnover tax	10.6	58.8	23.6	55.8	30.5	45.3	33.8	38.6	39.1	39.3
Deductions from profits	2.2	12.0	4.0	9.6	13.5	20.1	26.1	29.8	31.6	31.7
Social insurance*	1.4	7.7	2.9	6.7	5.9	8.8	19.8	22.6	21.0	21.1
Individual income tax	.9	5.2	3.6	8.5	5.2	7.7	6.3	7.2	7.3	7.3
Other**	2.9	16.3	8.2	19.3	12.3	18.3	1.6	1.8	.6	.6
Total expenditures	17.4	100	41.3	100	64.3	100	86.1	100	99.4	100
National economy	5.8	33.5	15.8	38.2	29.0	45.1	34.5	40.1	42.3	42.6
Social and cultural services	4.1	23.5	11.7	28.3	21.4	33.3	31.0	36.0	37.4	37.6
Military defense	5.7	32.5	8.3	20.0	9.4	14.6	13.9	16.1	12.8	12.9
Agencies of state administration	.7	3.3	1.4	3.4	1.2	1.9	1.1	1.3	1.1	1.1
Other***	1.2	6.6	4.2	10.1	3.3	5.2	5.6	6.5	5.8	5.8
Budgetary surplus	.6	3.3	1.0	2.3	3.0	4.6	1.5	1.7	.2	.2

* Includes income tax from collective farms and cooperatives, revenues from RMS (MTS), customs and other revenues.
** Includes income from savings deposits, reparations, fees, fines, etc.
*** Includes loan expenditures, military and economic assistance to other countries, reserve funds, etc.

+ Approved

[1]Sources: Vladimir Katkoff, The Soviet Economy 1940–1965 (Baltimore: Dangary Publishing Co., 1961), p. 249; A.G. Zverev, "Report to the Supreme Soviet," Pravda, Dec. 23, 1958; "Budget Law," Pravda, Dec. 24, 1958; V.F. Garbuzov, "On U.S.S.R. State Budget for 1963 and on Fulfillment of U.S.S.R. State Budget for 1961," Pravda, Dec. 11, 1962, pp. 4–6; V.F. Garbuzov, "On the U.S.S.R. State Budget for 1965 and on Fulfillment of the U.S.S.R. State Budget for 1963," Pravda, Dec. 10, 1964, pp.4–5.

constitutes the financial expression of the economic plan. Early in the year the Ministry of Finance prepares a preliminary budget indicating the amount of potential revenue and the allocation of revenue for All-Union expenditures and for the republican and local budgets. This rough draft, prepared without consultation with the republican and local authorities, is submitted to the U.S.S.R. Council of Ministers, the U.S.S.R. Council of the National Economy, the U.S.S.R. State Planning Committee, and the Council of Ministers of each Union Republic, each of which has the right to recommend modifications based on supplementary information submitted to the Ministry of Finance. During the course of the year the proposed economic plan and the proposed budget are adjusted to conform with each other. When both are in a more or less final stage they are examined jointly by the U.S.S.R. Council of Ministers which, when it approves them, submits them to the Economic Committee and Budgetary Committees of the Chambers of the Supreme Soviet. As a general rule, each of these Committees recommend changes of a relatively minor nature. Finally, the budget and the plan are submitted to the Supreme Soviet of the U.S.S.R. which formally approves them as law.

Table 1 presents the major sources of revenue and major expenditures in the U.S.S.R. for the years 1940, 1950, 1958, 1963 and 1965. The officially published figures have been adjusted to take into account the 1961 reevaluation of Soviet currency which made ten old rubles equivalent to one new ruble. In the succeeding pages all monetary amounts are expressed in terms of new rubles. The value of one new ruble fluctuates around 1.05 American dollars at the official exchange rate. Table 1 indicates that Soviet revenues and expenditures have increased more than fivefold during the twenty-five year interval. The summary budgets presented above do not include the vast sums of money retained by enterprises and organizations as their share of profits, capital investment funds and depreciation allowances which must be used in accordance with the national economic plan. For example, in 1965 the total planned investment in the national economy was 75.8 billion rubles, including the 42.3 billion listed in the national budget, and an additional 33.5 billion from funds belonging to enterprises and organizations. Funds retained by enterprises also supplement the national budget for education, science, culture, health, housing and welfare. The All-Union budget includes the republican budgets which, in turn, include the budgets for local agencies (Economic Councils and Soviets) within their jurisdiction.

SOURCES OF REVENUE

The most important source of revenue is the turnover tax which was introduced in 1930 to replace a variety of excise duties. Its relative importance as a source of revenue has declined from 1940 when it provided almost 60 percent of the total revenue in the national budget to 1965 when its planned contribution is slightly under 40 percent. The turnover tax is a form of sales tax which is levied in varying amounts on almost all consumer goods and, in negligible amounts or not at all, on producer goods with the exception of electricity, natural gas and oil. It is paid initially by the producing enterprise, and ultimately by the consumer, since the tax is included in the price of the commodity. In essence, the turnover tax amounts to the difference between the cost of production and distribution plus profit and the established retail price. For a few items, such as salt, vodka and matches, the tax is levied at a fixed rate. For most consumer items, it is expressed as a percentage of the retail price, which means that the consumer pays a much higher tax than is immediately apparent. For example, if the cost of production plus profit for an item were 4 rubles, and the turnover tax rate were set at 50 percent, the retail price would be 8 rubles, with the turnover tax amounting to 100 percent of the cost price.

The turnover tax has provided the Soviet government with convenient techniques to divert funds from consumption in order to subsidize industry and to equate supply and demand. The tremendous emphasis on industrialization has resulted in a perpetual shortage of consumer goods. Both wages and the number of wage earners in the U.S.S.R. have increased much more rapidly than the production of consumer goods. Discontent with the shortage of consumer goods would increase if the workers had ample funds lying idle; and non-utilization of funds would be uneconomical from the government's point of view. A downward adjustment of wages or lack of wage increments would have a negative motivating effect. The government has used the simple expedient of manipulating the turnover tax rate so that the workers can afford to buy little more than is available. Thus, supply and demand are roughly equated and, at the same time, the difference between the cost of production and the consumer's purchasing power is acquired by the State Treasury.

As a source of revenue, the turnover tax is both reliable and flexible. Its yield depends on the volume of production and the tax rate, both of which are controlled by the government. The severity of the tax on the same goods may be varied from region to region depending upon the goals of the government. Revenue from the turnover tax may be increased by increasing production or tax rates; the Ministry of Finance has modified turnover tax rates from time to time. Likewise, the government can, within limits, permit an increase in consumption by lowering the price or the tax rate or by increasing production. The cost of collecting the turnover tax is relatively small. Because the tax must be paid immediately after the goods are produced, the government has a steady source of revenue and a supplementary technique for checking on the output of enterprises.

The various practical advantages associated with the turnover tax account for its selection as a major source of revenue despite the fact that Marxist writers have consistently attacked indirect taxation as socially inequitable and regressive. It is for this reason that Soviet sources deny that the turnover tax is a tax at all and claim, instead, that it is merely a technique for transferring part of the "profit of the socialist economy" to the budget.[129] The major distinction between profit in the strict sense of the word and the turnover tax is that the former constitutes an index of the economic efficiency while the latter does not. As one economist put it:

> "It is necessary to consider briefly the difference . . . between *profits and turnover taxes.* The turnover tax represents a special form of mobilizing the centralized net income of the state. The form of the turnover tax has some positive aspects from the point of view of a guaranteed and quick flow of money into the centralized fund. Turnover rates are fixed in advance on each item of output. The mechanism for collecting the turnover tax also to a certain degree plays a role in control by the ruble. However, the turnover tax, unlike profit, does not serve the enterprise as an indicator of its profitability, an evaluator of its work, a stimulus and a source of material incentive. The rate of the turnover tax per unit of output does not change, no matter how much the unit's production cost may change; an increase in this rate does not depend on the enterprise. Profit per unit of output is another matter; its size depends on the quality of the enterprise's work, since achieving reductions in production costs increase profits."[130]

However, it is also argued that since the state owns industry, the difference between the cost of production and the retail price is a form of profit. If the turnover tax were indeed a form of profit, one might question why light industries are so profitable, as manifested by the high turnover tax rate, while heavy industries are relatively unprofitable, as manifested by a minimal tax rate. Khrushchev, of course, interpreted the turnover tax as economic profit rather than as a tax, when he stated to an American audience, "In the near future we are going to abolish, I repeat, to abolish— all taxation of the people."[131] His promise pertained only to the abolishment of income taxes, which have always been relatively low. Since the bulk of the revenue from the turnover tax is derived from the basic necessities, the combined effect of the low direct (income) tax and the high indirect (turnover) tax is such that the lower-income groups have had a disproportionately high percentage of their income diverted to the Treasury. In recent years, the increased availability of luxury items, which have an extremely high turnover tax rate, has increased the proportion of the turnover tax paid by the higher income groups. The claim by party leaders that the U.S.S.R. is able to raise almost all of its state revenue without recourse to taxation can be rejected as sheer propaganda.

The assumption made by many Western writers that the high price of consumer goods in the U.S.S.R. is due primarily to the high turnover tax rates is superficially correct, but a more basic reason should be examined. The primary long-range goals established by the party leadership require the allocation of vast material, financial and personnel resources to capital investment, industrial expansion, education, research, defense and health and other social services. The only available source of revenue to support these segments of the economy has been the surplus product produced by the workers. The effect on consumption and the amount of revenue channeled into the State Treasury would have been roughly the same had the state imposed heavy direct taxes, or had it set retail prices to correspond to the cost of production and simultaneously lowered wages, but the effect on morale and, hence, on the labor productivity might have been more detrimental. Given its long-range goals, the state cannot dispense with some technique to appropriate the surplus product. It can, of course, redistribute the burden by, for example, raising the turnover tax rate on household appliances and lowering it on food or clothing, but it cannot, at the present stage of economic development, allocate to the populace a major portion of the surplus product. Application of a high turnover tax rate on producer goods would have a negligible effect, because although the turnover tax on retail goods could be decreased correspondingly, the cost of their production would rise and retail prices would be substantially unchanged. Soviet economists point out that lower retail prices would reduce state revenue, while higher prices for the means of production would merely increase state revenues and expenditures simultaneously since the state is the chief consumer of the means of production.[132] If long-range goals were lowered or postponed a greater proportion of the surplus product could be assigned immediately to the populace. At present, standards of living are being permitted to rise somewhat, but the major portion of the surplus product is still being ploughed back into the economy because the eventual assignment of a large proportion of the surplus product to consumption requires realization of long-range goals. Thus, the reason for the high prices assigned to consumer goods is not the turnover tax *per se*, but rather the long-range economic goals espoused by the party leadership which, when they are eventually realized, are to guarantee the workers an adequate supply of consumer goods.

Deductions from profits are also an indirect tax, ultimately paid by the consumer. The contribution of profits to the state budget has been increasing steadily from 12 percent in 1940 to over 30 percent in 1965. In terms of billions of rubles the increase during the twenty-five year interval has been fourteenfold. In addition to the 31.6 billion rubles from deductions in profits listed in the state budget for 1965, approximately 8.4 billion are to be retained by enterprises for capital expansion and as part of the enterprise fund.[133] The revenues derived from profit deductions are obviously not an adequate reflection of the profits earned by Soviet enterprises since an enterprise which turns part of its "profit" over to the state may receive an even larger sum of money from the budget in the form of a subsidy. The rate of profit deductions varies in accordance with the state plan for expansion and has been as low as 10 percent for some heavy industries and as high as 90 percent for some consumer goods industries. Deductions from profit are set at a relatively low level for industries scheduled for rapid development so that money will be available for capital expenditure while industries that are not scheduled for development forfeit to the state almost the entire planned profit, plus a goodly share of the unplanned profit, if any. This permits the government to redistribute funds among industries in accordance with long-range goals for economic development.

The source of revenue labeled as social insurance in Table 1 incorporates a variety of taxes and levies including taxes on collective farms and cooperatives, revenues from Repair Machine Stations and customs. The social insurance levy, collected through payroll deductions, amounts to approximately 5 percent of the total state receipts.[134] These funds are earmarked for sickness and old age benefits. Revenues from compulsory collective farm crop and livestock insurance and optional personal property, life and accident insurance are substantial since contributions far exceed the payments. Collective farms which earn a profit of 15 percent or more are taxed at the rate of 12 percent of net income. [135] Individual plots are taxed on the basis of area possessed. Tax rates on production cooperatives increase progressively as a function of profits, and consumer cooperatives pay a tax of 25 percent of the total profit.[136] Prior to 1958 the Machine Tractor Stations provided a substantial source of revenue; revenues from the Repair Machine Stations which replaced them are of negligible importance. Revenues are also obtained from a number of miscellaneous sources including reparations, state loans, savings deposits, commercial licenses, automobile registration, passport fees, entertainment taxes, and fines.

Individual income taxes, together with a tax on single citizens and citizens with small families, have typically contributed less than 8 percent of the total revenue of the national budget. Prior to 1960 income tax rates for workers and employees earning less than 400 rubles and up to 3600 rubles per year ranged from zero to 11.4 percent. Writers, artists and cooperative artisans were taxed at slightly higher rates and independent artisans and professionals in private practice were taxed at discriminatorily high rates. As a wartime technique to increase revenues and reduce consumption discrepancies an additional tax of 6 percent of the income was imposed on all single adults and childless couples; couples with fewer than three children also paid the additional tax but at somewhat lower rates. In 1958, all single women and persons with children were exempted from this tax.

In 1960 a Supreme Soviet decree announced that all income taxes and taxes on single persons and small families would be completely abolished

by October, 1965.[137] Schedules were established to effect the gradual abolition of taxes beginning in October, 1960. The decree indicated that the
take-home pay of persons earning up to 1200 rubles would be increased
by the full amount of the tax reduction, but that in the highest income
brackets the increase in take-home pay would amount to only 10 percent
of the tax reduction because wage and salary scales would be lowered
simultaneously. Thus, the bulk of the benefit was designed to accrue to
the lower income groups, and the government built in a technique to
minimize its loss of revenue.

The reductions announced for 1960 and 1961 occurred as scheduled;
persons earning up to 720 rubles a year were completely exempted from all
income taxes by October, 1961, and taxes on incomes from 720 to 840
rubles were reduced by 40 percent. However, in September, 1962, a
decree of the Presidium of the Supreme Soviet resolved "to postpone
temporarily, pending a special announcement" the tax reductions scheduled
for October, 1962, and subsequent years.[138] Reasons provided for the
postponement included:

> ". . . important measures now being carried out by the U.S.S.R. for a
> further upsurge in agriculture and industry and for a substantial increase in
> the output of consumer goods and extensive housing construction, which call
> for additional budget allocations, and also . . . the intensification of the
> aggressive intrigues of imperialism and the need to strengthen the defense
> capacity of the Soviet Union."[139]

Since 1962 Soviet leaders have maintained almost complete silence with
respect to the abolition of income taxes. The promise to abolish the major
forms of direct taxation may eventually be honored, since the advantages
associated with such a move could more than offset the disadvantages. A
small increase in commodity taxation could replace the revenues currently
derived from direct taxation and concurrently simplify the collection procedure. Income taxes which have typically had only mildly progressive
rates have not been used as a major technique to reduce discrepancies between wage or consumption rates; if the state wanted to reduce such discrepancies, it could do so without recourse to income taxes. The initial
decree abolishing direct taxation had considerable propaganda effect both
in the Soviet Union and abroad; the lengthy postponement has fostered
disenchantment.

BUDGETARY EXPENDITURES

Well over one-third (42.6 percent in 1965) of the total budget of
the U.S.S.R. is ordinarily allocated to the national economy. The ruble
value of funds assigned by the central authorities for use in the national
economy has increased sevenfold from 1940 to 1965. As indicated previously, in 1965 a total of 75.8 billion rubles were earmarked for use in

the national economy, including 42.3 billion from the All-Union budget and 33.5 billion from funds retained by enterprises and organizations. The chief recipients of the budgetary funds are the capital goods and construction industries, as the major concentration has always been on growth-inducing investments in areas that constitute the basis of economic power—mining, metal processing, machine building, power plants, etc. In 1965 over half of the total allocation to the national economy (38.7 billion rubles, including 23.5 from the budget and 15.2 from enterprises) was assigned to capital investments, primarily to the chemical, oil and gas, metallurgical, power, machine building and light industries.[140] Funds allocated to agriculture amounted to 16 percent of the total economic budget (12.4 billion rubles, including 7.0 from the budget and 5.4 from agricultural enterprises). Funds from the budget are also used: to increase working capital; to purchase new equipment; for trade; for bonuses to enterprises; for subsidies to important enterprises which operate at a planned loss and for grants to enable unprofitable enterprises to rent housing to workers at less than cost. Such allocations from the budget are made in the form of grants and subsidies which the recipient enterprise or organization need not repay. Supplementary allocations may be made to specific sectors of the economy or to enterprises to cover unforeseen expenditures or to finance unplanned expansion. For this purpose contingency funds, which were set at 3.3 billion rubles for 1965, are retained by the Council of Ministers of the U.S.S.R. and each Union Republic.[141]

Funds allocated to social and cultural services represent the consumption categories of state expenditures. Soviet authorities point with pride to the disproportionate increase in allocations to social-cultural funds in relation to population growth. In recent years, well over one-third of the revenues of the national budget have been allocated to social-cultural funds and the ruble value of such funds has increased ninefold from 1940 to 1965. In 1965 state funds assigned to education amounted to 17 percent of the national budget (17.1 billion rubles), considerably more than the stated allocation for military defense. The funds for education are used to build and maintain children's institutions, schools, vocational training institutes, and universities, for the salaries of teachers and professors and stipends for students and to finance research. Since approximately one-third of the budget for education is used for research purposes, it is likely that many of the expenses associated with nuclear research and space exploration are paid for from the education budget.

Expenditures for public health and physical culture amount to 6.5 percent of the national budget. These funds are used to build, equip, staff, and operate medical institutions, to train medical personnel, to finance medical research, to provide the population with free medical and hospital care and some free drugs, to finance preventive medicine, to pay for funerals and to sponsor some athletic and recreational activities. Funds for social insurance and social security, which amount to approximately 14 percent of the national budget, are used for retirement and disability pensions, disability allowances, and allowances to mothers of large families, unmarried mothers and families which have lost their breadwinner. Also included in the consumption category of expenditures is housing construction; the 1965 budget allocated 4.7 billion rubles for this purpose.

Funds allocated from the state budget for military defense have varied as a function of the international situation from almost one-third of the total state budget in 1940 to less than one-sixth in 1965. Actual expenditures for military purposes may considerably exceed the figures listed in the state budget since stockpiling expenditures and investment in weapons factories may be included in "allocations to the national economy" and military research may be financed largely through "education" funds. Moreover, formally listed state expenditures for military purposes may greatly underestimate real expenditures because the state may set prices for military equipment well below cost.

Expenditures for agencies of state administration include the cost of maintaining the central, republican and local governmental apparatus and the judicial system. As the result of concentrated efforts to decrease the size and cost of the administrative apparatus, the percentage of the national budget used for this purpose has dropped from 3.4 percent in 1950 to 1.1 percent in 1965, and the number of administrative personnel declined from 13.8 percent of the total number of workers and employees in 1953 to 9.2 percent in 1963.[142] Unspecified "other" expenditures, which amount to somewhat over 5 percent of the state budget, include expenses associated with maintaining the police force, both secret and regular, interest payments, and economic aid to other socialist countries and to underdeveloped nations. The Ministry of Finance ordinarily allows for a substantial surplus of revenue receipts over scheduled expenditures. The surplus makes it convenient for the central authorities to modify the course of economic development by making supplementary allocations during the course of the plan's operation, to initiate unscheduled investments, to modify prices and to increase military and economic aid to other countries.

UNION REPUBLIC BUDGETS

The Union Republics have been granted considerably greater administrative responsibility for financial affairs during recent years, as indicated by Table 2 which shows the percentage of the national budget which has been allocated to the republics for selected years. Until 1955 the central authorities maintained direct control over approximately 75 percent of the national budget and authorized the budgets for all local administrative units as well as for the republics. Currently, over half of the total funds of the national budget are allocated to the budgets of the republics which in turn allocate the funds to subordinate organs (Autonomous Republics, Economic Councils and local Soviets) in accordance with the policy established by the national plan. The central authorities specify how much shall be spent by the Union Republics on the economy, social and cultural services and administration, and provide rather stringent guidelines on how funds are to be allocated within each of these broad categories.

All major decisions about sources of revenue and rates of taxation are made by the central authorities, but much of the revenue collection falls within the jurisdiction of the republics. Each republic is permitted to retain one-half of the income tax and some of the revenue from the agricultural, cooperative and turnover taxes which it collects. The amount which a given republic may retain depends on the central government's estimate of the need. Republics which are being developed rapidly, such as the Kazakh and Turkmenian S.S.R.'s, usually receive supplementary funds from the center. Although the republics have been allowed increased administrative responsibility and flexibility in the use of appropriations, the central government has retained firm control over fiscal affairs through direct control over almost one-half the funds in the national budget, and over the sources of revenue and general categories of expenditure.

TABLE 2

Revenues Assigned to the Union Republics*

(in Billions of Rubles)

Year	Total	Percent of All-Union Budget
1940	4.2	24.1
1950	9.6	23.2
1958	32.0	50.1
1962	44.7	55.7
1963	47.3	54.0
1964	49.9	54.4
1965	54.4	54.6

*Sources: Vladimir Katkoff, *The Soviet Economy 1940-1965, op. cit.,* p. 264; V. F. Garbuzov, "On the U.S.S.R. State Budget for 1962 and on Fulfillment of the Budget for 1960," *Pravda,* Dec. 7, 1961, pp. 4-5; V. F. Garbuzov, "On the U.S.S.R. State Budget for 1963 and on Fulfillment of the U.S.S.R. State Budget for 1961," *Pravda,* Dec. 11, 1962, pp. 4-6; V. F. Garbuzov, "On the U.S.S.R. State Budget for 1964-1965 and On the Fulfillment of the U.S.S.R. State Budget for 1962," *Pravda,* Dec. 17, 1963, pp. 4-6; V. F. Garbuzov, "On the U.S.S.R. State Budget for 1965 and On the Fulfillment of the U.S.S.R. State Budget for 1963," *Pravda,* Dec. 10, 1964, pp. 4-5.

The Union Republics serve as important administrative units of the central government rather than as relatively independent units which determine fiscal policy.

Prices

In the absence of free interaction between demand and supply, price control has played an important role in the Soviet economy.[143] A Soviet economist pointed out correctly that:

> "Frequently a whole conglomeration of different and often completely contradictory functions are assigned to price. Price is supposed to redistribute national income among branches of the economy and social groups of the population, to promote faster development of certain branches, to accelerate the introduction of new technology, to stimulate the use of new products and materials, and so on."[144]

Price control has not always served its designated functions well, and prices, perhaps more than any other feature in the Soviet economy, have contributed to imbalances and unplanned effects.

The system of pricing goods in the U.S.S.R. is incredibly complicated in that different principles are applied to establish prices for different categories of goods, and the same item may have several price tags depending upon the purpose for which it is purchased. Moreover, the system of establishing prices is currently in a state of flux, and major changes are likely, since Soviet leaders and economists are well aware that the illogical relationships which obtain between costs of production and planned prices, while useful for some purposes, are an impediment to the realization of some of the established goals for the smooth operation of the economy.

The party leadership is responsible for general decisions on price policy. Prices for the most important key products are fixed by the central planning agencies and confirmed by the U.S.S.R. Council of Ministers. Factors such as production and distribution costs, profit, goals for the redistribution of the national income, the importance of the item for expanding production or for consumption, supply and demand, etc., enter into the determination of price but the weight assigned to each factor varies from item to item. Since 1957, the republican governments have been allowed increased responsibility for price setting, and currently, about 40 percent of the prices for wholesale and retail items are determined at the republican level.[145] The price setting powers of the Economic Councils are extremely limited—they may establish temporary prices for new products and set prices for otherwise unpriced goods and services exchanged between enterprises within their jurisdiction and for unusual items which are made to order. The Economic Councils and enterprises have, however, virtually no role in determining the price which must be paid for raw materials or the price at which their products will be sold.

Prices fall into a number of general categories including factory wholesale prices, industrial wholesale prices, agricultural prices and retail prices. Factory wholesale prices, that is, the prices at which enterprises dispose of their products to wholesalers, are supposed to be based on the average production costs of all enterprises producing the commodity, plus the turnover tax, plus a margin of profit, and an allowance for the average cost of transportation to the delivery station. Some enterprises must necessarily produce a given item at a loss while other enterprises earn a profit because production costs vary with factors exclusive of economic efficiency, such as initial outlay of capital equipment, availability of raw materials and location and because transportation costs, which are paid by the producing enterprise, may vary considerably even within a given delivery zone. Sometimes large differences in natural conditions are offset by combining a differentiated price for producers with a single price for users, but this balancing mechanism is never very accurate and complicates planning and bookkeeping. The established prices for various items do not necessarily bear a logical relation to each other, and some enterprises must buy certain raw materials at prices which are excessively high (or low) in relation to the established price for the finished product. Enterprises which suffer losses on the production of such products must either compensate for the loss by producing other more profitable items or must receive a subsidy from the central or republican budget or from the Economic Council, which may redistribute profits and losses within the economic region.

Industrial wholesale prices, or the purchase prices for industrial goods, also vary with a number of factors. If the transfer is directly from one enterprise to another, and no turnover tax or differential for higher costs of production is involved, factory and industrial wholesale prices may be identical. If a wholesaling organization handles the transfer, a margin of profit is added to the factory price. If the item is subject to the turnover tax, state enterprises may purchase it without the tax while the tax is added for retail organizations and kolkhozy purchasers.

Theoretically, the policy for setting prices for industrial goods is supposed to encourage reductions in the cost of production, and at appropriate intervals, prices are supposed to be adjusted to reflect reduced costs. The ideal state of affairs for the Soviet economy would be for the price of capital goods to equal their cost of production. In practice, this has been far from the case and price changes, when they have been introduced, have as a rule been overdue and sufficiently radical to produce major imbalances during an extensive adjustment period.

Soviet authorities are paying increasing attention to the establishment of a logical price system, with major emphasis, at present, on wholesale prices. The Program of the C.P.S.U. states:

"Prices must, to a growing extent, reflect the socially necessary outlays of labor, ensure return of production and circulation expenditures and a certain profit for each normally operating enterprise. Systematic, economically justified price reductions based on growth of labor productivity and reduction of production costs are the main trend in the price policy in the period of communist construction."[146]

A Soviet professor described some of the disadvantages of the current pricing system as follows:

> "Prices that are not economically substantiated create for an enterprise 'paying' and 'non-paying' plan items, with some enterprises in a particular industry finding themselves in a privileged position solely as a result of a happy combination of the planned range of items to be produced by them; a weakening occurs in the planned utilization of the law of value; and there appear elements of planlessness and disproportions. In addition, . . . the heads of enterprises try to choose a version of the plan in which the highly profitable items make up the largest possible proportion of the total output. This results in the slow introduction of new items, which during the period of their introduction are most often insufficiently profitable or involve losses. . . . If the wholesale price is set at a level which ensures the plant a higher than normal profitability it also ceases to perform to a proper degree the role of a planned lever in improving the work of socialist enterprises . . . its management stops looking for new ways of cutting production costs. . . . At a plant where the plan envisages losses, most wholesale prices are below planned production costs. As a result, the losses are usually covered by the departments of the economic council by redistributing total profits within the industry. The amount of losses to be covered is calculated on the basis of 100 percent fulfillment of the planned marketable output. This practice leads to a situation in which enterprises operating with planned losses are not interested in overfulfilling the plan, since if they do the subsidy will not be enough to cover the simultaneously increased losses."[147]

The majority of retail prices are controlled by central and republican authorities. If the disparity between prices set by different republics is too great, the central government intervenes. For some commodities such as tea, tobacco, bicycles, automobiles and footwear, a uniform price is established throughout the country. To take transportation costs into account, three price zones have been established for a number of commodities such as sugar, salt, canned goods and furniture, with higher prices in zones remote from production centers. This procedure, of course, raises the cost of living in regions which do not specialize in the production of consumer goods. For some items retail prices are varied somewhat according to local production conditions and seasonal price changes may be authorized. In general, prices in rural areas and villages are set about 5 percent higher than in urban areas because of the higher cost of distribution. In March, 1965, Brezhnev announced that in May, 1965, the differential between rural and city prices would be removed for most items.[148]

The general principle underlying the establishment of retail prices, as indicated previously, is that the available goods should be priced to correspond closely with the purchasing power of the populace. If prices are such that the workers cannot afford to buy all of the goods which are produced or if purchasing power exceeds the monetary value of the goods, an imbalance results, in the first case, involving the unproductive use of resources and in the second, increased discontent with the limited supply of consumer goods. The retail price of most items includes the cost of production, the cost of wholesale and retail distribution, the producer's, wholesaler's and retailer's profit, and the turnover tax. By manipulating the turnover tax, the state can conveniently maintain prices more or less in line with purchasing power. "Errors" in price setting since the early 1950's have been in the direction of setting prices too low in relation to supply and purchasing power, as evidenced by the prevalence of queues and long waiting lists for durable items such as household appliances.

Theoretically, prices should be lowered when the economy can afford to divert more revenue into the production of consumer goods, or when the costs of production are substantially lowered. During World War II, acute shortages forced prices to an extremely high level, and during the early post-war period production of consumer goods increased more rapidly than purchasing power. Therefore, the marked price reductions which occurred between 1947 and 1950 were expedient to clear the market. Following Stalin's death, additional price reductions were made although purchasing power did not exceed available goods, and new imbalances developed. Since 1955, a number of consumer items have been reduced in price, apparently reflecting increased efficiency in production. In 1962, the retail prices for meat, meat products and butter were increased to cover the costs of production and to spur output; to make the increase somewhat more palatable, the prices for sugar and rayon goods were simultaneously reduced. During 1964 and 1965, there have been substantial reductions in the prices of a number of consumer goods including textiles, children's clothing, underwear, stockings, coats, shoes, radios, sewing machines, clocks, watches, photographic equipment, musical instruments, bicycles and a few foodstuffs.[149] In general, the trend over the past several years has been toward an increased supply of consumer goods, lower prices and higher wages. Consequently, the lot of the Soviet consumer, though still unenviable, has been improving.

One of the major problems which arises from the system of establishing retail prices is that no efficient mechanism exists to force production to reflect demand. The planning agencies may be reasonably well informed about overall demand but neither the planning agencies nor the producing enterprises have detailed information about consumer preferences for color, style and design. Retail stores could, of course, report to wholesalers who, in turn, could report to enterprises that certain items or styles sell well while others tend to be purchased only if there is no alternative. However, since prices and the margin of profit for both retail and wholesale organizations are fixed, and most products sell eventually because of the relative shortage of consumer goods, neither the retail nor the wholesale agency has much to gain by concerning itself with consumer preferences. Even if the manufacturer were fully informed, the impact of the information might be negligible, because fulfillment of the plan on the basis of the established success indicators might be inconsistent with consideration of consumer preferences, or because the system of allocating supplies might make it difficult to produce the preferred variant of the article. There is no spontaneously operating mechanism by which the price of the preferred of two interchangeable items could be raised, and even if the price of the preferred item were raised by the price setting authorities, the enterprise would not be encouraged, unless so instructed, to produce the higher priced variant, because the increased profit would be channeled to the state treasury by way of the turnover tax. Finally, because prices are established from above, rather than reflecting actual market conditions, the preferred items may be, as often as not, less profitable to produce than the non-preferred items. The fact that purchasing power has usually exceeded the available goods has, of course, decreased potential concern for consumer preference, since practically everything that is produced is sold eventually, even if the consumer would have preferred to purchase something else. Since 1962, when the Central Committee of the C.P.S.U. instructed planning agencies to explore ways to make production more responsive to demand, a number of innovations have been introduced or proposed. Of these innovations, the most important has been the right for selected trade organizations to negotiate directly with selected factories. The relatively enthusiastic response to this arrangement suggests that it might become a prototype.

Although the majority of consumer items are produced, priced and sold under the monopolistic control of the state, a relatively free interaction of supply and demand operates in the collective farm markets where surplus collective farm produce, produce from individual plots and a few other items are sold. The proportion of the total food trade handled by the collective farm market varies, of course, with factors such as state purchases and agricultural yields. Items which are scarce in state and cooperative retail stores generally sell for higher than the state established prices in the free market, while plentiful items sell for lower prices.

Trade

Marx described the role of the middle men in the exchange of goods as an intolerable, capitalist, profit-mongering technique. Since direct exchange is not feasible in a complex industrial society, the U.S.S.R. has evolved a system of marketing in which the state and state-controlled cooperatives execute most of the functions performed by middle men in other societies. Most producer goods are exchanged on the basis of the material-technical supply plan which was discussed previously. All consumer goods, plus producer goods used by cooperatives and collective farms, are marketed through state stores, consumer cooperatives and the collective farm market. Figure 2 outlines the organization of retail trade. Current and long-range plans are established for trade by the central planning agencies, the All-Union Chief Administration of Trade, the republican planning agencies and the republican Ministries of Trade. Each republican Ministry of Trade

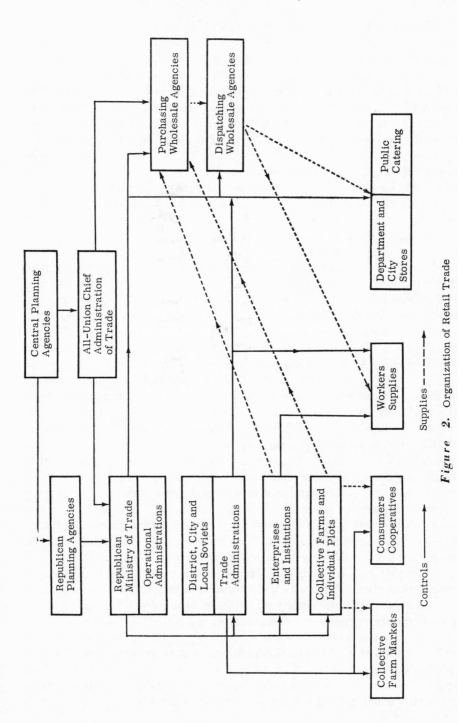

Figure 2. Organization of Retail Trade

Controls ⟶   Supplies ----⟶

is organized into departments dealing with planning, prices, wages, etc., and administrations which supervise the distribution of textiles, footwear, foodstuffs and other commodities within the republic. Purchasing and dispatching wholesale agencies are set up under the control of both the central and republican governments for key commodities, and under the control of the republican Ministry of Trade for all other commodities. The majority of urban stores and catering establishments are controlled by both the Ministry of Trade and the trade administration of the city Soviet. Consumer cooperatives, which are the main retail suppliers for rural areas, are also responsible to the Ministry of Trade and the trade administration as well as to superior organs in the cooperative hierarchy. Supply stores and canteens operated by an enterprise for its workers are supervised by the enterprise, the Economic Council and the republic. Collective farm markets are supervised by the local Soviets.

Purchasing wholesale agencies under the jurisdiction of either the republican or central authorities are established close to centers of production. Their purpose is to assemble a product from a number of enterprises and to facilitate its flow to wholesale dispatching centers and large institutional consumers. Wholesale dispatching centers, chiefly under republican jurisdiction, are located in retail centers. These dispatching centers obtain one or a number of lines of goods through the wholesale purchasing agencies for distribution to retail stores and catering services.

For centrally controlled products, the method of allocation is generally as follows: retail stores submit requests for items such as footwear through the trade administration of the city Soviet which submits a consolidated request through channels to Ministry of Trade. The request is resubmitted through the republican planning organs to the central planning organs which approve a certain allocation and use the information for subsequent planning. Eventually, the retail store is informed through channels of its allocation for a specific temporal period, and negotiations for the delivery of goods through the wholesale chain can be initiated. The same procedure in an abbreviated form is followed for goods controlled directly by the republic or the Economic Council. The lengthy and complicated allocation procedure is not well designed to reflect changes in demand.

State stores handle about 65 percent of Soviet retail trade, consumer cooperatives about 29 percent, and collective farm markets about 6 percent. State stores, which are located primarily in urban areas, include huge department stores, general stores, specialty stores, etc. The consumer cooperatives are financed chiefly through state loans and shares bought by the 4.3 million members.[150] Cooperative retail stores may purchase supplies from wholesale houses maintained by the central organ of the cooperative or from state wholesale agencies, collective farms, and individual peasants. Some cooperatives sell collective farm produce on a commission basis in urban areas, and provide sorting, processing, storage and transportation services. Cooperatives, as the primary retail organizations in rural areas, also operate bakeries, shoe repair shops and catering services. In 1962 consumer cooperatives operated 320,000 enterprises including 46,000 public catering services.[151]

The state supplies premises for collective farm markets in urban as well as rural areas in order to facilitate the distribution of goods, chiefly foodstuffs. A fee for use of the market facilities is based on the volume or value of produce sold. Local Soviets appoint farm market directors and inspectors. Although the free interaction of demand and supply is a paradox in a controlled economy, the state encourages sales in collective farm markets to free it from the need to establish additional retail stores, and to encourage the peasants to produce more.

Public catering services are supplied by consumers cooperatives and to a lesser extent, by the state, itself. Supervision is usually provided by the trade administrations of the local Soviets which, in conjunction with trade unions, appoint inspection committees. At present, public catering is underdeveloped in the U.S.S.R. because of the relatively small number of establishments, poor service, limited menus and the workers' lack of surplus funds. Recently, Soviet leaders recommended a great expansion of public catering in order to free women for employment, to utilize food more economically and to allow for its preparation according to scientific and hygienic principles. Future plans call for a hot meal for workers during the work day in an attempt to increase labor productivity, for public dining rooms in apartment houses and for hot meals to be delivered directly to homes. Because of wholesale purchases and quantity preparations, the price of meals prepared by public catering services is to be lower than home-cooked meals of the same quality. But these plans are for the future; present public catering services leave much to be desired.

Until recently, retail trade was definitely one of the neglected branches of the Soviet economy. Investments in buildings, stores and equipment have been limited, and inconveniently located, poorly equipped shops with unsanitary premises, poor storage facilities and lack of refrigeration have been common.[152] For a number of reasons trade enterprises were not forced to cater to the needs of consumers. However, efficiency in marketing is desirable from the point of view of the regime as well as the consumers, and a general trend toward improvement has been apparent. The central authorities have provided tangible evidence of their desire to improve services to customers by increasing budget allocations to trade and service organizations and, since 1963, by permitting these organizations to retain all profits for the expansion and improvement of their work.[153] Competition between enterprises for bonuses for overfulfillment of the retail turnover plan will be increasingly to the advantage of the consumer as consumer goods become more plentiful. "Progressive" methods such as packaged goods, self-service, automatic selling machines, home deliveries, installment buying and rental of items such as musical instruments and household appliances are becoming more common. Both wholesale and retail organizations have the right to reject goods of defective quality and enterprises which produce an excessive proportion of defective items are subject to fines and other disciplinary measures. A large number of items such as household appliances, television sets and watches are guaranteed, and defective goods may be returned within a specified time period. Some stores also permit the return of non-guaranteed items. As the supply of consumer goods has increased, customers have become more selective, and retail stores have been forced to obtain permission to reduce prices on low quality, unattractive or outmoded items in order to clear their stocks.

Wages

In the U.S.S.R. wage policy is determined by the party leadership, which acts through the central government; trade unions, as representatives of the workers, have no influence over the wage policy. Wage scales and monetary incentives have been designed to increase the productivity of labor, to encourage expansion in key industries and to redistribute the labor force according to the needs of the economy.[154] The total wage fund for a given period, wage scales and the overall remuneration policy are established by the central government. Major responsibility is delegated to the U.S.S.R. Council of Ministers State Labor and Wages Committee which coordinates its work with that of the U.S.S.R. State Planning Committee, the U.S.S.R. Council of the National Economy and the Ministry of Finance. Calculations entering into the determination of the total wage fund include incentive considerations, the projected size and qualifications of the labor force, planned output and labor productivity and planned relationships between the supply of consumer goods and retail prices. The total wage fund is subdivided through republican organs to the Economic Councils, which allocate funds to enterprises on the basis of the planned number of workers, their qualifications, and their pay entitlements under the centrally established wage scale. To preclude misuse of the wage fund by enterprises, the U.S.S.R. State Bank is given complete information about planned expenditures for wages, and is obligated to refuse wage payments in excess of the wage fund unless the plan is overfulfilled, in which case additional expenditures are allowed according to centrally determined regulations. Some Soviet administrators complain that "the existing system for registering staff with the financial agencies binds the director hand and foot," since it limits his right to reorganize production units and to reassign workers.[155]

Equalization of wages has never been a goal of the Soviet leaders. Soviet authorities state:

"Marxism does not understand equality to mean equality of physical and mental ability, or equality of the personal needs of people, but rather as the liquidation of exploitation and the private ownership of the means of production; equality means equal opportunity to use the social production means, equal obligation to work and for all an equal principle of remuneration according to work."[156]

Lenin, who stressed that the materialistic interests of the people must be stimulated to encourage greater productivity, was a firm advocate of a policy of differential payments based on productivity, skill and experience. Stalin stated that it is the "worth" of a worker in production that counts rather than his "needs." During the post-Stalin era Soviet leaders have decreased wage differentials and have attempted to provide a uniform minimum level for consumption through supplementation of income by comprehensive social welfare measures. However, they firmly reject wage equalization arguments as "petty bourgeois nonsense." Khrushchev pointed out that equality of incomes would work for the benefit of loafers, and the material incentive for people to work better to increase labor productivity and production would be lost.[157] According to one of the major "economic laws of socialism," rewards must vary with the quantity and quality of production during the period of transition to full communism.

Wage scales and methods of calculating the material rewards of labor have varied greatly from time to time, but the consistent underlying principle has always been that wages should be manipulated to assist in the achievement of the economic goals set by the party leadership. The first economic plan established wage differentials between skills, branches and regions in order to distribute labor according to planned output requirements and to encourage higher productivity through improved skill levels. Skilled labor was rewarded on the basis of a fixed multiple of the unskilled labor rate, with the multiple increasing with the importance of the skill. Wide differentials were encouraged and many skilled workers earned three to five times as much as unskilled laborers.[158] Workers in key branches of heavy industry were paid at higher rates because of the importance to the economy of the rapid development of these sectors, and regional wage differentials were introduced to attract workers to industries in remote areas. Additional benefits, such as better housing and more consumer goods for workers in preferred wage categories, increased actual wage differentials.

The basic wage pattern worked relatively efficiently for the distribution of labor, but its effect on increased labor productivity was not great, since productivity was not the basic index determining the amount of reward. Consequently, a second system of incentives based on piecework was combined with the basic wage scale. The policy of payment according to production had, in general, a beneficial effect on productivity, but the poorly coordinated combination of the two systems of payment had a number of unwanted effects. Wages of employees who worked solely on a salary basis remained stationary, except for statutory changes, while the income of workers in production tended to increase substantially in a chaotic and unplanned manner. Output norms were not always realistic, and some unskilled workers with low norms earned much more than highly skilled workers in other branches where the established norms were high. "Average-progressive" norms based on the production records of the above median enterprises in a given industry placed workers in less efficient or poorly equipped plants at an extreme disadvantage. Moreover, managers who had to compete for different types of labor adopted the practice of manipulating either grade level or labor norms within the framework of the allocated wage fund. By 1940 about 60 percent of the total income of industrial workers derived from piece rate incentives. The employment of marginal workers during the war made it necessary to lower work norms. When the skilled workers returned after the war, the lower work norms further increased the proportion of income derived from piecework, added to unplanned wage differentials, and forced wages up in an unplanned manner. To offset the discrepancies somewhat, the central authorities raised the incomes of low paid salaried workers in 1947 and at various times thereafter.

The Twentieth Party Congress of the C.P.S.U. concluded that the complex system of regulating income should be revised and simplified because it had become entirely too cumbersome and complex to assist most efficiently in the materialization of economic goals. The party decreed that excessive disparities in earnings should be reduced, more realistic work norms should be established, and time payments, rather than piecework payments, should constitute the major basis of income distribution. The emphasis on time payments rather than piece rate payments may have reflected in part the leadership's confidence that a modicum of the "socialist attitude" toward work had developed; however, the primary factor was probably the desire to establish a rational wage structure, more firmly subject to manipulation by the central authorities. Since the mid-1950's a vast reorganization of the wage system has been in progress in line with the party directive.

Table 3 summarizes information about current wage policies and differentials within a given branch and between branches. Ratio figures in Table 3 are taken from an official Soviet publication; wages in rubles were calculated from the ratio figures, and are based on the assumption that the lowest paid workers in the food industry earn 45 rubles per month, inasmuch as the minimum wage, as of January, 1965, is 40-45 rubles. Detailed job classifications on the basis of duties, education, experience and skill requirements have been established for each grade in each industry. For most industries the number of grades has been reduced to six. The disparity of income between grades one and six has been reduced so that in most in-

Table 3

Wage Differentials Within and Between Industries*

Industries	Number of Grades	Ratio of Extreme Rates in Scale	Ratio of First Grade Rate to First Grade Rate in Food Industry	Ratio of Top Grade Rate to Top Grade Rate in Food Industry	Basic Wage for First Grade +	Basic Wage for Top Grade +
Coal	8	3.75	1.33	2.78	60	225
Iron and steel	10	3.2	1.11	1.97	50	160
Machine building	6	2.0	1.24	1.38	56	112
Chemical	7	2.3	1.11	1.41	50	115
Textile	6	1.8	1.12	1.12	50	90
Food	6	1.8	1.00	1.00	45	81

* Ia. Gomberg, "Skilled Labor—a Factor in Wage Differentiation," Voprosy ekonomiki, 1964, No. 7 (Problems of Economics, Dec. 1964, Vol. VII, No. 8, pp. 36–44).

+ Calculated on the basis of a minimum wage of 45 rubles per month for workers in the food industry.

dustries a worker in the sixth grade receives approximately twice as much as a worker in the first grade. However, in some industries, as for example the coal industry, a worker with the highest grade may have a basic wage which is almost four times as much as that of a worker in the lowest grade. Higher basic wage rates for key industries and for certain regional zones have been maintained. A beginning worker in the coal industry has a basic salary which is one-third higher than that of a beginning worker in the food industry and a top level worker in the coal industry earns almost three times as much as a top level worker and five times as much as a beginner in the food industry. Remuneration rates are higher (normally about 15 percent) for work which requires strenuous physical effort or which must be performed under abnormal conditions such as extreme heat. The proportion of income determined by time rates has increased to between 70 and 80 percent,[159] but piece rate payments have not been eliminated, and in 1964 over 60 percent of the industrial workers received a substantial portion of their income on the basis of piecework payments.[160]

Since the Twenty-Second Party Congress posed the task of ". . . intensifying collective forms of material incentives that raise the interest of each employee in a high level of operation of the enterprise as a whole," piecework payment to the collective rather than to the individual has been the preferred form. Collective piecework payment is intended to encourage advanced workers to communicate their experience, skills and knowledge to less advanced workers and, in general, to implement the principle of "one for all and all for one" which is supposed to be part of the moral code of the builders of communism.[161] Since material incentives are designed to improve the quantity and quality of work, piece rate payment is distributed to the members of the work collective on the basis of qualifications, contributions and labor hours, rather than in equal amounts. If collective piecework payments are not appropriate, individual workers who exceed the established output norm may receive additional remuneration on either a direct or progressive piecework scale. Production norms are supposed to be periodically upgraded. Many workers complain that each time the output norm is overfulfilled, the norm is raised, thereby making it progressively more difficult for workers to fulfill the norm. Bonuses, either in combination with or as a substitution for piecework payment, may be awarded for the economical use of raw materials, lowered production costs, improved quality of products or innovations. Most workers in jobs which are not amenable to piecework payments are eligible for bonuses. Leading administrative, engineering and technical personnel are paid monthly salaries, differentiated on the basis of qualifications, experience and the size and importance of the enterprise. If the enterprise fulfills and overfulfills the plan according to the most important success indicators, these officials receive a bonus calculated as a percentage of a basic salary.

Although the basic remuneration policy worked out by the Soviet authorities facilitates the distribution of labor according to need and, in general, has increased labor productivity, the system is by no means flawless.[162] Centrally determined policies, no matter how rational, can never reflect accurately all aspects of the ever-changing and complex labor-market relations throughout the U.S.S.R. Directives to upgrade production norms are sometimes evaded by directors who have the concrete problem of recruiting workers; thus, productivity is not always adequately reflected by income, and piecework payments may still result in a chaotic, disproportionate and unplanned increase in the incomes of some workers. For example, in one plant fourth grade workers with easy norms earn on the average 142 rubles per month while more highly skilled sixth grade workers with more realistic norms average 120 rubles.[163] The labor force is not always distributed in accordance with the demands of the economy. For example, a manpower shortage in Siberia is one of the principal factors retarding its development. Despite the fact that the state has been using appeals for volunteers, organized recruitment, assignment of students and party members and a substantial pay differential to build up the labor force in Siberia, approximately half of the workers who transfer to Siberia leave within a three year period.[164] One of the chief reasons for the high labor turnover rate in this area is dissatisfaction with living conditions. Since 1956, workers have had the right to leave a job, with no penalty, if engaged in a new job within a month; consequently, workers tend to gravitate to areas with adequate housing and cultural facilities, and relatively low costs of living, and to those branches of industry which offer the best pay. Some industrial enterprises have been unable to recruit necessary engineers because engineers working in research institutes and design bureaus earn considerably more than their equally well-trained counterparts in industry.[165] Thus, even with careful planning, disproportions may arise between the number of workers required for a particular segment of the economy and the number trained and otherwise available to fill the positions. Other problems arise because youths under eighteen are entitled to work shorter hours and women are entitled to light work during pregnancy, maternity leave and other privileges, but must be paid at the same rate as other workers. Directors who have production norms to fulfill would naturally prefer not to hire persons with special privileges. This factor, combined with the problem of regional distribution of the labor force, results in less than total employment at all times, a not very significant, but highly undesirable, wastage of human resources from the Soviet point of view.

Since 1956, there has been a definite trend toward reducing wage differentials. In 1965, the minimum wage was increased from 27 to 35 rubles per month for rural workers and from 40 to 45 rubles per month for urban workers. The benefits of the income tax reduction which were effected in the early 1960's accrued almost entirely to workers in the lower wage brackets. The emphasis on time payments, and the elimination of some of the more extreme practices pertaining to piecework payments have also reduced disparities, and very high salaries, such as those of professors, bureaucrats and government officials, have apparently been reduced. In 1964, Khrushchev stated:

> "As the economy and public wealth grow and as the differences in the levels of workers' qualifications and labor productivity are reduced, the difference in the remuneration of the labor of high paid and comparatively low paid categories of workers will steadily be reduced. . . . This stems from Marxist-Leninist teaching, from the tasks set by the Party Program in perfecting the distribution of material goods."[166]

There is, however, absolutely no evidence that the U.S.S.R. intends to eliminate wage differentials. Material incentives are, Soviet leaders recognize, an indispensable necessity for the smooth operation of their economy.

Systematic data on average wages have not been published by Soviet authorities in recent years. In 1928 the average *annual* income was 70.3 rubles (703 rubles by the old scale), and in 1960 the average *monthly* income was approximately 80 (new) rubles, a more than twelvefold increase. Table 4, which presents approximate earnings for 1965 for selected types of workers, provides some information about wage differentials and the value placed by the Soviet regime on different types of qualifications. Within each profession or occupation, basic wage rates depend upon qualification, length of service and other factors, such as wage differentials for working in key industries or remote regions; for example, physicians with a work record of 25 years earn approximately 25 rubles per month more

TABLE 4
Approximate Basic Wage Rates in 1964-1965 for Selected Groups*

Minimum Wage workers	40 - 45
Unskilled workers	40 - 60
Semi-skilled workers	60 - 150
Skilled workers	80 - 225
Engineers	100 - 300
Physicians	90 - 125
Physicians Assistants	65 - 110
Nurses	60 - 110
Hospital attendants	45 - 50
Teachers	80 - 137
Professors	300 - 900
Enterprise Directors	300 - 900
Chairmen of rural Soviets	60 - 75
Secretaries of rural Soviets	50 - 65

*Sources: N. S. Khrushchev, "On Measures to Fulfill the C.P.S.U. Program in the Sphere of Increasing the Well-Being of the People," *Pravda,* July 14, 1964, pp. 1-5 (C.D.S.P., Vol. XVI, No. 29, pp. 4-21); Ia. Gomberg, "Skilled Labor—A Factor in Wage Differentiation," *op. cit.,* pp. 36-44; A. Korobov, "On the Tasks and Specific Features of the National Economic Plan for 1965," *Planovoe khozaistvo,* No. 1, Jan., 1965.

than beginning physicians; physicians in rural hospitals earn 10-15 rubles per month more than equally qualified physicians in urban hospitals; recognized medical specialists are paid an additional 30 rubles per month.[167] Take-home pay may be supplemented through above-quota piecework, overtime pay and bonuses; for example, teachers receive additional payments up to 23 rubles a month for class guidance and grading papers.[168] Table 4 indicates that most technical and professional workers have basic wage rates which are two to five times higher than those of unskilled laborers. Since purchasing power is more important than monetary income *per se* a few prices for the 1964-1965 period are provided in Table 5.

TABLE 5

Prices in 1963-1965 for Selected Commodities*

(in rubles)

meat (kg.)	1.80-2.50	practical shoes	8- 12
potatoes (kg.)	.22- .35	lightweight coat	60- 80
milk (lt.)	.40	raincoat	40- 60
butter (kg.)	3.6	wool suit	100-200
eggs (10)	1.2	cotton dress	10- 20
bread (kg.)	.13	necktie	1.4
green onions (kg.)	1.20	gaberdine (m.)	3.2
cabbage (kg.)	.60	vacuum cleaner	50- 60
sugar (kg.)	1.2	phonograph record	.4-.6

*Sources: "A Gain of 200,000,000," *Izvestia*, October 2, 1964, p. 2 (C.D.S.P., Vol. XVI, No. 40, p. 29); I. Abashkin and A. Michurin, "Why Some Places Favor the Speculator," *Ekonomicheskaya gazeta*, No. 27, July 6, 1963, pp. 40-41 (C.D.S.P., Vol. XV, No. 27, pp. 16-18); M. Ilyin, "Reporters Account of Reduced Price Shops," *Sovetskaya torgovlya*, December 3, 1964, p. 1. (C.D.S.P., Vol. XVI, No. 49, pp. 17, 29); A. Novoplyansky, "At Reduced Prices," *Pravda*, April 26, 1965, p. 4 (C.D.S.P., Vol. XVII, No. 17, pp. 12, 23); Ye. Liberman, "Prof. Ye. Liberman Reproves Bourgeois Propagandists," *Ekonomicheskaya gazeta*, May 30, 1964, p. 13 (C.D.S.P., Vol. XVI, No. 22, pp. 9-10); Anthony Sylvester, "Provincial Towns in Russia," *Problems of Communism*, Vol. XIII, No. 6, 1964, pp. 54-59.

The relationship between wages and prices suggests that workers and professionals in the higher income brackets might be able to afford a number of luxuries, whereas workers in the lower income brackets must necessarily lead a marginal type of existence. Of course, since almost all adults work, the income of a household may be two or more times greater than the income of the individual worker. Moreover, Soviet authorities emphasize that real income is considerably greater than wage and salary figures indicate, because of the comprehensive system of social welfare benefits.

Trade Unions

Trade unions are organized on the basis of industries; for example, the mining union represents all people who work in mining enterprises, including the director of the enterprise and his secretary. Primary units are established in factories and on farms, and intermediate organizations are established at the regional and republican levels. At the apex of the pyramid is the All-Union Central Council of Trade Unions (C.C.T.U.) which exercises authoritative control over all subsidiary units, and cooperates with the State Committee for Labor and Wages on questions related to labor legislation, labor conditions and wages. Each sector of the economy is represented by a Trade Union Committee at the All-Union, republican and regional levels, which is entitled to confer with governmental and economic organs with respect to the wage system, safety, employee rights, labor productivity and matters peculiar to the particular industry. At all levels, the trade unions are controlled by, and are the servants of, the party.

Trade union membership, which is voluntary, is generally advantageous to the worker. For an initiation fee of 1 percent of the monthly wage and a small monthly fee thereafter, union members receive larger sickness and disability payments, have priority in the use of rest homes, sanatoria and recreational and cultural facilities, and are entitled to legal assistance and grants and loans from funds administered by the union. Nevertheless, approximately 10 percent of Soviet workers, primarily temporary or seasonal workers, are not union members.

During the early years of the Bolshevik regime, the unions participated actively in the management of industrial enterprises and in the establishment of wage scales and norms. However, during the Stalin era, the active rights of the unions deteriorated progressively and they served primarily as "cheer leaders" for the party program in industry. Their major functions, according to the trade union statutes, were to mobilize the workers to ensure fulfillment of the economic plan and to participate in the ideological-political education of the workers.[169] On several occasions the party used the trade unions as a channel through which highly unpopular measures were introduced; for example, it was officially announced that the C.C.T.U. had requested the 1940 decrees which forbade workers to change employment and imposed heavy penalties for lateness and absenteeism. Apparently, the party believed that the workers would be more receptive to restrictive and otherwise unacceptable measures if it appeared that the measures had been sponsored, or at least approved, by their trade union representatives. Although the unions were expected to protect workers from local abuses and breaches of labor legislation, they performed this function very poorly, chiefly because the union officials, in their attempt to please party leaders, concentrated almost exclusively on the attainment of production goals. In fact, union officials usually overlooked, and often supported, labor violations in the interest of increased productivity. The justifiable lack of confidence of the workers in their unions tended to negate the efforts of the union leaders to organize socialist competitions and to introduce other measures to carry out the party program. Following Stalin's death the unions were subjected to severe official criticism, and a number of measures were introduced during the late 1950's to enable the unions to function more adequately with respect to the protection of the rights of workers and the mobilization of workers for increased productivity.

Currently, the trade unions are expected to assist the party and the government in five major spheres of activity: increased productivity; the protection of labor; the administration of social insurance benefits; mass cultural work; and the provision of cultural and recreational facilities and everyday services for the population. In the production sphere, the unions have retained all their former functions with respect to mobilization of the workers to ensure fulfillment of the economic plan. In addition, as part of the drive to involve the broad masses in economic organization and management, the unions are entitled to participate rather extensively in most spheres of the activity of the enterprise, including the drafting and execution of economic plans and the selection and control of managerial personnel. Much of the trade union work with respect to production is conducted through "permanent production conferences" which are organized by the union; membership in a production conference includes trade union leaders, advanced workers, engineers, scientists, employees and managerial personnel. The conference discusses questions and proposals relating to draft plans, the fulfillment of planned quotas, maximum utilization of internal production reserves, measures to increase labor productivity and measures to improve working and living conditions.[170] An American professor who studied Soviet trade unions reported that "relations between workers, union officers and management in many plants are self-respecting, friendly, and cooperative, promoting increases in production and jointly solving problems. . . ."[171] She concluded that the participation of trade unions in economic policy-making is truly functional and that "the encroachment on 'management prerogatives' goes surprisingly far and would shock most American managers and many trade unionists."[172] The more effective participation of trade unions in economic operations constitutes a clear gain for the party; union officials and members serve as a valuable source of initiative for improving economic efficiency and as watchdogs against abuses or inefficiency on the part of management. The party's satisfaction with this aspect of the work of the trade unions is indicated by a Party Central Committee proposal that trade union representatives should be granted voting rights in meetings of Economic Councils and department collegia.[173]

The second major function of Soviet trade unions is to protect the rights of the workers. This function does not include bargaining for better wages; in fact, the trade unions have no technique through which they could enforce demands for an increase in wages. Strikes are not expressly forbidden by law but, according to party logic, strikes are unnecessary because the interests of the workers and the employer (the state) are identical.

On rare occasions a minor strike has been staged, probably on the instiga-tion of the party as a technique to inform the world that Soviet workers have the right to strike, but are so well satisfied with employment conditions that they have no desire to use the right. An attempt to call a major strike would probably be suppressed ruthlessly, because a strike would seriously disrupt economic operations and provide visible evidence of lack of soli-darity. (Strikes by governmental employees in other countries are also rare and in some countries, such as the U.S.A., are illegal.) Wage increases in the U.S.S.R. are introduced by the government in relation to the overall economic policy dictated by the party; the trade unions can take no credit for the increases. Although the trade unions can do nothing to alter the total wage fund, they are permitted to "participate in planning and regulat-ing wages of workers and employees and in devising a system of wages guided by the socialist principle of pay according to amount and quality of work."[174] Their function is to contribute to the establishment of more rational and equitable wage scales with maximum incentive value to en-courage higher productivity.

Collective agreements entered into by the local trade union committee and the management of the enterprise have nothing to do with wage in-creases or hours of work. Rather, the collective agreement specifies the ob-ligations of management and workers with respect to improved organiza-tion of production and work, correct application of remuneration scales, increases in the productivity of labor, improvement of safety and health arrangements, and provision of housing and other facilities for the workers.[175] Thus, the workers promise to work more diligently and man-agement promises to treat the workers fairly and to provide them with cer-tain safety measures and welfare benefits. An important duty of the union is to protect members against faulty administration of labor legislation, in terms of unwarranted dismissals, incorrect assignments to grade levels, over-time and piece rate pay, the establishment of and adherence to output norms, the distribution of bonuses, holiday rights and shift assignments. An employee cannot be dismissed, except on grounds stated explicitly in labor legislation, without the consent of the trade union. Any employee who believes that any of his rights have been violated by management may appeal to the trade union for assistance. Most labor disputes are settled by a joint union-management board in which union and management have equal rights and status. The unions are expected to assume special respon-sibility for recommending and ensuring the implementation of health and safety measures.

The trade unions assist the state by handling the administration of social welfare benefits, including retirement pensions and disability pay-ments. The unions also build, operate and distribute passes to rest homes and sanatoria. Some of the funds for these activities derive from union dues but the bulk of the funds are allocated from the state budget. Other social welfare measures undertaken by the unions include participation in the distribution of housing to workers, supervision of dormitories maintained by the enterprise, the provision of everyday services, organization of political, educational and recreational activities, and sponsorship of Young Pioneer camps. In these capacities the unions have built a number of sports stadiums, gymnasiums, movie theaters, libraries and club rooms.

Like all other organizations in the U.S.S.R. the trade unions are expected to serve as propagators of Marxist-Leninist ideology and of the party program. The unions are obligated to take measures to raise the political-ideological consciousness of the masses, to conduct anti-religious campaigns, to encourage the workers to adopt a "socialist attitude toward work," to promote enthusiasm for fulfilling the goals of the party, to combat behavior which does not conform to the socialist moral code and, in general, to contribute to the molding of the "new Soviet man." In this capacity the local trade union leaders, along with the local party leaders, serve as wise parents who educate, guide and control the workers so that they might conform more adequately to the expectations of the party leadership.

Numerous complaints in the Soviet press indicate that the unions do not perform all their designated functions satisfactorily.[176] Complaints about union negligence with respect to violations of labor legislation and health and safety measures are particularly common. However, during the last several years the trade unions have met with increasing approval from both the party leadership and the workers. The improved operation of the trade unions does not derive from increased independence from the party. Rather, the trade unions have been restructured in such a way that they can implement the dictates of the party in a manner which is more acceptable to the workers, and can, according to party instructions, provide the workers with more adequate protection from abuses by the local management.

Labor Productivity

Lenin wrote: "Labor productivity is, in the final analysis, the most important and decisive point for the victory of the new social order";[177] Khrushchev frequently emphasized the importance of increased labor productivity; and Kosygin stated that the constant growth of labor productivity is a decisive condition for the victory of socialism over capitalism.[178] The long-range plan espoused by the Soviet leaders calls for industrial production to increase by six times and agricultural production to increase by two and one-half times between 1961 and 1980.[179] During this interval, the population of the U.S.S.R. is expected to increase by 30 percent. Hence, a tremendous increase in the productivity of labor is required for the materialization of production goals.

According to Soviet estimates, the productivity of Soviet industrial workers was less than 20 percent of that of workers in the U.S.A. in 1928 when the Five Year Plans were introduced. Outdated methods and the shortage of equipment, transportation facilities and technical experts severely hampered productivity. Work that could have been done by machine was done by hand, and many of the available machines were operated by novices. During the intervening years, concentrated efforts have been made to increase productivity. In almost every enterprise, modern machinery and technology have been introduced. Industrial experts and engineers have concentrated on effecting more efficient use of time and energy. Both negative and positive incentives have been used to encourage workers to improve their skills and the quality and quantity of output. The qualifications of the workers have been raised through extensive educational programs. Soviet officials claim that from 1928 to 1940 productivity per worker increased by more than three and one-half times and that, despite the disruption and devastation, it rose by another 40 percent during the war.[180] War-time increases occurred chiefly in the armament industries where high productivity was stimulated by patriotism, technological and material preferential treatment and substantial incentives to workers. After the war, productivity of labor fell and the pre-war level was not reattained until 1949.

Since 1949 labor productivity in the U.S.S.R. has been increasing steadily. Soviet sources state that the average annual increase in labor productivity in the U.S.S.R. and the U.S.A. amounted to 7.3 and 1.6 percent respectively for the total period from 1928 to 1958, including increases of 7.14 percent for the U.S.S.R. and 3 percent for the U.S.A. between 1950 and 1958.[181] From 1958 to 1963, according to Soviet statistics, U.S.S.R.'s industrial labor productivity increased by almost 40 percent in comparison to a 31 percent increase in the U.S.A.[182] In 1964 the U.S.S.R. reported a 4 percent increase in industrial labor productivity;[183] the planned increase for 1965 is 5.7 percent.[184] Since the U.S.S.R. started with, and has maintained, a much lower base figure, an increase of 1 percent represents a smaller absolute increase in labor productivity in the U.S.S.R. than in the U.S.A., and the absolute level of Soviet productivity has remained significantly below that of the U.S.A. In 1965 Kosygin estimated that the U.S.S.R. lags approximately two and one-half times behind the U.S.A. in labor productivity in industry.[185] If this is the case, it is almost certain that the U.S.S.R. will be unable to fulfill its plan to surpass the U.S.A. for labor productivity by 1970.

Although labor productivity in the U.S.S.R. is still much lower than that of advanced Western nations, both the achieved increases and the potential for additional increases are substantial. Progress has been retarded by a number of remedial factors. In non-key industries there has been a dearth of labor-saving tools. The chaos which is sometimes obtained in the establishment of wage scales and output norms has reduced the effectiveness of the material incentive to increase productivity. Fantastic amounts of time have been wasted because of organizational factors such as unrealistic plans, faulty allocation of resources, unnecessary meetings and complicated reports. Labor mobility, absenteeism and the production of defective goods have lowered productivity rates. Recent reorganizations of economic administration, planning techniques and incentive payments are designed to remove some of the barriers to maximum labor productivity. Since Soviet leaders are now emphasizing that increased labor productivity is a major goal, additional remedial measures can be expected. Currently, efforts are being directed toward improved management and labor organization and increased automation and mechanization. The attitude toward the utilization of labor is also undergoing a change. For many years, the U.S.S.R. was able to treat labor as an abundant resource. However, at present, extensive economic expansion requires increased labor resources at the same time as the supply of new labor has been decreased by the abnormally low birth rates of the war years and the male-female imbalance which followed the war. The discrepancy between the supply of new workers and the needs of the economy requires that the available labor force must be used most efficiently. Under-utilization of labor resources can be reduced by the substitution of machine power for manpower, improved regional distribution of labor, elimination of slack work periods and in other ways. Continued upgrading of the qualifications of workers is also used as a technique to increase labor productivity. Thus, many factors contribute to the likelihood that the U.S.S.R. will be able to retain its capacity for a progressive increase in labor productivity over a considerable period of time.

Industrial Output

A consistent goal of the Soviet leaders has been to maximize industrial productivity. To this end, the state has used all resources at its command: nationalization of industry, economic planning, subsistence consumption rates to allow for enormous capital investments in industry, distribution of the labor force, price and wage manipulations, educational policy, etc. The results of all these efforts have been remarkable. Since 1917 the U.S.S.R. has moved from fifth to second place in the ranking of nations according to industrial production. In 1959 when the Seven Year Plan was adopted, Soviet leaders announced: "In the next fifteen years the U.S.S.R. will rise to the first place in the world, not only for overall volume of production but also for 'per capita' output, and the material and technical basis for communism will be established in our country."[186] The overwhelming desire is to surpass the United States which has held a significant, but steadily declining, lead.

Soviet authorities claim that the growth rate for industrial production in the U.S.S.R. has been approximately 10 percent per year since 1918 (16.5 percent for 1930-1940; -1.7 percent for 1941-1945; 15.9 percent for 1947-1957; 9.7 percent for 1958-1963; 7.1 percent for 1964); during the same period, Soviet sources say, the growth rate for industrial production in the U.S.A. has been slightly over 3 percent (1.2 percent for 1930-1940; 9.8 percent for 1941-1945; 4.3 percent for 1947-1957; and 3.3 percent for 1958-1963).[187] American estimates of average annual increments in the U.S.A. correspond fairly well to the Soviet estimates.[188] Western estimates of the Soviet rate of growth vary from a conservative 6.5 percent to 12 or 13 percent.[189] There is general agreement that the rate of growth of industrial production in the U.S.S.R. has been much higher than in the U.S.A. Nevertheless, the U.S.S.R. still lags far behind the U.S.A. in absolute volume of industrial production. According to Soviet estimates, by 1953 Soviet industrial output amounted to only 33 percent of the output of the U.S.A.; by 1957 it amounted to 47 percent; and by 1963 it reached 65 percent.[190] Some Western authorities doubt whether the U.S.S.R. has already attained 65 percent of the American industrial output, but even the most conservative suggest that current Soviet output must be at least 50 percent of American output.

If it were assumed that Soviet-United States output ratio was about 63:100 in 1965 and that the per annum growth rates in the two countries were maintained at about 8 percent and 3 percent respectively, it could be predicted that Soviet industrial output would indeed reach that of the United States in the mid-1970's. Even the assumption of a Soviet-United States output ratio of 50:100 with constant per annum growth rates of 7 percent and 3 percent respectively leads to the prediction that the U.S.S.R. would overtake the U.S.A. in the relatively short period of nineteen years. Whether the hopes of the Soviet leaders, which are based on such predictions, will be materialized depends on a large number of factors, including the absence of war and the relative rates of economic growth. Factors affecting the growth of industrial output in the U.S.A. are beyond the scope of this book; however, it is pertinent to consider whether the U.S.S.R. can be expected to maintain its current high rate of growth during the ten to twenty year period which Soviet leaders consider crucial in the "peaceful competition" between the U.S.S.R. and the U.S.A.

Some of the factors which have contributed appreciably to the rapid expansion of the Soviet economy can be expected to have an increasingly reduced effect. First, the U.S.S.R. started from such a low level that small absolute increases have been registered as highly impressive percentage increases. For example, between 1928 and 1955, steel production increased by 150 and 100 percent in the U.S.S.R. and the U.S.A. respectively; however, the absolute increase was almost twice as great in the U.S.A. as in the U.S.S.R. Secondly, throughout the years the U.S.S.R. has transferred a labor reserve from agriculture to industry to such an extent that the rural-urban population ratio changed from 85:15 in 1914 to 52:48 in 1963. As the new labor force acquired rudimentary skills, it contributed to substantial increases in industrial output. Currently, the agricultural labor reserve has been reduced markedly, and the skill of the majority of industrial workers has been raised to such an extent that percentage increases in industrial output, comparable to past performance, cannot be expected from these sources. The introduction of advanced technology could, of course, compensate for a relative decline in growth rate caused by other factors.

Initially, Soviet expansion was facilitated by the opportunity to borrow technical ideas from the West. Before and immediately following the revolution, machinery and almost all scientific and technical instruments were imported. During the 1920's and 1930's large numbers of foreign technicians were brought to the U.S.S.R. to superintend the construction of new factories, power projects and mines, to introduce new production processes and to train Soviet technicians. Thus the fledgling U.S.S.R. was able to advance much more rapidly than if technological advances had had to come solely from internal sources. Now, the U.S.S.R. has its own technological experts and the Soviet scientific and technical achievements which have been astonishing the world since the 1950's suggest that major industrial expansion deriving from the discoveries and innovations of Soviet scientists and engineers is likely. Moreover, the regime is able to concentrate heavily on research, to introduce technological advances into key industries rapidly and to enforce the spread of innovations without fear of inter-enterprise competition. One of their chief goals is to control thermonuclear energy as a source of industrial energy. Achievement of this goal by any nation will open up incredibly vast avenues for industrial growth and may be the determining factor in the economic competition between socialist and Western countries.

A number of factors peculiar to the Soviet political regime tend to contribute to continued rapid industrial expansion. Most important is the ability to divert a very large proportion of the available resources to develop a strong economic superstructure with emphasis on growth-inducing industries. Because of the dictatorial nature of the regime, the Soviet people have not been able to register effective protests against the investment policy of the government. Trade unions have played an inconsequential part in protecting the interests of the people, and economic decisions have not been influenced by their potential for attracting votes. The allocation of resources, and the manipulation of wages, incentives, prices and taxes can be used to encourage and, in fact, to guarantee the rapid development of the growth-inducing sectors of the economy in comparison to the consumption sectors. A factor unrelated to the political regime, which contributes to economic growth, is an ample supply of almost all basic raw materials. When it is too uneconomical to transport the materials to the centers of high population density, measures can be taken to redistribute the labor force.

On the other hand, a number of features deriving from the political regime have tended to impede industrial expansion. Several such features have been mentioned in the preceding sections. Included are over-centralization, errors in planning, a multitude of checks and balances which limit the opportunities of a director to run the enterprise in the most rational manner, inadequate success indicators, an illogical price system and a poorly operating profit motive. Should the regime manage to remove a number of these problems without introducing new problems, industrial growth would be accelerated.

The rate of growth of industrial output may be slowed down, at least temporarily, by a number of factors. The decision of the party leadership to devote a greater proportion of national resources to the development of agriculture, though perhaps not requiring diversion of resources away from industrial expansion, may retard the rate of investment in industry. Man hours available for industrial production, though increasing in terms of absolute numbers, will increase at a slower rate because of the reduction in the labor reserve and shorter working hours. Soviet authorities, of course, maintain that increases in labor productivity will much more than counteract this trend. The increased years of compulsory education, which will likewise cut into production time, may be more than offset by increases in skill. Finally, increased pressures for higher living standards are forcing the Soviet leaders to divert funds away from industrial expansion. Although the Soviet masses have neither an effective vote nor trade union protection, their leaders cannot totally ignore their wishes, if centrally determined economic goals are to be materialized. For example, improved living conditions in remote regions is a prerequisite for recruiting and maintaining the necessary labor force. The relationship between lack of adequate housing and a high rate of labor turnover in many areas may have contributed to the decision of the leadership to allocate substantial resources for the construction of housing. In order to obtain increased agricultural production, the leaders had to grant more independence to the peasants, provide them with more adequate everyday services and consumer goods and raise prices for agricultural produce. Numerous other examples of concessions to the people could be cited. Whether the underlying motivation on the part of the leadership is to fulfill long standing promises or to increase the productivity of workers is irrevelant to the present discussion. What is relevant is that diversion of significantly greater proportions of the nation's resources away from growth-inducing industries and into consumer industries would initially change the content of industrial output, and eventually, if not counteracted by other factors, reduce the rate of industrial growth. Since both pronouncements and practice indicate that the needs of the population are being given increasing, albeit by Western standards inadequate, attention and at the same time plans for industrial growth are not being curtailed, Soviet leaders apparently believe that counteracting factors are sufficiently strong to warrant at least some diversion of resources from industry.

When all the evidence is weighed, it seems safe to conclude that the Soviet rate of growth of industrial output will decline somewhat during subsequent years. Even Soviet officials make this prediction. However, the Soviet Union possesses the potential to sustain a rate of industrial growth considerably higher than the rates now prevalent in highly developed Western nations. The Soviet leaders were completely in earnest when they made their peaceful economic competition challenge to highly developed Western countries. They believe that through economic accomplishments, they will win adherents to their ideology and social order.

Addendum: Major Changes in Industrial Organization and Planning

In September, 1965, Kosygin, member of the Presidium of the C.P. S.U. Central Committee and Chairman of the U.S.S.R. Council of Ministers, introduced a number of proposals designed to improve industrial management and planning and to enhance the effectiveness of economic incentives in industrial production.[191] The proposals were approved immediately by the Central Committee of the C.P.S.U.,[192] and in October and December, 1965, by the Supreme Soviet of the U.S.S.R.[193] Because the post-Khrushchev leadership tends to act somewhat less precipitously than Khrushchev, all of the approved changes have not, as yet (February, 1966), been introduced. It is anticipated that the reorganization will not be accomplished completely until 1967. Since all of the details of the reorganization have not been announced, sections of this chapter, which present the organizational structure of Soviet industrial management and planning prior to the initiation of the current reorganization, will be left intact. Although the organizational structure is changing, the general outline of the approach to industrial planning and management, and the types of problems which have plagued the Soviet economy, as presented in the earlier sections of the chaper, are still relevant. In view of the unfinished status of the reorganization, a comprehensive analysis of Soviet economic practices would be impossible without reference to the industrial structure which is now in the process of being remodelled.

The reorganization involves three major aspects of economic operations: (1) The branch principle of industrial management is to be substituted for the territorial principle. (2) Measures are being introduced to expand the economic independence and initiative of enterprises. (3) The system of cost accounting is to be strengthened and production is to be stimulated with the help of such means as price, profit, bonuses and credit. The overall goal is to stimulate industrial productivity by providing a more rational system of management and planning, by removing unnecessary barriers such as the excessive number of restrictions, which were often unreasonable, under which enterprises have operated, and by increasing the interest of workers and employees in improving the overall results of the work of their enterprises.

The re-introduction of the branch principle of industrial management requires major changes in the organs which supervise economic operations. All industrial enterprises are to be removed from supervision by Economic Councils and are to be placed under the supervision of industrial Ministries. A number of industrial Ministries have already been established; more than thirty Ministries will be formed during the course of the reorganization. The Economic Councils are to be retained until all industrial enterprises are placed under ministerial control. Approximately ten All-Union Ministries are to be established to assume responsibility for various branches of the machine-building industry. Enterprises of the machine-building industry are being placed under national control to ensure standardization of design, units and parts, and to guarantee uniform, high quality production. The majority of the state industrial committees are also to be transformed into All-Union Ministries (e.g., All-Union Ministries for Defense Industry, Aviation Industry, etc.). Until the new Ministry is fully functional, the state committee is to continue to discharge its duties. Approximately a dozen new Union-Republican Ministries are to be formed to exercise jurisdiction over chemical, food, and woodworking industries, and over the various branches of mining. In addition to these Ministries which are being formed at the national level, the Union Republics are forming a number of Republican Ministries to supervise industries within their own borders.

A number of major structural changes have been required in conjunction with the establishment of the industrial Ministries. As indicated above, the Economic Councils and the industrial state committees are to be abolished as soon as the new organs are prepared to take over their duties. The Supreme Council of the National Economy, the U.S.S.R. Council of the National Economy and the Councils of the National Economy of the Union Republics are to be disbanded, and organs, such as the U.S.S.R. State Committee for Construction Affairs and the U.S.S.R. State Planning Committee, which were previously responsible to the Supreme Council of the National Economy, are now directly responsible to the U.S.S.R. Council of Ministers. The powers of the State Planning Committee, at both the national and Union Republic levels, have been expanded considerably. A new Union-Republican State Committee on Material and Equipment Supply has been charged with responsibility for realization of supply plans, securing interbranch deliveries involving production cooperation and control over the fulfillment of output plans.

A First Vice-Chairman of the U.S.S.R. Council of Ministers summarized reasons for the return to the branch principle of industrial organization and management as follows:

". . . major shortcomings appeared in the system of managing industry through the economic councils, and as industrial production grew these made themselves felt more and more and had a negative effect on the qualitative indices of operation of our industry. Enterprises of a single branch of industry became cut off from one another. The management of a branch of industry as a single production-technical complex was disrupted.

"The republic Councils of the National Economy, the U.S.S.R. Council of the National Economy, the Supreme Council of the National Economy and the state committees for branches of industry, all of which were set up later, did not eliminate the shortcomings present in the territorial system of managing industry. The committees and the research, design and drafting organizations under their jurisdiction were cut off from the industrial enterprises subordinate to the economic councils. This lowered the quality of planning, weakened the technical guidance of industry and slowed down the utilization of production capacities and the introduction of new technological processes.

"Departure from the branch principle caused extraordinary complications in the management of industry, which became multistage and unwieldly. Many production questions, even questions of an operational nature, before receiving a final answer had to be agreed upon in numerous state agencies. . . ."[194]

Brezhnev indicated that signatures from representatives of from fifteen to thirty organizations might be required for the resolution of a simple question.[195] It is emphasized that the formation of industrial Ministries does not constitute a readoption of the methods of planning and management which were in effect prior to 1957, since the new Ministries will be functioning in conditions in which the rights of enterprises have been considerably expanded and their managerial-economic independence has been increased.[196]

The new measures to increase the rights, independence and responsibility of the enterprises might well be more important in terms of materialization of Soviet economic goals than the readoption of the branch principle of industrial management because the major weakness of the Soviet economic system has centered around related problems such as the inability of enterprise directors and personnel to make independent decisions in view of the concrete situation, a strict cost accounting system was not used, indices on which rewards to the enterprise were based frequently did not reflect economic efficiency, and material incentives were not adequate to encourage workers and managerial officials to strive for increased production efficiency. A recent series of decrees and resolutions are aimed at removing these problems. Of these the most important is the Statute on the Socialist State Production Enterprise.[197]

According to the new regulations, enterprises are to be relieved of a

number of restrictions which hitherto hampered their work. Instead of receiving four labor indices from the supervising agencies (productivity of
labor, number of personnel, average level of wages and the size of the wage
fund), enterprises will be given only one index, the wage fund, and the
director will be entitled to use this wage fund as he sees fit, as long as he adheres to centrally established wage policies. In the future, the major production indices will be the main assortment of goods (to ensure that necessary
items are produced in sufficient quantity) and volume of goods to be sold.
The right to establish direct ties between enterprises is to be expanded, and
enterprises will have to take demand for their products into account if they
are to fulfill the plan for volume of goods to be sold. Other indices which
will be established from above include payments into the budget and allocations from the budget; volume of centralized capital investment and commissioning of production capacities and fixed assets; main targets for introducing new technology; indices for supplying materials and equipment;
and the sum of profits and profitability.[198]

Major use is to be made of the index of profitability in evaluating the
work of an enterprise and in rewarding enterprise personnel. Prerequisites
for the use of profit as a meaningful index are the establishment of a rational price system and the enforcement of a strict cost accounting system in
which managers bear full responsibility for the economic results of the work
of their enterprises. Preliminary measures to revise the price system are
underway,[199] and a number of measures are being introduced to make cost
accounting practical. The most important of these are measures designed
to give the enterprises greater independence in dealing with production
problems, and greater interest in making maximum use of the fixed assets
assigned to them. Payments into the budget from the enterprise are to vary
in accordance with the fixed assets assigned to it by the state; this measure
is intended to curb the tendency of enterprises to purchase equipment for
which they have no need, merely to spend all the money allocated to it.
Over a period of years, enterprises will pay for their own fixed assets,
through their contributions to the state budget. Instead of making free
supplements to the circulating assets of enterprises from the state budget,
credit will be extended in order to encourage enterprises to use their assets
more thriftily. Enterprises which make better use of fixed and circulating
assets will be allowed to retain a higher percentage of profits for setting up
incentive funds.

Each enterprise is to be allowed to retain a reasonable proportion of
its profits, which it may use as it sees fit for development, introduction of
technical improvements, bonuses, awards and measures to improve living
conditions and cultural facilities for workers. The proportion of profits
which may be retained by given enterprises will, during the transition
period, be established by the responsible Ministry in order to take into

account the influence of anomalies in the price system and different levels of profitability due to circumstances over which the enterprise has no control. The plan, however, is that all enterprises which are functioning at a reasonable level of efficiency will be allowed to retain a substantial sum, and the more efficient the enterprise, the larger the sum which it will retain. The goal is to encourage all employees to strive for growth of production, reduced production costs, better utilization of assets, improved quality and greater profitability of production. The greater the profit, the greater the reward to workers and employees, in terms of bonuses, lump-sum payments at the end of the year and various welfare and cultural measures.

On the surface it would appear that the new Soviet leaders are taking constructive action to eliminate many of the most serious problems which have plagued their economic operations. If their new measures would, indeed, give the management of enterprises effective independence in making economic decisions, and at the same time make managers fully responsible for their economic decisions, if contractual ties can be set up between enterprises so that supply will be directly influenced by demand, and if workers and employees receive rewards in direct relation to their economic productivity, then the Soviet economic system will have eliminated most of the barriers to economic productivity which have traditionally been a source of trouble to it. In fact, if the system were to work in accordance with the intentions of its originators, it would be operating on many of the same principles which are inherent in a free enterprise system of economy. However, the changes do not suggest that the U.S.S.R. is adopting an economic system which is modelled on Western practices. State or "socialist" ownership of the means of production is and will remain the characteristic feature of the Soviet economic system. Utilization of the profit motive as a technique for enhancing economic efficiency does not in any way augur the gradual return of the Soviet economy to capitalism. In spite of the enthusiasm which Soviet economists and theoreticians have expressed for the "creative socialist principles" which are being introduced, it is unlikely that the innovations will fulfill their intended purposes completely. It is likely that the Ministries will set up a complicated series of administrations or other supervisory organs which will limit the independence of enterprise directors. Because of continuing irrational features in the price system, profits will not reflect economic efficiency adequately; in many enterprises the incentive fund will be so small or administered so poorly that it will not serve as a spur to economic efficiency; and other problems of a similar nature will arise. Over the years Soviet leaders have introduced numerous changes in industrial administration, each of which was intended to solve many of the problems which precipitated this reorganization. It is probable that this reorganization will, like its predecessors, solve some problems, and will, at the same time, introduce new problems, which will, within a relatively few years, encourage the party leaders to engage in another major reorganization.

The New Five Year Plan (1966-1970)

At the Twenty-Third Congress of the C.P.S.U. which met in March, 1966, L. I. Brezhnev, General Secretary, and A. N. Kosygin, Chairman of the U.S.S.R. Council of Ministers, summarized economic progress during the preceding period and issued the general directives of the party for economic development during the period 1966-1970.[200] It was reported that during the period of the Seven Year Plan national income, used for accumulation and consumption, rose by 53 percent; the volume of industrial output, by 84 percent; fixed production assets, by 92 percent; and the average earnings of workers and employees, by 19 percent. However, the goals for a number of branches of industry and construction were not fulfilled; the volume of agricultural output rose by only 14 percent during the seven-year period, and the average annual rise in labor productivity from 1961-1965 was only 4.6 percent in comparison to 6.5 percent from 1956-1960. The quantity and quality of consumer goods and housing also fell far short of the planned norms.

According to party directives, from 1966-1970 gross social product is to increase by 40 percent; fixed production assets, by more than 50 percent, including 60 percent in industry and 90 percent in agriculture; national income, by 38 percent to 41 percent; and real income of the working people, by 30 percent. Industrial and agricultural output are to increase by 50 percent and 25 percent, respectively. Great emphasis is to be placed on the development of agriculture; capital investment in agriculture is to increase by almost 100 percent. A larger proportion of economic resources are to be used for increased production of consumer goods. Whereas in the last five-year period production of the means of production increased by 58 percent, and production of consumer goods increased by 36 percent, planned figures for the new five-year period are for a 49 percent to 52 percent increase in the production of producer goods and a 43 percent to 46 percent increase in the production of consumer goods. Thus, the party has decreed that heavy industry is still to be given priority, but that the lag in the production of consumer goods is to be reduced. Various measures are to be introduced in an attempt to increase economic efficiency and thus to fulfill the major economic task—the creation of the material and technical base for communism.

Several directives, in addition to the increased emphasis on the production of consumer goods, should, if actually implemented, affect the material well-being of many Soviet citizens. It was announced that during the five-year period minimum wages are to be raised from 45 rubles to 60 rubles per month; wages for production and office workers are to increase to about 115 rubles per month, excluding benefits from public consumption funds; income tax reductions (decreed for the last plan period and then postponed) are to be put into effect. The system of material incentives, based on quantity and quality of output, is to be greatly improved, and collective farmers are to be given guaranteed payments, backed up by state loans if necessary, after July 1, 1966. Retirement pensions and disability allowances for collective farmers and certain other categories of workers are to be increased. There is to be a gradual transition to a five-day work week with, however, no reduction in the hours of work per week. Benefits from public consumption funds are to increase by at least 40 percent.

Impact on the Individual and Society

Since the implications of Soviet economic policy have been mentioned several times throughout the course of this book, only a few additional comments will be made at this point. The economic deprivation which Soviet citizens have suffered as a result of the emphasis on industrial expansion has, no doubt, given rise to a considerable amount of resentment against the regime. The resentment, however, has been tempered by a number of factors, including propaganda statements designed to convince the people of the necessity and the value of their sacrifices, the virtual elimination of unemployment and the determination of the people to contribute to the achievement of economic goals. The majority of the people apparently agree with the party leaders that the improved welfare of society as a whole, and its individual members, depends largely on the increased economic might of the U.S.S.R. There are indications that the majority of the people are enthusiastic about the rapid industrialization of their country, determined that plans will be fulfilled, involved in the economic competition between the U.S.S.R. and the advanced Western nations and proud of the prestige which the U.S.S.R. has earned for its scientific and technological achievements. Because of factors such as these, a large proportion of the people apparently experience a sense of teamwork with the party in the economic sphere; the sense of teamwork has probably increased as the people have begun to reap more tangible rewards for their contributions to the economy. On the other hand, state control over all economic matters places the regime at a unique disadvantage in its relation to the people. As in any other social order, a large number of Soviet workers experience frustration in conjunction with their employment. In Western societies, workers ordinarily direct their resentment toward the "boss," the company, fellow workers or even toward the policies of the government; few, however, attribute their difficulties to private enterprise or the democratic social order. In the Soviet Union, where enterprises are state owned, managers are representatives of the state, and workers have no choice but to work for the state, most of the resentment which is experienced in conjunction with employment is focused directly on the state and the regime. Thus, Soviet workers tend to blame the regime for all their employment woes, including problems due to interpersonal conflicts and other factors which are not unique to the Soviet system, at the same time as they thank the regime for their improved social status, and work with it to fulfill economic goals.

REFERENCES

1 G. Glezerman, "V. I. Lenin and the Interrelation of Economics and Politics in the Construction of the New Society," *Kommunist,* No. 7, May, 1963, pp. 30-40.

2 *Ibid.*

3 George B. Cressey, *Asia's Lands and Peoples,* (2nd ed.), (New York: McGraw-Hill Book Co., Inc., 1951), p. 257.

4 Emil Truog and Dimitry T. Pronin, "A Great Myth: The Russian Granary," *Land Economics,* Vol. XXIX, 1953, p. 200.

5 *Fundamentals of Marxism-Leninism, op. cit.,* p. 700.

6 *Ibid.,* pp. 695-700.

7 *Ibid.,* pp. 700-1.

8 *Ibid.,* p. 700.

9 *Ibid.,* p. 695.

10 I. Yevenko, *Planning in the U.S.S.R.,* (Moscow: Foreign Languages Publishing House, no date), p. 8.

11 *Fundamentals of Marxism-Leninism, op. cit.,* p. 694.

12 *Ibid.,* p. 696.

13 Lenin, *Works,* Vol. 24, *op. cit.,* p. 430.

14 V. I. Lenin, Miscellany, (Moscow-Leningrad, 1931), Vol. XI, p. 382.

15 *Fundamentals of Marxism-Leninism, op. cit.,* p. 701.

16 *Ibid.,* p. 704.

17 N. I. Lialikov, *Economic Geography of the U.S.S.R.,* (Moscow: State Educational-Pedagogical Publishers, 1957), p. 5.

18 *The Large Soviet Encyclopedia,* Vol. 50, p. 307.

19 *Ibid.,* Vol. 50, p. 198.

20 P. Liashchenko, *History of the National Economy of the U.S.S.R.,* Vol. II, (Moscow: State Publishers of Political Literature, 1956), p. 585.

21 For a brief history of the expansion of state control and of successive economic plans see Harry Schwartz, *Russia's Soviet Economy,* (New York: Prentice-Hall, Inc., 1954), pp. 103-29.

22 *National Economy of the U.S.S.R.,* (Moscow: State Statistical Publishers, 1956), p. 45.

23 *Ibid.*

24 *The Large Soviet Encyclopedia,* Vol. 50, *op. cit.,* p. 236.

25 *Ibid.*

26 Liashchenko, *History of the National Economy,* Vol. III, *op. cit.,* p. 562.

27 *Economics of Socialist Industry,* (Moscow: State Publishers of Political Literature, 1962), p. 48.

28 *Target Figures for the Economic Development of the U.S.S.R. from 1959 to 1965,* Soviet Booklet No. 49, (London: May, 1959), pp. 21-3.

29 Khrushchev, Report to the Twenty-First Congress of the C.P.S.U., Jan. 27, 1959.

30 A. Kursky, "Some Problems in the Improvement of National Economic Planning," *Voprosy ekonomiki,* (Problems of Economics, Vol. II, June, 1959, pp. 43-5).

31 Yevenko, *Planning in the U.S.S.R., op. cit.,* p. 31.

32 "On Forming a U.S.S.R. Supreme Council of the National Economy of the U.S.S.R. Council of Ministers," *Pravda,* March 14, 1963, p. 1.

33 G. Mironov, "How the Management of Industry and Construction Is Organized," *Ekonomicheskaya gazeta,* Nov. 23, 1963, p. 30. (C.D.S.P., Vol. XVI, No. 3, pp. 3-5)

34 *Ibid.*

35 "In the U.S.S.R. Council of Ministers U.S.S.R. Supreme Council of the National Economy," *Pravda,* March 27, 1963, p. 1.

36 Mironov, "How the Management of Industry and Construction Is Organized," *op. cit.,* p. 30.

37 "Session of the U.S.S.R. State Planning Committee," *Pravda,* March 30, 1963, p. 1.

38 G. Ivanov, "How Our National Economy Is Managed," *Planovoe khozaistvo,* No. 11, Nov., 1963, pp. 87-8. (C.D.S.P., Vol. XVI, No. 3, pp. 6-7)

39 "Session of the U.S.S.R. State Planning Committee," *op. cit.,* p. 1.

40 Yevenko, *Planning in the U.S.S.R., op. cit.,* p. 44.

41 V. Dymshits, "Realization of Plans Is the Main Task of the U.S.S.R. Council of the National Economy," *Pravda,* April 6, 1963, pp. 2-3.

42 "Session of the U.S.S.R. State Planning Committee," *op. cit.,* p. 1.

43 Dymshits, "Realization of Plans Is the Main Task," *op. cit.,* p. 2.

44 Mironov, "How the Management of Industry and Construction Is Organized," *op. cit.,* p. 30.

45 Yevenko, *Planning in the U.S.S.R., op. cit.,* pp. 48-9.

46 I. Novikov, "Capital Construction at a New Stage," *Pravda,* June 5, 1963, pp. 2, 5.

47 *Ibid.*

48 *Ibid.*

49 Yevenko, *Planning in the U.S.S.R., op. cit.,* p. 49.

50 "Session of the U.S.S.R. State Planning Committee," *op. cit.,* p. 1.

51 Yevenko, *Planning in the U.S.S.R., op. cit.,* p. 23.

52 S. Tokarev and P. Alampiev, "Problems of Development of Economic Regions," *Planovoe khozaistvo,* No. 7, July, 1961.

53 P. Alampiev and V. Kistanov, "Large Economic Areas of the U.S.S.R.," *Ekonomicheskaya gazeta,* May 28, 1961.

54 *Ibid.*

55 *Ibid.*

56 "In the Interests of the National Economy," *Pravda,* Feb. 23, 1962, p. 1.

57 V. Pavlenko, "Economic Regions in New Conditions," *Ekonomicheskaya gazeta,* Oct. 19, 1963, pp. 12-13. (C.D.S.P., Vol. XV, No. 42, pp. 3-5, 18)

58 *Ibid.*

59 *Ibid.*

60 Khrushchev, "The Development of the U.S.S.R. Economy and Party Guidance of the National Economy," *op. cit.,* p. 12.

61 "Map and Description of the New Economic Regions," *Ekonomicheskaya gazeta,* Feb. 16, 1963, pp. 12-3.

62 "The Economic Regions of the Russian Federation," *Sovetskaya Rossia,* Dec. 28, 1962, p. 2. (C.D.S.P., Vol. XV, No. 2, pp. 14-16)

63 *Pravda,* Dec. 23, 1964, p. 4.

64 Khrushchev, "The Development of the U.S.S.R. Economy and Party Guidance of the National Economy," *op. cit.,* pp. 1-8.

65 "The Apparatus of the Economic Council of an Economic Region," *Ekonomicheskaya gazeta,* No. 3, Jan. 1964, p. 31. (C.D.S.P., Vol. XVI, No. 3, pp. 7-8)

66 Yevenko, *Planning in the U.S.S.R., op. cit.,* p. 57.

67 *Ibid.,* p. 53.

68 *Ibid.*

69 *Ibid.,* p. 59.

70 A. Nove, *The Soviet Economy,* (New York: Frederick A. Praeger, 1961), p. 71.

71 Ch. Touretski, "Regional Planning of the National Economy in the U.S.S.R. and its Bearing on Regionalism," *International Social Science Journal,* UNESCO, Vol. XI, No. 3, 1959, p. 382.

72 Ivanov, "How Our National Economy Is Managed," *op. cit.,* p. 88.

73 Yevenko, *Planning in the U.S.S.R., op. cit.,* p. 60.

74 Cf. Lynn Turgeon, *The Contrasting Economies,* (Boston: Allyn and Bacon, Inc., 1963), pp. 211-32.

75 M. Alexeyev, "Free the Enterprise from Petty Tutelage," *Pravda,* Dec. 7, 1964, p. 2. (C.D.S.P., Vol. XVI, No. 50, pp. 13-14)

76 A. N. Kosygin, "On the State Plan for the Development of the U.S.S.R. National Economy in 1965," *Pravda,* Dec. 10, 1964, pp. 1-4. (C.D.S.P., Vol. XVI, No. 49, pp. 3-13)

77 "Direct Ties Are Expanding," *Ekonomicheskaya gazeta,* No. 3, Jan. 20, 1965, pp. 33-4. (C.D.S.P., Vol. XVII, No. 7, pp. 27-8)

78 *Ibid.*

79 *Ibid.*

80 *Ibid.*

81 *The Soviet Economy 1959-1965,* (New York: International Arts and Sciences Press, 1959), pp. 43-4.

82 *Ibid.,* p. 41.

83 V. I. Lenin, *Works,* (Prague: Svoboda, 1952), p. 65.

84 University of Prague, Department of Economics, Collective of the Chair of National Planning, "Planning of the National Economy," (Prague: State Pedagogical Publishers, no date), p. 65.

85 Yevenko, *Planning in the U.S.S.R., op. cit.,* pp. 60-1.

86 V. Nemchinov, "Socialist Economic Management and Production Planning," *Kommunist,* No. 5, March, 1964, pp. 74-87. (C.D.S.P., Vol. XVI, No. 18, pp. 3-11)

87 S. Vezirov, "The State Planning Committee and the Economic Council," *Izvestia,* May 17, 1962, p. 3.

88 Yevenko, *Planning in the U.S.S.R., op. cit.,* pp. 84-5.

89 F. Khiliuk, "Some Questions on Improving the Organization of Planning," *Planovoe khozaistvo,* 1962, No. 7, pp. 14-18.

90 Yevenko, *Planning in the U.S.S.R., op. cit.,* p. 87.

91 Quoted from *Readings on the Soviet Economy,* Franklyn D. Holzman, (ed.), (Chicago: Rand McNally & Co., 1962), p. 176.

92 Khrushchev, "The Development of the U.S.S.R. Economy and Party Guidance of the National Economy," *op. cit.,* pp. 1-8.

93 Nemchinov, "Socialist Economic Management and Production Planning," *op. cit.,* pp. 74-87.

94 M. Eidelman, "The First Interindustry Balance Sheet of Labor Input in the U.S.S.R.'s National Economy," *Vestnik statistiki,* 1962, No. 10.

95 Yevenko, *Planning in the U.S.S.R., op. cit.,* p. 141.

96 *Ibid.*

97 F. Artamonov, "On the Scattering of Resources and Wretched Planning," *Sovetskaya Rossia,* Nov. 11, 1962, p. 2.

98 "Planning of the National Economy," *op. cit.,* p. 60.

99 Lenin, *Works, op. cit.,* p. 65.

100 Cf. Nove, *The Soviet Economy, op. cit.,* pp. 145-194.

101 *Ibid.,* pp. 161-2.

102 B. L. Goncharenko and I. V. Maevskii, "Improving the System of State Plan Indices," *Voprosy ekonomiki,* 1962, No. 3, p. 55. (Problems of Economics, 1962, Vol. V, No. 6, pp. 49-58)

103 *Ibid.,* p. 57.

104 Khrushchev, "The Development of the U.S.S.R. Economy and Party Guidance of the National Economy," *op. cit.,* pp. 1-8.

105 "Voracious Ton-Kilometers," *Izvestia,* Dec. 23, 1962, p. 3.

106 I. Novikov, "How Grain Was Procured in Grodno Province," *Pravda,* Nov. 26, 1963, p. 3.

107 Goncharenko and Maevskii, "Improving the System of State Plan Indices," *op. cit.,* pp. 53-4.

108 *Izvestia,* Jan. 6, 1957, quoted in P. J. Wiles, *The Political Economy of Communism,* (Cambridge, Mass.: Harvard University Press, 1962), p. 131.

109 Goncharenko and Maevskii, "Improving the System of State Plan Indices," *op. cit.,* p. 50.

110 O. Antonov, "Let Us Calculate Better," *Izvestia,* May 25, 1962, p. 3.

111 Goncharenko and Maevskii, "Improving the System of State Plan Indices," *op. cit.,* p. 55.

112 V. Shkatov, "What Is Useful for the Country Is Profitable for Everyone," *Pravda,* Sept. 1, 1964, p. 2.

113 A. Zverev, "Against Oversimplification in Solving Complex Problems," *Voprosy ekonomiki,* 1962, No. 11. (Problems of Economics, Vol. V, No. 12, pp. 15-18)

114 Goncharenko and Maevskii, "Improving the System of State Plan Indices," *op. cit.,* p. 56.

115 B. Sukharevskii, "On Improving the Forms and Methods of Material Incentives," *Voprosy ekonomiki,* 1962, No. 11. (Problems of Economics, Vol. V, No. 12, pp. 3-12)

116 Goncharenko and Maevskii, "Improving the System of State Plan Indices," *op. cit.,* p. 56.

117 L. Pekarsky, "Labor and Its Incentives," *Pravda,* July 11, 1964, p. 2.

118 Shkatov, "What Is Useful for the Country Is Profitable for Everyone," *op. cit.,* p. 2.

119 L. Gatovskii, "The Role of Profit in a Socialist Economy," *Kommunist,* 1962, No. 18.

120 Khrushchev, "The Development of the U.S.S.R. Economy and Party Guidance of the National Economy," *op. cit.,* pp. 1-8.

121 Kosygin, "On the State Plan for the Development of the U.S.S.R. National Economy in 1965," *op. cit.,* pp. 1-4.

122 Ye. Liberman, "Improve Economic Management and Planning," *Pravda,* Sept. 9, 1962, p. 3. (C.D.S.P., Vol. XIV, No. 36, pp. 13-15)

123 E.g., Ye. Liberman, "Once More on the Plan, Profits and Bonuses," *Pravda,* Sept. 20, 1964, p. 3; G. Kulagin, "Operational Autonomy of an Enterprise," *Pravda,* Sept. 15, 1964; V. Shkatov, "What Is Useful for the Country Is Profitable for Everyone," *op. cit.,* p. 2; O. Volkov, "Urgent Questions," *Pravda,* August 23, 1964, p. 2; R. Belousov, "The Chief Thing Is Economic Effectiveness," *Pravda,* Nov. 13, 1964, p. 2; L. Leontyev, "The Unity of Economics and Politics," *Pravda,* March 7, 1965, pp. 2-3.

124 Ia. Ofmanis, "The Wholesale Price of the Enterprise and Profitability," *Nauchnye doklady vysshei shkoly, ekonomicheskie nauki,* 1962, No. 3, p. 20. (Problems of Economics, Vol. V. No. 10, pp. 19-23)

125 Kosygin, "On the State Plan for the Development of the U.S.S.R. National Economy in 1965," *op. cit.,* pp. 1-4.

126 Goncharenko and Maevskii, "Improving the System of State Plan Indices," *op. cit.,* p. 58.

127 Khrushchev, "The Development of the U.S.S.R. Economy and Party Guidance of the National Economy," *op. cit.,* pp. 1-8.

128 Kh. Karzhaubayev, "Botchers Called to Account," *Pravda,* March 9, 1965, p. 4.

129 M. Postolovsky, *Why Taxation of the People can Be Abolished in the U.S.S.R.,* (Washington, D. C.: Embassy of the Union of Soviet Socialist Republics, Press Department, 1960), p. 3.

130 L. Gatovsky, "The Role of Profits in Socialist Economics," *Kommunist,* Dec. 1962, No. 18, pp. 60-72. (C.D.S.P., Vol. XV, No. 2, pp. 3-6)

131 *Ibid.*

132 Lev Maizenberg, "Revision of Wholesale Prices in Heavy Industry and Some Problems of Price Formation in the U.S.S.R.," *Voprosy ekonomiki,* 1961, No. 1. (Problems of Economics, Vol. V, No. 2, pp. 42-51)

133 Garbuzov, "On the U.S.S.R. State Budget for 1965 and on Fulfillment of the U.S.S.R. State Budget for 1963," op. cit., pp. 4-5.

134 Nicholas Spulber, The Soviet Economy, (New York: W. W. Norton & Co., 1962), pp. 181-2.

135 "Decree of the Presidium of the U.S.S.R. Supreme Soviet on Collective Farm Income Tax," Pravda, April 11, 1965, p. 2.

136 Nove, The Soviet Economy, op. cit., p. 43.

137 "Law of the U.S.S.R. on Abolishing Taxes on Wages of Workers and Employees," Pravda, May 8, 1960, p. 1.

138 "On Postponing the Dates for Exempting Workers and Employees from Taxes on Wages," Izvestia, Sept. 25, 1962, p. 1. (C.D.S.P., Vol. XIV, No. 39, p. 3)

139 Ibid.

140 Garbuzov, "On the U.S.S.R. State Budget for 1965 and on the Fulfillment of the U.S.S.R. State Budget for 1963," op. cit., pp. 4-5.

141 V. F. Garbuzov, "On the U.S.S.R. State Budget for 1964-1965 and on the Fulfillment of the U.S.S.R. State Budget for 1962," Pravda, Dec. 17, 1963, pp. 4-6.

142 V. F. Garbuzov, "On the U.S.S.R. State Budget for 1963 and on Fulfillment of the U.S.S.R. State Budget for 1961," Pravda, Dec. 11, 1962, pp. 4-6.

143 Turgeon, The Contrasting Economies, op. cit., pp. 177-201.

144 I. Malyshev, "Planning Is an Important Link in Socialist Management," Pravda, Feb. 7, 1963, p. 2.

145 Ofmanis, "The Wholesale Price of the Enterprise and Profitability," op. cit.

146 "Program of the Communist Party of the Soviet Union," op. cit., p. 83.

147 Ofmanis, "The Wholesale Price of the Enterprise and Profitability," op. cit., p. 19.

148 L. I. Brezhnev, "On Urgent Matters for the Further Development of Agriculture in the U.S.S.R.," Pravda, March 27, 1965, pp. 2-4. (C.D.S.P., Vol. XVII, No. 12, pp. 3-11)

149 "In the C.P.S.U. Central Committee and the U.S.S.R. Council of Ministers," Pravda, April 25, 1965, p. 1.

150 A. Klimov, "Concerns of the Rural Cooperatives," Izvestia, May 17, 1962, p. 3.

151 Ibid.

152 P. Mikhailov, "Paragon of Reticence," Izvestia, Feb. 13, 1963, p. 3.

153 Garbuzov, "On the U.S.S.R. State Budget for 1963 and on Fulfillment of the U.S.S.R. State Budget for 1961," op. cit., pp. 4-6.

154 Cf. Nove, The Soviet Economy, op. cit., pp. 115-144.

155 A. Gromov, "Technology, Labor and Wages," Pravda, April 9, 1962, p. 2.

156 Political Economy, (Moscow: State Publishers of Political Literature, 1958), p. 535.

157 Khrushchev, Report to the Twenty-First Party Congress, Jan. 27, 1959.

158 Vladimir Katkoff, The Soviet Economy 1940-1965, (Baltimore, Md.: Dangary Publishing Co., 1961), p. 282.

159 A. Volkov, "Consistently Implement the Principle of Material Incentives," Pravda, April 4, 1962, pp. 2-3. (C.D.S.P., Vol. XIV, No. 14, pp. 6-8)

160 Y. Yagodkin, "Material Incentive as a Mighty Factor," Pravda, Nov. 23, 1964, p. 2. (C.D.S.P., Vol. XVI, No. 47, pp. 3-4)

161 Volkov, "Consistently Implement the Principle of Material Incentives," op. cit., pp. 2-3.

162 Ye. Manevich, "Economic Labor Incentives and the Forms of Transition to Communist Distribution," Voprosy ekonomiki, No. 5, May, 1961, pp. 76-85. (C.D.S.P., Vol. XIII, No. 33, pp. 10-14)

163 Volkov, "Consistently Implement the Principle of Material Incentives," op. cit., pp. 2-3.

164 Ye. Lazutkin, "Conference of Economists of Siberia and the Far East," Voprosy ekonomiki, No. 12, Dec., 1964, pp. 140-4. (C.D.S.P., Vol. XVII, No. 6, pp. 16-18)

165 Gromov, "Technology, Labor and Wages," op. cit., p. 2.

166 Khrushchev, "On Measures to Fulfill the C.P.S.U. Program in the Sphere of Increasing the Well-Being of the People," *op. cit.,* pp. 1-5.

167 *Ibid.*

168 *Ibid.*

169 *Statutes and By-Laws of Soviet Trade Unions,* (C.D.S.P., May 31, 1949, pp. 26-32)

170 A. Piatakov, "The Purpose and Functions of Trade Unions in the U.S.S.R.," in Shaffer, *The Soviet Economy, op. cit.,* p. 245.

171 Emily Clark Brown, "The Local Union in Soviet Industry: Its Relation with Members, Party and Management," in Shaffer, *The Soviet Economy, op. cit.,* p. 239.

172 *Ibid.*

173 D. Chesnokov, "The November Plenary Session of the Party Central Committee and Questions of State Construction," *Kommunist,* No. 2, Jan., 1963, pp. 11-20. (C.D.S.P., Vol. XV, No. 10, pp. 27-8)

174 *Statutes and By-Laws of Soviet Trade Unions, op. cit.,* pp. 26-32.

175 Piatakov, "The Purpose and Functions of Trade Unions in the U.S.S.R.," *op. cit.,* p. 245.

176 Cf. I. F. Shkuratov, "The Collective Farm Trade Union Committee: What Are Its Functions?" *Trud,* March 16, 1965, p. 2; M. Zholzhaksynov, "Contrary to Law and Authority," *Izvestia,* April 13, 1965, p. 3; "In the U.S.S.R. Council of the National Economy; Strictly Observe Labor Laws," *Pravda,* March 2, 1965, p. 2.

177 V. I. Lenin, *The Great Initiative, Works,* Vol. 29, (Prague: S.N.L.B., 1955), p. 421.

178 A. N. Kosygin, "Increasing the Scientific Soundness of Plans Is the Most Important Task of Planning Bodies," *Planovoe khozaistvo,* No. 4, April, 1965, pp. 3-10. (C.D.S.P., Vol. XVII, No. 18, pp. 17-20)

179 V. Starovsky, "The Productivity of Social Labor and Problems of Population," *Izvestia,* May 23, 1963, p. 3. (C.D.S.P., Vol. XIV, No. 23, pp. 14-17)

180 St. Turetsky, *Productivity of Labor and Lowering of Production Costs,* in *The New Five Year Plan,* (Moscow: State Publishers of Political Literature, 1947), p. 49.

181 G. I. Samborsky, *The Soviet Economy 1959-1965,* (New York: International Arts and Sciences Press, 1959), p. 29.

182 V. Starovsky, "Victorious Strides in the Soviet Economy and the Sorry Efforts of Unscrupulous 'Experts'," *Pravda,* March 14, 1964, pp. 2-3. (C.D.S.P., Vol. XVI, No. 11, pp. 3-4, 20)

183 "On Results of Fulfillment of the State Plan for Development of the U.S.S.R. National Economy in 1964," *Pravda,* Jan. 30, 1965, pp. 1-2. (C.D.S.P., Vol. XVII, No. 4, pp. 3-6)

184 Kosygin, "On the State Plan for the Development of the U.S.S.R. National Economy in 1965," *op. cit.,* pp. 1-4.

185 Kosygin, "Increasing the Scientific Soundness of Plans Is the Most Important Task of Planning Bodies," *op. cit.,* pp. 3-10.

186 *Target Figures for the Economic Development of the U.S.S.R. from 1959 to 1965, op. cit.,* p. 6.

187 Samborsky, *The Soviet Economy 1959-1965, op. cit.,* p. 22; Dymshits, "On the State Plan for Development of the U.S.S.R. National Economy in 1963," *op. cit.,* p. 1; Khrushchev, "On Measures to Fulfill the C.P.S.U. Program in the Sphere of Increasing the Well-Being of the People," *op. cit.,* pp. 1-5; "On Results of Fulfillment of the State Plan for Development of the U.S.S.R. National Economy in 1964," *op. cit.,* pp. 1-2.

188 Allen Dulles, *New York Times,* April 9, 1959; R. V. Grunstade and Phyllis A. Wallace, *The American Economic Review,* Sept., 1959, p. 693; M. J. Rathbone, "United States Foreign Trade and Investment in a Changing World," Speech to Economic Club of Detroit, April 9, 1962.

189 Norman M. Kaplan and Richard H. Moorsteen, "An Index of Soviet Industrial Output," *American Economic Review,* No. 3, June, 1960, pp. 295-318.

190 Khrushchev, "On Measures to Fulfill the C.P.S.U. Program in the Sphere of Increasing the Well-Being of the People," *op. cit.,* pp. 1-2.

191 A. N. Kosygin, "On Improving Industrial Management, Perfecting Planning, and Enhancing Economic Incentives in Industrial Production," *Pravda,* Sept. 28, 1965, pp. 1-4.

192 "Resolution of the Plenary Session of the C.P.S.U. Central Committee on Improving the Management of Industry, Perfecting Planning and Strengthening Economic Incentives in Industrial Production," *Pravda,* Oct. 1, 1965, pp. 1-2.

193 "On Ratification of the Decrees of the U.S.S.R. Supreme Soviet," *Pravda,* Oct. 3, 1965, pp. 2, 5; "Law of the Union of Soviet Socialist Republics on Introducing Changes in and Additions to Article 70 of the U.S.S.R. Constitution," *Pravda,* Dec. 10, 1965, p. 2.

194 K. T. Mazurov, "On Improving the Management of Industry," *Pravda,* Oct. 2, 1965, pp. 2-3. (C.D.S.P., Vol. XVII, No. 40, pp. 4-9)

195 L. I. Brezhnev, "Address to the Plenary Session of the Central Committee of the C.P.S.U., *Pravda,* Sept. 30, 1965, pp. 1-3.

196 Mazurov, "On Improving the Management of Industry," *op. cit.,* pp. 2-3.

197 "Statute on the Socialist State Production Enterprise," *Ekonomicheskaya gazeta,* No. 42, Oct., 1965, pp. 25-9.

198 Kosygin, "On Improving Industrial Management, Perfecting Planning, and Enhancing Economic Incentives in Industrial Production," *op. cit.,* pp. 1-4.

199 V. Sitnin, "Price Is an Important Tool of Economic Management," *Pravda,* Nov. 12, 1965, p. 2.

200 L. I. Brezhnev, "Report of the C.P.S.U. Central Committee to the Twenty-third Congress of the Communist Party of the Soviet Union," *Pravda,* March 30, 1966, pp. 2-9; A. N. Kosygin, "The Directives of the Twenty-third C.P.S.U. Congress for the Development of the U.S.S.R. National Economy in 1966-1970," *Pravda,* April 6, 1966, pp. 2-7.

CHAPTER IX

AGRICULTURE

Historical Background

The Soviet leadership has yet to work out a satisfactory agricultural policy; agriculture has consistently been the weak link in the chain of Soviet economic development.[1] The growth of agricultural productivity has lagged far behind that of industry; the farms have been unable to provide the population with an adequate supply of foodstuffs; and the farmers themselves have lived and worked under unenviable conditions. The backwardness of agriculture has constituted a major barrier to the realization of the overall economic, political and social goals of the Soviet regime. Progress in agriculture has been retarded by a number of factors. First, climatic variables and the nature of agricultural operations do not allow agriculture to be as responsive to the dictates of the regime as other branches of the economy; nevertheless, Soviet leaders have attempted, most unsuccessfully, to impose the same types of rigid controls on agriculture which have been used with some success in industry. Second, the traditionally conservative peasants, who could be neither controlled nor indoctrinated as easily as the workers and who have suffered even more than the workers, have not been enthusiastic builders of the new communist society. Third, most policy decisions pertaining to agriculture have been based on political expediency rather than sound economic considerations involving long-range perspectives. Fourth, the farms have been required to make compulsory deliveries to the state at prices which sometimes did not even cover costs of production. Consequently, the incentive to increase production has been lacking, living standards have been abysmally low and agriculture has been deprived of internal resources for expansion. Fifth, the state has not provided agriculture with adequate support in terms of machinery, fertilizers, research and technical assistance. In short, the surplus products of agriculture have been appropriated by the state to support industrial expansion, and agriculture has been given nothing positive in return: neither financial support, enlightened leadership, independence nor an incentive to increase production. Khrushchev's successors are making a concentrated attempt to rectify the unsatisfactory situation. Since the problems which they face in this attempt are the aftermath of unsatisfactory

437

and unenlightened policies of the past, past policies will be traced in broad outline.

Initially, Lenin's chief interest in the peasants involved using them as tools to facilitate the attainment of his political goals. His ultimate goal for agriculture was large, highly mechanized farms, either state owned or based on an extensive cooperative movement. However, in order to attain the support of the peasants who were much more interested in acquiring land than in Bolshevik ideology, he encouraged them, in 1917, to appropriate large agricultural estates. Concurrently, he urged the local Soviets to distribute the land equitably, and preferably, to establish collective farms. However, very few collective farms were established because the peasants preferred independent holdings.

During the chaotic period of War Communism, the peasants were not able to reap the advantages of their newly gained land. Their produce was either appropriated by the armies and cities or paid for with money that was almost worthless because of the extremely limited industrial output and galloping inflation. When the peasants retaliated by refusing to produce except for their own use, they were punished by having their own supplies and even their seed grain requisitioned by force. Lenin attempted unsuccessfully to neutralize the political reaction of the peasants by fomenting intra-village strife between the poor and rich peasants; Committees of Poor Peasants were given governmental sanction to suppress the rich peasants. By 1921 the majority of peasants were so thoroughly disillusioned with the Bolshevik regime that a number of peasant rebellions were staged. Lenin acknowledged: "The peasants are not content with our attitude toward them and they will not tolerate it any longer."[2] His corrective action, the New Economic Policy (N.E.P.), which legalized private enterprise in agriculture and small scale industries and shops, was absolutely contrary to Marxist dogma. The N.E.P. was a tactical retreat which pacified the peasants, maintained agricultural production during a difficult time and allowed the inexperienced Bolsheviks to concentrate on industrial development. The N.E.P. did not, however, constitute an ideal solution to the agricultural problem. The incentive to produce continued to be relatively low because of high state requisitions at low prices, and the inability of industry to supply the peasants with machinery and other manufactured goods. In addition, the majority of the farms were small, lacked machinery and used inefficient farming techniques. Increases in productivity occurred chiefly on the larger farms. As a consequence, the more prosperous peasants grew richer and the poor peasants grew poorer. Class antagonisms, encouraged by Lenin's divide and rule tactics, increased. To the very numerous subsistence farmers who had to borrow implements, animals and money at exorbitant rates from the well-to-do kulaks, the prospect of collectivization in which the property of the prosperous and the poverty stricken would be pooled began to have some appeal. The government was not satisfied because instead of a strong agricultural sector which provided an adequate and reliable food supply to support progress in industry, there were millions of inefficient farmers, many of whom were unable to make, or tried to evade, the compulsory deliveries to the state. Moreover, there was no place for a large free enterprise agricultural segment in the type of economic organization envisaged by the Bolshevik leaders.

In 1927, the government initiated a drive to encourage voluntary collectivization and to limit the "exploitative tendencies of the kulaks." By 1929 the battle cry was "liquidation of the kulaks as a class," and in January, 1930, the government announced the goal of the complete liquidation of the kulak and complete collectivization within three years. Thousands of party members were sent from the cities with instructions to crush both actual and potential resistance to collectivization. Within a short time approximately five million prosperous farmers were dispossessed of their property, and most of them were dispersed to remote regions. Thousands were killed for resisting collectivization. Classification as a kulak was based on property and income status, but the criteria were sufficiently vague to allow for discrimination on political or personal grounds. Millions of poor peasants, eager to share the property confiscated from the kulaks, submitted willingly to collectivization. Stern measures were taken to force unwilling peasants to join the collectives and to pool all property including garden plots and domestic fowl. Within a few weeks, over half the peasants were herded into collective farms. However, neither the party, the state nor the peasants had been adequately prepared for rapid transition to a collective form of agriculture. Anarchy prevailed. By March, 1930, the party realized that the situation was getting well out of hand, and some measures were taken to limit the excessive and often brutal zeal of the organizers. The state decreed that no more than three percent of the peasantry were to be treated as kulaks (in comparison to the 15 and even 20 percent that had already been dispossessed and dispersed in some regions), and that five percent of the surplus product of the farm was to be distributed to members in proportion to the value of property contributed to the farm. Members were not to be forced to pool living arrangements and incomes, and were to be remunerated in accordance with the number of work days done by each. Finally, the "voluntary" character of collective farm membership was stressed and over half of the members hastened to withdraw.[3] In March, 1931, the party again made it clear to the peasants that collectivization was inevitable through official statements such as: "The poor and average individual peasant who helps the kulak to combat the kolkhoz undermines the collectivization movement . . . he is in fact an ally of the kulak. . . . The poor and average peasant has only one way . . . joining the kolkhozy."[4] Since many peasants who had resisted collectivization had already been treated as kulaks, the majority of peasants realized that resistance to collectivization would be futile. By July, 1931, 1934, 1935, 1936, and 1938 the respective percentages of peasant households which were collectivized were 53, 71, 83, 90 and 94.[5] Since 1938 economic pressure (high taxes, lack of machinery and supplies, etc.) has been used to eliminate most of the few remaining independent farmers. By the early 1960's approximately 60,000 isolated farms were still operated on an individual basis.[6] State farms (sovkhozy) have been established in new agricultural areas and from amalgamated collective farms.

The number and size of the kolkhozy and sovkhozy have varied from time to time. In 1959, after a drive to convert to the state farm system and to combine smaller farms into larger units, there were 54,000 kolkhozy and 6,500 sovkhozy. Kolkhozy in the lower and upper quartiles for size averaged around 1,000 acres and 4,400 acres respectively. Over half of the collective farms included fewer than 300 peasant families. State farms tend to be much larger, with a 1959 average of 58,000 acres and approximately 600 workers. Some of the largest state farms include more than 480,000 acres, and state grain farms, considered separately, average 80,000 acres. (American farms average around 310 acres.) In 1965 there were over 39,500 collective farms and 9,000 state farms.[7]

The kolkhozy and sovkhozy system of agricultural organization did not solve the problems of Soviet agriculture, and in fact introduced a host of new problems. The force and brutality associated with collectivization produced widespread resentment which the new conditions did little to dispel. Because of the poor organization of the new farms, the lack of material support and the high demands of the state in terms of low priced compulsory deliveries, the majority of the peasants lived and worked under conditions which were no better and, in fact, were often worse than the conditions which had obtained previously. Many factors militated against an upsurge in agricultural productivity. During the early stages of collectivization many of the peasants had slaughtered their livestock, for several reasons including a desire to undermine the collective movement or to realize personal profit prior to entering the collective, fear of being treated as a kulak and the naive belief that the government would provide animals for the collective. The effects of the wholesale slaughter in terms of reduced supplies of meat, milk, wool, draft power and manure were felt for many years; in fact, the pre-collectivization level was not reached until 1955. The enlargement of the farms facilitated mechanization, but an adequate supply of machinery was not available. With the liquidation of the kulaks, the best farmers were removed from agriculture. The majority of the peasants who joined the collective farms had been unsuccessful farmers and knew little about agronomy, machinery and administration. The need for expert guidance was crucial.

The government's attempt to deal with the problems associated with collectivization and its rapid introduction proved to be totally inadequate. In the main, the government relied on strong central control and petty tutelage from local party and state officials. The independence of the farms was drastically curbed; they were told what to produce, and even assigned specific dates to begin seeding and harvesting operations. The orders from above often violated good agricultural practices or were totally unrealistic with reference to the potential of the farms. The unreasonable state procurement system appropriated the entire surplus product of the majority of farms; many farms had no excess whatsoever to invest in capital improvements or even to pay the members of the collective a pittance for their work.

One rather ingenious, but totally inadequate, technique used by the Stalin regime to cope with some of the agricultural problems involved the establishment of an institution known as the Machine Tractor Stations (M.T.S.) Almost all of the inadequate supply of machinery was allocated to the M.T.S., which rented the machinery to the collectives for stipulated fees paid in kind. Central control was designed to maximize the use and minimize the damage to machines. Assigned to each M.T.S. were agronomists, veterinarians and other agricultural specialists who were expected to serve, guide and instruct the farm personnel, and party workers who were responsible for the political education of the peasants. Thus the M.T.S. were designed to distribute machinery, to foster increased productivity through agricultural guidance and direction, to act as a state procurement agency and to serve as the political agents of the Communist Party. In 1958, a variety of factors, including an attempt to reduce the amount of petty tutelage over farms, the increased expertness of the peasants in the use of machinery and the growing strength of party organizations on the farms, contributed to the decision to abolish the M.T.S. They were replaced by Repair and Technical Stations (R.T.S.) which supply the farms with spare parts, major repair services, fertilizer, fuel and other production supplies.

After Stalin's death, the new leadership expressed deep concern over the sorry state of affairs in agriculture and, particularly, over the fact that agricultural output was so low that the needs of the population for foodstuffs and of industry for agricultural raw materials were not being met. During the early post-Stalin period and the period of Khrushchev's dominance, a number of remedial measures were introduced. The desired effects were not achieved primarily because none of the measures went far enough. Promises to provide agriculture with an adequate supply of machinery, fertilizer, insecticides and other material supports were only partially fulfilled. Reorganizations intended to increase the independence of the farms in the spheres of planning and production, to reduce petty tutelage and to ensure that the necessary leadership would be provided by enlightened experts, familiar with concrete conditions on the farms, had relatively little effect. Pricing and procurement policies were made somewhat less disadvantageous to the farms but were not sufficiently drastic to enable the farms to retain the necessary funds for capital investment and to pay farm members adequately. Thus, under Khrushchev the farms still suffered from inadequate material support, poor guidance and restrictive controls, and the incentive to increase productivity was missing. Moreover, some of the new policies introduced by Khrushchev, such as overemphasis on the production of corn and additional restrictions on private auxiliary farming, were economically unwise. During the Khrushchev era increases in agricultural productivity were far below planned quotas. The average annual rise in gross output of agriculture from 1958-1964 was only 1.9 percent.[8] Khrushchev's failure to solve the agricultural problem may have contributed substantially to his downfall.

The post-Khrushchev leadership acted immediately in an attempt to rectify the unsatisfactory situation in agriculture. Within a few months after Khrushchev's dismissal, the procurement prices for agricultural products were raised substantially, the incentive system for agricultural personnel was improved, the farms were promised greater independence in planning and organizing production, more adequate material support from the state was promised, farm indebtedness to the state was lowered and some of the restrictions on auxiliary farming were lifted. Agriculture, the long-time Cinderella of the Soviet economy, is apparently being given *de facto* recognition by the new Soviet leaders as the junior partner, rather than as the handmaiden of industry. However, even if, and this still remains to be seen, the barriers which have impeded progress in Soviet agriculture are removed, many years will be required to eliminate the effects of the long period of misuse and abuse to which agriculture has been subjected.

Administration

Throughout the years the Soviet regime has tried, without notable success, to develop organizational forms which will place agriculture under firm state control and, at the same time, guarantee maximum productivity.[9] The post-Khrushchev leaders, who have criticized Khrushchev for engaging in "numerous and sometimes ill-conceived reorganizations"[10] seem to be willing to retain, at least temporarily, the major features of the organizational framework for state control over agriculture which was established in 1962. The organization of agricultural management, as of the summer of 1965, is outlined in Figure 1. Participation of party officials, as well as state officials, is mandatory in all administrative organs.

At the apex of the agricultural hierarchy is the U.S.S.R. Agriculture Committee, composed of a vice-chairman from each of the U.S.S.R. Coun-

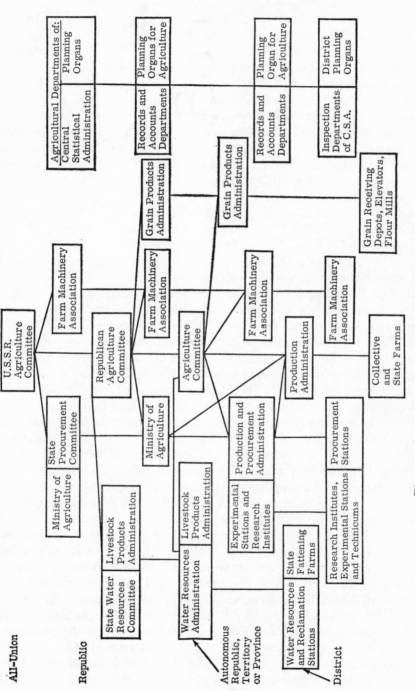

Figure 1. Organization of Agricultural Administration.

cil of Ministers and the U.S.S.R. State Planning Committee, the Director of the Department of Agriculture subordinate to the Central Committee of the Party, and chairmen of all major organs subordinate to the Agriculture Committee. This Committee exercises general supervision over all agencies concerned with agriculture throughout the U.S.S.R. It is responsible for ensuring the fulfillment of all production and procurement plans, for evaluating long range and current plans for agriculture, for determining agricultural needs for capital investment, equipment, supplies and specialists, and for ensuring that industry provides the necessary material support for agriculture. During the first three years of its operation, the Committee did not fulfill its responsibilities satisfactorily.

Supervisory and administrative responsibility for agriculture is parcelled out to a number of agencies subordinate to the U.S.S.R. Council of Ministers and the U.S.S.R. Agriculture Committee. The Ministry of Agriculture, a Union-Republican organ, has been awarded increased power by the new leadership. Under Khrushchev the Ministry was primarily a scientific organ which worked with the Academy of Agricultural Sciences and through research institutes and experimental stations on problems such as the development of new varieties of grain, livestock feeding techniques, insect and disease control and the correct use of fertilizers. In 1965, it was announced that the Ministry will continue its work with respect to agricultural science but that its main functions will relate to "the correct planning and distribution by zones of the country of the output and procurement of agricultural products."[11] The Ministry will ascertain the need for, and will distribute, machinery, fertilizers and other material resources, deal with questions concerning labor productivity, production costs and zonal prices and will supervise the training of agricultural specialists.[12] The Minister of Agriculture stated that within the Ministry there will be formed a chief collective farm administration and a chief state farm administration which will be charged with strengthening the economies of the state and collective farms and with the analysis of their production and economic activities.[13] Each republic is to have a Ministry of Agriculture which will establish territorial and district agricultural administrations to exercise direct guidance over the local collective and state farms.[14] The R.S.F.S.R., which had abolished its Ministry of Agriculture in 1963, announced in 1965 that its Ministry of Production and Procurement of Farm Products had been transformed into a Union-Republic Ministry of Agriculture.[15] This transformation suggests that the U.S.S.R. Ministry of Agriculture and the subordinate organs may be assuming major responsibility for the production and procurement of farm products. As of the summer of 1965, there has been no announcement of the formation of territorial and district administrations under the Ministries of Agriculture of the republics, but it is probable that the Production Administrations will be made subordinate to the Ministries of Agriculture.

The U.S.S.R. Farm Machinery Association, also a Union-Republican organ, is responsible for the design, sale and repair of farm equipment. Organization of the procurement of farm products has been the responsibility of the State Procurement Committee. The State Planning Committee has an Agricultural Department charged with developing plans for agriculture in cooperation with the other federal agencies, particularly the State Procurements Committee and the Farm Machinery Association. The Agricultural Department of the Central Statistical Administration keeps records and accounts, and commands an inspection apparatus which serves as a major control organ for the state and the party.

The All-Union apparatus, including an Agriculture Committee composed of leading party and government officials, is replicated at the republican level. Some republics have additional agencies such as a State Water Resources Committee, a Grain Products Administration and a Livestock Procurement and Fattening Administration. Branch administrations of each Union-Republican organ are established in the Autonomous Republics, territories and provinces. Grain receiving depots, elevators, grading plants, flour mills, mixed fodder enterprises, agricultural institutes and technicums, farm machinery associations, etc. are established at the district level, under the supervision of the appropriate republican Ministry or Committee and its counterpart at the territorial or provincial level.

In 1962 Collective Farm-State Farm Production Administrations were established to serve as the chief administrative unit to supervise both state and collective farms. Ordinarily, a Production Administration embraces several districts and is responsible for from 30 to 60 farms. The chief executive body of a Production Administration is a Council composed of the Director, the chief party-organizer and the chief Y.C.L. organizer of the Production Administration, the First Secretaries of the district Party Committees, the chairmen of the Executive Committees of the district Soviets, the collective farm chairmen and state farm directors, and representatives from Farm Machinery Associations, Procurement Agencies and scientific institutions. Each Production Administration employs a staff of experts and a number of inspector-organizers, each of whom is assigned to work with a limited number of farms. The Production Administrations are expected to provide concrete, practical guidance to the state and collective farms, with the overall goal of substantially increasing productivity. The inspector-organizers, who are expected to spend a great deal of their time directly on the farms and in the brigades and livestock sections, are authorized to make concrete recommendations to the farm administrators about plans, farming methods and the organization of production. The Production Administration supervises planning, production activities, procurement, norm setting and labor payments, and participates in the selection of farm specialists and administrators. Attached to each Production Administration are Party and Y.C.L. organizers, most of whom have been appointed by the Party or Y.C.L. Central Committee of the Union Republic. Each organizer is provided with a staff of instructors who assist the primary party and Y.C.L. organizations with organizational and mass-political work, and organize socialist competitions for the fulfillment of production and procurement plans.

Collective farms, according to the Collective Farm Statutes, are supposed to operate on the basis of democracy and equality. Theoretically, the highest authority on the collective farm is the general assembly of farm members. The general assembly is entitled to elect the collective farm chairman, an Executive Committee and a Control Committee which constitutes the management of the farm. In actuality, the candidate for the collective farm chairmanship is usually selected by state or party officials. The general assembly dutifully admits the proposed candidate to membership in the collective and elects him as their chairman. Unfortunately for the collective, the position has sometimes been used as a reward for loyal, but not necessarily competent, party members. The Executive Committee of five to nine members is usually selected by the chairman and then duly elected for a two year term by the general assembly. The Executive Committee, which shares responsibility for the management of the farm with the chairman, is required to meet at least twice a month. It appoints, from among members of the collective, the brigadiers who are given responsibility for production within a specific segment of the farm economy. The brigade, which is usually composed of 40 to 60 members, may be divided into smaller units called squads (zveno). Brigadiers and squad leaders assign duties to their members and are responsible for the fulfillment of subplans. The term of a brigade varies with the nature of the work; for example, on grain farms the term is the full period of the crop rotation. The Control Committee inspects the financial and economic activities of the chairman and the Executive Committee and is required to report irregularities to higher state authorities.

The organizational structure of a state farm resembles that of an industrial enterprise. It is headed by an appointed director who is held responsible to higher authorities (the Production Administration and the party) for its efficient operation. He selects the assistant director and the main agricultural specialists for appointment by higher authorities, and directly hires all other subordinate personnel. A number of functional and operational departments such as finance, personnel, livestock and grain are formed, along with brigades and squads.

The decree on the reorganization of the management of agriculture stated explicitly that inspector-organizers from the Production Administrations are not to usurp the authority of the collective farm chairman and the state farm director and that "the collective farm boards and state farm directors are directly responsible for the production, financial and economic state of the farms, and they have the final decision in the solution of production questions."[16] However, the same decree stated that the inspector-organizers, as representatives of the state and the party, "will decide on the spot questions of production and procurement."[17] Despite statements to the contrary, the doctrine that collective farms are autonomous co-operatives governed by their members does not correspond to reality. Both state farm directors and collective farm chairmen are required to do as they are told, and what they are told to do does not always make sense.

The 1962 and 1965 reorganizations have the potential for a number of distinct advantages over the preceding system. Since the Agriculture Committees include leading party officials and representatives from all major state agencies concerned with agriculture, policy decisions and directives to agriculture should be coordinated more effectively than in the past. The proximity of the well-staffed Production Administrations to the farms should allow for the provision of more adequate positive assistance, including better coordinated, more realistic and down-to-earth guidance. Moreover, agricultural efficiency should be increased by the elimination of a number of negative features such as directives from agriculturally naive officials which run counter to good agricultural practice. Since the Production Administrations are responsible for both state and collective farms, cooperation in the development of irrigation projects, food processing stations, etc. is more feasible, and the uneconomical duplication of such projects could be eliminated. Perhaps one of the most important features of the reorganization is the unification of party and state supervision of agriculture, which is effected by the inclusion of ranking party officials in the state supervisory and administrative organs at all levels. The intention of the party is to maintain strict control over agriculture but, at the same time, to eliminate the confusion resulting from a dual hierarchy of party and state control organs, along with outright interference by uninformed party officials. However, both Khrushchev and his successors have had to reprimand party officials for issuing unauthorized directives to the Production Administrations, and Production Administrations for adopting a bureaucratic approach to the farms. (E.g. all farms subordinate to a given Production Administration were instructed to ensure that output of milk per animal reached a specified level within a ten day period, although many of the animals were dying of starvation, and the Production Administration did nothing about providing the urgently needed fodder.) The post-Khrushchev organizational revisions seem to be designed primarily to simplify and streamline the organizational framework which was established in 1962, and to establish conditions which will enable agricultural organs to function in accordance with their intended purposes.

Planning, Procurement and Prices

During the Stalin era, organs of the central government prepared plans, targets and output quotas for almost every phase of farm operations. Individual farms were provided, through channels, with directives which specified compulsory deliveries to the state, output, livestock productivity, crop and pasture acreages and even planting dates. Often the planners were totally unfamiliar with the potential of the farm for which the plans were developed, and typically, unrealistically high output quotas were established by planning organs at all levels. In many cases, rather than serving as a lever to encourage increased productivity, the plan disrupted progress in agriculture by forcing farms to engage in agricultural operations for which they were poorly suited. Moreover, it proved to be a poor instrument with respect to its major purpose—ensuring adequate deliveries of agricultural products to the state—because many farms were unable to meet their quotas for compulsory deliveries. Numerous errors were perpetuated on a large scale, such as the universal adoption of a system of rotating crops with perennial grasses, which removed from active production thousands of acres of land which should never have been involved in the grasslands plan.

Until 1958, all collective farms were required to make compulsory deliveries to the state, the size of the quota being determined by factors such as the number of hectares of tillable land. For most products, state prices were well below production costs, and in some cases prices did not even cover the transportation costs to the delivery point which had to be paid by the collective farm. Such prices hardly provided an adequate incentive to increase productivity. For sales to the state over and above the compulsory delivery quota, the state paid an over-quota price which usually amounted to two to four times the fixed price for quota deliveries. The over-quota prices were, however, well below the retail prices which consumers had to pay for agricultural products. Thus, almost all collective farms were required to subsidize the state as producers as well as consumers. The greatest hardship was inflicted on farms which had low yields, regardless of the reason since all, or almost all, of their produce had to be delivered to the state at the low fixed price. In addition to making it difficult, if not impossible, for most farms to make investments which would eventually improve their production potential, this system of pricing and procurement caused average prices to be higher in years of good crops than in years of bad crops. The system was complicated by concessions in terms of lower retail prices to farms which specialized in certain scarce products or made over-quota deliveries to the state. Moreover, the relationship between prices was so illogical that a number of highly uneconomical practices developed; for example, peasants fed bread bought at retail stores to their privately owned livestock because it was cheaper than fodder. Finally, local officials frequently forced the more productive farms to turn over to the state, at quota prices, products over and above their assigned quotas to compensate for other farms which were unable to meet the quota. In this way, the local party and state officials could receive credit for having ensured plan fulfillment within the area of their jurisdiction. State farms were (and are) obligated to deliver all their produce to the state except for seed grain, feed for livestock and some foodstuffs for consumption on the farm. Initially, the state farms received only the low quota delivery price paid to the collective farms. Beginning in 1940, state farms were paid higher delivery prices than collective farms, but even so, the majority of state farms were unable to meet production costs and had to be subsidized by the state. The entire system governing planning, pricing and procurement was chaotic, complicated, irrational and detrimental to the development of agriculture. Immediately following Stalin's death and particularly during the period of Khrushchev's dominance, a large number of measures were introduced in the attempt to evolve a rational system of control over agriculture and to foster increased productivity. The first step was taken in 1953 when the quota and over-quota prices for most goods were increased.

In 1955, the regulations governing planning underwent a major revision which was intended to introduce a significant amount of decentralization. The 1955 planning regulations, which have remained in effect without substantial changes (as of the summer of 1965), granted the state and collective farms extensive rights, on paper, to establish their own production plans and to govern their own production activities. Central authorities prepare an overall plan for agricultural output, state procurement of agricultural products, capital investment in agriculture and the production and distribution of agricultural supplies. With the exception of a few scarce agricultural products which are crucial to key industries, necessary to meet export obligations or to build up central reserves, the central government delegates major responsibility for the implementation of the overall agricultural plan to the republics, which are responsible for procurement and distribution within their own areas. The agricultural management chain of command outlined in Figure 1 is followed in the preparation, confirmation and supervision of plan fulfillment. Each collective and state farm is given a minimum quota for compulsory delivery to the state. Each farm is required to organize its production activity to ensure fulfillment of the compulsory delivery quota. In all other respects the farm is, in principle, entitled to plan and organize its own production activities. However, in reality, state and party authorities have maintained rigid control over agriculture, and the independence of the farms has been highly circumscribed. Each farm is expected to prepare both perspective and current plans which are submitted to the Production Administration for guidance with respect to output targets, planning patterns and investments. The Production Administration, in turn, receives directives from superior organs which govern the guidance conveyed to the farm. The farm's long-term plan includes crop rotations, stock breeding and fodder supply, soil improvement and water conservation projects, capital investment in buildings and machinery, long-range output goals, measures to increase labor productivity, etc. Yearly plans are very detailed: acreages to be sown to specific crops, plans for plowing, sowing, harrowing and harvesting, livestock increase, fodder supply, farm building construction, the purchase of machinery, fuel, repairs, fertilizer, the cost of production including the purchase of supplies and payments for labor, capital investment and cultural expenditures. The inspector-organizer from the Production Administration has the right to suggest modifications of any aspect of the plan.

The farms have never been allowed to exercise their rights to regulate their own planning and production operations. A 1964 resolution of the C.P.S.U. Central Committee and the U.S.S.R. Council of Ministers reaffirmed these rights and, at the same time, revealed clearly that state and party officials continued to interfere in all aspects of farms activities. The resolution stated:

> "The composition of plans for the development of agricultural production must begin directly on the collective and state farms and must be carried out with an eye to the concrete conditions and possibilities of each farm.
>
> "The collective and state farms must be given an assignment for the quantities and types of products they are to sell to the state, but what crops to plant and in what amounts, the number of livestock to be maintained and how to use the land most rationally to obtain the largest amount of produce and successfully fulfill the state plans for its purchase are the concern of the collective farmers and state farm workers themselves. . . .
>
> "Recently, however, a number of provinces, territories and republics have tolerated the practice of stereotyped planning from above, which the Party has long condemned; plans for sown areas and the yields of farm crops and for the size and productivity of livestock herds have been unceremoniously thrust upon the farms, and the entire work of the collective and state farms has been regimented through directives. . . .
>
> "Certain local agencies frequently display a disdainful attitude toward the plans and proposals that have been worked out by the collective and state farms, compel the farms' leaders to revise their plans for no reason and do not take the real possibilities and economic expediency into account. . . .
>
> "In determining the assignments for a farm, the officials of the production administrations proceed not from the farm's possibilities but from the level of production that has actually been achieved. As a result, farms located in the same zone and having the same soil and climatic conditions are assigned different plan targets . . . we must not be guided by the principle 'A smaller plan for those who work worse and a bigger plan for those who work better.'
>
> "The C.P.S.U. Central Committee and the U.S.S.R. Council of Ministers

have data indicating that local Party, Soviet and agricultural agencies are forcing collective and state farms to extend the plantings of some crops and to reduce the plantings of others, to increase the herd of this or that type of livestock simply to maintain a certain percentage in the plan for show purposes. . . .

"Serious shortcomings have been permitted in the planning of state purchases of farm products. The production orientation of the farm, its specialization, is not always taken into account in fixing the plans for the sale of products to the state by the collective and state farms."[18]

During the last few months of the Khrushchev era, the top party leadership evidenced increasing concern about the negative effects of the lack of independence of the state and collective farms. The post-Khrushchev leadership has increased the tempo of the attack against "petty tutelage" and unnecessary interference. It is possible that the farms may finally be allowed a small measure of the independence which has been their technical right since 1955 and which is a necessary prerequisite for sensible agricultural operations.

In 1958 the entire system of pricing was revised. An attempt was made to establish prices which bore a rational relation to each other and to the costs of production. The system of quota and over-quota prices was replaced by a single zone price for each product. The differential in state prices between zones was intended to compensate for regional variations in production and delivery costs. Delivery quotas for basic produce (grain, milk, meat, etc.) were assessed by regions but the norms for each farm were set according to specialization. Regions not well suited for grain growing were to have lower norms for grain than other regions and, within a region, some of the farms could be exempted from the obligation to make grain deliveries to the state. This represented an attempt to enable the state to buy the bulk of its agricultural produce at low prices from regions with low production costs and to allow for reasonable specialization on individual farms.

The single zone price for each product was set considerably above the old fixed quota price. The average price increase from 1952 to 1958 was approximately threefold for the aggregate of agricultural products.[19] By 1963 agricultural prices averaged approximately four times higher than in 1952.[20] In 1961 and 1962, additional concessions were made to the collective farms through reduced prices for farm machinery, fuel, spare parts and building materials and the establishment of a more favorable income tax rate.[21] In spite of these relatively sensible changes which were introduced during the Khrushchev era, the agricultural management, planning, pricing and procurement systems did not fulfill their intended purposes. State prices were too low to permit the majority of farms to cover production costs and allocate sufficient funds for extended reproduction; many farms were still required to engage in agricultural operations for which they were poorly suited; the farms had neither the independence nor the incentive required for an upsurge in productivity. Collective farm members continued to bear the brunt of the burden in terms of reduced consumption. The minimal gains in agricultural productivity constituted a source of deep concern for the party leaders because successful solution of the agricultural problem is mandatory if overall political, economic and social goals are to be achieved.

The post-Khrushchev leadership devoted immediate attention to agriculture. Brezhnev, in a major speech on agriculture, stated that from 1959 to 1964 agriculture had, to all intents and purposes, merely marked time.[22] He listed a number of basic reasons for the agricultural lag. First, Khrushchev and his agricultural advisors had ignored, or applied inadequately, the laws and principles relating to expanded socialist reproduction, planned and proportional development, the combination of public and personal interest and material incentives. He stated that "actions of a purely willful nature, especially in the field of planning, price formation, financing and the extension of credits, increasingly came to the fore in the practice of agricultural guidance."[23] Second, the numerous reorganizations gave rise to confusion, and the "practice of administration by fiat, of issuing commands to collective and state farms was often permitted."[24] Third, agriculture was not given the necessary material support particularly in terms of "the correct determination of the level of prices for agricultural products and goods needed for production, the allocation of appropriate capital investments and the improvement of the material and technical supply."[25] Fourth,

> ". . . practically nothing was done to raise farming standards or increase fertility. . . . The central agencies issued various kinds of stereotyped instructions on tilling the soil, on determining the structure of sown areas and replacing one farming system by another, and on caring for and feeding livestock, without taking into account natural-economic and production conditions or local experience. All this prevented the planned management of farms, reduced the role of the land agencies and did not contribute to the productive utilization of the land."[26]

Finally, the party, Soviet and agricultural agencies did not perform their functions in agriculture with maximum efficiency, partly because of the frequent organizational changes which presumably made it difficult for individuals and agencies to know what their tasks were and to work consistently toward designated goals. Brezhnev stated:

> ". . . *an upsurge in agriculture is something that is vitally necessary to us for the successful construction of communism. In order to resolve this nationwide task, we must put a firm economic foundation under agriculture.* . . . We must correct the mistakes that have been made in agriculture more quickly and put an end to subjectivism. We must utilize on a broad economic basis material and moral incentives for the development of production. Great efforts and a decisive change in methods of work is demanded of Party, Soviet and economic agencies, of all of us."[27]

By April, 1965, a number of decisive actions were taken by the U.S.S.R. Council of Ministers acting on instructions from the C.P.S.U. Central Committee. The most important measure was designed to improve the system of procurements and purchase of agricultural products which, as Brezhnev pointed out, was inadequate because purchase prices frequently did not cover production expenses, and because the farms did not know from one year to the next what their assignment for deliveries to the state would be. Purchase prices for a number of agricultural products including wheat, rye, rice, buckwheat, millet, sunflower seeds, sugar beets, meat and milk were raised substantially.[28] The new price schedules incorporate zonal price differentials, higher purchase prices for collective farms in comparison to state farms for some products, such as wheat and rye, and markedly higher above-quota purchase prices for a number of items. Concurrently, it was decreed that a fixed, unalterable plan for state purchases of agricultural products should be established for a six year period for each republic, province, district and state and collective farm.[29] The shift to a "firm" or long-term plan for procurements is intended to enable the farms to organize production activities in a more rational manner since each farm will know well in advance what will be expected of it in the succeeding years. Brezhnev emphasized that there must be firm agreement that no one will have the right to change the plans.[30] Quotas for compulsory delivery of agricultural products to the state have been set more realistically. Thus, the plan for total state purchases of grain for each of the years 1965 to 1970 is lower than the plan which was originally prepared for 1965. The state plan for procurement of livestock and poultry products was also reduced for 1965 and increases of approximately twenty-five percent are planned by 1970. With lower compulsory delivery quotas for a number of products, there conceivably could be an excess of produce which the farms could sell to the state at above-quota purchase prices.

A new system of supplementary payments designed to encourage collective farm members and state farm workers to increase productivity has also been developed. The amount of the bonus is tied directly to productivity. Detailed schedules for supplementary payments have been worked out for a variety of products. The plan for bonus payments for persons engaged in the growing of sugar beets is illustrative. All workers who participate in the production of sugar beets are entitled to buy sugar at substantially reduced prices in amounts which vary with work output.[31] If the plan is overfulfilled by amounts up to 5 percent, then for each centner of sugar beets sold above the plan, the farm chairman or director receives 4 kopeks and the brigade leader receives 5 kopeks. If the plan is overfulfilled by more than 5 percent or more than 10 percent, the bonus per centner is doubled or tripled respectively. Farm specialists and technicians receive a bonus amounting to 80 percent of the director or chairman's bonus, or if they worked directly in the sugar beet segment, a bonus amounting to 80 percent of the brigade leader's bonus. These bonuses are not to exceed the regular salary for a six month period. Specialists in the Production Administrations are awarded bonuses of up to three months of their regular salaries depending upon the degree of over-fulfillment of the plan. Workers engaged in the production of rice are to receive supplementary payments of up to 10 percent of the gross harvest of rice within the limits of the plan for the brigade and of from 25 to 50 percent of the gross harvest above the plan.[32] An all-out effort is being made to make it worth while for every worker, specialist and administrator to strive to increase production.

A number of rather significant measures have been introduced to improve the financial status of the collective farms. Fundamental improvements of collective farm lands, including measures to improve drainage, to reduce the acid or alkaline content of the soil and other land reclamation operations are to be paid for from state budget funds. A large portion of the indebtedness of the collective farms to the State Bank has been written off, and all debts of collective farms for equipment, tools and premises acquired from the Machine and Tractor Stations have been cancelled.[33] Whereas, previously, collective farms had to pay income tax on total gross receipts, a new decree stipulates that income tax will be levied at the rate of 12 percent of the net income which exceeds a profit level of 15 percent. Farms with a profit rate of less than 15 percent pay no income tax and other farms pay the tax only on the net income which exceeds the indicated profit rate.[34] The C.P.S.U. Central Committee has promised impressive capital investment by the state in argiculture, substantial increases in the supply of trucks, tractors and other farm machinery, adequate facilities for the repair of machinery, elimination of price differences for industrial and agricultural purchasers of equipment, materials and electrical power, a program for the widespread electrification of agriculture, and a number of other improvements. Brezhnev pointed out, with justifiable realism, that a considerable amount of time would be required to complete all the projected plans.[35]

On paper, it would appear that the measures introduced by the post-Khrushchev leadership should culminate in a fairly adequate solution of the Soviet agricultural problem. However, Khrushchev also attempted to achieve exactly the same goals through a program which was designed to eliminate the very barriers that his successors are attacking. Khrushchev's agricultural program was, perhaps, not quite as impressive as the current program, but it too, on paper, had the potential to foster substantially increased productivity. A number of weaknesses in his program, including inadequate price increases and lack of emphasis on personal incentives, contributed to his failure. However, the chief reason for his failure may have been that the program, as it was planned, was never actually implemented; for example, the farms were never given the independence nor the material support which they were promised. Perhaps the new leaders, unlike Khrushchev, will be able to carry their new program through to fruition. However, they too may find that they have promised more than they can deliver.

Operation of Collective Farms

The party would prefer if all members of collective farms lived in modern, well-equipped, semi-urban centers so that schools, hospitals, utilities and other community facilities could be shared. However, the majority of peasant families continue to live in primitive, individual dwellings, grouped in farm villages, much as they did before collectivization. Many collective farms include a number of rural settlements; a few very large collective farms incorporate fifty or more small villages. A great deal of time may be wasted because of poor transportation and communication facilities between settlements.

New members may be admitted to a collective farm by action of a general meeting of the collective. New members who own property must surrender it to the collective. Approximately half of the contributed property becomes the indivisible property of the collective; the remainder, which is considered to be the member's invested share, may be retrieved in the form of a cash payment, at low prices, if the member withdraws from the collective. Members may withdraw with the approval of the kolkhoz management, and superior party and state authorities, to take a position in industry, to transfer to another kolkhoz or sovkhoz, or even in rare cases to engage in individual farming. Members may be expelled from the collective for failure to participate sufficiently in communal work, for serious infringements of the rules of the collective or for criminal offenses.

The state, which owns all land, permits each collective farm to hold its land in perpetuity. The land cannot be leased or sold by the kolkhozy, and may be taken by the state for important public needs only if proper compensation is made. Illegal leases or sale of land to individuals and institutions, and the illegal seizure of land by party or government officials for public or private use does, however, occur on occasion. With the exception of the small individual plots which are allotted to the households of the collective, all original peasant holdings have been consolidated into large fields for the use of the collective. The capital assets of the collective, called the indivisible fund, are composed of barns, storage buildings, machinery, collective livestock, seed, forage supplies, etc. The indivisible fund has been augmented by the original contributions of the members, natural growth, deductions from the current income and long-term state credits.

The organization of the work of a kolkhoz is more similar to that of a large factory than to small scale farming in a private enterprise system. As previously indicated, management of the farm is delegated by the farm members to an "elected" chairman and an Executive Committee. The acquisition of competent chairmen has constituted a persistent problem for the collective farms; many of the chairmen imposed from above have been incompetent or unable to operate efficiently within the framework of directives and interference from the party and the state; competent chairmen tend to be transferred to other farms or positions where there is supposedly a more urgent need for their talents. Recent measures have been designed to increase the autonomy of farm chairmen with respect to the internal operation of the farms, and to improve the training and qualifications of persons assigned to serve as farm chairmen. The labor force consists of the collective farm members who are subject to the orders and supervision of the management. The Executive Committee may supplement the labor force, if necessary, by employing outside specialists and seasonal laborers.

Cash revenues of the collective farms derive from three sources: sale of farm produce to the state; sale of farm produce on the collective farm market; and from other enterprises. The state is the first claimant to the collective's output. Surplus produce, over and above that required for deliveries to the state and for seed and forage, may be sold to members of the collective at reduced rates or on the free market. In the past a number of collectives attempted to supplement their meager incomes through subsidiary revenue producing activities, such as the production of bricks, food processing, handicrafts, and supplying transportation services to other enterprises. State and party authorities were not too well pleased with these sideline activities which removed members of the collective from agricultural production. However, dire economic necessity forced many collectives, which relied primarily on the subsidiary industries for revenue, to retain them despite official disapproval. Since 1958 the small scale industrial operations have become increasingly less important as a source of income.

The state is the first claimant to the revenue of the collective farm as well as to the output. Until the 1965 collective farm income tax revision, the tax burden was very severe. Insurance of collective farm property and crops against fire, hail and other natural disasters, though not entirely compulsory, is necessary, because the kolkhozy are not subsidized by the state. From 15 to 20 percent of gross cash revenues must be assigned to the indivisible fund for the purchase of machinery, breeding stock, the construction of farm buildings and other capital improvements.

Amounts of up to two percent of the gross revenue are supposed to be assigned to the cultural fund to be used for educational and recreational purposes. All too frequently, no funds have been available for this category of expenditures. Administrative expenses including the salaries of administrative personnel are not supposed to exceed two percent of the gross revenues. Many collectives exceed this limit because of unreasonably large administrative staffs which sometimes illegally include local party officials who make no contribution to the work of the farm. After all unavoidable expenses have been met, the collective farm members are the residual claimants to the cash revenue and surplus products of the farm.

The typical practice is for residual income of the farm to be subdivided among the members on the basis of number of work day units or trudodni which have been earned during the course of the year. Each job is rated in terms of the amount of effort and skill required for its performance. Theoretically, average work of average quality is graded at one trudoden per day norm. For most types of work, the trudoden measure is based on work performed rather than hours expended. Thus, a tractor driver might earn three trudodni for plowing one hectare of land in ten hours, while a janitor might earn only one trudoden for cleaning a building in eight hours. Brigades that exceed production plans are given supplementary credits which are divided among brigade members in proportion to the annual total of trudodni that each accumulates. Deductions are made when plans are not fulfilled, and have, at times, amounted to 25 percent of the earned trudodni. The complicated system of remuneration is illustrated by considering the computation of the salary of the kolkhoz chairman. His basic pay consists of a specified number of trudodni credits plus a monthly cash salary based on the size and type of farm, and his qualifications, seniority and production record. If the kolkhoz overfulfills the approved plan, the chairman receives a bonus which may amount to 50 percent of his basic salary. If the plan is underfulfilled, he is penalized by a deduction of work day credits. At the end of the year all trudodni earned by all members, including those awarded as bonuses or deducted for non-fulfillment of production quotas, are summed, and divided into the revenue and surplus product available for distribution.

The system of allocating the income of the kolkhoz has a number of obvious disadvantages. The number of trudodni earned by an individual member depends less upon his willingness to work than upon the type and volume of work assigned to him by the managerial staff or the brigade leader. The collective is not obligated to assign work to all members at all times, especially during the slack winter season, or to ensure that the work which is assigned is commensurate with skill and qualifications. Trudodni credits are assigned on the basis of the job rather than on the skills of the individual who performs the job. There is ample leeway for unfair treatment or favoritism in the assignment of jobs. Since bonuses and the distribution of surpluses are based on trudodni credits, the individual who earns the smallest number of trudodni receives the smallest bonus. Although this may be just in the majority of cases, it increases income inequalities within the collective. Members may be penalized by a reduction in trudodni for failure to fulfill planned quotas, even if the poor results have been due to natural conditions, rather than to inefficiency or negligence. The collective farmer cannot determine the value of his work until after the harvest or until the end of the year when the produce has been marketed and final accounting has been made. Because, all too often, income from the collective farm has been pitifully small, the remuneration system has had a detrimental effect on morale and motivation. The actual value of a trudoden varies from collective to collective and from year to year, depending on prices, yields, production expenses, etc. On a few of the more prosperous collective farms, members have typically earned as much as, and sometimes considerably more than, industrial workers of comparable skill; on less well located or efficiently managed collectives, the value of the trudoden has typically been so low that the remuneration which able bodied, hard working peasants received from the collective farm has been a mere fraction, sometimes less than one-fourth, of that earned by industrial workers of comparable skill. It has not been uncommon for collective farm workers to receive absolutely nothing for their work on the collective farm.[36] During the last few years, the value of the trudoden has risen somewhat. Nevertheless, in 1964 most collective farm members were still earning substantially less than similarly qualified state farm and industrial workers.[37]

Leading party and state officials have repeatedly expressed dissatisfaction with the remuneration practices on collective farms, primarily on the basis that more efficient techniques must be developed to encourage increased labor productivity. However, because of the complexity of the problem, and the wide differences between collectives with respect to income, labor force and types of operation, the central authorities have not yet been able to design a comprehensive material incentive system which would be appropriate for universal application. Consequently, the Production Administrations and the collective farms have been encouraged to develop and adopt remuneration systems which are feasible with respect to local conditions. Some of the more prosperous collectives have established definite monetary wages for each task and guarantee the members minimum earnings regardless of harvest conditions. This system, when combined with supplementary payments of the type outlined by the 1965 price, procurement and incentive decrees, is favored by the regime as a technique to increase labor productivity and to advance toward the basic communist goal of transforming the peasant into a wage earner. Most collectives, however, have been unable to guarantee minimum cash incomes. Some collectives allow members to receive monthly cash advances in proportion to earned trudodni in amounts not to exceed 50 percent of the current cash receipts of the collective. Previously, collective members received payment from the collective only annually. Even prior to the 1965 decrees, a number of farms experimented with techniques such as awarding members or brigades a percentage of the gross output or net income over and above the planned quota for the specific sector which is the responsibility of the member or the brigade.[38] The majority of farms have retained the trudoden as the basic technique for subdividing the surplus product of the collective farm because of lack of a suitable substitute.

Since these lines were written, the central authorities have decreed that after July 1, 1966, all collective farmers must receive a guaranteed monthly wage.* Work norms are to be set with regard for specific conditions and with relation to work norms for similar jobs on state farms. Collective farms which do not have the funds to guarantee payments will be entitled to borrow money from the State Bank. Collective farmers are also to be guaranteed certain payments in kind.

The income of the collective farm member is derived from three sources; his portion of the cash income of the kolkhoz; his portion of the surplus product of the kolkhoz; and the produce grown on his own individual plot of land. Each household is permitted to use from .5 to 2.5 acres, usually adjacent to the dwelling place, as a privately operated garden plot. The plots are allotted to the whole family, not to individual members. Because many members found it more profitable to work on the private plot than for the collective, a policy of varying the size of the plot according to the labor which each able bodied member of the household contributes to the collective was introduced. The household is allowed to raise potatoes, vegetables, sunflower seed and other crops and to possess a small number of livestock.

Surplus produce awarded to the peasant by the kolkhoz provides much of the feed for the livestock. Any remaining surplus produce, plus produce from the household plot not required for individual consumption, may be sold in the collective farm market. For many years the household plots have provided the major source of cash income and of food for the majority of collective farmers. In fact, it is probable that a large number of collective farmers would not have been able to subsist without the food supply derived from their own plots. Moreover, the house-

---

* "In the C.P.S.U. Central Committee and the U.S.S.R. Council of Ministers," *Pravda,* May 18, 1966, p. 2.

hold plots have constituted an indispensable source of food supplies for non-agricultural workers, in that until the early 1960's approximately one-half of all milk, meat and vegetables produced in the U.S.S.R. came from auxiliary farms.[39]

The existence of millions of very small household plots operated on a free enterprise basis is something of an anomaly in the Soviet economy. The ultimate goal of the regime is to eliminate them. The Party Program states:

> "At a certain stage the communal production of collective farms will achieve a level at which it will be possible to satisfy the collective farmers' requirements fully out of its resources. On this basis individual supplementary farming will gradually become economically obsolete. When collective farm communal production is able to replace in full the collective farmers' individual supplementary farming and when the collective farmers see for themselves that it is unprofitable for them to have personal plots, they will give them up of their own accord."[40]

In 1963, Khrushchev apparently assumed that the state could dispense with the produce of the household plots and that the time spent by the peasants on their private farming operations could be used more advantageously in communal labor. Definite limits were placed on the permissible number of privately owned livestock and other restrictions designed to reduce the importance of auxiliary farming were introduced.[41] Khrushchev's successors did not agree with his analysis of the current importance of auxiliary farming. Three weeks after his demotion, all of the restrictions which he had placed on subsidiary husbandries were removed and collective and state farms were instructed to support auxiliary farming in a variety of ways including the sale of surplus fodder at reduced prices and the loan of draft animals and machinery for use on household plots.[42] The State Bank was also instructed to extend credit to individuals for the purchase of personal livestock. Apparently, private auxiliary farming will continue to make a substantial contribution to the food supply of the U.S.S.R. and to the economic well-being of collective farm members.

A number of collective farm workers also supplement their incomes by obtaining part-time employment in industrial or construction enterprises or on state farms. This practice is officially sanctioned, within limits, because many collective farms are unable to provide full-time employment for all members during the slack seasons and their gainful employment elsewhere adds to the overall productivity of labor. However, work on collective farms has sometimes been disrupted because so many members have taken advantage of the opportunity to work elsewhere for higher wages. For a number of years, farm members have been required to receive permission from the management prior to engaging in outside work.

State Farms

State farms (sovkhozy) are described as representing a higher level of socialist production since they are owned and operated entirely by the state. An ultimate goal of the regime is to convert all agriculture to the state farm model. State farms are established on all new land, including the 90 million acres of virgin land which was first cultivated in the mid 1950's, and, from time to time, measures have been taken to merge collective farms with state farms or to convert collective farms to state farms. A number of the poorer collective farms have welcomed the opportunity to convert to the state farm system primarily because of the more acceptable remuneration policy. State farm workers are paid regardless of yields and profit levels, whereas collective farm members receive only the residual income of the farm, after all other expenses have been paid, and bear the brunt of all the risks involved in farming with few of the associated advantages. The wages of state farm workers are determined by means of trade scales similar to those used in industry with established work norms for an eight hour work day. Approximately 80 percent of the workers' annual salary is paid on a monthly basis according to the established norms. Bonuses based on quality of work, overfulfillment of quotas, etc., may be added periodically or at the end of the year. Administrative personnel receive a guaranteed annual salary, equivalent to the salaries of persons of comparable skill in industry, with bonuses or penalties computed annually in proportion to the overfulfillment or underfulfillment of the plan. Each permanent state farm worker is permitted to use a household garden plot and to rent state-owned housing at a minimum fee. State farm workers do not, however, receive payment in kind as collective farm workers do, nor are they permitted to market the produce raised on their household plots.

Throughout the years, state farms have been given highly preferential treatment in comparison to collective farms. Whereas the kolkhoz has been required to pay out its own revenues for almost all of its investments in machinery, livestock and buildings, meet insurance and tax expenses, support its aged and sick members and support educational and cultural institutions, most of these items have been provided by the state for the state farms. Major state farm investments are budget-financed, and losses, which have been substantial, are covered by subsidies. State farm workers, like industrial workers, have always been eligible for old age and disability pensions and other social service benefits; it was not until 1964 that collective farmers were covered by a state sponsored social security program. Until the price revisions of the 1950's, collective farms received lower purchase prices for their produce and had to pay higher retail prices for their supplies. According to the 1965 price revisions, the collective farms will receive somewhat higher prices for a few products. The best agricultural equipment and the best qualified workers have been channeled by the state to the state farms. The majority of state farms are better equipped and more highly mechanized than collective farms and a greater proportion of them are supplied with electric power. State farms also have an advantage with respect to control over the labor force; workers may be hired or released on the basis of the need for their labor, whereas collective farms have to manage with a more or less stationary labor force which might be too small during peak rush seasons, but too large during slack seasons.

Since the mid 1950's state farms have been required to operate on a cost accounting system. The overall mode of operation resembles that of an industrial firm. The state appointed director is held responsible for the internal operation of the farm, subject to the directives and guidance of the Production Administration and superior state and party officials. The farm establishes its own detailed plans, in accordance with state and regional planning directives, for output, deliveries, cost, wages and capital expenditures. Budgetary limits are established by the republican authorities, and the details of the plan, especially output targets, may be revised by planning organs up to the republican level. The Production Administration bears the same relation to the state farm as to the collective farm, and may suggest revisions in the plan or modifications in actual farm operations. The state reserves the right to purchase all the produce of the state farms, except that needed for internal use. Many of the state farms are highly specialized and raise only grain, corn, cotton, sugar beets or livestock, while others engage in diversified production.

Agricultural Output

Agriculture has, with good reason, made a very sorry showing throughout the entire Soviet regime. Increases in agricultural output have been markedly below the expectations of the Soviet leaders and the needs of the Soviet population. According to figures presented by the U.S.S.R. Central Statistical Administration, from 1913 to 1963 the annual output of meat, milk and eggs increased by 102, 108 and 142 percent respectively, and grain output increased by approximately 75 percent.[43] During the same 50 year period the population increased by 42 percent. Considered independently from all other data, the figures for percentage increases in output are relatively impressive. However, when the low level of production during the base period, the emphasis on increased output, and population growth are taken into consideration, it is apparent that increases in agricultural output have been rather insignificant. For example, from 1913 to 1963 the annual output of eggs increased from 74 to 127 per member of the population and the output of meat products increased from 63 to 90 pounds per person; in 1963 Soviet farms produced approximately 2.5 eggs and 1.75 pounds of meat products per week per Soviet citizen.

According to the target figures for the Seven Year Plan (1959-1965), the gross output of agriculture should have risen by 70 percent during the seven year interval. Brezhnev stated flatly that during the first six years of the plan, the increase of gross agricultural output amounted to only 10 percent.[44] Current Soviet agricultural accomplishments are particularly unimpressive in view of the announcement in 1960 that agricultural output would increase by two and one-half times from 1961 to 1980, and Khrushchev's boast that within a few years the U.S.S.R. will surpass the United States in per capita production of all major agricultural products.

The post-Khrushchev leaders tend to be setting the goals for agriculture at a more realistic level and, at the same time, are attempting to provide agriculture with the necessary prerequisites for an upsurge in productivity. There is a potential for a very significant growth in the agricultural sector of the economy, and it is probable that at least some of this potential will be realized under the new agricultural program. After the long period of the neglect, abuse and impoverishment of agriculture, Soviet leaders have finally introduced some relatively realistic measures to remove the negative factors which impeded its natural growth and to apply positive, constructive measures to accelerate its expansion.

Even the powerful totalitarian regime of the Soviet Union can do nothing to manipulate basic soil and climatic conditions which are generally much less favorable to agriculture in the U.S.S.R. than in the U.S.A. However, the regime can manipulate a number of the factors which have impeded agricultural progress, many of which have been the result of the unenlightened policy of the regime itself. In the past, the price and procurement policy was such that the more a farm produced of certain products, the bigger the losses it suffered, and consequently, the smaller the earning of agricultural workers.[45] The new policies are designed to allocate some of the advantages of increased productivity to the farm workers, specialists and administrators. Labor productivity in agriculture has typically been excessively low; in 1958 Khrushchev stated that labor productivity on state and collective farms was approximately three and six times lower respectively than on American farms;[46] in 1964, a Soviet expert placed labor productivity in Soviet agriculture three to three and one-half times lower than in the United States.[47] The agricultural labor force in the U.S.S.R. averages one worker per 15 acres of sown area in comparison to one worker per 60 acres in the U.S.A. A number of interrelated factors have contributed to the low labor productivity in Soviet agriculture: shortages of machinery, spare parts, fertilizer, irrigation and other forms of material support; unenlightened interference; the system of remuneration; and the poor utilization and organization of the labor force. Many operations which could be mechanized are performed by manual labor. The system of assigning tasks and pay often results in a serious wastage of potential labor; for example, a worker responsible for serving a few motor vehicles may have long periods of inactivity during a time when there is a shortage of labor in the harvest fields. Periods of inactivity could be, but seldom are, used for productive work such as in the vegetable gardens or the orchards of the collective. However, better facilities for transporting vegetables to urban areas would be required to make the production of vegetables profitable for the farms. In short, with improved organizational forms, incentive systems, mechanization and transportation and marketing facilities, there could be a marked upsurge in labor productivity, and agricultural output could be increased substantially with no increase in the labor force.[48]

The regime can and probably will eventually provide adequate material support for agriculture. Currently, there is a great shortage of all kinds of farm machinery, and the available machinery is not used with maximum efficiency because spare parts are frequently not available, there are not enough repair shops, and in spite of or perhaps because of the numerous agencies responsible for the allocation of machinery, it is not unusual for grain farms to be supplied with all kinds of machinery for cotton growing while the cotton farms are burdened with grain combines. Tremendous losses result from extended sowing and harvesting operations due to equipment shortages.[49] In spite of the substantial funds which have been allocated to the chemical industries, agriculture has received totally inadequate supplies of fertilizer and insecticides. At present, both labor and produce are wasted because of lack of adequate storage facilities, processing plants and transportation. Grain rots in unprotected piles on the ground, and milk and vegetables that could be processed or distributed in urban areas to add to the cash revenues of the farm and the urban food supply are fed to livestock or discarded. Whenever the party leaders initiate a campaign for or against something, as for example, Khrushchev's campaign for increased emphasis on corn and his successors' campaign to reduce the emphasis on corn, pressures are brought to bear on the farms, through party and state channels, for the universal adoption of the proposal, even if local conditions make it highly inappropriate. Officials at all levels are eager to demonstrate that the farms under their jurisdiction are operating in accordance with the directives of the party leaders, even if the farms have to be cajoled into adopting unproductive practices. Moreover, the agricultural campaigns are usually initiated prior to the establishment of an adequate material basis for their fulfillment. For example, during the Khrushchev era, plans for increased production of machinery and fertilizer coincided with, rather than pre-ceded, the plans for the great upsurge in agricultural productivity, and the farms were expected to operate as if the material support were already available.

The post-Khrushchev leadership seems to be making a relatively sensible attack on the innumerable barriers which have impeded progress in agriculture. However, even if the new measures are implemented fully in accordance with the intended purposes, and even if no new barriers are imposed by the regime, and both of these events are rather unlikely in view of the regime's handling of agricultural matters in the past, Soviet agriculture cannot be expected to reach its maximum potential for a number of years. Time will be required to eradicate the effects of past abuses and to put into effect some of the proposed improvements such as land reclamation projects and increased mechanization. However, if a growth pattern in agriculture is finally established, it can be expected to have a strong cumulative effect because success in agriculture tends to be self-reinforcing; for example, higher prices and lower taxes should enable the farms to buy more machinery and fertilizer, which should in turn increase yields and income and encourage the farm workers to in-crease output. It would appear that the basic prerequisites for a spiral effect in agriculture have been or are being established. If no new burdens are imposed a significant progressive upsurge in the agricultural sector is likely within the next decade.

Impact on the Individual and Society

On the whole, the peasants have had little reason to feel grateful to the C.P.S.U., and hostility toward the regime has always been con-siderably stronger in rural than in urban areas. Despite the number of decades which have intervened, the resentment aroused by the forced collectivization, with its associated brutality, is still strong among the peasants. One of the major reasons for the persistence of the resentment is that when the state forced the peasants to join the collective, it did nothing to improve their economic and material situation, removed none of the risks associated with private farming, but deprived them of the independence and freedom of action that, to many, compensated for the risks and the hardships. The peasants still have a number of highly legiti-mate gripes against the regime, which has consistently given them the "short end of the stick." The party and the state have demanded as much from the collective farmers as from the workers, but have given them less in return. The collective farmers have been expected to work diligently in the communal economy, in spite of the fact that they re-ceived little, and sometimes next to nothing, in exchange for their labor. In general, the standard of living in rural areas has been even lower than in urban centers. Most of the collective farm households have had to get along without electricity, running water and other conveniences. Educational, medical and cultural facilities in rural areas have been markedly inferior to urban areas. The peasants have been singled out for the most intensive anti-religious indoctrination and, in general, have been less willing than the workers to give up their religious beliefs. During the early years of the regime, the peasants were placed under the tutelage of the workers, and the party leaders have always treated them as a less "advanced group." The prestige of a collective farmer in Soviet society is ordinarily considerably lower than that of a worker of comparable skill. In short, the peasants have borne more than their fair share of the hardships associated with the economic and social restructuring of society, and have been given less than their share of the credit and of the material rewards. Although policy changes introduced by the post-Khrushchev party leadership may alleviate the problems of the collective farmers, it is likely that several decades will be required to eradicate the major reasons for the antipathy of the peasants toward the regime.

REFERENCES

1 For an excellent article on the problems of Soviet agriculture, see Alec Nove, "Soviet Agriculture Marks Time," in Shaffer, *The Soviet Economy, op. cit.,* pp. 155-172.

2 V. I. Lenin, "Speech to the Tenth C.P.S.U. Congress," March 15, 1921, *Sochinenia,* IV ed., Moscow, 1952, Vol. XXXII, pp. 192-3.

3 L. E. Hubbard, *The Economics of Soviet Agriculture,* (London: Macmillan and Co., Ltd., 1939), p. 309.

4 Quoted in Naum Jasny, "Early Kolkhozy and Big Drive," in Holzman, *Readings on the Soviet Economy, op. cit.,* p. 309.

5 Kolkhozy in the Second Stalin Five Year Period, Gosplan, (Moscow, 1939), pp. 4-5.

6 Spulber, *The Soviet Economy, op. cit.,* p. 76.

7 V. V. Matskevich, "Tasks Posed by Life," *Trud,* April 4, 1965, p. 2. (C.D.S.P., Vol. XVII, No. 17, pp. 10-11)

8 L. I. Brezhnev, "On Urgent Measures for the Further Development of Agriculture in the U.S.S.R.," *Pravda,* March 27, 1965, pp. 2-4. (C.D.S.P., Vol. XVII. No. 12, pp. 3-11)

9 Cf. Lazar Volin, "Agricultural Policy of the Soviet Union," in Holzman, *Readings on the Soviet Economy, op. cit.,* pp. 285-318.

10 Brezhnev, "On Urgent Measures for the Further Development of Agriculture in the U.S.S.R.," *op. cit.,* pp. 2-4.

11 Matskevich, "Tasks Posed by Life," *op. cit.,* p. 2.

12 *Ibid.*

13 *Ibid.*

14 *Ibid.*

15 "In the Presidium of the Russian Republic Supreme Soviet," *Pravda,* March 3, 1965, p. 4.

16 "On Reorganization of the Management of Agriculture," *Pravda,* March 24, 1962, p. 1. (C.D.S.P., Vol. XIV, No. 13, pp. 10-13)

17 *Ibid.*

18 "Resolution of the C.P.S.U. Central Committee and U.S.S.R. Council of Ministers," *Pravda,* March 24, 1964, p. 1. (C.D.S.P., Vol. XVI, No. 12, pp. 10-11)

19 A. Komin, "Economic Substantiation of Purchase Prices of Agricultural Produce," *Planovoe khozaistvo,* 1962, No. 7. (Problems of Economics, Vol. V, No. 9, pp. 29-36)

20 Khrushchev, "On Measures to Fulfill the C.P.S.U. Program," *op. cit.,* pp. 1-5.

21 Komin, "Economic Substantiation of Purchase Prices," *op. cit.,* pp. 29-36.

22 Brezhnev, "On Urgent Measures for the Further Development of Agriculture in the U.S.S.R.," *op. cit.,* pp. 1-3.

23 *Ibid.*

24 *Ibid.*

25 *Ibid.*

26 *Ibid.*

27 *Ibid.*

28 "In the U.S.S.R. Council of Ministers," *Pravda,* April 11, 1965, p. 1; *Pravda,* April 15, 1965, p. 1. (C.D.S.P., Vol. XVII, No. 15, pp. 3-6)

29 Brezhnev, "On Urgent Measures for the Further Development of Agriculture in the U.S.S.R.," *op. cit.,* pp. 1-3.

30 *Ibid.*

31 "In C.P.S.U. Central Committee and U.S.S.R. Council of Ministers," *Pravda,* April 12, 1965, pp. 1-2. (C.D.S.P., Vol. XVII, No. 15, pp. 4-5)

32 "In the U.S.S.R. Council of Ministers," *op. cit.,* p. 1.

33 "In C.P.S.U. Central Committee and U.S.S.R. Council of Ministers," *Pravda,* April 20, 1965, p. 1. (C.D.S.P., Vol. XVII, No. 15, p. 6)

34 "Decree of the Presidium of the U.S.S.R. Supreme Soviet: On Collective Farm Income Tax," *Pravda,* April 11, 1965, p. 2. (C.D.S.P., Vol. XVII, No. 16, pp. 3-4)

35 Brezhnev, "On Urgent Measures for the Further Development of Agriculture in the U.S.S.R.," *op. cit.,* pp. 1-3.

36 M. D. Belous, "At the Foundation Lies Material Incentive," *Selskaya zhizn,* Nov. 15, 1964, p. 1. (C.D.S.P., Vol. XVI, No. 48, pp. 8-9)

37 *Ibid.*

38 I. Semenov, "Thoughts on Material Incentives," *Izvestia,* May 15, 1962, p. 3.

39 V. Venzher, "Supplementary Plots—An Additional Source of Agricultural Products," *Voprosy ekonomiki,* No. 7, July, 1962, pp. 58-69.

40 *Program of the Communist Party of the Soviet Union,* (Moscow: Foreign Languages Publishing House, 1961), p. 77.

41 "On Norms of Livestock in the Personal Possession of Citizens Who Are Not Members of Collective Farms," *Vedomosti Verkhovnovo Soveta R.S.F.S.R.,* No. 18, May, 1963, pp. 445-6. (C.D.S.P., Vol. XV, No. 22, pp. 25-6)

42 "In the C.P.S.U. Central Committee Bureau for the Russian Republic and the Russian Republic Council of Ministers," *Sovetskaya Rossia,* Nov. 14, 1964, p. 1. (C.D.S.P., Vol. XVI, No. 44, p. 3)

43 "Some Indices of the Living Standards in Our Country," *Izvestia,* July 25, 1964, p. 3.

44 Brezhnev, "On Urgent Measures for the Further Development of Agriculture in the U.S.S.R.," *op. cit.,* pp. 1-3.

45 *Ibid.*

46 N. S. Khrushchev, in a speech made Dec. 15, 1958. Figures are also summarized in an article by Artemy Shlikhter. (C.D.S.P., Vol. XI, No. 36, pp. 3-18, 31)

47 V. Starovsky, "Victorious Strides of the Soviet Economy and the Sorry Efforts of Unscrupulous 'Experts'," *op. cit.,* pp. 2-3.

48 Cf. Volin, "Agricultural Policy of the Soviet Union," *op. cit.,* pp. 285-318.

49 Brezhnev, "On Urgent Measures for the Further Development of Agriculture in the U.S.S.R., *op. cit.,* pp. 1-3.

CHAPTER X

INTERNATIONAL RELATIONS

Relations with Western Nations

Soviet foreign policy is designed to serve two distinct and sometimes incompatible goals. First, Soviet leaders are committed to the Marxist-Leninist goal of the establishment of a communist social order on a world-wide basis. The internationalist goals of Marxism-Leninism commit Soviet leaders to exert themselves unceasingly to weaken and discredit all governments and social orders which are opposed to communism, to foment revolutions and to provide ideological "guidance" and other support for any social movement which has the potential to undermine the strength of opponents to communism. As the self-appointed leaders, or rather propagators, of an international communist movement, the Soviet leaders have believed themselves to be entitled to disregard the accepted norms in international relations, and have, through their attempts to undermine other governments and social orders, earned well-deserved hostility. Second, Soviet foreign policy is designed to serve the national goals of the U.S.S.R. In this respect the foreign policy of the U.S.S.R. has resembled that of other great powers.[1] Its actions have been designed to protect its security, to expand its sphere of influence and to establish and retain its position as a great power. To achieve these goals it has, like other major nations, pursued balance of power tactics, established buffer states and exploited any opportunity to strengthen and extend its influence in any part of the world. It has, when expedient with respect to its own national purposes, co-operated with nations with diametrically opposed ideologies. Like other nations, in its own self-interest, it signs alliances and treaties and participates in summit meetings with its ideological opponents, joins world organizations and engages in international exchanges and trade.

From a very long-range view, the goals of the Soviet leaders for communizing the world and for the U.S.S.R. as a national power coincide in that the stronger the U.S.S.R. is in relation to other nations, the greater the probability that the international goals of communism will eventually be achieved, and, it might be added, the greater the probability that the U.S.S.R. would be able to dominate the movement. However, on a short range basis, the national and the international goals of the Soviet leaders do not always coincide. For example, overt support by the U.S.S.R. of a communist movement in a given nation could conceivably upset a precarious balance of power between the socialist and Western blocs and, thus, endanger Soviet national security; Soviet support of the expansionist policies of the Chinese communist leadership might bolster the international communist movement but, at the same time, endanger the Soviet position of hegemony over the movement. When forced to choose between national and international goals, the choice has typically been in favor of the national interests of the U.S.S.R. Regardless of whether a particular policy is designed primarily to serve national or international interests or if it reflects a genuine combination of the two, it is invariably presented as a faithful application of Marxist-Leninist ideology.

Like all other nations, the U.S.S.R. has from time to time modified the details of its foreign policy to take into account the actions of its allies and adversaries and its own changed status as a world power. Throughout the years, it has adhered to the Marxist-Leninist premise that there is a life and death struggle between capitalism and socialism for world supremacy. At the same time, in the interests of national security, it has almost as consistently adhered to the doctrine of peaceful coexistence of states with different social systems. Lenin, as ardent proponent of world revolution, was, during his tenure as leader of the Soviet state, anxious to avoid armed conflict with the Western powers, because he was well aware of the fact that the U.S.S.R. did not have the military strength to emerge as the victor, and also that peace was an indispensable prerequisite to solidify the gains of socialism in one country. Peaceful co-existence was for Lenin, as it has been for all Soviet leaders, a doctrine of national expediency. The doctrine of peaceful co-existence, however, did not prevent Lenin or any of his successors from fomenting revolution or trouble for capitalist nations whenever it was possible to do so without endangering the security of the Soviet Union. For example, the abortive socialist uprising in Germany in 1918 was Soviet inspired and supported. During the early years of his dictatorship, Stalin's assessment of the U.S.S.R.'s relative strength made it expedient for him to pursue a relatively isolationist foreign policy while he concentrated on building socialism at home. As it became increasingly evident that the fascist powers would precipitate the outbreak of a major war, the national security of the U.S.S.R. took precedence over the goals of the international communist movement. Stalin approached his ideological opponents, Britain and France, with the intention of entering into defensive alliances. The Western powers, however, rebuffed his overtures primarily on the basis of the vain hope that the fascist war machines could be turned away from themselves and against the U.S.S.R., and that Hitler and his allies would wear themselves out in a prolonged conflict against the U.S.S.R., thereby ridding the world of the fascist and the communist threats simultaneously. Stalin reacted to the rebuff by negotiating a mutual non-aggression pact with Hitler. Although his primary goal was to protect the U.S.S.R., he also hoped that the fascist and democratic countries would destroy each other and that the U.S.S.R. would be able to emerge as the most powerful nation in the world. This would, of course, have been an extraordinarily efficient approach for materializing both the national and international goals of the Soviet leadership since, if the U.S.S.R. had been able to remain neutral while the major Western countries had engaged in mutual destruction, the U.S.S.R. would have enjoyed unique advantages in its attempts to impose its social order on the rest of the world.

When Germany and its allies unleashed their war machines against both the Western democracies and the U.S.S.R., ideological differences posed no barrier to mutual co-operation. For both the Western allies and the U.S.S.R., national security took precedence over ideological differences. Although mutual co-operation was the keynote of the wartime relationships, none of the members of the anti-fascist alliance refrained from operations and negotiations designed to enhance the strength of the individual nation. Both the U.S.S.R. and the Western allies regarded the alliance as one of convenience. As soon as the mutual enemy was annihilated and the victory was assured, there was nothing to hold the alliance together. Even before the final victory, the alliance began to disintegrate; each of the major allies began to act primarily on the basis of its own national interests, and ideological differences, which had been played down or totally overlooked during the period of mutual danger, again emerged in major proportions.

During the last stages of the war and the early post-war period, relations between the U.S.S.R. and her Western allies deteriorated rapidly for the simple reason that both sides were engaged in jockeying for power. The U.S.S.R. sought to reward itself for its wartime sacrifices by extending its sphere of influence over all the territories which it had either occupied or liberated, and in as far as possible, by making ideological advances in the areas which had been occupied by Western troops. The Western powers, though much less eager to extend their military domination, were equally determined that Western ideology should not be replaced by Marxist ideology and that the Western-style, democratic, private enterprise social orders should not be replaced by Soviet-style socialism. Soviet foreign policy during this period was characterized by a strong expansionist drive; the U.S.A. and her allies reacted with an equally strong policy designed to resist Soviet expansion, the policy of "Soviet containment." By 1947 the wartime alliance had degenerated into the Cold

War with mutual hostility characterizing all points and all levels of contact between the U.S.S.R. and the U.S.A.[2]

The Cold War developed primarily because the U.S.S.R. and the U.S.A. were pursuing roughly identical national and international goals, and because each served as a barrier to the fulfillment of the goals of the other. Each sought to ensure its own national security, to enhance its own national stature, to extend its own sphere of influence and to increase the probability that its own social order and ideology would be adopted by as many nations as possible. The early post-war techniques varied, however, in that the U.S.S.R. tended to rely more heavily on force, threat and subversion, whereas the Western allies placed more emphasis on persuasion, example, democratic processes and the beneficial effects of economic aid. Neither side has hesitated to use any technique that was potentially safe and effective with reference to its overall goals. Both sides have entered into defensive alliances, established buffer states and built up their military might in order to deter the advance of the other side.

The techniques of Soviet foreign policy have been modified slightly from time to time with changing circumstances, but the goals have remained essentially the same from the post-war Stalin era through the Khrushchev era and into the post-Khrushchev era. The chief change in technique during the post-Stalin era was the greater emphasis on the policy of peaceful co-existence between nations with different ideologies. Khrushchev's emphasis on peaceful co-existence did not herald a basic change in policy, but rather represented an attempt to facilitate the materialization of long standing goals. His successors almost immediately indicated their continued commitment to the policy of peaceful co-existence.[3]

Soviet post-war aims have been to consolidate the gains that the U.S.S.R. made during the war and to exploit any opportunity that might offer itself to strengthen and extend Soviet influence in any part of the world. However, the American policy of containment has stymied Soviet progress and has placed definite limits on the techniques which the Soviet Union has been able to use. Initially, the U.S.S.R. was forced to proceed with considerable caution because the United States had nuclear weapons while it did not. Even since the U.S.S.R. has built up its own powerful nuclear arsenals, it has been adamantly opposed to military conflict because it realizes that there would be no victor in a thermo-nuclear war. Nevertheless, the U.S.S.R. has tended to pursue its expansionist policies as boldly as it dares, and to withdraw, always under the cloak of the very moral desire for peace, when its policies are challenged. The Cuban situation in 1962 was a clear-cut example of a bold military expansion tactic which was hastily withdrawn when pressure was applied. Actually, since the early post-war period, the Soviet Union has relied relatively little on the direct use of military force as an expansion technique because of the tremendous danger involved. Instead, it has attempted to attain its national and international goals through a number of approaches which are little affected by the containment policy and are not subject to military challenge. Techniques to expand Soviet influence have included the attempt to demonstrate the economic advantages of socialism, heavy emphasis on indoctrination and the development of ideological conflict and class struggle, subversion, assistance to national liberation movements and to underdeveloped countries, fomenting trouble where it can for its adversaries, particularly the U.S.A., and the creation of a favorable world image for itself and an unfavorable image of Western states.

Soviet foreign policy during the post-war years and to the present may be summarized by saying that no method short of armed conflict between the major world powers is ruled out in the drive of the U.S.S.R. to protect its own security, to expand its own influence and power, to weaken its opponents, and to pave the way for the eventual emergence of a world-wide socialist order. Soviet leaders have carefully avoided such inferences, but their actions indicate that an integral part of their goal is Soviet domination of a communized world.

Although Soviet foreign policy may be directed primarily toward the attainment of the national goals of the U.S.S.R., Soviet statements of foreign policy are couched predominantly in terms of Marxist-Leninist international goals. Obviously, there is not a one to one relationship between Soviet statements of foreign policy and Soviet actions in the international sphere; often noble words are followed by base actions, or as in the case of the 1956 Hungarian revolution, base actions are followed by noble words. Equally obvious, leaders in other nations also engage in the practice of saying one thing about foreign policy and doing another. In spite of the fact that the foreign policy statements of Soviet leaders do not accurately reflect either the goals or the practices of the Soviet Union in international affairs, it is interesting to examine these statements because of their potential propaganda value, and because the pronouncements are not entirely divorced from **reality.**

The goals of Soviet foreign policy with respect to Western nations, stated in the simplest terms, are twofold: first, to protect and strengthen the U.S.S.R.; second, to weaken and, if possible, destroy the existing order in the Western states. Because the goal of national security and aggrandizement can be more or less subsumed under the goal of destroying the Western social order, official statements by Soviet leaders tend to emphasize the conflict between social orders. According to a Soviet-dictated statement of the Moscow Conference of Communist Parties, "The development of international relations in our time is determined by the struggle of the two social systems—the struggle of the forces of socialism, peace and democracy against the forces of imperialism, reaction and aggression. . . ."[4] Khrushchev, himself, expressed Soviet goals for the Western social order in more earthy language. He commented that during the Civil War the Red soldiers used to say that the basic dispute between the Whites and the Reds was over the land question since "the Whites want to bury us in the land and we want to bury the Whites. Who will bury whom first? That is our small dispute." According to Khrushchev the same kind of small dispute exists between socialism and capitalism.

> "It wants to bury the socialist system, while we want—and not only want, but have even dug quite a deep hole, and will exert further efforts to dig this hole deeper and bury forever the capitalist system, the system of exploitation, war and plunder. And capitalism will fall—of this there can be no doubt. But it will not fall by itself."[5]

At the same time as the Soviet leaders talk about burying capitalism, they stress their adherence to the policy of peaceful co-existence of states with different social systems which, according to Brezhnev:

> ". . . is aimed at preventing a thermo-nuclear world war, at settling disputes among nations by negotiations, respecting the right of each people to choose for itself the social and state system that it wishes, at deciding itself the questions of the internal development of its country."[6]

Taken at face value, the Soviet doctrine of peaceful co-existence could be interpreted as a policy of "live and let live," as a plea for the peaceful and parallel development of divergent social orders, and as an ideological retreat from Marxist-Leninist internationalism. Of course, the doctrine means none of these things. On the contrary, it is an attempt on the part of the Soviet leaders to provide a social climate which will facilitate materialization of their plans to "bury capitalism."

Soviet leaders are completely sincere in their desire to avoid a major military conflict with the Western powers. Their reasons are manifold. In a nuclear holocaust, both sides would be destroyed, and even if the socialist forces were to emerge as the "victors," socialism would have to be built from the ashes of a ruined civilization. They assert that permanent peace is one of the goals for which they are striving, since their goals for mankind can be achieved only if peace can be maintained. Moreover, they draw on the Marxist-Leninist proposition that internal contradictions within the capitalist system make its downfall inevitable, and therefore, the socialist countries need not undertake the risks involved in destroying capitalism through war. In their official statements, they purposely gloss over the internal strengths of the Western states, but in their subversive activities they do their utmost to undermine the very strengths which are treated as non-existent from an official point of view. Peace is a prerequisite for the achievement of the economic and social goals through which the Soviet leaders hope to demonstrate the superiority of socialism and to encourage working people throughout the world to "rise up against their oppressors" and demand a social system modelled along Soviet lines. Soviet leaders have reiterated, with realism, that if the demands of the people of the non-socialist nations are to contribute to the victory of socialism, socialism must demonstrate its advantages through concrete evidence rather than utopian promises. Khrushchev proclaimed:

> "No matter what ardent and passionate speeches are made, how many oaths are sworn that socialism is the best social system, if these words are not backed up by deeds, things will not change. The people judge by what socialism gives them, not according to speeches and promises but according to how their situation changes with the victory of socialism, what kind of political rights, what kind of freedom socialism brings them, how their material situation improves—that is, how much bread, meat, butter and other products a person can get for his labor, how many clothes he has and of what quality, how he can use his working time, how he can rest, how his spiritual needs are more and more fully satisfied. And if socialism does not provide this, does not give the people greater advantages than capitalism, then those who advocate such socialism will be windbags and not revolutionaries."[7]

To date, the U.S.S.R. has failed dismally in its attempt to demonstrate that socialism gives the people greater advantages than private enterprise systems, and therefore, can have no justifiable hope that "oppressed" workers in advanced Western nations will attempt to overthrow their government in order to attain standards of living and personal freedoms commensurate with those attained by citizens of the U.S.S.R. Their potential success with this gambit in the underdeveloped and new nations is somewhat greater; for people who are leading a marginal existence under a harsh dictatorial regime, the example of the U.S.S.R.'s rapid industrial progress, and the rising standards of living may have some appeal, particularly when skillful Soviet propaganda overrates Soviet accomplishments and grossly distorts reality with respect to Western societies. Moreover, the Soviet Union's extremely vocal stand on world peace, which is ordinarily combined with highly derogatory statements about the war mongering nations of the West, has been used as a fairly effective technique to gain sympathy for the communist cause. The Soviet leadership, well aware of the fact that the majority of mankind does not want, and is profoundly afraid of, a nuclear war, builds up the fear by participating fully in the arms race and by emphasizing the dangers of war, and at the same time, tries to earn the gratitude of people of all nations through the firm Soviet stand against war and as the guardian of peace.

As part of its policy of peaceful co-existence, the U.S.S.R. has been negotiating with Western powers since 1946 on arms control and disarmament. In nearly every conference, the Soviet Union has made sweeping proposals for general disarmament, abandonment of nuclear testing or some arms control device. Its disarmament proposals are always accompanied by moving propaganda statements: the interests of all mankind, they point out, will be served if economic resources are used for constructive purposes and if the fear of war is reduced by a reduction in the stockpile of arms along with a stabilization in the balance of terror at a lower level of destructive power. The U.S.S.R., they assert, can be fully sincere in its disarmament overtures, since no group within Soviet society gains from the arms race; military expenditures are an unmitigated economic liability for the U.S.S.R. since the growth of the entire economy is hampered by the need to divert financial, material and labor resources away from growth-inducing industries for military purposes. Soviet propaganda statements assert that the Western powers are unwilling, or unable, to enter into an effective disarmament agreement, in spite of the good intentions and reasonable proposals of the U.S.S.R., because of the militaristic aspirations of Western reactionary groups, particularly in the U.S.A. and Western Germany, the imperialistic motives of the Western nations, and the political power of military groups and the manufacturers of military weapons who have a vested interest in maintaining the arms race. However, in spite of its highly moral stand and its sweeping disarmament proposals, the U.S.S.R. has, with full co-operation from the Western nations, effectively blocked the adoption of any major measure to limit the arms race. The U.S.S.R.'s major obstruction technique has been her refusal to agree to any enforceable provision to police or ensure enforcement of a potential agreement.

Several factors have probably contributed to the Soviet refusal to submit to enforcement techniques which would be acceptable to the Western nations. First, the U.S.S.R. apparently considers that its sovereignty would be violated, and that it would be almost inviting espionage activity if it were to agree to admit outsiders with inspection control functions. Soviet spokesmen argue that instruments which detect nuclear explosions are sufficient to check on the fulfillment of nuclear testing agreements, and that additional inspections are superfluous. In a sense, agreement to an international inspection agency might represent capitulation of Soviet aims to the Western conception of international order. Second, the U.S.S.R., which can manipulate the implied risk of war with somewhat more flexibility than the Western democratic nations, is not above using the uncertainties of the thermo-nuclear balance of terror as an instrument to produce pressures for accommodation in the West. For example, one of the Soviet gains from the Cuban situation was the expressed, or implied, indignation of many Western nations that the United States should have led them to the brink of a nuclear war. Third, the U.S.S.R.'s drive for "general and complete disarmament" is a political instrument designed to enlist the support of all peace loving people from all classes and all nations. Of course, for this weapon to have continued effectiveness the

U.S.S.R. must either demonstrate that it has contributed materially to disarmament agreements or must place the blame for lack of agreement squarely and unequivocally on the shoulders of the Western nations. The Soviet propaganda machine has done its utmost to achieve the latter goal. However, the U.S.S.R.'s fairly skillful use of the prolonged arms race may merely reflect a relatively sensible, self-interested adjustment to the reality situation. The fact of the matter is probably that the U.S.S.R., like the Western nations, sincerely desires to limit or terminate the arms race, but that neither side is willing to agree to anything which does not either improve or maintain its relative position in the balance of power. The Limited Test Ban Treaty, which was signed in 1963, constitutes the first major step toward a disarmament agreement between the two opposed blocs. In this case, it was apparently possible to reach a mutually satisfactory understanding without affecting the established balance of power.

Khrushchev summarized the official Soviet propaganda line on relations with Western powers in the following terms:

". . . the greater our economic successes, the higher is the prestige of the Soviet state in the international arena and the more attractive to the peoples of the world is the policy of peace and peaceful co-existence that our party's Central Committee and the Soviet government are constantly pursuing.

"It is precisely because our general line in international affairs is in the course toward peaceful co-existence between states with different social systems, toward economic competition between them, . . . that the Soviet state . . . has waged and will continue to wage a tireless struggle to solve the problems of disarmament. . . . The course toward economic competition and the course toward disarmament stem in equal measure from the social nature of our society. Since we are convinced that the socialist system is demonstrating its advantages over the capitalist system in the field of peaceful economic competition and is gaining victory over it—and we are as sure of this as we are sure that spring always follows winter—we do not have and cannot have any incentive toward the arms race.

"And if the Soviet Union is perfecting its defenses, . . . we are doing it only because we must do it in the face of the armed imperialist states and the military preparations of the aggressive blocs. . . .

"The Soviet people are peaceful people. We are engaged in carrying out majestic creative plans. But we want to warn those who place their hopes on the force of arms in their relations with socialist states, who have been poisoned by the revanchist fumes: The day they dare to unleash aggression will be their last day. The Soviet Union has everything necessary and in sufficient supply to restrain any aggressor, to ensure the safety of our people and the peoples of the socialist countries.

"But, I repeat, the Soviet Union proposes competition not in preparations for war but in the sphere of peace. We are opposed to the arms race. . . . The Soviet Union is convinced that there is a more realistic approach to the question of how states with different social systems can live together on the same planet."[8]

Thus, the Soviet Union asserts that it will consistently strive for peace, but that as long as it perceives danger of aggression from the West, it will maintain its massive military machine as a deterrent to aggression; that it has no need for war because it will eventually demonstrate so much economic and social superiority that the peoples of the world will demand adoption of a social order which emulates the Soviet system.

The Soviet doctrine of peaceful co-existence of states with different social systems does not incorporate an acceptance on their part of the status quo. The Soviet leaders are dedicated to the perfection, defense and promulgation of their version of a world order through the use of all available resources and techniques. By the same token, the Western leaders are equally dedicated to the containment, or preferably the elimination, of communist based societies, and to the extension of the democratic, private enterprise social order. The attempts of both sides to avoid a major military conflict do not reflect a rapproachment of goals, or a partial capitulation on the part of either. The conflict between systems involves all aspects of life and all resources of both contestants, and is waged in the economic and ideological spheres, through diplomatic channels, by subversion, with propaganda tactics, with military and economic assistance to less developed areas, support for friendly or pliable political leaders in other nations and through limited military engagements. In the continuing, long-range struggle between the two competitors for a world order, the Soviet Union has attempted to maintain an offensive strategy, which permits it to determine the time, place and weapons to be used in a crucial engagement. Its policy of peaceful co-existence is one of attempted extension of the sphere of Soviet influence and weakening of its competitors through any means short of a military conflict between the major powers.

Marxism-Leninism is used as a major ideological weapon for the extension of Soviet influence. Soviet leaders are very explicit that the doctrine of peaceful co-existence does not apply to the ideological sphere. The Central Committee of the C.P.S.U. stated:

> "Peaceful co-existence does not mean reconciling socialist and bourgeois ideologies. . . . Peaceful co-existence of states with different social systems assumes an unrelenting ideological, political and economic struggle between the two social systems; class struggle by the working people within the countries of the capitalist system, including armed struggle when the people deem that necessary; and the steady broadening of the national-liberation movement of the peoples in colonial and dependent countries."9

Khrushchev elaborated:

> "To agree to peaceful co-existence of the communist and bourgeois ideologies—this means to give the enemy an opportunity to blacken everything most dear to us, to encourage slander, to facilitate corruption of the people's consciousness, to destroy our self-discipline and in every way to retard our advance. We have fought and will continue with all implacability to fight not only against corrupt bourgeois ideology, but against its agents in our midst, as agents of our class enemies."10

Soviet leaders are diligent in their attempts to discredit and limit the potential influence of "bourgeois" ideology and to gain adherents in other nations to Marxism-Leninism. All the familiar techniques to gain support are used: propaganda, timely economic or military assistance, political support, free Soviet education for potential national leaders, etc. Concurrently, expedient measures are taken to encourage intensification of class struggle within national states. Soviet leaders have frequently expressed the belief that peaceful co-existence creates a favorable climate for the development of class struggle in capitalist countries and in emerging or underdeveloped national states. Khrushchev proclaimed:

> "From the first days of the birth of the socialist world there has been competition between it and the capitalist world. The question of which system will stand in this competition and which will suffer defeat . . . is being decided in the international arena. Peaceful co-existence between states with different social systems does not at all mean that there is any slackening of the class struggle in the international arena, and since class struggle is under way, peaceful co-existence in the field of ideology is impossible. . . . The successes of the Soviet Union in Communist construction and the successes of the other socialist countries strengthen the faith of the working class in every country in its own strength, they arouse the oppressed peoples to the struggle for freedom, act on the consciousness of the intelligentsia in the various countries of the world and arm the fighters for the cause of socialism in the ideological struggle against the forces of imperialism. . . . Our successes will inspire the working class of all the capitalist countries to more resolute and active revolutionary class struggle. . . . The people of the various countries who are struggling for their freedom and independence are receiving our help today, while tomorrow there will be even greater possibilities for rendering assistance of a different character as well."[11]

Needless to say, the U.S.S.R. has been doing its utmost to aid and abet the development of internal dissension, particularly in new and underdeveloped nations. Its "guidance" in Cambodia, Laos, Ghana, Mali, Guatemala, Cuba, Panama, North Korea, North Vietnam, the Congo and many other states has been designed to weaken or destroy pro-American regimes, to lay the groundwork for the eventual establishment of communist or pro-communist regimes, or simply to discredit or embarrass the Western powers. Although these activities have not attained any concrete victories for the U.S.S.R., they have constituted a continual nuisance-type annoyance for the United States and her allies, who have been forced to divert attention, resources and military forces to areas which without Soviet "guidance" would not have been troublesome from the Western point of view. At the same time, in a number of these countries, the internal chaos has been used to advantage by Soviet-trained native politicians in their attempts to win converts to Marxism-Leninism and the Soviet style social order.

In its drive to achieve its national and international goals, the U.S.S.R. has engaged itself in an all-out struggle of indefinite duration to bring about the triumph of socialism over capitalism and is willing to use any weapon short of a nuclear attack to achieve its goals. Although it is convinced that historical processes are working in its favor, it has assumed responsibility for accelerating the historical process. Its doctrine of peaceful co-existence is a tactical weapon which is intended to yield a number of advantages in addition to decreasing the probability of the outbreak of a thermo-nuclear war which neither bloc wants. Peace is a prime prerequisite for the economic growth of the U.S.S.R. and for it to exert its maximum ideological influence on the peoples of other nations. The U.S.S.R. maintains diplomatic and trade relations with Western nations in its own best interests and encourages scientific and cultural exchanges as a demonstration of the Soviet willingness to cooperate, and in order to draw Soviet accomplishments to the favorable attention of other nations. All its dealings with Western nations are intended to influence the balance of power or world opinion in favor of the Soviet Union and the socialist social order. Through its proposals for complete disarmament, its consistent stand on peace, its apparent willingness to negotiate, its anti-colonial pronouncements and its support for the political and economic aspirations of the less developed countries, the Soviet Union is attempting to advance its goals by creating a favorable image of itself as the helpful, progressive, peace-loving friend of the masses. Concurrently, it does its utmost to distort the image and weaken the prestige of the Western democracies.

National Liberation Movement

The C.P.S.U. "considers the national liberation movement to be a component part of the world revolutionary process, a mighty force acting against imperialism."[12] By posing as the champion of all oppressed peoples and providing assistance to revolutionary movements and new national regimes, even those that are not sympathetic to the communist cause, the Soviet Union hopes to detract from the strength of the anti-communist bloc, and eventually to increase the size of the socialist bloc. The position of the Soviet Union is that any change in the non-communist world is potentially advantageous to the Soviet cause. The Central Committee of the C.P.S.U. stated:

> "Socialist revolutions, national liberation, anti-imperialist, anti-colonial revolutions, popular democratic revolutions, broad peasant movements, the struggle of the masses for the overthrow of fascist and other tyrannical regimes and the general democratic movements against national oppression—these are all merging in our time into a single world revolutionary torrent that is undermining and destroying capitalism."[13]

Needless to say, Soviet leaders are constantly seeking ways to gain from uprisings, forces seeking social change and internal problems in other states. Their support for newly emerging nations does not constitute a denial of the internationalism of Marxism-Leninism, but rather involves a realistic assessment of the strength of nationalistic sentiments among the former colonial peoples. Support of nationalistic movements is a stepping stone, a device to gain the sympathy of and influence over the population of the new states, to weaken Western influence and to increase the likelihood that eventually the new nations can be lured into the socialist camp.

Soviet support for national liberation combines economic, military and political assistance with a powerful battery of propaganda designed to encourage the people to chafe under the "yoke of colonialism," to demand new rights, to have faith in their own strength, to rise up against the political regime, to discredit the capitalist countries and to portray the U.S.S.R. as a solicitous and helpful ally, willing to make unselfish sacrifices because of its overwhelming concern for the welfare of all mankind. A statement of the Central Committee of the C.P.S.U. summarizes and illustrates several of the most important features of the Soviet propaganda line and the professed Soviet policy in this sphere:

> "The CPSU looks upon its fraternal alliance with the peoples who have thrown off the colonial yoke and with semi-colonial peoples as one of the cornerstones of its foreign policy. Our party considers it its internationalist duty to assist peoples who are on the road to achieving and consolidating national independence, all people who are fighting for the total abolition of the colonial system. . . . Our party regards the national liberation movement as an integral part of the world revolutionary process, as a potent force that is smashing the imperialist front. . . . The growing strength of the socialist system is actively contributing to the liberation of oppressed peoples and their achievement of economic independence, to the further development and expansion of the national liberation movement, of its struggle against all forms of colonialism, new and old. . . . The compelling tasks of national rebirth in countries that have cast off the colonial yoke can be successfully accomplished only if an all-out struggle is waged against imperialism and the vestiges of feudalism, if all patriotic forces of a nation—the working class, peasantry, national bourgeoisie and democratic intelligentsia—have been lined up in a united national front.
> ". . . The attainment of full independence by the underdeveloped countries would mean a serious new weakening of imperialism, for the whole present international division of labor, a predatory and inequitable system, would be wrecked, and the foundation on which the exploitation of the 'world village' by capitalist monopolies rests would be undermined."[14]

Soviet goals with respect to the national liberation movement are clear cut: to weaken Western influence and strengthen and extend Soviet influence. Soviet tactics, however, vary with the phase of the movement and with local conditions. During the earliest phases of a national liberation movement, an attempt is made to unite all groups, classes and forces to work together in an attempt to overthrow the existing social order. Marxist-Leninist Parties are advised to "call for the creation of states of national democracy whose political basis is a bloc of all progressive, patriotic forces that fight for the full insurance of national independence, for broad democracy, for pursuing the anti-imperialistic, anti-feudal and democratic revolution to its end."[15] The U.S.S.R. is completely willing to support a movement led by a strongly anti-communist national bourgeois faction, since the initial goal is to strike a blow against capitalism and to encourage the development of a new state which might eventually be brought into the socialist camp. The establishment of a new state, the Soviet leaders say, "is a form of the transition of the liberated countries from colonial dependency to the path of non-capitalist development."[16]

After a new state is established, the U.S.S.R. is ordinarily willing to provide it with military, economic, cultural or other assistance, regardless of the class or political ideals of the new leadership. Soviet goals during this phase involve an attempt to weaken Western influence on the new regime, to win admiration for the U.S.S.R. and its social order and to establish conditions for a proletarian victory in a class struggle which the communists believe is inevitable. Soviet theoreticians assert that, although several classes unite against a common enemy during a liberation struggle, the former allies diverge after independence is achieved because each class has different goals for the structure of the new society. The bourgeois nationalists, they say, attempt to impede the development of workers' movements toward socialism in order to protect their own class interests. "The only class," Soviet writers state, "that fights consistently against imperialism and capitalism as systems and that remains interested in their final liquidation is the proletariat, and only under the leadership of the world proletariat and in close alliance with it can the objective anti-capitalist potential of the national liberation movement be revealed."[17]

Theoretically, as the "class struggle emerges" in the new national states, the U.S.S.R. would be expected to throw the weight of its support behind the local Communist Parties which serve as the self-appointed leaders of the working class. However, in practice, the Soviet leadership has more frequently decided that its immediate goals would be achieved best through active support of a national regime, including regimes which refused to co-operate with the local Communist Party. A case in point is Soviet assistance to Nasser of Egypt, despite the fact that Nasser outlawed the Egyptian Communist Party. The Soviet rationale in such cases has been that more is to be gained by substantially weakening the prestige and influence of the Western nations, particularly the U.S.A., than by supporting a local Communist Party which could, almost certainly, not gain control over the state. When the U.S.S.R. supports an anti-Communist or neutral regime, its dual role as a nation and as the head of a revolutionary party which seeks to overthrow existing regimes may decrease the effectiveness of its endeavors in both roles. Its position as the leader of the international communist movement is weakened when it supports regimes antagonistic to local Communist Parties, and the psychological effect of its assistance to a non-communist regime is reduced because Marxist-Leninist ideology stands for the ultimate overthrow of the regime, and because the local party, unless specifically restrained by Moscow, usually engages in harassment.

The C.P.S.U. asserts that, at the same time as it is striving to avert a world war, it "considers it to be the sacred right of every people to undertake a war of liberation or a popular uprising against oppressors."[18] According to communist logic, the people who live within the socialist camp have no justification for exercising this "sacred right" because they are not subjected to oppression. The 1956 Hungarian uprising, for example, is described by Soviet authorities as an attempt on the part of counterrevolutionary forces to reintroduce oppression of the masses, rather than as a popular uprising against the oppressors. Soviet intervention is described as a "humanitarian response" to a request for assistance from the leadership which most adequately represented the "true interests of the Hungarian people" and the "help" which was given to the "Hungarian people" in defending "their socialist gains" is presented as a "worthy example of the fulfillment of international duty and proletarian solidarity."[19] According to Soviet leaders, uprisings in areas beyond the Soviet sphere of control are fundamentally different in that they constitute a struggle for freedom and independence from "capitalist exploiters." "Wars of liberation," Khrushchev said,

> ". . . will occur while imperialism still exists and while colonialism still exists. These are revolutionary wars. These wars are not only permissible but inevitable because the colonialists will not grant the peoples independence voluntarily. Therefore, it is only through struggle, including armed struggle, that the peoples can win their freedom and independence."[20]

Although Soviet leaders state that to be successful, revolutions should be internally inspired and supported, the U.S.S.R. uses all techniques available to it, short of actually initiating hostilities, to encourage uprisings. It encourages local leaders to incite and indoctrinate the masses, and is eager to provide military, economic or moral support to any faction or group that is willing to engage in armed conflict or any other action that would be troublesome to a Western state or has potential to weaken the strength or prestige of the non-communist world. During the early 1960's, Soviet military and economic assistance and propaganda played an important role in the civil wars in Algeria, the Congo, Laos and Vietnam; in the controversies between Pakistan and Afghanistan, and Israel and the Arab states; in the revolutions in South Korea, Angola, Cuba and Madagascar; and most dramatically, in the controversy between the United States and Cuba. The U.S.S.R. always justifies its military assistance on highly moralistic and humanitarian grounds: it is providing comradely assistance to weak and oppressed peoples who are waging a just battle against well-armed capitalist oppressors. In fact, the U.S.S.R. misses no opportunity to divide and destabilize the non-communist world, to detract from the strength of the powerful Western nations and to gain support for its own policies.

The U.S.S.R. contends that even after political freedom has been attained, the new states must struggle to free themselves from the neo-colonial bonds of economic dependence on capitalist countries. Consequently, after a new national regime is established, either following armed conflict as in the case of Algeria and Cuba, or through a peaceful transition as in the case of the majority of the former British colonies, the U.S.S.R. pays particular attention to extending its influence through economic, technical and cultural assistance. Economic assistance has taken a variety of forms, including outright gifts, long term credits and loans at low interest rates (usually 2 or 2.5 percent), trade relations, support for growth-inducing industries, geological surveys and technical guidance. Soviet foreign aid to new and underdeveloped countries is carefully integrated with other aspects of foreign policy to support fulfillment of political aims. A continued barrage of propaganda statements make unfavorable comparisons between Western and Soviet foreign aid. Soviet sources contend that:

> "Whereas imperialist loans serve as instruments of colonial expansion and enslavement of underdeveloped countries, the aid of socialist states is called upon—and herein lies its principal importance—to further the economic liberation of the countries of Asia, Africa and Latin America from the fetters of foreign monopoly capital, to help these countries create a national economy."[21]

According to Soviet propagandists, the United States and her allies demand from the recipient, in exchange for assistance, the right to intervene in the politics of the nation including specification of the form of government and selection of major governmental officials; to control foreign policy; to establish military bases; and to forbid trade relations with recalcitrant states such as Cuba. They argue that it matters little to the capitalist nations if the funds which they assign to an underdeveloped nation such as the Dominican Republic are used almost exclusively for the personal gratification of the elite, politically powerful clique while the masses starve, provided that the leadership of the recipient nation is subservient to its benefactor. Soviet foreign aid, on the other hand, is described by Soviet propagandists as unselfish, comradely assistance provided without political strings and motivated solely by the desire to improve the welfare of the people. The recipients, they say, are not required to adopt the Soviet social order, to permit Soviet military bases to be established on their soil or to submit to Soviet direction of their internal or foreign policies.

The Soviet analysis of motivation underlying Western and Soviet aid to new and developing countries is obviously one-sided and biased, and the claim that the U.S.S.R. has no ulterior motives is grossly untrue. However, the U.S.S.R. does possess some unique advantages in its relations with these countries which enable it to reap disproportionately high advantages for a monetary expenditure in foreign aid which has been only a fraction of the expenditures of the Western allies. The U.S.S.R.'s greatest advantage is that it bears no responsibility for the existing social orders in the new and underdeveloped countries and has no desire to maintain the *status quo*. It can, on the other hand, exploit the violent anti-colonial and anti-Western sentiments that have gripped many of these countries, identify itself with the national aspirations of the population, disparage Western assistance and encourage the local populace to engage in almost any action directed toward change. To accomplish its goals, the U.S.S.R. has absolutely no need to interfere directly in the internal or foreign policies of the new nations. In the main, all that it has to do is to give a little well placed aid here and there, build a favorable image of itself and its social order, discredit Western nations, foster local dissatisfaction and internal conflict without direct intervention and then sit back and wait. The Western powers are in a much less enviable position. In most nations, current woes are blamed on the past policies of the West, and Western nations frequently must apply their foreign aid policies against a backdrop of intense hostility. Even more important, because the Western nations do take responsibility for the welfare of recipient nations and are interested in maintaining some kind of stability, they sometimes have no choice but to involve themselves in the internal and foreign policies of the recipients of their aid. Soviet propagandists naturally exploit to the hilt their relative advantages in this sphere.

The U.S.S.R. has placed considerable emphasis on educational assistance to the new states. Technological and other educational institutions have been built with Soviet aid in India, Burma, Guinea, Tunis, Cambodia, Ethiopia, Mali and other countries.[22] Soviet leaders, fully cognizant of the pride of the people of the developing nations and their desire for independence in all spheres, have charged Soviet engineers and technicians who assist in the establishment of Soviet-sponsored economic projects to train local personnel to manage and operate them. Soviet citizens who participate in educational or economic aid missions are selected carefully and are instructed that they are to fraternize with the local population, and must under no circumstances adopt a patronizing attitude. Thousands of students from the developing states have been invited to study in the U.S.S.R. These students pay no tuition and are granted stipends comparable to, and in some cases larger than, those awarded to Soviet students. In view of the extreme shortage of educational facilities and well-educated personnel in the majority of the underdeveloped nations, the almost fanatic desire of many of the youth in these nations to add to their knowledge so that they might serve their country better, and the crucial need for educated people to guide the government, economy and social institutions of the new nations, the U.S.S.R. can anticipate rewards in terms of gratitude, admiration and political converts in return for its educational outlays. Since the leadership potential of the young students who are sent to the U.S.S.R. to study is generally high, one political convert from among this group may eventually result in thousands of converts among his fellow countrymen.

The reward which the U.S.S.R. hopes to reap ultimately for its "unselfish" military, economic and cultural assistance to the developing countries is new converts to socialism. Referring specifically to economic aid, a Soviet authority stated:

> "This aid is important support in their struggle for complete independence and against imperialist exploitation. The U.S.S.R.'s economic aid strengthens the state sector in the liberated countries, which serves as an important instrument in smashing the imperialist economy. The U.S.S.R.'s economic aid furthers the growth of the proletariat and strengthens it as counterweight to the forces of internal reaction."[23]

The message is clear: the U.S.S.R. hopes that the new nations will decrease their economic dependence on the West, expand the state-owned economic sector, and develop an increasingly strong and radical working class. These factors, the U.S.S.R. anticipates, in combination with political indoctrination, hostility toward the West, and admiration for the U.S.S.R. and its economic and social progress, will contribute to the demands of the local populace for the adoption of a social order based on the Soviet pattern.

The U.S.S.R. is doing everything in its power to encourage the new nations to adopt the non-capitalist course of development. It, however, deems it advantageous to its own purpose to act cautiously, to follow a policy of non-interference combined with assistance designed to influence the internal political climate and to lead and mold the people of the new nations to struggle for socialism rather than to impose it upon them. Although the power of the United States and its allies is the major factor contributing to the Soviet caution, the U.S.S.R. has reasons to proceed slowly. Time is required for the development of its own economy and for the forces it is manipulating or supporting in the newly established states to develop according to the Moscow plan. Its propaganda line against the export of revolution and for the rights of all peoples for self-determination has a highly moral tone designed to appeal to the new states. At the same time, it is doing everything in its power to prepare conditions for a socialist revolution in each of the new and underdeveloped states.

The Soviet leaders assert that a socialist revolution, rather than being "nudged" into being by other socialist countries, must be based on the development of class struggle within each country. Although peaceful transition to socialism is not ruled out, they predict that in most cases civil war will be inevitable. The Central Committee of the C.P.S.U. stated:

". . . the socialist revolution is brought about as a result of the internal development of the class struggle in each country, its forms and methods are determined by the concrete conditions of the given country. The general law is the revolutionary overthrow of the power of capital and the establishment of the dictatorship of the proletariat in the one form or another. The task of the working class and the Communist Party is *to take maximum advantage of the presently existing opportunities for a peaceful path to socialist revolution, not connected with civil war, and at the same time to be prepared for non-peaceful paths, for the armed suppression of the resistance of the bourgeoisie;* . . . The working class and its vanguard, the Marxist-Leninist parties, are eager to effect the socialist revolution peacefully, without a civil war. At the same time . . . if the exploiter classes resort to violence against the people, the working classes will be compelled to use non-peaceful means to win power. Everything depends on the specific conditions, on the alignment of class forces within the country and in the world arena."[24]

Soviet authorities predict that in the majority of the underdeveloped and newly liberated states internal conditions, the desires of the people to gain political and economic independence, the contrast between poverty, disease and ignorance of the masses and the affluence of their economic overlords, admiration for the U.S.S.R., timely assistance and guidance from socialist countries, the intensification of class struggle and the emerging strength of the proletariat will contribute to the development of revolutionary movements directed toward the establishment of socialism. Thus, the U.S.S.R. expects that it will eventually reap a rich harvest in terms of the expansion of socialism and weakening of capitalism in return for its military, economic, political, psychological and cultural support of the national liberation movement. Fortunately, Soviet expectations and accomplishments seldom coincide. Despite Soviet propaganda claims, the attempts of the U.S.S.R. to manipulate the national liberation movement have been fairly effectively curbed by Western policies and have been weakened further by the split among the Communist Parties. During the last fifteen years only Cuba and North Vietnam have been enticed into the socialist camp.

Relations with Soviet Bloc States

One of the most important and complicated tasks which has concerned the Soviet leadership during the last several years is the development of a feasible, and preferably mutually satisfactory, set of principles to govern relations between socialist states and between fraternal parties. The importance of the task derives in part from the Soviet belief that the rate of progress by each of the socialist states toward higher stages of socialism, and perhaps more important, the rate of expansion of the socialist bloc is affected significantly by relations maintained between socialist states. Soviet leaders would like to be able to point realistically to relations within the socialist bloc as a model of international cooperation, mutual benefit, and solidarity. The U.S.S.R. does, of course, make extravagant claims about the voluntary and mutually advantageous nature of relations within the socialist camp, but it is occasionally admitted that not all problems have been solved satisfactorily. The establishment of mutually satisfactory relations has been complicated by a number of factors. First, the U.S.S.R., despite its claims to the contrary, is determined to maintain effective control over the countries of Central-Eastern Europe, and to use them as instruments of Soviet national policy. Second, the people of Central-Eastern Europe did not adopt the Soviet style social order or join the socialist camp willingly. Communist regimes in these countries were imposed and have been maintained almost exclusively through Soviet support. Third, the post-Stalin leadership of the U.S.S.R. has had to cope with a strong heritage of resentment which resulted from the forceful imposition of socialism and from Stalin's high-handed treatment of socialist regimes of Central-Eastern Europe. Fourth, the strong nationalist sentiments of the people and the leaders of the smaller socialist states, which run counter to the international ideology of Marxism-Leninism, must be handled cautiously by the Soviet leaders. They want to avoid at all costs another armed uprising which would demonstrate to the world the discontent of the people with their Moscow-directed leaders and the lack of solidarity within the Soviet Union's own Central-European Empire.

The U.S.S.R. can credit itself with full responsibility for the communization of Eastern Europe during the early post-war period. The political and spiritual vacuum and economic exhaustion and chaos that were the aftermath of the war, combined with the presence and threat of the Red Army, made it relatively easy for the local communists to seize control, in spite of lack of popular support. In not one of the new socialist countries did the communists acquire power by legal methods. The communist takeover in Rumania is illustrative of the "assistance" given by the U.S.S.R.[25] In February, 1945, the U.S.S.R. gave the King of Rumania a two hour ultimatum demanding the dismissal of the pro-Western government, and supported the demand with a massive display of Soviet military might in the streets of Bucharest. Since resistance would have been futile, a National Democratic Front Government was formed under the leadership of a Moscow puppet. The U.S.S.R. soon made it clear that the Rumanian Constitution was invalid, and that there could be no change in government without consent from Moscow. Opposition parties were nominally allowed to operate, but the post-war election (November, 1946) was manipulated to give the communists and groups collaborating with them in the Bloc of Democratic Parties a very strong majority. During the following year, all opposition parties were either paralyzed or liquidated through intimidation, false accusations, and police terror. The Soviet army remained on hand to render assistance if necessary, but primarily to demonstrate the complete futility of resistance. Late in 1947, the Rumanian king was forced to abdicate, and in April, 1948, the Rumanian People's Republic was established officially. Soviet direction and Soviet military might enabled a Communist Party which in 1945 numbered around one thousand members[26] to attain absolute control over the Rumanian governmental machinery and to operate it on orders from Moscow. The details of the communist take-over in Bulgaria, Albania and Czechoslovakia, Hungary, Poland and East Germany varied with local conditions, but the overall approach was identical: the people were given absolutely no choice but to submit to the imposition of a Moscow puppet regime, since an armed uprising would have been crushed by the Red Army. Only in Yugoslavia, whose relations with the U.S.S.R. will be discussed in detail subsequently, was Soviet influence in the communist take-over relatively unimportant.

Once he had established puppet governments in the states of Central-Eastern Europe, Stalin proceeded to use the satellite status of these states to the advantage of the U.S.S.R. Each of the states was granted all the external attributes of independence and sovereignty, but both foreign and domestic policies were controlled by the Soviet Union. The Soviet army, which continued to be stationed on satellite territory, provided a guarantee that the local populace would submit to the dictates of their communist overlords who were completely subservient to Stalin. Stalin's domination of his underlings in the satellites was not, however, based entirely on force. Loyalty to Stalin, as the recognized leader of the world communist movement, was a natural outgrowth of the voluntary discipline and unity of the Communist Parties. Moreover, the satellite communist leaders owed a strong debt of gratitude to Stalin for having placed them in their positions of authority, and they realized that he could topple them from their pinnacles of power even more readily than he had placed them there. Stalin's authority over his local lieutenants was accepted without question and was almost complete. He summoned them to Moscow to invest them with power, to instruct them and to call them to account for their activities. Although a *Pravda* editorial was generally all that was required to bring back into line any local communist leader who strayed slightly from the Moscow-dictated policy, Stalin did not completely trust his puppets and consequently maintained a cumbersome apparatus directly in the satellite capitals to fortify his absolute control. Departments of the Central Committee of the C.P.S.U. maintained close supervision over the corresponding departments of the Central Committees of the "fraternal" parties; Soviet ambassadors, acting almost as proconsuls, gave detailed "advice" to the governments of the satellite states on matters concerning both internal and foreign policy; the Soviet army and security organizations maintained representatives in the local ministries of defense and interior; and a comprehensive spy network operated by Soviet intelligence services provided Moscow with detailed information about the political and social climate in the socialist states. Soviet policy was effectively designed to maintain the subservience of the satellite puppets to their Soviet overlords.

To facilitate the post-war reconstruction of the Soviet Union, former enemies within the socialist camp (Rumania, Hungary and East Germany) and also non-socialist countries under Soviet domination (Finland and the Soviet zone in Austria) were required to pay heavy reparations. Former allies (Poland, Czechoslovakia and Yugoslavia) were required to pay economic tribute chiefly through joint-stock companies to which the U.S.S.R. contributed confiscated German assets and the satellites were required to contribute their resources. All satellite countries were forced to participate in trade agreements whereby they paid for imports from the U.S.S.R. on the basis of world prices, but sold their products to the U.S.S.R. at disadvantageous prices. In several countries the Soviet army dismantled industrial enterprises for transfer to the U.S.S.R. Moreover, the satellite countries were required to maintain armed forces under Soviet control larger than their economies could legitimately support in order to bolster the military might of the socialist camp. In 1955, the form of Soviet military control over the satellites was changed with the establishment of the Warsaw Pact, which provided for a unified command of the satellite armies and the Soviet army units in satellite territory under a Soviet officer and a Moscow controlled Political Consultive Committee.

As if these various forms of political subjugation and economic tribute were not adequate payment for the honor of belonging to the socialist camp, the satellite nations were burdened with a number of unpopular, economically unsound and repressive measures. Some of these measures were introduced on direct orders from Moscow and others were introduced on the initiative of local leaders who deemed it advisable to imitate Stalin and to copy mechanically the social and economic order which he had established. For example, each of the satellite states sought to emulate the U.S.S.R. by attempting to industrialize rapidly and to attain economic inclusiveness. For a variety of reasons, including the fact that the smaller states did not have the breadth and quantity of economic resources which were at the disposal of the U.S.S.R., their attempts resulted in economic regression. A multitude of factors, including low standards of living, repressive police measures, suppression of religious expression, the absolute absence of political liberties, anti-Soviet sentiments which were strengthened by the frequent brutalities of the "liberating Red Army" and Stalin's dictatorial policies, and strong nationalistic sentiments, contributed to the general discontent of the peoples of the socialist states of Central-Eastern Europe. Popular demonstrations or uprisings in Czechoslovakia and the German Democratic Republic in 1953 and in Poland and Hungary in 1956, convinced Stalin's successors that it was absolutely necessary to modify drastically the relations between the U.S.S.R. and the Soviet satellites.

Stalin's immediate successors attempted to maintain the satellite status of the Central-Eastern European states and, at the same time, to reduce somewhat the control from Moscow. The net result was to give the impression of Soviet vacillation without giving the people the increase in freedom which they so urgently desired. The de-Stalinization movement apparently caused an upsurge of hope among the subjugated people since, if the former dictator was dethroned and his policies were subjected to harsh criticism, the basis of the power and authority of his successors was questionable. The Polish reaction to the changed situation in Moscow was relatively subdued since the party was able to retain control. In the intra-party struggle which was touched off by the popular uprisings, the pro-Stalinist leadership was replaced by an anti-Stalinist faction headed by Gomulka. Gomulka, by playing on the Soviet leaders' fear of having to use brute force to suppress a more massive uprising, was able to wring several concessions from Moscow including the right to pursue a "Polish road to socialism" and to allow the intensely religious population slightly greater freedom of religious expression. The Hungarian Revolution constituted a much more serious problem for Moscow in that it was directed against communism rather than against a group of unacceptable communist leaders. In Hungary, under the revolutionary onslaught, the Communist Party actually lost effective control for a few days; power was preempted by revolutionary workers' councils, and a coalition government was formed. Hungary withdrew from the Warsaw Pact and proclaimed neutrality. The U.S.S.R. had to intervene with its massive military machines to prevent Hungary from deposing the communist regime and seceding from the socialist camp. The Hungarian Revolution, more than any other single factor, shocked Khrushchev and his associates into realizing the tenuous nature of the ties, other than fear, which bound the peoples of Central-Eastern Europe to the socialist way of life and to allegiance to the Soviet Union.

During the Khrushchev era, relations between the U.S.S.R. and the Soviet bloc states underwent a kind of metamorphosis during which the smaller states emerged from an essentially colonial status to the status of junior partners of the U.S.S.R. The metamorphosis is, of course, far from complete; despite Soviet statements to the contrary, the U.S.S.R. continues to intervene in the affairs of other socialist states, and the ties that bind them to the U.S.S.R. are not entirely based on comradely love. The changes in Soviet policy toward the erstwhile satellites have been dictated by expediency. Another popular uprising against a communist dictatorship and Soviet domination would almost completely destroy the image of harmonious socialist relations and of the U.S.S.R. as the benevolent friend of the smaller socialist states, which the U.S.S.R. has sought so diligently to establish. Total destruction of this image might well cancel out the effects of other Soviet policies designed to foster the spread of socialism. By the same token, the lack of economic progress in the smaller states was hardly a good advertisement for socialism. The economic backwardness of the satellite states could be attributed to the fact that they were required to subsidize Soviet industrialization, and at the same time were operating under unwise economic policies which were imposed by Moscow or by the local leaders in their attempt to imitate the U.S.S.R. The Khrushchev leadership realized that if the boast that the socialist bloc would surpass the capitalist bloc in the economic sphere were to be realized, remedial action was imperative; in fact, the economic advantages to the U.S.S.R. of exacting economic tribute from the satellites would be minimal in comparison to the tactical advantages to be derived from being able to point to the smaller states as showcases of economic prosperity. Moreover, changes in economic policy were necessary in order to neutralize the discontent of the populace. Consequently, the leaders of the states of Central-Eastern Europe were given considerably more leeway to adapt socialist economic programs to local circumstances, and the U.S.S.R., instead of exacting economic tribute, began to pour vast amounts of economic aid into the socialist bloc states. Another major factor which has affected relations within the Soviet bloc is the Sino-Soviet dispute. The violent Chinese campaign against the U.S.S.R. and the C.P.S.U. for their dictatorial relations with fraternal parties and states has made it imperative for the Soviet leaders to make additional concessions to the former satellites and to intensify the propaganda campaign to convey the impression that a model of harmonious relations has been established. On the whole, the Chinese attack has served the smaller states well; it has brought into the open some of the deleterious features of Soviet policy and, at the same time, by offering the smaller states an alternate protector, has increased their bargaining leverage.

Khrushchev recognized that the unity and solidarity of the socialist camp is more important in terms of long-range goals than complete Soviet hegemony over the less powerful states, and that overtures toward equality are a prerequisite for harmonious relations within the socialist camp and for the establishment of a world image which will contribute to the advancement of the socialist movement. It is almost ironical that it was during Khrushchev's period of leadership that the facade of socialist unity and solidarity was rudely shattered by the Sino-Soviet dispute.

Soviet propaganda statements imply that relations between fraternal Communist Parties and the states which they control are characterized by equality, the effort to achieve unified goals, comradely mutual assistance and the concern of each for the welfare of all. According to the Statement of the 1960 Conference of Communist and Workers' Parties to which the Soviet leaders subscribe:

"All the Marxist-Leninist parties are independent and have equal rights; they shape their policies on the basis of the specific conditions in their countries, guided by the principles of Marxism-Leninism, and lend each other support. The success of the cause of the working class in each country demands the international solidarity of all Marxist-Leninist parties. Each party is responsible to the working class, the working people of its country and to the international workers' and Communist movement as a whole."[27]

The Program of the C.P.S.U. describes inter-state socialist relations as:

"A social, economic and political community of free sovereign peoples pursuing the socialist and communist path, united by an identity of interests and goals and the close bonds of international socialist solidarity. . . . The world socialist system is a new type of economic and political relationship between countries. The socialist countries have the same type of economic basis—social ownership of the means of production; the same type of political system—rule of the people with the working class at their head; a common ideology—Marxism-Leninism; common interest in the defense of their revolutionary gains and national independence from encroachments by the imperialist camp; and a great common goal—communism. This socio-economic and political community constitutes the objective groundwork for lasting and friendly inter-governmental relations within the socialist camp. The distinctive features of the relations existing between the countries of the socialist community are complete equality, mutual respect for independence and sovereignty and fraternal mutual assistance and co-operation. In the socialist camp, or which is the same thing, in the world community of socialist countries, none have, nor can have, any special rights or privileges."[28]

Soviet leaders disclaim any special leading role for the C.P.S.U. and the U.S.S.R. in the international communist movement. Nevertheless, the delegates to the 1960 Conference of the Communist and Workers' Parties were allowed to:

". . . unanimously declare that the Communist Party of the Soviet Union has been and continues to be the universally recognized vanguard of the World Communist Movement, being the most experienced and most thoroughly tempered detachment of the international Communist movement."[29]

Khrushchev insisted, with purposeful modesty, that the Soviet Union by no means "directs" other countries, but on the basis of its rich experience, merely provides examples of the successful solution of the most intricate problems of socialist and communist construction. "As for the Soviet Union," he stated, "everyone knows that its role consists not in controlling other countries, but in having pioneered the way to socialism for mankind, in being the most powerful country in the world socialist system and the first to enter the period of full-scale communist construction.[30] Thus, all Soviet discussions of relations between Communist Parties and between socialist states are based on the questionable premise that "there are no 'superior' and no 'subordinated' parties, just as there are no 'hegemon' states or 'satellite' states in the socialist camp."[31]

Although relations between the U.S.S.R. and the socialist states of Central-Eastern Europe do not approach the ideal depicted by Soviet propagandists, a definite liberalizing trend was apparent during the Khrushchev era, and the relative status of the small states has improved markedly.[32] In an attempt to counteract the discontent that had culminated in the Polish and Hungarian uprisings, local communist leaders were allowed to make a number of concessions to the populace. Terroristic methods and purges have been abandoned and the power of the secret police has been curbed; efforts have been made to improve standards of living through wage raises, increased social security benefits, better housing and greater emphasis on the production of consumer goods; and there has been some relaxation of cultural orthodoxy. The basic communist aim of economic development through rapid industrialization and collectivization was retained but the smaller states were granted increased independence of decision in the economic sphere; Poland, for example, was allowed to decentralize industrial management to a considerable extent and even to abandon collectivization as a temporary expedient. The Council for Mutual Economic Aid (COMECON) which had been established in 1949, and had been used primarily to the advantage of the U.S.S.R., was revitalized and transformed into an organ of mutual economic assistance. During the past several years the COMECON has been used to co-ordinate the long-range plans of the various states, and to organize international co-operation and specialization which has relieved each state from the need to strive for autarchy. Trade within the socialist bloc has increased markedly on the basis of relationships which are ordinarily mutually advantageous. The U.S.S.R. has given very tangible economic assistance to the smaller bloc members in terms of easy credit, loans, technical assistance and production designs. In exchange, the U.S.S.R. has bolstered her supply sources of a number of scarce raw materials and has received some technical assistance and industrial goods, primarily from Czechoslovakia and East Germany. The former satellites have been allowed to increase their trade and cultural contacts with Western nations, and some of them have even accepted economic aid from the United States. Currently, the U.S.S.R. apparently does not object to increased ties with the Western world as long as these ties do not in any way endanger the allegiance of the socialist bloc countries to the U.S.S.R. Although Soviet garrisons are still stationed in most of the smaller states, the threat of military suppression has been played down. A number of concessions have been made to the nationalistic sentiments of the local populace, including the important principle that "the roads of socialist development are different in different countries." The Soviet propaganda line has sought to reassure the smaller states that they are in no danger of being engulfed against their will into a super-state. The Soviet solution to the dialectical contradiction of support for nationalism within the international socialist movement is simple: "Only when the nations are really free and equal, when no one nation encroaches on the independence of another, only in that case do they deeply trust each other, and voluntarily enter into close relations dictated by the interests of developing the economy, defense and foreign policy."[33]

As a result of the changes which have taken place in the U.S.S.R.'s relations with the smaller states in the Soviet bloc, the term Soviet satellite has lost much of its validity. The smaller states are enjoying a degree of freedom from Soviet control that was unthinkable during the Stalin era. The relaxation of control has gone so far that the small, powerless state of Albania has dared to withdraw totally from the Soviet sphere of influence, albeit under the protective cloak of China, and Rumania has refused to align herself firmly with the U.S.S.R. in the Sino-Soviet dispute. Nevertheless, the ties that bind the majority of the former satellites to the U.S.S.R. are far from severed. In almost all of these states, the ruling communist leaders are completely dependent on Soviet support to maintain their control over the people who did not elect them and, in all probability, would like to oust them and their social order. The leaders are, moreover, bound to the U.S.S.R. by a common ideology and common goals. Because of the close economic relations which the U.S.S.R. at first imposed and then sponsored, a considerable degree of economic chaos and regression would follow any attempt on the part of one of the smaller states to assert complete independence from Soviet influence. Some of the states, notably Poland and Czechoslovakia, have an allegiance or dependence to the U.S.S.R. which is based on national interest since they realize that if Germany were ever again to attack them, Soviet assistance would be indispensable. Thus, from 1957 until 1965, the U.S.S.R. has progressively relaxed its firm grip on Central-Eastern Europe and, for some of her former satellites, allegiance to the U.S.S.R. is based on self-interest.

Future relations between the U.S.S.R. and the smaller socialist states of Central-Eastern Europe can not be predicted with any degree of certainty. A number of factors could conceivably maintain or accelerate the centrifugal trend which began during the Khrushchev era. The smaller states are unlikely to relinquish willingly the limited independence which they have gained from Moscow, and the Soviet emphasis on "equality, sovereignty and independence" within the socialist camp will make it difficult, but not impossible, for the U.S.S.R. to reimpose complete domination. The ideological confusion which resulted from the split between the U.S.S.R. and Communist China continues, at present, to weaken the ideological ties that have helped to hold the smaller states in the Soviet orbit, and at the same time, makes it tactically easier for them to assert independence. It is conceivable that some of the smaller states might attempt to emulate Yugoslavia's successful independent stand. It is improbable, however, that any of these states will attempt to turn away from Soviet-style socialism; a popular uprising would be crushed ruthlessly, and the leaders would certainly not initiate an anti-socialist movement because they are, after all, Marxists-Leninists, and because their positions of power depend on maintenance of the "socialist" regime. On the other hand, it is not inconceivable that the Soviet grip on the smaller states in Central-Eastern Europe might be tightened. The fact that the immediate post-Khrushchev leadership has shown no signs of attempting to reimpose Soviet domination may mean relatively little from the long-range point of view. The new leaders are themselves in a precarious position, and are, moreover, preoccupied with internal problems and the Sino-Soviet dispute. Settlement of the differences between the U.S.S.R. and China could set the stage for a concentrated drive to reestablish socialist solidarity and discipline. If a new Soviet strongman were able to consolidate his power firmly within the U.S.S.R., he could manipulate policy toward the Central-Eastern European states in either direction: the smaller states could be granted increased independence, or Khrushchev's policy could be described as a grave error, and Soviet domination could be increased sharply. The Soviet leaders could even, particularly if Communist China did not object, decide that the smaller socialist states should enter into a political and economic union with the U.S.S.R. The Sino-Soviet dispute could, on the other hand, serve as the motivation for the unification of all European socialist states. Such a drastic move could be facilitated if strongly nationalistic leaders in the smaller states were replaced by dedicated Marxist-Leninist internationalists. Even now, the U.S.S.R. has adequate techniques to effect a change of command, and there are within the smaller states a minority of communists who would favor union with the U.S.S.R. There is, finally, a third alternative to a progressive weakening of ties within the Soviet bloc or to a tightening of the Soviet grip. It is possible, but perhaps not too probable, that if the U.S.S.R. were to continue and accelerate her current program of fairer treatment for the former satellites and if these states were to make rapid progress in the economic sphere, that anti-Soviet and anti-socialist sentiments would gradually die out and a genuine socialist solidarity with the U.S.S.R. could develop on a voluntary basis.

Soviet-Yugoslav Relations

Of all the European socialist countries, only Yugoslavia has been able consistently to demand and maintain functional independence from Moscow. The U.S.S.R. has alternately tried to force and to woo the Yugoslavs to adhere to the policy dictated by Moscow. At no time has its efforts been marked by more than partial success, and Yugoslavia, a socialist country lead by a dedicated communist, Marshal Tito, continues to stand apart from the other socialist countries, independent from both Moscow and Peking, but not without influence on the development of the socialist movement.

The difficulties between the U.S.S.R. and Yugoslavia, according to Yugoslavian sources, began even before the end of World War II when it became evident to the Yugoslavian communists that Stalin's tactical aims and hegemonistic ambitions did not coincide with the national interests of Yugoslavia. Subsequently, the Yugoslavs were angered by inadequate Soviet support for their claim to Trieste. Stalin was severely provoked when Tito made it increasingly clear that Yugoslavia's internal and foreign policy would be determined exclusively in Belgrade, and that although Yugoslavia was a faithful member of the socialist camp, it would not be a satellite to the U.S.S.R. The Central Committee of the C.P.S.U. demanded that the Yugoslav communists admit mistakes such as: slandering the C.P.S.U. and the Soviet army; deviating from the Marxist-Leninist course in the question of the leading role of the working class; identifying the foreign policy of the U.S.S.R. with the foreign policy of the imperialists; collaboration with the imperialists; establishing a police state ruled by military leadership which suppressed democracy and criticism within the party, etc. When the Yugoslavian communists refused to submit to Soviet domination, Stalin's wrath was so great that all military and economic ties between the Soviet bloc and Yugoslavia were severed. In 1948 Stalin had Cominform, an internationalist Marxist-Leninist organization, expel Tito and his party from the fraternal organization because of nationalistic attitudes, doctrinal errors and hostility to the Soviet Union.[34] The resolution declared that the Yugoslav communists followed "an incorrect line on the main questions of home and foreign policy, a line which represents a departure from Marxism-Leninism." Yugoslav communists were instructed that if Tito's group did not change its line, it was their duty "to replace them and to advance a new international leadership of the party." A full scale propaganda attack against Tito was launched and anti-Tito Yugoslavs were organized both within and outside of Yugoslavia. Typical of Soviet statements at that time was one by Bulganin in 1949:

> "Judas Tito and his helpers—these malevolent deserters from the camp of socialism to the camp of imperialism and fascism—have converted Yugoslavia into a Gestapo prison where every reflection of free thought and human rights is put down, where the advanced representatives of the working class, the toiling peasantry, and the intelligentsia are brutally murdered. All progressive humanity looks with loathing upon these despicable traitors, agents and aides of imperialism who fulfill the will of their masters."[35]

Soviet condemnation of Tito for the use of repressive methods was a clear cut case of the pot calling the kettle black. Stalin and his colleagues were certainly not motivated by a desire to foster increased civil liberties in

Yugoslavia. What the attacks on Tito do demonstrate clearly is that regardless of what Soviet leaders were saying at the time, the Soviet Union was attempting to establish its complete and unquestioned hegemony over all the socialist countries.

Tito, who unlike the leaders of the Soviet satellites, felt that his control over his party and state was sufficiently strong that it could withstand Soviet attacks, adhered to his position of independence. His stand was bolstered materially by considerable economic aid from the Western countries, particularly the U.S.A. Yugoslavia's responses to Soviet denunciations have typically been marked by restraint. Even after expulsion from Cominform, Tito reaffirmed his country's solidarity with the Soviet Union and the other People's Democracies. His long-range position seems to have been one of refusal to be bullied into submitting to Soviet demands or conversely, of being shoved into the Western camp against his will. He has consistently maintained his loyalty to the communist cause, but at the same time persistently asserted the right of Yugoslavia to develop her own line of advance toward socialism. A statement by the Minister of Foreign Affairs of Yugoslavia describes the Yugoslav leaderships' version of the issues of conflict which dominated relations between the two states during the early post-war period. He said:

"The meeting of the Cominform in Bucharest where the Yugoslav Communist Party was tried and condemned *in absentia* . . . marked the beginning of a violent campaign of political, ideological, economic and even military pressure against Yugoslavia. While resisting the pressure—and this demanded considerable determination and no small sacrifice on the part of the people—Yugoslavia affirmed certain basic views, certain fundamental tenets of her political philosophy, concerning relations between Socialist states and within the international labor movement in general. The Stalinist view was based on the concept of the leading role of the Soviet Union within the Socialist camp. Since the latter was equated with socialism as a system, the interests of the Soviet Union became both identical and co-extensive with those of socialism, and transcended those of the other Socialist countries and of the working class movement as a whole. This was the Stalinist understanding of 'proletarian internationalism' which was but a very thin disguise for Soviet Great Power hegemony.

"In resisting this hegemony, the Yugoslavs had of necessity to combat the ideological guise under which it was presented. Yugoslavia thus denied the concept of a 'leading nation' within socialism and insisted instead on full equality—political, economic and ideological—among Socialist countries. The Yugoslavs also rejected any uniform pattern or blueprint, either for the working class movement or for the construction of socialism. They demanded instead for each country the right to build socialism through a creative rather than a dogmatic application of Marxism and in accordance with its specific needs and conditions. In the Yugoslav view, a rigid pattern or a centralized leadership for the international working class movement would only stultify the general advance toward socialism for which the times called. In other words, a country's independence, a nation's right to self-determination, necessarily meant its right to elect its own form of government, and to choose its particular line of progress toward socialism."[36]

Tito's greatest crime from the point of view of the Stalin leadership was his open and effective rejection of Soviet domination. His independence was manifested in a variety of ways. His solution of internal problems did not follow the pattern established by Moscow: A system of "workers' management" was adopted in industry and production was put on a profit basis; control over heavy industry and farming was partially decentralized, and participation in collectivization was made voluntary, with the result that the majority of the collective farms were dissolved; freedom of worship was granted; and in general, Tito relied more than Stalin on persuasion and less on compulsion. Yugoslavia accepted economic aid from Western nations, and did not hesitate to form free trade relations with them. Tito has consistently pursued a policy of non-alignment with either of the major military blocs. The Yugoslav position has been that socialism will eventually be adopted by the majority of countries but that the struggle for socialism has to be fought within each country, and not on the international level between countries or groups of countries. Yugoslavia has supported a doctrine of peaceful co-existence which emphasizes the concept of active cooperation rather than the passive state of living side by side. As part of his stand for national self-determination, Tito stresses that one of the tenets of co-existence is "respect for the obligation of non-interference in the internal affairs of other nations and states, and the right of every nation and state to organize its own life."[37]

Stalin feared, not without reason, that Tito's heresy, if uncurbed, might find imitators among the other satellites. He was so accustomed to using dictatorial methods to his own satisfaction that he apparently believed that he had only to shake his little finger at Tito to bring the Yugoslavs back into line. The Yugoslavs, however, refused to capitulate and continued to pursue their course of national socialism with considerable success. To counteract the potential attraction of Yugoslavia's successful assertion of independence, the Soviet economic, military and ideological grip over the satellites was tightened, and Stalin used his influence over Cominform to initiate a general purge of communist leaders who showed the slightest signs of independence. The blind obedience of the satellite communists was insured for the time being.

Stalin's successors, for reasons which probably included a realistic assessment of Stalin's errors and recognition of Yugoslavia's growing influence among the non-aligned nations, took the initiative to improve relations between Moscow and Belgrade. Concurrently, some minor concessions were made to the satellite regimes which were showing increased signs of wanting, if not the degree of independence from the U.S.S.R. which Yugoslavia had attained, at least greater freedom from Soviet intervention. During 1955 and 1956 visits were exchanged between the leading officials of Belgrade and Moscow and in February, 1956, Khrushchev apologized publicly for the 1948 break in relations, assigning the blame for the break to Stalin. He stated:

> " 'The Yugoslav affair' contained no problems which could not have been solved through Party discussions among comrades. There was no significant basis for the development of this 'affair'; it was completely possible to have prevented the rupture of relations with that country. This does not mean however that the Yugoslav leaders did not make mistakes and did not have shortcomings. But these mistakes and shortcomings were magnified in a monstrous manner by Stalin, which resulted in a break of relations with a friendly country."[38]

Khrushchev's statement exemplifies the post-Stalin Soviet attitude toward Yugoslavia. Yugoslavia has erred and is erring, and must be brought back into line, but the "big stick" approach is no longer considered feasible. Soviet rapproachment and admission of errors constituted a significant victory for the Yugoslav "heretics." Later in 1956, Yugoslavia wrested a major ideological concession from the U.S.S.R. when Khrushchev and Tito issued a joint declaration which stated that "the roads of Socialist development are different in different countries" and reaffirmed the equality and sovereignty of socialist states.[39] Thus, the Kremlin leaders formally conceded that all socialist countries were not bound to follow blindly the lead and example set by Moscow.

The unwavering stand taken by the Yugoslavs and the limited Soviet recognition of Yugoslavia's independence encouraged the satellite states, particularly Poland and Hungary, to make a bid for emancipation from Soviet control. Although none of the satellite communist leaders were able to duplicate Tito's feat, the Yugoslavian declaration of independence and the 1956 uprisings contributed appreciably to the partial relaxation of Soviet domination in Central-Eastern Europe. The U.S.S.R., smarting under the loss of prestige occasioned by the Hungarian Revolution and anxious to curb the spread of "Titoism," renewed its attacks on Yugoslav "revisionism" and Tito retaliated by making some highly uncomplimentary but truthful statements about the Soviet treatment of the smaller socialist states.

Soviet anger was aroused anew in 1957 when Tito issued a Program for the Yugoslav Communist Party which again denied the Soviet Union's claim to leadership in the communist world, accused the Soviet state of violating some of the basic concepts of Marxism-Leninism, reaffirmed the correctness of his own position and blamed the East as much as the West for the international tension of the Cold War. Again, the Soviet leaders treated Tito as a traitor to socialism, but again, a partial reconciliation was effected. Since the late 1950's the Chinese have been particularly virulent in their attacks on the "traitorous Yugoslav revisionists" and it was they who insisted that the 1960 Congress of Representatives of Communist and Workers' Parties condemn the Yugoslavs in the following terms:

> "The Communist Parties have unanimously condemned the Yugoslav variety of international opportunism, which is a concentrated expression of the 'theories' of the present-day revisionists. The leaders of the Yugoslav League of Communists, having betrayed Marxism-Leninism and declared it to be obsolete, have counterposed their anti-Leninist revisionist program to the 1957 Declaration and the Yugoslav League of Communists to the entire international Communist movement and have severed their country from the socialist camp, making it dependent on the so-called 'aid' of the American and other imperialists and thereby jeopardizing the revolutionary gains won by the heroic struggle of the Yugoslav people. The Yugoslav revisionists are engaged in subversive work against the socialist camp and the world Communist movement. Under the pretext of pursuing an 'outside-of-blocs' policy, they are developing activity that harms the cause of the unity of all peace-loving forces and states. Further exposure of the leaders of the Yugoslav revisionists and a vigorous struggle to safeguard the Communist movement and the workers' movement from the Yugoslav revisionists' anti-Leninist ideas continue to be the essential task of the Marxist-Leninist parties."[40]

By the time the statement was approved, relations between Belgrade and Moscow were again on the upgrade, and in fact, since then, Moscow has maintained a fairly conciliatory attitude toward the Yugoslavs. "The line of the C.P.S.U." has consisted "not of perpetuating the departure of the League of Communists or Yugoslavia from the international communist movement but of helping it to correct its errors and take its place in the ranks of our movement."[41]

Why has the U.S.S.R., the most powerful state of the socialist camp, tried so persistently to woo Yugoslavia, between intervals of threats and retaliatory measures? What is the tremendous significance of Yugoslavia to the Soviet leaders? First and foremost, Yugoslavia has been a thorn in the side of the Soviet leaders. Tito's successful insistence on national socialism, different paths to socialism and national independence have forced the Kremlin to loosen its hold on the satellites. He has asserted that there is no reason for the division of the world into blocs, that honest cooperation and friendship between all nations is the true Marxist-Leninist reaction to reality in view of the "objective tendency" for all nations to move toward socialism because of internal forces. Since Tito does not believe that the socialist world is menaced by a "capitalist conspiracy," he argues that there is no reason for the socialist countries to band together and take orders from Moscow, or from any other center. Thus, he has not only asserted his own independence, but in addition has assumed a position which deprives the U.S.S.R. of its major justification for binding the smaller socialist states so closely to it. Tito's ideas have considerable appeal to socialist states that have been under Soviet domination, to a goodly number of Soviet citizens and to many of the underdeveloped and newly liberated states. Having failed in their attempts to force Tito to capitulate, the Soviet leaders would, no doubt, like to persuade him to modify those views which run counter to Soviet interests. At the same time, they would like to capitalize on the appeal which his brand of socialism has for non-aligned states and on the considerable influence which he has among neutral nations. A minor but perhaps not unimportant reason for courting Tito is the fact that he is the anti-Stalinist *par excellence*. The post-Stalin Soviet leaders have maintained that they disapproved of Stalin's tactics but remained silent because they were powerless to act, but Tito was an anti-Stalinist while Stalin was alive. Rapprochement with Tito is, in a sense, a way for the Soviet leadership to demonstrate to the world that Stalin's techniques are, indeed, a thing of the past. Finally, Yugoslavia and Albania for a considerable time served as convenient mediums through which Sino-Soviet political dispute was conducted. By using the two small countries as "fronts," the U.S.S.R. and Communist China and their respective Marxist parties were able to hurl insults at each other, and engage in ideological warfare while avoiding direct conflict and situations from which it would be difficult to withdraw with dignity.

The Sino-Soviet Dispute

The Sino-Soviet dispute which poses the major threat to the unity of the communist movement has long standing antecedents. Throughout the nineteenth and early twentieth centuries, Imperial Russia directed constant expansionist pressure against the Chinese, particularly on the border areas of Manchuria, Mongolia and Sinkiang. The most common techniques for expansion were through commercial penetration and intrigue, but military force was used on occasion. In conflicts between China and Japan, Russian assistance was granted sometimes to one side, sometimes to the other, on a self-interest basis. After the termination of the Civil War, the Bolsheviks adopted the Tsarist policy of extending Russian influence in China as far as possible, and at the same time, attempted to limit the influence of other powers over China. Soviet control over Outer Mongolia was established in 1924 and in Sinkiang in the early 1930's. Stalin favored the establishment of a unified central Chinese government which would be strong enough to prohibit Western intervention in Chinese affairs, but would at the same time be amenable to Russian influence. This goal, and perhaps also fear that a communist revolution in China would result in Western intervention against the communist movement, influenced Stalin to support the Nationalist Kuomintang, led first by Sun Yat-Sen and later by Chiang Kai-shek, rather than the Chinese communists. The Chinese communists, led by Mao Tse-tung, were thus relegated to a secondary position by their fraternal brothers in Moscow, and were eventually expelled by Chiang from all positions of power. Other policies which Moscow urged on the Chinese communists proved to be disastrous to their cause, and ultimately, Mao Tse-tung began to pursue independent policies which were sometimes at variance with the advice of Stalin. After the Japanese occupation of Manchuria in 1932, the Nationalist Kuomintang and the Chinese communists formed a partnership which continued on a somewhat tenuous basis throughout the Sino-Japanese conflict. Stalin continued to support Chiang Kai-shek as the leader of the resistance to Japanese aggression. He also used the Chinese preoccupation with the Japanese to extend Soviet influence at their expense, and the limited Soviet action in World War II on the Japanese front to justify Soviet claims for territory in the Far East.

The Chinese communists had gained considerable strength during the 1940's and by 1945 Mao Tse-tung was ready to launch an all-out effort to wrest control from the Nationalists. Stalin, however, continued to support the Nationalist government and advised the Chinese communists to cooperate with Chiang Kai-shek. It has been suggested that Stalin would have preferred China to remain under Nationalist control so that he could, without ideological scruples, continue to pursue an expansionist policy at the expense of China. Mao, however, acted on his own initiative, and against Stalin's advice: by 1949 he had defeated the Kuomintang and proclaimed the Chinese People's Republic. With considerable justification, Mao's forces took full credit for their victory which had been achieved with only minimal assistance from the U.S.S.R. Thus, Mao Tse-tung, like Tito, felt that he was not obligated to kowtow to Moscow in return for past favors, nor dependent on Moscow for support to retain political power. Stalin had not provided the basic prerequisites to force the new Chinese People's Republic into satellite status. Stalin's continuation of the Tsarist expansionist policy with respect to China, his apparent disregard of Chinese national ambitions, his subordination of the Chinese communist movement to the Nationalist Kuomintang and his inept advice to the Chinese communists contributed to Mao's determination to maintain some independence from Moscow, and his unwillingness to trust the Russians to look after his interests.

Nevertheless, the Chinese had to turn to Moscow for help. The success of the Chinese communist regime depended ultimately on its ability to overcome the technical backwardness and appalling poverty of China. The U.S.S.R. was the legitimate and, in fact, the only source of help. From the Chinese point of view, the U.S.S.R. was not overly generous. Following Mao's visit to Moscow in 1949, the Chinese received a loan of $300 million, considerably less than had been granted to Poland earlier. The U.S.S.R. promised to return some of the traditionally Chinese territory which it had acquired from the Japanese at the end of World War II. Some joint Soviet-Chinese companies were established with the maximum advantage accruing to the U.S.S.R. Soviet military and technical advisors made a significant contribution to China's development and, at the same time, provided a means through which the U.S.S.R. could influence Chinese policy. Trade agreements were established which, while necessary to China, increased her dependence on the U.S.S.R. During the course of the Sino-Soviet conflict, the Chinese have indicated that they felt that their fraternal brothers in the U.S.S.R. did far less than could and should have been done to assist them in their reconstruction tasks in the early 1950's, and that they were humiliated by the arrogant and patronizing attitude taken by the Russians. Mao, no doubt, felt that he deserved greater rewards for having led 500 million people into the socialist camp. The Chinese's dissatisfaction was increased even more when Stalin used a variety of techniques to delay the transfer of territory and property to Chinese control. Stalin's successors, thus, inherited Chinese antagonism against the Russians which dated back to the Tsarist era and was augmented by Stalin's treatment of the Chinese communist movement.

The post-Stalin leadership took immediate steps to improve relations between Moscow and Peking. Soviet economic aid was advanced on an unprecedented scale and the U.S.S.R. committed itself to assist in China's industrial development, even to the point of retarding its own advances. The Chinese were accorded the status of joint or at least secondary leaders in the socialist camp; Chinese pride was protected by careful adherence to protocol measures such as the pilgrimage of top Soviet leaders to Peking; and Mao was treated as a leading Marxist theoretician. The U.S.S.R. offered no objection to the extension of Chinese influence in the Far East and South East Asia, and it appeared that the two major socialist countries had achieved a mutually satisfactory division of spheres of responsibility and influence. The Soviet Union was recognized by the Chinese as the leader of the socialist camp, the vanguard of the socialist revolution and the friend and protector of all fraternal socialist countries, including the Chinese People's Republic. The Chinese leaders appeared to be fully willing to accord leadership status to the Soviet leaders, provided the latter were open to influence and made decisions which conformed with the interests of the Chinese. By 1956 the Sino-Soviet alliance seemed firm, unbreakable and mutually advantageous; there were no overt indications of a potential conflict.

During the late 1950's relations between Moscow and Peking, though on the surface full of mutual amicability, deteriorated progressively; and by 1963 the Sino-Soviet cleavage was so great that the fraternal communist parties engaged in public and abusive polemics. Major incidents in the dispute have included Khrushchev's attack on Stalin and his proclamation of fundamental changes in the Marxist doctrine at the Twentieth Congress of the C.P.S.U. and subsequently, without prior consultation with Mao and other communist leaders; the sharp curtailment of Soviet aid to China in 1960, after a period of significantly high assistance; the Soviet attack on the Albanian communist leaders and the Chinese support for the renegades; the Chinese attack on the Yugoslav "revisionists" whom Khrushchev was openly courting; the expulsion of Chinese diplomats from Moscow for alleged anti-Soviet activities; the abrupt withdrawal of the Chinese delegation from the Twenty-Second Congress of the C.P.S.U. in 1961; anti-Soviet propaganda, openly sponsored by the Chinese Communist Party, both at home and abroad; Chinese disapproval of the Soviet handling of the Cuban situation; and Soviet disapproval of China's aggression against India. Until 1963 both sides maintained a formal front of unity within the communist movement. Unpleasant incidents occurred but neither side chose to make a public issue of them. Both sides reserved the right to withdraw with dignity by conducting the dispute through semi-intermediaries, Albania and Yugoslavia; Moscow attacked Albania and "other dogmatists" (China) and Peking attacked Yugoslavia and "other revisionists" (the U.S.S.R.). The Chinese had a slight edge in the use of intermediaries in that the Albanians served them as willing spokesmen while the Yugoslavs did not serve as a mouthpiece for Moscow. Although the dispute has been phrased in ideological terms, its origin lies in more basic factors such as the hegemonistic aspirations of both sets of leaders and their desire to dominate the world communist movement, and the different historical backgrounds, world power status and stages of economic development of the two states. The personalities of Khrushchev and Mao, and their general ideological values have not been without influence in the conflict, but the effect on the conflict of the overall political, economic, historical and social milieu from which they operate is greater than that of personalities or ideological positions *per se*.

The histories of the peoples who occupy the U.S.S.R. and the Chinese People's Republic serve as background for the dispute. The Chinese, keenly aware that their ancestors had a highly developed civilization when most of the white race were barbarians, operate from a highly ethnocentric position which is enhanced by resentment of their subjugation by the whites during the nineteenth century. In spite of the fact that the notion of national and racial superiority is foreign to Marxist-Leninist ideology, the Chinese simultaneously feel superior to and resent the white race, including the Russians, and harbor goals for a Chinese-led yellow race domination of the world. The traditional attitude of superiority has made it less easy for the suave, scholarly Chinese leaders to accept with equanimity the intellectual leadership of proletarians such as Khrushchev, whom they objected to particularly for his crudity.

The Chinese and Soviet leaders both espouse the internationalism of Marxism-Leninism, yet their relations with each other and with all foreign states are influenced markedly by their nationalist aspirations. It was partly by building up and appealing to strong nationalist aspirations that the Communist Party of China was able to achieve power. Once having attained power, Mao Tse-tung's group has acted as the leaders of a potentially powerful nation: they have attempted to define, defend and if possible extend the boundaries of the Chinese People's Republic; to extend its sphere of influence to neighboring states; and to win world recognition, prestige and a share of the global decision-making commensurate with its power. A number of factors have impeded realization of the nationalistic aims of Communist China: strong American support for Chiang Kai-shek; American opposition to its membership in the United Nations; and most important in this context, a certain amount of conflict with the hegemonistic aims of the Soviet Union. Moreover, when the Soviet leaders have presumed to make unilateral decisions which affect all socialist states, the Chinese self-concept of superiority and the Chinese national pride is wounded. These factors, combined with a heritage of anti-Russian sentiment from the Tsarist and Stalin eras, contribute to a low frustration tolerance level for the Chinese.

Economic factors loom large in this conflict, as in the majority of conflicts between nations. China is still an underdeveloped "have not" nation; the U.S.S.R. has entered the camp of the most economically and politically powerful "have" nations. Although China has made considerable economic progress, partly because of the 1953-1960 Soviet economic aid program, much greater economic strength is a prerequisite for great power status. The Chinese have resented what they consider to be minimal Soviet assistance to a comradely nation, and were angered by the 1960 Soviet cutback in aid which was in part motivated by a desire to show the Chinese that the Soviet purse would be opened widest to those who were most amenable to Soviet influence. The Chinese have adopted the position that the U.S.S.R. is violating Marxist international ideology by concentrating on its own rapid development, and thereby, increasing the gap between the Soviet Union and other socialist states. The Soviet view of the situation is, however, altogether different. The U.S.S.R. did, in fact, assume considerable responsibility for the economic development of Communist China, probably more than it could legitimately afford in terms of the low standard of living of the Soviet people themselves. Had the Soviet Union attempted to raise China to its own level of economic development, its own position as a major world power would have been seriously jeopardized, and discontent among the Soviet people might have reached major proportions. Khrushchev pointed out that the Soviet people must be given some rewards for their sacrifices; Soviet aid on the scale expected by the Chinese would have postponed these rewards indefinitely, and would have destroyed the Soviet hope to win the peaceful economic competition with the West. Equally important was the fact that the Soviet leaders did not feel that they were getting fair returns for their economic aid. With each economic advance that the Chinese People's Republic experienced, the Chinese leaders felt freer to assert their independence from Moscow. Moreover, while the U.S.S.R. was pumping its economic resources into China, the Chinese were expending considerable sums to extend their influence over the socialist nations of Asia and over new and underdeveloped states. In short, Soviet resources were being used to extend Chinese influence, at least in part, to the detriment of Soviet influence. The Russians also recognized that if China with its huge population (approximately 760 million) were to equal the U.S.S.R. in economic development, it could pose a real threat to the security of the Soviet Union. The Soviet leaders have had good reason to assume that by adding appreciably to China's economic strength, they were building up a potential rival which, when it became strong enough, would attempt to dominate them. Chinese references to the superiority of the East over the West, and the yellows over the whites did nothing to allay such suspicions. Had the Chinese demonstrated more of the diplomacy, sensitivity and patience at which they assume they excel, they could perhaps have postponed the Sino-Soviet cleavage for a period of years, and thereby benefited from Soviet economic assistance for a longer time.

The Chinese also deeply resent their relative "have not" status in the military sphere. They have been angered and humiliated by the Soviet refusal to share nuclear secrets with them and claim that in 1959 the U.S.S.R. unilaterally broke a 1957 Sino-Soviet defense technology agreement and "refused to give China models of an atomic bomb and the technical documents for its production, making a present of this on the occasion of the . . . trip by the Soviet leader to the U.S.A. in September, 1959."[42] They were particularly bitter when the U.S.S.R. agreed with the Americans and British on a test ban in 1963 against very strong Chinese protests. The test ban treaty, the Chinese said, ". . . bears witness only to the fact that the foreign policy line being conducted by the Soviet leaders is capitulation in the full sense of the word. The imperialists, of course, eagerly accede to co-existence with those who capitulate to them, but this is capitulation, not co-existence."[43] The Soviet agreement to the pledge that nuclear powers should not give nuclear weapons or the technical information necessary for their production to non-nuclear states and that non-nuclear states should not accept such weapons or technical information involved, according to the Chinese, a gross violation of China's

sovereignty. The Chinese added that "The Soviet leaders long before today began to enter deals with American imperialism, trying to bind China
hand and foot."[44] In 1964 the Chinese, apparently without Soviet assistance, exploded an atomic bomb of their own construction. Although
this feat was tremendously important from the point of view of the Chinese
self-concept, it did little to change Communist China's immediate status as
a world power or its relative position of power among the socialist countries, since China's nuclear power is infinitesimal in comparison to that
of the U.S.A. and the U.S.S.R., and even to that of Britain and France.
The Chinese have been furious because the U.S.S.R., as the only effective
nuclear power among the socialist states, can and does formulate policies
which regulate interaction between the socialist and Western blocs, almost
completely independent of Chinese influence. The situation could be
fraught with frustration for the Chinese even if they agreed with Soviet
decisions concerning inter-bloc relations. Since they are adamantly opposed to the Soviet "revisionist" approach to communist world strategy,
their subordinate role as a non-effective nuclear power is doubly hard
to take.

The frustration of the Chinese is compounded by the fact that Communist China is excluded from the United Nations, and even after its
recognition by France in 1964, is ignored by most of the Western powers.
Although the U.S.S.R. is not responsible for the inferior status accorded
to the Peking regime in the international arena, since it has repeatedly
made sincere and strenuous efforts to have the United Nations admit Communist China, the different world status of the two largest communist
states is a reason for conflict over foreign policy, which in turn contributes
to their overall irritation with each other. The U.S.S.R. is treated as a
super-power by Western powers, and is in a position to negotiate with
them. Communist China, on the other hand, is ignored, belittled and
denied channels of negotiation; as a consequence, it regards most of the
rest of the world as the "enemy" and frames its foreign policy and its
diatribes accordingly. Moreover, Soviet leaders, while acting in general
for the international communist movement in negotiations with other
powers, are at the same time serving primarily as the leaders of the
U.S.S.R. The Chinese, with their nationalistic aspirations, different world
view, lower status and, by the same token, lower level of responsibility,
can hardly be expected to agree with all Soviet decisions concerning relations between socialist and Western states. The Soviet leaders, on the
other hand, are hampered in their attempts to stabilize relations with the
Western powers by the constant needling and the denunciatory harangues
which the Chinese direct toward the U.S.S.R. as well as toward the
Western bloc.

Differences between the Chinese and Soviet approaches arise also because of the different ages of their respective revolutions. The Communist Party has controlled the U.S.S.R. for almost a half century, and the contemporary Soviet leadership is made up of second and third generation communists, who were not themselves engaged in a militant revolution, and whose main task has been the defense and extension of the revolutionary gains. Contemporary Chinese leaders, on the other hand, led their militant revolutionary movement and think in terms of the "revolutionary battles" which are yet to be fought. The Chinese leaders, because they are so much closer to the revolution, show much more revolutionary ardor, militarism and bitterness than the Soviet leaders. The Soviet revolution has acquired maturity, status, power and possessions. The Chinese revolution, which is still in the stage of raw, militant adolescence, has yet to prove itself. Generally speaking, the Soviet Union is satisfied with her accomplishments in terms of world power and status, and her potential for internal development. Because she wants to maintain and extend what she has gained, she cannot afford adventurism in her dealings with the Western states. The U.S.S.R. has also acquired the caution which befits a well-developed state with global responsibility. Rather than to risk losing what she has by involvement in a military conflict, she prefers to rely on long-range political and economic competition. Communist China, on the other hand, is generally dissatisfied with its world status, its status in the communist movement and its own economic development. The Chinese, who in comparison to the U.S.S.R. have relatively little to defend, tend to emphasize the extension rather than the defense of revolutionary gains. It has fitted the purposes of the Chinese to blame "the imperialists" for the majority of their difficulties and to mobilize the energies of their people against the external challenge symbolized by the United States. China, unlike the U.S.S.R., cannot think realistically in terms of military or economic competition with the United States within the twentieth century, and hence, its preferred tactic is to foment a world revolution. They believe that if all the peoples of the world were to rise up against the "capitalist imperialists," both the internal and external status of China would be improved immeasurably. Thus, the Chinese leaders, because of their personal experience with revolutionary tactics and the relative "have not" status of their nation, tend to be much more revolutionary and militant than the Soviet leaders, and are severely provoked by the "peaceful capitulation" policy which they attribute to the U.S.S.R.

Against the background of these and other factors the Soviet and Chinese leaders have conducted their bitter "ideological" dispute. Initially, both sets of leaders maintained the pretense that the basis of their disagreement was, above all else, ideological. By 1964, however, the pretense had worn thin and each side began openly to accuse the other of using the ideological dispute as a cover for "great power schemes," "hegemonism" and "nationalistic policies."[45] There are, of course, real and important ideological differences, but the ideological dispute is best viewed as a derivative and expression of more basic differences. The essence of the dispute does not lie in their different interpretations of Marxism-Leninism, but rather in practical politics, and the desire of each, if not to dominate the other, at least not to be dominated.

In the course of the lengthy and bitter polemics, representatives of the Soviet and Chinese Communist Parties have expressed ideological differences in almost every conceivable sphere. A clear cut statement of the issues and the positions of the adversaries is confounded by a number of factors: neither party has attempted to present its position with maximum conciseness or clarity; differences have been exaggerated because each party attributes to the other positions which it did not take; at times, both sides argue belligerently from essentially the same position; on some issues neither party has maintained ideological consistency; both sides issue insulting and irrelevant taunts and engage in self-aggrandizement. In some respects, the dispute between the world's two leading communist parties could be likened to a sophisticated version of an argument between two small school boys over who will be the captain of the team. However, although the exchange abounds in trivialities, basic differences are involved which center around interrelated issues such as the correct interpretation of Marxism-Leninism and who has the right to interpret it; decision-making within the socialist bloc; the strategy of the world communist movement including tactics and policies toward the West and toward emergent and non-aligned nations; intra-socialist bloc relations; and internal policies for the development of communism.

Since Marxism-Leninism is held to be a complete political, philosophical, economic, social and moral doctrine, the need for the "correct" interpretation of the ideology permeates and, in fact, clutters the discussion of all points of difference. Each party claims that its interpretation of Marxism-Leninism is correct and that the other has espoused an erroneous and dangerous interpretation which it attempts to impose on all other communist parties. The Chinese charge that the Soviet "revisionists," usually referred to as "certain people," have, under the pretext of "creatively developing Marxism-Leninism" cast aside "universal Marxist-Leninist truths" and have tried to force on others their own erroneous "prescriptions which are based on nothing but subjective conjectures and are divorced from reality and from the masses."[46] According to the Chinese, the leaders of the C.P.S.U., as "modern revisionists, are opposing Marxism-Leninism under the pretext of opposing dogmatism, and are renouncing revolution under the pretext of opposing 'Left' adventurism, and are advocating unprincipled compromise and capitulation under the pretext of flexibility in tactics."[47] The Soviet leaders deny the charge that they have been guilty of revisionism; they declare with full self-righteousness that "The C.P.S.U. has always sacredly guarded the purity of Marxist-Leninist teaching, creatively developing it under new historical circumstances."[48] At the same time, the C.P.S.U. charges the Chinese with two equally despicable, but opposite, errors; the Chinese have not recognized the correctness of the creative interpretations developed by the C.P.S.U., and have dared to introduce their own incorrect interpretations. Soviet theoreticians state: "Marxist-Leninist theory . . . constantly develops on the basis of the Communist and the entire liberation movement and is enriched by new conclusions. To approach the theory as a collection of congealed rules, as they are now doing in Peking, is to break with the very spirit of Marxist-Leninist teaching. . . ."[49] It is the Chinese, according to the C.P.S.U., who are guilty of destroying the purity of Marxism-Leninism: "In their struggle for hegemony the Chinese leaders are more and more openly replacing Leninism with Mao Tse-tungism, letting it be known that Mao Tse-tungism is the chief thing and Leninism is subordinate."[50] Soviet spokesmen add that "defending the ideological legacy" is

" . . . especially important now, when Communists throughout the world have come into conflict with the hegemonistic desires of the Chinese leaders who, distorting Marxist-Leninist teaching, are attempting to drive the Communist Parties from the true path, to subordinate the revolutionary movement to their own nationalist purposes and aspirations."[51]

The Communist Party of China (C.P.C.), which has been no more pleased with Khrushchev's theoretical innovations than the C.P.S.U. is with Mao's, stated:

" There are certain persons who assert that they have made the greatest creative contributions to revolutionary theory since Lenin and that they alone are correct. But it is very dubious whether they have ever really given consideration to the extensive experience of the entire world Communist movement, whether they have ever really considered the interests, the goals and tasks of the international proletarian movement as a whole, and whether they really have a general line for the international Communist movement which conforms to Marxism-Leninism."[52]

One of the chief concerns of the Chinese has been that the Soviet interpretation of "peaceful co-existence" covers "relations between colonial and semi-colonial people on the one hand and imperialists and colonialists on the other," and, as such, asks "oppressed nations to 'co-exist peacefully' with their colonial rulers . . . rather than to resist or wage struggles for independence."[53]

The criticisms which each side has directed at the other have carried a high degree of validity; for example, each side has interpreted Marxism-Leninism to suit its own purposes; the Soviet leaders, long accustomed to

their position of dominance, have more or less assumed that their interpretation would be accepted without question by the other communist
parties; the Chinese have inserted strong nationalist and racist overtones
into the ideology, and have practically deified Mao; the C.P.S.U. has been
relatively uninformed about the Asian situation and, consequently, the
Chinese claim that the Soviet doctrine is not suitable for the international
proletarian movement as a whole is justified. Both sides agree that "the
cause of Socialism cannot move forward successfully without a decisive
struggle for the purity of Marxism-Leninism."[54] However, each reserves
for itself the right to legislate on the purity of the ideology, to develop it
creatively along the "correct lines" in terms of new historical conditions,
and to expect other parties to adopt its interpretation. Since the interpretation offered by each party is influenced by the current conditions and
goals under which that party operates, neither party can offer an interpretation that is wholly acceptable to the other.

Much of the ideological dispute has centered around issues related
to the strategy for the extension of the socialist system. It should be stressed,
however, that although the C.P.S.U. and the C.P.C. are arguing violently
over general issues of world strategy, they agree completely that one of
the most important goals of the communist movement is to eradicate
capitalism and to extend socialism. There is consensus that capitalism
must be "buried"; there is disagreement over the choice of techniques to
hasten its burial. Also, although neither side openly admits it, one of the
issues in the dispute is whether the U.S.S.R. or the C.P.R. shall benefit
more from the anticipated demise of capitalism. In general, the preferred
technique of the U.S.S.R. is to rely on long-range political and economic
competition between the two blocs without military encounters. The
U.S.S.R. believes that in its negotiations with Western powers it must
argue from a position of military and economic strength, but that armed
conflict is unnecessary because socialism will eventually demonstrate its
superiority under conditions of peaceful competition. The general tenor of
the Chinese position is much more revolutionary, action-oriented and
violent. The Chinese have, in some respects, a more realistic evaluation
of the internal strengths of the Western social orders, and are of the
opinion that more pressure than is advocated by the U.S.S.R. will be
required to ensure the victory of socialism. Moreover, they are afraid that
the U.S.S.R., in its desire to avoid a thermo-nuclear war, is following a
policy of appeasement which is endangering the opportunities for socialist
gain, and may "end up burying the cause of the proletarian revolution."[55]

The C.P.S.U. has repeatedly criticized the Chinese for having adopted
a position toward war which is erroneous from both the ideological and
tactical points of view. Whatever the true position of the Chinese, the
Soviet leaders have attributed to them a position which borders on war-

mongering for the purpose of advancing the socialist revolution and particularly Chinese national goals. A Soviet editorial described the "special platform that has been created in Peking in the area of foreign policy" as:

> ". . . an orientation toward maintaining international tensions, which is regarded as a favorable atmosphere for implementing hegemonistic plans, masked in the slogan of 'world revolution'. If one follows the course that is being imposed from Peking concerning the world thermo-nuclear war that might be provoked, it would seem that this is not a hindrance but, on the contrary, a good thing for the revolution."[56]

The Chinese, Soviet spokesmen assert, "prefer to repeat the ideas that war cannot be done away with while imperialism exists, that peaceful co-existence is only an illusion and is not a general principle of the foreign policies of the socialist countries, and that the struggle for peace allegedly impedes the revolutionary struggle."[57] The U.S.S.R. claims that far from representing capitulation to the Western powers, its policy of peaceful co-existence strengthens the cause of socialism:

> "The slogan 'A world without weapons, a world without war' in the hands of the Communist Parties is a mighty weapon for the consolidation of the popular masses for an active struggle against the shameless militarist imperialist circles. . . . Isn't it clear that the rejection of this slogan could only weaken the Communists' influence on the popular masses, which would play into the hands of reaction?"[58]

Peaceful co-existence, Soviet theoreticians say, is a wise policy, not because the "imperialists" have become more "complaisant" or "peace-loving," but because their fear of the "devastating rebuff," which could be administered to them by the military might of the socialist countries, forces them to pursue a relatively peaceful policy, and under conditions of peace, a favorable atmosphere is provided for an increase in strength of "mighty workers' and democratic movements in the capitalist countries."[59] At the same time, according to the C.P.S.U., the national liberation movements, which are strengthened by the policy of peaceful co-existence, steadily weaken the position of the Western nations.

The U.S.S.R. has adopted a highly moralistic attitude toward the alleged Chinese disregard of the loss of life which would result from war between the socialist and Western blocs. According to a Soviet government statement:

> "While certain persons in Peking are prepared to sacrifice the lives of half their country's population and the lives of half mankind, the CPSU Central Committee and the Soviet government cherish not only the lives of half the population of the Soviet Union, but the life of every Soviet person and they are by no means indifferent to the fate of other peoples of the world."[60]

Soviet spokesmen have pointed out, perhaps with justification, that the Chinese leaders may feel that they can afford to heighten international tension and to act "with irresponsibility" since the U.S.S.R. rather than China would be the first target for nuclear bombs from the West:

> "Are they not counting on the fact that 'others'—those against whom the most reactionary imperialist forces would like to direct their nuclear weapons in the first place—will have to pay for the thoughtless and irresponsible provocation of imperialism? Perhaps the final meaning of the twaddle about 'the paper tiger' and the profuse talk about the 'self-sacrifice' of true hero-revolutionaries lies here?"[61]

The most crucial Soviet criticism is that the Chinese have betrayed the goals of proletarian internationalism. The U.S.S.R. argues that the Chinese have abandoned the thesis of a socialist victory through class struggle and instead are inciting the peoples of Asia, Africa and Latin America to engage in a racial struggle which is directed against the entire white race, regardless of class affiliation. The C.P.S.U. suggests that the position taken by

> ". . . the Chinese comrades may give rise to justified suspicion that what we have here is no longer a class approach in the struggle for the destruction of capitalism but some sort of completely different aims . . . it is impossible not to direct attention to the fact that, instead of the class internationalist approach as expressed in the slogan 'Proletarians of all countries, unite!', the Chinese comrades are stubbornly propagandizing the slogan, lacking all class content, 'The wind from the East will prevail over the wind from the West'."[62]

The Chinese are further accused of abandoning the division of the world into two opposing social systems, the socialist and capitalist, and of having substituted in its stead a division of the world into geographical zones with the peoples of Asia, Africa and Latin America representing a "special community of interests." This approach, according to the C.P.S.U., totally ignores the social system and the class structure of the component countries, and is dictated solely by "the purposes of the great-power policy of the C.P.C. leaders" who, in their attempts to attain "hegemony over the national-liberation movement" are "trying to separate this movement from the world system of socialism."[63]

The Chinese, in turn, assail the U.S.S.R. for adopting a "non-revolutionary" line, betraying the vital interests of the people of the whole world, "capitulating to the imperialists," "paralyzing the revolutionary will of the proletariat" and "caring only for their own well-being."[64] They argue that by over-emphasizing peaceful competition with the capitalist states, the Soviet leaders have renounced their position as true revolutionaries. "Certain persons," according to the Chinese,

> ". . . have one-sidedly exaggerated the role of peaceful competition between socialist and imperialist countries in their attempt to substitute peaceful competition for the revolutionary struggles of the oppressed peoples and nations. According to their preaching, it would seem that imperialism will automatically collapse in the course of this peaceful competition and that the only thing that the oppressed peoples and nations will have to do is to wait

quietly for the advent of this day. What does this have in common with Marxism-Leninism?"[65]

The Chinese maintain that:

"The proletarian party must never base its thinking, its policies for revolution and its entire work on the assumption that the imperialists and reactionaries will accept peaceful transformation. The proletarian party must prepare itself for two eventualities—while preparing for peaceful development of the revolution, it must also fully prepare for a non-peaceful development."[66]

They add that though they would "prefer to bring about the transition to socialism by peaceful means," as true revolutionaries devoted to the cause of Marxism-Leninism, they are prepared to make inevitable "sacrifices."[67] "To abandon revolution on the pretext of avoiding sacrifices," they say, "is in reality to demand that the people should forever remain slaves and endure infinite pain and sacrifice. . . ."[68] The Chinese vehemently reject the Soviet allegation that they have adopted an adventuristic position toward war between states as "nothing but imperialist and reactionary slander" designed "to hide the fact that they are opposed to revolutions by the oppressed peoples and nations of the world and opposed to others supporting such revolutions."[69] They assert that the abolition of war is their ideal and that as true Marxists-Leninists they believe that world war can be averted.[70] However, they argue that to lump together "just and unjust wars" and to oppose them all indiscriminately is a "bourgeois pacifist" not a Marxist-Leninist approach. Wars of national liberation and revolutionary civil wars, the Chinese say, are "just" wars, and are absolutely necessary. Peaceful transition is rejected by the Chinese as a "new world-wide strategic principle of the international Communist movement" because:

"Marxism-Leninism consistently holds that the fundamental question in all revolutions is that of state power. . . . The old government never topples even in a period of crisis, unless it is pushed. This is a universal law of class struggle . . . the prophets who pin all their hopes on 'peaceful transition' proceed from historical idealism, ignore the most fundamental contradictions of capitalism, repudiate the Marxist-Leninist teachings on class struggle, and arrive at a subjective and groundless conclusion. . . . The proletarian party must never base its thinking, its policies for revolution and its entire work on the assumption that the imperialists and reactionaries will accept peaceful transformation."[71]

The Chinese claim that the Soviet leaders, in their desire to maintain world peace, have adopted a "pacifist" approach which is extremely detrimental to the world socialist movement. They imply that the C.P.S.U. is asking the people of the world to believe in the "assurances" and "good intentions" of the imperialists and to place their hopes for world peace on "mutual conciliation" and "mutual accommodations" with imperialism.[72] By begging imperialism for peace, the U.S.S.R. has purportedly thrown overboard revolutionary principles.[73] According to the Soviet stand on peaceful co-existence, the Chinese say, oppressed peoples and nations should not wage struggles against "imperialism" and "reactionaries" for fear of disturbing world peace.[74] The Chinese also express grave doubts that communist aims can be advanced through Soviet support to "national bourgeois" regimes in ex-colonial countries such as Egypt and India, particularly if these regimes refuse to co-operate with and even outlaw the local Communist Party as Nasser has done. What the U.S.S.R. has been doing, the C.P.C. asserts, is to substitute class collaboration for class struggle on a world wide scale, and to advocate, in effect, a fusion of the socialist and capitalist systems.[75] The over-emphasis on peaceful co-existence and peaceful transition to socialism, according to the Chinese, will benumb the revolutionary will of the proletariat, result in ideological disarmament, and political and organizational unpreparedness, and will eventually "bury" the proletarian revolution.[76] The Chinese alternative to Soviet pacificism is to inculcate in the masses of the people "the revolutionary confidence, the revolutionary courage and the revolutionary spirit to defeat imperialism and the reactionaries" and "to resolutely combat every trace of weakness and capitulation" since "otherwise there will be no hope for any revolution."[77]

The difference in emphasis on the best techniques to speed the transition from capitalism to socialism and to capitalize on the national liberation movement derive in part from, and are augmented by, differences in world status and national goals. The Chinese fear that the Soviet emphasis on peaceful transition reflects a willingness to collaborate with and even to capitulate to capitalist powers, in order to protect Soviet gains while endangering the entire communist movement. The C.P.S.U. fears that the Chinese policy of "prodding revolutions" could increase international tension to such an extent that a thermo-nuclear war would be inevitable. The Soviet Government has criticized the Chinese leaders for

> ". . . trying to impose on the international working class and the national liberation movement the theory of prodding revolution through 'revolutionary wars' . . . in obvious violation of Lenin's tenet that revolution is an internal matter for the working people of each country and that revolution cannot be imported from abroad."[78]

Moreover, "in the course of prodding revolutions, the C.P.C. leaders irresponsibly assume that revolution is possible always, . . . ignore the correlation of class forces . . . and fail to take the international situation into account."[79] This is condemned as a "serious mistake" since "local wars might be the spark that ignites the flames of a world war."[80] Moreover, the Soviet statement continued, it is doubtful whether the C.P.C. leaders are really "zealous revolutionaries," since "the facts show that the Chinese leaders, far from giving first place to the interests of the peoples who are fighting for socialism and national liberation, are pursuing their own great power aims." The Chinese Government countered by saying that the Soviet leaders have indulged in "national egoism," "permitted themselves to be at one with the American imperialists," and at a time when millions of "oppressed peoples are . . . waging a majestic struggle for their independence and freedom," the Soviet leaders have cared "only for their own well-being."[81] The Soviet leaders are thereby responsible for "paralyzing the fighting will of the peoples of all countries and undermining the cause of peace throughout the world."[82] Moreover, according to the Chinese, the U.S.S.R. has misinterpreted the national liberation movement and has failed to support it adequately. The C.P.C. stated:

> "Certain persons in the international Communist movement are now taking a passive or scornful or negative attitude toward the struggles of the oppressed nations for liberation. They are in fact protecting the interests of monopoly capital, betraying those of the proletariat and degenerating into social democrats."[83]

Soviet spokesmen retorted that they have supported the national liberation movement fully but that unlike the Chinese, they do not believe that capitalism will be destroyed on the basis of this movement. According to the Soviet analysis:

> "The national liberation movement . . . is not a class movement; various classes united in the struggle against the common enemy, imperialism, take part in it. Objectively, however, this movement because of its anti-imperialist nature, helps the cause of the world socialist revolution. . . . Communists have never considered the national liberation movement to be the main factor leading to the collapse of world capital, have not equated this movement with the class struggle of the proletariat of all countries against the bourgeoisie, have not placed it in opposition to the international working class and its principle offspring—the world socialist system."[84]

Soviet theoreticians say that it is correct for the working class to co-operate with the national bourgeoisie who are usually at the forefront of a national liberation movement, and for socialist states to encourage and support such movements since the liberation of oppressed people weakens the capitalist social order and some of the new states adopt the "non-capitalist" path of development.[85] The Chinese are, in turn, criticized for giving priority to the national liberation movement over the international workers' movement, substituting a "petty-bourgeois approach" for the proletarian and class approach and for preaching that "it is not the working class but the national bourgeoisie that must have hegemony over the world struggle against imperialism."[86] The C.P.S.U. charged that by adopting an erroneous ideological position "the C.P.C. is gambling on the national liberation movement, hoping to bring it under its own hegemony, to isolate it from the international working class and the world socialist system."[87] Chinese attempts to incite national and racial egoism are described as reflecting:

". . . neither concern for the world revolution nor . . . for the national liberation movement. . . . They are simply attempts to earn cheap popularity among the peoples of Asia, Africa and Latin America through flattering words, to establish their hegemony over them and use them for egotistical, great power goals."[88]

The constant repetition of the accusation that the other party to the dispute is pursuing great power goals indicates clearly that although there are real ideological differences concerning the world strategy of the socialist movement, the ideological and practical positions adopted by each of the two socialist giants may be governed more by their desire to enhance their own power than by genuine differences in their interpretation of Marxism-Leninism.

The importance of the power motive is clearly demonstrated in the Sino-Soviet exchange concerning relations between socialist states. Communist China is spear-heading a struggle, which in some respects resembles that waged by what the Chinese refer to as the "Yugoslav traitors," against Soviet monolithism. The Soviet leaders are able, from an intellectual point of view, to accept the necessity for sharing decision-making power within the socialist bloc. However, partly because of the habit of the long standing recognition of the Soviet leadership as the final source of authority in the communist world, and partly because of a genuine reluctance to share their power, particularly with non-subservient fellow communists such as the leaders of the C.P.C., the men in Moscow do sometimes act as if unilateral decisions made in Moscow should be adopted without question by fraternal parties and states. Each set of leaders maintains that it adheres completely to the principles of complete equality, respect for territorial integrity, sovereignty and independence, non-interference in each other's internal affairs, mutual support and mutual assistance in accordance with proletarian internationalism.[89] Each side accuses the other of violating these principles in a number of ways. The Soviet leaders assert that the Chinese have attempted to impose their erroneous theories and policies on other socialist states and parties, have actively supported factions which have been expelled from parties in other states, have engaged in schismatic and underhand dealings, and have even attempted to interfere with Soviet domestic and foreign policies and to violate the territorial integrity of the U.S.S.R.[90] The Chinese claim that the C.P.S.U. has attempted to impose its program and resolutions on other fraternal parties as the "common program" of the international communist movement, the U.S.S.R. has used economic pressure on fraternal countries and has interfered with their internal and domestic policies, and that among other gross violations, the C.P.S.U. and the U.S.S.R. have posed as the "superior" party and state in the communist movement.[91] Each of the accusations, whether made by the Soviet or the Chinese authorities, is based on more than a kernel of truth. Although each of the adversaries claims complete innocence and describes itself in the most virtuous terms, both have engaged in practices within and outside of the socialist bloc which are greatly at variance with the noble motives which each ascribes to itself.

The cleavage in relations within the socialist bloc is based on real issues. If the Soviet Union does not or cannot maintain a leadership role, what should be the relationship between communist powers and between fraternal parties? By what means are decisions affecting relations between the socialist and the Western camps to be made if there is no one leading state or no socialist international organization which has authority to act for all socialist states? In the absence of an international organization, is it the duty of each state or party to consult with its counterparts before engaging in any policy of potential importance to the entire communist movement? If there were an international organization, what authority would it have over fraternal parties in non-socialist states? Should the more advanced states within the socialist camp be obligated to render substantial assistance to the less advanced ones, so that all would advance more or less equally toward communism? Questions such as these, though generally not phrased so explicitly, are interwoven into the Sino-Soviet dispute. The statements and the solutions proposed by the Chinese to questions of this nature are typically those of a "have not" state and party; the Soviet position reflects its "have" status.

The U.S.S.R., though by no means willing to relinquish its hold over the states in its own "camp," denies its status as the "leading" state. It refuses to enter into any international communist organization which would obligate it to assume responsibility for the world communist movement, or enable other communist parties, in combination, to dictate policy to it, or even to influence its policy. The U.S.S.R. and its C.P.S.U. (perhaps it would be more accurate to say the C.P.S.U. and its U.S.S.R.) have little to gain and could lose much through a close knit international communist organization. As the most powerful member of the socialist bloc, it can to a very large extent determine policy for the entire bloc without the fetters that would be imposed by an international organization. Under the present arrangements it can attempt to advance its own national goals or the goals of the world communist movement by rendering support to socialist countries or to national liberation movements which meet with its approval, without consulting other states or parties. If an international communist organization were established in which all states or parties had an equal voice, the U.S.S.R. might be placed in the unenviable position of serving as the economic and military base for all the less developed socialist countries. The levelling-off process which would follow would soon destroy whatever advantage the U.S.S.R. might have retained because of its superior economic and military strength.

The Chinese, on the other hand, whose status within the international communist movement was until recently that of a voice in the wilderness, would have stood to gain from the beginning of their participation in the movement if there had been a formal organization. Such an organization could have curbed the Soviet propensity for unilateral decision-making and would have allowed the Chinese to exert a much stronger influence on overall socialist strategy. The smaller socialist states, too, would prefer decision-making between parties by consensus because it would protect them, at least to a certain extent, from domination by either the U.S.S.R. or Communist China. International control over the economies of the member states might also have been a tremenuous asset to the Chinese, since a much larger portion of the U.S.S.R.'s economic gains might have been channeled southward to bolster the lagging Chinese economy.

Since the dissolution of the Third International, the closest facsimile that the communist parties have had to an international policy-making organization has been the international conferences of Communist and Workers' Parties which were held in Moscow in 1957 and 1960. The 1957 conference conferred on the C.P.S.U. the authority to convene conferences of Communist and Workers' Parties "in consultation with the fraternal parties." During the initial phases of the Sino-Soviet dispute, the Soviet leaders took no steps to call an international conference. Apparently they believed at that time that their advantages might have been minimized in an international conclave, and that therefore it would be preferable to continue the Sino-Soviet discussions on a bilateral basis. By 1964, the Soviet leaders decided that an international conference would be advisable; the change of tactics might have reflected a belief that the Chinese would be forced to yield ground under pressure from the majority of fraternal parties since, despite the fact that the C.P.C. has a number of firm supporters among the fraternal parties, it could not match the C.P.S.U. for votes in a showdown. Khrushchev might, on the other hand, have intended to use the authority of the international conference to expel the C.P.C. from the world communist movement. Whatever the Soviet intentions, the Chinese were wary. They reacted to Soviet overtures concerning a conference by retorting that:

". . . it is impermissible that one party or group of parties, in violation of the principle of consulting and achieving unity among fraternal parties, should make a unilateral decision to convene a conference of representatives of all Communist and Workers' Parties, since such action would be illegitimate and completely mistaken and would entail serious consequences."[92]

They added that a successful international conference would require a great deal of preparatory work which, to judge from the present situation, might take four or five years, or even longer. Despite the C.P.C.'s rejection, the C.P.S.U. invited a number of parties to participate in a consultive meeting which was intended to engage in preparation for a conference of representatives of all fraternal parties. The consultive meeting which was held in Moscow in March, 1965, was virtually boycotted by all parties which have aligned themselves with the C.P.C. After the meeting, a communique was issued which reflected the Soviet position, stressed that what unites the Communist Parties is much stronger than what disunites them, and called for collective efforts to improve relations among the parties and to strengthen the solidarity of the international communist movement.[93] On the whole, the accomplishments of the consultive meeting with respect to solving the Sino-Soviet dispute were nil; if anything was accomplished, it was by the Chinese who confirmed their right to remain aloof from a Soviet dominated fraternal conclave.

The Chinese have apparently decided that the Soviet propensity for making unilateral decisions which affect the entire communist movement must be curbed sharply. One example from many, of a unilateral Soviet decision which angered the Chinese was Khrushchev's de-Stalinization campaign. The attack on Stalin had implications for all communist parties and socialist states because Stalin had been the recognized leader of the communist international movement; after his fallibility was publicized, a re-organization of relations within all parties was indicated. Had the C.P.S.U. consulted with the C.P.C. and other fraternal parties before the Twentieth Party Congress the Chinese, who had little reason to love Stalin, might possibly have approved the de-Stalinization movement, and at any rate, would have had time to prepare for it. The Soviet denunciation of Stalin, without prior consultation, was interpreted subsequently as a violation of proper decision-making power and as an example of Soviet high-handedness and crudity. The Chinese managed, however, to phrase their objections in ideological terms. The C.P.C. stated:

> "Over the past few years, certain persons have violated Lenin's integral teachings about the interrelations of leaders, party, class and masses, and raised the issue of 'combatting the cult of the individual'. This is erroneous and harmful. . . . To raise the question of 'combatting the cult of the individual' is actually to counterpose the leaders to the masses, undermine the Party's unified leadership which is based on democratic centralism, dissipate its fighting strength and disintegrate its ranks. . . . The Communist Party of China has always disapproved of exaggerating the role of the individual."[94]

The ideological objections were bolstered by a blunt, and not entirely unjustified, attack on Khrushchev:

> "While loudly combatting the so-called cult of the individual, certain persons are in reality doing their best to defame the proletarian party and the dictatorship of the proletariat. At the same time they are enormously exaggerating the role of certain individuals, shifting all errors onto others and claiming all credit for themselves.
> "What is more serious is that under the pretext of 'combatting the cult of the individual' certain persons are crudely interfering in the internal affairs

of other fraternal parties and fraternal countries and forcing other fraternal parties to change their leadership in order to impose their own wrong line on these parties. What is all this if not great-power chauvinism, sectarianism and splittism? What is all this if not subversion?"[95]

By the same token, the Soviet attack on the Albanian leaders, Khrushchev's analysis of their errors and the attempts of the C.P.S.U. to "guide" the Albanian Workers' Party to adopt a "correct" Marxist-Leninist course were regarded by the Chinese as gross interference in the affairs of a fraternal party. The absence of appropriate discussion and reconciliation gestures and the publicity of the attack, according to the Chinese, violated proper relations between fraternal parties and fraternal states, damaged proletarian internationalism and weakened the world communist movement. The Chinese are probably right in this respect, but the damage to the world communist solidarity caused by the Soviet-Albanian quarrel would appear to be infinitesimal in comparison to that caused by the Sino-Soviet dispute.

The discrepancies in the economic advances of the two countries is reflected in the ideological dispute about goals for the welfare of the people during the current stage of development. The Chinese imply that the goal of the C.P.S.U. to provide a better life for the Soviet people is a manifestation of the "bourgeoisification" of the Soviet leaders and the degeneration of Soviet society. The Soviet leaders, in turn, imply that the Chinese have a very distorted notion of communism. The C.P.S.U. has stated scornfully that, according to the logic of the Chinese leaders, "if people walk about in bast sandals and drink thin cabbage soup from a common bowl, this is communism, but if a working people lives well today and wants to live still better tomorrow, this is all but a restoration of capitalism."[96]

The most purely ideological aspect of the entire Sino-Soviet dispute is the Chinese allegation that the C.P.S.U. committed an ideological blunder when it announced that in the U.S.S.R., the state of the dictatorship of the proletariat had evolved into a state of the entire people and that proletarian democracy had evolved into socialist democracy of all the people. The Chinese quote innumerable statements from Marx and Lenin to the effect that "the dictatorship of the proletariat will inevitably continue for the entire historical period of the transition from capitalism to communism, that is, for the entire period up to the abolition of all class differences and the entry into a classless society."[97] According to the Chinese, the concept of a state of the entire people is meaningless: "In the view of Marxists-Leninists, there is no such thing as a non-class or super-class state. So long as the state remains a state, it must bear a class character; as long as the state exists, it cannot be a state of the 'entire people'. As soon as society becomes classless, there will no longer be a state."[98] The C.P.C. pointed out that bourgeois spokesmen usually refer to a bourgeois state as a "state of all the people," and that by doing likewise, without adequate justification, the C.P.S.U. had replaced the Marxist-Leninist concept of a state by a bourgeois concept. The Chinese assert that the dictatorship of the proletariat is indispensable for the struggle against the enemies of the proletariat and the people, the remolding of society, the building of socialism and the transition to communism.[99] It cannot be dispensed with, they say, until a classless society is established and, they add, "certain people" are entirely wrong when they claim that "their society is already one without classes," because remnants of the old exploiting classes, new capitalists, parasites, speculators and other undesirable elements still exist.[100] The C.P.C. charged that the announcement "halfway before entering the higher stage of Communist society that the party of the proletariat has become the 'party of the entire people'" and the repudiation of its "proletarian class character" disarms "the proletariat and all the working people, organizationally and ideologically" and is "tantamount to helping to restore capitalism."[101]

The leaders of the C.P.S.U. retorted that the "malicious attacks" by the Chinese theoreticians are nothing but "slanderous fabrications" which are "inconsistent, confused, reactionary" and "testify to the break of the C.P.C. with revolutionary theory."[102] In the first place, according to the C.P.S.U., when Marx and Lenin talked about the necessity of the proletarian state and the dictatorship they were referring to the transition from capitalism to socialism, and not to the transition from socialism to capitalism. "The Chinese comrades," they say, "are mechanically applying the laws of development of society in the period of transition from capitalism to socialism to the period of transition from socialism to communism."[103] During the earlier stage, the dictatorship of the proletariat is necessary to suppress antagonistic classes. However, according to the C.P.S.U., with "the complete and final victory of socialism" in the U.S.S.R., class conflict has been eliminated and the need for the dictatorship of the proletariat has disappeared.[104] They add that no Soviet communist has ever asserted that a classless society has already been created in the U.S.S.R.; Soviet society still consists of two basic classes, the workers and the peasants but "the relations between all the social sections of Soviet society are not the relations of class struggle but relations of solidarity, comradely co-operation and mutual aid, fraternal unity and a community of interests and goals."[105] They reject as "ridiculous" the notion that the dictatorship of the proletariat is necessary to cope with parasitical elements and "other bearers of bourgeois survivals" and categorically deny the Chinese charge that "new bourgeois elements are constantly making their appearance in the U.S.S.R."[106]

The C.P.S.U. countercharged that, although the dictatorship of the proletariat is indispensable in Communist China where antagonistic class relations still prevail, the C.P.C. has over-emphasized its suppressive nature and under-emphasized the essential fact that the dictatorship of the proletariat "is a democracy for the working class, a socialist democracy."[107] The C.P.S.U. asserted that there is no justification for the Chinese suggestion that the U.S.S.R. is no longer a socialist state because it has adopted the theses of the "state of all the people" and "the party of all the people." What has happened, they say, is that since the "victory of socialism" there have been "no exploiter classes and no one to suppress" and, consequently, the state has been transformed "from a weapon of class supremacy into an agency expressing the will of the entire people";[108] and, since "all groups in society, with the working class in the leading role, are fighting for the construction of Communism" the Communist Party is able to express and represent the interests "of the entire people."[109]

In the dispute over the dictatorship of the proletariat and the state and party of all the people, as in other segments of the Sino-Soviet dispute, neither side is arguing from an entirely logical position. The Chinese, for example, have been unnecessarily rigid in their interpretation of statements by Marx about the continued necessity of the dictatorship of the proletariat, and the C.P.S.U. has, no doubt, exaggerated the harmony of relations among different groups in Soviet society. Had the C.P.S.U. and C.P.C. not been at each other's throats for a number of other reasons, their ideological differences about the dictatorship of the proletariat and the state of all the people could have been settled without undue difficulty. No great violation of Marxism-Leninism would have been required to admit that class structure, class relations and relations between the party and the masses could change as society progresses from a lower to a higher stage of socialism. This is, in effect, what the C.P.S.U. has proposed, while the Chinese seem to be arguing that relations between classes and between the party and the masses remain relatively fixed throughout the entire stage of socialism. The unilateral decision of the Soviet leaders to reinterpret Marxism-Leninism and the generalized feelings of hostility probably contributed more to the wrath of the Chinese than their actual disagreement with the Soviet interpretation. The "revisionistic error" is a club with which to beat the C.P.S.U. rather than a reason for administering a beating.

These, then, are some of the issues over which the Sino-Soviet dispute has raged. There has been considerable speculation over the effect of the Sino-Soviet cleavage on the world communist movement.[110] The immediate effect appears to be one of considerable damage. Whereas, previously, the communist movement, with the exception of the Yugoslav "revisionists," appeared to be speaking with one voice and acting with united purpose, communism now speaks with several voices, each of which claims authenticity. Its monolithic nature and its unified centrally-directed policy has been destroyed. Weaknesses and errors within the movement have been loudly and vindictively proclaimed, not by "imperialistic enemies" but by fraternal parties. The infallibility of the ideology, and the policies which the leaders have purportedly based on ideology, have been questioned. The solidarity of the socialist camp has been disrupted by the movement of Albania, North Korea and North Vietnam into the Chinese camp. Moreover, the Sino-Soviet cleavage has resulted in new or widened splits in a number of Communist Parties such as those of India, Burma, Brazil and Australia. Because there is a division on ideology, internal policy and world strategy, the entire movement is weakened. However, in the long run, it is conceivable that the world communist movement may be strengthened through its division. The U.S.S.R., unfettered by obligations to assist in the development of the Chinese economy, may be able to forge ahead more rapidly in its peaceful economic competition with the West. The Chinese, unrestricted by the Soviet fear of nuclear war, may be able to pursue more vigorously their policy of "nudging" socialist revolutions in the "have not" nations and may be able to capture and use more effectively the nationalist movement. As Professor Scalapino has pointed out:

> ". . . when the international movement was monolithic and centered in Moscow it was difficult for a foreign Communist party to take on the image of nationalism and independence or to follow pragmatic and realistic policies suited to local conditions. . . . Now . . . in many parts of the world Communism is developing a greater rapport with its own society and increased flexibility in tactics and strategy, while at the same time retaining its thorough commitment to internationalism."[111]

In some respects, Communist China is a more appropriate model than the U.S.S.R. for aspiring Asian communists, and Chinese tactics, including the use of the peasantry as a mass base for the socialist revolution, and emphasis on national aspirations, have the potential to advance the communist cause. Finally, Tito's brand of communism may be attractive to nations that wish to pursue simultaneously policies of socialism and non-alignment. Instead of one rigid and immutable brand of communism, there may be a variety of communist approaches to suit the taste of all comers.

The future course of Sino-Soviet relations remains a matter of speculation. In spite of the fact that, at times, the Chinese have acted as if Khrushchev bore personal responsibility for all of the Soviet "errors," Khrushchev's dismissal did not materially change Sino-Soviet relations, because the reasons for the dispute were unaffected. The new Soviet leaders have given no indication that they intend to modify substantially their stand on the Sino-Soviet conflict, or for that matter on any aspect of foreign policy, and the Chinese have already criticized them for their adherence to "Khrushchevism." The two parties did exchange relatively friendly greetings to mark the fifteenth anniversary of the Sino-Soviet Treaty of Friendship, Alliance and Mutual Aid, but this isolated example of cordiality was intended to inform the United States that neither of the two major socialist powers is indifferent to the Vietnam situation and as such, the exchange had little bearing on Sino-Soviet relations. In view of the exchange of personal insults and taunts, the possibility that relations could be "smoothed over" would increase if there were a marked turnover in the leadership of both parties more or less simultaneously, and if each of the new sets of leaders were to display maximum tact and to emphasize the unifying rather than the disunifying aspects of the relationship. A total change of leadership would not, however, affect the power relations between the two states and parties, and therefore would leave the basis of the conflict unchanged. Since disagreements over ideological interpretations and world communist strategy, though not unimportant, are subordinate to the underlying power struggle, the differences cannot be resolved around the conference table. Increased mutual fear of the Western powers and outside pressure which would endanger the expansion of the communist movement could, however, make it expedient for both nations to abandon temporarily the intra-socialist power struggle in order to present a united front. In spite of their differences, the U.S.S.R. and Communist China have much more in common with each other than either has with the Western world. The major common uniting themes are that both are committed to the expansion of communism and the destruction of the Western social order, and that neither would want to stand without the other in any serious confrontation with the West. Neither nation has another major potential ally to which it could turn if a complete break within the socialist camp were precipitated. Each might attempt to impose its policies on the other, but neither will take any action that would jeopardize the existence of the communist regime in the other state or in any socialist country. Whether communist solidarity, mutual goals for the expansion of the communist movement and the destruction of capitalism and mutual fear of the Western powers can provide a sufficient basis for permanent Soviet-Chinese co-operation only the future will show. In view of the factors which divide and unite the two contenders for national glorification and control over the international communist movement, an uneasy tension-filled alliance directed toward the protection and expansion of the communist movement may co-exist with attempts on the part of each to strengthen and extend its own sphere of influence.

Impact on the Individual and Society

The Soviet leadership has used consummate skill in describing its foreign policy to the world in general, and to the citizens of the U.S.S.R. and the socialist bloc. People in non-socialist countries have access to information which demonstrates the discrepancies between the stated and real goals and actions of the Soviet leadership in their relations with other states. Soviet citizens, however, and to a somewhat lesser extent citizens in other socialist states, have few channels through which to check the validity and reliability of Soviet foreign policy pronouncements. Soviet leaders paint a very pretty picture of their own policy and motives, and a very ugly picture of the policy and motives of the "Western imperialists."

Briefly, the analysis of the world situation which is presented to Soviet citizens is approximately as follows: Soviet foreign policy is directed toward peace and the welfare of mankind. The socialist states, however, have to contend with hostile imperialist forces which are ready to unleash an aggressive war against the socialist states on the slightest pretext. Only the military strength of the U.S.S.R. and the wise policies of its leaders have saved the world from a thermo-nuclear holocaust. The powerful owners of the means of production in capitalist states enjoy the fruits of the labor of the masses who live in a state of political and economic subjugation. Millions of down-trodden and oppressed people in colonies, former colonies, new and underdeveloped states are suffering under the colonial and neo-colonial policies of the imperialists. Only under socialism do the masses have a true opportunity to live without oppression. Working people the world over are striving to overthrow their capitalist overlords, but because the capitalists have firm control over the means of production, the state and military power, this is an extremely difficult, and under some of the circumstances, an impossible task. One of the missions of the U.S.S.R. and all socialist states is to remove forever from the face of the earth the "cancer of capitalism." The U.S.S.R. could accomplish this task with dispatch if it chose to use military methods, but the cost of such a victory to the peoples of the entire world, and the humanitarian principles of Marxism-Leninism preclude the use of destructive techniques. Instead, the U.S.S.R. has challenged the capitalist powers to agree to complete disarmament, and to rely solely on peaceful techniques of competition. Although the U.S.S.R. accepts the moral obligation to maintain world peace under all circumstances short of an aggressive attack by the "imperialists" on a socialist state, it is also morally obligated to assist all oppressed peoples and to arouse their "proletarian consciousness" so that they will be more firm in their resolution to escape from the capitalist yoke. The assistance which the U.S.S.R. gives to the Cubans, Algerians, North Koreans and other groups striving to gain or maintain national independence is motivated by humanitarianism, i.e., the desire to assist oppressed peoples and to weaken capitalism. In short, all that the U.S.S.R. does is good; all that the "imperialists" do is bad. A clear-cut example of the "goodness" of the U.S.S.R. is its firm stand on complete disarmament; if it were not for the militaristic, expansionistic aspirations of the capitalist states, the peoples of the world would not have to fear war, and the resources used for building up military power could be used for the welfare of mankind.

Obviously, the Soviet description of the world situation, conditions in non-socialist countries, conditions in socialist countries and the motivation underlying Soviet strategy is a far cry from the truth. However, the Soviet people are generally much less skeptical about the foreign policy pronouncements of their leaders than about propaganda with respect to domestic policy. Marxist-Leninist ideology, constant anti-imperialistic propaganda, a long tradition of suspicion of Western nations, the lack of access to non-Soviet analyses of international relations and world events, a sincere desire for peace and a number of other factors contribute to their credulousness. The majority of Soviet people, apparently, do believe that capitalism represents an evil force which threatens their peace and security, and are appreciative of the firm stand which their leaders have taken against war between the blocs. Although many of them may be relatively disinterested in the ideological aspects of the conflict between socialism and capitalism, few if any are indifferent to the prospect of war. By standing firmly for peace and peaceful competition the Soviet leaders have endeared themselves to their people, confirmed their wisdom, and strengthened the resolution of the people to compete with the "hostile forces of capitalism" along the lines selected by the leadership. The hostility between socialism and capitalism, as interpreted to the Soviet people by their leaders, thus serves as a unifying force within Soviet society, and the common desire for peace serves as an important positive link between the masses and the leadership.

The Sino-Soviet dispute, however, has introduced some disharmonious elements. Through blunt challenges and taunts, the Chinese have more or less forced the Soviet leaders to publish Chinese statements criticizing the policies of the U.S.S.R. government and the C.P.S.U. The Soviet people have been informed by the Chinese that their leaders are not infallible, and that their true motives are sometimes far different from their stated motives. It is logical to assume that some skepticism within the U.S.S.R. must have resulted from the Chinese attacks on the Soviet leadership. However, in some respects, the Chinese diatribes may serve primarily to reinforce and confirm what the Soviet leaders have already told their people. In general, the Chinese position on the "rottenness" of the capitalist system, the aggressive intentions of the capitalists and their oppression of the world's masses is even more extreme than that taken by the Soviet leadership. On the other hand, the apparent lower level of reluctance of the Chinese to engage in a military conflict may, to a certain extent, cancel the effects of the justified criticism proffered by the Chinese. The downright nastiness and pettiness of some of the Chinese pronouncements, the Chinese attitude of racial superiority, and the incidents in which Soviet nationals have been abused in China may contribute to a heightened Soviet patriotism in contra-distinction to allegiance to the international socialist movement. Had the Chinese been somewhat more tactful and less vindictive in their attacks, had they been less war-like and more sympathetic to the doctrine of the overthrow of capitalism through peaceful competition, their criticisms of the Soviet leadership might have seriously affected the faith of the Soviet people in their leaders. However, the Soviet people are so firmly behind their leaders in the desire for peace that the militaristic stance of the Chinese has, more than anything else, aroused their anger and their fear, and confirmed the wisdom of their own leaders.

REFERENCES

1 Cf. Hans J. Morgenthau, "The Real Issue Between The United States and The Soviet Union," in Robert A. Goldwin (ed.), *Readings in Russian Foreign Policy,* (New York: Oxford University Press, 1959), pp. 423-32.

2 For a good short summary of Cold War relations between the U.S.S.R. and the West, see Harry Schwartz, *The Red Phoenix,* (New York: Frederick A. Praeger, 1961), pp. 228-303.

3 L. I. Brezhnev, "47th Anniversary of the Great October Socialist Revolution," *Pravda,* No. 7, 1964, pp. 1-3. (C.D.S.P., Vol. XVI, No. 43, pp. 3-9)

4 "Communique on Conferences of Representatives of Communist and Workers' Parties," *Pravda,* Dec. 2, 1960, p. 1, and *Pravda,* Dec. 6, 1960, pp. 1-4. (C.D.S.P., Vol. XII, No. 48, pp. 3-9, and No. 49, pp. 3-7)

5 N. S. Khrushchev, "Marxism Is Our Banner, Our Fighting Weapon," *Pravda,* June 21, 1963, pp. 1-4. (C.D.S.P., Vol. XV, No. 25, pp. 3-11)

6 Brezhnev, "47th Anniversary of the Great October Socialist Revolution," *op. cit.,* pp. 1-3.

7 N. S. Khrushchev, "Speech at Hungarian-Soviet Friendship Rally," *Pravda,* July 20, 1963, pp. 2-4. (C.D.S.P., Vol. XV, No. 27, pp. 3-7)

8 N. S. Khrushchev, "Use All the Forces of the Party and the People for Fulfilling Plans of Communist Construction," *Pravda,* Dec. 15, 1963, pp. 1-3. (C.D.S.P., Vol. XV, No. 49, pp. 3-13)

9 "Letter from the C.P.S.U. Central Committee to the Central Committee of the Communist Party of China," *Pravda,* April 3, 1963, pp. 1-2. (C.D.S.P., Vol. XV, No. 14, pp. 3-9)

10 Khrushchev, "Marxism-Leninism Is Our Banner," *op. cit.,* pp. 1-4.

11 *Ibid.*

12 "Open Letter from the Central Committee of the Communist Party of the Soviet Union to Party Organizations, to All Communists of the Soviet Union," *Pravda,* July 14, 1963, pp. 1-4. (C.D.S.P., Vol. XV, No. 28, pp. 16-30)

13 "Letter from the C.P.S.U. Central Committee to the Central Committee of the Communist Party of China," *op. cit.,* pp. 1-2.

14 *Ibid.*

15 L. Shernov, "Ideological Intrigues of Neocolonialists," *Pravda,* June 14, 1963, p. 3. (C.D.S.P., Vol. XV, No. 24, pp. 24-5)

16 *Ibid.*

17 G. Mirsky, "Socialism, Imperialism and Afro-Asian Solidarity," *Izvestia,* July 16, 1963, p. 2. (C.D.S.P., Vol. XV, No. 29, pp. 11-13)

18 "For the Triumph of Creative Marxism-Leninism, Against Revising Course of World Communist Movement," *Kommunist,* No. 11, July, 1963, pp. 3-36. (C.D.S.P., Vol. XV, No. 35, pp. 10-24)

19 *Fundamentals of Marxism-Leninism, op. cit.,* p. 773.

20 "For the Triumph of Creative Marxism-Leninism," *op. cit.,* pp. 3-36.

21 "Powerful Mainstay of Movement Against Colonialism," *Pravda,* August 7, 1963, pp. 4-5. (C.D.S.P., Vol. XV, No. 32, pp. 3-5)

22 "An Important Form of Aid," *Pravda,* August 7, 1963.

23 "In the Name of Complete Independence—Facts and Figures Speak," *Pravda,* Aug. 7, 1963, p. 4. (C.D.S.P., Vol. XV, No. 32, pp. 5-6)

24 "Open Letter from the Central Committee of the Communist Party of the Soviet Union to Party Organizations, to All Communists of the Soviet Union," *op. cit.,* pp. 1-4.

25 Cf. Jan Librach, *The Rise of the Soviet Empire,* (New York: Frederick A. Praeger, 1964), p. 165.

26 *Ibid.*

27 "Communique on Conferences of Representatives of Communist and Workers' Parties," *op. cit.,* pp. 1-4.

28 "Program of the C.P.S.U.," *op. cit.,* pp. 21-2.

29 "Communique on Conferences of Representatives of Communist and Workers' Parties," *op. cit.,* pp. 1-4.

30 N. S. Khrushchev, *Control Figures for the Economic Development of the U.S.S.R. for 1959-1965,* (Moscow: Foreign Languages Publishing House, 1960), p. 111.

31 *Fundamentals of Marxism-Leninism, op. cit.,* p. 775.

32 Cf. Hugh Seton-Watson, "Eastern Europe After Hungary," in Swearer and Longaker, *Contemporary Communism, op. cit.,* pp. 366-74.

33 *Fundamentals of Marxism-Leninism, op. cit.,* p. 771.

34 "Cominform Resolution," Bucharest, June 28, 1948.

35 Marshal Bulganin, "Speech in Sophia, Bulgaria," Sept. 8, 1949, quoted in Schwartz, *The Red Phoenix, op. cit.,* p. 307.

36 Dyura Nincic, "The Foreign Policy of Yugoslavia," in Joseph E. Black and Kenneth W. Thompson, (eds.), *Foreign Policies in a World of Change,* (New York: Harper and Row, 1963), pp. 266-7.

37 Josip Broz Tito, "Speech at the Fifteenth Session of the General Assembly of the United Nations," Sept. 22, 1960.

38 N. S. Khrushchev, Feb., 1956, quoted in Schwartz, *The Red Phoenix, op. cit.,* pp. 307-8.

39 "Joint Declaration of the Communist Parties of the Soviet Union and Yugoslavia," quoted in Hans W. Gatzke, *The Present in Perspective,* (Chicago: Rand McNally Co., 1962), p. 122.

40 "Communique on Conferences of Representatives of Communist and Workers' Parties," *op. cit.,* pp. 1-4.

41 "For Marxist-Leninist Unity of the Communist Movement, for Solidarity of the Countries of Socialism," *Pravda,* Feb. 10, 1963, pp. 2-3. (C.D.S.P., Vol. XV, No. 15, p. 3-9)

42 "Statement of Representatives of the Chinese Government," *Pravda,* August 21, 1963, pp. 3-4. (C.D.S.P., Vol. XV, No. 34, pp. 3-8)

43 *Ibid.*

44 *Ibid.*

45 Cf. "C.P.S.U. Central Committee's Letter of June 15, 1964, to the Central Committee of the Communist Party of China," *Kommunist,* No. 10, July, 1964, pp. 9-20. (C.D.S.P., Vol. XVI, No. 30, pp. 5-10); May 7, 1964, "Letter of the C.P.C. Central Committee to the C.P.S.U. Central Committee," *Kommunist,* No. 10, July, 1964, pp. 20-4. (C.D.S.P., Vol. XVI, No. 30, pp. 3-5)

46 "Letter of the Central Committee of the Communist Party of China to the Central Committee of the Communist Party of the Soviet Union," *Pravda,* July 14, 1963, pp. 5-7. (C.D.S.P., Vol. XV, No. 28, pp. 3-15)

47 "The Differences Between Comrade Togliatti and Us," *Renmin Riboa,* reprinted in Swearer and Longaker, *Contemporary Communism, op. cit.,* pp. 320-31.

48 "For Marxist-Leninist Unity of the Communist Movement, for Solidarity of the Countries of Socialism," *op. cit.,* pp. 2-3.

49 "For The General Line of the World Communist Movement, Against Left Opportunism, Nationalism and Adventurism," *Kommunist,* No. 15, Oct., 1963, pp. 13-47. (C.D.S.P., Vol. XV, No. 43, pp. 3-14)

50 Yu. V. Andropov, "Leninism Illuminates Our Path," *Pravda,* April 23, 1964,

pp. 1-2. (C.D.S.P., Vol. XVI, No. 17, pp. 15-17)

51 *Ibid.*

52 "Letter from the Central Committee of the Communist Party of China to the Central Committee of the Communist Party of the Soviet Union," *op. cit.,* pp. 5-7.

53 "The Differences Between Comrade Togliatti and Us," *op. cit.,* pp. 326-31.

54 "For The General Line of the World Communist Movement, Against Left Opportunism, Nationalism and Adventurism," *op. cit.,* pp. 13-47.

55 "The Differences Between Comrade Togliatti and Us.," *op. cit.,* pp. 326-31.

56 "For The General Line of the World Communist Movement, Against Left Opportunism, Nationalism and Adventurism," *op. cit.,* pp. 13-47.

57 Nikolai Tikhonov, Alexander Korneichuk and Yury Zhukov, "The Rallying of All Peace-Loving Forces Is the Primary Task in the Struggle to Avert a World War," *Pravda,* July 15, 1963, pp. 3-4. (C.D.S.P., Vol. XV, No. 29, pp. 10-11)

58 M. A. Suslov, "On the Struggle of the C.P.S.U. for the Solidarity of the International Communist Movement," *Pravda,* April 3, 1964, pp. 1-8. (C.D.S.P., Vol. XVI, No. 13, pp. 5-16)

59 *Ibid.*

60 "Soviet Government Statement," *Pravda,* Aug. 21, 1963, pp. 1-3. (C.D.S.P., Vol. XV, No. 34, pp. 8-13)

61 A. Chernyayev, "Socialism Is the Main Force of World Revolutionary Development," *Pravda,* Aug. 3, 1963, pp. 5-6. (C.D.S.P., Vol. XV, No. 31, pp. 8-11)

62 "Open Letter from the Central Committee of the Communist Party of the Soviet Union to Party Organizations, to All Communists of the Soviet Union," *op. cit.,* pp. 1-4.

63 "Concerning Mao Tse-tung's Talk with a Group of Japanese Socialists," *Pravda,* Sept. 2, 1964, p. 2. (C.D.S.P., Vol. XVI, No. 34, pp. 3-7)

64 "Statement of Representatives of the Chinese Government," *Pravda,* August 21, 1963, pp. 3-4. (C.D.S.P., Vol. XV, No. 34, pp. 3-8)

65 "Letter from the Central Committee of the Communist Party of China to the Central Committee of the Communist Party of the Soviet Union," *op. cit.,* pp. 5-7.

66 *Ibid.*

67 *Ibid.*

68 *Ibid.*

69 *Ibid.*

70 *Ibid.*

71 *Ibid.*

72 "The Differences Between Comrade Togliatti and Us," *op. cit.,* pp. 326-31.

73 *Ibid.*

74 *Ibid.*

75 *Ibid.*

76 *Ibid.*

77 *Ibid.*

78 "Statement of the Soviet Government," *Pravda,* Sept. 21, 1963, pp. 1-2, and Sept. 22, 1963, pp. 1-2. (C.D.S.P., Vol. XV, No. 38, pp. 3-15)

79 *Ibid.*

80 *Ibid.*

81 "Statement of Representatives of the Chinese Government," *op. cit.,* pp. 3-4.

82 *Ibid.*

83 "Letter from the Central Committee of the Communist Party of China to the Central Committee of the Communist Party of the Soviet Union," *op. cit.,* pp. 5-7.

84 Tikhonov, Korneichuk and Zhukov, "The Rallying of All Peace-Loving Forces Is the Primary Task in the Struggle to Avert a World War," *op. cit.,* pp. 3-4.

85 "For the Triumph of Creative Marxism-Leninism, Against Revising Course of World Communist Movement," *op. cit.,* pp. 3-36.

86 *Ibid.*

87 *Ibid.*

88 "For The General Line of the World Communist Movement, Against Left Opportunism, Nationalism and Adventurism," *op. cit.,* pp. 13-47.

89 "Letter from the Central Committee of the Communist Party of China to the Central Committee of the Communist Party of the Soviet Union," *op. cit.,* pp. 5-7.

90 "C.P.S.U. Central Committee's Letter of June 15, 1964, to the Central Committee of the Communist Party of China," *op. cit.,* pp. 9-20.

91 "To the Central Committee of the Communist Party of the Soviet Union," *op. cit.,* pp. 5-7.

92 "Letter from the Central Committee of the Communist Party of China to the Central Committee of the Communist Party of the Soviet Union," *op. cit.,* pp. 20-4.

93 "Communique on the Consultive Meeting of Representatives of the Communist and Workers' Parties in Moscow," *Pravda,* March 10, 1965, p. 1.

94 "Letter from the Central Committee of the Communist Party of China to the Central Committee of the Communist Party of the Soviet Union," *op. cit.,* pp. 5-7.

95 *Ibid.*

96 "Open Letter from the Central Committee of the Communist Party of the Soviet Union to Party Organizations, to All Communists of the Soviet Union," *op. cit.,* pp. 1-4.

97 "Letter from the Central Committee of the Communist Party of China to the Central Committee of the Communist Party of the Soviet Union," *op. cit.,* pp. 5-7.

98 *Ibid.*

99 *Ibid.*

100 *Ibid.*

101 *Ibid.*

102 "On the Dictatorship of the Proletariat," *Izvestia,* May 17, 1964, p. 3. (C.D.S.P., Vol. XVI, No. 21, pp. 3-6)

103 "For the Triumph of Creative Marxism-Leninism, Against Revising Course of World Communist Movement," *op. cit.,* pp. 3-36.

104 "Open Letter from the Central Committee of the Communist Party of the Soviet Union to Party Organizations, to All Communists of the Soviet Union," *op. cit.,* pp. 1-4.

105 "The Socialist State of all the People," *Izvestia,* May 23, 1964, p. 3. (C.D.S.P., Vol. XVI, No. 21, pp. 6-8, 42)

106 *Ibid.*

107 "On the Dictatorship of the Proletariat," *op. cit.,* p. 3.

108 "The Socialist State of all the People," *op. cit.,* p. 3.

109 "For the Triumph of Creative Marxism-Leninism, Against Revising Course of World Communist Movement," *op. cit.,* pp. 3-36.

110 Cf. Donald S. Zagoria, "Implications of the Sino-Soviet Conflict," and Robert A. Scalapino, "Moscow, Peking and Asia," in Swearer and Longaker, *Contemporary Communism, op. cit.,* pp. 310-22.

111 Scalapino, *ibid,* pp. 317-22.

CHAPTER XI

THE STATE AND THE INDIVIDUAL

Soviet leaders have consistently stressed their desire to develop a society in which each individual member, regardless of race, sex, parentage or social origin, will have the opportunity to lead a full and rich life and all material and spiritual needs will be met adequately. In almost every policy statement the concern of the party for the people is emphasized. "The policy and the entire practical activity of the Communist Party and the Soviet Government," they say, "are determined in the final analysis by the most important, the chief thing—concern for the welfare of the people."[1] Goals for the welfare of the people purportedly incorporate the desire to provide an opportunity for "the all-round free development of the personality of every member of society."[2]

The concern which the party leaders express for the welfare and freedom of the individual conflict markedly with a number of the repressive measures which the Soviet regime has sponsored. Many Western spokesmen have charged, not without justification, that the Soviet regime "sacrifices the individual to the state," "devaluates human personality," "submerges the individual in the collective" and "destroys human freedom."[3] From the point of view of Western ideologies the majority of the derogatory charges about the Soviet regime's treatment of the individual are completely legitimate. However, most of the Soviet policies toward the individual make a certain amount of sense when viewed within the framework of the ideology to which the party leaders subscribe. There are notable exceptions; even the most skillful Soviet propagandists have been unable to justify the brutal excesses of the Stalin era as a manifestation of the regime's concern for the welfare of mankind.

According to Marxist-Leninist ideology, true and universal freedom can be attained only in a society in which the common interests of the collective are given priority over the interests of the individual members of the collective. The cornerstone of their collective ideology is that the individual can be emancipated only through the emancipation of the working masses. True freedom and social justice for all, they say, is unobtainable in a society which includes a "privileged class." They argue that "the existence of classes lies at the root of social injustice. . . .It is not the 'will of God' and not man's nature as an individual . . . but membership in a particular class which explains the dominating privileged position of some and the oppression, poverty and lack of rights of others."[4] One of the indispensable prerequisites for the emancipation of the working masses and the eventual establishment of social justice for all, according to the Marxists-Leninists, is that all individuals and groups must be deprived of special privileges which they had "preempted" by a variety of techniques and particularly by virtue of their favored position in relation to the ownership of the means of production. Therefore, they hold that an initial and absolutely necessary step in freeing the masses is the acquisition of political power by the working people under the leadership of the Communist Party, and the transfer of the means of production to public ownership. They concede that a socialist revolution is not in the best interests of privileged individuals and classes since it deprives them of their special position in society but this, they say, is justified since the existence of a privileged class prohibits the establishment of "true democracy" and runs counter to the interests of the majority of members of society.

Marxists-Leninists point out that whereas private ownership of the means of production gave rise to the classes, state structure, code of laws, customs and ethics which characterize capitalist society, public ownership of the means of production must inevitably give rise to a different set of institutions, customs and morals. However, they concede that even after the radical change in the political and economic superstructure of society, a rather prolonged period is required to establish the economic basis for material plenty and to restructure political and social relations, ideological and moral values, customs and modes of behavior. During the interim period the interests of the collective and all its individual members do not form an identity; what the individual deems best for himself is not always best for the collective. Soviet theoreticians analyze this aspect of the development of their society in the following way:

> "The objective possibility of the harmonious combination of the interests of society and the individual is established in the socio-economic and political structure of our Soviet society. But, needless to say, the transformation of this possibility into reality is no simple matter. It does not happen of itself smoothly and evenly, without the overcoming of difficulties and contradictions between the individual and the collective. Side by side with the united public interests of the different social groups, strata and nationalities there also exist various specific social, national, local, vocational, cultural and everyday interests and needs. Various vital contradictions and even conflicts between the individual and the collective, between the individual and society can also arise under certain conditions. It is impossible to forget the existence of survivals of the past in the consciousness and everyday life of the people, survivals of bourgeois individualism, nationalism, egoism and careerism, religious survivals, etc."[5]

One of the tasks which has been assumed by the party leaders is to establish the conditions under which contradictions between the interests of the individual and society are eliminated. It is the party leaders, of course, in their role of omnipotent parents made wise by virtue of their understanding of Marxism-Leninism, who have established the goals for society and have decided that these goals can be achieved only if the interests of the collective are given priority over the interests of the individual members.

The party leaders have assumed that the goal of establishing a society in which the interests of society as a whole and its individual members form one harmonious unit, a society in which all can enjoy equal rights and freedoms, has justified and, in fact, necessitated a number of measures which have restricted the rights of individuals. Such restrictions are described as entirely legitimate "because individual freedom does not mean freedom to do as one wishes, regardless of the consequences on others . . . unrestricted freedom results ultimately in freedom for the few and oppression for the masses."[6] Their choice, they say, is to impose restrictions on the selfish demands of the few and to train people to subordinate self-interest to the interest of society in order to pave the way for "true freedom" for the masses. According to communist logic, the interests of society demand that restrictions must be placed on the freedom of anyone who opposes the construction of socialism, attempts to maintain the privileges of a particular class or ethnic group, clings to religious beliefs, does not strive diligently for the construction of communism, puts personal interests before the interests of the collective or engages in any activity which is not condoned by the regime. Party spokesmen assert that these kinds of restrictions are indispensable for the emergence of the type of society which the Soviet people are striving to build.

According to the Kremlin leaders, public ownership of the means of production, the formal reorganization of social relations, the abolition of all special privileges, restrictions on the rights of the few in the interests of the majority, massive educational and indoctrinational programs and other measures have established the groundwork for a new and higher type of social relations in which most individuals willingly subordinate their own interests to the interest of the collective. As society is perfected, they assert, the harmony between the interests of the collective and its members becomes ever more complete until eventually the interests of the collective and all its members are virtually identical. In that "higher" stage of society, each individual is to work willingly and selflessly for the good of society, and in so doing is to improve his own well-being since what is good for the collective is good for each and every member of society.

Soviet authorities stress that their emphasis on the welfare of the collective does not constitute a denial of the importance of the individual; their position, they say, is not that the individual is unimportant but rather that equal and extensive rights and freedoms can be guaranteed to all members of society only if the rights of the collective are given priority over the rights of any individuals or social group within society. They claim that their social order opens up new vistas to all members of society. An official of the Soviet government stated:

> "The fundamental economic and political transformations wrought by the Soviet system brought into being a new type of relation that had never existed before among people and between people and the state. By abolishing unemployment, poverty and want, by eliminating all national, racial and sexual discrimination, the Soviet state opened up unlimited opportunities for the development of the individual. The principles of socialist humanism, of profound concern for man, of fraternal relations between the people have become the salient features of Soviet society, and of the activity of the state. In the Soviet Union concern for human welfare has ceased to be one's own private affair; it is a collective matter assisted by the state which has made it the cornerstone of its policy."[7]

The Constitution of the U.S.S.R. lists as the fundamental rights of citizens, the right to work, the right to rest and leisure, the right to maintenance in old age and in case of sickness or loss of capacity to work, the right to education, sex equality, absence of discrimination on account of race or nationality, freedom of conscience, freedom of speech, freedom of the press, freedom of assembly including the holding of mass meetings, freedom of street processions and demonstrations, inviolability of the person and the homes of citizens, and privacy of correspondence. It is ironical that the formal statement of these rights (1936) coincided with a reign of terror which violated even the most elementary concepts of individual liberty. Moreover, in spite of the invidious comparisons which Soviet publicists make between the extensive freedoms which are "guaranteed" to Soviet citizens and the alleged oppression of the masses in non-socialist countries, the rights which are formally granted to Soviet citizens have been enjoyed in substantial measure for decades by citizens in most Western nations. Finally, Soviet leaders do not subscribe to the doctrine that there are certain natural or inalienable rights of man; personal liberties or rights in the U.S.S.R. are treated as a gift from the regime to the people. Obviously, what the state can give, the state can also take away, withdraw temporarily or modify to suit its purposes. Much more important than the formal list of rights which Soviet leaders say are accorded to the people is how these rights are translated into practice.[8]

The Right to Work

Soviet publicists point with great pride to the fact that unemployment has been virtually eliminated in the U.S.S.R. Not all Soviet citizens are necessarily satisfied with their employment status either in terms of job assignments, location, working conditions, hours of work or pay scales, and there is a certain amount of under-employment on collective farms. However, months of enforced and unpaid idleness are not inflicted upon Soviet workers through no fault of their own. Some Western scholars have pointed out that the guaranteed right to work is not an unmixed blessing; for example, Professor Fainsod commented:

> "The right to work is not a right to choose one's work freely, but a duty to work in disciplined subordination to state and party regulations. It frequently means working at the post to which one is assigned, at wages and in conditions which are determined by higher authorities over whom one has no control. There is no right to strike, and trade unions function essentially as glorified state company unions."[9]

Although there can be no disagreement with this analysis of the Soviet work situation, fairness requires admission of the fact that many of the disadvantages under which Soviet workers labor are equally prevalent, for somewhat different reasons, in advanced Western nations. For example, although most Soviet citizens are able to exercise some choice in the selection of a job, many are required to accept assignments on orders from higher authorities, regardless of whether the type of work, wages and working conditions are according to preference; by the same token, the majority of citizens in Western societies are able to exercise some choice in the selection of a job but some, and usually a sizeable proportion, are required, because of economic necessity, to take whatever work is available. The majority of workers in all societies work in "disciplined subordination" to one authority or another so there is nothing exceptionally unique about the disciplined subordination of the Soviet worker to state and party regulations. Soviet workers are at a disadvantage since they cannot take concerted action through their trade unions to demand higher wages, shorter hours or better working conditions; the state, or rather the party, decides when the interests of the collective will be served by the introduction of changes along these lines.

Soviet critics also point out that the guaranteed right to work amounts to no more than a doctrinal commitment to a socio-economic policy of full employment and argue that the positive features of this policy have been offset by enforcement of the duty to work with the ensuing "witch hunt" against parasites and vagabonds.[10] Enforcement of the duty to work, part of the Soviet drive to create the "new Soviet man" who will have a "communist attitude toward labor," is in some respects an example of the rather ludicrous extremes in which Soviet leaders sometimes indulge; very few individuals in the U.S.S.R. could survive long without working unless they were engaging in illegal activities such as speculation, robbery or embezzlement. The point is sometimes made that the right to work provides no evidence that the regime is concerned with the welfare of the individual since full employment is a prerequisite for the materialization of the economic goals of the regime. This is true, but regardless of the motivation of the party leaders, the ability of the regime to provide full employment is undoubtedly highly valued by Soviet citizens who, at least as far as employment is concerned, have been, as Soviet authors stated, delivered from "oppressive anxiety and uncertainty over the morrow."[11]

Budgetary Expenditures

Table 1 presents the social-cultural budget of the U.S.S.R. for representative years. Funds allocated to social-cultural services amounted to approximately one quarter of the entire state budget during the Stalin era and have risen to well over one-third of the budget since the early 1960's. The social-cultural program is often presented as a concrete example of the identity of the interest of the individual and the collective. A Soviet author stated: "The public consumption funds are a great achievement of our socialist system. They enable any Soviet family, regardless of income, number of children or number of able-bodied members, to obtain the most important social and cultural benefits free of charge."[12] The explicit assumption is that social and cultural services should not be the prerogative of a privileged few. The authorities also state with equal explicitness that an educated, cultured and healthy populace is "a source of strength for the state, a way to multiply public wealth, to accelerate progress."[13] A former U.S.S.R. Minister of Finance explained, "Man is a social being. He cannot exist outside the collective, in isolation from social production. He works for the benefit of all society and society satisfies his requirements."[14] He might have added that the workers' contribution to society would be lower if society did not ensure the satisfaction of basic social-cultural requirements.

Table 1
U.S.S.R. Social-Cultural Budget*
(In Billions of Rubles)

Item	1940	1950	1959	1963	1965
Social Insurance and Social Security		3.59	9.37	12.0	13.8
Health and Physical Culture		2.14	4.40	5.2	6.5
Education, Science and Culture		5.69	9.43	13.8	17.1
Total Social-Cultural Budget	4.09	11.67	23.20	31.0	37.4
Total State Budget	17.44	41.27	70.76	80.5	99.4
Allocation to Social-Cultural Measures	23%	28%	33%	38%	38%

* Sources: "Expenditures for Social-Cultural Measures in the State Budget of the U.S.S.R.," Moscow, 1958; V. F. Garbuzov, "On the U.S.S.R. State Budget for 1963 and on Fulfillment of the U.S.S.R. State Budget for 1961," *Pravda,* Dec. 11, 1962, pp. 4-6; V. F. Garbuzov, "On the U.S.S.R. State Budget for 1965 and on the Fulfillment of the U.S.S.R. State Budget for 1963," *Pravda,* Dec. 10, 1964, pp. 4-5.

Since the funds allocated to social-cultural services are derived from the surplus product of labor, party leaders cannot legitimately claim that these services constitute a gift from the state to the people. The state could have allowed each worker to retain a greater proportion of his own earnings and concurrently to assume greater financial responsibility for the provision of social-cultural services for himself and his family. Such a procedure would, however, run counter to Soviet ideology and the paternalistic attitude of the party and the state to the people; the party has decreed that the welfare of the collective is served more efficiently and justly if the state assumes responsibility for dispensing the benefits.

Social Insurance, Social Security and Pensions

According to Article 120 of the Constitution: "Citizens of the U.S.S.R. have the right to maintenance in old age and also in case of sickness and disability." A pension plan for employees of state enterprises was enacted in 1930 and revised in 1956. Prior to 1965, collective farm workers were not covered by a state insurance and retirement plan; a few prosperous collective farms had inaugurated a formal social insurance program but on the majority of the farms the elderly and disabled had to rely on support from relatives and relief payments from collective farm funds. The 1965 law on pensions and allowances for collective farmers provides collective farmers with social security benefits at a level which is generally lower than the benefits which accrue to state employees.[15]

State pensions are granted on retirement, for disabilities and when the breadwinner dies. Males who have worked for at least 25 years may retire at the age of 60 if they have been state employees or at the age of 65 if they have been collective farm members; for women the retirement ages are 55 for state employees and 60 for collective farm members and the required period of service is 20 years. State workers who have been engaged in hazardous occupations may retire 10 years earlier. Women who have reared five or more children and have been employed for at least 15 years may retire at 50 or 55 depending on whether they have worked for the state or a collective farm. Minimum and maximum monthly pensions are 30 and 120 rubles for state employees, and 12 and 102 rubles for collective farm members. In "exceptional" cases (presumably involving high ranking officials) retirement pensions may be larger.[16] The size of pension is determined by preretirement earnings. State workers earning up to 35 rubles per month receive pensions amounting to 100 percent of their earnings; the pensions of workers in higher income brackets are determined on a percentage basis; on the average the pension of state workers amounts to 60 percent of preretirement wages.[17] Collective farm members are granted pensions in the amount of 50 percent of earnings up to 50 rubles per month plus 25 percent of the remainder of their earnings. Pensioners are entitled to accept employment at the established wage rates, and, while employed, are awarded 50 percent of their normal pension but not less than the minimum old age pension.[18]

Disability pensions depend upon degree of incapacitation, predisability earnings, length of service, and whether the disability is the result of an occupational injury or disease. Minimum monthly payments for a total disability are 30 rubles for urban state employees, 27 rubles for rural state employees and 15 rubles for collective farm members. Trade union members receive twice as much as non-union members. Grants for the support of the dependants of a pensioner vary with the number of dependants, the degree of disability, whether the pensioner was employed by the state or a collective farm and whether he had been a member of the armed forces. Recipients of disability pensions are entitled to work for remuneration but, if the combined pension and wages exceed predisability earnings or 120 rubles per month, the pension is decreased. The size of the pension awarded to families who have lost their breadwinner depends on whether the breadwinner's death was related to his occupation, the length of his employment, the amount of his earnings, and the number of unemployable persons who had been dependent on him. When a breadwinner dies for reasons not related to his occupation, his family, if it includes three or more unemployable persons, receives a pension which corresponds to the amount the breadwinner would have received on retirement.

Prior to 1960, an attempt was made to minimize labor turnover by making full rates of sick pay and disability benefits contingent upon a six month minimum period of work for the same enterprise, except for those workers who were transferred under official orders. Current regulations specify that temporary disability benefits are to be awarded on a common basis regardless of the amount of time a worker has been employed by a particular enterprise.[19] Retirement and permanent disability rights are retained without interruption by workers who change jobs on their own initiative if they are reemployed within one month. Workers who discontinue their employment temporarily to continue their education, to join a spouse who has transferred to a new location, to care for an infant, or because of sickness, disability or pregnancy retain uninterrupted seniority if a new job is taken within a reasonable time period.[20]

It is generally conceded, even by opponents of the Soviet system, that the U.S.S.R. has made considerable progress toward the development of a comprehensive and reasonable pension system. However, Soviet authorities admit that the state has not yet assumed full responsibility for the maintenance of pensioners and in many cases financial hardships inevitably accrue either to the pensioner or his family. Subsistence standards of living cannot be maintained on the basis of minimum pension allowances. One of the goals of the regime is to provide for the complete and adequate maintenance of all elderly and disabled persons through public consumption funds.[21] The size of pensions is to increase gradually "to a level sufficient for consumption benefits and services meeting scientific and rational standards" and the network of boarding houses for the aged and incapacitated is to be increased to meet completely the needs of all who wish to use them.[22]

Health Protection

Since its inception, the Soviet regime has exerted vigorous efforts to expand and improve medical and health services. Its accomplishments are impressive. No Soviet citizen has to pay directly for medical or dental care or for hospitalization; drugs which are not provided by the state are relatively inexpensive. Almost all physicians and dentists, like other professional workers, are state employees. The private practice of medicine is not prohibited although the earnings of private practitioners are taxed heavily. Some people in the higher income brackets apparently feel that better or more convenient medical care can be obtained for a fee, but private practitioners render an almost negligible proportion of medical services in the U.S.S.R. Party leaders point with great pride to the fact that no matter how ill a Soviet citizen may be, medical expenses need not constitute a financial catastrophe for him or his family. Soviet authorities report that by 1963 the U.S.S.R. had 87 hospital beds and 20 physicians per 10,000 members of the population; they claim that their physician-population ratio is equal or superior to that of the most advanced Western nations.[23] Life expectancy has been more than doubled since 1913, and preventive medicine practices and the control of contagious diseases are comparable with Western standards.

The U.S.S.R. Ministry of Health is responsible for planning, coordinating and supervising health services for the entire nation. The U.S.S.R. Academy of Medical Sciences works closely with the Ministry with respect to medical research. Each Union Republic has its own Ministry of Health which supervises the Health Administration at the district level. Each local Soviet has administrative responsibility for the provision of adequate health services within its locality. All local Soviets have standing committees on public health and the party has attempted to obtain "the broad creative participation of the people" to implement "measures of sanitation and health promotion and to improve the people's health protection."[24] Most urban areas are reasonably well supplied with hospitals, health centers, sanitary inspection agencies and other health care institutions and services. Many large industrial enterprises employ several physicians and other medical personnel and some enterprises support fully equipped hospitals for use by the enterprise workers. Medical facilities available to collective farmers, however, often leave much to be desired, since the collective farms have been expected to assume considerable responsibility for health services, usually on an inter-collective farm cooperative basis. Many collective farmers travel long distances to large urban centers with the hope of obtaining superior medical care.

Soviet authorities recognize that much must yet be done to achieve the universal excellence in health care standards to which they aspire. Official condemnatory statements such as the following one by the Party Central Committee and the U.S.S.R. Council of Ministers are common:

> "Despite gains registered in the field of public health, medical services are not yet adequate to meet the growing needs of the public, especially in areas of new industrial construction, the virgin lands and the far north and in mountainous localities. The working people are provided with too few out-patient polyclinics and, in particular, with inadequate dental and denture services. There are grave shortcomings in the organization of in-patient care for the population, especially in hospitals with a small number of beds; these hospitals find it difficult to provide patients with skilled care. Many medical institutions are inadequately supplied with up-to-date medical equipment and special furniture. . . . Some party, Soviet and trade union agencies pay inadequate attention to the problems of medical services for the population . . . and have exercised feeble control over the carrying out by economic organizations of measures for providing sanitation facilities in population centers and industrial enterprises. The organization of water supply, sewage disposal and the cleaning of streets, squares and yards is unsatisfactory in a number of cities, worker's settlements and villages."[25]

Steps are being taken to eliminate these and other shortcomings, and it can be expected that standards of health care will improve progressively.

The fact that the quality of medical care accorded to Soviet citizens depends little on the size of their bank accounts has provided the party with powerful grist for the propaganda mill. The following statement which was made in 1951 provides an excellent example of the propaganda line, except that now credit would be assigned to the party instead of to Stalin.

> "The Soviet Union is the first country in the world where the principle of free and socialized medical-sanitary assistance for everyone is realized. This is one of the many manifestations of the Stalinist concern for the individual . . . all efforts of medical science are used in our country to protect the health of the workers. . . . In the capitalist countries medical assistance is available only to the rich . . . this is what happens when the working man does not count . . . where all is done for profits."[26]

Education

From the very outset, the Soviet government and the C.P.S.U. have placed great emphasis on education as a technique of national and personal advancement. During the Tsarist era the population was preponderately illiterate or semi-literate and higher education was reserved for the Russian upper classes. Approximately 80 percent of the peasants, the most numerical class within the population, were illiterate, and only one woman out of eight knew how to read and write. Members of the national minorities had almost no opportunity to acquire a higher education. Approximately 40 percent of the students in secondary schools and 60 percent of the students in institutions of higher learning were children of the privileged classes who made up approximately 3 percent of the total population.

The new Soviet regime launched an attack on illiteracy immediately. In 1919 a state decree required all people from 8 to 50 years of age to learn to read and write either in their native language or in Russian. The educated were instructed to help the uneducated in the interest of the common cause. Soviet sources report that by 1935 approximately 50 million people had become literate and that by 1939 the illiteracy rate had dropped to about 9 percent.[27] Since then illiteracy has been virtually eliminated. In 1962 compulsory eight-year schooling was made universal throughout the U.S.S.R. More than 68 million people were engaged in various types of study in 1964; of these, almost 47 million were enrolled in general-education schools.[28] For a few years during and after World War II students in secondary schools and higher educational institutes were charged a small tuition fee. During most of the Soviet era, no tuition fees have been charged and educational opportunities have been available on a more or less equal basis to all Soviet citizens who are able and eager to study, regardless of sex, nationality or the socio-economic status of parents. Competent students in higher educational institutions receive stipends from the state and extensive arrangements have been made to enable persons who are engaged in full or part-time work to improve their educational qualifications. The legal status of education in the U.S.S.R. is summarized in Article 121 of the Constitution which states:

> "Citizens of the U.S.S.R. have the right to education. This right is ensured by universal compulsory eight-year education; by extensive development of secondary general polytechnical education, vocational technical education, and secondary specialized and higher education based on close links between school, and life and production; by utmost development of evening and extramural education; by free education in all schools; by a system of state grants; by instruction in schools being conducted in the native language, and by the organization in the factories, state farms and collective farms of free vocational, technical and agronomic training for the working people."

Although many of the rights which are guaranteed to Soviet citizens by the Constitution of the U.S.S.R. are poorly materialized, the regime has gone to great lengths to ensure the fulfillment of the right to education.

The right to education has been honored more fully than most of the other constitutional rights because a well-educated populace is indispensable for the materialization of party goals. All Soviet authorities have agreed with the thesis elaborated by Marx, Engels and Lenin that the establishment of full communism requires that productive capacity must be increased sufficiently to allow for material abundance for all, and that man must be transformed into a new kind of social being whose chief desire is to serve society. Education has been assigned a major role in bringing about both of these two primary conditions. Increased economic productivity and scientific progress, indispensable prerequisites for the establishment of the economic base for communism, depend largely on the availability of an adequate supply of well-trained specialists and highly skilled workers. Educational institutions are also expected to contribute substantially to the rearing of Soviet citizens who will participate actively and efficiently in the construction of the communist society and to assist in the molding of the "new Soviet man" who is to live in the communist utopia. In the educational sphere the interests of the party leaders, or, as Soviet spokesmen would say, the interests of society, and the interests of the majority of Soviet citizens coincide; both the leaders and the people are committed to education. To the party leaders, the provision of adequate educational facilities is an indispensable stepping stone for the materialization of full communism; to the individual Soviet citizen, education is a basic tool for personal advancement. In the Soviet Union, a citizen's income and status depends chiefly on what he does rather than on what he owns, and therefore, the acquisition of an education which will prepare him for higher level positions is highly valued. Full utilization by the people of the extensive educational opportunities which have been provided by the state is a technique through which the individual can achieve a better future for himself and, at the same time, make an acceptable contribution to society.

All educational policy decisions in the U.S.S.R. are made by the leaders of the C.P.S.U. Major policy statements are issued jointly by the Central Committee of the C.P.S.U. and the U.S.S.R. Council of Ministers. State control of education is effected by the U.S.S.R. Ministry of Higher and Specialized Education, corresponding ministries in Union and Autonomous Republics, and departments of education established by the intermediate and local Soviets. The Central Committee of the C.P.S.U. has a Department for Science, Education and Schools which has subordinate sections at each level of the administrative hierarchy. Funds for education are allocated from the U.S.S.R. budget through the Union Republics to the local Soviets. Although the Union Republics are purported to have "complete independence" to decide "questions of major importance" in the educational sphere, the Union Republics invariably adopt the decisions of the central state and party apparatus with only minor variations to suit local conditions.

The three major areas of emphasis in the Soviet educational system have been academic education, polytechnical education and moral education. Apart from the fact that all academic subjects must be studied from a "Marxist-Leninist point of view," Soviet educators approach academic problems in essentially the same manner as academic matters are dealt with in other educational systems. Since the mid 1950's increased emphasis has been placed on polytechnical education which is designed to prepare young people for work; Soviet educators state that polytechnical education "provides a knowledge of the scientific fundamentals of modern production, acquaints pupils with its major branches, arms them with basic skills in the use of modern tools, involves pupils in socially useful productive labor, and shapes a communist attitude to work.[29] Schools in all countries are expected to inculcate devotion to the prevailing ideology and to influence the morals, beliefs and values to the younger generation; Soviet schools are required to emphasize political and moral education more strongly than schools in other nations because the party leaders want all members of society to accept Marxist-Leninist ideology fully and without question, and because they are attempting to effect substantial changes in moral and value norms. Soviet schools are required to serve as a major vehicle for the indoctrination of youth. In the political sphere the schools are supposed to instill dedication to Marxist-Leninist theory and the goals of the Communist Party; Soviet patriotism and proletarian internationalism; disdain for anything associated with "bourgeois capitalist societies"; understanding of the course and perspectives of world development; a correct view (i.e. the view determined by the party leaders) of international and domestic events; and determination to participate fully in the construction of communism.[30] The "communist morality" which the schools are supposed to foster is discussed and described in the Party Program as follows:

"The Communists reject the class morality of the exploiters; in contrast to the perverse, selfish views and morals of the old world, they promote communist morality, which is the noblest and most just morality, for it expresses the interests and ideals of the whole of working mankind. Communism makes the elementary standards of morality and justice, which were distorted or shamelessly flouted under the rule of the exploiters, inviolable rules for relations both between individuals and between peoples. Communist morality encompasses the fundamental norms of human morality which the masses of the people evolved in the course of millenniums as they fought against vice and social oppression. . . .

"The Party holds that *the moral code of the builder of communism* should comprise the following principles: devotion to the communist cause; love of the socialist motherland and of the other socialist countries; conscientious labour for the good of society—he who does not work, neither shall he eat; concern on the part of everyone for the preservation and growth of public wealth; a high sense of public duty; intolerance of actions harmful to the public interest; collectivism and comradely mutual assistance: one for all and all for one; humane relations and mutual respect between individuals—man is to man a friend, comrade and brother; honesty and truthfulness, moral purity, modesty, and unpretentiousness in social and private live; mutual respect in the family, and concern for the upbringing of children; an uncompromising attitude to injustice, parasitism, dishonesty, careerism and money-grubbing; friendship and brotherhood among all peoples of the U.S.S.R.; intolerance of national and racial hatred; an uncompromising attitude to the enemies of communism, peace and the freedom of nations; fraternal solidarity with the working people of all countries, and with all peoples."[31]

Thus Soviet schools are expected to turn out "morally pure," dedicated communists, who have an academic and polytechnical background which will enable them to function adequately in the economy with a minimum of extra training or to continue their education in a higher educational institute. Although, on the whole, the regime has been relatively well satisfied with the accomplishments of its educational system, it is admitted that achievements have fallen far short of goals.

Throughout the years the educational system has been reorganized a number of times as the party leaders have decided to use first one organizational form and then another in their attempts to maximize excellence in education or as one or another of the tasks of education have been given priority. Figure 1 summarizes the major units in the Soviet educational system as of 1965. Preschool child-care and education is provided by nurseries which are established by enterprises for the convenience of working mothers and by kindergartens which are established by the state or by enterprises and collective farms. A shortage of both types of facilities is reported in the Soviet press. Most nurseries and kindergartens are open 24 hours a day; children may be left there only during the work hours of the mother or may be taken home only for weekends. As a general rule, no charge is made for child care in a nursery, but a small tuition, prorated according to wages and size of family, is paid for enrollment in a kindergarten. Kindergarten teachers are required to "instill in the child love of the Soviet homeland, its leaders, and the Soviet Army" and to develop the "spirit of collectivism." Moral and political indoctrination starts early.

At present, eight years of formal education from the age of seven to fifteen or sixteen is compulsory. The majority of children spend these eight years in a general educational day school; the mentally retarded, physically handicapped or the artistically gifted may attend special schools; approximately 2.4 million children attend boarding schools or extended day schools.[32] Several party spokesmen have referred to boarding schools as "the new school of communist society"; alleged advantages of the communal system of living include the greater influence of the school over the children, intensification of the spirit of collectivity, the opportunity for children of different nationalities to live and work together, increased cultural opportunities and, as some Soviet authorities stress, the provision of adequate care for orphans and children who are neglected by their parents. In the eight-year school children study the usual academic subjects; reading, literature, history, mathematics (in-

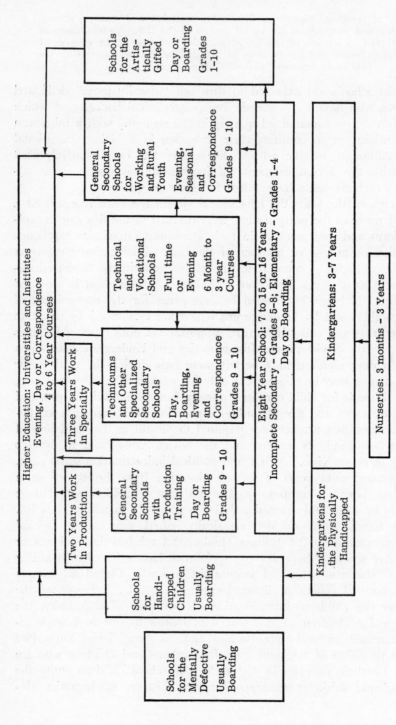

Figure 1. The Educational System of the U.S.S.R.*

*Source: Adapted From: "The Educational System of the U.S.S.R.," U.S.S.R. *Illustrated Monthly*, Oct., 1963, p. 4; and Elizabeth Moos, "Education in the Soviet Union," Reproduced in Harry G. Shaffer (ed.), *The Soviet System*, op. cit, p. 272.

cluding simple algebra and geometry starting in the sixth grade), geography, biology and a foreign language (starting in the fifth grade), and physics and chemistry (starting in the sixth and seventh grades respectively).[33] Instruction is always given in the native language of the area; many children study Russian as a second language. Physical education and training in music and art are given in all grades. Since 1958, when the emphasis on polytechnical education was increased, from two to four hours per week of school time have been allocated to polytechnical education, and students have been required to devote extra-curricular time to "socially useful labor" such as keeping the school grounds clean and attractive. Students in the elementary grades raise laboratory animals, work in a garden plot or make large numbers of various useful objects such as cardboard boxes, toys or flower pots; enterprises have been asked to cooperate with the schools by providing materials or piecework projects. Children in grades five to eight study woodworking, metal working, technical model making, electrical assembly, sewing and handicrafts, and may spend some time actually working in a factory or on a farm. When the work of the children has commercial value the proceeds are usually used to purchase materials for new projects and to finance school excursions. It is argued that, in addition to learning skills and techniques and about production processes, the children develop healthy attitudes toward work and derive satisfaction from producing well-made objects which have social value.

The Soviet educational system does not allow school children very much leisure or free time. The length of the academic year varies from 210 days for elementary school to 231 days in secondary school, and the school week varies from 24 to 33 hours. All children attend classes six days per week. Ten to twelve-day winter and spring vacations are scheduled. Homework assignments are given from the second grade up and vary from two to four hours per day. In addition to their school work, children are expected to participate in Pioneer or Y.C.L. activities and to devote time to "socially useful" labor projects. Many educators, parents and health officials have expressed concern about the overburdening of children and attempts are underway to reduce the amount of required homework by deleting unnecessary material in textbooks and by improving the subject matter and methodology training of teachers so that material can be covered more efficiently in the classroom. Because of the shortage of buildings and other school facilities, many schools still operate on a two-shift basis.

A number of alternatives are open to the graduate of the eight-year school. He may become a full-time worker immediately, or he may enroll in one of the following institutions: (1) *General Secondary Polytechnical Schools with Production Training:* These schools are the usual choice of students who intend to enroll eventually in an institute of higher education. From 1958 until 1964 a total of 11 years or 3 years beyond the eight years of compulsory education were required for graduation from secondary school. In 1964 a transition from the 11-year program to a 10-year program was initiated on the grounds that with more efficient organization the required academic and polytechnical work could be mastered within a shorter time. Academic subjects taught in the general secondary polytechnical schools include Soviet and foreign literature, mathematics including solid geometry and elementary calculus, history, economic geography, advanced physics, inorganic and organic chemistry, introduction to astronomy, a foreign language, and the fundamentals of philosophy, political economy, ethics and morality.[34] Nine to twelve hours per week are devoted to polytechnical or production training, and students are expected to obtain designated amounts of work experience during their summer vacations. The techniques and even the goals of the polytechnical training have varied considerably from one school to another. A large number of schools have provided narrow vocational training in a limited number of relatively low level specialties; students have been required to choose one of the available specialties whether or not they have had any desire to work in that area after graduation; permission could, however, be obtained to transfer to another school which offered a different set of specialties. Vocational training has been provided in school workshops or directly in enterprises under the joint supervision of enterprise workers and teachers. By 1965 criticisms of the vocational training functions of the general secondary schools reached a crescendo; it has been pointed out that this form of vocational training is inordinately expensive in terms of time and material resources; the vocational training sponsored by the schools could be given to novice workers in a fraction of the time and at a much lower cost per trainee; moreover, a large number of students do not elect to work in the specialty in which the school has trained them. The current trend is to de-emphasize vocational training in the general secondary schools; instead, the schools are expected to provide the students with a broad background of knowledge and experience which will enable them to master rapidly the specialty which they choose after graduation. According to the new trend, students will continue to spend a considerable amount of time directly in factories and workshops but the goal will be to understand a variety of production processes rather than to learn a narrow set of skills. After the completion of secondary education in a general secondary school with polytechnical education, the student may become a full-time worker immediately, or he may take additional training as a middle-grade specialist in a technicum or a vocational institute on a full time, evening, or correspondence basis. The most proficient students are allowed to enroll directly in a higher educational institution.

(2) *Technicums and Specialized Secondary Schools:* These schools offer semi-professional training in selected specialties in addition to a general secondary education, which is supposed to be comparable in level and scope to that provided by the general secondary polytechnical schools. The majority of specialized secondary school students, including part-time and correspondence students, receive a stipend from the state during the training period if their grades are acceptable. In return for the stipend, they are required by law to accept employment in their field of specialization for three years following graduation. Outstanding graduates are exempted from the mandatory three-year job assignment if they enroll immediately in a higher educational institution. Other graduates may, if they pass the competitive entrance examinations, enroll in a higher educational institute after working for three years, or may participate in correspondence or part-time programs while they are working full time. However, because graduates of specialized secondary schools tend to do less well on entrance examinations than graduates of regular secondary schools, a relatively small proportion of them are admitted to higher educational institutions.

(3) *Vocational Training Schools:* These schools train graduates of the eight-year schools as semi-skilled or skilled workers. The period of training ordinarily varies from six months to three years. Because major emphasis is placed on vocational training, only about 20 percent of the instructional time is devoted to general educational subjects. Graduates of these schools are not eligible for enrollment in a higher educational institution.

(4) *Schools for Working and Rural Youth:* These schools are designed to enable graduates of the vocational training schools and young people who engage in full-time employment immediately after graduation from the eight-year school to obtain a secondary education in conjunction with employment. Schools for working and rural youth are considered to be the equivalent of the general secondary polytechnical schools and students are entitled to transfer from one school to the other. In schools for working youth the academic term is of ten months duration and classes are held for four to five hours per evening four evenings per week; consultation periods are arranged for the fifth evening. Schools for rural youth operate only from November 1 to May 1, the slack season in agriculture. Emphasis is placed on general academic subjects, and in view of the shorter periods of instruction and the fact that these students are already engaged in production, additional work experience is not required of them by the schools. Nevertheless, it is generally conceded that academic standards in the schools for working youth and particularly the schools for rural youth are lower than in the regular secondary schools. Students in these schools are granted leave with pay on examination days

and twenty working days with pay to prepare for and take the state examinations at the end of the senior year.

(5) *Correspondence Courses:* Correspondence secondary schools are designed to meet the needs of people in isolated areas and people who, for one reason or another, are unable to attend a full-time secondary school or a school for working or rural youth. Study consultation centers, staffed by teachers who review written work and are available for consultation for a few hours per week, are supposed to be established in areas where forty or more students are enrolled in the correspondence program. Apart from the fact that work experience and physical education are not required, correspondence students are expected to meet the same basic requirements as students in the regular secondary schools. Students who have completed grade ten by correspondence or in a school for working youth and have passed the state matriculation examinations are entitled to seek admission to a university or institute on the same basis as graduates of the regular ten-year schools.

Soviet figures indicated marked yearly increases in the number of students enrolled in each of these various types of schools. In 1964, four million pupils graduated from the eight-year schools and 1.4 million from the general education secondary schools. More than 3.3 million students were enrolled in technicums and specialized secondary schools; approximately half of these students (1.7 million) were combining study and employment. Another million young people enrolled in technicums during 1964, and 900,000 completed their training in vocational schools.[35]

Because of the strong emphasis on education in the U.S.S.R., a large percentage of the students who complete secondary education attempt to enter an institution of higher learning. It is not unusual for an institution to have a rejection-acceptance ratio of six to one and ratios of fifteen to one have been reported. The number of admissions is governed largely by the needs of the economy; if the authorities decide that more physicists and chemists are required, the enrollment quotas for those fields are increased and stipends are raised. Since 1958 the procedure for selecting candidates for higher education has been in a state of flux. At that time it was decreed that all but a few of the openings in higher educational institutions would be reserved for applicants who had at least two years of production experience. Primary among the reasons for this decision was the concern of the party leaders that higher education was "divorced from life" and that many secondary school graduates had a disdainful attitude toward physical labor, a paradox in a proletarian society in which the demarcation between physical and mental labor is supposed to disappear. Almost immediately, the party had reason to regret its decision to give high priority to production workers for admission to higher educational institutions. A large proportion of the production workers performed poorly on the rigorous entrance examinations which were administered, as always, to all applicants for higher education. However, the preferential treatment of workers with production experience required that many new graduates from secondary schools who performed brilliantly on the entrance exams were rejected, while many production workers who barely passed the entrance exams had to be admitted to fill the quota. Many of these marginal candidates were unable to complete their program of studies and the low caliber of the persons who were admitted initiated a trend toward downgrading standards in a few institutions. In 1963 the rules for admission to higher schools were modified to guarantee no fewer than 20 percent of the available places to new graduates of secondary schools; production workers and new graduates were selected separately on the basis of secondary school grades and entrance examination scores on the Russian language, a foreign language and subjects required for the technical specialty.[36] These rules did little to rectify the problems associated with the admission of poorly qualified production workers, and some people complained that applicants who had performed brilliantly on the entrance exams were rejected because of a poor record in secondary school which had been completed years earlier. In 1964 the foreign language entrance exam was discarded except for foreign language majors and students whose specialty makes considerable use of a foreign language. In 1965 it was announced that the procedure of reserving 80 percent of the places in higher educational institutions for production workers did not justify itself.[37] Henceforth, higher schools are to accept new graduates and production workers in proportion to the number of applications received. Thus, if 75 percent of the applications received by a particular institute come from new graduates, new graduates will be granted 75 percent of the places. The number of fields covered by the entrance examination has been reduced, and more emphasis is being placed on the candidates qualifications to perform well in his chosen specialty. The U.S.S.R. Minister of Higher and Specialized Education indicated that the 1965 revision is designed to raise entrance requirements.[38]

The U.S.S.R. has three types of higher schools: traditional universities which offer training in a variety of disciplines; polytechnical institutes which provide training in a number of specialties within a given field such as engineering or agriculture; and specialized institutes which ordinarily educate specialists for a definite industry such as metallurgy or mining. The vast majority of higher schools are financed by the state. There are, in addition, a few institutes which are operated by the trade unions or the Y.C.L. and a number of party schools; the latter offer training to selected individuals in politics, economics, law, the humanities and general science. The universities and most of the polytechnical institutes come under the jurisdiction of the Ministry of Higher and Specialized Secondary Education. A number of the specialized institutes are under the jurisdiction of other ministries; for example, agricultural and medical institutes are under the jurisdiction of the Ministries of Agriculture and Public Health respectively. The U.S.S.R. Ministry of Higher Education exercises general guidance over all educational institutions, irrespective of jurisdiction, to ensure uniformity in standards and policy.[39]

The period of training in Soviet universities and institutes ordinarily ranges between four to six years, depending on the specialization. In 1964 the period of instruction for most specializations was reduced by several months; for example, students in most medical specialties will now complete their training in five and one-half years instead of six, and in law, journalism, and history the training period has been reduced from five and one-half to five years.[40] Many higher schools have three sections: a day department, for full-time study; an evening department for employed people who work in the vicinity of the school; and a correspondence department for people who come to the school at regular intervals for consultation and to take examinations. Ordinarily, slightly more than half the students who are enrolled in higher education programs combine work and study. For example in 1964, of the 3.6 million who were enrolled in higher schools, two million (55 percent) were studying without leaving production.[41] Students who take higher education by correspondence or on a part-time basis are not expected to complete their program of studies within the temporal period which is established for the full-time students.

In general, the universities train the theorists and the scholars, while the institutes train specialists and professionals in applied fields to meet the needs of the economy. The training provided by Soviet higher schools in the initial program is roughly comparable to the training given by American universities up to the Masters degree or the first professional degree. However, most training programs in the U.S.S.R. are much more narrowly specialized than in the United States. Thus, the graduate of a Soviet higher school might well be more highly trained in his specialization than his American counterpart but his education is lacking in breadth. At the end of the period of training, Soviet students must pass rigorous state examinations and most of them are required to present and defend a diploma project or thesis. Degrees are not awarded to graduates of higher schools. A few of the most talented graduates are selected on the basis of highly competitive examinations for a three-year post graduate program. The "aspirant" works for two years with professors in his field of specialization and devotes the third year to the preparation of a dissertation. If the program is completed successfully, the academic title or degree, Candidate of Sciences, is awarded. The Soviet Candidate of Sciences degree is more or less the equivalent of the American Ph.D. degree. Outstanding Candidates of Sciences may be allowed to enroll in one of the few universities and research institutes which are entitled to confer the Doctor of Sciences degree. In order to earn a D.Sc. degree, the candidate must defend an entirely original dissertation on a major scientific problem at a public hearing before an Academic Council. The Soviet D.Sc. is not comparable to any Western degree.

Detailed arrangements are made to enable Soviet citizens to acquire a higher education in conjunction with full-time work. Admission requirements for part-time and correspondence students are roughly the same as in the day institutions, i.e. graduation from secondary school and satisfactory performance on entrance examinations. However, students whose entrance examination scores would not be high enough to justify admission to the full-time program are sometimes accepted as part-time students. Highly competent part-time students may eventually transfer to the full-time program. There is no age limit for students in evening and correspondence courses but persons over 35 years of age are rarely accepted as full-time students. Special correspondence institute consultation centers where students may receive help, attend lectures and do laboratory work are established in regions where there are many correspondence students. Students in remote areas may receive help from specialists who have a contract with the parent institution. Part-time and correspondence students are granted generous, paid leaves from work for consultation, to prepare diploma projects and to study for and take state examinations: for example, correspondence students are granted 30 calendar days leave for each of the first two years and 40 days for subsequent years, 30 days to prepare for state examinations, four months to prepare and defend the diploma project, and during the last 10 months, one day per week at half pay for work on the diploma project. Students do not pay tuition fees and books are provided free of charge. Even travel expenses to and from the institute are covered in part by the state or by the enterprise which employs the student. In spite of all these complex arrangements, Soviet authorities generally concede that the training acquired by the part-time students and particularly the correspondence students is of a lower caliber than that acquired by the full-time students. The regime has been experimenting with a number of other approaches to the acquisition of a higher education in combination with full-time work. One of the most favored of these has been the factory school, a number of which have been established since 1960. The factory schools offer advanced training, through evening courses taught by factory personnel or by professors, in a few fields related to the major specialization of the factory. In some factories instruction is offered during the day as well as in the evening; two student workers are assigned to one job and spend alternate weeks as full-time workers and full-time students. Regular wages are paid for the work week and student stipends are awarded for the week of studying. The goal of the factory colleges is to relate higher education more closely to practical work and to extend higher educational facilities to a greater number of industrial workers.

All students who graduate from a specialized secondary school, technicum or institution of higher learning are required to accept a three-year assignment where their services will be of particular value to the economy. Requests for specialists are sent to the educational institution by ministries, Economic Councils, and enterprises several months prior to the graduation date. A committee composed of representatives of the faculty, ministries, enterprises and youth organizations examines the requests and provides information to students about available positions, job descriptions, salaries and living conditions. Prospective candidates for a position are supposed to be interviewed by the committee. Superior students who have an acceptable political record may be allowed to choose from among several potential positions. However, the needs of the economy have priority over the personal preferences of the students; for example, graduates of the factory schools are usually returned to their home factory, because it is politically advantageous to demonstrate that a former bench worker can become an engineer; some of the best students may be assigned to the least desirable jobs on the grounds that lagging enterprises and remote areas have the greatest need for the most competent specialists. The assignment procedure sometimes leaves much to be desired; Soviet officials complain that assignments are sometimes made without any real attempt to match the qualifications of the student to the requirements of the job; electrical engineers are assigned to civil engineering positions; teachers who specialized in Russian literature are assigned jobs as teachers of physics or are sent to schools where the language of instruction is not one in which they are proficient.[42] A number of enterprises submit inflated requests for specialists with the result that some of the specialists who are sent to them are used for jobs requiring relatively low levels of training.[43] Before reporting for work all graduates are entitled to a one month vacation during which the student stipend is continued. Moving expenses for the graduate and his family are paid by the employing enterprise. After three years of employment, new positions may be sought.

On the whole, Soviet educational policies have served both the regime and the individual citizen well. The general educational-cultural level of the population has been increased markedly and the majority of Soviet people are dedicated to increasing their educational qualifications. The economy has been supplied with the specialists which were indispensable for rapid industrialization and the rate of training specialists in various applied fields such as engineering, agriculture and medicine currently exceeds the rate in other advanced countries. The outstanding achievements of Soviet scientists during the last decade provide a glowing testimonial to the quality of scientific training in the U.S.S.R. The official Soviet doctrine stresses that educational services are based on the principle of equal opportunity for all and to a very large extent the regime has remained faithful to its official pronouncements. As in other societies, higher education is available to only a relatively small proportion of the population (in 1964 enrollment in higher schools amounted to 3.6 million or approximately 1.6 percent of the population), and only the most talented are enrolled in higher schools. However, the financial status of the family is rarely a factor which limits the educational opportunities of a highly talented individual. The majority of Soviet youth are trained for service in the lower ranks of industrial and agricultural work, but opportunities and financial support are available to those who have the talent and desire to advance through education.

Naturally, there are a number of weaknesses and problems associated with the Soviet educational system. One of the major problems has resulted from the penchant which the party leaders have for reorganization. As a general rule, major reorganizations such as the 1958 emphasis on production training have been introduced without adequate preparation and have resulted in a considerable amount of chaos and wastage of time and resources. Various regulations are changed so frequently that often neither students nor school authorities know what is expected of them. Moreover, party control over education and the requirement that all educational practices and scientific dissertations must conform to Marxist-Leninist ideology has tended to stifle initiative in a number of academic disciplines. Finally, the tremendous emphasis on education has had some results which were unexpected and unwanted. Because education is one of the major tools for personal advancement, and opportunities for higher education are not available to all, some people have attempted to use parental influence and even bribes to gain admission to a higher school, practices which hardly conform with the moral code of communism.[44] Some Soviet spokesmen suggest that too much emphasis is being placed on education; too many people, who would serve both themselves and society better if they were to settle for being competent workers or technicians, are striving to earn accreditation as engineers and specialists; a great deal of time and money is being spent to give production workers advanced training which they do not require to perform their jobs well.[45] Since education is the major channel through which well-paid positions of responsibility and prestige can be attained, it is not surprising that a large proportion of Soviet citizens are highly motivated to improve their educational qualifications.

Rest and Leisure

Article 119 of the Constitution states:

"Citizens of the U.S.S.R. have the right to rest and leisure. The right to rest and leisure is ensured by the establishment of a seven-hour day for industrial, office and professional workers, the reduction of the working day to six hours for arduous trades and to four hours where conditions of work are particularly arduous; by the institution of annual vacations with full pay for industrial, office and professional workers and by the provision of a wide network of sanatoriums, holiday homes and clubs for the accommodation of the working people."

Western authors have commented that workers in most advanced countries have equal or superior rights without the impressive-sounding constitutional guarantee.[46]

From 1940 until 1956, the majority of Soviet workers were required to work eight hours a day, six days a week, excluding overtime. In 1956 a seven-hour work day was introduced in selected branches of the economy and Saturday work was reduced to six hours. By 1960, the standard work week was reduced to forty-one hours, seven hours five days a week plus six hours on Saturdays. Corresponding reductions in work hours were made for workers in hazardous and high priority occupations. Plans announced in 1959 to reduce working time to forty hours per week in 1962 and to thirty-five hours per week in 1964 have apparently been shelved, since official statements no longer allude to them. Complaints in the Soviet press suggest that legal limits on work hours and overtime are frequently ignored by enterprise directors who are pressed to meet plan quotas.

All Soviet workers are granted at least twelve days paid vacation per annum and approximately one third, primarily workers in high priority or hazardous occupations, have twenty-four or more days of paid vacation. Vacations are distributed throughout the year, partly because of emphasis on maximum production and partly because vacation facilities, including the low priced sanatoria and rest homes operated by the trade unions, would be totally inadequate if the majority of workers took their vacations during the summer months. The U.S.S.R. has six state holidays. The day off during the week is usually, but not necessarily, Sunday. Sick leave, excluding leave for pregnancy, averages about seven days per year; employees are also allowed to be absent with pay for educational reasons and to perform public duties such as serving as people's assessors. Approximately five million people per year are given passes to receive medical treatment or to relax in sanatoria or rest homes. The pass may cover all expenses or the recipient may have to pay a portion of the expenses, the amount depending on his financial status and the reason that the pass was given. Most passes are granted as a form of reward for outstanding performance in production, education, culture or public work. Usually, sanatoria and rest homes are located in beautiful surroundings and have excellent facilities for relaxation and entertainment. The competition to obtain passes is keen and cases of favoritism and even bribery in the granting of passes have been reported. The trade unions have been urged by the party to increase the number of sanatoria and rest homes and to build resort towns "for the relaxation of the working people."[47] Local Soviets, enterprises and collective farms have been authorized by the party to build groups of small dachas in desirable locations for use by members of the work collective.[48] Families are able to rent holiday accommodations in these dachas for a small fee. A few prosperous families vacation in privately owned dachas which are officially sanctioned, but are not encouraged.

More than seven million children spend part of their summer vacations at camps run by Young Pioneers or other organizations. Parents, who can afford to do so, pay for the camping expenses, but children from low income families are subsidized. Many students and young people participate in organized hiking and camping expeditions and low cost tours. A shortage of hotel accommodations and travel facilities limits the opportunities for private travel. Like people in other countries, many Soviet citizens spend their vacations at home or with relatives and friends in other areas. Restrictions on travel to other countries have been reduced somewhat in recent years.

Because of the "enormous political and practical significance" of the use of off-work time by the working people, Soviet authorities have been

Table 2
Working Peoples Expenditures of Off-Work Time on
Week Days Averaged for Several Cities*

	Men		Women	
	Time	Percentage	Time	Percentage
Connected with production including travel	1:58	12	1:12	8
Meals including lunch break	1:08	7	:59	6
Housework, personal needs and child care	2:46	17	4:44	29
Free time	3:16	20	1:47	11
Sleep	6:51	42	6:41	41
Other	:19	2	:49	5
Total	16:17	100	16:17	100

* Calculated from materials presented by G. Petrosyan, "On the Rational Use of the Off-Work Time of the Working People," *Voprosy ekonomiki,* No. 6, June, 1963, pp. 32-41. In the Soviet publication the data were presented separately for each of several cities and territories. This table presents the unweighted average for the data from all cities and territories. The study was based on time-budgets for approximately 48,000 man-days.

devoting considerable attention to what people do when they are not on the job. The results of an extensive time-budget study are summarized in Table 2. The study indicated that the absolute magnitude of the off-work time is relatively constant and ranges around sixteen hours per day for all workers. However, there is wide variability in how the time is used, depending on the age and family situation of the worker, the composition of his family and the age of his children, the presence of "helping" members of the family (usually pensioners who help with the housework and supervision of children), the amount of income and housing space per person, educational level, occupation, availability of communal services, distance between home and work, etc.[49] The survey indicated that workers in large cities ordinarily have more "free time" than workers in smaller centers. On the average women have to devote much more time than men to housework and as a result have markedly less "free time" than men.

Soviet authorities stress the need to increase "free time" by eliminating or reducing irrational expenditures of off-work time on travel to work, waiting for services, shopping, cooking and other housework. They offer a number of concrete suggestions: the one to two hours which many people spend in connection with production and travel to work could be reduced considerably by streamlining briefings and shift changes, improving elevator service and urban transport, simplifying the exchange of housing and building more houses close to enterprises; trade and service organizations should be improved so that people should no longer have to stand in line or otherwise waste a lot of time in connection with shopping and everyday services; time spent on housework should be reduced through the provision of better catering services, more household conveniences, etc. The people would, no doubt, be highly gratified if there were a substantial reduction in the number of inconveniences, and the regime would stand to gain in that it would presumably have a more productive, inventive and satisfied populace under its control; thus, Soviet officials are able to present the drive to improve the conveniences of everyday living as an example of harmony between the interests of the individual and the collective. What the Soviet leaders never mention is the fact that the Soviet people have long had to put up with dozens of inconveniences which are non-existent or relatively unimportant in advanced Western societies. Many of the inconveniences which characterize everyday life in the U.S.S.R. are a natural by-product of the social and economic system which the party has imposed on the people; the Soviet planners have been unable to cope with the problem of arranging facilities for the convenience of the people, and in the absence of free enterprise and economic competition, the people have had no choice but to tolerate the inconveniences to which they have been subjected. In any other system, the people have considerable choice about the location of living quarters in relation to their place of employment—in the U.S.S.R. they must accept with gratitude the living space that is assigned to them by the state authorities, even if the assigned apartment is many miles from the place of work; in other societies competition forces each establishment to attempt to maintain its services at a high level since if a particular establishment gives poor service the people take their business elsewhere—in the U.S.S.R. all everyday service establishments are operated by the state or cooperatives and competition does not serve as a lever to maintain high standards; in other societies private entrepreneurs are on the alert for areas which have a need for a particular type of service—in the U.S.S.R. the decision to provide a service is made by state officials who are not always well-informed and are not obligated to give immediate priority to the needs of the populace. Thus, the official emphasis on the removal of inconveniences amounts to an attempt to cope with some of the disadvantages which are inherent in the Soviet economic system.

The party officials are apparently sincere in their desire to provide the people with more free time but their interest is not in free time to be frittered away frivolously according to individual inclination; rather, the emphasis is on the "rational use of free time for the important task of communist construction."[50] A Soviet authority commented:

> "It must be kept in mind that leisure is not merely the idle passing of time, not merely engaging in entertainment or amusing activities. Its chief task is to provide conditions for the fuller disclosure of the spiritual and physical aptitudes of the Soviet people, for the education of the working people, particularly the younger generation."[51]

According to the official dogma, free time may be used "to rest in preparation for new work," to study and improve political, cultural and skill qualifications, to fulfill public duties, to enhance the individual's own spiritual and physical development, to visit with family and friends or for leisure and relaxation "on the basis of free choice of one means or another of employing it."[52] The most rational use of free time purportedly involves the use of a large portion of it for the purpose of gradually reforming the Soviet citizen to conform to the ideal of the "new Soviet man." Although Soviet authorities stress the importance of the "organization of more rational and purposeful relaxation for the working people,"[53] the government does not dictate specifically how individuals should use their free time; emphasis is, however, placed on ensuring the availability of facilities for leisure time activities which are condoned by the regime.

Soviet citizens engage in the same general types of recreational activities that are common in Western societies: sports, movies, TV, theatre, dancing, amateur groups, lectures, etc. The Soviet leaders consider athletic activities to be valuable for building disciplined characters as well as strong bodies. A very large number of sports grounds, stadiums, gymnasiums, swimming pools, skiing and boating stations and other facilities have been built at state expense, and trade unions, the Komsomol and other organizations are urged to add to the existing facilities, to organize sports events and to encourage widespread participation. More than 20 million people are enrolled in sports clubs where athletic training is directed by instructors and coaches trained and usually paid by the state.[54] Almost all of the sports club members are "enthusiasts" who participate regularly in the rigorous training and undergo a series of graded tests. In most clubs, the emphasis is on developing general athletic proficiency, rather than expertness in one sport only. Although the regime appears to be relatively well satisfied with the athletic programs, there has been some concern about the number of people who are merely spectators rather than activists. Also, the Y. C. L. and other organizations have been criticized because too many young people engage in petty hooliganism, loafing, drunkenness and "even" attend church instead of participating in sports.

Soviet authorities point to the large number of social and cultural clubs which have been established by the state, trade unions, industrial enterprises and collective farms as material evidence of the regime's concern that the working people should be provided with adequate facilities for the rational use of their free time. In major urban areas the clubs or Palaces of Culture are generally large and well equipped; most of them have lecture, dance and concert halls, a movie theatre, a large library, rehearsal rooms for amateur dramatic and musical activities, physical education facilities and even rooms for playing pool or cards. At the other end of the extreme, a club in a rural area might be little more than a small hut with a few comfortable chairs, a few books and a radio. All but the very small clubs have special children's sections. A very large number of people participate in folk dancing, choral singing and orchestral groups and other amateur activities, and hobbies, such as painting, photography and electronics, which are generally conducted on a high level. The authorities complain that the political and cultural lectures are not well attended; the blame is placed on the poor quality of the lectures as well as on the lassitude of the people. For many, particularly in the rural areas, the club serves as a community center where people meet to visit, dance, watch television or a movie, and perhaps also to escape from their own crowded living quarters. The value of the clubs to the people is sometimes marred by over zealous organizers who seek to dictate to the patrons the form and content of their leisure time activities, but in the main, the clubs apparently provide highly appreciated facilities for "rational" but relatively free use of leisure time.

Parks of Culture and Rest provide an outdoor counterpart to the Palaces of Culture. In the more elaborate parks open-air dance halls, stages, movie theatres, skating rinks and restaurants or snack bars are surrounded by formal gardens, political statues, cement walks and park benches. Here for a small fee, Soviet citizens may dance, skate, watch amateur dramatic, dance or choral performances, engage in group games, or simply visit or walk. Communities sometimes vie with each other with respect to the beauty of their parks and even most small communities have a park which, though it may include little more than playground and a few flowers and benches, constitutes an integral part of the life of many residents.

All works of art and entertainment productions must conform with official ideology. Pleasing the officials and the people at the same time has posed a severe problem; according to some observers, ideological restrictions have effected a decline in both the quality and popularity of the theatre. Ballet, which by its very nature is freer from regimentation, continues on a very high level, and although the majority of rural and small town residents never see a professional ballet performance, it is a legitimate source of national pride. Concerts also tend to be of high quality and are well attended. Movie makers, after dull and stultifying efforts during the Stalin regime, have produced a fairly large number of films that have met official approval and, at the same time, have been highly popular with the people. Naturally, not all movies have met the double criteria. Because of their mass consumption, the officials demand that movies glorify the Soviet way of life and the kinds of virtues that are to characterize the "new Soviet man." Films which do not conform fully with official standards and foreign films, including excellent productions and mediocre Hollywood westerns, may be shown. The Soviet press frequently carries a careful analysis of popular movies to inform the public about ideological and artistic weaknesses. The number of movie theatres is insufficient to meet the demands of the population, and many are poorly heated and ventilated. However, people often travel many miles and stand in long lines to get tickets, tangible evidence that going to the movies is a popular form of entertainment, even if many of the films are designed to provide ideological indoctrination in a palatable form.

Leisure time in the U.S.S.R. is, of course, used in a multitude of other ways, common to most societies: family activities, picnics, reading, visiting friends and relatives, walks, street dancing, fairs, spectator sports, etc. Most observers of the Soviet social scene have been impressed by the strong interest of the Soviet people in cultural matters. Museums, libraries, concerts and art galleries are typically crowded; writers, musicians and artists are praised lavishly by the authorities and the public for acceptable accomplishments and are criticized sharply for poor quality productions. Television, with approximately 12 million sets available, is extremely popular and has effected a major change in the leisure time activities of the Soviet populace. Needless to say, a considerable amount of time and money is devoted to the consumption of alcoholic beverages. The regime disapproves of the excessive use of alcohol, but has considered it impractical to introduce prohibition because speculators, who are generally more disparaged than alcoholics, might flood the market. Therefore, the sale of alcoholic beverages is condoned by the state, and indeed, apart from bootlegged and homebrewed liquor, beverages are sold exclusively through cooperative or state operated enterprises. Recently, more stringent measures have been taken to enforce regulations prohibiting the sale of alcoholic beverages to adolescents. The state and party leaders indicated their willingness or need to cater to the population, even contrary to their own admonitions, when arrangements were made to import the ingredients for vodka from Canada and the U.S.A. when the 1963 crop failure reduced the vodka production potential.

Thus, as the Soviet Union has progressed industrially, the government has allowed the people an increased amount of leisure time; additional increases are likely within the foreseeable future. The individual and the regime apparently do not agree completely on the best use of the free time. The majority of individuals probably want genuine free time to be used as they see fit, whereas the regime wants the free time to be used to refashion the individual as a worthy citizen in the communist society. Apparently, the party leaders, cognizant of the futility of the use of dictatorial methods in this sphere, have settled for a compromise which is relatively acceptable to the people. The government is providing more adequate facilities for the people to engage in recreational and other leisure time activities which are in harmony with party-dictated objectives, and the people are allowed to choose among various alternatives, the majority of which are to their liking. Regardless of the motivation of the party leaders, individual Soviet citizens are reaping benefits from the increased availability of time and facilities for leisure time activities.

The Family and Emancipation of Women

The Soviet system has attempted to manipulate its policy toward the family to serve a number of goals simultaneously: to emancipate women from various forms of political, religious, paternal and economic subjugation; to involve women as fully as possible in economic production; to ensure a rapid population growth; and to arrange for the upbringing of children in conformity with party-dictated goals. Legal norms and theoretical pronouncements about the role of the family in society have varied from time to time depending upon the priority status assigned to emancipation, productivity, population growth or upbringing. Policy changes have also been introduced in an attempt to eradicate unanticipated and unwanted effects of earlier policies.

A consistent ideological theme which has influenced Soviet family policy is the Marxist premise that formal legal rights for women are relatively meaningless unless women are freed from economic, ecclesiastical, social and traditional shackles. Engels argued:

> "With the patriarchical family and still more with the simple monogamous family . . . the wife became the head servant, excluded from all participation in social production. . . . The modern individual family is so founded on the open or concealed domestic slavery of the wife. . . . In the great majority of cases today, at least in the possessing classes, the husband is obliged to earn a living and support his family and that in itself gives him a position of supremacy, without any need for special legal titles and privileges. . . . The wife differs from the ordinary prostitute only in that she hires out her body not by the hour, like a daily woman, but sells it once and for all into constant slavery . . . the first condition for the liberation of the wife is to bring the whole female sex back into public industry . . . and this in fact demands the abolition of the monogamous family as the economic unit of society."[55]

The extraordinary attention devoted by the Soviet regime, at its inception, to the rights of women and to family relationships in general was due, in part, to the extreme subjugation of women in the preceding era. In Tsarist Russia the church had jurisdiction over all matrimonial affairs; wives were legally subordinated to their husbands; divorce was almost completely prohibited; in Mohammedan areas polygamy was sanctioned and girl children were given in marriage for a bride price; very few women were allowed a modicum of education; women workers received low wages for working long hours under deplorable conditions; in short, women had almost no legal or social rights. The egalitarian principles of Marxism-Leninism and the desire to involve women more fully in production made it necessary for the new Bolshevik regime to take immediate action to change the status of women in society.

Within a few months after the Bolsheviks took over, decrees were issued which directly affected the status of women, the family and the church.[56] Civil marriage was substituted for religious marriage and a signed statement that the marriage was contracted voluntarily was required. Spouses were allowed to assume jointly the surname of the husband, the wife or a combined surname. Divorce was permitted without a statement of grounds upon the request of either spouse. Provisions were made for payment of alimony to the wife. Children born out of wedlock were given equal rights in all respects to children born in wedlock. Co-education from elementary school to university was introduced early in 1918 as a preliminary condition for the actual equality of women in professional and industrial work. A more complete Family Law passed in October, 1918 confirmed and expanded the provisions in the original decrees.[57] In accordance with the principle that "Birth itself shall be the basis of the family," fathers were held jointly responsible for the maintenance of children born out of wedlock, *de facto* marriages were recognized, and authorities spoke of the rightness of a dissoluble marriage rather than a life long union. In

1919 pregnant women were granted a sixteen week maternity leave with full pay, free medical care and other benefits.[58] The intent of the regime was elaborated in the 1919 Party Program which stated:

> "Bourgeois democracy through the ages proclaimed equality of persons, irrespective of religion, race or nationality and the equality of the sexes, but capitalism prevented the realization of this equality. . . . The Soviet government, by being the authority of the toilers, for the first time in history could in all spheres of life realize this equality, destroying the last traces of woman's inequality in the sphere of marriage and the family. . . . The Party's aim is not to limit itself to the formal proclamation of woman's equality, but to liberate woman from all the burdens of antiquated methods of housekeeping, by replacing them by house communes, public kitchens, central laundries, nurseries, etc."[59]

The party has adhered consistently to the policy of attempting to establish complete equality for women; the 1961 Party Program stated: "The remnants of the unequal position of women in domestic life must be totally eliminated."[60] The goal of equality for women has been one of the major determinants of all legislation pertaining to the family.

The government soon recognized that the militant feminist movement which it encouraged, its policy of weakening family ties, its tacit sanction of "free love," and economic conditions, under which the birth of another child often resulted in severe hardships for the family, had greatly increased the number of illegal abortions. The state did not have the material resources to establish a large number of children's institutions or to give substantial financial assistance to parents. A decree which legalized abortions to "protect the health of women" made explicit the regime's disapproval of abortions and its recognition of the futility of prohibiting them under the given circumstances.[61] A Marriage and Divorce code issued in 1926 sustained the policies established by the earlier legislation.[62]

During the initial years of Soviet rule, the consensus of opinion among party spokesmen was that the family in its traditional form would wither away, the state would assume responsibility for the upbringing of children, women would gladly relinquish domestic and child rearing responsibilities in order to function in the economy in complete equality with men, the duty of mutual support within the family would be replaced by social security measures, and the union between a male and a female would be based solely on mutual attraction and comradely feelings. Madam Kollontay, a leading propagandist of Bolshevik views on the family, wrote in 1920:

> ". . . the old type of family has seen its day. . . . *The Family is ceasing to be a necessity of the State,* as it was in the past; on the contrary, it is worse than useless, since it needlessly holds back the female workers from more production and from more serious work. Nor is it any longer necessary to the members of the family themselves, since the task of bringing up children . . . is passing more and more into the hands of the collective. But on the ruins of the former

family we shall see a new form rising which will involve altogether different relations between men and women, and which will be a union of affection and companionship, a union of two equal members of the communist society, both of them free, both of them independent, both of them workers."[63]

Sabsovich, writing in 1929, reiterated that the elimination of the individual household was a prerequisite for the cultural revolution and the refashioning of man: he asserted that "individual upbringing given to children in each family separately is a bad thing"; all able-bodied women should be involved in production; and the individual household should be replaced by communal establishments.[64]

By the early 1930's unwanted consequences of the family legislation and the doctrine of the withering away of the family became painfully apparent. Multiple marriage and divorce rates rose excessively and in the larger cities well over 30 percent of all pregnancies culminated in abortions.[65] Free love and casual cohabitation were widely practiced; cases of men having five or six wives simultaneously or within a short time were common, and at least one "scoundrel" was reported to have had sixteen wives.[66] Although a large proportion of Soviet citizens attempted to maintain traditional family relationships, the authority of parents was undermined by the official ideology, by what the children were taught in school, and by the encouragement children were given to report parents who expressed deviant political views. The instability of marriages, the inadequate facilities for the upbringing of children by the state, the weakened parental authority and the general chaos contributed to a disruption of social values and to inadequate upbringing of the younger generation. In 1935, parents were made responsible for the disorderly conduct of their children, an indication that the official attitude toward the family was changing.

In 1936, family legislation was revamped.[67] A number of measures were introduced to improve the material position of mothers and abortion was prohibited, except for strict medical reasons. The network of medical and children's institutions was expanded; labor legislation to protect the rights of pregnant women and mothers of small children was strengthened; state allowances for mothers of six or more children were introduced. Alimony payments were established at the rate of one-fourth of the wages of the defendant for one child, one-third for two children and one-half for three or more children, and the procedure for the collection of alimony was improved. Fathers of children born out of wedlock were held responsible for their support. Divorce was made more expensive and both parties had to report to the Registry office; the fact of divorce was entered on the passports of both divorcees as a slight measure of social sanction.

The consensus of published opinion coinciding with the 1936 decree was that "Assertions that socialism leads to the extinction of the family are profoundly mistaken and harmful. . . . The family does not become extinct under socialism: it merely grows stronger,"[68] and ". . . what takes place is not the complete abolition of the family, to be replaced by extra family sex relations . . . but the disappearance of the old form of the family in which woman was enslaved and subjugated."[69] A Pravda editorial stated:

> ". . . a blow will be dealt at the light hearted, negligent attitude toward marriage. When we speak of strengthening the Soviet family, we are speaking precisely of the struggle against the survivals of a bourgeois attitude toward marriage, women and children. So-called "free-love" and all disorderly sex life are bourgeois through and through, and have nothing to do with either socialist principles or the ethics and standards of conduct of the Soviet citizen. . . . More than once the enemies of the people suggested to us the foul and poisonous idea of liquidating the family and disrupting marriage. . . . Marriage and divorce are, of course, private affairs—but the state cannot allow anyone to mock at women or to abandon his children to the mercy of fate. . . . Marriage is a serious, responsible business and one that must not be approached light heartedly. . . . We must safeguard our family and raise and rear healthy Soviet heroes!"[70]

Thus, in 1936 the concept of the "withering away of the family" was replaced by the concept of a new "freer and stronger" family based upon the socialist transformation of economics and the emancipation of women. Conditions were purportedly created to "allow woman to combine harmoniously an active participation in productive and social life with the performance of her family functions, her duties as a mother."[71] Monogamy was allegedly stabilized under socialism, but divorce was a right if mutual love were alienated.[72] Parenthood was treated as a virtue with honorable rights and obligations, and the identity of the interests of the family and society was stressed. A Soviet official commented:

> "Under socialism personal and family interests are not in conflict with social interests, as is the case under capitalism. In socialist society, personal interests and those of the family are combined harmoniously with the interests of the whole society . . . the welfare of the Soviet family depends on the welfare of the whole of society and on the honest, conscientious work of the members of the family in the socialist enterprises and Soviet establishments. Social ownership is, therefore, the economic basis for the existence and prosperity of the Soviet family."[73]

Concurrently, the authorities suggested that love should not be apolitical: "Sexual love between men and women is under socialism . . . essentially different from the ordinary sex attraction. . . . This love gains strength from the common ideological and political interests . . . and the common struggle for the common Communist ideal."[74] Potential mates were to be evaluated for political reliability and for the value of their contribution to society.

In 1944 the marriage and family law was again revised.[75] The 1944 code, with minor amendments, is still in force, but since 1964 proposals for a new marriage and family law have been under consideration

by the Legislative Committees of the chambers of the U.S.S.R. Supreme
Soviet.[76] The 1944 legislation was designed to achieve two almost incompatible goals: to foster stable family relationships and to increase the birth
rate by encouraging both married and unmarried women to produce a
large number of children. Although the philosophy underlying the 1944
code was roughly the same as that which had shaped the 1936 code, rather
drastic legal changes were introduced in an attempt to cope with concrete
problems which resulted from the war devastation and the tremendous loss
of life. A high birth rate was a prerequisite for maintaining and expanding
the military and economic might of the U.S.S.R.; the abnormal male-
female ratio influenced the decision to sanction and encourage unmarried
motherhood, and to provide substantial state assistance for the upbringing
of children born out of wedlock; the material damage caused by the war
and other economic factors made increased assistance to mothers of large
families advisable.

Measures designed to foster stable family relations included increased
advantages associated with registered marriages and decreased ease of
obtaining divorces. The code specified that only marriages registered in the
Civil Registry Office would produce the rights and obligations of husband
and wife, including the rights to maintenance if in need, community of
property and inheritance. *De facto* marriages have no legal status whatsoever; the mother of a child born in an unregistered marriage has no legal
claim on the father of the child and men have been relieved of all legal
and financial responsibility for children born out of wedlock. Provisions
were made for the registration of *de facto* marriages which were in existence before the decree was issued.

The procedure for dissolving a marriage has been made rather involved and costly, a far cry from the early days of the regime when one
party could inform the Registry Office that he wanted to discontinue the
marriage and the Registry Office would merely send the other party a
postcard to inform him that his marital status had changed. Divorce procedure is now initiated by a petition to the People's Court with a statement of grounds and a ten ruble filing fee. Notice of the proceedings
is next advertised in the press at the expense of the petitioner, a process
which may take several months. The court then calls in the parties and
witnesses in order to establish the motives for the divorce and to attempt
to affect a reconciliation. If the reconciliation efforts are ineffective, the
petitioner next appeals to a higher court which hears the case in public
unless there are well founded reasons for granting a request that the hearing be *in camera*. The law provides no statutory grounds for divorce and
the higher court may, on the basis of its instructions to "strengthen family
ties," deny the divorce petition even if mutual consent is involved; non-
contested divorces are, however, usually granted. Before a divorce can be

registered a fee of 50 to 200 rubles must be paid, usually by the "guilty" party. The court settles questions concerning custody, alimony, maintenance and property.

To encourage large families the state established allowances for mothers on the birth of the third and all subsequent children, according to the scale presented in Table 3. An unmarried mother is given a monthly allowance of 5 rubles for her first child, 7.5 rubles for the second, and 10 rubles for the third until the child reaches the age of 12; for each additional child she receives an allowance as a mother of a large family. If the unwed mother marries she retains the right to state assistance; if she elects to have her child brought up in a state institution at state expense, she does not receive the allowance, but she does retain the right to remove the child from the institution. In 1964 about six million mothers of large families and unwed mothers received state allowances.[77] Both married and unmarried women qualify for medals and titles of honor on the birth of the fifth and all subsequent children; the mother of ten children is made a "Mother-Heroine" and is given a certificate of recognition by the U.S.S.R. Supreme Soviet.

Other measures introduced in 1944 entitled expectant mothers and mothers of small children to special privileges on the job, including rest periods and assignments to light work, extended the network of institutions for the protection of mothers and children, and reduced creche and kindergarten fees for children from large families. The tax on single people and small families, which was introduced in 1941 and extended in 1944, was used as a further incentive to encourage large families and to help the state support them. In 1962 this tax was reduced substantially. Maternity leave

Table 3
Allowances to Mothers of Large Families*

To Mothers	Monthly Allowance From Age 1 to 5	Single Grant
With 2 children on birth of 3rd	—	20 r.
With 3 children on birth of 4th	4 r.	65 r.
With 4 children on birth of 5th	6 r.	85 r.
With 5 children on birth of 6th	7 r.	100 r.
With 6 children on birth of 7th	10 r.	125 r.
With 7 children on birth of 8th	10 r.	125 r.
With 8 children on birth of 9th	12.5 r.	175 r.
With 9 children on birth of 10th	12.5 r.	175 r.
With 10 children on birth of each subsequent child	15 r.	250 r.

* "Decree of Presidium of the Supreme Soviet of the U.S.S.R. on Less Aid to Mothers of Large Families," November 25, 1947, Reproduced in James H. Meisel and Edward S. Kozera, *The Soviet System, op. cit.,* pp. 409-10.

which had been reduced to 63 days in 1938, as a war preparation measure, was increased in 1944 to 77 days, and was subsequently extended to 112 days. In 1956 abortion was again legalized because the number of illegal abortions had increased markedly.

The changes which have been proposed for the marriage and family law do not reflect any basic change in philosophy. Apparently, the reform will be directed chiefly toward the removal of "certain flaws in a number of the provisions of the existing law."[78] One of the chief problems has been the fact that the unmarried father has not been required to assume responsibility of any kind for his children. The authorities had apparently assumed that women would be more likely to insist on a registered marriage if the unmarried father were relieved of all responsibility. However, regardless of the intention of the authorities and of the women involved, the result of the law has apparently been to encourage some males to be casually promiscuous, since they could not be held financially or legally responsible for children born out of wedlock, and others to be excessively cautious as manifested by the number of relatively permanent unregistered marriages. Many stable *de facto* marriages have, of course, been unregistered because of the rather lengthy and expensive procedure involved in dissolving a previous marriage. One of the proposed changes is to simplify and shorten the divorce procedure, to abolish public announcements in the newspapers and to settle divorce suits in the People's Courts instead of in a higher court. Second, provision is to be made for the voluntary admission of paternity and in certain cases for the determination of paternity through court action. These proposed changes should reduce the number of unregistered marriages and enable the regime to force a large number of unmarried fathers to assume responsibility for their children. The new law will probably also introduce an abbreviated birth certificate in order to eliminate the practice of placing a dash through the entry "Father" in the birth certificates of children born out of wedlock. It has also been suggested that the new legislation should provide additional guarantees for the prompt collection of alimony.[79]

The current attitude of the regime toward the family differs little from that expressed in the 1944 legislation. An official stated that the tasks of the new legislation on marriage and the family include:

> ". . . the further strengthening of the Soviet family, the building of family relationships upon a voluntary marital union of a woman and a man based on mutual love, friendship and respect and free of material considerations; final elimination of harmful vestiges and customs of the past in family relations; and an increased feeling of responsibility for the creation of a family."[80]

The family, rather than withering away, is still regarded as the primary unit of socialist society and efforts are made to strengthen family ties. The monogamous marriage is favored; divorce, though allowed, is not encouraged, and divorced men are required to contribute to the support of their children. Although birth out of wedlock is officially sanctioned, the regime would apparently prefer, now that the male-female imbalance caused by the war is no longer a major problem, to increase the number of registered unions. Soviet spokesmen, however, insist that both the unwed mother and the illegitimate child are totally free from social stigma and that the extra-marital child is as well off economically as the child born in wedlock. Requests from the populace to change the procedure for registering births out of wedlock suggest that social stigma is not entirely absent. Also, the state allowance to the unwed mother is less than obligatory child-support payments of a divorced man who earns the minimum wage. Parents, though guided and assisted by the party, state, school and youth organizations, are expected to assume considerable responsibility for the upbringing of their children and the shaping of the "new Soviet man." Children are taught in school that they must respect and obey their parents and the parents of children who flaunt the social mores are berated in public. As the parents themselves have become more accepting of Soviet ideology, the regime is apparently less concerned that parents would attempt to inculcate political deviationist ideas into the children. However, parents who force their children to perform "religious rituals" may be deprived of their parental rights by court action, since "such children grow up to be inferior people, morally unstable, incapable of becoming full members of society. . . ."[81] In general, the regime prefers not to apply legal sanctions against parents "who are guilty of incorrect, anti-social upbringing of children,"[82] since it would be extremely difficult to prepare a code which would cover every eventuality. Instead, it relies heavily on the "moral influence" of the community; Comrades' Courts, apartment house and street committees, youth and other public organizations are entitled to advise and criticize parents with respect to their upbringing techniques.

Although the official attitude toward the family is almost the antithesis of that which was espoused during the early years of the regime, the attitude toward women, which has to a large extent shaped family policy, has been remarkably consistent. The only major change in the attitude toward women is that, initially, the importance to the regime and to the woman herself of her role as a worker was given official priority over all else. Subsequently, the value and social distinction associated with motherhood was sharply upgraded. The regime has remained faithful to its promise to uphold the constitutional statement that women have absolutely equal rights with men in all spheres of economic, cultural, political and other activities. Soviet accomplishments with regard to women's rights must be regarded as substantial, especially if the low status of women in Tsarist Russia is taken into consideration. In as far as such matters can be controlled by the regime, Soviet women have equal educational opportunities, equal opportunities for advancement in their careers, equal pay rates and all other objective manifestations of equality. Women account for approximately half of the total labor force and half of the total enrollment in higher educational institutions. Most female workers, like most male workers, are assigned to work in low income and low status jobs, but women have full equality with respect to high level jobs; more than one-third of all Soviet lawyers and engineers, one-half of the leading officials and specialists in the national economy, and more than three-quarters of all physicians are women.[83] However, as Soviet authorities point out, "conditions for the growth of women, for their promotion to posts of leadership, have not yet been created everywhere."[84] Full equality of opportunity has not been achieved simply because, in general, female students and workers must devote more of their off-duty time than their male counterparts to child care and household tasks. As a consequence, most women have less time than men for study and "self-improvement" and public duties, and some may approach their work and educational duties with less vigor.

The regime has been deeply concerned about the "vestiges of inequality" under which women must still operate. Soviet officials consistently emphasize the need to increase the number of children's establishments and to decrease the amount of time women must spend doing housework, and as the economy progresses it can be anticipated that increasingly large funds will be used for these purposes. One of the most important planned measures to improve the life of women and of entire families is to provide more adequate housing. The majority of Soviet people have always had to put up with extremely limited and inconvenient living quarters. Millions of families still live in a single room or share an apartment with another family. Newlyweds often consider themselves lucky if they can move into the crowded quarters of one of their parents. As late as 1958 it was reported that even in Moscow only 39 percent of the apartments had a private bathroom and only 10 percent had hot running water.[85] The housing situation has improved considerably during the last few years, but not as rapidly as had been planned. According to official reports over 100 million people received new apartments or improved their living conditions between 1956 and 1965.[86] The amount of living space per capita has increased to approximately 6.3 square meters (about 67 square feet).[87] The party plans that by 1975 each family should be provided with a separate apartment with a floor space of approximately 45 square meters (about 480 square feet). Under present circumstances, home life may be more than a little lacking in peace, quiet and privacy; all Soviet citizens, but particularly women, should find life much more pleasant when each family can have its own small apartment with modern conveniences and at least a modicum of privacy.

The regime has attempted to provide conditions under which women can effectively combine work in the economy with motherhood. Because of the multitude of demands on material resources, these measures have been far from adequate as witnessed by the insufficient supply of children's institutions, poor housing and the inconveniences of everyday living. A number of critics of the Soviet system have condemned the regime for forcing women to assume the dual role of workers and homemakers, but Soviet women themselves do not appear to feel unduly oppressed. The system of children's institutions, inadequate though it is, the high praise which they get for their contributions to the economy, the doctrine that everyone should strive to contribute to the welfare of society and a number of other factors contribute to the ease with which the Soviet woman is able to adjust to her dual role. She suffers a minimum of conflict because social expectations and the social structure facilitate the combination. A woman in the U.S.S.R. may devote herself exclusively to the upbringing of her children if she wants to do so and if the income of other members of the family is sufficient. As in other societies, many women in the Soviet Union work because of economic necessity; however, it is likely that the majority of Soviet women would prefer to work even if economic necessity were not a factor.

Soviet officials are fond of stating that in the U.S.S.R. a woman is honored as a mother and for the work that she does, rather than for physical beauty or because of "the last name of her husband." Soviet newspapers and magazines feature stories about "Mother-Heroines" and women who have excelled in industry, agriculture, science or the arts, but not about beauty queens and glamour girls. However, during the last few years measures have been introduced to enable women to dress and groom themselves more attractively; more beauty parlors and cosmetics are available and more attention has been devoted to the color, style and quality of clothing.

The regime's treatment of women has contributed appreciably to the economic progress of the state. However, the consistency of the attempts to materialize the rights of women suggest that, in this case, ideological considerations have contributed as much as economic considerations to the shaping of official policy. The rewards have been shared by women and the regime. In exchange for their improved status women have, no doubt, rewarded the regime with appreciation which influences their indoctrination of the younger generation, and the regime, in addition to its economic gains, can use the fact that it has effected almost complete emancipation of women as a powerful propaganda weapon at home and abroad.

Religion

The Communist Party of the Soviet Union has consistently pursued a policy deliberately designed to eliminate all vestiges of religious influence. Hostility toward religion is deeply rooted in communist ideology; Marx referred to religion as "the opium of the people" and Lenin asserted that "Marxism has always viewed all contemporary religion and churches, all and every kind of religious organization as agencies of bourgeois reaction, serving as a defense of exploitation and the drugging of the working class."[88] Communists argue that: religion is anti-scientific; belief in God destroy's man's faith in himself and his will to break the shackles that bind him unnecessarily; the doctrine that meek, obedient and patient persons will receive their reward in heaven serves merely to mislead the masses and to support and defend the exploiting classes. The official party line has never varied from the thesis that religion must be rejected permanently and without reservations.

When the Bolsheviks acquired power, they would have liked to have prohibited all formal religious worship. Religious institutions were regarded, rightly, as enemies of communism and impediments to the realization of communist goals. However, Lenin recognized that over-zealous repressive action against religion could have disasterous consequences for the new regime, since the majority of people, regardless of their religious affiliation, simply would not tolerate the abrupt denial of the right to engage in religious practices and to express religious beliefs. Consequently, he ruled that the campaign against religion should be waged rather cautiously with major emphasis on indoctrination, persuasion and education, bolstered by relatively mild legislative action. His goal was to destroy all religious beliefs as quickly as possible, but he recognized that several years or perhaps decades would be required for "ultimate victory" over religion.

The formal battle against religious institutions was initiated in February, 1918, when the new regime issued a decree which separated the church from the state and the school from the church. [89] This decree nationalized all church property, including the extensive rental lands owned by churches, the church buildings and even sacramental vestments and vessels. Buildings and articles specially designated for religious services could be allocated by local or state authorities for use by religious groups, but the authorities were free to deny or withdraw use of such facilities, and many local Soviets designated church buildings for use as clubs or offices and even as warehouses or stables. All acts of a civil nature such as marriage, divorce and birth registration were removed from the jurisdiction of the church. The teaching of religious doctrines in all educational institutions in which general subjects were taught was forbidden, and all religious oaths were abolished. Concurrently, certain concessions were made to the doctrine that religion is a private affair. Every citizen was given the right to profess any religion or none at all. Free observance of religious customs was guaranteed, provided that public order was not disturbed and the rights of citizens were not violated. Citizens were allowed to study and teach religion privately. Local laws or regulations which would restrict or limit freedom of conscience or establish any kind of privileges or advantages on the basis of religious affiliation were prohibited. The 1918 Constitution assured to every citizen freedom of religious and anti-religious propaganda and "genuine liberty of conscience"; at the same time monks and priests of all religious denominations were disfranchised.

The regime's enduring attitude toward religion is stated clearly in the following quotation which states what the government hoped to accomplish through its initial decree on the church:

> ". . . the Soviet Decree concerning the Separation of the Church from the State and the School from the Church was from the beginning directed *against religion*. In the question of religion, the Soviet Government never carried a double-dealing policy of equal cooperation with religion and atheism. It would be wrong to represent the whole matter as if our government kept away from the problems of religion, washed its hands and left the matter to its natural course . . . this decree cannot be considered otherwise than as *a measure deliberately directed against religion*. . . . Soviet power fights against religion: . . . first, by means of separation of all Churches from the State and then by means of organization of *anti-religious education* in the schools and anti-religious education of the people at large. If . . . our government would not have developed . . . by all means at its disposal anti-religious propaganda, then . . . religion would have developed and to an extent strengthened in new refined forms . . . it would be treason to the dictatorship of the proletariat . . . to fail to organize the fight against religion on a union-wide scale by the force and means of the government itself . . . the analysis of the decree may be summarized as follows: . . . the Soviet separation of the Church and State leads to the free and final death of religion." [italics added][90]

During the 1920's a series of decrees designed to weaken the influence of the church were passed: to provide private religious instruction to groups composed of more than three children was made a criminal offence; the right to conduct religious propaganda was withdrawn but the right to anti-religious propaganda was retained; religious associations were denied the right to function as charitable or social organizations.[91] The regime was determined to limit and, if possible, abolish religious education for children, and to cut down the activities and influence of religious groups to a bare minimum.

Concurrently, the regime sponsored violently anti-religious indoctrination campaigns. Militant atheist groups were formed under the auspices of the party and the state, and the people were subjected to a deluge of anti-religious literature and lectures. Schools were instructed to ensure an "anti-religious upbringing" of students. Those who remained faithful to their beliefs were subjected to scorn and, not infrequently, to abuse; persons who wanted to attain or retain positions of power had to disavow any religious sympathies. Religious groups did not submit passively to the restrictive treatment; most of the churches strongly supported the counter-revolutionary forces during the October Revolution and the Civil War, and issued counter-propaganda against the new Bolshevik regime. During the early years, the conflict between the church and the state often erupted into violence; a governmental order to the local Soviets to remove from the churches all articles of value which were not absolutely essential for the performance of religious rites aroused particularly strong resistance. The motivation underlying this order was financial as well as anti-religious; zealous local officials stripped churches of objects of value, and then proceeded to destroy large quantities of religious books, ikons and even consecrated relics. There were many bloody incidents and large numbers of church leaders and laymen were imprisoned; several were executed. During the imprisonment of the Patriarch of the Russian Orthodox Church for his defense of consecrated objects, splinter groups subservient to the party formed within the Orthodox Church. The Patriarch apparently decided that active opposition to the regime was futile; he was released without trial after he announced that "henceforth I am not an enemy of the Soviet Power."[92] This marked the beginning of the capitulation of the Orthodox Church to an "attitude of loyalty to the Soviet regime."[93] However, the restrictive measures against all religious groups continued in full force. When the Patriarch died in 1925, a Metropolitan who was completely subservient to the dictates of the party was allowed to assume titular leadership of the Orthodox Church. Despite the fact that the Metropolitan did as he was told, pledged wholehearted support for the Soviet government and used the church as a platform to instill loyalty to the regime in the believers, no concessions were made to the Orthodox Church, or any other religious group, with the sole exception that members of religious orders were granted the franchise in 1936. Many churches were closed and atheistic propaganda was intensified.

The 1936 Constitution, which is still in effect, reads:

> In order to ensure citizens freedom of conscience, the church in the U.S.S.R. is separated from the state and the school from the church. Freedom of religious worship and freedom of anti-religious propaganda is recognized for all citizens.

Again, the emphasis was on the freedom of anti-religious propaganda. Individuals had the right to go to the church of their choice, if one were available, and churches had the right to perform religious ceremonies, but there the matter ended. Parents had to send their children to schools which ridiculed religious beliefs, and all members of society were subjected to a barrage of atheistic propaganda. However, the party discovered that religious beliefs were extremely resistant to change. The massive anti-religious campaign, though not without effect, was not achieving the "death of religion." By 1940 it was admitted publicly that probably half or even more of the population still believed in God.

During World War II the party used the churches, particularly the Orthodox Church, to rally the people to defend the motherland; limited concessions were granted in exchange for loyal support of the Soviet state. A limited number of religious books were published, seminaries were opened for the training of a few theologians, and in 1943 a Patriarch of the Orthodox Church was elected. Two official organs, the Council of Affairs of the Russian Orthodox Church (1943) and the Council of Affairs of Religious Cults (1944), which represents all other religious associations, were formed under the U.S.S.R. Council of Ministers to maintain contact between religious orders and the government. The state conducted its anti-religious campaign chiefly through persuasion and education rather than by active persecution. However, none of the concessions were legalized, and hence could be withdrawn at any time.

The period of relative quiescence in the tensions between the state and the church which began during the war years was disrupted in the early 1950's. During the relatively non-oppressive period the hold of the church over the people had increased sufficiently to constitute a source of alarm to the party.[94]. In 1954 the party launched a frantic anti-religious campaign which did not confine itself to persuasion and atheistic indoctrination. Zealous local groups engaged in a number of excesses, including repressive acts against religious leaders and the abrupt closing of churches and synagogues. The state, cognizant of the latent power of church forces, eventually found it expedient to intervene and to reemphasize the priority of ideological weapons in the struggle against religion. In the early 1960's the party deemed it necessary to reinforce the anti-religious campaign and in the fall of 1963 the Ideological Commission of the C.P.S.U. Central Committee introduced a number of "measures for intensifying the atheistic indoctrination of the people."[95] A new Institute of Scientific Atheism, attached to the Central Committee's Academy of Social Sciences, was established to coodinate all anti-religious research and teaching; universities have been instructed to establish scientific atheism departments and a regular quota of students are to be trained as professional propagators of atheism; all students in universities and in higher medical, agricultural and pedagogical schools are required to take a course on the principles of scientific atheism; atheistic indoctrination in party, Y.C.L. and secondary schools has been intensified; party and Y.C.L. activists have been charged with the involvement of the entire population in seminars, courses and circles for the study of atheism; the publication of atheistic literature is to be stepped up and an attempt is to be made to have anti-religious literature which will be appropriate for all sections of the population; radio and television networks are to put on more anti-religious programs; prizes will be offered for the best artistic works on atheistic themes in the fields of literature, drama, films and painting. No stone is to be left unturned in the regime's attempt to destroy religious faith and to make "militant atheists" out of every member of society. The party even plans "to organize atheistic work in Houses of Health Education, hospitals, maternity homes and women's and children's consultation clinics."[96] Much more important than the provision of atheistic indoctrination on maternity wards is the plan to strengthen control "over the protection of children and adolescents from the influence of churchgoers and from parental coercion of children to perform religious rites."[97] Apparently there has been an increase in the number of cases in which children have been taken away from parents who have required them to participate in religious activities or have forbidden them to engage in activities deemed desirable by the authorities. The regime is using every persuasive and indoctrinational weapon at its command to eliminate all religious beliefs among Soviet citizens.

Religious communities serve as the only large and fairly vocal opposition groups to the Soviet regime; they offer resistance in varying amounts to official policy and advocate rival philosophies and sets of values. The party cannot tolerate opposition of any kind, particularly opposition groups which have a firm grip on the allegiance of millions of Soviet citizens and which teach them that they must believe in an ideology which conflicts sharply with the communist doctrine. Soviet officials admit with chagrin that religious beliefs have been retained by a significant but unspecified proportion of the population. Estimates by Western authorities as to the number of "believers" in the U.S.S.R. range between twenty and a hundred million; Soviet authorities seldom give estimates of the number of persons with religious affiliations and beliefs, but they do concede that many people who are not committed to religious beliefs can not qualify as militant atheists; occasionally, they also concede that, whereas most of the believers are elderly or poorly educated people, there are a few intellectuals and even party members who have not discarded all religious beliefs. The majority of believers in the U.S.S.R. subscribe to the Russian or Georgian Orthodox religion or to the Islamic faith; the Roman Catholic, Lutheran, Methodist and Baptist churches are particularly strong in some areas; the Judaic and Buddhist faiths have remained strong; and there are a number of religious associations, such as the Jehovah Witnesses and the Seventh Day Adventists, which have only a few members.

The Soviet government is adamantly opposed to all religious affiliations and religious beliefs and is determined to destroy all "vestiges of religion." All religious faiths are condemned equally on ideological grounds; but some religious communities, because they pose more important practical or political problems for the regime, are held in greater disfavor than others. The Roman Catholic Church has been the object of particularly strong hostility because of its international character, its allegiance to the Pope, its international political influence and its militantly anticommunist stand. Political considerations have also colored the Soviet reaction to Judaism; the party has been concerned about the international force of Zionism and has attempted to destroy in Soviet Jews the sense of cultural and ethnic affiliation with the world Jewish community. The Islamic faith has constituted an entirely different problem for the Soviet government in that it has served as a focal point for nationalism among the peoples of Central Asia and has encouraged the people to cling to customs and mores which have been condemned by the party. The Orthodox Church has no international affiliations which conflict with the universalist pretentions of the regime, and its leaders profess loyalty to and acceptance of the social ideals of the party in all spheres except the abolition of religion; therefore, the Orthodox Church, the largest religious community in the U.S.S.R., is objected to chiefly on religious grounds. The regime's greatest hostility is reserved for small groups such as the Jehovah Witnesses which have encouraged believers to engage in civil disobedience and have countered anti-religious propaganda with anti-Soviet teachings. The overt, militant resistance to state authority by these groups may have been the most important reason for the current intensification of the anti-religious campaign. Thus, although the regime considers one set of religious beliefs to be as bad as another, its harassment techniques have been directed most strongly against the Roman Catholics and the Jews whose religion can be construed as involving international political connections which are incompatible with the goals of the Soviet state, and the small sectarian groups whose religious teachings and practices have internal political importance.

Soviet authorities claim that all religious cults enjoy the same rights and in their propaganda statements they attempt to convey the impression that these rights are rather extensive. Thus it is pointed out that:

> "Religious associations have the right to hold congresses and meetings of the clergy and representatives of believers, to publish ecclesiastical journals, liturgical books, church calendars and other religious books, for which purpose the State puts presses and paper at their disposal. There are special ecclesiastical teaching establishments for training ministers of religion."[98]

These rights do exist, but in a most circumscribed manner. Vital religious texts are published in token quantities only, and very few students are trained in theological seminaries; atheist groups are required to try to dissuade applicants for theological training from proceeding with their plans and even to persuade seminary students to discontinue their training. Religious associations are allowed to hold congresses and meetings but do not have the right to express themselves freely. Freedom of antireligious propaganda is a constitutional right; the exercise of religious propaganda, except in officially approved places of worship, is a criminal offense. Religious organizations have been deprived of their economic base; the state, naturally, does not subsidize religious communities, and only strictly voluntary donations can be accepted to pay priests, ministers and rabbis, and to construct and maintain religious buildings and property; to solicit financial support in any way would constitute a criminal offence. Many of the pre-revolutionary religious buildings are used for non-religious purposes and neither funds nor material have been readily available for the construction of new premises; some of the large new industrial centers do not have a single church, synagogue or mosque. Congregations do not have the right to hold services in buildings which have not been designated for that purpose by the state. In short, the rights, activities and the opportunity of the church to influence the populace have been cut to an absolute minimum. A Soviet author commented, "All that it has retained is the only function that belongs to it alone; the performance of religious rites."[99]

At the same time as it has restricted the rights of all religious groups, the regime has conducted a fantastically thorough, many faceted, militant campaign against religion. Every media of mass communication is used to combat religion and to instill atheistic beliefs. Newspapers carry articles and cartoons which debunk religion; schools and higher educational institutions are required to teach all subject matter from an atheistic point of view, and since 1964 courses on the principles of scientific atheism are obligatory for some students; lecturers on atheism make the rounds of factories and collective farms, and the masses are required to attend; special emphasis is placed on the production of interesting movies and television shows with anti-religious themes. These rather mundane methods are bolstered by a number of invidious techniques designed to force the believer to capitulate; students who are faithful to their religious beliefs are given academic grades lower than their work merits, and are not recommended for admission to higher educational institutions; work brigades are given bonuses for converting a believer to atheism; workers are sometimes threatened with dismissal and are often denied promotion because of their religious beliefs; ruthless interference in the family lives of believers is encouraged to "save" children from "destructive" religious influences; Y.C.L. groups patrol places of worship in order to dissuade children from attending services and see to it that those who do attend are subjected to special indoctrination in youth groups and at school; children are required to participate in atheist circles, and to watch atheist films; high school students put on comedy acts which are intended to discredit all religious miracles; all believers are subjected to individual attention from professional atheists and from their public-spirited neighbors; various subtle and not-so-subtle forms of social pressure are applied.

Recently, much emphasis has been placed on undermining the influence of religion by providing secular substitutes for traditional church activities; efforts are being made to develop ceremonies to mark birth, marriage and death that will satisfy the needs of the people and yet will be "completely devoid of the slightest elements of religious worship,"[100] and to substitute a Christmas tree celebration and a Russian Winter Festival for the religious celebration of Christmas and Shrove Tuesday; activities in club houses are to be arranged to compete with religious ceremonies; one author commented: "If every evening at the local club is gay, interesting and entertaining, many believers will stop going to church, youngsters will not go to prayer houses for want of anything better to do and girls with good voices will prefer to sing good Soviet songs rather than psalms."[101] Religious groups are even denied the right to reconcile religious teachings with communist ideology; a Soviet author reported scornfully that:

> "Religionists are now advocating an "alliance" of science and religion. They are advancing the thesis that religion and science not only do not contradict, but on the contrary supplement each other, and that therefore, their link is natural and necessary. The Christian ideologists assert that Christianity is related to communism, that Christ was allegedly the first to summon people to freedom, equality and morality."[102]

Attempts by religious groups to "adapt themselves to the new conditions in the life of society" are condemned as a "dangerous subterfuge" designed "to cloak their harmful activity in all sorts of patriotic slogans and appeals" and "to veil the reactionary essence" of their teachings.[103] The party is unwilling to allow religion to survive, regardless of the magnitude of the compromises offered by the religious groups; as one author asserted "a willingness to accept compromises . . . is incompatible with genuine atheism, which sees its task in overcoming religion completely and cannot permit any ideological compromises or any ideological peaceful co-existence with it."[104] Believers and religious groups in the U.S.S.R. have almost no weapon of defense, other than pure faith, against the massive anti-religious campaign.

Since the regime is so hostile to religion, why, now that its power is firmly consolidated, does it tolerate formal religious observances of any kind? A Soviet author commented that people often question ". . . why are religious associations permitted? Would it not be better to prohibit them and close the churches?" His reply, typical of Soviet propaganda statements, was "No, the socialist state because of its democratic nature cannot act this way. We still have believers and they are our own Soviet people. Their feelings and aspirations cannot be ignored. Freedom of conscience is an inalienable property of our society."[105] The comment of another author is much more germane: "If administrative agencies violate the rights of believers, this will greatly damage anti-religious propaganda and will produce the opposite effect."[106] The party leaders would probably heave a sigh of relief if they could abolish religious beliefs and practices by administrative fiat; the oft reiterated statements that the religious beliefs and practices of individual citizens must be protected are meaningful only from a propaganda and tactical point of view. It is almost certain that as far as religion is concerned, the party has been little interested in protecting the rights of the individual, except in as far as protection has been necessary to ensure attainment of the party's ultimate goal for religion—its complete eradication. The few limited rights which Soviet citizens have in the sphere of religious beliefs and practices have been granted not because the party leaders believe that freedom of conscience is an inalienable right, but rather because the party has recognized that religion constitutes a strong social force which must be handled with caution; drastically repressive anti-religious measures might foment a religious revival, could impede progress toward other goals and would be condemned by world opinion. The party leaders apparently believe that with the repressive legislative and administrative measures which were introduced during the early years of the regime to serve as a supportive background, a prolonged intensive ideological campaign will eventually, and with accelerating speed as one generation succeeds another, lead to the "full and final death of religion." Progress toward that goal has, however, been much slower than the founders of the Soviet regime had anticipated. In the religious sphere, the interests of the collective, as dictated by the party leaders, and the interests of the individual, as decided by individuals themselves and by parents for children, have not approached "harmony." Although millions may have acquiesced to the party-sponsored atheism, millions of Soviet citizens have put up a stubborn fight to retain the faith of their fathers. No final resolution of the battle for and against religion can be expected during the next few decades.

Freedom of Speech and of the Press

The Soviet Constitution states that citizens of the U.S.S.R. are guaranteed freedom of speech, freedom of the press, freedom of assembly and freedom of demonstrations. As is the case with other constitutional rights, a distinction must be made between formal stipulations and actual practice. Soviet citizens are entitled to exercise these guaranteed freedoms only "in conformity with the interests of the working people and in order to strengthen the socialist system." Marxists argue that true personal freedom can be attained only after all relations within society have been restructured and communism has been attained. If individuals were given license to act contrary to the interests of society, they say, progress toward communism would be impeded. Therefore the party, which has reserved for itself exclusive determination of the interests of society, has deemed it necessary to place rigid limitations on the exercise of individual rights in order that the "interests of all" might be served. Use of any of the constitutionally guaranteed freedoms for the purpose or with the effect of undermining the prestige or authority of the Communist Party, the Soviet state or the socialist order is a criminal offence.

The party and state organs have established an effective bulwark which prevents Soviet citizens from using their guaranteed freedoms in opposition to the established order. The press and all other media of information are owned and operated either by the party, the state, or organizations such as the trade unions and the Y.C.L., which are completely subservient to the party. All media of communication are supervised by the Chief Administration of Literary and Publishing Affairs (Glavit), a state agency, and by the Department of Agitation and Propaganda of the Central Committee of the C.P.S.U. Reporters, editorial writers and publishers are carefully selected and trained by the party; Khrushchev emphasized the importance of placing the information media "in the hands of the most faithful, most trustworthy, most politically steadfast people devoted to our cause."[107]

A Soviet editorial stated:

> "It is the sacred duty of our entire press and radio to assist the Party actively in rearing the working people in the spirit of Marxism-Leninism, Soviet patriotism and proletarian internationalism, in the spirit of friendship and revolutionary solidarity with the peoples of the socialist countries and with all peoples struggling for their social and national liberation. . . . To assist the Party in shaping the new man, in overcoming survivals of the past and combating the influence of bourgeois ideology with all possible force is a vital task of our newspapers and magazines."[108]

Every effort is made to ensure that the press, the radio, and the theatre perform these functions to the fullest extent. A fantastically thorough system of censorship is practiced to guarantee that no article, book, movie or play conveys ideas or attitudes which conflict with, or do not support, the official ideology. The most effective censorship is exercised by the authors themselves since they are well aware of the limits within which they must work. Before any production is made available to the public it is scrutinized by one or several censors who are held responsible for passing judgment on the ideological purity and political timeliness of the item. Censors and editors are authorized to instruct authors to delete or revise objectionable passages and to add sections to support the required viewpoint. Apparently it is not uncommon for rather extensive changes to be made without permission from the author. Many works are not approved by the censors. All kinds of efforts are exerted to protect the public from literary, artistic or informational works which would "not be good for the people" or which might undermine the materialization of party goals. Many books and plays, including the classics, are banned; the majority of those which are available have fallen under the heavy hand of the censors. Foreign newspapers and magazines are virtually prohibited in the U.S.S.R. and although the writings of non-communist social scientists are published occasionally, textual changes are usually made or companion articles point out and rebut the "ideological errors" in the articles. Books and articles that no longer conform to the party line are withdrawn from circulation or revised substantially. After Stalin's denunciation, the majority of social science books were rewritten, and after Beria was executed, subscribers to the *Bolshaia sovetskaia entsiklopediia* (Great Soviet Encyclopedia) were given new pages to replace those which had been devoted originally to the "enemy of the people." Since October, 1964, the Soviet press has totally ignored the hitherto much lauded contributions of that "staunch builder of communism, N. S. Khrushchev," a very large number of books and articles about Khrushchev were withdrawn from circulation and many textbooks have been rewritten. Authors are encouraged to keep their works "up to date" by the fact that a substantially revised version is treated as a "new" production and, as such, earns new royalties. Freedom of the press and freedom of artistic expression in the U.S.S.R. amounts to nothing more or less than freedom to print or express ideas and information that meet with the approval of the party. Severe chastisement would be the reward given to any person who would dare to make a speech, write an article or produce a play which criticized socialism, ridiculed Soviet institutions or leaders, questioned the authority of the party to exercise complete control over society, inferred that other social and political orders might have some merit or failed to support or glorify the Soviet system.

By the same token, freedom of assembly is limited to groups which are authorized and licensed by the state and the party: trade unions, co-operative societies, youth organizations, sports and defense organizations, volunteer activist groups, and cultural, technical and scientific societies. No political organization other than the C.P.S.U. is tolerated, and since party members are instructed to "supervise" the activities of all non-party organizations, it would be impossible for any organization to survive if its activities did not conform with the dictates of the party leaders; religious organizations constitute the sole exception to this general rule, and as indicated previously, the regime is doing its utmost to ensure their demise. Citizens who do not want to join one of the authorized public organizations which must promote the official ideology must refrain from exercising the constitutionally prescribed freedom of assembly, since to organize without official sanction could be interpreted as criminal conspiracy. In short, only those individuals who subscribe fully and completely to Marxist ideology, as interpreted by the party leaders, and to the system of social values which the party leaders have imposed on the Soviet people, are able to exercise a modicum of freedom of speech, freedom of assembly and freedom of the press. Individuals who oppose or do not fully accept the party-dictated value system are denied the right to exercise the freedoms which are guaranteed by the Constitution.

Personal Property

Although abolition of the private ownership of the means of production is a cornerstone of the Marxist program, Marx and Engels did not advocate abolition of the individual ownership of all personal property. In the *Communist Manifesto* they stated:

> "The distinguishing feature of Communism is not the abolition of property in general but the abolition of bourgeois property. . . . We communists have been reproached for wanting to abolish personally acquired property earned by one's own labor. . . . We by no means intend to abolish this personal appropriation of the products of labor that serve directly for the reproduction of human life. . . ."[109]

Regardless of ideological considerations, Soviet leaders have not been oblivious to the fact that if ownership rights to personal property were curtailed too drastically, the people would not work sufficiently well to establish the material base for communism. Consequently, Soviet citizens have always been entitled to own items of personal property. According to Article 10 of the Constitution:

> "The personal property right of citizens in their incomes and savings from work, their dwelling-houses and subsidiary husbandries, in articles of domestic economy and use and articles of personal use and convenience, as well as the right of citizens to inherit personal property, is protected by law."

The early Marxists referred to inheritance as a bourgeois institution which entitled the recipients to enjoy the benefits of unearned income. The Soviet regime has made a number of gestures toward abolishing inheritance rights but in practice its inheritance laws have always been fairly liberal. A 1918 decree announced that inheritance was abolished and that the property of the deceased person would accrue to the state; however, the decree indicated that if the value of an estate did not exceed 10,000 (old) rubles it was to pass directly to the designated or legal heirs, and that if the value of the estate exceeded 10,000 rubles, close relatives were to be allotted funds necessary for their support. This law did not place serious limitations on inheritance rights, because after the nationalization of the means of production, few estates were valued at more than 10,000 rubles. In 1926 a progressive inheritance tax, up to 90 percent of the value of the estate, was substituted for the 10,000 ruble limitation. Since 1943 the government has appropriated only a small fee, not to exceed 10 percent of the value of the estate, for issuing an inheritance certificate. Thus, there is actually no limit placed on the amount which can be inherited in the U.S.S.R.; since some people earn very high incomes, fairly large estates could be bequeathed to heirs. Of course, no one can accumulate or inherit excessive wealth because of the public ownership of the means of production; and although a few heirs may receive enough interest from inherited money to live in comfort, no one is freed from the duty to work.

Although the Soviet citizen can own and inherit money, bank accounts, a dwelling place, and household equipment and if he can afford them, may even acquire luxury items such as a television set, car and dacha, the regime has placed definite limits on what the citizen can do with his personal property and, in some cases, how much he may acquire. It is strictly against the law to use privately owned property as a "source of unearned income." A Soviet citizen who hires out his private automobile, builds a house larger than necessary for personal use and rents the excess space, or even sells too much surplus produce from a large kitchen garden is liable to criminal prosecution, since it is illegal to use private property as a means of production with the intent to make profit. No person is entitled to own more than one dwelling place and even that must be limited to 60 square meters of living space. If a person who already owns a house inherits another one, the second house must be sold within a year; in the absence of a buyer it is confiscated without compensation by the state. During the 1950's as a stimulus to private initiative in meeting the housing shortage, the state offered subsidies to finance private home construction. The subsidies were discontinued in 1960, apparently because the regime began to view the expansion of home ownership as a threat to the advance toward communism in that too many people were manifesting signs of "private property psychology." The most horrendous sign of the emergence of the "private property psychology" was the number of private dwelling places which had been financed by funds acquired through speculation, bribe taking or embezzlement or built from materials stolen from the state. The state decreed that all such dwelling places should be confiscated without compensation, and as is usual in the U.S.S.R., the campaign against illegal ownership was carried to extremes; an unknown number of innocent citizens were deprived of the private dwelling places which they might have saved and worked for years to finance and construct. A 1965 decree, which entitled collective farmers to credit for the construction of homes, suggests that the authorities are somewhat more confident that problems associated with "private property psychology" are being reasonably well controlled.

Soviet authorities predict that in the future communist society, public forms of satisfying needs will prevail; personally owned property will be relegated to a very minor role; inheritance rights are to become superfluous; the absence of scarcity should weaken the motivation for accumulation; and members of a communist society will work willingly and without need for supplementary motivation such as the opportunity to acquire property for their own use or to bequeath to offspring. In the meantime, the personal property and inheritance rights of citizens in the present Soviet society serve as an indispensable incentive to work. Soviet people, like people in other countries, strive to improve their material standards of living, to be able to afford better food, nicer furniture, more conveniences, more luxurious vacations and to have something to bequeath to their children. However, even at the present stage of Soviet society, an ostentatious display of material wealth is of negative social value. Social prestige derives from accomplishments in work and in education and from behavioral characteristics rather than from property ownership.

Impact on the Individual and Society

The Soviet leaders have been engaged in a vigorous attempt to restructure society. The direction of their efforts has been determined by two major factors: Marxist-Leninist ideology and the social environment of Tsarist Russia which provided the material from which the new society was to be built. From Marxist-Leninist ideology the Soviet leaders derived the goal of restructuring society to ensure social equality and economic security for all. Accordingly, one of the major tasks which they have taken upon themselves is to eliminate all vestiges of class structure and differential privileges associated with property ownership, social origin, race or sex. From the Tsarist era they inherited a society with a rigid social structure and a number of other characteristics which were the diametrical opposite of the Marxist ideal. The pre-revolutionary society of the Russian empire had an archaic social structure that was out of harmony with the aspirations of its most dynamic classes, groups and individuals. Tsarist autocracy drew its support from an aristocracy of landlords, civil and military bureaucrats and officers and the higher clergy which monopolized political power and dominated the economy. The aristocracy formed a highly privileged and largely parasitical social elite which contributed little or nothing to improve the condition of the masses whom it regarded as little more than beasts of burden. A rigid censorship prevailed and opposition against the regime was squelched with systematic ruthlessness. The conformist clergy preached blind obedience to the Tsar and his officials. The masses were kept in a condition of poverty and ignorance so that they might know their place in society and accept their lowly status as natural and in keeping with the will of God.

The Bolsheviks took immediate action designed to introduce a new set of social relationships and social values. Their goal has been to create a classless society in which all people have equal rights, duties and privileges, and social harmony prevails. The socialist value system aims to develop a new type of individual and social psychology; it stresses the security and social integration of the individual rather than the development of his unique individuality; each individual is to develop and use his talents for the good of the entire society rather than for his own personal advancement; society, in turn, is to protect the individual against economic want, exploitation, social discrimination and ignorance. Marxists-Leninists believe that social equality and economic security constitute the foundation of personal freedom and that these can be attained only in a society which gives priority to the interests of the collective; personal freedom, they say, is the end product of social harmony.

The traditional class structure of the Tsarist society was disrupted irrevocably when the new Bolshevik state appropriated all means of production and abolished all hereditary titles and privileges. However, the party leaders recognized that these measures, in themselves, were not sufficient to establish the desired state of classlessness and social harmony. Consequently, the regime has directed massive efforts in a variety of directions in its attempt to restructure social relations. Although these efforts included a number of repressive measures and many brutal excesses which were totally unnecessary in relation to the party's goals for society, on the whole, the party's program in the social-cultural sphere has been relatively constructive when viewed within the framework of Marxist-Leninist ideology. Social welfare measures have been introduced to ensure that educational and employment opportunities, medical care, retirement and disability benefits are available to all members of society. The regime has occasionally violated its own decrees with respect to equal rights and privileges for all races and nationalities but it has, nevertheless, probably succeeded better than any other major multinational state in minimizing racial discrimination. Women enjoy essentially equal rights with men. The educational policy, which obligates all youth to obtain a modicum of formal education and offers vast opportunities for specialized and higher education to the able and the highly motivated, has been an extremely important factor in eliminating vestiges of class privileges. Soviet leaders claim that as a result of these and other measures, exploiting classes and class privileges have been eradicated and that Soviet society is now composed of workers, peasants, and the intelligentsia who are united in a harmonious pattern of common interests.

Although the Soviet regime has succeeded in destroying the traditional class structure with its differential system of privileges, it has not achieved, or even approached, its ideal of social equality. Contemporary Soviet society is made up of a number of distinct social strata. At the apex of the social pyramid are the most important party and government officials, the ruling elite, and a few military and economic leaders and very prominent scientists, professors, writers and artists. On the next rung of the social ladder are the intelligentsia; within this category there are several gradations of social status—for example, the prestige of a university professor is vastly greater than that of physicians or lawyers. Generally below, but overlapping, with the lower levels of the intelligentsia is the working class "aristocracy" composed of the most highly skilled and productive workers. The white collar group including petty bureaucrats, clerks and secretaries tends to have lower social status than the working class "aristocracy" and is usually classified at about the same level as average workers and leading peasants. Below these groups are collective farm members of average skill and workers of marginal skill and productivity and finally, at the bottom of the social ladder, are the lazy, the social outcasts, the parasites and the criminals.

This social stratification is determined by a complex of factors including educational attainments, skill, productivity, occupation and functions performed in the economy or the party or state apparatus. Hereditary factors, apart from genetic inheritance, and factors related to social origin are of inconsequential importance, since all members of society have approximately equal opportunities in relation to the factors which determine social position. The value placed by the party on the services rendered to society by the various strata is a major determinant of both social position and income. Although the incomes of the various strata overlap, income and, therefore, standard of living tends to vary directly with social position. A twenty-fold difference between the incomes of members of the upper and lower strata has not been uncommon. Added rewards such as bonuses and housing priorities are conferred upon outstanding workers in any field of endeavor; citations such as a "Hero of Socialist Labor" confer economic rewards as well as social prestige.

In many respects the hierarchy of social strata in the U.S.S.R. resembles the class structure of various Western societies. Soviet officials usually deny that their society has developed its own variety of stratification, and when it is conceded that social gradations do exist, they argue that these are different from the traditional class structure in that Soviet society promotes social mobility. At the present stage of Soviet development, the principle of equality is interpreted as the equal right of all citizens to improve the quantity and quality of their output through educational and professional advancement, and to be remunerated on the basis of their contributions to society. The Soviet spokesmen who admit to the existence of social gradations present official encouragement of upward social mobility as an example of the identity of the interests of society and the individual; the individual benefits from rising from a lower strata to a higher one through higher standards of living and increased prestige, and society benefits because members of the higher strata usually contribute more to the achievement of the goals of the party. The Soviet system has fostered one of the most competitive societies in the world. The three major channels of upward social mobility are through education, high productivity and the party apparatus. Almost any person of average or better than average intelligence, irrespective of race, social origin or sex, is able to improve his professional and social status through education since the rapid pace of economic growth has created a permanent demand for qualified specialists and the regime has provided extensive opportunities for free education. Party membership creates a less reliable vehicle of upward social mobility. Contrary to popular assumptions, few party members achieve social elite status unless party membership is coupled with advanced education and outstanding contributions in a profession or in the party bureaucracy. Tireless and devoted service to the party may be rewarded by appointment to the professional apparatus of the party bureaucracy, but advancement is generally slow until the functionary has proved his competence as a political worker. A party career offers an insecure future and is replete with risks, but those who survive its competitive struggle and become members of the ruling elite are rewarded with power, prestige and substantial incomes.

The Soviet regime has not eliminated social stratification and has not completely abolished social privileges. Members of the political and intellectual elite enjoy higher standards of living and greater social prestige and although, theoretically, all members of society start their lives at the same level, the elite are able to confer special advantages to their children in terms of bequests and somewhat better opportunities to develop their talents. A greater proportion of children of the upper income families are able to proceed directly from secondary school to full-time study in a higher educational institution. The party has sometimes found it necessary to campaign against nepotism and favoritism in the allocation of educational privileges and professional jobs, an indication that a certain amount of occupational parasitism persists. However, children from high status families are able to retain the status of their parents only if, in maturity, they are able to make acceptable contributions to society; playboys and socialites are not tolerated, regardless of the eminence, prestige and status of the parents. With the exception of the fact that the offspring of members of the elite do in some cases enjoy unique advantages, the social stratification in Soviet society at its present stage of development does not constitute a gross violation of the Marxist dictum of equality for all. Most of the members of the upper strata have earned their social elite status and although a few individuals may enjoy some unearned privileges, there are few barriers other than innate ability, lack of motivation and non-acceptance of Marxist ideology which prevent a member of a lower strata from rising to a higher strata.

Although the policies of the regime have resulted in the development of social strata and favored professions and categories of workers, effective counter measures have prevented the formation of a privileged class and the crystallization of class consciousness and in-group cohesiveness. The growth of any form of *esprit de corps* among the officer groups of the armed forces has been combated since this might imperil the elite status of the party which cannot tolerate the existence of a rival elite. All professional organizations are infiltrated by party members who must anchor these associations firmly to the party. As in the Tsarist era, a rigid system of censorship prevails and all channels for the development of opposition to the regime are closed.

How free is the Soviet citizen? He is relatively free from the restrictions which flow from the threat of unemployment, the difficulty of getting an education, fear of crippling medical expenses and inability to maintain himself in old age, social discrimination based on ethnic group, race or sex, and a class structure which assigns him a permanent position in life on the basis of his social origin. He is free to acquire an education commensurate with his natural abilities and motivation and to better his economic and social status by improving his skills and working diligently and productively. Within broad limits he may select his own occupation and transfer from one to another. He may save his money or spend it as he sees fit, on the somewhat limited, but increasing, supply of consumers goods. He may travel fairly freely within the U.S.S.R. but is permitted to visit a non-socialist country only under exceptional circumstances. Because of the extreme shortage of housing, he is not free to move from one dwelling place to another and frequently, but less often than in the past, he must share his limited living space with another family. He is probably much less fearful than he was in the Stalin era that he will be subjected to arbitrary arrest and summary punishment without the due process of law, but it is unlikely that all fear of arbitrary arrest has been eliminated. His freedom in a number of spheres which are taken for granted by citizens of the Western world is extremely limited. He is entitled to attend the church of his choice if one is available, but if he does, he is subjected to a barrage of anti-religious propaganda, social disparagement and harassment; he is not entitled to attempt to win converts to his faith, and even his rights with respect to the religious upbringing of his children are extremely limited. In his family and personal life his activities are subjected to constant scrutiny by representatives of the regime; if he oversteps prescribed limits his neighbors and fellow workers are obligated to attempt to influence him to act in accordance with the socialist value system. He is, of course, not allowed to engage in any form of private enterprise including the use of property for rental purposes; he may improve his economic status only through job advancement.

In the political sphere the Soviet citizen has remarkably few rights. From the Western point of view, his right to elect and be elected to public office is relatively meaningless because of the mode of selection of unopposed candidates and the complete subservience of elected officials to the dictates of the party. He is entitled, within rather narrow limits, to criticize local party or state officials for lack of efficiency or failure to adhere to the party program, to participate in a public discussion of draft legislation, to make minor proposals through the party, trade union or youth organizations and to perform various public duties. The most basic limitation is his complete lack of right to question the party's claim to power and the correctness of party policy. He has no right, whatsoever, to join an alternate political organization or to advocate an alternate political program. He must accept docilely the absolute power of the party to organize, manage and restructure society, and hence, his own personal life. All political, social and economic decisions of consequence are made exclusively by the party leaders, and the Soviet citizen who is under constant surveillance must never express a dissenting opinion. He is not free to examine and evaluate the merits of alternate political and social systems and ideologies. Freedom of speech and freedom of assembly are strictly limited. The Soviet citizen is totally subservient to the state against which he has no protection since all institutions are controlled by the party oligarchy.

Are the social welfare benefits provided by the Soviet state adequate to compensate the Soviet citizen for his lack of political freedom? Because of the innumerable variables which influence the reaction of the Soviet citizen to his regime, no clear cut answer can be given to this question; speculative evaluations must be made with reference to the Soviet social milieu rather than on the basis of Western standards. In the first place, it should be recognized that because the majority of Soviet citizens have grown up under the Soviet system and have been subjected to constant indoctrination, their system of values differ radically in many respects from the value systems held by members of other social orders; many features of the Soviet social system which are considered objectionable from the Western point of view may not constitute a source of distress to most Soviet citizens. Secondly, Soviet citizens have been subjected to an intensive, consistent, and long-term propaganda campaign designed to convince them that their social order is highly superior in almost all respects to all other social systems. The party propaganda machine informs the Soviet populace that life in the West in characterized by class privileges; economic exploitation; unemployment; unequal wages for women; racial discrimination; educational opportunities, legal rights, and medical facilities which vary with income; and magnificent homes surrounded by slums. They are told that under these circumstances legal and political rights are meaningless and that the whole political and social structure of Western society is designed to preserve the interests of the small rich and powerful capitalist class. Roughly the same criticisms are directed against the social order of the Tsarist era. There is evidence to suggest that the party propaganda has been so effective that many Soviet citizens, far from envying Westerners their political freedom, actually pity them as objects of economic, social and political oppression. Some Westerners who have visited the U.S.S.R. have reported with considerable surprise that it is not uncommon for educated Soviet citizens to express the apparently sincere opinion that they enjoy greater freedom and a higher form of democracy than citizens in any Western nation.[110] A large number of Soviet citizens do, however, envy the material affluence of Western societies. It is probable that many defectors from the Soviet orbit have been influenced less by the hope of political freedom than by the hope of attaining riches and luxury. Most Soviet citizens are apparently much more impressed by the notion that common people in other countries have spacious homes with gardens, private cars, and a choice of fashionable clothes and luxury items than they are by the political heritage of the Americans or British which few understand because of their limited experiences and the distorted information which is given to them. The constant barrage of propaganda which glorifies the Soviet system may fairly effectively conceal from the average man active awareness of the fact that his political freedoms are virtually non-existent, and it is not unlikely that a large proportion of Soviet citizens are relatively unperturbed about their lack of political freedom. The party leaders have consistently told the Soviet people that their major concern is for the welfare of all members of society, and have recently provided material evidence of their concern. Improved standards of living and the cumulative effects of indoctrination on each succeeding generation may make it increasingly less likely that many Soviet citizens will question the rightness of the party dictatorship. Political rights are primarily a vehicle through which the individual can exert some influence over the manner in which society is governed; if the party is able to convince Soviet citizens that it is governing according to their best interests, the lack of political rights may not be perceived as a deprivation.

It has been suggested by a number of authors that as the educational level of the Soviet population increases, the party leaders may be confronted with increasingly insistent demands from the people for participation in political decision-making, since as a general rule a well-educated populace is less likely to submit willingly to a dictatorship. There are, of course, exceptions to this generalization; the well-educated Germans acquiesced to Hitler's dictatorship when he offered them material well-being and world domination in exchange for personal freedom; moreover, although Hitler's program required the German people to risk their lives in an aggressive war and to commit atrocities, he gained their cooperation without the many years of skillful indoctrination which has strengthened the power of the Communist Party over the Soviet people. Although it is unlikely that the Soviet leaders will relinquish their great power voluntarily, it is possible that as a result of pressure from the population a modification toward democratic practices within the communist framework may follow a future struggle for leadership. The Soviet government has been non-democratic since its inception, but the totalitarian heritage is not an absolute indication of its unchangeability.

Soviet leaders express confidence that in a relatively short time they will be able to demonstrate the superiority of their social system in terms of its ability to meet the fundamental needs of the people. Obviously, the outcome of the peaceful competition does not depend only on what happens in the U.S.S.R. Three of the major ingredients in the struggle of the two types of social orders for favorable world opinion are social welfare measures, standards of living and political freedom. Western social orders have the advantage of a definite, but diminishing, lead in terms of standards of living and a very definite and probably permanent lead in terms of political freedom. The Soviet system has a diminishing advantage in terms of social welfare measures. It seems likely that standards of living and social welfare measures will eventually be more or less equalized, or if not, that superiority in one sphere will be offset by inferiority in the other. If this is the case, political freedom would determine the outcome of the peaceful competition and the Western social order would emerge as the victor. If, however, the U.S.S.R. were to attain a standard of living equivalent to that of Western nations and were to improve and extend its social welfare measures, it is possible that the importance of political freedom might be underrated. It is this possibility which poses the greatest threat to Western political and economic systems.

Because the party leaders have been determined to build a society which corresponds to their interpretation of the Marxist-Leninist ideal, Soviet citizens have been forced to make many sacrifices. The official propaganda line has always maintained that all the hardships which the Soviet people have suffered have been necessary for the ultimate good of society and, hence, for the ultimate good of the individual members of society. An integral part of the Marxist principle of the priority of the interests of the collective is the proposition that until a higher stage of social organization is attained, the people of one generation must make sacrifices so that the next generation may live in a more nearly perfect society. In fact, the Soviet people have been required to make many sacrifices which, even from the Marxist frame of reference, were unnecessary, avoidable and worse than useless; the sacrifices which have resulted from errors, mismanagement, the Stalinist terrorism, and the many brutal excesses which have characterized the party dictatorship have obviously been against the interests of the individual and, at the same time, have tended to impede materialization of the party goals for the collective. During the early years of the regime talk about the identity of interests of the individual and the collective had little validity except through projection to future decades; the regime had to use coercive and persuasive techniques to ensure that the interests of the collective, as determined by the party leaders, prevailed. In a number of areas party leaders are now able to claim that individuals are reaping the benefits of the long-term emphasis on the interests of the collective; for example, because, for decades, resources have been channeled into the production of producer goods in the interests of the collective instead of into consumer goods in the interests of the individual, the U.S.S.R. has made rapid economic progress and the state now is able to provide the members of society with increased material benefits. After years of subverting individual interests to the welfare of the collective the regime has achieved a number of subsidiary goals, and as a result of these achievements, many of the contradictions between the interests of the individual and the collective have been reduced. Currently, there are a number of areas in which the interests of the individual and the collective are in relative harmony, e.g. the drive to improve standards of living, legal guarantees, social welfare benefits, educational opportunities, recreational facilities and the quest for peace. There are, of course, a great number of areas in which the party-designated interests of the collective conflict with the interests of large numbers of individuals, e.g. all members of religious communities must resent the vigorous anti-religious campaign which the party leaders have deemed necessary for the good of society; a number of artists, writers, scientists and academicians must resent the rigid limitations which the regime places on their intellectual freedom; many families and individuals must resent the "comradely guidance" which the regime entitles various public volunteer organizations to offer; the list of legitimate reasons that some members of Soviet society have for resentment against official decisions could be extended almost indefinitely. Even the party leaders admit that the majority of Soviet citizens live under conditions which are far from ideal; nevertheless, it may be fairly concluded that the Soviet citizens of today are better off in most respects than either they or their ancestors, excluding members of the former privileged classes, have ever been. Whether or not the regime has been interested in the welfare of the individual *per se* or merely in the collective welfare, the individual has gained as the contradictions between the individual and the collective interest have decreased and the initial goals of the party have been realized.

REFERENCES

1 N. V. Podgorny, "In the Friendly Family of Peoples of the U.S.S.R.: Toward New Successes in the Building of Communism," *Pravda,* May 22, 1965, pp. 1-2.

2 A. Rumyantsev, "The Party and the Intelligentsia," *Pravda,* Feb. 21, 1965, pp. 2-3.

3 Cf. Ezra Taft Benson, "No Freedom Under Communism," reprinted in Shaffer, *The Soviet System, op. cit.,* pp. 334-6.

4 *Fundamentals of Marxism-Leninism, op. cit.,* pp. 184-5.

5 M. Kammari, V. Podmarkov and C. Tselikova, "The Individual and Society Under Socialism," *Izvestia,* June 15, 1965, p. 5, and June 16, p. 3. (C.D.S.P., Vol. XVII, No. 24, pp. 12-13)

6 *Fundamentals of Marxism-Leninism, op. cit.,* p. 741.

7 A. G. Zverev, *The Soviet Standard of Living: Social Benefits,* (New York: International Arts and Sciences Press, 1959), p. 1.

8 Cf. Frederick L. Schuman, "The Rights of Man," in Randolf L. Braham, (ed.), *Soviet Politics and Government,* (New York: Alfred A. Knopf, 1965), pp. 400-6; and Alec Nove, "Social Welfare in the U.S.S.R.," in Samuel Hendel, (ed.), *The Soviet Crucible, op. cit.,* pp. 549-63.

9 Fainsod, *How Russia Is Ruled, op. cit.,* p. 376.

10 George Ginsburgs, "Rights and Duties of Citizens," *Problems of Communism,* March-April, 1965, Vol. XIV, No. 2, pp. 22-8.

11 *Fundamentals of Marxism-Leninism, op. cit.,* p. 741.

12 N. Buzlyakov, "What Do Public Funds Give Us?" *Izvestia,* June 2, 1962, p. 3. (C.D.S.P., Vol. XIV, No. 22, pp. 19-20)

13 *Fundamentals of Marxism-Leninism, op. cit.,* p. 742.

14 Zverev, *The Soviet Standard of Living: Social Benefits, op. cit.,* p. 2.

15 "Law of the U.S.S.R. on Pensions and Allowances for Collective Farm Members," *Pravda,* July 16, 1964, pp. 1-2.

16 Zverev, *The Soviet Standard of Living: Social Benefits, op. cit.,* p. 14.

17 Buzlyakov, "What Do Public Funds Give Us?" *op. cit.,* p. 3.

18 "In the U.S.S.R. Council of Ministers," *Pravda,* March 6, 1964, p. 1.

19 "Decrees of the Presidium of the Supreme Soviet on Temporary Disability Benefits for Workers and Employees Who Have Left Their Former Jobs of Their Own Will," *Vedomosti Verkhovnovo Soveta SSSR,* No. 4, Jan. 28, 1960, p. 56.

20 *Ibid.*

21 Buzlyakov, "What Do Public Funds Give Us?" *op. cit.,* p. 3.

22 *Ibid.*

23 "In the Name of Man," *Pravda,* Nov. 4, 1963, p. 2.

24 "On Measures for Further Improving Medical Care and Public Health Services for the U.S.S.R. Population," *Pravda,* Jan. 20, 1960, pp. 1-2. (C.D.S.P., Vol. XII, No. 3, pp. 10-13)

25 *Ibid.*

26 "Persistently Improve Medical Care of Toilers," *Trud,* July 5, 1951.

27 *The U.S.S.R. as It Is,* (Moscow: State Publishers of Political Literature, 1959), p. 286.

28 "On Results of Fulfillment of the State Plan for Development of the U.S.S.R. National Economy in 1964," *Pravda,* Jan. 30, 1965, pp. 1-2.

29 S. Shapovalenko, "Once Again About Polytechnical Education," *Uchitelskaya gazeta,* March 2, 1965, p. 1. (C.D.S.P., Vol. XVII, No. 13, pp. 3-6)

30 Cf. "Program of the Communist Party of the Soviet Union," *op. cit.,* pp. 106-7.

31 *Ibid.,* pp. 108-9.

32 "On the Results of the Fulfillment of the State Plan for the Development of the U.S.S.R. National Economy in 1963," *Pravda,* Jan. 24, 1964, pp. 1-2.

33 "Content of Soviet Elementary and Secondary Education," *U.S.S.R. Illustrated Monthly,* Oct., 1963, pp. 6-7.

34 *Ibid.*

35 "On Results of Fulfillment of the State Plan for Development of the U.S.S.R. National Economy in 1964," *op. cit.,* pp. 1-2.

36 V. P. Yelyutin, "What Is New in Admission to Higher Schools," *Izvestia,* March 13, 1963, p. 2.

37 V. P. Yelyutin, "Higher Educational Institutions Await Good Entering Class," *Pravda,* March 20, 1965, p. 6.

38 *Ibid.*

39 Cf. V. Yelyutin, *Higher Education in the U.S.S.R.,* (New York: International Arts and Sciences Press, 1959), p. 15.

40 V. Yelyutin, "Prepare Outstanding Specialists in Shorter Periods of Time," *Pravda,* June 20, 1964, p. 4.

41 "On Results of Fulfillment of the State Plan for Development of the U.S.S.R. National Economy in 1964," *op. cit.,* pp. 1-2.

42 P. Barkov, "The Institute and Its Charges," *Izvestia,* Feb. 9, 1962, p. 4.

43 A. Agranovsky, "Against Waste in Education," *Izvestia,* May 5, 1963, p. 3.

44 S. Morozov, "How I Was Offered a Bribe," *Izvestia,* Sept. 28, 1963, p. 4.

45 Agranovsky, "Against Waste in Education," *op. cit.,* p. 3.

46 Cf. Ginsburgs, "Rights and Duties of Citizens," *op. cit.,* pp. 22-8.

47 Ts. Stepanyan, "Communism and Property," *Oktyabr,* No. 9, Sept., 1960, pp. 3-12.

48 *Ibid.*

49 G. Petrosyan, "On the Rational Use of Off-Work Time of the Working People," *Voprosy ekonomiki,* No. 6, June, 1963, pp. 32-41.

50 *Ibid.*

51 *Ibid.*

52 *Ibid.*

53 *Ibid.*

54 Zverev, *The Soviet Standard of Living: Social Benefits, op. cit.,* p. 19.

55 Friedrich Engels, "The Origin of the Family and of Society," quoted in Rudolf Schlesinger, *The Family in the U.S.S.R.,* (London: Routledge and Kegan Paul, Ltd., 1949), p. 8.

56 "Marriage, Children and Registration of Civil Status," Dec. 31, 1917; "Revolutionary Divorce Law," Dec. 31, 1917, in Meisel and Kozera, *Materials for the Study of the Soviet System, op. cit.,* pp. 39-43.

57 "Code of Laws Concerning Civil Registration of Deaths, Births and Marriages," Oct. 17, 1918, in "Collection of Laws and Decrees of the Workers and Peasants Government," 1918, Nos. 76-7.

58 "Program of the All-Russian Communist Party (Bolsheviks) Adopted at the Eighth Congress," March 18-23, 1919, in Meisel and Kozera, *Materials for the Study of the Soviet System, op. cit.,* p. 120.

59 *Ibid.,* p. 106.

60 "Program of the Communist Party of the Soviet Union," *op. cit.,* p. 88.

61 "Decree on the Legalization of Abortions," Nov. 18, 1920, reproduced in Schlesinger, *The Family in the U.S.S.R., op. cit.,* p. 44.

62 "Decree on Marriage and Divorce," Nov. 19, 1926, in Meisel and Kozera, *Materials for the Study of the Soviet System, op. cit.,* pp. 172-6.

63 A. M. Kollontay, *Communism and the Family,* (London: Workers' Socialist Federation, 1920), quoted in Schlesinger, *The Family in the U.S.S.R., op. cit.,* pp. 67-8.

64 A. M. Sabsovich, *The U.S.S.R. After Another 15 Years,* 1929, reproduced in

Schlesinger, *The Family in the U.S.S.R., op. cit.,* pp. 169-71.

65 G. M. Szerdukov, "Artificial Abortions as Biological Trauma," reproduced in Schlesinger, *The Family in the U.S.S.R., op. cit.,* p. 175.

66 V. Svetlov, "Socialist Society and the Family," *Pod Znamenem Marxisma,* 1936, reproduced in Schlesinger, *The Family in the U.S.S.R., op. cit.,* pp. 315-47.

67 "Decrees on the Prohibition of Abortions, the Improvement of Material Aid to Women in Childbirth, the Establishment of State Assistance to Parents of Large Families, and the Extension of the Network of Lying in Homes, Creches and Kindergartens, the Tightening up of Criminal Punishment for the Non-payment of Alimony, and on Certain Modifications of Divorce Legislations," June 27, 1936, reproduced in Schlesinger, *The Family in the U.S.S.R., op. cit.,* pp. 269-79.

68 S. Wolffson, "Socialism and the Family," *Pod Znamenem Marxisma,* 1936, reproduced in Schlesinger, *The Family in the U.S.S.R., op. cit.,* pp. 280-315.

69 Svetlov, "Socialist Society and the Family," *op. cit.,* pp. 315-47.

70 *Pravda,* May 28, 1936, reproduced in Schlesinger, *The Family in the U.S.S.R., op. cit.,* pp. 251-4.

71 Wolffson, "Socialism and the Family," *op. cit.,* p. 296.

72 *Ibid.*

73 Svetlov, "Socialist Society and the Family," *op. cit.,* pp. 320-1.

74 *Ibid.*

75 "Decree of the Presidium of the Supreme Soviet of the U.S.S.R. on Increased State Aid to Expectant Mothers, Mothers of Large Families and Unmarried Mothers; On Strengthening Measures for the Protection of Motherhood and Childhood; On the Establishment of the Title 'Heroine Mother'," July 8, 1944, reproduced in Meisel and Kozera, *Materials for the Study of the Soviet System, op. cit.,* pp. 373-80.

76 O. P. Kolchinaya, "Birth of a New Law," *Trud,* Feb. 16, 1964, p. 3. (C.D. S.P., Vol. XVI, No. 11, p. 10)

77 N. S. Khrushchev, "On Measures to Fulfill the C.P.S.U. Program in the Sphere of Increasing the Well-Being of the People," *Pravda,* July 14, 1964, pp. 1-5.

78 Kolchinaya, "Birth of a New Law," *op. cit.,* p. 3.

79 R. Kallistratova and L. Lesnitskaya, "Peregrinations of a Court Order," *Izvestia,* Jan. 8, 1965, p. 3. (C.D.S.P., Vol. XVII, No. 1, pp. 25-6)

80 Kolchinaya, "Birth of a New Law," *op. cit.,* p. 3.

81 Yu. A. Korolev, "The Integration of Morality and Law in Marital and Family Relations," *Voprosy filosofii,* No. 11, 1963, pp. 75-85. (C.D.S.P., Vol. XVI, No. 11, pp. 10-13)

82 *Ibid.*

83 N. Muravyeva, "Tireless Toilers, Active Fighters for Peace," *Pravda,* March 8, 1963, p. 2.

84 *Ibid.*

85 "Moscow, the Development of City Economy and Culture," *Stroitelnaya gazeta,* June 8, 1960.

86 B. Svetlichny, "Improved Housing for Soviet People," *Kommunist,* No. 6, April, 1965, pp. 41-51.

87 "100 Family Budgets," *Ekonomicheskaya gazeta,* Jan. 4, 1964, pp. 21-2.

88 V. I. Lenin, *Collected Works,* Vol. 14, (2nd Russian Ed.) (Moscow: 1926), p. 68.

89 "On Separation of the Church from the State and the School from the Church," Feb. 5, 1918, quoted in Meisel and Kozera, *Materials for the Study of the Soviet System, op. cit.,* pp. 63-4.

90 "Anti-religious Movement in the U.S.S.R. and Abroad," quoted from Vladimir Gsovski, "Survey of State-Church Relations," in Alex Inkeles and Kent Geiger, (eds.), *Soviet Society, a Book of Readings,* (Boston: Houghton Mifflin Co., 1961), p. 415.

91 "Law Concerning the Religious Associations of the R.S.F.S.R.," April 8, 1929, reproduced in Meisel and Kozera, *Materials for the Study of the Soviet System, op. cit.,* pp. 179-80.

92 *Izvestia,* June 23, 1923.

93 Ye. F. Muravyev and Yu. V. Dmitriyev, "On Concreteness in Studying and Overcoming Religious Prejudices," *Voprosy filosofii,* No. 3, March, 1961, pp. 63-73. (C.D.S.P., Vol. XIII, No. 20, pp. 3-8, 12)

94 *Ibid.*

95 "On Measures for Intensifying Atheistic Indoctrination of the Population," *Partiinaya zhizn,* No. 2, Jan., 1964, pp. 22-6. (C.D.S.P., Vol. XVI, No. 9, pp. 3-7)

96 *Ibid.*

97 *Ibid.*

98 Robert Maxwell, (ed.), *Information U.S.S.R.,* (New York: The Macmillan Co., 1962), p. 654.

99 P. Kolonitsky, "Reason and Mysticism Are Irreconcilable," *Izvestia,* Feb. 18, 1961, p. 4.

100 I. Kryvelev, "An Important Side of Everyday Life," *Kommunist,* No. 8, May, 1961, pp. 65-73.

101 Yu. Feofanov, "Persistently, Flexibly, Intelligently," *Sovety deputatov trudyashchikhsya,* No. 10, Oct., 1961, pp. 19-26. (C.D.S.P., Vol. XII, No. 51, pp. 36-8)

102 Muravyev and Dmitriyev, "On Concreteness in Studying and Overcoming Religious Prejudices," *op. cit.,* pp. 63-73.

103 M. S. Bezhayev, "Conference on Urgent Problems of Scientific Atheism," *Vestnik vysshei shkoly,* No. 3, March, 1961, pp. 86-8. (C.D.S.P., Vol. XIII, No. 20, pp. 7-8)

104 G. Simonov, "Do Not Flirt With God," *Izvestia,* Oct. 25, 1963, p. 4. (C.D.S.P., Vol. XV, No. 43, pp. 33-4)

105 Kolonitsky, "Reason and Mysticism Are Irreconcilable," *op. cit.,* p. 4.

106 Feofanov, "Persistently, Flexibly, Intelligently," *op. cit.,* pp. 19-26.

107 *Pravda,* August 28, 1957.

108 "Tribune of the People," *Pravda,* May 5, 1965, p. 1. (C.D.S.P., Vol. XVII, No. 18, p. 21)

109 *A Handbook of Marxism,* (New York: International Publishers, 1935), p. 38.

110 Cf. Konrad B. Krauskopf, "Russia, a Land of the Free?" in Shaffer, *The Soviet System, op. cit.,* pp. 337-42.

CHAPTER XII

THE TRANSITION TO THE FUTURE COMMUNIST SOCIETY

The ultimate goal of all communist parties is the establishment of a world communist order. Early Marxists believed that the "revolutionary break-up of imperialism" would occur more or less simultaneously in all capitalist countries, and that formerly oppressed colonies, "freed from their capitalist oppressors," would follow the lead of the revolutionary proletariat in the more advanced countries. Engels wrote:

> ". . . the Communist revolution will be not merely a national phenomenon but must take place simultaneously in all civilized countries, that is to say, at least in England, America, France and Germany. It will develop in each of these countries more or less rapidly according as one country or the other has a more developed industry, greater wealth, a more significant mass of productive forces. . . . It will have a powerful impact on the other countries of the world and will radically alter the course of development which they have followed up to now, while greatly stepping up its pace. It is a universal revolution and will accordingly have a universal range."[1]

When the Bolshevik revolution was not followed by a series of socialist revolutions in Western nations, Lenin set the stage for the theory of socialism triumphing first in one country taken singly. Although Trotsky and some other members of the old Bolshevik guard argued that the Russian Marxists should devote considerable attention to the fomenting of proletarian revolutions in other countries, Stalin elaborated the thesis of the development of socialism in one country, and concentrated on solidifying the socialist gains in the new Soviet state. At no time, however, has the goal of the establishment of a world-wide communist society been abandoned.

Marxists assert that the development of society as a whole is a forward movement from lower to higher forms of social organization; according to their hierarchy of values, capitalism represents a higher form of social relations than feudalism, but is infinitely inferior to socialism which is a necessary stage in the development of the more perfect communist society. The Marxist laws of social development stipulate that within each of these stages the evolutionary process continues; thus, from the initial imperfect form of socialism there emerges first a higher stage of socialism and eventually communism which, in turn, must undergo a process of development and perfection. The rate of progress between and within stages purportedly varies from one society to another because of a number of "historical conditions"; the Marxists point out that the rate of transition from capitalism to socialism may be affected by factors such as the sharpness of class struggle, the political consciousness of the masses, the skill of the exploiting class in maintaining its power and in appeasing the masses, and opportunities to make concessions to the oppressed classes in one nation by imperialistic exploitation of entire subject states; the rate of transition from the lower to the higher stages of socialism and from socialism to communism depends, they say, on factors such as the correct interpretation of Marxist laws by the party leadership, the active participation of the masses, the elimination of internal and external enemies and emphasis on goals of crucial importance, such as the development of a strong production base, the elimination of competing ideologies and social distinctions, and the introduction of universal education. It is the thesis and hope of the leaders of the C.P.S.U. that the transition from capitalism to socialism and from socialism to communism in all other countries will be more rapid because concrete forms for "progress" have been worked out by the Soviet people and their party, and because the Soviet system will soon demonstrate such a superior capacity to meet more of the needs of more of the people that people all over the world will rise up and demand a society modelled according to the Soviet pattern. The duty and the goal of all Marxists is the acceleration of what they believe to be the inevitable progress of all mankind toward communism.

The Development of Socialism

Lenin asserted that a communist society can be developed only after socialism is fully entrenched. He stated:

> "From capitalism, mankind can pass directly only to socialism, i.e. to the public ownership of the means of production and the distribution of goods according to the work performed by each individual. Our party looks farther ahead: inevitably socialism must gradually turn into communism upon the banner of which is inscribed the motto, 'From each according to his ability, to each according to his needs.' "[2]

The party leadership has always affirmed that:

> ". . . to pass prematurely to distribution according to needs when the economic conditions for this have not yet been created, when an abundance of material goods has not been achieved and when people have not been prepared to live and work in a communist society would harm the cause of building communism."[3]

Marxists point out that although the basis for the development of a socialist society is established by revolution, thereby involving a "leap," a long and tortuous series of evolutionary changes are required to restructure society according to the socialist pattern. As Lenin wrote shortly before his death, "We, too, lack sufficient civilization to enable us to pass straight on to socialism, although we have the political requisites for it."[4]

The Marxist analysis of the processes involved in the development of a socialist society have been discussed elsewhere and will be reviewed only briefly here. The initial prerequisite, the Marxists say, is for the proletariat under the leadership of a Marxist party to preempt political power and use it to curb the opposition of the overthrown exploiting classes and to establish the material and social structure necessary for socialism. Public ownership of the means of production and measures designed to change man's social consciousness are considered indispensable. The proletariat, though purportedly more advanced than other segments of the population, lacks the required political consciousness, acumen, knowledge of Marxist-Leninist principles, purposefulness and organization; hence, decisive leadership must be provided by the party which is guided by the "scientific" theory of Marxism-Leninism. Marxists say that the dictatorship of the proletariat is absolutely necessary at this stage of social development since coercive measures are required to effect the changes which the party deems necessary and because opposition to the development of socialism is inevitable. Marxists argue that the dictatorship of the proletariat represents a step toward more perfect democracy because, although it uses oppression, it oppresses only those classes and individuals who oppose the Marxist program, and, in doing so, it acts for the benefit of the majority of the population. The fact that the people were never given an opportunity to delegate to either the proletariat or the party the right to act for them and in their interest is irrelevant, or perhaps it would be more accurate to say, necessary from the Marxist point of view. The party assumes that until the goals, values and attitudes of the people have been changed, they simply cannot know what is best for themselves, and therefore, decisions must be made for them. During the initial phase of socialism, one of the important tasks assumed by the party and its helper, the proletariat, is to provide the economic, social and ideological framework to force a radical, but necessarily gradual, change in the consciousness of the people so that they will eventually know what is best for themselves, i.e. adopt Marxist goals, and will be prepared to participate in a higher form of democracy. This follows from the Marxist dictum that "It is not the consciousness of men that determines their existence, but, on the contrary, their social existence that determines their consciousness."

In 1936 Stalin announced "the complete victory of the socialist system in all spheres of the national economy" and concluded that "in the main we have already achieved the first phase of communism-socialism."[5] Soviet theoreticians point out that his announcement meant only that the basic framework for socialism had been developed in that all but a negligible proportion of the means of production were owned by the public, the exploiting classes had been eradicated, internal opposition to the regime no longer constituted a major threat to its stability and the majority of the people had developed the rudiments of the required attitude toward the new social relations. Progress toward a higher stage of socialism, according to Soviet spokesmen, required that these accomplishments be followed by new achievements such as rapid growth of economic productivity, elimination of the vestiges of capitalism and of social distinctions, and the gradual transformation of the dictatorship of the proletariat into a higher form of socialist democracy. During the period of advancing from a lower to a higher form of socialism the people were to exert themselves under the leadership of the party in order to solidify and perfect the gains of the socialist revolution, to develop the material basis for the transition to communism, and to prepare themselves as worthy citizens of the new society.

At the Eighteenth Party Congress in 1939 it was announced very prematurely that the stage was set for the gradual transition to communism. The war and the war restoration required a long period of diversion, but the Rules of the C.P.S.U. adopted by the Nineteenth Party Congress in 1952 again set as the major task of the party the gradual transition from socialism to communism. After the effects of the post-Stalin revision had been more or less stabilized, the emphasis on the transition to communism gained momentum. At the Twenty-First Congress in 1959, the party announced that the Soviet Union, as a result of the victory of socialism and extensive changes in all spheres of social life, had entered a new period in its development, the period of the full scale construction of a communist society. Since then, major efforts in all spheres have been directed toward propelling society toward the new and higher phase. The fundamental task of the Seven Year Plan adopted in 1959 was that of "accelerating the economic advance toward Communism, of gaining in the shortest possible time in the peaceful competition between socialism and capitalism"; it was announced at that time that within the next fifteen years "the material and technical basis for Communism will be established in our country."[6] The goals and tasks of the party and the people during the transition period were outlined by the Party Program adopted by the Twenty-Second Congress of the C.P.S.U., and the Soviet press has published many articles on problems to be solved during the transition and on the probable organization of the new society. The 1939 and 1959 announcements of the gradual transition to communism had a vastly different meaning. In 1939, the party leaders probably did not expect substantial progress beyond a higher stage of socialism during the following decade, in view of the threatening international situation and the lack of preparation for communism in the economic and social spheres.

By 1959 the party leaders, working from a much more adequate economic and social base, may actually have believed that their predictions and promises concerning the transition to communism could be fulfilled within the foreseeable future and that they would finally be able to deliver the long-promised communist utopia to the Soviet people.

The Transition to Communism

The Soviet socialist society, according to Soviet spokesmen, is infinitely superior to Western societies because of the elimination of exploitation of man by man, class conflicts, discrimination based on social origin, race or sex, unemployment, economic crises, war mongering, illiteracy and other conditions which militate against the well-being of mankind, and the concurrent development of related positive measures such as equality of opportunity, humanitarian welfare benefits, social and economic democracy and the priority of the interest of the collective over the interest of the individual. Obviously, not all of the claims are justified, many of the innovations are not unmixed blessings and the shortcomings of the Soviet social order, in comparison to Western social orders, are glossed over or denied. What the Soviet authorities do admit is that in comparison to communism, socialism is a highly imperfect form of social organization both from the point of view of meeting the needs of members and from the attributes of the members of society. Socialism falls far short of the projected goals in a number of major ways: at the present level of production there are not enough material goods to satisfy fully the requirements of all the people; the distribution system is necessarily based on socialist rather than communist principles; social distinctions have not been totally eliminated; conditions are not right for the exercise of the highest form of democracy; socialist morality is not practiced fully and communist morality has yet to be developed; conflicting ideologies and social systems flourish and are accepted by the majority of mankind. The solution of these and other problems is the major task set by the C.P.S.U. for the period of the transition to communism.

All Soviet theoreticians emphasize that the transition must be gradual rather than leap-like. There is to be no sharp dividing line between socialism and communism; rather communism is to grow out of socialism and to be its direct continuation. Soviet writers say that even contemporary Soviet society has "shoots of communism" or communist features which are to be developed and improved; specific reference is made to "shoots of communism" such as communist forms of labor and industrial organization, public participation in the administration of justice, and socio-cultural measures including child care institutions, pensions and free education and medical care. It is conceded that none of these exist completely in its higher communist form, and that even the rudiments of other features of communist society have not been introduced. The general plan is to introduce new features on a limited scale and to strive for the gradual development and perfection of all features. For example, the party leaders have always completely rejected the possibility of an abrupt change from distribution according to work to distribution according to need. Even in the early stages of socialism certain welfare benefits such as health measures and mothers' allowances were distributed according to need while other benefits such as pensions were distributed on a combination of the need and work principles. As the Soviet society has reached a higher stage of socialism, the principle of distribution according to work has retained priority but increased emphasis has been placed on distribution according to need. The party intends to extend gradually the application of the principle of distribution according to need by increasing the number of free boarding schools, nurseries, and health and vacation resorts, supplying one free meal a day at work or at school, etc. Only one or a few of these measures are to be introduced at a time and the use of differential wages and salaries as a technique for enabling individuals to acquire what they need or want is to be decreased gradually. The gradualness of the transition to communism is deemed necessary for a number of reasons. The party leaders believe that if the advantages which are granted to the people coincide with the potential of society, the material base for communism can be developed more rapidly, organizational forms necessary for the new communist society can be established, and the people can be prepared to live under a new set of social relations. They assert that if all features of communism were withheld until the material and technical base is prepared completely, economic progress would be retarded, and the change-over from socialism to communism would be chaotic because neither the organizational forms nor the social consciousness of the people would be prepared for the radical changes.

The gradualness of the transition to communism is not, according to the party leaders, to be interpreted as slow movement. Khrushchev stated that, on the contrary, the period of transition is ". . . a period of rapid development of modern industry and large scale mechanized agriculture, rapid progress in all of the economy and culture with the active and conscious participation of millions of builders of Communist society."[7] The transition is to be distinguished by high rates of development in all spheres of social life from the growth of production to the advance of culture and the political consciousness of the people.[8] The development is to be accelerated by a number of factors; the long-term emphasis on growth-inducing industries and new technical developments are to permit a "big leap" in the growth of the productive forces; as "society increasingly masters the laws of its own development," it is able "to choose the shortest way to advance not gropingly but with certainty, achieving maximum results with the least effort"; and far from unimportant is the "constructive endeavor of the masses themselves, their conscious participation in the expansion of social production, in the advance of culture, and in the administration of state and economic affairs."[9] The party leaders assert that since a strong base of socialism has been established, rapid economic advances, wise leadership of the party, and a highly motivated populace will enable the U.S.S.R. to achieve the major goals of communism within a relatively short time.

Tasks During the Transition Period

THE ESTABLISHMENT OF THE MATERIAL AND TECHNICAL BASIS FOR COMMUNISM

Because material affluence is a prerequisite for communism, Soviet leaders must continue to assign high priority to economic goals. In 1959 Khrushchev stated: "Our country's basic practical task at this time is to establish the material and technical base of a Communist society, to secure a great new expansion of socialist productive forces."[10] The aim is to accomplish the "main economic task of the Party and the Soviet people within two decades," i.e. by 1980. Some of the economic goals established by the C.P.S.U. are summarized in Table 1. One of the stated goals is to increase industrial and agricultural output by 500 and 250 percent respectively from 1960 to 1980 in order to meet adequately the requirements of the expanded population. According to Soviet authorities fulfillment of the economic goals will require a highly developed modern industry, complete electrification of the country, scientific and technical progress in all branches of industry and agriculture, mechanization and automation of all production processes, maximum utilization of all natural resources, a higher cultural and technical level of all the working people, better organizational forms and higher labor productivity. Since the chapters on economics and agriculture carried detailed discussions of economic goals, programs and problems it is sufficient to restate at this point that the party leaders are directing a massive effort to establish the economic basis of communism, but some of their goals are unreasonably high in relation to the objective situation and the temporal interval which has been set for their accomplishment. Most analysts of the Soviet economy have concluded that very substantial economic progress can be expected, but that not all of the economic goals established by the party can be accomplished within the specified time; and even the post-Khrushchev leaders themselves have suggested that the goals for agriculture are unreasonably high. However, in the long run, it may make little difference whether the U.S.S.R. accomplishes its economic goals by 1980 or not until 1990 or even 2000 if it does indeed succeed in building the economic base for communism within a relatively few decades. Whether the U.S.S.R. is able to demonstrate economic superiority to Western nations within a few decades is much more important than whether it meets its 1980 deadline.

Table 1
Planned Economic Growth by 1980*

Item	Percentage Increase from 1960 Base			
	by 1970		by 1980	
National Income		150		400
Total Industrial Output		150		500
of which:				
electric power	approximately	240	approximately	900
steel	—		approximately	300
Agricultural Output		150		250
of which:				
grain	—		more than	100
milk	more than	100	approximately	200
meat	approximately	200	approximately	300
Labor Productivity:				
industry		100		300-350
agriculture		150		400-500
Real Income:				
per capita			more than	250
per employed person	almost	100		
per lowest paid worker	approximately	200		
per collective farmer	more than	100	more than	300

* *Program of the Communist Party of the Soviet Union, op. cit.,* pp. 64-85.

Party leaders state that the U.S.S.R. does not consider the U.S.A. to be its "yardstick of economic development" since, they point out with glee, there are millions of unemployed and marginal workers in the United States whose most elementary needs are not fully satisfied, whereas the goal of the party is to ensure that all reasonable requirements of all members of society can be met all of the time. The Soviet leaders believe that if they are able to surpass the U.S.A. in the economic sphere, they will have reached a milestone on the road to communism and will have gained a powerful propaganda weapon to influence other societies in favor of their system. They assert that full communism can be intro-duced only after the economic might of the U.S.S.R. is substantially greater than that attained to date by any Western nation since communism requires that society is able to provide the full abundance of material goods and cultural benefits to meet the growing requirements of all of the people. Only then can the principle of "to each according to his needs" be applied. Since the present level of socialist production is entirely inadequate to meet the reasonable needs of all the people, extensive economic development is an absolute necessity if communism is to be attained.

A related reason for the need to expand economic productivity was provided by Engels who wrote:

> "So long as it is not possible to produce so much that there is enough for all, with more left over for expanding the social capital and extending the forces of production—so long as this is not possible, there must always be a ruling class directing the use of society's productive forces, and a poor, oppressed class. How these classes are constituted depends on the stage of development."[11]

Soviet leaders would admit that living standards in the U.S.S.R. are still relatively low, and that the highest stage of socialist democracy has not been attained because the necessary prerequisites of economic abundance and advanced social consciousness have not yet been developed. They would claim that in the higher stage of social development which they have purportedly achieved class conflict has been eliminated and equality of opportunity has been established. They would vigorously deny that the masses of the Soviet people are oppressed since, they would say, all sacrifices have been made for the ultimate good of the entire society rather than for the benefit of an exploiting minority. Their denial would, of course, be weakened by the indubitable fact that some of the sacrifices which the Soviet people have been required to make were of no value whatsoever with reference to the goals of the party for society.

One of the chief hopes of the Soviet leaders is that if they develop an economy strong enough to meet adequately the needs of all Soviet citizens, the majority of people in all nations will perceive the advantages of the socialist system and will strive with revolutionary zeal to force the adoption of Soviet-style socialism in their own countries. Khrushchev articulated this goal clearly in an address to the C.P.S.U. Central Committee in December, 1963. He stated:

> "Here, in the sphere of material production . . . the advantages of socialism over capitalism are being irrefutably confirmed. In present day conditions the struggle to create the economic base for Communism in our country and to build socialism in other countries constitutes one of the chief forms of class struggle in the international arena. Firm foundations for a full victory over capitalism will not be built by ultra-revolutionary phrases but by the unflagging labor of millions in the sphere of material production, which strengthens the common front of socialism, multiplies its forces in the revolutionary struggle of the peoples of all countries. *'We exert our chief effect on the international revolution by our economic policy'*, V. I. Lenin stressed. . . . *'Let us solve this*

task—and then we will win on an international scale surely and finally.' (Works [in Russian], Vol. XXXII, p. 413) (Italics original).

"The successes of Communist construction in the U.S.S.R. are a great contribution of our Leninist party, of the entire Soviet people to the common revolutionary cause of strengthening the world socialist system, the struggle of the working class of all countries against exploitation and oppression, a contribution to the people's struggle against imperialism and colonialism, for their freedom and national independence, for social progress. This is our contribution to the struggle for the cause of peace, democracy and socialism.

"Our achievements in building Communism are showing what the working class, the working people, can accomplish when they have taken power into their hands. The peoples of the Soviet country, under the leadership of the Communist Party, have turned backward Russia into the most advanced and powerful socialist state. *The stronger the economy of the Soviet Union, of all socialist countries, the more will the advantages of the socialist system become clear, the greater will be their revolutionizing, inspiring influence on the minds and hearts of the working people of the whole world. . . ."*[12] [Italics added]

The emphasis which the party leaders place on economic progress as a powerful weapon in the struggle for world communism is only partially justified. First, they tend to overestimate the potential of the Soviet economy for rapid growth and simultaneously to underestimate the growth potential of Western economies. Second, they grossly exaggerate the disadvantages and underestimate the advantages of the private enterprise system to the majority of members of Western societies and, at the same time, exaggerate the advantages and grossly understate the disadvantages of their own economic and social order to the majority of members of their society. Finally, they overlook the possibility that before the Soviet economic system can support full communism, Western economic orders might be able to provide most of the members of society with many of the material advantages promised by full communism, and if so, these advantages will be given without all the intervening hardships which have been associated with the revolution, the dictatorship of the proletariat and the construction of socialism. In short, given a long period of peace, it is possible that economic affluence could be achieved under a system of planned economy or under a private enterprise system; if economic affluence can be achieved under both economic systems, the majority of mankind might well prefer a variant of the Western economic order as the least painful path to plenty.

THE ELIMINATION OF SOCIAL DISTINCTIONS

Since a basic tenet of the Marxist doctrine is that as society advances toward communism all class and other social distinctions are to be obliterated, one of the tasks of the transition period is the approximation of actual equality for all. Soviet authorities delineate several areas in which progressive action is required: chief among these are elimination of differences due to state and collective ownership, between town and country, between mental and physical labor, the remnants of inequality in the status of women, and improvement of the distribution system.

Soviet authorities point to the existence of two forms of social property—state property and cooperative-collective farm property—as one of the chief current sources of inequality. Although prosperous collective farms are able to provide their members with material and cultural benefits roughly comparable to those provided by the state for state workers and employees, the majority of collective farm members are not as well-off as state workers. In general, the peasants work longer hours for a lower monetary income, and are at a disadvantage with respect to medical facilities, pensions, child care institutions, paid vacations and opportunities for educational and cultural advancement. Because Marxist ideology accords a higher status to public ownership, Soviet authors attribute major responsibility for the disadvantages of the peasants to the continued existence of collective rather than public ownership of the means of production. The very real disadvantages which the peasants have suffered as a result of party policy are glossed over, or blamed on Stalin. Although collective ownership is held to be vastly superior to private ownership, it is described as a lower form of social organization than public ownership, in that it does not permit optimal levels of productivity or optimum satisfaction of the needs of the people. Hence, the party has announced that the eventual evolution of collective ownership into public ownership is inevitable.[13]

During the transition period the task is not to eliminate collective ownership of property entirely, but rather to strengthen its productive base and to pave the way for its gradual conversion into public property, and at the same time to increase the proportion of property which is publicly owned. The emphasis is to be on a party-directed, evolutionary transformation rather than on change dictated by administrative fiat. The party and the state have promised to promote the growth of the productive forces of the kolkhoz system by providing adequate material support, streamlining the system of state direction and procurement, adjusting prices, and by training a sufficient number of agricultural specialists. The kolkhozy are expected to improve organization, productivity and incentive systems, and to extend continuously their commonly owned assets for production, insurance, cultural and community needs. Eventually all collective farms are to be sufficiently productive to permit transition to a guaranteed monthly wage and to develop community services to such an extent that the disadvantages that the majority of collective farmers now have in comparison to state workers will be eliminated. In 1964, the state took action to remove in part one of the major disadvantages by instituting a nationwide pension system for collective farmers; state workers, however, still receive superior pension benefits. The strengthening of collective farms is part of the policy designed to encourage a progressive advance toward the higher stage of socialist ownership. When collective farms are able to satisfy fully the requirements of the members, supplementary farming plots are to be relinquished voluntarily; collective farms may elect to merge with state farms; and increasing numbers of inter-collective farm or collective-state farm projects are to be constructed. Thus, the difference between public and collective ownership and the associated inequalities are to disappear gradually.

Related to the differences between collective and public ownership are the differences between town and country. Party theorists say that the Soviet Union still has to overcome the great backwardness of the country that was inherited from capitalism which, they say, typically allows the towns to exploit the countryside ruthlessly. One of the tasks of the transition period is to reshape the lives of the peasants and to bring them the benefits of the achievements of science, technology and culture. A most important measure is the further development of mechanization and automation of agriculture which will make the labor of the collective farmer increasingly similar to that of the skilled urban worker. In addition to increasing agricultural output, this measure is to teach the collective farmer the "rules of socialist labor discipline and the higher form of socialist cooperation of labor." The reorganization of agricultural production is expected to lead to a complete change in the traditional aspect of the village. Mechanization will require an increased number of garages and repair shops; local processing plants will be established; the population will increase and new demands will be made for better facilities. The need will arise for more and better roads, hospitals, children's institutions, schools, shops, catering establishments and cultural institutions, and for living quarters with modern conveniences. Thus, the cultural institutions and amenities in agricultural areas are to be comparable to those in urban areas. Soviet officials say that at the same time measures will be introduced to limit the size of cities and to distribute industry to avoid urban congestion. The distinctions which remain between labor in industry and agriculture are to be no more than those which exist between different branches of industry and are not to lead to or support social stratification or inequalities. The program of the C.P.S.U. states: *"Elimination of the socio-economic and cultural distinctions between town and country and of differences in their living conditions will be one of the greatest gains of communist construction."*[14]

Marxists attach extraordinary importance to the antithesis of brain workers and manual workers which they maintain arose as an inevitable result of the division of society into oppressors and oppressed. They say that under the "old division of labor" all forms of mental work became a hereditary privilege of the propertied classes, while the non-propertied, oppressed classes were forced to work so long and strenuously in heavy manual labor or as "mere appendages of the machine" that all their productive and creative propensities and endowments were suppressed. Under communism all people are to participate in, and to enjoy, both mental and manual labor. Lenin wrote in 1920 that ". . . communism is moving toward, must be moving toward and will attain to . . . the abolition of the division of labor among people, the rearing, instruction and training of *comprehensively developed* and *comprehensively trained* people who can do *everything.*"[15] However, he recognized that the obliteration of the distinctions between the intelligentsia and the workers and peasants would require a long time and predicted that the intelligentsia would remain a special stratum "which will persist until we have reached the highest stage of development of communist society."[16]

Marxists say that under socialism the antithesis between mental and physical workers is eliminated, because the manual workers no longer labor for the benefit of the propertied classes, and physical and mental workers alike work for the common cause of building and extending socialism. Nevertheless, a distinction remains because a multitude of factors have prevented the workers and peasants from achieving the level of technical knowledge and culture acquired by the intelligentsia. A well-educated intelligentsia was necessary for the rapid development of society. The distinctions between manual and mental work are to be eliminated primarily by raising the cultural and technical level of the workers and the peasants to that of the intelligentsia. A two-way process is to be involved. Shorter working days and increased educational opportunities and requirements are to enable the workers and peasants to engage in the intellectual, technical and cultural activities that have traditionally been reserved for members of the intelligentsia and privileged classes. At the same time, the intelligentsia are to remove themselves from their ivory towers and to participate more fully in the practical work of society. The combination of theoretical and practical training is to do much to eliminate attitudinal distinctions between mental and physical work, particularly on the part of the "white collar workers" who in the recent past have been accused of adopting a superior attitude toward manual workers. An important factor is a change in the very nature of labor which, to an increasing extent, is to demand "constant intellectual development, a broad outlook, great knowledge and a creative approach."[17] Much of the work which involves heavy, unskilled labor, and repetitive and monotonous operations which are fatiguing to the worker is to be done by machines. Strumilin asserted that even now "the old division of labor is losing specific odious features" and that with the advent of mechanization and automation

". . . a new type of worker of broad qualifications, embracing functions of physical and mental work with the mental clearly dominant is already growing up here. . . . The content and character of labor are changing fundamentally and the worker is emerging not as a person who performs manual, physical labor but as an organizer, . . . a manipulator of machine processes, which will require predominantly mental work; on the automatic lines this type of worker is already starting to bear a greater resemblance to the engineer and technician, to the toiler of the future communist society."[18]

The elimination of the remnants of inequality in the status of women and the reduction of the working day are considered to be vital prerequisites for enabling manual workers to raise their knowledge and culture. Strumilin visualizes that under communism about four hours will be needed for obligatory work; sleep and meals will take up about ten hours; and every person will have about ten hours of free time at his disposal.[19] He anticipates that on the average about two hours will be used for relaxation at the television set, a concert or the movies, about four hours for active participation in sports and amateur arts, and about four hours on reading or mental work of interest to the person. Under such circumstances it is anticipated that individuals can become proficient and even expert in a number of spheres; a machine operator could also be an amateur botanist, a civic leader, an author or a professional athlete; an academician could operate factory machines or plow a field. Strumilin asserted that ". . . all working people reach out for knowledge as a flower turns to the sun . . . in a society that has overcome class antagonisms and property barriers."[20] He continued:

> "And if it does not surprise us even now when a piano tuner sometimes tops off the performance of his mechanical function with Beethoven's 'Moonlight Sonata', like a true musician, even more natural will such combinations of functions be with the shortened working day under communism, when in hours off-work hundreds of thousands of workers will turn to invention or reinforce the ranks of public figures, scientists and scholars, writers, inspired musicians and artists. And all these millions of replenishments from the worker groups, supplanting the onesided worker of the old division of labor system, will create the society that we shall call communist."[21]

It is explicity assumed that, as the higher stage of society is approached, work will constitute more and more the "primary vital need and even a pleasure" for all healthy people who will use their off-work time enthusiastically for the good of society and for self-development.

Women are to be relieved of household drudgery and public forms of child rearing are to be extended. Strumilin apparently favors a program which would virtually separate children from their parents. He wrote:

> "Giving public forms of upbringing absolute preference over all others, we shall have to expand these forms constantly in the next few years, at a pace that will enable us in 15 to 20 years' time to make them available to the entire population of the country from the cradle to secondary school graduation certificate. Immediately upon leaving the maternity hospital, each Soviet citizen will be assigned to a nursery and from there to a kindergarten with round-the-clock maintenance or to a children's home; next he will go to a boarding school from which he will graduate to life on his own."[22]

He recommended that parents should be permitted to "call at the children's quarters" only now and then or "as many times as the established regulations provide for. . . ."[23] Other theoreticians suggest that in the future society both forms of rearing children—in the family and in public institutions—will co-exist and complement each other.[24] Even the Party Program states that in the future children and adolescents may be kept free of charge in children's establishments if the family "so desires." In the more ideal society parents should have more time to assist the state in the upbringing of children and the danger that parents would attempt to inculcate into children attitudes which are at variance with the official ideology should be minimal. Even if full communism were achieved the regime would probably not find it convenient to dispense with the family.

An important prerequisite for the establishment of full communism is the elimination of inequality in the distribution of material benefits. During the initial stages of the transition to communism a number of factors preclude the introduction of an egalitarian system of distribution: the economy is not sufficiently developed to satisfy fully the requirements of all of the people; the attitude toward labor has not been perfected to the extent that material incentives for work can be discarded; the distinction between manual and mental work remains and the more highly skilled intelligentsia receive higher remuneration than workers and peasants; remuneration differs widely from collective farm to collective farm, because of different levels of efficiency and productivity, and even between industrial branches because of party-determined priorities. Consequently, there are wide differences in standards of living: a few people live in relative luxury while many are hard pressed to pay for basic food and clothing requirements.

As society progresses toward communism, differences in living conditions and material benefits are to be eliminated gradually, and eventually, all are to enjoy equal, but high standards of living. Present plans do not suggest that the equalization will be effected through the introduction of equal remuneration for labor. Party theoreticians predict that the premature introduction of such a policy would be disruptive and would lower the average productivity of labor because the majority of Soviet citizens do not have the desired attitude toward work; and it might be added, they could hardly be expected to work most diligently for the joy of working and for the privilege of contributing to society when society is unable to satisfy many of their legitimate desires. A prominent Soviet economist stated categorically, "Every worker participating in socialist production is interested in the highest possible remuneration for his labor."[25] However, as the technical and cultural level of the population grows, the distinction between manual and mental labor is eradicated, and all collective farms are brought up to a high level of productivity, there are to be few, if any, people whose labor is not worth a substantial amount to society and a leveling-up of the rates of remuneration is to occur. Tangible evidence of the leveling-up process was provided when the minimum wage was increased in 1964. Prices, particularly of the basic necessities, are to be lowered, but price-lowering, taken by itself, is described as an inadequate equalization technique because persons in the higher income brackets receive a disproportionate share of the benefits. At the Twenty-First Party Congress Khrushchev stated:

> "It goes without saying that the Party and the Government will consistently adhere to the charted course of increasing wages and reducing prices. But that is only one of the ways. . . . There is a really communist way of promoting the prosperity of the people, of creating better living conditions for all society and for each member of it. It includes good housing and public catering, better public services, more kindergartens and nurseries, an improved system of education, more recreation and holiday facilities, better medical services, more cultural establishments, etc."[26]

The majority of Soviet economists seem to agree that "personal and social incentives to labor will be harmoniously combined over a long period of time" and that "two forms of distribution according to work and according to needs—will exist, complementing each other over an equally long period."[27] Although Soviet theorists have not reached agreement on whether distribution according to work should continue to have priority during the period of the full scale building of communism, all are agreed that, "As our country forges on to Communism, the role of the public consumption funds, as shoots of the new public forms for the common satisfaction of the needs of society's members, will increase."[28] It is generally assumed that one of the most important initial measures will be to relieve the working people gradually of financial responsibility for family members who are unable to work, i.e. society will assume full responsibility for the maintenance of the aged and incapacitated, and will assume increased financial responsibility for the support of children from families with relatively low incomes. Adequate pensions are to be provided for all elderly and incapacitated citizens regardless of length of service and occupational status. These projected policies are intended to eliminate some of the current inequalities that do not derive directly from distribution according to work.

As abundance is approached an increased number of material benefits are to be distributed according to need. Khrushchev stated in 1959, "Full satisfaction of the food, housing and clothing needs of all Soviet people, within necessary and sensible limits can probably be brought about in the not too distant future."[29] In 1963, he suggested that in the near future arrangements should be made to provide children in kindergartens and nurseries with free food, to serve free breakfasts and lunches in schools and to issue free school uniforms and shoes, and that the time will come when workers will be given free breakfasts and then free lunches at enterprises.[30] At the same time, he emphasized that ". . . the growth of public funds will be combined with a direct increase in wages, with a reduction in the price of goods. All factors contributing to an advance in the standard of living will be brought into play, directed toward the good of the people."[31] After the initial measures of distribution according to need have been worked out, the populace will, presumably, be able to obtain all meals free; at some stage free repair and laundry services, and free access to places of entertainment are to be introduced, and eventually the people are not to have to pay for any service or material which is required for their well-being. Soviet theorists stress, however, that the principle "From each according to his ability, to each according to his needs" cannot be practiced fully until all material goods are available in abundance, and the people have perfected their attitude toward work.

There is general agreement that during the transition period personal property will be retained as an important economic incentive to work. However, under full communism when the law of distribution according to work becomes totally inoperative, the people are to have no need to accumulate, retain or augment personal property. Strumilin commented:

> ". . . generally speaking, these articles of personal property have no future. The people themselves will throw away personal cars and dachas and individual plots like so much excess baggage when modern boarding houses with all the conveniences spring up in the best and most picturesque locations, offering separate rooms, yachts, motor scooters for pleasure rides, helicopters for excursions, etc., and when excellent cars of all models and colors (just pick one to suit your taste) are lined up in public garages, just waiting for passengers. Only when man draws abundantly from 'ours' will he gladly give up 'mine'."[32]

Much emphasis is placed on the assumption that the people will realize the superiority of public forms of ownership; for example, Khrushchev commented that under communism transportation facilities, including the use of cars for private outings, will be excellent and the individual will be relieved of such annoyances as assuming responsibility for the upkeep of a private car; several authors have remarked that vacations in publicly-owned model resorts will be preferred to vacations in a private dacha because the vacationer will be freed from housekeeping chores, repair jobs and other labor associated with home ownership.[33]

Soviet authorities stress the need for material and psychological preparation for the transformation of property ownership norms and emphasize that the process must necessarily be a gradual one. According to one theorist:

> "The new public forms of satisfaction of steadily growing and reasonable needs, disclosing their superiority more fully, are inexorably squeezing out the old individual forms of the use of material and cultural goods. But this process cannot take place spontaneously, of course. Only by ensuring the preponderant development of public forms and gradually restricting individual forms is it possible to accelerate the complete victory of communist methods of satisfying the needs of the entire population and of each individual. This will be the achievement of complete material equality characteristic of communism."[34]

The party must not anticipate comprehensive limitations on personal ownership in the immediate future since the Party Program states, that within
20 years, "public consumption funds will total about half the aggregate
real income of the population."[35] Moreover, according to Strumilin:

> "The abundance of the public funds of consumption does not by any
> means sound the death knell for personal property in general. It would seem
> that goods having the most intimate connection with the individuality and
> personality of the consumer can become articles of personal consumption.
> These include clothing and footwear chosen according to taste and size, articles
> of personal use, a hunter's time-tested rifle, a musician's piano and violin,
> cherished books that a person is accustomed to having at hand and many other
> things necessary for man's diversified individual inclinations, habits and
> needs."[36]

When asked about the future of inheritance, Strumilin replied:

> "Judge for yourself; in such a society, what can be transmitted through
> inheritance to one's offspring, outside of things that are cherished as souveniers?
> And besides, who needs a full inheritance when each new generation through
> its own labor wins the right to all things the previous generations have used,
> only on a still broader scale and in still more perfect forms?"[37]

Soviet theorists maintain that there is no real danger that under communism, when everything is accessible to all, that "some people will grab
out of all proportion and nothing will be left for others."[38] Persons who
raise such questions are accused of projecting their own "private property
psychology" to the citizens of the future communist society who, instead of
manifesting traits "inculcated by capitalism such as greed, selfishness and
egotism . . . will be highly conscientious, truly cultured, free of the 'earmarks'
of the evil past and filled with the spirit of collectivism, public duty and
nobility."[39] Moreover, it is held that excessive personal accumulation would
be senseless and that if, perchance, an imperfect communard were to engage
in hoarding, social sanctions would soon cause him to change his behavior.

Thus, during the transition period the importance of personal property is to decline gradually, and under communism people are to have a
number of items for personal use, but such items are not to constitute personal property in the sense that they cannot be accumulated, sold, bequeathed or even given away since there is to be no need for such practices. A Soviet economist provided the following analysis of the impact of
the transformation of ownership norms:

> "With the abolition of personal property, the basis of the contradictions
> between personal and public interests will have been removed and economic
> inequality among the members of society for once and for all eliminated. This
> will be feasible only at a definite stage of the highest phase of communism,
> when the sole principle of distribution will be according to needs. Society will
> then have no need to resort to any forms or types of material encouragement
> to work. Society will also dispense with commodity-money relations. The level
> of people's social consciousness, their psychology, habits and customs will have
> become altogether different in that phase of communism. The communards

will differ in many ways from our contemporaries for labor will have become a genuine and profound necessity of life for every individual."[40]

The doctrine demands that when the abundance of communism has been attained ". . . all people, voluntarily and irrespective of the share of the material goods that they receive, will work to the full of their ability, knowing that this is necessary to society."[41] One Soviet writer expressed apprehension that under communism when work has become a source of joy to all and all people have a number of areas of expertness an "unreasonable person" might consider that: "you rise in the morning and you begin to reflect: where shall I go to work today—to the factory as the chief engineer, or shall I gather and lead the fishing brigade? Or perhaps fly to Moscow to conduct an urgent session of the Academy of Sciences?"[42] Khrushchev roundly condemned the "vulgarized conception of Communist society as a loose, unorganized, anarchic mass of people"; he stressed that on the contrary, under communism there must be:

". . . planned and organized allocation of labor among the various branches of production and social regulation of working time in accordance with the specific requirements of various production processes. . . . Operation of machinery requires that each person perform his job and meet his social obligations at definite times and in definite ways."[43]

Obviously each communard is to take his obligations to society seriously.

EDUCATION FOR COMMUNISM

The importance attached by the party to refashioning human nature and creating a "new Soviet man" has been mentioned so often in previous sections that the topic would not be reintroduced if it were not that one of the major tasks of the transition from socialism to communism is to effect extensive changes in the minds, morals and manners of the people and the entire spiritual superstructure of society. Success in this task is crucial to the attainment of communism since under communism the goals and behavior of people are to be vastly different than under any other social order, including socialism. If the party is not able to reshape human nature, to modify the most basic motives of mankind, application of the communist principle of "From each according to his ability, to each according to his need" would produce chaos and regression of the social and economic order, which could be precluded only by rigid organizational and perhaps coercive measures that would, in turn, violate other basic tenets of communist ideology. Only if all members of society willingly and fully put the interest of society above self-interest, work to the best of their ability on any job where their services are needed, and "cast aside all survivals of bourgeois psychology" can communism be made to work. The essential questions seem to be whether the powerful weapons at the command of the totalitarian regime are sufficient, whether all prerequisites are included, whether the party has both the techniques and the skill to effect the projected changes in human behavior, morals and motives. Can human nature and social mores be changed as the party wants to change them?

Most Western critics have described the goals of the party for re-shaping human nature as completely utopian, and even the majority of those scholars who predict that the party will achieve many of its other goals have concluded that the goal of developing a "new" man for the communist society is one of the weakest links in the entire program of the party. The party leaders, too, recognize that it is much more difficult to change human nature than, for example, to increase economic productivity manifold. They concede also that all of the changes which they demand in human nature cannot be accomplished within a few years or even a few decades, and that even after the other prerequisites for full communism have been attained, the people will not be prepared completely to live in a communist society. Despite their recognition of the obstacles, the party leaders cling persistently to the assumption that basic, central changes in human nature will occur, that the members of the future communist society will have motives, goals and behavior which differ in essential respects from those which have prevailed throughout the recorded history of mankind, that the interests of individuals and society will coincide, and that because people will be different and the social organization will be different, full and complete happiness will be attainable on earth.

Ever since the party has been in power it has been working on the problem of modifying the behavior and attitudes of people to conform with the type of society which it has attempted to build. However, what the party has wanted the people to be like under socialism and its goals for human nature under communism are two vastly different matters. The motives of the "ideal" person under Soviet socialism do not differ in most essential respects from those of the "ideal" person in Western societies. Under both systems, the ideal individual works diligently, assumes social obligations, is considerate of others, adheres to the values of society, etc., because it is in his own best interest to do so. Self-interest, self-preservation and personal gratification are among the basic motivating forces which play a dominant role in both types of society. True, under socialism, people have been encouraged more strongly to put the welfare of the collective above personal welfare, but even when they have done so, self-interest may have been far from unimportant, since social rewards are meted out to individuals for demonstrations of selflessness. Under socialism the majority of rewards, both tangible and intangible, have been distributed on the basis of what the individual has done, his contribution to society, his de-meanor, his overall behavior, and this is more or less as it has been under all hitherto existing social systems. The changes in attitudes, morals and behavior which the party has attempted to introduce have been of a peripheral nature and in many respects have constituted nothing more than an attempt to encourage consistent adherence to traditional values such as honesty, diligence, hard work, unselfishness and concern for the welfare of others.

Under communism the situation is to be vastly different. People are to work diligently and to give their best to society, not because their material and social well-being depends on their behavior, but simply because human nature will have changed for the better, and because there will be no barriers in the new society to impede the expression of the innate goodness of mankind. Each individual is to give precedence willingly to the needs of society and self-interest is no longer to be a prime motivating factor. The Marxists believe that in the long run the submerging of self-interest will not constitute a problem because of the identity of the interests of the individual and society. Consequently, their goal is two-fold and circular, to perfect social organization so that the members of society may be perfected gradually, and at the same time to transform people into higher social beings who will participate actively in the process of perfecting society. Major progress along these lines is to be achieved during the period of transition to communism. The Party Program states:

> "The party considers that the paramount task in the ideological field in the present period is to educate all working people in the spirit of ideological integrity and devotion to communism, and to cultivate in them a communist attitude to labor and the social economy; to eliminate completely the survivals of bourgeois views and morals; to ensure the all-round harmonious development of the individual; and to create a truly rich spiritual culture."[44]

The party has at its command a large and diverse number of techniques which it uses in its attempt to change human nature. Among the most important of its assets are its control over the social, economic and legal structure of society, its direction of the educational system, its monopoly over all media of communication, its assumed right to stipulate what is acceptable or unacceptable behavior and its control over the dispensation of rewards and punishments. It is probable that the party has an absolutistic type of control over more variables which affect human behavior than any other leadership group has ever had in the history of mankind. However, in its messianic task, the party faces a number of impediments and perhaps impenetrable barriers: the basic motives and characteristics of human nature may not prove to be malleable; tradition, though not unchangeable, changes slowly; human perfection presumably requires perfection of social organization which in turn depends on people; even if human nature is malleable, the party may not invariably select the techniques necessary to bring about the changes it wants; its manipulations may produce either no or minimal changes, or entirely unintended and unwanted changes; the restrictive aspects of the party's policy and the emphasis on conformity may prohibit the development of some of the sought-after characteristics. Whatever the outcome of the party's program to change human nature, it constitutes an extraordinarily fascinating experiment of unprecedented complexity, and it is regretable that few, if any, of the current observers, participants and experimenters will live long enough to evaluate even the preliminary results. However, consideration of the initial methodology and speculation about its possible effects is not precluded.

The most pervasive of the educational tasks which the party has assumed during the transitional period is the fullest development of "communist consciousness." All currently available techniques are to be directed toward the accomplishment of this goal. Naturally, much emphasis is placed upon ideological indoctrination. The people are not only to know about and to understand Marxism-Leninism; they are to believe in it, to live by it and to strive for the complete fulfillment of the Marxist-Leninist program. In order to ensure that the ideology will be fully assimilated by the masses, propaganda is to be designed to explain the theory, to make it personally meaningful and to show the people how to apply it, i.e. propaganda is to be "connected with life—with the practical work of building communism." Education for communism is not to be left only to the party, the school and the family, but is to be the responsibility of all. Every work and residential collective, court, trade union, scholar, artist and scientist, in short, every group and individual is expected to be a propagandist, to strive to conform to the wishes of the party and to ensure that all members of society conform. According to the Party Program, "Communist ideas and communist deeds should blend organically in the behavior of every person and in the activities of all collectives and organizations."[45]

One of the most important facets of the desired communist morality is a universal love for work and a willingness to work to the best of one's ability, not because of the differential material and prestige rewards that are provided for differential accomplishments, but because of "moral stimuli," the desire to contribute to society. From a non-communist standpoint, it seems likely that a complete transformation in this direction is improbable. If no one has to be concerned about providing the material necessities for himself and his family, saving for the future or against unexpected catastrophies, financing the education of his children, paying medical bills, or indulging in conspicuous consumption, will all the people, or even a majority of them, work to the utmost of their abilities for the benefit of society when each one might assume that if he, and perhaps, even a few others took life a little easier, society would still be able to provide him with the good things of life? In other words, can interest in the collective welfare assume the same motivating role as self-interest has in other societies? Communists counter doubts by saying that moral stimuli will have completely superseded material incentives for work, and that the individual will have fully assimilated the principle that what is good for the collective is good for himself, since individual and collective interests will coincide. Moreover, they point out that under communism such "bourgeois" forms of satisfaction and sources of prestige as conspicuous consumption will be completely eliminated; the person who will be highly respected and admired will not be the socialite, the prosperous financier, or the person who lives in the most impressive house, but rather the person who contributes most to society; admiration is to be accorded for accomplishments commensurate with abilities, and social group and affluence are to cease to be relevant since all will be equal in these respects. Incidentally, though the Soviet leaders are attempting to create a society of equality, they concede that all people are not created equal in terms of strength and talents. Their position is that he who has more strength or talent is obligated to contribute more, though all are to have equal rights with respect to distribution. Herein, perhaps, lies another paradox: is it not likely that the talented individual whose accomplishments are high will be accorded more prestige than the person of average or below average talent who may also work to the utmost of his ability? In theory all are to be honored equally if each contributes fully within the limits of his capabilities. Anyone who manifests signs of laziness or negligence is to be brought into line through social ostracism.

As society draws nearer to communism, more people are to receive secondary and higher education, and the highly-educated populace with ample time for self-development is to effect a new cultural revolution in which millions will contribute to scientific and artistic developments and in various social and governmental spheres. Higher educational levels with polytechnical emphasis are to assist in the "solution of a cardinal social problem, namely, the elimination of substantial social distinctions between mental and physical labor."[46] All people are to have increasing opportunities to widen their horizons, to develop their talents, and to become physically strong and morally pure. Gradually, as the other prerequisites for communism are attained, the Soviet people are to develop a universal code of ethics based on "devotion to Communism and irreconcilability toward its enemies, awareness of public duty, active work for the good of society, voluntary observance of the basic norms of human behavior, comradely mutual assistance, truthfulness, and an intolerance of the violators of public order."[47] All "survivals of capitalism" such as greediness, egotism, rudeness, envy, laziness, dishonesty and religious piety are to be eliminated. Again, the complete elimination of these traits or attitudes seems to be an unrealistic goal. For example, after almost five decades during which the party has conducted an energetic campaign against religion, there are still millions of believers in the U.S.S.R.; the party can, of course, claim that the marked increase in the number of atheists indicates that substantial progress has been made toward "stamping out religion." Or consider envy: even in a society which practices distribution according to need, is it not likely that there might still be reason for one individual to envy another because of his greater innate ability or more handsome physique, his brighter or healthier children, his prettier or more congenial wife or even because society has accorded him more recognition for his accomplishments? The party leaders may perhaps believe that they will be able to handle manifestations of envy and other "non-communist" emotions and forms of behavior under the concept of mental illness since they do concede that under full communism there may be a few mentally ill people who deviate from the norms of society. Certainly the definition of mental illness does vary from one culture to another; for example, an anthropologist reported that in the Dobuan society the only individual who was considered to be mentally ill was also the only one who was not highly suspicious, did not fear evil spirits and was willing to help others.[48] Under full communism any person who puts self-interest before the interest of society, expresses religious beliefs, does not demonstrate the communist attitude toward labor or fails to conform to the moral code of communism in any other way may be considered mentally ill and may perhaps be required to undergo intensive treatment.

Whereas skepticism with reference to the ambitiousness of the party's program for modifying human nature is justified, it is, however, possible that a number of peripheral, but not necessarily insignificant, changes will occur in attitudes and behavior. According to the principle that man's consciousness is determined by his social existence, which has received considerable support by psychological and sociological research, substantial changes in social mores and behavior can be expected as a result of the ideological indoctrination and the formal economic and social changes which have been, or are to be, introduced. Moreover, these changes are likely to have a cumulative effect. This point would hardly need elaboration if it were not for the rather prevalent tendency for each social group to assume that its way of doing things is the normal and natural way, often without taking into account the extent to which its way is determined by tradition and by objective factors in the past and current situation. It is generally agreed that inhabitants of the northern and southern parts of the United States tend to have somewhat different mores, customs and attitudes as a result of a complex of rather subtle factors including tradition, past history and current social problems. If the relatively minor historical and objective differences between the north and south of the United States can produce differences in the behavior and attitudes of the people, then it is inconceivable that the much greater differences between the Western and Soviet social orders, including private versus public ownership of the means of production, should not produce substantial differences in the mores, customs and attitudes of the people. Obviously, what is possible, appropriate and goal-satisfying behavior under one set of objective circumstances may not be adequate under a very different set of circumstances; as the situation changes, so do the people who function in the situation. The "social consciousness" of the Soviet people is different from that of their ancestors and from that of people in Western societies, simply because they live in a social environment which is very different in certain crucial ways from that of Tsarist Russia and of Western nations.

The various objective and ideological measures introduced by the party including socialist ownership, emphasis on collectivity and conformity, intolerance for competing ideologies, the anti-religious campaign, the rule of terror, the drive to expand production, the educational and cultural programs, the social welfare measures, the participation of the public in the administration of justice, and the promises for a glorious future could not but have some effect on the attitudes, values and behavior of the people. Many of the changes may be of a very peripheral nature and the changes may not correspond with the intentions of the party leaders, but it is almost axiomatic that each major measure introduced by the party produces an associated attitudinal or behavior change. Therefore, it may be assumed that as the ideological, social, economic and legal structure of the Soviet social order diverges more markedly from that of Western social orders, the "social consciousness" of the Soviet people will become increasingly different from that of the members of Western societies.

Has the party had any success so far in its attempt to fashion the "new Soviet man?" In some areas a beginning may have been made. At least some Soviet citizens seem to be convinced of the superiority of socialism and of these many could probably be described as enthusiastic builders of communism. Social barriers, though not eliminated, have been broken down very considerably and the status of women has been improved markedly. Millions of people have involved themselves in education and cultural pursuits with apparent enthusiasm. Many people apparently give precedence to the collective interest, at least part of the time. These examples of partial success apply to only some of the people, and do not involve the basic changes which are required for the creation of the "new" man. Moreover, many of the types of behavior which the party leaders point to as signs of progress toward the perfection of man are far from unique to the Soviet social order; many members of other societies also work selflessly for a common cause, accord equal status to all people regardless of race, sex or social background, and engage themselves enthusiastically in educational, cultural and civic affairs. In many areas the party leaders can point to no evidence of progress. The Soviet Union still has criminals, loafers, wife-beaters, drunkards and other types of social deviants. The majority of people apparently still put self-interest first most of the time. It is likely that countless people would gladly exchange the opportunity to assist in the construction of communism for a few more tangible rewards in the present. Even the party leaders concede that the communist attitude toward labor is so poorly developed in the majority of Soviet citizens that there can be no thought of eliminating material incentives for work for decades to come. In short, although the party has had partial success in preparing some of the prerequisites for the changes which it desires, there is no tangible evidence to support the hypothesis that it will be able to mold human nature in accordance with its goals. However, neither the partial successes, nor the partial failures which are evident at this stage constitute a legitimate basis for predictions about the eventual outcome of the party's campaign to create the "new Soviet man." The factors which are to be the most decisive in effecting the changes have not yet been introduced. The potential effectiveness of factors which have been introduced may have been limited by the absence of other crucial factors and by the relatively short time since their introduction. At this stage predictions are hazardous. Intuition, common sense and knowledge of history all suggest that the hope to effect basic changes in human nature is the most utopian part of the communist program. Yet, the experience of science indicates that one is seldom justified in drawing conclusions about the results of an experiment before the experiment is concluded, particularly if one does not have exact knowledge about the form of the major variables, the circumstances under which they are to be introduced, and the order of their introduction.

THE POLITICAL ORGANIZATION OF SOCIETY

Party spokesmen say that during the period of building communism the party is confronted with "world-historic tasks in the political sphere" since "conditions are being prepared for the gradual transition in the future to stateless organization of society, to communist public self-government."[49] Marxism-Leninism teaches that under communism the state will wither away and that the functions of public administration will lose their political character and will turn into management of society's affairs directly by the people. The doctrine of the withering away of the state did not pose a very serious problem for the party leadership during the initial four decades of party rule, because its implementation in practice was temporally remote. Lenin had emphasized that it would be impossible to define the exact moment of the future withering away of the state, especially since the process would necessarily be a lengthy one. Stalin decreed that a strong state was indispensable as long as internal enemies existed causing an inevitable intensification of class struggle during the advance toward socialism, and as long as hostile external forces encircled the solitary socialist state. Khrushchev, however, had to deal somewhat more concretely with the potential prospects of the withering away of the state, in view of the claim that class struggle has been eliminated, a "socialist commonwealth" has been established, and the period of full scale communist construction has begun.

Khrushchev's treatment of this subject was justifiably cautious. He pointed out that "one cannot over-simplify and conceive of the process of the withering away of the state as something like the turning of leaves in autumn when the branches are left bare as the leaves fall."[50] Under Khrushchev's leadership the party concluded that during "the entire stage of the transition from socialism to Communism the state is not only to be retained but strengthened" and that concurrently, socialist democracy is to be extended and perfected and the entire society is to assume increased responsibility for public self-government.[51] The Party Program states:

> "The state as an organization of the entire people will survive until the complete victory of communism. Expressing the will of the people, it must organize the building up of the material and technical basis of communism, and the transformation of socialist relations into communist relations, must exercise control over the measure of work and measure of consumption, promote the people's welfare, protect the rights and freedoms of Soviet citizens, socialist law and order and socialist property, instill in the people conscious discipline and a communist attitude to labor, guarantee the defense and security of the country, promote fraternal cooperation with the socialist countries, uphold world peace, and maintain normal relations with all countries."[52]

A stronger state is thus considered indispensable for preparing the social and economic base for communism, for extending socialist democracy, and for molding the new man for a self-governing society. And even after communism is established fully in one country or in a bloc of countries, the state is to retain in full force its defense functions as long as the danger of aggression from other countries exists. However, the party authorities point out that the strengthening of the state

> ". . . does not mean that in this entire stage the state remains unchanged. . . . The historical stage has now begun in which democracy is being developed to the fullest and the need for coercion is diminishing more and more and will gradually disappear. The Communist Party is carrying out a whole system of measures aimed at the further comprehensive development of socialist democracy."[53]

These measures fall into three major categories: first, expanding the role of the Soviets and increasing the participation of the masses in their work; second, transfer of many of the functions performed by government agencies to public organizations; and third, and perhaps most important, training the people and modifying their social consciousness so that they will be competent to administer the affairs of society and so that no form of state coercion will be necessary.

The Party Program specifies a number of ways, some of which have already been introduced formally, through which the operation of democratic principles in state organs is to be improved. The Soviets are to operate more and more like social organizations with the masses participating extensively and directly in their work. The people are to involve themselves more actively in the selection of the most suitable candidates for the Soviets; there is to be a systematic renewal of membership in the Soviets and their leading bodies so that fresh millions of people may learn to govern the state. Soviets and deputies are to be held strictly accountable to their constituents who are to exercise the right to advise, criticize and recall. The standing committees of the Soviets are to exercise extensive control over the administrative and executive branches of the state apparatus (ministries, departments, Economic Councils, etc.). The local Soviets are to have increased control over all questions of local significance. The Soviet government apparatus is to be simple, inexpensive, efficient, and free of bureaucracy, formalism and red tape. The establishment of public control bodies is to be used as an effective means to draw large sections of the people into the management of state affairs, to ensure the strict observance of legality, and as a technique to perfect the governmental apparatus, to eradicate bureaucracy and to realize promptly the proposals of the people. Gradually all leading officials of state bodies are to be elected and held accountable to the electorate. Broad democracy is to be combined with strict observance of comradely discipline. The transition to communism is to be characterized by the fullest extension of the personal freedom and rights of Soviet citizens and by the further promotion of socialist law and order. Finally, according to the Program, the whole system of government and social organizations is to educate the people in a spirit of voluntary and conscientious fulfillment of their duties and to lead to a natural fusion of rights and duties to form single standards of communist behavior.

Concurrent with the proposed expanded role of the Soviets and the increased participation of the masses in their work, many of the functions performed by government agencies are to pass gradually to public organizations. All social and public organizations, including the trade unions, Y.C.L., cooperatives, scientific, professional, artistic, and athletic associations, are to strive to "promote labor emulation in every possible way, to encourage Communist forms of labor, to stimulate the activity of working people in building a Communist society, to work for the improvement of the living conditions of the people and the satisfaction of their growing spiritual requirements."[54] The Party Program suggests that:

> "Mass organizations should be given a greater part in managing cultural, health and social insurance institutions; within the next few years they should be entrusted with the management of theatres and concert halls, clubs, libraries and other state-controlled cultural-education establishments; they should be encouraged to play a greater part in promoting law and order, particularly through the people's volunteer squads and comradely courts."[55]

Khrushchev pointed out that the transfer of the functions of state agencies to public organizations requires that the people should be prepared adequately for the assumption of greater responsibilities.[56] The Party Program also suggests that social organizations should be given the right to take legislative initiative, all important draft legislation should be presented for public discussion, and the most important draft laws should be put to a nation-wide referendum. Thus, according to official statements, as socialist statehood develops, it "will gradually become *communist self-government,* which will embrace the Soviets, trade-unions, cooperatives and other mass organizations of the people."[57]

The Party Program points out that "communist society will be a highly organized community of working men" and that "public functions similar to those performed by the state today will be retained under communism."[58] However, the "character of the functions and the way in which they are carried out" are to change, in that instead of government organs there will be organs of public self-government in charge of planning, accounting, economic management and cultural advancement.[59] Moreover, as society approaches the "higher stage of perfection" the need for compulsion is to be eliminated gradually because "universally recognized rules of the communist way of life will be established whose observance will become an organic need and habit with everyone."[60]

Soviet theoreticians are faced with what would appear to be two related theoretical contradictions: first, between the eventual disappearance of the state and its immediate strengthening; and second, between the principle of the withering away of the state with the concurrent extension of public administration and the principle that under communism society will be highly organized. Khrushchev, however, resolved these "non-antagonistic" contradictions by substituting the ruling party for the state. As public organizations assume more of the functions traditionally assigned to the state, control by the party over public organizations is to become more complete. Soviet authors comment:

> "It is not difficult to see that the Party's guidance . . . decides the success of the matter, and the farther we go the more it should be strengthened. . . . The policy of public participation expressed in all spheres of our life . . . provides the basis for a further growth of the role of the Party. Indeed, who except the Communist Party can unite and coordinate the multifaceted activity of the entire ramified system of public organizations? The Party is the highest form of public organization, and only it can give and does give correct political direction to the work of all other organizations. In contrast to all other organizations, the Party is not bound by any professional, departmental or local interests . . . and it always proceeds from public interests. The processes now taking place—the growth of the public principle, the narrowing of the sphere of coercion and the corresponding reduction in the state apparatus, and the transfer of a number of administrative functions to public organizations—are leading to a gradual disappearance of the socialist state system. The Communist Party is able to direct these complex processes in the necessary channel because it is armed with a scientific, Marxist-Leninist understanding of the course and perspectives of our development. . . ."[61]

Thus, the state is to wither away as the people are increasingly prepared to participate in public forms of self-government by administering society through their public organizations. But the control of these organizations by the party is to be complete. Therefore, the major change is not to be the transfer of authority from the state to the public organizations, but rather a change in the organizations through which the party exerts its control. In the past, the party has controlled society via its control over the state organs which held the formal reigns of power; in the future, it is to control society via its control over the public organizations. The fact that the locus of power is not to change, does not, however, mean that no significant changes are intended. The two most important projected changes are increased participation by the masses in the administration of society, under the guidance and control of the party; and the substitution of persuasion for coercion as a control technique. Under communism the methods of persuasion are to become the sole regulator of relations among people; according to Soviet dogma:

> "It is precisely the Party which commands enormous prestige and relies in all its work on the method of persuasion, that can ensure the development and effectiveness of public opinion in the struggle against the survivals of the old, against various anti-social crimes, against all that impedes our progress. It is precisely the Party that is able, on the one hand to eliminate manifestations of conservatism and attempts to impede the development of the public principle, and on the other, to prevent the underestimation of measures of state coercion."[62]

The authors might have added that it is precisely the party which knows what is best for society, and will continue to use whatever measures are necessary, though the method of persuasion is preferred, to maintain its complete control over society while it attempts to shape society to fit the mold which it has designed.

The Khrushchev principle of the gradual substitution of the party for the state is extraordinarily convenient for a number of reasons. It meets the demands of an ideology which forecasts continuing change in the social order as society progresses toward communism. It allows for the strengthening of the state in preparation for its eventual disappearance. It permits the party leaders even now to point to some beginnings of the withering away of the state through the transfer of some state functions to public organizations. It paves the way for the gradual elimination of the duality of party-state guidance of society in favor of increasingly monistic rule by the party. And most important, it preserves the party leadership's monopoly of power. Finally, it allows the party time without limit to work toward the stateless society, in that the state is to maintain some of its functions even after full communism is established, and as long as imperialism exists. There appears to be no conceivable point of time in the future at which critics could claim that the communist program has failed on the basis of the continued existence of the state, because the party leaders can extend ad infinitum the period of transition to a stateless society. However, whether there is or is not a partial withering away of the state, there is no question whatsoever about the withering away of the party. The party's strength and its monistic control over society is to increase steadily, and the promised democracy is to consist of rule by the party over a populace which is expected to agree with and participate actively in carrying out the party program.

The Future Communist Society

Soviet scholars point out that since the "birth" of communism "is a matter of the not very distant future . . . the question as to what communism is has become of great practical interest for millions of working people. They want to know, and should know, what kind of society will arise as a result of their efforts, their day to day endeavors—big and small, heroic and prosaic."[63] Soviet people, and people of other nations as well, would no doubt like to examine the blueprint of the Soviet leaders for the new communist society. The blueprint, however, proves to be disappointingly vague, fuzzy and sketchy, perhaps because the Soviet leaders themselves, though they may be able to visualize the short run tactics required to bring them closer to an ultimate goal, have not been able to perceive clearly many of the details of the final goal toward which they are striving. Perhaps at this stage in the development of society Soviet leaders may feel that it is unwise to bind themselves to specific details of a plan which would surely be subject to modification in the course of unfolding events; perhaps also, despite their overt optimism and many promises, they may not actually believe that the stage of full communism will ever be achieved.

Soviet literature abounds with eulogies about the glory of the future communist society, and many general statements have been made in the form of Marxist platitudes about the principles which will operate in the future. There has been wide discussion in the Soviet press about specific problems such as techniques of distribution, the communist attitude to labor, and the fate of personal property, but the tentative solutions offered to these problems have been based on the assumption that the "new Soviet man" with all the required qualities will emerge. Since even Soviet leaders themselves admit that they foresee long-range problems in the creation of the "new Soviet man," the proposed solutions are based on a high element of uncertainty. All Soviet authors affirm that the future communist society is to be a "glorious" society of abundance and harmony; the plans for the materialization of abundance are presented but the details of the organization and functioning of the glorious and harmonious society are, in the main, left to the imagination of the reader and the ingenuity of another generation of Soviet leaders and scholars.

The following paragraphs summarize a description of the future communist society which was prepared by a group of Soviet scholars, party officials and publicists under the leadership of the late O. W. Kuusinen, member of the Presidium of the Central Committee of the C.P.S.U. and old-time Bolshevik.[64] The summary of their presentation is included more as a demonstration of the superficial, descriptive nature of Soviet analyses of the projected social order than for its positive informative value. Instead of analyzing how the new society is to function, these theoreticians, and other Soviet authorities, tend to do little more than to describe the communist society in general terms and to add a generous dose of propaganda. Their presentation is essentially devoid of evidence of a serious attempt to come to grips with the basic dynamics, the *modus operandi* of the projected social order.

According to Kuusinen and his colleagues:

> "Communism is a society that puts an end to want and poverty for once and for all, assuring the well-being of all its citizens. The working man's age-old dream of abundance comes true under communism. The way to this is opened by the socialist remaking of society, which puts an end to private ownership of the means of production, to the exploitation of man by man and the unjust social order.
> ". . . the successes of socialist science, technology and the organization of production will . . . enable all members of society to have an abundance of healthy, tasty and varied food . . . convenient and spacious homes, high-quality beautiful clothes, diverse household articles which make daily life more convenient and beautiful, . . . convenient means of transport and articles needed for cultural recreation (books, wireless and TV sets, musical instruments, athletic gear), and many other things. . . .
> "Under communism . . . human labor remains the sole source of all values. 'Communism will bring man not a lordly life in which laziness and idleness prevail, but a life of labor, an industrious, cultured and interesting life!' (N. S. Khrushchev). Hence, the slogan 'from each according to his abilities' will remain the immutable principle of the communist system. . . . Communism, however, introduces deep changes into the content of the formula. . . . In socialist society material stimuli (payment according to work), operating in combination with moral stimuli, are of decisive significance. Under communism, all members of society will work, prompted solely by moral stimuli, a high sense of consciousness. In other words, this will be labor without payment, and the satisfaction without payment of all the needs of workers. . . . Under communism human labor will be entirely freed from everything that made it an onerous burden for a thousand years. It will not only be free, but also genuinely creative. . . . An approximate picture of what labor will be like under communism . . . [is] as follows: each worker . . . performs functions for which a trained engineer is required in present-day production; people work 20-25 hours a week (i.e. approximately 4-5 hours a day) and, in time, even less; each person can choose an occupation in conformity with his or her inclinations and abilities and can change it at will; all talents and abilities inherent in people are fully developed . . . ; while working, a man does not have to think about his livelihood, or how much he will get for his labor, because society has assumed all responsibility for satisfying his requirements; labor enjoys the highest respect in society and becomes in the eyes of all the chief measure of a man's worth.
> "Communism introduces a mode of distribution of material and spiritual benefits which is based on the principle of "to each according to his needs"

. . . each man, irrespective of his position, of the quantity and quality of labor he can give to society, receives from society gratis everything he needs. . . . Together with the disappearance of the need to control the amount of labor and consumption, together with the abolition of money and the disappearance of commodity-money relations, the very nature of the connections between man and society are radically changed. These connections are completely freed from selfish considerations, from everything introduced in them by quest for an income, for material gain. The opportunity to obtain at any time gratis from the public stocks everything needed for a cultured and carefree life will have a wholesome effect on man's mind, which will no longer be weighted down with concern for the morrow. In the new psychology and the new ethics there will be no room for thought of income and private property. . . . Man, at long last, will receive the opportunity to dedicate himself to lofty interests, among which social interests will take a foremost place."[65]

The theorists add that whereas distribution according to need meets the humanitarian dictates of Marxism it is also a "direct economic necessity" in that it creates the best conditions for the further development of society's main productive force, the working man, and "for the flowering of all his abilities." "This," they say, "will benefit both the individual and society in equal measure." They reject as "slander to the citizens of the future communist society" such "absurd suppositions" as the possibility that attempts to engage in conspicuous consumption will constitute a problem. It is conceded that "a certain amount of time will be needed to develop in all citizens a reasonable attitude toward consumption" and that "the communist system naturally cannot undertake to satisfy all whims and caprices." Should there be people who would make "unjustifiably high claims" they would be placed "in a ridiculous light before public opinion." The theorists predict that the people will adjust with relative ease "to communist forms of consumption since it does not require of them any artificial self-restriction or asceticism." They say that from the very beginning, communist society will be sufficiently rich "to satisfy generously" the needs of all citizens for the prime necessities of life and "to place at their disposal everything that an intelligent and cultured person needs for a full and happy life." Under communism the "possession of things and the level of consumption" will not constitute a "criteria of man's position in society," and things will be restored to "their real purpose: to ease and beautify man's life." An attempt is to be made "to satisfy the highest requirements of all the people," but the rationality of the system is to prohibit the wastage of human labor and public wealth on the production of consumption items which serve a senseless or unworthy purpose.

They assert that "Communism . . . the most just social system . . . will fully realize the principles of equality and freedom, ensure the development of the human personality and turn society into a harmonious association, a commonwealth of men of labor." The "historic task" of establishing *"universal actual equality of people,"* in contradistinction to mere formal equality, is to be "fully accomplished by communism." They point out that "communist equality presupposes the eradication of not all distinctions between people but only of such distinctions and such conditions as would give rise to a difference in the social position of people." It is stressed that "the disappearance of these distinctions in no way signifies a leveling of individualities. . . . Communism is not a barrack inhabited by persons who lack individuality." On the contrary, "the supreme goal of communism is to ensure *full freedom of development of the human personality,* to create conditions for the boundless development of the individual. . . ."

Communism is to bring with it the "final triumph of *human freedom,*" since it "ensures the full fusion of the social and economic interests of all members of society . . . the grounds for any measures of coercion disappear. The relations of domination and subordination are finally replaced by free cooperation"; there is to be "no need for the state" and "the need for legal regimentation" is to "wither away." This is to be possible because:

> "For cultured people imbued with lofty ideas and high moral standards, as people will be under communism, the observance of the norms of human behavior in the community becomes a habit, a second nature. . . . Man . . . in everything will act freely in accordance with his convictions and his moral duty."

The theorists point out that "the freedom which communism gives man" does not presuppose a society that lacks organization. Some form of organization will be necessary "for social production to function normally and develop, for culture and civilization to advance, ensuring all people well-being, and a free and happy life." When the state withers away, instead of anarchy, there is to be a system of public self-government. The people are to display a high degree of civic responsibility and a deep interest in the public affairs. Disputes may arise over the conduct of society's affairs, but since differences of opinion will not be based on "insoluble contradictions," the divergencies will be resolved "in conditions of a deep-seated community of interests, aims and world outlook." They conclude that:

> "All these features of communist public self-administration will be wholly in accord with the nature of the relations between people in the future society, relations of cooperation, brotherhood and fellowship. The communist man is not an egotist, not an individualist; he will be distinguished by conscious collectivism and deep concern for the common good. The main-spring of the morality of this man is devotion to the collective, readiness and ability sacredly to observe the public interests. It is these qualities of the free and equal citizens of the new society that will make communism a highly organized and harmonious community of people, real masters of creative communist labor."

The principles of communism are to extend to relations between states. Actual equality, mutuality of interest, socialist internationalism and lofty moral principles are to rule out forever the possibility of war. Communism is to "impart a new, lofty meaning to the very concept of 'mankind,' turning the human race which for thousands of years was torn asunder by discord, quarrels, conflicts and wars, into one world-wide commonwealth." No longer will "the life of each man individually and the life of society as a whole" be shaped by "alien forces, natural and social, . . . beyond man's control." In addition to enabling people to produce in abundance everything necessary for their life, the victory of communism is to "free society from all manifestations of inhumanity: wars, ruthless struggles within society and injustice, ignorance, crime and vice. Violence and self-interest, hypocrisy and egoism, perfidy and vainglory, will vanish forever from relations between people and between nations."

In its first stages the communist system is to realize "the most cherished aspiration of mankind, its dream of general sufficiency and abundance, freedom and equality, peace, brotherhood and cooperation of people." This accomplishment, however, is to be only a beginning:

> "The victory of communism does not mean a halt in its historical development: communist society will change and improve continuously. . . . The advance to the shining heights of communist civilization will always engender in people unusual power of will and intellect, creative impulses, courage, and life-giving energy."

This, then, is the essence of the Soviet blueprint for the structure, operation and development of the future communist society.

Quo Vadis?

A number of related questions emerge from Soviet descriptions of the society toward which they are purportedly aspiring. Of these, the most important question of all concerns the feasibility of the goal of establishing a communist society. Can the basic prerequisites for the establishment of a communist society be met? Can people be remolded to such an extent that a communist society could function? Can the leadership and the party modify their mode of operation sufficiently so that they themselves will not constitute a barrier which impedes progress toward the goals which they have elaborated? Are the Soviet leaders really trying to lead the people to communism, or is what they are aspiring toward only a more advanced form of socialism? What is the most probable course of development of the social order within the U.S.S.R.?

The thesis that the goal of establishing communism is unrealistic, and that Soviet society will move toward a more advanced form of socialism rather than full communism, is supported by logical considerations, as well as by an examination of the changes which are likely and possible during the next few years and decades. A multitude of factors converge to lend credence to the thesis of the improbability of the achievement of communism. The absolute goals for the organization and operation of society, and the characteristics of the individuals who will live in the society, are so high that it will be virtually impossible to attain them. Numerous barriers are operating, and will continue to operate, against materialization of the basic prerequisites for the transition from the stage of socialism to the stage of communism. Full communism requires, among other things, a society composed of industrious, unselfish, non-individualistic, non-egotistic, highly cultured, civic-minded people who perceive their interests to be in harmony with each other and with society as a whole, the elimination of social distinctions, economic abundance, the withering away of the state, the establishment of a perfect direct democracy and the elimination of nationalism and conflict of interests between states. Each individual is to work for the good of society with no thought of personal gain or aggrandizement, and society is in return to meet his highest needs. Soviet officials describe the communist society as a perfection of harmony, a utopia on earth, characterized by true freedom, and universal happiness. All sources of personal frustration are to be removed. Apparently, the only negative emotions which should be experienced at any time are grief over the death of a loved one, fear and frustration that derive from illness and physical disabilities and regret that one should eventually be required to leave the earthly paradise.

Some of the prerequisites for full communism may well be attained. The goal of economic abundance is not unrealistic. As the Soviet economy expands, it is most likely that increasing attention will be devoted to satisfying the material needs of the people. Within a relatively short time all Soviet people may be able to eat well, dress well, live in comfortable and attractive apartments and have ample facilities to enjoy a considerable amount of leisure. The proportion of these benefits which are distributed on the basis of the principle of "to each according to his need," instead of "to each according to his work," may increase considerably. But economic abundance is merely a prerequisite for rather than the earmark of communism. Economic abundance and distribution of a number of benefits on the basis of need can be attained under a number of social orders, including Soviet-style socialism, other brands of socialism and by social orders which do not use the label socialism. Full adherence to the principle of "from each according to his ability, to each according to his need" would be an earmark of communism, but there are many reasons to suggest that no attempt will be made to adhere fully to this principle, and that if such an attempt were made, the resulting disruption in the social order would lead to a retraction.

Soviet officials have announced that for a long time distribution will be based on both work and need. In all probability distribution according to need will increase substantially; the state may well assume major responsibility for the care of all the sick, disabled, feebleminded, and elderly people, provide housing and public transportation free of charge, arrange for free meals at work and at schools, increase the number of free recreational and cultural facilities, and extend welfare benefits in a number of other ways. Although such measures will be presented as evidence of progress toward communism, the mode of distribution will be socialistic, in contradistinction to communistic, until all distribution is based on need rather than work.

The Soviet leaders recognize that until the "new Soviet man" emerges fully, a material incentive will be indispensable to maintain a high level of economic productivity. Economic abundance is an absolute requirement for the establishment of the communist society, and until all or at least the majority of the people have developed the "communist attitude toward labor" either payment in accordance with work or coercion will be necessary to maintain and extend the productivity of labor. It is most unlikely that the Soviet leaders would make the blunder of substituting coercion for material incentives for work, since the former would be a less efficient technique and would constitute a step backward from the established goals. However, the communist attitude toward work is not expected to develop fully until the "new Soviet man" emerges. In short, even the architects of the communist society do not anticipate that material incentives for work can be dispensed with before many other changes, which are remote in time, have occurred. Most non-communists are of the opinion, and not without reason, that distribution completely on the basis of need will remain unrealistic. The vagueness of the analysis of the problems of communist distribution by Soviet theoreticians suggests that perhaps Soviet experts, too, are, if not convinced, at least doubtful that the communist dream can be translated into reality.

No attempt has been made to deal theoretically with the numerous problems that would arise if material incentives for work were to be discontinued. The apparent assumption is that problems would not arise if society is inhabited by the "new Soviet man" who has the "communist attitude toward work." However, even if one were to assume that people did change fundamentally in accordance with the plans of their leaders, would the economy function at its optimum level if neither material incentives nor coercion were used? For example, how would the labor force be distributed most efficiently in relation to the needs of the economy? What would happen if a disproportionate number of people felt strongly that they could make their maximum contribution to society by working in the Crimea where the climate tends to be pleasant, and at the same time, almost no one wanted to work in northern Siberia? Even if automation eliminates the most arduous and unpleasant features of most types of work, some types of work may still appeal to fewer people than are required, and other types of work may attract more people than are necessary for the most efficient functioning of the economy. Under socialism, such problems are solved more or less to the satisfaction of the majority of people, and to the benefit of the economy, through the use of differential material incentives. What would happen under communism? It is a foregone conclusion that the needs of the economy will be given priority over the personal preferences of the individual; there will have to be some technique for rationing the pleasant jobs and directing labor to the unpleasant ones. Presumably the communard is to be so devoted to serving the interests of society that he will gladly accept a position as a hog-raiser in Siberia and will display a communist attitude toward labor on this job, in spite of a strong preference to function as a musician in the Sochi area where he has close family and cultural ties. In reality, if material incentives to work were abolished, the communard would probably work with a reasonable degree of competence at an assigned job but might, at the same time, resent strongly assignment to a job low on his hierarchy of preferences if someone else, no more competent than he, is assigned to the preferred job. Under such circumstances, less than perfect harmony between the interests of the individual and society and between individuals would exist. In the less than perfectly harmonious society, the people might well experience such negative emotions as resentment, envy, jealousy, and frustration; and people who experience such emotions do not meet the basic criteria for the "new Soviet man." In short, the abolition of material incentives for work would require that people be assigned to jobs on the basis of the needs of the economy. Since it would not be feasible to give every individual the job which he would most prefer, and the mitigating effect of material incentives would be removed, society would not be perfectly harmonious. Therefore, the members of society could not attain the perfection required of the "new Soviet man." All kinds of problems which the Soviet leaders have not discussed, at least in public, would arise. However, problems of this nature may never have to be dealt with in their concrete form because the Soviet leaders most likely will never see fit to dispense entirely with distribution according to work. Rather, distribution according to need is likely to be extended, but not to the extent that it replaces distribution according to work entirely. As long as distribution is, in part, based on work, certain inequalities will exist and the criteria for full communism cannot be met. Distribution entirely on the basis of need would create new disharmonies which would likewise violate the basic presuppositions of communism. Thus, regardless of whether the Soviet leaders decide to retain distribution according to work, or whether they rely entirely on distribution according to need, less than the full perfection of communism will be achieved. It is most probable that the lesser of the two evils, distribution partially on the basis of work, will be chosen, in which case Soviet society will remain in the stage of socialism rather than communism.

One of the basic prerequisites for the establishment of full communism in the U.S.S.R. is the march of all nations of the world toward communism and the development of world-wide internationalism. The assumption of the Soviet leaders has been that the U.S.S.R. will demonstrate its economic superiority to the most advanced Western nations by 1980, or at least in a relatively few decades, and that this accomplishment will serve as the stimulus for the working people all over the world to strive toward socialism. If the U.S.S.R. were able to demonstrate economic superiority, which is far from a foregone conclusion, it would not be surprising if a number of the less developed countries were to move in the direction of the Soviet social order. However, regardless of how great the economic accomplishments of the U.S.S.R., the probability that the majority of the people in any of the more advanced nations would want to emulate the Soviet Union is very small. Innumerable factors augur against the fulfillment of the Soviet prediction that the working people of the advanced industrial nations will choose in favor of communism. Among these factors are powerful and widespread anti-communist sentiments which are supported and built up by all the major sources of power and authority within each of the industrial nations; almost equally strong anti-Soviet sentiments which derive in part from conflict of interests with the U.S.S.R. in the international arena and great distaste for many of the past and present domestic policies of the Soviet regime; the power of each of the governments to prevent the development of an internal movement in favor of communism, and the deterrent of American military might; the distorted perception which the Soviet leaders have concerning the relative advantages of the two types of social orders to the working people; and strong nationalistic and religious sentiments among the majority of the peoples of the world. In short, it is extremely unlikely that the majority of the working people in the economically advanced nations will act in accordance with Moscow's plans for them simply because they believe that, in comparison to the Soviet system, other social systems are vastly superior in almost all crucial respects including the economic rights of the individual, political and religious freedom, freedom of speech and assembly, legal rights and personal privacy.

As long as the peoples of the advanced Western nations stand firmly opposed to the adoption of a Soviet-type social order and as long as the Soviet leaders pursue their policy of exporting communism, and the probability of a substantial change in either of these spheres is remote, sharp antagonisms will persist between the Soviet Union and the Western nations. As long as these antagonisms persist, the U.S.S.R. cannot dispense with its state and military machinery and, therefore, cannot meet the conditions for full communism. In fact, adherence to Marxist ideology seems to have forced the Soviet leaders into a circular and self-defeating course of action. Marx totally underestimated the power of nationalism and the potential of non-communist social orders to meet most of the needs of most of the people, and he was absolutely wrong when he predicted that proletarian revolutions would occur in the most advanced industrial nations. The ideology demands that the entire world must be communized, and this requires the Soviet Union to follow a policy which arouses extreme antagonism on the part of the peoples and the leaders of other nations. This antagonism serves as an effective deterrent against communist advances and, at the same time, makes it necessary for the U.S.S.R. to divert a large proportion of its resources to strengthen its military might at the expense of some of its goals for communist construction. Thus, the antagonism aroused by the Soviet attempt to communize the world offsets the psychological advantage of Soviet economic advances, and, at the same time, because it necessitates vast military expenditures, it impedes the very economic advances through which the Soviet Union hopes to demonstrate the superiority of its system. Moreover, the antagonism which is generated by the Soviet policy precludes Soviet progress toward the stateless society.

Another reason for predicting that the Soviet goals for full communism cannot be achieved centers around the problem of nationalism. According to the Marxist plan, national consciousness in all non-socialist countries is to be replaced by class consciousness, the working class is to effect the transition to socialism, classes are to be eliminated and class consciousness is to be replaced by goals for the solidarity of all mankind. The plan with respect to non-socialist countries is, as was indicated previously, highly unrealistic; moreover, even within the socialist countries, nationalistic aspirations and antagonisms remain strong and serve as a powerful deterrent to the establishment of the international solidarity which is a prerequisite for the attainment of full communism. Although Lenin predicted that national sentiments would be relatively resistant to change, he and his successors apparently underestimated their tenacity. The Soviet leaders claim that, within the Soviet state and the socialist camp, great progress has been made in the removal of national antagonisms. There is some evidence that the strong central Soviet government has been able to remove some of the basis for antagonism between the national groups of the U.S.S.R. and that at the very least it has effectively curbed expressions of national antagonisms. However, the party is indulging in exaggeration when it claims that it has "solved the problem of relations between nations, a most complicated problem that has troubled mankind for centuries and persists to this day in the capitalist world."[66] Neither nationalistic sentiments nor religious beliefs have been eliminated within the U.S.S.R. to the degree that the party anticipated and claims.

Even if application of the powerful techniques which the monolithic party machine has at its command were to eradicate nationalistic sentiments within the U.S.S.R., the problem of national aspirations and antagonisms within the socialist bloc and in the entire international arena would still constitute a barrier to the realization of the international goals of communism. It is well-known that many of the peoples of the socialist states of Eastern Europe are highly nationalistic, and that strong anti-Soviet sentiments are far from uncommon. The Sino-Soviet dispute is a glaring example of the lack of international solidarity within the socialist bloc, and of the propensity of the leaders of socialist states and fraternal parties to place national interest above the international goals of the communist movement. If even the Soviet leaders themselves, as the architects of the future communist society, are unable to substitute internationalism for nationalism, it is most unlikely that full international solidarity can be established among the masses. Less than complete harmony between states, and hence nationalism will be a reality as long as national states exist. Even if socialism were to be established in every state on earth, and the probability of such an event is infinitesimal, the blueprint for worldwide communism still allows for the retention of national boundaries. Thus state machinery would be necessary to govern international relations. But under full communism, the state is to wither away. Soviet leaders leave the solution to this paradox to future generations. Perhaps they have come to the wise conclusion that it would be foolish for them to waste their time speculating about how to handle a situation that will almost certainly never materialize. When they talk about the withering away of the state, they are referring to the very remote future. Their emphasis on remoteness seems to be fully justified.

Another prerequisite for the establishment of full communism is the development of a form of "communist public self-government" in which all public affairs are decided by the people, all of whom have an equal voice. The probability that this prerequisite will be met is also very small. There may, indeed, be a marked extension of democratic rights, as defined by Marxist-Leninist ideology, in the social and economic spheres and the people may participate more extensively, *under the leadership of the party,* in the administration of society. However, it is improbable that there will be any marked development of democratic rights in the political sphere.

Marxists have always maintained that rulers who wield enormous power are unwilling to relinquish or share that power voluntarily. The only exception to this rule, they say, is that the working class, which wields political power for the benefit of all the working people after a socialist revolution, has no interest in perpetuating the power after it has been used to establish a more perfect social order. Since it is purportedly the working class which has been governing the U.S.S.R. through its vanguard, the Communist Party, there is apparently to be no problem about transferring the power to all the people who, since the Bolshevik Revolution, have supposedly been undergoing training in preparation for full self-government. These notions are, of course, highly divorced from reality. The Soviet state has not been ruled by the working class any more than it has been ruled by the former aristocrats or by the clergy; it has been ruled by the self-selected party leadership which has not been responsible to the Soviet people, the working class or even to the party members. There is no evidence to suggest that the party elite will be any more willing to relinquish or share its power than any other ruling group has ever been.

In the Program of the Communist Party and the pronouncements of the party leaders there is no indication of any serious intention, even in the form of verbal promises, to transfer fundamental decision-making power to the people. The party leaders could not, for various ideological and practical reasons, consider the formation of an actual opposition party, which most non-Marxists consider to be essential for the operation of a democratic government; an opposition party would be deemed totally unnecessary in a classless society, and more than that, it would be regarded as a disruptive force, a traitorous, heretical clique. Party spokesmen have not, however, even discussed possible channels through which decision-making power could be transferred to the people within the confines of the one-party system. Progress toward materialization of the democratic tenets of Marxism-Leninism could be made if the party were to be transformed from an elitist organization (it now incorporates approximately 5 percent of the population) into a mass organization, which would incorporate the majority of the population, and if the party leaders would actually be elected by the party members. The party leaders, however, have typically opposed the formation of a mass-based party, and they cannot suggest that political democracy should be expanded through the election of party leaders because they insist, quite untruthfully, that even now the leaders are elected by the party members. If the party were a mass organization and if the party members were really to elect party officials and leaders, there could be a meaningful competition between candidates, party officials could be held responsible to the people since their reelection would depend on public support, and the people could participate meaningfully in decision-making. The fact that all candidates would have to espouse Marxist-Leninist goals for society, and could differ only with respect to proposed techniques for the accomplishment of these goals, would impose limitations on the decision-making power of the people if society were composed of various disharmonious elements, but this limitation would presumably be unimportant in the monolithic classless society toward which the Soviet people purportedly aspire. If other basic goals of the party were achieved, then all members of society would presumably embrace identical social goals, and decisions would concern the resolution of "non-antagonistic" differences of opinion concerning techniques to achieve these goals. Such an extension of political rights within the one-party system would be consistent with the democratic tenets of Marxist-Leninist ideology and could conceivably facilitate the achievement of other goals of the party for society.

However, no Soviet authority has suggested that the people are eventually to be allowed to select their leaders within the one-party system or that any other technique will be used to transfer decision-making power to the people. Under communist public self-government the people are to perform the administrative functions of government through their mass organizations and under the guidance of the party but the fundamental decisions will be made by the party leaders. Thus, political control over society will be retained by a party elite, who will be responsible for but will not be responsible to the people, and the democratic prerequisite for full communism will not be met.

These, then, are some of the reasons for predicting with almost complete confidence that Soviet society will not reach the stage of full communism. The Soviet people have been promised a prosperous, egalitarian, democratic communist society; instead, they will probably get a prosperous, non-egalitarian, authoritarian socialist society. It is, of course, impossible to predict with a high degree of confidence the future development of Soviet society because the whole trend of development could be modified by a major change in the international situation, a nuclear war, or several other factors, including a struggle for power among the top party leaders. If the chief contenders for supreme leadership of the party and the state were hopelessly deadlocked, and if one of them had fairly substantial support from the army, the police or the air force, it is conceivable that he could attempt to use force to gain dominance. If a civil war were to follow, the party could lose control over society; the leaders who would emerge from such a struggle would not necessarily be the leaders who initiated it, and they could decide to modify the organization of society drastically. Given that some such event of major significance does not intervene, the general outline and direction of movement of Soviet society within the next several decades is likely to be approximately as follows: unless the party disintegrates because of an internal struggle for power, its leaders will maintain an effective monopoly of control over society. Several factors make it likely that no segment of the population will attempt to wrest control from the party leaders: such an attempt would be doomed to failure unless it were led by top military officers because the unarmed populace would be helpless against the military might at the command of the regime; the party leaders have effective techniques to prevent the development of any form of organized resistance; the identification of the people with the regime is likely to increase as the economy matures and standards of living are raised. The masses will participate much more extensively than at present in the administration of society but decision-making power will be retained by the party leaders. The trend toward control by persuasion, or "social control" by public organizations which carry out the dictates of the party leaders, will be continued but the latent threat of coercion will be retained to ensure the effectiveness of the persuasive techniques.

It is probable that the Soviet Union will continue to make rapid economic advances and that as the economy matures its organization, and in fact, the organization of the entire society will become more rational and efficient. Living standards will be raised very appreciably and within two or three decades will be roughly equivalent to current living standards in the United States. The party will not find it expedient to dispense with material incentives for work and, therefore, there will not be equality of consumption. However, the distribution of an increased number of materials and services "according to need" will establish a basic minimum standard of living. Thus, although all members of society should be provided with the necessities of life, and most people should have more than the necessities, there will probably continue to be a few who, by virtue of their special contributions to society, will be able to afford luxuries which will not be available to the majority. Because of differential rates of remuneration and levels of consumption, society will remain stratified to a certain extent.

As the organization and operation of economic and social institutions become more efficient, the people should be relieved of many of the inconveniences and sources of frustration which currently characterize their everyday life. Considerable progress will probably be made toward the fulfillment of several of the socio-cultural goals: educational levels will be generally high; rural areas will be provided with amenities and cultural, educational, medical, and recreational facilities on a more or less equivalent basis with urban areas; the majority of the people will have convenient living quarters; the working day will be shortened and the people will probably have considerably more time for leisure, self-improvement and civic affairs. It is improbable that religious beliefs will be eliminated entirely within the foreseeable future, but the number of believers may well decrease with each succeeding generation. It is not unlikely that the various national groups within the U.S.S.R. will achieve actual equality of status and that internal national antagonisms will decrease markedly. The antagonism generated against the regime for various measures such as forced collectivization, the reign of terror, the anti-religious campaign and ideological restrictions will probably evaporate as one generation replaces another and as standards of living increase, inconveniences are removed and the socio-cultural goals of the regime are fulfilled. The party leaders will make skillful use of the reduction of antagonisms, and increased welfare measures and standards of living as a basis for encouraging the people to identify their own well-being with the preservation of the existing order.

Thus, it is predicted that the citizens of the future Soviet society will enjoy many economic and social advantages which are not available at present. However, their society will fall far short of the communist ideal in a number of significant ways: the "new Soviet man" will not emerge; perfect harmony between individuals, between individuals and society, and between societies will not be established; the communist attitude toward work will not prevail; equality of consumption will not be established, and, hence, perfect social equality cannot be materialized; political rights will be extremely limited. Neither man nor the organization of society will approach the ideal, and social distinctions, crime, greediness, envy and selfishness will not be eradicated. These predictions give rise to a number of related questions. Are the Soviet leaders sincere in their promises with respect to full communism, or are they aware of the impossibility of achieving the goal toward which they say they are leading their people? How will the Soviet leaders handle the non-delivery of the promised utopia? How will the Soviet people react if they are given a more advanced form of socialism instead of the promised communism?

Some of the more cynical observers of Soviet affairs have suggested that Soviet leaders have, from the very beginning, had no intention of ever attempting to introduce full communism, but have used the promise of a future utopia as a convenient device for manipulating the population into obeying more willingly the dictates of their political superiors. Such cynicism is probably not justified. What seems more likely is that the leaders of the C.P.S.U., from pre-revolutionary days until recently, entered into their revolutionary struggle with full messianic zeal and enthusiasm, complete with the belief that the ultimate goal of communism will eventually be achieved. During most of the history of the C.P.S.U. and the U.S.S.R., the leaders have been so overwhelmingly engaged in the solution of concrete problems of immediate consequence that there has been little time to study in detail the multitude of problems that would emerge if attempts were made to establish full communism. Long-range plans have been made, it is true, but these have been in the form of glittering generalities rather than carefully thought out details. For example, the Soviet leaders have necessarily been more preoccupied with the numerous problems associated with the establishment of the prerequisites for abundance than with the problems which might arise in the organization of society if distribution were based on need. Until it was reasonable to expect that abundance could be achieved in the foreseeable future, it was perhaps pointless to concentrate on problems of communist distribution. However, since it has been announced that society is now in the period of transition to communism, general statements about the glory of the communist society are no longer sufficient. If the assumption that society is undergoing a transition to communism is to be maintained, detailed plans for the operation and functioning of society under communism must be formulated.

During the last few years Soviet leaders and theoreticians have apparently devoted increasing attention to some of the many problems which would have to be solved if communism were to be a reality. Although no Soviet official has said so, there are suggestions that there is a dawning awareness that some of the problems are insoluble, and that there are certain other problems, such as the emergence of direct democracy versus continued control by the party leaders, which the leaders do not want to solve in accordance with the tenets of communist ideology. Official pronouncements to the effect that distribution according to work and according to need will be used simultaneously "for a long time to come," that the state will not wither away "for a long time to come," and that "the new Soviet man" will not emerge "for a long time to come" suggest that party leaders are beginning to realize that goals for the improvement of socialism are realistic, but that the goal of introducing full communism is not. If this is the case, the Soviet leaders are not necessarily, as yet, guilty of intentional deception. It is possible that they have, from the beginning, sincerely believed in the possibility of building a communist society, and that only now, as they begin to ponder over the concrete problems associated with the introduction of communism, are they becoming aware of the impossibility of achieving their goals. History is full of examples of societies, organizations and individuals who have exerted themselves for decades to achieve goals which became obviously unrealistic only after the initial problems were mastered.

Whether or not the past and present Soviet leaders have been sincere in their promise of communism, it seems likely that future Soviet leaders will have to deal in one way or another with the impossibility of materializing communist goals. One or a combination of several alternatives may be used. Marxist-Leninist ideology might be reinterpreted either to justify or to correspond with reality. Certainly there have been many precedents for the reinterpretation of the ideology. The transition to communism may be extended indefinitely, and increased welfare benefits and material prosperity may be pointed to as tangible evidence of progress toward communism. The announcement may even be made that communism has been achieved, and the presence of non-communist features such as distribution according to work, economic inequalities, authoritarianism and a populace which falls far short of the criteria for the "new Soviet man" may be ignored, glossed over or treated as minor imperfections which are to be rectified as the communist society moves to ever higher planes. It would, of course, be possible to deal with the failure to achieve communist goals in a straightforward, honest manner, by announcing that what has been or is to be achieved is a higher stage of socialism. Although such an announcement would constitute an ideological retreat, which would evoke the wrath of the Chinese and weaken the world communist movement, it is likely that it would not have a very disruptive effect on Soviet society if the people were provided with material abundance, and considerable personal freedom. In spite of all the propaganda, indoctrination, and training to make every Soviet citizen an "enthusiastic builder of communism," most Soviet citizens would probably be quite satisfied with peace, high standards of living, extensive welfare benefits, freedom from coercion, more free time, preferably increased political rights and other benefits which could be provided by a society which aspired to or called itself socialism in a higher form rather than communism. If international peace can be maintained, it seems likely that Soviet society will indeed progress to a more advanced form of socialism, and that Soviet citizens will enjoy increasing socio-economic benefits which will, if not compensate for, at least offset their relative lack of political fredom. The transition to full communism will, however, continue to be a utopian dream.

REFERENCES

1 Friedrich Engels, *Principles of Communism,* quotation from a translation by Paul M. Sweezy, *Monthly Review,* Pamphlet Series, No. 4, (New York: 1952), p. 13.

2 Lenin, *Works,* Vol. 24, *op. cit.,* p. 62.

3 N. S. Khrushchev, "New Stages in Communist Construction and Some Problems of Marxist-Leninist Theory," *Pravda,* Jan. 28, 1959, pp. 2-10. (C.D.S.P., Vol. XII, No. 5, pp. 13-19)

4 V. I. Lenin, *Selected Works,* Vol. 2, (Moscow: Foreign Languages Publishing House), p. 853.

5 Stalin, *Problems of Leninism, op. cit.,* p. 548.

6 *Target Figures for the Economic Development of the U.S.S.R. from 1959 to 1965,* (London: Soviet Booklet No. 49), May, 1959, p. 6.

7 Khrushchev, "New Stages in Communist Construction and Some Problems of Marxist-Leninist Theory," *op. cit.,* pp. 2-10.

8 *Fundamentals of Marxism-Leninism, op. cit.,* p. 789.

9 *Ibid.*

10 Khrushchev, "New Stages in Communist Construction and Some Problems of Marxist-Leninist Theory," *op. cit.,* pp. 2-10.

11 Engels, *Principles of Communism, op. cit.,* p. 13.

12 N. S. Khrushchev, "Accelerated Development of the Chemical Industry Is a Major Condition for an Upsurge of Agricultural Production and a Rise in the People's Well-Being," *Pravda,* Dec. 10, 1963. (C.D.S.P., Vol. XV, No. 48, pp. 4-24)

13 *Fundamentals of Marxism-Leninism, op. cit.,* p. 813.

14 *Program of the Communist Party of the Soviet Union, op. cit.,* p. 79.

15 Lenin, *Works,* Vol. 31, *op. cit.,* p. 32.

16 Lenin, *Selected Works,* Vol. 2, *op. cit.,* p. 624.

17 *Fundamentals of Marxism-Leninism, op. cit.,* p. 817.

18 S. Strumilin, "What Communism Is: Thoughts About the Future," *Oktyabr,* No. 3, March, 1960, p. 140-6. (C.D.S.P., Vol. XII, No. 15, pp. 11-14)

19 *Ibid.*

20 *Ibid.*

21 *Ibid.*

22 S. Strumilin, "The Workers Way of Life and Communism," *Novy mir,* No. 7, 1960, p. 208.

23 *Ibid.*

24 Ye. Manevich, "Economic Labor Incentives and the Forms of Transition to Communist Distribution," *Voprosy ekonomiki,* No. 5, May, 1961, pp. 76-85. (C.D.S.P., Vol. XIII, No. 33, pp. 10-14)

25 *Ibid.*

26 N. S. Khrushchev, *Control Figures for Economic Development of the U.S.S.R. for 1959-1965,* (Moscow: Foreign Languages Publishing House, 1960), p. 56.

27 Manevich, "Economic Labor Incentives and the Forms of Transition to Communist Distribution," *op. cit.,* pp. 76-85.

28 *Ibid.*

29 Khrushchev, "New Stages in Communist Construction and Some Problems of Marxist-Leninist Theory," *op. cit.,* pp. 2-10.

30 N. S. Khrushchev, "Use All Forces of the Party and the People for Fulfilling Plans of Communist Construction," *Pravda,* Dec. 15, 1963, pp. 1-3.

31 *Ibid.*

32 S. Strumilin, "For All, in the Interests of Each," *Izvestia,* Aug. 30, 1961, p. 3. (C.D.S.P., Vol. XIII, No. 35, pp. 24-5)

33 Ts. Stepanyan, "Communism and Property," *Oktyabr,* No. 9, Sept., 1960, pp. 3-12. (C.D.S.P., Vol. XII, No. 42, pp. 17-20)

34 *Ibid.*

35 *Program of the Communist Party of the Soviet Union, op. cit.,* p. 90.

36 Strumilin, "For All, in the Interests of Each," *op. cit.,* p. 3.

37 *Ibid.*

38 *Ibid.*

39 *Ibid.*

40 Manevich, "Economic Labor Incentives and the Forms of Transition to Communist Distribution," *op. cit.,* pp. 76-85.

41 Khrushchev, "New Stages in Communist Construction and Some Problems of Marxist-Leninist Theory," *op. cit.,* pp. 2-10.

42 *Kommunist,* No. 12, August, 1960, p. 117.

43 Khrushchev, "New Stages in Communist Construction and Some Problems of Marxist-Leninist Theory," *op. cit.,* pp. 2-10.

44 *Program of the Communist Party of the Soviet Union, op. cit.,* p. 106.

45 *Ibid.,* p. 107.

46 *Fundamentals of Marxism-Leninism, op. cit.,* p. 808.

47 *Ibid.,* p. 832.

48 R. F. Fortune, *Sorcerers of Dobu,* (New York: Dutton Press, 1943).

49 V. Ivanov, V. Pchelin and M. Sakov, "The Party's Growing Role in the Building of Communism," *Kommunist,* No. 17, Nov., 1959, pp. 3-20. (C.D.S.P., Vol. XII, No. 1, pp. 3-7)

50 Khrushchev, "New Stages in Communist Construction and Some Problems of Marxist-Leninist Theory," *op. cit.*, pp. 2-10.

51 Ivanov, Pchelin and Sakov, "The Party's Growing Role in the Building of Communism," *op. cit.*, pp. 3-20.

52 *Program of the Communist Party of the Soviet Union, op. cit.*, p. 92.

53 Ivanov, Pchelin and Sakov, "The Party's Growing Role in the Building of Communism," *op. cit.*, pp. 3-20.

54 *Program of the Communist Party of the Soviet Union, op. cit.*, pp. 98-9.

55 *Ibid.*

56 Khrushchev, "New Stages in Communist Construction and Some Problems of Marxist-Leninist Theory," *op. cit.*, pp. 2-10.

57 *Program of the Communist Party of the Soviet Union, op. cit.*, p. 99.

58 *Ibid.*

59 *Ibid.*

60 *Ibid.*

61 Ivanov, Pchelin and Sakov, "The Party's Growing Role in the Building of Communism," *op. cit.*, pp. 3-20.

62 *Ibid.*

63 *Fundamentals of Marxism-Leninism, op. cit.*, p. 855.

64 *Ibid.*, pp. 856-77.

65 *Ibid.*, pp. 856-63.

66 Khrushchev, "Report on the Program of the Communist Party of the Soviet Union," *op. cit.*, p. 13.

BIBLIOGRAPHY

Abramovitch, Raphael R., *The Soviet Revolution, 1917-1939*. New York: International Universities Press, 1962.

Adams, Arthur E., *Bolsheviks in the Ukraine: The Second Campaign, 1918-1919*. New Haven, Conn.: Yale University Press, 1963.

Adams, Arthur E., ed., *Readings in Soviet Foreign Policy: Theory and Practice*. Boston, Mass.: D. C. Heath and Co., 1961.

―――― *The Russian Revolution and Bolshevik Victory—The Why and How*. Boston, Mass.: D. C. Heath and Co., 1960.

Adams, Henry Packwood, *Karl Marx in His Earlier Writings*. London: George Allen and Unwin, Ltd., 1940.

Adoratsky, Vladimir V., *Dialectical Materialism: The Theoretical Foundation of Marxism-Leninism*. New York: International Publishers, 1934.

Alampiev, P., *Where Economic Inequality Is No More—Progress of the Soviet Eastern Republics as Exemplified by Kazakhstan*. Moscow: Foreign Languages Publishing House, 1959.

Allen, W. E. D., *The Ukraine: A History*. New York: Cambridge University Press, 1941.

Almond, Gabriel Abraham, Krugman, H., Lewin, E. and Wriggens, H., *The Appeals of Communism*. Princeton, N. J.: Princeton University Press, 1954.

Anderson, Paul B., *People, Church and State in Modern Russia*. New York: Macmillan Co., 1944.

Anderson, Thornton, ed., *Masters of Russian Marxism*. New York: Appleton-Century-Crofts, 1963.

The Anti-Stalin Campaign and International Communism. New York: Columbia University Press for the Russian Institute, 1956.

Arakelian, A., trans. by Ellsworth L. Raymond, *Industrial Management in the U.S.S.R.* Washington, D.C.: Public Affairs Press, 1950.

Arendt, Hannah, *The Origins of Totalitarianism*. London: G. Allen and Unwin, 1958; New York: Meridian Books, 1960.

Armstrong, John A., *Ideology, Politics and Government in the Soviet Union*. New York: Frederick A. Praeger, 1962.

―――― *The Politics of Totalitarianism: The Communist Party of the Soviet Union from 1934 to the Present*. New York: Random House, 1961.

―――― *The Soviet Bureaucratic Elite: A Case Study of the Ukrainian Apparatus*. New York: Frederick A. Praeger, 1959.

―――― *Ukrainian Nationalism 1939-1945*. New York: Columbia University Press, 1955.

Ashby, Eric, *Scientist in Russia*. Harmondsworth, Middlesex, England-New York: Penguin Books, 1947.

Avtorkharov, Abdurakhman, *Stalin and the Soviet Communist Party: A Study in the Technology of Power*. New York: Frederick A. Praeger, 1959.

Babb, Hugh Webster, trans., *Soviet Legal Philosophy*. Cambridge, Mass.: Harvard University Press, 1951.

Bach, Marcus, *God and the Soviets*. New York: Thomas Y. Crowell, 1958.

Baldwin, Roger Nash, *Liberty Under the Soviets*. New York: Vanguard Press, 1928; and Macmillan Co., 1929.

Balzak, S. S., Vasyutin, V. T., and Teigin, Yar. G., *Economic Geography of the U.S.S.R., ACLS Translation Project*. New York: Macmillan Co., 1949.

Baransky, Nikolai N., *Economic Geography of the U.S.S.R.* Moscow: Foreign Languages Publishing House, 1956.

Barghoorn, Frederick C., *The Soviet Cultural Offensive.* Princeton, N. J.: Princeton University Press, 1960.

―――― *The Soviet Image of the United States, A Study in Distortion.* New York: Harcourt, Brace and World, Inc., 1950.

―――― *Soviet Russian Nationalism.* New York: Oxford University Press, 1956.

Baron, Samuel H., *Plekhanov: the Father of Russian Marxism.* Stanford, Cal.: Stanford University Press, 1963.

Basili, Nikolai Aleksandrovich, *Russia Under Soviet Rule: Twenty Years of Bolshevik Experiment.* London: G. Allen and Unwin, Ltd., 1938.

Batsell, Walter Russell, *Soviet Rule in Russia.* New York: Vanguard Press, 1928; and Macmillan Co., 1929.

Bauer, Raymond A., *et al., How the Soviet System Works: Cultural, Psychological and Social Themes.* Cambridge, Mass.: Harvard University Press, 1956.

―――― *The New Man in Soviet Psychology.* Cambridge, Mass.: Harvard University Press, 1952.

――――, and Wasiolek, Edward, *Nine Soviet Portraits.* Cambridge, Mass.: Mass. Institute of Technology Press and John Wiley and Sons, Inc., 1955.

――――, and Inkeles, Alex, *The Soviet Citizen: Daily Life in a Totalitarian Society.* Cambridge, Mass.: Harvard University Press, 1959.

Baykov, Alexander, *The Development of the Soviet Economic System, An Essay on the Experience of Planning in the U.S.S.R.* Cambridge, England: The University Press, 1946.

Beck, F., and Godin, W., trans. from German by Mosbacher & Porter, *Russian Purge and the Extraction of Confession.* New York: Viking Press, 1951; and London: Hurst & Blackett, 1951.

Beloff, Max, *Soviet Policy in the Far East, 1944-1951.* London: Oxford University Press, 1953.

―――― *The Foreign Policy of Soviet Russia,* Vol. I: 1929-1936; Vol. II: 1936-1941. New York: Oxford University Press, 1947-1949.

Belov, Fedor, *The History of a Soviet Collective Farm.* New York: Published for Research Program on U.S.S.R. by Frederick A. Praeger, 1955.

Berdiaev, Nikolai A., *The Russian Revolution.* Ann Arbor, Mich.: University of Michigan Press, 1961.

Berdyaev, Nicolas, trans. from Russian by R. M. French, *The Origin of Russian Communism.* Ann Arbor, Mich.: University of Michigan Press, 1937, 1948 and 1960.

Bereday, George Z. F., Brickman, William W. and Read, Gerald H., eds., *The Changing Soviet School: The Comparative Education Society Field Study in the U.S.S.R.* Boston: Houghton Mifflin Co., 1960.

――――, and Pennar, Jaan, eds., *The Politics of Soviet Education.* New York: Frederick A. Praeger, 1960.

Berg, L. S., *Natural Regions of the U.S.S.R.* New York: Macmillan Co., 1950.

Bergson, Abram, *Economic Trends in the Soviet Union.* Cambridge, Mass.: Harvard University Press, 1963.

―――― *The Economics of Soviet Planning.* New Haven, Conn.: Yale University Press, 1964.

―――― *The Real National Income of Soviet Russia Since 1928.* Cambridge, Mass.: Harvard University Press, 1961.

――――, ed., *Soviet Economic Growth.* Evanston, Ill.: Row, Peterson & Co., 1953.

―――― *Soviet National Income and Product in 1937.* New York: Columbia University Press, 1953.

――――, and Heymann, Hans, Jr., *Soviet National Income and Product 1940-1948.* New York: Columbia University Press, 1954.

―――― *The Structure of Soviet Wages, A Study in Socialist Economics.* Cambridge, Mass.: Harvard University Press, 1944.

Berlin, Isaiah, *Karl Marx, His Life and Environment*. New York: Oxford University Press, 1948.

Berliner, Joseph S., *Factory and Manager in the U.S.S.R.* Cambridge, Mass.: Harvard University Press, 1957.

Berman, Harold J., *Justice in Russia: An Interpretation of Soviet Law*. Cambridge, Mass.: Harvard University Press, 1950.

———— *The Russians in Focus*. Boston: Little, Brown and Co., 1953.

————, and Kerner, Miroslav, *Soviet Military Law and Administration*. Cambridge, Mass.: Harvard University Press, 1955.

Bienstock, Gregory, Schwartz, Solomon M., and Yugow, Aaron, *Management in Russian Industry and Agriculture*. London-New York: Oxford University Press, 1944.

Billington, James H., *Mikhailovsky and Russian Populism*. Oxford, England: Clarendon Press, 1958.

Bishop, Donald Gordon, *Soviet Foreign Relations: Documents and Readings*. Syracuse, N. Y.: Syracuse University Press, 1952.

Black, Cyril E., ed., *Rewriting Russian History: Soviet Interpretations of Russia's Past*. New York: Frederick A. Praeger, 1956.

————, ed., *The Transformation of Russian Society, Aspects of Social Change Since 1861*. Cambridge, Mass.: Harvard University Press, 1960.

Blake, Patricia, and Hayward, Max, eds., *Dissonant Voices in Soviet Literature*. New York: Pantheon Books, 1962.

Bober, Mandell Morton, *Karl Marx's Interpretation of History*. Cambridge, Mass.: Harvard University Press, 1948.

Bochenski, I. M., *Soviet Russian Dialectical Materialism*. Dordrecht, Holland: D. Reidel Publishing Co., 1963.

Boffa, Giuseppe, *Inside the Khrushchev Era*. New York: Marzani and Munsell, Inc., 1959; London: G. Allen and Unwin, 1960.

Boorman, Howard L., *et al.*, *Moscow-Peking Axis: Strengths and Strains*. New York: Published for the Council on Foreign Relations by Harper, 1957.

Borkenau, Franz, *European Communism*. London: Farber & Farber, Ltd., 1953.

———— *World Communism: A History of the Communist International*. New York: W. W. Norton & Co., 1939.

Braham, Randolph L., ed., *Soviet Politics and Government: A Reader*. New York: Alfred A. Knopf, 1965.

Brameld, T. B. H., *A Philosophic Approach to Communism*. Chicago: Chicago University Press, 1933.

Brandt, Conrad, *Stalin's Failure in China, 1924-1927*. Cambridge, Mass.; Harvard University Press, 1958.

Browder, R. P., and Kerensky, A. F., eds., *The Russian Provisional Government 1917: Documents*. Stanford, Cal.: Stanford University Press, 1961

Brown, Edward James, *The Proletarian Episode in Russian Literature, 1928-32*. New York: Columbia University Press, 1953.

Brumberg, Abraham, ed., *Russia Under Khrushchev—An Anthology from Problems of Communism*. New York: Frederick A. Praeger, 1962.

Brzezinski, Zbigniew K., *Ideology and Power in Soviet Politics*. New York: Frederick A. Praeger, 1962.

———— *The Permanent Purge: Politics in Soviet Authoritarianism*. Cambridge, Mass.: Harvard University Press, 1956.

————, ed., *Political Controls in the Soviet Army*. Based on reports by former Soviet officers. New York: Research Program on the U.S.S.R., 1954.

———— *The Soviet Bloc, Unity in Conflict*. Cambridge, Mass.: Harvard University Press, 1960.

————, and Friedrich, Carl J., *Totalitarian Dictatorship and Autocracy*. Cambridge, Mass.: Harvard University Press, 1956.

Budurowycz, Bohdan B., *Polish-Soviet Relations, 1932-1939*. New York: Columbia University Press, 1963.

Bukharin, Nikolai I., *Historical Materialism*. New York: International Publishers, 1925; and London: G. Allen & Unwin, Ltd., 1926.

————, *et al., Marxism and Modern Thought*. New York: Harcourt, Brace and World, Inc., 1935.

Bunyan, James, and Fisher, H. H., *The Bolshevik Revolution, 1917-1918: Documents and Materials*. Stanford, Cal.: Stanford University Press, 1961.

———— *Intervention, Civil War, and Communism in Russia, April-December, 1918*. Baltimore, Md.: John Hopkins Press, 1936.

Burns, Emile, ed., *A Handbook of Marxism*. New York: Random House, 1935.

Campbell, Robert W., *Soviet Economic Power: Its Organization, Growth and Challenge*. Boston: Houghton Mifflin Co., 1960.

Carr, Edward Hallett, *A History of Soviet Russia*, (Vols. I-VI on the years 1917-1926). New York: Macmillan Co., 1951-1960.

———— *A History of Soviet Russia*, (3 Vols.). London: Macmillan and Co., Ltd., 1950-1953.

———— *The Soviet Impact on the Western World*. New York: Macmillan Co., 1947.

———— *Studies in Revolution*. London: Macmillan and Co., Ltd., 1950.

Carson, George Barr, *Electoral Practices in the U.S.S.R.* New York: Frederick A. Praeger, 1955.

Casey, Robert Pierce, *Religion in Russia*. New York: Harper and Brothers, 1946.

Chamberlin, William H., *The Russian Enigma*. New York: Charles Scribner's Sons, 1944.

———— *The Russian Revolution, 1917-1921*, (2 Vols., reissue). New York: Macmillan Co., 1952.

———— *Russia's Iron Age*. Boston: Little, Brown and Co., 1934.

Chapman, Janet G., *Real Wages in Soviet Russia Since 1928*. Cambridge, Mass.: Harvard University Press, 1963.

Chernov, Viktor Mikhailovich, trans. and abridged by P. E. Mosely, *The Great Russian Revolution*. New Haven, Conn.: Yale University Press, 1936.

Clarkson, Jesse Dunsmore, *A History of Russia*. New York: Random House and Co., 1961.

Cobban, Alfred, *Dictatorship: Its History and Theory*. New York: Charles Scribner's Sons, 1939.

Cole, George Douglas Howard, *Communism and Social Democracy, 1914-1931*, (2 Vols.). New York: St. Martin's Press, 1958; London: Macmillan and Co., Ltd., 1958.

———— *A History of Socialist Thought*. New York: St. Martin's Press, 1953.

———— *The Meaning of Marxism*. Ann Arbor, Mich.: University of Michigan Press, 1964.

———— *What Marx Really Meant*. New York: Alfred A. Knopf, Inc., 1934, 1937.

Communist Party of the Soviet Union, Central Committee, *History of the Communist Party of the Soviet Union* (Bolsheviks). New York: International Publishers, 1939.

Communist Party of the Soviet Union, Eighteenth Congress. *Land Of Socialism Today and Tomorrow. Reports and Speeches at the Eighteenth Congress of the C.P.S.U., March 10-21, 1939*. Moscow: Foreign Languages Publishing House, 1939.

Comparisons of the United States and Soviet Economies: Hearings Before the Joint Economic Committee, Congress of the United States. Washington, D.C.: United States Government Printing Office, 1960.

Comparisons of the United States and Soviet Economies: Papers Submitted By Panelists Appearing Before the Sub-Committee on Economic Statistics, Part II and Part III. Washington, D.C.: United States Government Printing Office, 1960.

Condoide, Mikhail V., *The Soviet Financial System: Its Development and Relations With the Western World*. Columbus, Ohio: Ohio State University Press, 1951.

Conquest, Robert, *Power and Policy in the U.S.S.R.: The Study of Soviet Dynastics*. New York: St. Martin's Press, 1961.

———— *Russia After Khrushchev*. New York-Washington-London: Frederick A. Praeger, 1965.

Conforth, Maurice C., *Dialectical Materialism: An Introductory Course,* (3 Vols.). New York: International Publishers, 1953-1954.

———— *In Defense of Philosophy Against Positivism and Pragmatism.* New York: International Publishers, 1950.

———— *Philosophy for Socialists.* London: Lawrence & Wishart, 1959.

Counts, George S., *The Challenge of Soviet Education.* New York: McGraw-Hill Book Co., Inc., 1957.

Crankshaw, Edward, *Khrushchev's Russia.* Baltimore, Md.; Penguin Books, Inc., 1959.

———— *The New Cold War: Moscow vs. Peking.* Baltimore, Md.: Penguin Books, Inc., 1963.

———— *Russia and the Russians.* New York: Viking Press, 1948.

———— *Russia Without Stalin: The Emerging Pattern.* London: Michael Joseph, 1956; New York: Viking Press, 1956.

Cressey, George B., *The Basis of Soviet Strength.* New York: McGraw-Hill Book Co., 1945.

———— *Soviet Potentials: A Geographical Appraisal.* Syracuse, N. Y.: Syracuse University Press, 1962.

———— *How Strong Is Russia? A Geographical Appraisal.* Syracuse, N. Y.: Syracuse University Press, 1954.

Crossman, Richard, *The God That Failed.* New York: Bantam Books, Inc., 1963.

Curtiss, John Shelton, *Church and State in Russia, 1900-1917.* New York: Columbia University Press, 1940.

———— *Essays in Russian and Soviet History* (In Honor of Geroid Tanquary Robinson). New York: Columbia University Press, 1963.

———— *The Russian Church and the Soviet State, 1917-1950.* Boston: Little, Brown and Co., 1953.

———— *The Russian Revolutions of 1917.* Princeton, N. J.: D. Van Nostrand Co., Inc., 1957.

Dallin, Alexander, Harnis, Jonathan and Hodnett, Grey, eds., *Diversity in International Communism: A Documentary Record, 1961-1963.* New York: Columbia University Press, 1963.

————, ed., *Soviet Conduct in World Affairs, A Selection of Readings.* New York: Columbia University Press, 1960.

———— *The Soviet Union at the United Nations: An Inquiry into Soviet Motives and Objectives.* New York: Frederick A. Praeger, 1962.

Dallin, David J., *The Changing World of Soviet Russia.* New Haven, Conn.: Yale University Press, 1956.

Dallin, David Yulevich, and Nicolaevsky, Boris I., *Forced Labor in Soviet Russia.* New Haven, Conn.: Yale University Press, 1947.

————, trans. by Joseph Shaplen, revised and enlarged edition, *The Real Soviet Russia.* New Haven, Conn.: Yale University Press, 1947.

————*Soviet Espionage.* New Haven, Conn.: Yale University Press, 1955.

———— *Soviet Russia's Foreign Policy, 1939-1942.* New Haven, Conn.: Yale University Press, 1942.

Daniels, Robert Vincent, *The Conscience of the Revolution: Communist Opposition in Soviet Russia.* Cambridge, Mass.: Harvard University Press, 1960.

————, ed., *A Documentary History of Communism.* New York: Random House and Co., 1960.

———— *The Nature of Communism.* New York: Random House and Co., 1962.

Davies, Robert William, *The Development of the Soviet Budgetary System.* Cambridge, England: Cambridge University Press, 1958.

Deane, J. R., *The Strange Alliance.* New York: Viking Press, 1947.

Degras, Jane Tabrisky, *Calendar of Soviet Documents on Foreign Policy, 1917-1941.* New York: Royal Institute of International Affairs, 1948.

————, ed., *The Communist International, 1919-1943.* London-New York: Oxford University Press, 1956.

————, ed., *Soviet Documents on Foreign Policy,* (3 Vols.). New York: Oxford University Press, 1951-1953.

DeKoster, Lester, *Vocabulary of Communism.* Grand Rapids, Mich.: Wm. B. Eerdmans, 1964.

Denikin, A. I., *The Russian Turmoil; Memoirs: Military, Social and Political.* London: Hutchinson and Co., 1922.

Denisov, A., and Kirichenko, M., *Soviet State Law.* Moscow: Foreign Languages Publishing House, 1960.

Dennett, R., and Johnson, J. E., eds., *Negotiating With the Russians.* Boston: World Peace Foundation, 1951.

Deutscher, Isaac, *The Great Contest: Russia and the West.* New York: Oxford University Press, 1960.

———— *The Prophet Armed: Trotsky, 1879-1921.* New York: Oxford University Press, 1954.

———— *The Prophet Outcast: Trotsky, 1929-1940.* New York: Oxford University Press, 1963.

———— *The Prophet Unarmed: 1921-1929.* London-New York: Oxford University Press, 1959.

———— *Russia in Transition, and Other Essays.* New York: Coward-McCann, Inc., 1957.

———— *Russia: What Next?* New York: Oxford University Press, 1953.

———— *Soviet Trade Unions: Their Place in Soviet Labor Policy.* London-New York: Royal Institute of International Affairs, 1950.

———— *Stalin, A Political Biography.* New York: Oxford University Press, 1949.

Dewar, Margaret, *Labor Policy in the U.S.S.R., 1917-1928.* London-New York: Royal Institute of International Affairs, 1956.

DeWitt, Nicholas, *Education and Professional Employment in the U.S.S.R.* Washington, D.C.: National Science Foundation, 1961.

———— *Soviet Professional Manpower.* Washington, D.C.: National Research Council, 1954; National Science Foundation, 1955.

Dinerstein, Herbert Samuel, and Goure, Leon, *Communism and the Russian Peasant.* Glencoe, Ill.: Free Press, Inc., 1955.

———— *War and the Soviet Union: Nuclear Weapons and the Revolution in Soviet Military and Political Thinking.* New York: Frederick A. Praeger, 1959.

Djilas, Milovan, *Conversations With Stalin.* New York: Harcourt, Brace and World, Inc., 1962.

———— *The New Class: An Analysis of the Communist System.* New York: Frederick A. Praeger, 1957.

Dmytryshyn, Basil, *U.S.S.R.: A Concise History.* New York: Charles Scribner's Sons, 1965.

Dobb, Maurice Herbert, *Soviet Economic Development Since 1917.* London: Routledge and Kegan Paul, Ltd., 1958.

Drachkovitch, Milorad M., ed., *Marxism in the Modern World.* Stanford, Cal.: Stanford University Press, 1965.

Dudintsev, Vladimir, *Not By Bread Alone.* New York: E. P. Dutton and Co., 1957.

Dunayevskaya, Raya, *Marxism and Freedom: from 1776 Until Today.* New York: Bookman Associates, 1958.

Dux, Dieter, ed., *Ideology in Conflict: Communist Political Theory.* Princeton, N. J.: D. Van Nostrand Co., Inc., 1963.

Eastman, Max, *Marxism: Is It Science?* New York: W. W. Norton and Co., Inc., 1940.

Education in the U.S.S.R. New York: International Arts and Sciences Press, 1963.

Ehrenburg, Ilia, *The Thaw.* London: MacGibbon and Kee, 1961.

Engels, Friedrich, *Anti-Dühring: Herr Eugen Dühring's Revolution in Science.* Moscow: Foreign Languages Publishing House, 1962.

———— *Dialectics of Nature.* Moscow: Foreign Languages Publishing House, 1954; and New York: International Publishers, 1960.

———— *Ludwig Feuerbach.* New York: International Publishers, 1941.

———— *The Origin of the Family, Private Property and the State.* New York: International Publishers, 1942.

———— *Socialism, Utopian and Scientific.* New York: International Publishers, 1935.

Erickson, John, *The Soviet Command: A Military-Political History, 1918-1941.* New York: St. Martin's Press, 1962.

Erlich, Alexander, *The Soviet Industrialization Debate, 1924-1928.* Cambridge, Mass.: Harvard University Press, 1960.

Fainsod, Merle, *How Russia Is Ruled,* (2nd ed.). Cambridge, Mass.: Harvard University Press, 1963.

———— *Smolensk Under Soviet Rule.* Cambridge, Mass.: Harvard University Press, 1958; and London: Macmillan and Co., 1959.

Federn, Karl, *The Materialist Conception of History: A Critical Analysis.* London: Macmillan and Co., Ltd., 1939.

Fedotov, White Dmitri, *The Growth of the Red Army.* Princeton, N. J.: Princeton University Press, 1944.

Feis, Herbert, *Churchill, Roosevelt, Stalin: The War They Waged and the Peace They Sought.* Princeton, N. J.: Princeton University Press, 1957.

Field, Mark G., *Doctor and Patient in Soviet Russia.* Cambridge, Mass.: Harvard University Press, 1957.

Fischer, George, *Russian Liberalism from Gentry to Intelligentsia.* Cambridge, Mass.: Harvard University Press, 1958.

———— *Soviet Opposition to Stalin, A Case Study in World War II.* Cambridge, Mass.: Harvard University Press, 1952.

Fischer, Louis, *The Life of Lenin.* New York: Harper & Row, 1964.

———— *The Soviets in World Affairs, 1917-1929,* (2nd ed., 2 Vols.), Princeton, N. J.: Princeton University Press, 1951; *History of the Relations Between the Soviet Union and the Rest of the World,* (abridged by author). New York: Vintage Books, 1960.

Fisher, H. H., *The Famine in Soviet Russia, 1919-1923: The Operations of the American Relief Administration.* New York: Macmillan Co., 1927.

Fisher, Ralph Talcott, *Pattern for Soviet Youth: A Study of the Congresses of the Komsomol, 1918-1954.* New York: Columbia University Press, 1959.

Fitzsimmons, Thomas, *et al.,* *U.S.S.R.: Its People, Its Society, Its Culture.* New Haven, Conn.: Human Relations Area Files Press, 1960.

Florinsky, Michael T., *The End of the Russian Empire.* New York: Collier, 1961.

———— *Russia: A History and an Interpretation,* (2 Vols.). New York: Macmillan Co., 1953.

————, *et al.,* eds., *Encyclopedia of Russia and the Soviet Union.* New York: McGraw-Hill Book Co., Inc., 1961.

———— *Towards an Understanding of the U.S.S.R.: A Study in Government, Politics, and Economic Planning,* (rev. ed.). New York: Macmillan Co., 1951.

Floyd, David, *Mao Against Khrushchev—A Short History of the Sino-Soviet Conflict.* New York: Frederick A. Praeger, 1963.

Footman, David, *Civil War in Russia.* New York: Frederick A. Praeger, 1961.

Freedman, Robert, ed., *Marx on Economics.* New York: Harcourt, Brace and Co., 1961.

Freund, Henry Alexander, *Russia from A to Z: Revolution, State and Party, Foreign Relations, Economic System, Social Principles and General Knowledge.* London: Angus and Robertson, Ltd., 1945.

Friedrich, Carl J., and Brzezinski, Zbigniew K., *Totalitarian Dictatorship and Autocracy.* Cambridge, Mass.: Harvard University Press, 1956.

Friedman, Israel E., *Co-operatives in the Soviet Union.* London: Soviet News Booklets, No. 36, 1958.

Fromm, Erich, *Marx's Concept of Man.* New York: Frederick Ungar Publishing Co., 1961.

Fundamentals of Marxism-Leninism, Manual. Moscow: Foreign Languages Publishing House, no year.

Galenson, Walter, *Labor Productivity in Soviet and American Industry.* New York: Columbia University Press, 1955.

Gallagher, Matthew P., *The Soviet History of World War II: Myths, Memories and Realities.* New York: Frederick A. Praeger, 1963.

Garthoff, Raymond L., *Soviet Military Doctrine.* Glencoe, Ill.: Free Press, 1953.

——— *Soviet Strategy in the Nuclear Age.* New York: Frederick A. Praeger, 1958.

Gibian, George, *Interval of Freedom—Soviet Literature During the Thaw.* Minneapolis, Minn.: University of Minnesota Press, 1960.

Glezerman, G., *The Laws of Social Development.* Moscow: Foreign Languages Publishing House, 1962.

Gliksman, Jerzy, *Tell the West.* New York: Gresham Press, 1948.

Goldberg, Ben Zion, *The Jewish Problem in the Soviet Union: Analysis and Solution.* New York: Crown Publishers, Inc., 1961.

Golder, F., trans. by E. Aronsberg, *Documents of Russian History 1914-1917,* New York-London: Century House, 1927.

Goldwin, Robert A., *et al.,* eds., *Readings in Russian Foreign Policy.* New York: Oxford University Press, 1959.

Goodall, G., ed., *Soviet Russia in Maps: Its Origins and Development.* Chicago: Denoyer-Geppert, 1942.

Goodman, Elliot, *The Soviet Design for a World State.* New York: Columbia University Press, 1960.

Gordon, Manya, *Workers Before and After Lenin.* New York: E. P. Dutton and Co., Inc., 1941.

Gorer, Geoffrey, and Rickman, John, *The People of Great Russia: A Psychological Study.* New York: Chanticleer Press, 1950.

Gorky, M., *et al.,* eds., *The History of the Civil War in the U.S.S.R.,* (2 Vols.). New York: International Publishers, 1938-1947.

Goure, Leon, *The Siege of Leningrad.* Stanford, Cal.: Stanford University Press, 1962.

Granick, David, *Management of the Industrial Firm in the U.S.S.R.: A Study in Soviet Economic Planning.* New York: Columbia University Press, 1954.

——— *The Red Executive: A Study of the Organizational Man in Russian Industry.* Garden City, N. Y.: Doubleday and Co., Inc., 1961.

Gregory, James S., *Land of the Soviets.* Harmondsworth, Middlesex, England-New York: Penguin Books, Inc., 1946.

Grierson, Philip, *Books on Soviet Russia 1917-1942.* London: Methuen and Co., Ltd., 1943.

Gripp, Richard C., *Patterns of Soviet Politics.* Homewood, Ill.: Dorsey Press, 1963.

Grossman, Gregory, *Soviet Statistics of Physical Output of Industrial Commodities, Their Compilation and Quality.* Princeton, N. J.: Princeton University Press, 1960.

Gruliow, Leo, ed., *Current Soviet Policies: The Documentary Record of the Nineteenth Communist Party Congress and the Reorganization After Stalin's Death.* New York: Frederick A. Praeger, 1953.

———, ed., *Current Soviet Policies: The Documentary Record of the Twentieth Communist Party Congress and Repercussions of De-Stalinization.* New York: Frederick A. Praeger, 1957.

Grzybowski, Kazimierz, *Soviet Legal Institutions: Doctrines and Social Functions.* Ann Arbor, Mich.: University of Michigan Press, 1962.

——— *The Socialist Commonwealth of Nations—Organizations and Institutions.* New Haven, Conn.-London: Yale University Press, 1964.

Gsovski, Vladimir, and Grzybowski, Kazimierz, *Government, Law and Courts in the Soviet Union,* (Vols. I-VI). New York: Frederick A. Praeger, 1959.

——— *Soviet Civil Law, Private Rights and Their Background Under the Soviet Regime,* (2 Vols.). Ann Arbor, Mich.: University of Michigan Law School, 1948-1949.

Guins, George Constantine, *Communism on the Decline*. New York: Philosophical Library, 1956.
—— *Soviet Law and Soviet Society*. The Hague: Mijhoff, 1954.
Gunther, John, *Inside Russia Today*. New York: Harper and Brothers, 1958.
Gurian, Waldemar, *Bolshevism: An Introduction to Soviet Communism*. South Bend, Ind.: University of Notre Dame Press, 1952.
——, ed., *The Soviet Union: Background, Ideology, Reality*. South Bend, Ind.: University of Notre Dame Press, 1951.
Gyorgy, Andrew, *Communism in Perspective*. Boston: Allyn and Bacon, Inc., 1964.

Haimson, Leopold H., *The Russian Marxists and the Origins of Bolshevism*. Cambridge, Mass.: Harvard University Press, 1955.
Hammond, Thomas T., *Lenin on Trade Unions and Revolution, 1893-1917*. New York: Columbia University Press, 1957.
—— *Soviet Foreign Relations and World Communism: A Selected and Annotated Bibliography of 7,000 Books in 30 Languages*. Princeton, N. J.: Princeton University Press, 1965.
Harcave, Sidney S., *Russia: A History*. Chicago: J. B. Lippincott Co., 1959.
Hare, Richard, *Pioneers of Russian Thought: Studies of Non-Marxian Formation in 19th Century Russia and its Partial Revival in the Soviet Union*. London-New York: Oxford University Press, 1951.
Harper, Samuel N., *Civic Training in Soviet Russia*. Chicago: University of Chicago Press, 1929.
——, and Thompson, Ronald, *The Government of the Soviet Union*. New York: D. Van Nostrand Co., 1949.
Hazard, John Newbold, *Law and Social Change in the U.S.S.R.* Toronto: Carswell, Co., 1953.
—— *Settling Disputes in Soviet Society*. New York: Columbia University Press, 1960.
—— *Soviet Housing Law*. New Haven, Conn.: Yale University Press, 1939; London: H. Milford, Oxford University Press, 1939.
—— *The Soviet System of Government*. Chicago: University of Chicago Press, 1960.
Hendel, Samuel, ed., *The Soviet Crucible: Soviet Government in Theory and Practice*. Princeton, N. J.: D. Van Nostrand Co., Inc., 1959.
Hindus, Maurice, *House Without a Roof: Russia After 43 Years of Revolution*. New York: Doubleday and Co., 1961.
—— *Red Bread*. New York: Cape and H. Smith, 1931.
Hodgkinson, Harry, *Doubletalk: The Languages of Communism*. London: George Allen & Unwin, 1955; published in U.S.A. as *The Language of Communism*. New York: Pitman, 1955.
Hodgman, Donald R., *Soviet Industrial Production, 1928-1951*. Cambridge, Mass.: Harvard University Press, 1954.
Holzman, Franklyn D., ed., *Readings on the Soviet Economy*. Chicago: Rand, McNally and Co., 1962.
—— *Soviet Taxation: The Fiscal and Monetary Problems of a Planned Economy*. Cambridge, Mass.: Harvard University Press, 1955.
Hook, Sidney, *From Hegel to Marx: Studies in the Intellectual Development of Karl Marx*. Ann Arbor, Mich.: University of Michigan Press, 1962.
—— *Marx and the Marxists*. Princeton, N. J.: D. Van Nostrand Co., Inc., 1955.
—— *Towards the Understanding of Karl Marx*. New York: John Day Co., 1933.
——, ed., *World Communism: Key Documentary Material*. Princeton, N. J.: D. Van Nostrand Co., 1962.
Horecky, Paul L., ed., *Russia and the Soviet Union: A Bibliographic Guide to Western-Language Publications*. Chicago: Chicago University Press, 1965.
Hubbard, Leonard, *The Economics of Soviet Agriculture*. London: Macmillan Co., 1939.
Hudson, G. F., *The Sino-Soviet Dispute*. New York: Frederick A. Praeger, 1961.
Hudson, P. S., and Richens, R. H., *The New Genetics in the Soviet Union*. Cambridge, England: School of Agriculture, 1946.

Hunt, Robert Nigel C., *Books on Communism, A Bibliography.* London: Ampersand, Ltd., 1959.
———— *A Guide to Communist Jargon.* New York: Macmillan Co., 1957.
———— *Marxism: Past and Present.* New York: Macmillan Co., 1955.
———— *The Theory and Practice of Communism.* New York: Macmillan Co., 1958.

Inkeles, Alex, *Public Opinion in Soviet Russia, a Study in Mass Persuasion.* Cambridge, Mass.: Harvard University Press, 1950.
————, and Bauer, Raymond A., *The Soviet Citizen.* Cambridge, Mass.: Harvard University Press, 1959.
————, and Greiger, Kent, eds., *Soviet Society: A Book of Readings.* Boston: Houghton Mifflin Co., 1961.

Jacobs, Daniel Norman, *The New Communist Manifesto and Related Documents.* Evanston, Ill.: Row, Peterson and Co., 1961-1962.
Jasny, Naum, *Essays on the Soviet Economy.* New York: Frederick A. Praeger, 1962.
———— *The Socialized Agriculture of the U.S.S.R.* Stanford, Cal.: Stanford University Press, 1949.
———— *The Soviet Economy During the Plan Era.* Stanford, Cal.: Stanford University Press, 1951.
———— *Soviet Industrialization, 1928-1952.* Chicago: University of Chicago Press, 1961.
———— *The Soviet Price System.* Stanford, Cal.: Stanford University Press, 1951.
Jorausky, David, *Soviet Marxism and Natural Science, 1917-1932.* New York: Columbia University Press, 1961.
Jorré, Georges, trans. by E. D. Laborde, *The Soviet Union, the Land and Its People.* London-New York: Longmans, Greene and Co., 1950.

Kammari, M. D., *Socialism and the Individual.* Moscow: Foreign Languages Publishing House, 1950.
Karlgren, Anton, trans. from Swedish by A. Barwell, *Bolshevist Russia.* London: G. Allen and Unwin, Ltd., 1927.
Karpinsky, V., *The Social and State Structure of the U.S.S.R.* Moscow: Foreign Languages Publishing House, 1950.
Karpovich, Michael, *Imperial Russia 1801-1917.* New York: Henry Holt and Co., 1932.
Kassof, Allen, *The Soviet Youth Program.* Cambridge, Mass.: Russian Research Center Studies, 49, Harvard University Press, 1965.
Katkoff, Vladimir, *Soviet Economy 1940-1965.* Baltimore, Md.: Dangary Publishing Co., 1961.
Kautsky, Karl, *The Dictatorship of the Proletariat.* Ann Arbor, Mich.: University of Michigan Press, 1964.
Kellen, Konrad, *Khrushchev: A Political Portrait.* New York: Frederick A. Praeger, 1961; and London: Thames and Hudson, 1961.
Kelsen, Hans, *The Communist Theory of Law.* New York: Frederick A. Praeger, 1955.
———— *The Political Theory of Bolshevism.* Berkeley, Cal.: University of California Press, 1948.
Kennan, George F., *The Decision to Intervene.* Princeton, N. J.: Princeton University Press, 1958.
———— *Russia and the West.* Boston: Little, Brown and Co., 1960.
———— *Russia Leaves the War.* Princeton, N. J.: Princeton University Press, 1956.
———— *Soviet Foreign Policy, 1917-1941.* Princeton, N. J.: D. Van Nostrand Co., Inc., 1960.
Kerensky, Alexander Fedorovich, *The Catastrophe: Kerensky's Own Story of the Russian Revolution.* New York-London: D. Appleton and Co., 1927.
———— *The Crucifixion of Liberty.* New York: John Day Co., 1934.
Kerner, R. J. *Northeastern Asia: A Selected Bibliography and a Guide to Reading.* Berkeley, Cal.: University of California Press, 1939; and London: Methuen, 1943.

———— *Slavic Europe: A Selected Bibliography in the Western European Languages.* Cambridge, Mass.: Harvard University Press, 1918.

Khrushchev, Nikita S., *For Victory in Peaceful Competition With Capitalism.* New York: E. P. Dutton and Co., Inc., 1960.

———— *On Peaceful Co-existence.* Moscow: Foreign Languages Publishing House, 1961.

———— *Report on the Program of the Communist Party of the Soviet Union.* New York: Crosscurrents Press, 1961.

———— *Report to the Central Committee of the CPSU to the Twenty-Second Congress of the Communist Party of the Soviet Union.* New York: Crosscurrents Press, 1961.

———— *Target Figures for the Economic Development of the Soviet Union, 1959-1965.* London: Farleigh Press, Ltd., 1959; Soviet Booklet No. 47.

Kirchner, Walther, *A History of Russia,* (3rd ed.). New York: Barnes and Noble, 1963.

Kline, George Louis, ed., *Soviet Education.* New York: Columbia University Press, 1957.

Klyuchevsky, V. O., *A History of Russia,* (5 Vols.). New York: Dutton, 1911-1931.

———— *A History of Russia.* New York: Russell and Russell, 1960.

Kochan, Lionel, *The Making of Modern Russia.* Harmondsworth, Middlesex, England: Penguin Books, Ltd., 1963.

Koestler, Arthur, *Darkness at Noon.* New York: Macmillan Co., 1948.

Kohn, Hans, *Basic History of Modern Russia.* New York: Anvil Books, D. Van Nostrand, Co., Inc., 1957.

————, ed., *The Mind of Modern Russia: Historical and Political Thought of Russia's Great Age.* New Brunswick, N. J.: Rutgers University Press, 1955.

———— *Nationalism in the Soviet Union.* London: G. Routledge and Sons, Ltd., 1933.

Kolarz, Walter, *The Peoples of the Soviet Far East.* New York: Frederick A. Praeger, 1954.

———— *Religion in the Soviet Union.* London-New York: Macmillan Co., 1961.

———— *Russia and Her Colonies.* New York: Frederick A. Praeger, 1952.

Konstantinovsky, Boris A., *Soviet Law in Action: The Recollected Cases of a Soviet Lawyer,* ed. by H. J. Berman. Cambridge, Mass.: Harvard University Press, 1953.

Korbel, Josef, *Poland Between East and West: Soviet and German Diplomacy Toward Poland, 1919-1933.* Princeton, N. J.: Princeton University Press, 1963.

Kornilov, Alexander, *Modern Russian History from the Age of Catherine the Great to the End of the 19th Century.* New York: Alfred A. Knopf, Inc., 1943.

Korol, Alexander G., *Soviet Education for Science and Technology.* Cambridge, Mass.: Technology Press of MIT, 1957.

Kosa, John, *Two Generations of Soviet Man: A Study in the Psychology of Communism.* Chapel Hill, N. C.: University of North Carolina Press, 1962.

Kostin, Leonid A., *Wages in the U.S.S.R.* Moscow: Foreign Languages Publishing House, 1960.

Kovalevsky, Maxime, *Russian Political Institutions.* Chicago: University of Chicago Press, 1902.

Koznacheev, Aleksandr, *Inside a Soviet Embassy: Experiences of a Russian Diplomat in Burma.* New York-Philadelphia: J. B. Lippincott Co., 1962.

Kropotkin, Peter, *Fields, Factories and Workshops.* New York-London: G. P. Putnam's Sons, 1913.

Kruglak, Theodore Edward, *The Two Faces of Tass.* Minneapolis, Minn.: University of Minnesota Press, 1962.

Kulski, Wladyslaw W., *The Soviet Regime: Communism in Practice.* Syracuse, N. Y.: Syracuse University Press, 1959.

Kunitz, Joshua, ed., *Russian Literature Since the Revolution.* New York: Boni and Gaer, 1948.

Kursky, Alexander D., *The Planning of the National Economy of the U.S.S.R.* Moscow: Foreign Languages Publishing House, 1949.

Kuusinen, O. V., ed., *Fundamentals of Marxism-Leninism.* Moscow: Foreign Languages Publishing House, 1961.

Labedz, Leopold, ed., *Revisionism: Essays on the History of Marxist Ideas*. New York: Frederick A. Praeger, 1962.

Laird, Roy D., *Collective Farming in Russia: A Political Study of the Soviet Kolkhozy*. Lawrence, Kan.: University of Kansas Publications, Social Science Studies, 1958.

————, Sharp, D. E., and Sturtevant, R., *The Rise and Fall of the MTS as an Instrument of Soviet Rule*. Lawrence, Kan.: University of Kansas Government Research Center, 1960.

Lamont, Corliss, *The Peoples of the U.S.S.R.* New York: Harcourt, Brace and World, Inc., 1946.

———— *Soviet Civilization*. New York: Philosophical Library, 1952, 1955.

Langer, William L., *Foreign Affairs Bibliography: A Selected and Annotated List of Books on International Relations, 1919-1932*. New York: Published for Council on Foreign Relations by Harper and Brothers, 1933.

La Pira, Giorgio, *et al.*, *The Philosophy of Communism*. New York: Fordham University Press, 1952.

Laquer, Walter, and Labedz, Leopold, eds., *The Future of Communist Society*. New York: Frederick A. Praeger, 1962.

————— eds., *Polycentrism, the New Factor in International Communism*. New York: Frederick A. Praeger, 1962.

————, and Lichtheim, G., eds., *The Soviet Cultural Scene, 1956-1957*. New York: Frederick A. Praeger, 1962.

Laserson, Max M., ed., *The Development of Soviet Foreign Policy in Europe, 1917-1942: A Selection of Documents*. New York: Carnegie Endowment for International Peace, 1943.

Laski, Harold Joseph, *Communism*. New York: H. Holt & Co., 1927.

Lederer, Ivo J., ed., *Russian Foreign Policy: Essays in Historical Perspective*. New Haven, Conn.: Yale University Press, 1962.

Lee, Asher, ed., *The Soviet Air and Rocket Forces*. New York: Frederick A. Praeger, 1959.

Leites, Nathan C., *The Operational Code of the Politburo*. New York: McGraw-Hill Book Co., Inc., 1951.

————, and Bernaut, Elsa, *Ritual of Liquidation: The Case of the Moscow Trials*. Glencoe, Ill.: Free Press, Inc., 1954.

———— *A Study of Bolshevism*. Glencoe, Ill.: Free Press, Inc., 1953.

Lengyel, Emil, *The Soviet Union: The Land and Its People*. New York: Oxford Book Co., 1960.

Lenin, V. I., *A Letter to American Workers*. New York: International Publishers, 1934.

————, *et al.*, *The Soviet Union and the Cause of Peace*. New York: International Publishers, 1936.

———— *Selected Works*. Moscow: Foreign Languages Publishing House, 1952.

———— *Selected Works,* (Vols. I-XII). Moscow: Co-operative Publishing Society of Foreign Workers in the U.S.S.R., 1934.

———— *What Is to Be Done?* Moscow: Foreign Languages Publishing House, 1952.

Lensen, George Alexander, ed., *Russia's Eastward Expansion*. Englewood Cliffs, N. J.: Prentice-Hall, Inc., 1964.

Leonhard, Wolfgang, *Child of the Revolution*. Chicago: H. Regnery Co., 1958.

———— *The Kremlin Since Stalin*. New York: Frederick A. Praeger, 1962.

Leroy-Beaulieu, Anatole, *The Empire of the Tsars and the Russians*. New York-London: G. P. Putnam's Sons, 1896.

Liberman, Simon Isaevich, *Building Lenin's Russia*. Chicago: University of Chicago Press, 1945.

Librach, Jan, *Rise of the Soviet Empire: A Study of Soviet Foreign Policy*. New York: Frederick A. Praeger, 1964.

Lichtheim, George, *Marxism: An Historical and Critical Study*. New York: Frederick A. Praeger, 1961.

Liddell Hart, Basil H., *The Red Army: The Red Army 1918-1945, The Soviet Army, 1946 to the Present*. New York: Harcourt, Brace, 1956.

Littlepage, J. D., and Bess, D., *In Search of Soviet Gold*. New York: Harcourt, Brace and Co., 1938.

London, Kurt, *The Seven Soviet Arts*. New Haven, Conn.: Yale University Press, 1937.

————, ed., *Unity and Contradiction: Major Aspects of Sino-Soviet Relations*. New York: Frederick A. Praeger, 1962.

Lorimer, Frank. *The Population of the Soviet Union*. Geneva: League of Nations, 1946.

Luckyj, George Stephen Nestor. *Literary Politics in the Soviet Ukraine, 1917-1934*. New York: Columbia University Press, 1956.

Luxemburg, Rosa. *The Russian Revolution and Leninism or Marxism?* Ann Arbor, Mich.: University of Michigan Press, 1961.

McClosky, Herbert, and Turner, John E., *The Soviet Dictatorship*. New York: McGraw-Hill Book Co., Inc., 1960.

McKenzie, Kermit E., *Comintern and World Revolution, 1928-1943: The Shaping of Doctrine*. New York: Columbia University Press, 1963.

MacKintosh, J. M., *Strategy and Tactics of Soviet Foreign Policy*. London-New York: Oxford University Press, 1962.

McLane, Charles B., *Soviet Policy and the Chinese Communists, 1931-1946*. New York: Columbia University Press, 1958.

McLean, Hugh, and Vickery, Walter N., eds., *The Year of Protest, 1956*. New York: Vintage Russian Library, 1961.

McNeal, Robert H., *The Bolshevik Tradition: Lenin, Stalin, Khrushchev*. Englewood Cliffs, N. J.: Prentice-Hall, 1963.

————, ed., *Lenin, Stalin, and Khrushchev: Voices of Bolshevism*. Englewood Cliffs, N. J.: Prentice-Hall, 1963.

MacLeod, Joseph Gordon, *The New Soviet Theater*. London: G. Allen and Unwin, Ltd., 1943.

Mager, N. H., and Katel, Jacques, eds., *Conquest Without War*. New York: Simon and Schuster, 1961.

Malia, Martin E., *Alexander Herzen and the Birth of Russian Socialism, 1812-1855*. Cambridge, Mass.: Harvard University Press, 1961.

Malyshev, I., *The Social Accounting of Labour and Price Under Socialism*. New York: International Arts and Sciences Press, 1960.

Marcuse, Herbert, *Reason and Revolution: Hegel and the Rise of Social Theory*, (part 2). New York: Humanities Press, 1954.

———— *Soviet Marxism*. New York: Columbia University Press, 1958.

Marx, Karl, *Capital*, (3 Vols.). Chicago: G. H. Kerr & Co., 1906-1909.

———— *Capital: A Critique of Political Economy*. Moscow: Foreign Languages Publishing House, 1954-1959.

———— *Economic and Philosophic Manuscripts of 1844*. Moscow: Foreign Languages Publishing House, n.d.; New York: International Publishers, 1964.

———— *A Contribution to the Critique of Political Economy*. Chicago: G. H. Kerr & Co., 1904.

———— *Critique of the Gotha Program*, (rev. trans.). New York: International Publishers, 1938.

———— *Early Writings*. New York: McGraw-Hill, 1964.

————, and Engels, Friedrich, *The German Ideology*, (parts 1 and 3). New York: International Publishers, 1939-1947.

————, and Engels, Friedrich, *The Holy Family: or, Critique of Critical Critiques*. Moscow: Foreign Languages Publishing House, 1956.

———— *The Poverty of Philosophy*. Moscow: Foreign Languages Publishing House, n.d.

————, and Engels, Friedrich, *Selected Correspondence, 1846-1895*. New York: International Publishers, 1942.

———— *Selected Works*, (2 Vols.) (ed. by V. Adoratsky). London: Lawrence & Wisehart, Ltd., 1942; New York: International Publishers, 1942.

Masaryk, Thomas G., *The Spirit of Russia: Studies in History, Literature, and Philosophy*, (2 Vols.). New York: Macmillan Co., 1919-1959.

Mavor, James, *An Economic History of Russia,* (2 Vols.). London-Toronto: J. M. Dent and Sons, Ltd., 1925; New York: E. P. Dutton and Co., 1925.

—— *The Russian Revolution.* New York: Macmillan Co., 1929.

Maynard, Sir John, *Russia in Flux: Before October 1946 and The Russian Peasant and Other Studies.* New York: Macmillan Co., 1948.

—— *The Russian Peasant and Other Studies.* London: Victor Gollancz, Ltd., 1942; New York: Macmillan Co., 1948.

Mayo, Henry B., *Introduction to Marxist Theory.* New York: Oxford University Press, 1960.

Mazour, Anatole G., *The Rise and Fall of the Romanovs.* Princeton, N. J.: Anvil Books, D. Van Nostrand Co., Inc., 1960.

—— *Russia: Tsarist and Communist.* Princeton, N. J.: D. Van Nostrand Co., Inc., 1962.

Mead, Margaret, *Soviet Attitudes Toward Authority.* London: Tavistock Ltd., 1955.

Medinsky, Evgeny N., *Public Education in the U.S.S.R.* Moscow: Foreign Languages Publishing House, 1950.

Medlin, William K., Lindquist, Clarence B., and Schmitt, Marshall L., *Soviet Education Programs—Foundations, Curriculums, Teacher Preparation.* Washington, D.C.: Dept. of Health, Education & Welfare, Office of Education, Government Printing Office, 1960.

Mehnert, Klaus, *Peking and Moscow.* New York: G. P. Putnam's Sons, 1963.

—— *Soviet Man and His World.* New York: Frederick A. Praeger, 1961, 1962.

Mehring, Franz, trans. by Edward Fitzgerald, *Karl Marx.* London: G. Allen and Unwin, Ltd., 1948.

Meisel, James H., and Kozera, Edward S., eds., *Materials for the Study of the Soviet System,* (2nd rev. and enlarged ed.). Ann Arbor, Mich.: George Wahr Publishing Co., 1953.

Meissner, Boris, *The Communist Party of the Soviet Union,* (ed., with a chapter on the Twentieth Party Congress, by John S. Reshetar, Jr.). New York: Frederick A. Praeger, 1956.

Meyer, Alfred G., *Communism.* New York: Random House, 1960.

—— *Leninism.* Cambridge, Mass.: Harvard University Press, 1956.

—— *Marxism.* Cambridge, Mass.: Harvard University Press, 1954.

—— *The Soviet Political System, An Interpretation.* New York: Random House, 1965.

Meyer, Frank S., *The Moulding of Communists: The Training of the Communist Cadre.* New York: Harcourt, Brace and World, Inc., 1961.

Miliukov, Paul, *Outlines of Russian Culture,* (3 Vols.). Philadelphia: University of Pennsylvania Press, 1942.

Miller, Wright W., *Russians as People.* New York: E. P. Dutton & Co., 1961.

—— *U.S.S.R.* Cambridge, England: Published for the National Book League at the University Press, 1961.

Mills, C. W., *The Marxists.* New York: Laurel Editions, Dell Publishing Co., 1962.

Milosz, Czeslaw, *The Captive Mind.* New York: Vintage Books, 1955.

Mitrany, David, *Marx Against the Peasant.* New York: Collier, 1961.

Monnerot, Jules, *Sociology and Psychology of Communism.* Boston: Beacon Press, 1960.

Moore, Barrington, Jr., *Soviet Politics—The Dilemma of Power.* Cambridge, Mass.: Harvard University Press, 1950.

—— *Terror and Progress., U.S.S.R.* Cambridge, Mass.: Harvard University Press, 1954.

Moore, Harriet L., *Soviet Far Eastern Policy, 1931-1945.* Princeton, N. J.: Princeton University Press, 1945.

Moore, Stanley W., *The Critique of Capitalist Democracy: An Introduction to the Theory of the State in Marx, Engels, and Lenin.* New York: Paine-Whitman, 1957.

Moorehead, Alan, *The Russian Revolution.* New York: Harper & Row, 1958.

Moorsteen, Richard H., *Prices and Production of Machinery in the Soviet Union, 1928-1958.* Cambridge, Mass.: Harvard University Press, 1962.

Moos, Elizabeth, *Soviet Education Today and Tomorrow*. New York: National Council of American-Soviet Friendship, 1959.

Morgan, Glenn G., *Soviet Administrative Legality: The Rule of the Attorney General's Office*. Stanford, Cal.: Stanford University Press, 1962.

Mosely, Philip E., *The Kremlin and World Politics: Studies in Soviet Policy and Action*. New York: Vintage Books, 1960.

———, ed., *The Soviet Union, 1922-1962—A Foreign Affairs Reader*. New York: Published for Council on Foreign Affairs by Frederick A. Praeger, 1963.

Neumann, Sigmund, *Permanent Revolution: The Total State in a World at War*. New York: Harper and Brothers, 1942.

North, Robert Carver, *Moscow and Chinese Communists,* (2nd ed.). Stanford, Cal.: Stanford University Press, 1962.

Nove, Alec, *The Soviet Economy,* New York: Frederick A. Praeger, 1961.

Nutter, G. Warren, *Growth of Industrial Production in the Soviet Union*. Princeton, N. J.: Princeton University Press, 1962.

Oakeshott, Michael, *The Social and Political Doctrines of Contemporary Europe*. Cambridge, England: Cambridge University Press, 1939.

Olgin, Moissaye Joseph, *The Soul of the Russian Revolution*. New York: Henry Holt and Co., 1917.

Page, Stanley W., *Lenin and World Revolution*. New York: New York University Press, 1959.

———, ed., *Russia in Revolution: Selected Readings in Russian Domestic History Since 1855*. Princeton, N. J.: D. Van Nostrand Co., 1965.

Paloczi-Horvath, Gyorgy, *Khrushchev: The Making of a Dictator*. Boston: Little, Brown and Co., 1960.

Pares, Sir Bernard, *The Fall of the Russian Monarchy*. New York: Alfred A. Knopf, 1939.

——— *A History of Russia*. London: Jonathan Cape, Ltd., 1926; New York: Alfred A. Knopf, 1937.

——— *Russia,* (rev. ed.). New York: New American Library, 1949.

Paris Peace Conference 1946, Selected Documents, (U. S. Dept. of State Publication 2868, Conference Series 103). Washington, D.C.: Government Printing Office, 1947.

Park, Alexander G., *Bolshevism in Turkestan, 1917-1927*. New York: Columbia University Press, 1957.

Parry, Albert, *Russia's Rockets and Missiles*. Garden City, N. Y.: Doubleday, 1960.

Payne, Pierre Stephen Robert, *The Life and Death of Lenin*. New York: Simon and Schuster, 1964.

Pentony, Deveu Edwin, ed., *Soviet Behavior in World Affairs: Communist Foreign Policies*. San Francisco, Cal.: Chandler Publishing Co., 1962.

Perlo, Victor, *U.S.A. and U.S.S.R.: The Economic Race*. New York: International Publishers, 1960.

Perov, G. V., *For the Benefit of the People: The Distribution of Wealth in the U.S.S.R.* London: Soviet Booklets, 1960.

Petrov, Vladimir Mikhaelovich, *Empire of Fear*. New York: Frederick A. Praeger, 1956.

Philipov, A., *Logic and Dialectic in the Soviet Union*. New York: Research Program on the U.S.S.R., 1952.

Pipes, Richard, *The Formation of the Soviet Union: Communism and Nationalism 1917-1923*. Cambridge, Mass.: Harvard University Press, 1954.

———, ed., *The Russian Intelligentsia*. New York: Columbia University Press, 1961.

——— *Social Democracy and the St. Petersburg Labor Movement, 1885-1897*. Cambridge, Mass.: Harvard University Press, 1963.

Pistrak, Lazar, *The Grand Tactician: Khrushchev's Rise to Power*. New York: Frederick A. Praeger, 1961.

Plamenatz, John, *German Marxism and Russian Communism*. London-New York: Longmans, Green and Co., Ltd., 1954.

Plekhanov, George, *Essays in Historical Materialism*. New York: International Publishers, 1940.

———— *Selected Philosophical Works*, (Vol. I.). Moscow: Foreign Languages Publishing House, 1961.

Ploss, Sidney I., *Conflict and Decision Making in Soviet Russia: A Case Study of Agricultural Policy 1953-1963*. Princeton, N. J.: Princeton University Press, 1965.

Pokrovskii, M. N., *History of Russia from the Earliest Times to the Rise of Commercial Capitalism*. New York: International Publishers, 1931.

Ponomaryov, B. N., *et al.*, eds., *History of the Communist Party of the Soviet Union*. Moscow: Foreign Languages Publishing House, 1960.

Popper, Karl R., *The Open Society and Its Enemies*. Princeton, N. J.: Princeton University Press, 1963.

Programme of the Communist Party of the Soviet Union: Adopted by the Twenty-Second Congress of the CPSU, October 31, 1961. Moscow: Foreign Languages Publishing House, 1961.

Pundeff, Marin, *Recent Publications on Communism: A Bibliography of Non-Periodical Literature, 1957-1962*. Los Angeles, Cal.: University of Southern California, Research Institute on Communist Strategy and Propaganda, 1962.

Radkey, Oliver H., *The Agrarian Foes of Bolshevism: Promise and Default of the Russian Socialist Revolutionaries, Feb. to Oct., 1917*. New York: Columbia University Press, 1958.

———— *The Election to the Russian Constituent Assembly of 1917*. Cambridge, Mass.: Harvard University Press, 1950.

———— *The Sickle under the Hammer: The Russian Socialist Revolutionaries in the Early Months of Soviet Rule*. New York: Columbia University Press, 1963.

Rauch, Georg von, trans. by Peter and Annette Jacobsohn, *A History of Soviet Russia*. New York: Frederick A. Praeger, 1957.

Reavey, George, *Soviet Literature Today*. New Haven, Conn.: Yale University Press, 1947.

Reed, John, *Ten Days That Shook the World*. New York: Modern Library, 1935.

Reshetar, John S., Jr., *A Concise History of the Communist Party of the Soviet Union*. New York: Frederick A. Praeger, 1960.

————, and Niemeyer, Gerhart, *An Inquiry into Soviet Rationality, or An Inquiry into Soviet Mentality*. New York: Frederick A. Praeger, 1956.

———— *The Ukrainian Revolution 1917-1920: A Study in Nationalism*. Princeton, N. J.: Princeton University Press, 1952.

Riasanovsky, Nicholas V., *A History of Russia*. New York: Oxford University Press, 1963.

Ritvo, Herbert, ed., *The New Soviet Society*. New York: The New Leader, 1964.

Roberts, Henry L., *Foreign Affairs Bibliography, 1942-1952*. New York: Published for Council on Foreign Relations by Harper, 1955.

———— *Russia and America, Dangers and Prospects*. New York: Published for Council on Foreign Relations by Harper, 1956.

Robinson, Geroid T., *Rural Russia Under the Old Regime*. New York: Macmillan Co., 1949.

Romashkin, Peter S., *Fundamentals of Soviet Law*. Moscow: Foreign Languages Publishing House, 1961.

Rosenberg, Arthur, *A History of Bolshevism*. London-New York: Oxford University Press, 1934.

Rostow, Walt W., Levin, Alfred, and Daniels, Robert, *The Dynamics of Soviet Society*. New York: W. W. Norton and Co., Inc., 1953.

———— *The Stages of Economic Growth*. Cambridge, England: Cambridge University Press, 1960.

Rubinstein, Alvin Z., ed., *The Foreign Policy of the Soviet Union*. New York: Random House, 1960.

Ruhle, Otto, *Karl Marx*. Garden City, N. Y.: Garden City Publishing Co., Inc., 1936; Viking Press, 1929.

Runes, D. D., *The Soviet Impact on Society, A Recollection*. New York: Philosophical Library, 1953.

Rush, Myron, *Political Succession in the U.S.S.R.* New York: Frederick A. Praeger, 1955.

―――― *The Rise of Khrushchev*. Washington, D.C.: Public Affairs Press, 1958.

Russell, Bertrand, *The Practice and Theory of Bolshevism*. New York: Simon and Schuster, 1964.

Sabine, George H., *Marxism*. Ithaca, N. Y.: Cornell University Press, 1958.

Salisbury, Harrison E., *American in Russia*. New York: Harper, 1955.

―――― *A New Russia?* New York: Harper & Row, 1962.

―――― *To Moscow—and Beyond*. New York: Harper & Row, 1960.

―――― *Moscow Journal: The End of Stalin*. Chicago: University of Chicago Press, 1961.

Salvadori, Massimo, *The Rise of Modern Communism: A Brief History of the Communist Movement in the Twentieth Century*. New York: Holt, Rinehart and Winston, 1952.

Samborsky, G., *The Soviet Economy, 1959-1965*, (A Short Statistical Handbook). New York: International Arts and Sciences Press, 1959.

Schapiro, Leonard B., *The Communist Party of the Soviet Union*. New York: Random House, 1960; London: Eyre and Spottiswoode, 1960.

―――― *The Origin of the Communist Autocracy*. Cambridge, Mass.: Harvard University Press, 1955.

―――――, ed., *The U.S.S.R. and the Future: An Analysis of the New Program of the CPSU*. New York: Frederick A. Praeger, 1962.

Schlesinger, Rudolf, ed., *Changing Attitudes in Soviet Russia*—(Vol. I: *The Family in the U.S.S.R.*, Vol. II: *Social Conditions*, Vol. III: *Politics and Government*). London: Routledge and Kegan Paul, Ltd., 1949.

―――― *Marx, His Time and Ours*. London: Routledge and Kegan Paul, Ltd., 1950.

―――――, ed., *The Nationalities Problem and Soviet Administration*. London: Routledge and Kegan Paul, Ltd., 1956.

―――― *Soviet Legal Theory, Its Social Background and Development*. London: Oxford University Press, 1945.

―――― *The Spirit of Post-War Russia: Soviet Ideology 1917-1946*. London: D. Dobson, 1947.

Scholmer, Joseph, *Vorkuta*. London: George Weidenfeld and Nicolson, Ltd., 1954; New York: Holt, Rinehart and Winston, Inc., 1955.

Schueller, George K., *The Politburo*. Stanford, Cal.: Stanford University Press, 1951.

Schuman, Frederick L., *Government in the Soviet Union*. New York: Thomas Y. Crowell Co., 1961.

―――― *Russia Since 1917*. New York: Alfred A. Knopf, 1957.

―――― *Soviet Politics, at Home and Abroad*. New York: Alfred A. Knopf, 1946.

Schwartz, Benjamin Isadore, *Chinese Communism and the Rise of Mao*. Cambridge, Mass.: Harvard University Press, 1951.

Schwartz, Harry, ed., *The Many Faces of Communism*. New York: Berkeley-Medallion, 1962.

―――― *The Red Phoenix: Russia Since World War II*. New York: Frederick A. Praeger, 1961.

―――― *Russia's Postwar Economy*. Syracuse, N. Y.: Syracuse University Press, 1947.

―――― *Russia's Soviet Economy*. Englewood Cliffs, N. J.: Prentice-Hall, 1958.

―――― *The Soviet Economy: A Selected Bibliography of Materials in English*. Syracuse, N. Y.: Syracuse University Press, 1949.

Schwarz, Solomon M., *The Jews in the Soviet Union.* Syracuse, N. Y.: Syracuse University Press, 1951.

———— *Labor in the Soviet Union.* New York: Frederick A. Praeger, 1952.

Scott, Derek J. R., *Russian Political Institutions.* New York: Frederick A. Praeger, 1961.

Scott, John, *Behind the Urals, an American Worker in Russia's City of Steel.* Boston: Houghton Mifflin Co., 1942.

Selsam, Howard, *Philosophy in Revolution.* New York: International Publishers, 1957.

————, and Martel, H., eds., *Reader in Marxist Philosophy.* New York: International Publishers, 1964.

————*What Is Philosophy? A Marxist Introduction.* New York: International Publishers, 1963.

Seton-Watson, Hugh, *The Decline of Imperial Russia.* New York: Frederick A. Praeger, 1956.

———— *The East European Revolution,* (3rd ed.). New York: Frederick A. Praeger, 1956.

———— *From Lenin to Khrushchev, the History of World Communism.* New York: Frederick A. Praeger, 1960.

———— *Neither War Nor Peace: The Struggle for Power in the Postwar World.* New York: Frederick A. Praeger, 1960.

Shabad, Theodore, *Geography of the U.S.S.R.: A Regional Survey.* New York: Columbia University Press, 1958.

Shaffer, Harry G., ed., *The Soviet Economy: A Collection of Western and Soviet Views.* New York: Appleton-Century-Crofts, 1963.

————, ed., *The Soviet System in Theory and Practice—Selected Western and Soviet Views.* New York: Appleton-Century-Crofts, 1960, 1965.

Shapiro, Leonard, ed., *Soviet Treaty Series,* (Vol. I: 1917-1928). Washington, D.C.: Georgetown University Press, 1950.

Shimkin, Demitri Boris, *Minerals, A Key to Soviet Power.* Cambridge, Mass.: Harvard University Press, 1953.

Shore, Maurice Joseph, *Soviet Education, Its Psychology and Philosophy.* New York: Philosophical Library, 1947.

Shotwell, James T., and Laserson, Max M., *Poland and Russia, 1919-1945.* New York: King's Crown Press, 1945.

Shteppa, Konstantin Feodosevich, *Russian Historians and the Soviet State.* New Brunswick, N. J.: Rutgers University Press, 1962.

Shub, David, *Lenin.* New York: Doubleday, 1948.

Shulman, Marshall D., *Stalin's Foreign Policy Reappraised.* Cambridge, Mass.: Harvard University Press, 1963.

Simmons, Ernest J., ed., *Continuity and Change in Russian and Soviet Thought.* Cambridge, Mass.: Harvard University Press, 1955.

———— *Through the Glass of Soviet Literature: Views of Russian Society.* New York: Columbia University Press, 1953.

Slonim, Mark L'vovich, *Modern Russian Literature, from Chekov to the Present.* New York: Oxford University Press, 1953.

Slusser, Robert M., and Triska, Jan F., *A Calendar of Soviet Treaties, 1917-1957.* Stanford, Cal.: Stanford University Press, 1959.

Smekhov, B., *The Planning of Capital Investments.* New York: International Arts and Sciences Press, 1963.

Sokolovsky, Vasilii D., *Military Strategy, Soviet Doctrine and Concepts.* New York: Frederick A. Praeger, 1963.

Somerville, John, *Soviet Philosophy, A Study of Theory and Practice.* New York: Philosophical Library, 1946.

Sontag, R. J., ed., *Nazi-Soviet Relations, 1939-1941: Documents from the Archives of the German Foreign Office.* Washington, D.C.: U.S. Department of State, 1948; New York: Didier Press, 1948.

Souvarine, Boris, *Stalin: A Critical Survey of Bolshevism.* London: Secker and Warburg, 1940.

Soviet Commitment to Education—Report of the First Official U.S. Education Mission to the U.S.S.R. Washington, D.C.: U.S. Government Printing Office, 1959.

Soviet Handbook 1959-1965—Statistics and Data Relating to the Soviet Seven-Year Plan. London: Soviet Booklets, No. 57, 1959.

Soviet Political Agreements and Results, U.S. Congress, Senate Committee to Investigate the Administration of the Internal Security Act and Other Security Laws, 84th Congress, Second Session, Doc. No. 125. Washington, D.C., 1955.

Soviet Political Treaties and Violations, U.S. Congress, Senate Committee on the Judiciary Subcommittee to Investigate the Administration of the Internal Security Act and Other Security Laws, 84th Congress, First Session, Doc. No. 85. Washington, D.C., 1955.

Spector, Ivar, *An Introduction to Russian History and Culture.* Princeton, N. J.: D. Van Nostrand Co., 1961.

———, and Spector, Marion, eds., *Readings in Russian History and Culture.* Boston: Allyn and Bacon, Inc., 1965.

Spinka, M., *Christianity Confronts Communism.* New York: Harper, 1936.

Spulber, Nicholas, *The Soviet Economy,* New York: W. W. Norton and Co., 1962.

Stalin, Joseph, *Economic Problems of Socialism in the U.S.S.R.* New York: International Publishers, 1952.

——— *From Socialism to Communism in the Soviet Union.* New York: International Publishers, 1939.

——— *The Great Patriotic War of the Soviet Union.* New York: International Publishers, 1945.

——— *Leninism: Selected Writings.* New York: International Publishers, 1942.

——— *Marxism and the National Question: Selected Writings and Speeches.* New York: International Publishers, 1942.

——— *The October Revolution: A Collection of Articles and Speeches.* New York: International Publishers, 1934.

——— *Problems of Leninism.* New York: International Publishers, 1934; Moscow: Foreign Languages Publishing House, 1953.

——— *Problems of Leninism,* (11th ed.). Moscow: Foreign Languages Publishing House, 1947.

Steinberg, Isaac N. *In the Workshop of the Revolution.* New York: Holt, Rinehart and Winston, Inc., 1953.

Steinberg, Julien, ed., *Verdict of Three Decades: From the Literature of Individual Revolt Against Soviet Communism.* New York: Duell, Sloan and Pearce, 1950.

Stewart, George, *The White Armies of Russia: A Chronicle of Counter-Revolution and Allied Intervention.* New York: Macmillan Co., 1933.

Stillman, Edmund O., ed., *Bitter Harvest: The Intellectual Revolt Behind the Iron Curtain.* New York: Frederick A. Praeger, 1959.

Strakhovsky, Leonid, ed., *A Handbook of Slavic Studies.* Cambridge, Mass.: Harvard University Press, 1949.

Strumilin, Stanislaw, *Problems of Socialism and Communism in the U.S.S.R.* New York: International Arts and Sciences Press, 1961.

Struve, Gleb, *Soviet Russian Literature, 1917-1950.* Norman, Okla.: University of Oklahoma Press, 1951.

Sukhanov, Nicholai N., *The Russian Revolution, 1917: A Personal Record.* London-New York: Oxford University Press, 1955.

Sumner, Benedict H., *A Short History of Russia.* New York: Harcourt, Brace and World, 1949.

Swayze, Harold, *Political Control of Literature in the U.S.S.R., 1946-1959.* Cambridge, Mass.: Harvard University Press, 1962.

Swearer, Howard R., and Longaker, Richard P., eds., *Contemporary Communism: Theory and Practice.* Belmont, Cal.: Wadsworth Publishing Co., 1963.

——— *The Politics of Succession in the U.S.S.R.—Materials on Khrushchev's Rise to Leadership.* Boston: Little, Brown and Co., 1964.

Talmon, Jacob Leib, *Political Messianism—The Romantic Phase*. New York: Frederick A. Praeger, 1961.
——— *The Rise of Totalitarian Democracy*. Boston: Beacon Press, 1952.
Taracouzio, T. A., *The Soviet Union and International Law*. New York: Macmillan Co., 1935.
——— *War and Peace in Soviet Diplomacy*. New York: Macmillan Co., 1940.
Tertz, Abram, trans. from Russia by Max Hayward, *The Trial Begins*. New York: Pantheon Books, 1960.
Theil, Erich, *The Soviet Far East: A Survey of its Physical and Economic Geography*. New York: Frederick A. Praeger, 1957.
Timasheff, Nicholas S., *The Great Retreat: The Growth and Decline of Communism in Russia*. New York: E. P. Dutton Co., 1946.
——— *Religion in Soviet Russia: 1917-1942*. New York: Sheed and Ward, Inc., 1942.
Timoshenko, Vladimir P., *Agricultural Russia and the Wheat Problem*. Stanford, Cal.: Food Research Institute, 1932.
Towster, Julian, *Political Power in the U.S.S.R., 1917-1947: The Theory and Structure of Government in the Soviet State*. New York: Oxford University Press, 1948.
Treadgold, Donald W., *Lenin and His Rivals: The Struggle for Russia's Future, 1898-1906*. New York: Frederick A. Praeger, 1955.
——— *Twentieth Century Russia*. Chicago: Rand, McNally and Co., 1959.
Triska, Jan F., ed., *Soviet Communism: Programs and Rules*. San Francisco: Chandler Publishing Co., 1962.
———, and Slusser, Robert M., *The Theory, Law, and Policy of Soviet Treaties*. Stanford, Cal.: Stanford University Press, 1962.
Trotsky, Leon, *The History of the Russian Revolution*. Ann Arbor, Mich.: University of Michigan Press, 1957.
——— *Lenin*. New York: Milton, Balch and Co., 1925.
——— *My Life*. New York: Charles Scribner's Sons, 1930.
——— *The Revolution Betrayed*. Garden City, N. Y.: Doubleday, Doran and Co., Inc., 1937.
——— *Stalin*. New York: Harper and Row, 1941.
Tucker, Robert, *Philosophy and Myth in Karl Marx*. Cambridge, England: Cambridge University Press, 1961.
——— *The Soviet Political Mind: Studies in Stalinism and Post-Stalin Change*. New York: Frederick A. Praeger, 1963.
Turgeon, Lynn, *The Contrasting Economies: A Study of Modern Economic Systems*. Boston: Allyn and Bacon, Inc., 1963.
———, and Bergson, Abram, *Prices of Basic Industrial Goods in the U.S.S.R.* Santa Monica, Cal.: The Rand Corporation, 1957.

Ulam, Adam B., *The New Face of Soviet Totalitarianism*. Cambridge, Mass.: Harvard University Press, 1963.
——— *The Unfinished Revolution: An Essay on the Sources of Marxism and Communism*. New York: Random House, 1960.
Ullman, Richard H., *Intervention and the War: Anglo-Soviet Relations, 1917-1921*. Princeton, N. J.: Princeton University Press, 1961.
U.S. Department of State, Division of Library and Reference Services, *Soviet Bibliography*. Washington, D.C.: May 6, 1949.
——— *Foreign Relations of the United States: Diplomatic Papers, The Soviet Union, 1933-1939*. Washington, D.C.: U.S. Government Printing Office, 1952.
——— *Papers Relating to the Foreign Relations of the United States, 1918, Russia*, (3 Vols.). Washington, D.C.: U.S. Government Printing Office, 1931-1932.
U.S. Library of Congress, Division of Bibliography, *Soviet Russia: A Selected List of Recent References*. Washington, D.C.: 1943.
U.S. Senate, *World Communism: A Selected Annotated Bibliography*, prep. by Joseph Whelan. Washington, D.C.: Government Printing Office, 1964, 88th Congress, 2nd Session, Doc. No. 69.

Utechin, S. V., *Russian Political Thought: A Concise History.* New York: Frederick A. Praeger, 1964.

Vakar, Nicholas P., *Byelorussia: The Making of a Nation, A Case Study.* Cambridge, Mass.: Harvard University Press, 1956.
———— *The Taproot of Soviet Society.* New York: Harper & Row, 1962.
Venable, V., *Human Nature: The Marxian View.* New York: Alfred A. Knopf, 1945.
Venturi, Franco, *Roots of Revolution: History of the Populist and Socialist Movements in 19th Century Russia.* New York: Alfred A. Knopf, 1960.
Vernadsky, George, and Karpovich, Michael, *A History of Russia,* (3 Vols.). New Haven, Conn.: Yale University Press, 1943.
———— *A History of Russia.* New Haven, Conn.: Yale University Press, 1961.
Vickery, Walter N., *The Cult of Optimism: Political and Ideological Problems of Recent Soviet Literature.* Bloomington, Ind., Indiana University Press, 1963.
Volin, Lazar, *A Survey of Soviet Russian Agriculture.* Washington, D.C.: U.S. Government Printing Office, 1951.
Von Laue, Theodore H., *Why Lenin? Why Stalin: A Reappraisal of the Russian Revolution.* Philadelphia-New York: J. B. Lippincott, 1964.
Voyce, Arthur, *Russian Architecture: Trends in Nationalism and Modernism.* New York: Philosophical Library, 1948.
Vucinich, Alexander, *Soviet Economic Institutions.* Stanford, Cal.: Stanford University Press, 1952.
Vyshinsky, Andrei Y., *The Law of the Soviet State.* New York: Macmillan Co., 1948.

Walsh, Warren B., *Russia and the Soviet Union, a Modern History.* Ann Arbor, Mich.: University of Michigan Press, 1958.
———— *Readings in Russian History.* Syracuse, N. Y.: Syracuse University Press, 1959.
Webb, Sidney, and Webb, Beatrice, *Soviet Communism: A New Civilization?,* (2 Vols.). New York: Charles Scribner's Sons, 1936.
Weissberg, Alexander, *The Accused.* New York: Simon and Schuster, 1951.
Werth, Alexander, *Russia at War, 1941-1945.* New York: E. P. Dutton and Co., 1964.
———— *Russia Under Khrushchev.* New York: Hill and Wang, 1962.
———— *The Year of Stalingrad: An Historical Record and a Study of Russian Mentality, Methods and Policies.* London: Hamilton, 1946.
Wetter, Gustavo A., *Dialectical Materialism: A Historical and Systematic Survey of Philosophy in the Soviet Union.* New York: Frederick A. Praeger, 1959.
Wheeler-Bennett, J. W., *Munich: Prologue to Tragedy.* New York: Duell, Sloan and Pearce, 1948.
Whiting, Allen S., *Soviet Policies in China, 1917-1924.* New York: Columbia University Press, 1954.
Whiting, Kenneth R., *The Soviet Union Today: A Concise Handbook.* New York: Frederick A. Praeger, 1962.
Wiles, Peter John D., *The Political Economy of Communism.* Cambridge, Mass.: Harvard University Press, 1962.
Wilson, Edmund, *To the Finland Station: A Study in the Writing and Acting of History.* Garden City, N. Y.: Doubleday and Co., 1955.
Wolfe, Bertram D., *Communist Totalitarianism.* Boston: Beacon Press, 1961.
———— *Khrushchev and Stalin's Ghost.* New York: Frederick A. Praeger, 1957.
———— *Six Keys to the Soviet System.* Boston: Beacon Press, 1956.
———— *Three Men Who Made a Revolution.* New York: Dial Press, Inc., 1948.
Wolfe, Thomas W., *Soviet Strategy at the Crossroads.* Cambridge, Mass.: Rand Corporation Research Study, Harvard University Press, 1964.
Wolff, Robert Lee, *The Balkans in Our Time.* Cambridge, Mass.: Harvard University Press, 1956.
Wolin, Simon, and Slusser, Robert M., eds., *The Soviet Secret Police.* New York: Frederick A. Praeger, 1957.

Woolbert, Robert Gale, *Foreign Affairs Bibliography: A Selected and Annotated List of Books on International Relations, 1932-1942*. New York: Council on Foreign Relations, by Harper & Brothers, 1945.

Wren, Melvin C., *The Course of Russian History*. New York: Macmillan Co., 1958.

Wu, Aitchen K., *China and the Soviet Union: A Study of Sino-Soviet Relations*. New York: J. Day Co., 1950.

Yarmolinsky, Avrahm, *The Jews and Other Minor Nationalities Under the Soviet Union*. New York: Vanguard Press, 1928.

—— *Road to Revolution: A Century of Russian Radicalism*. New York: Macmillan Co., 1959, and Collier Books, 1962.

Yevenko, Ivan A., *Planning in the U.S.S.R.* Moscow: Foreign Languages Publishing House, 1961.

Yugow, Aaron, *Russia's Economic Front for War and Peace*. New York-London: Harper and Brothers, 1942.

Zagoria, Donald S., *The Sino-Soviet Conflict, 1956-1961*. Princeton, N. J.: Princeton University Press, 1962.

Zaitsev, Y., and Poltorak, A., *The Soviet Bar*. Moscow: Foreign Languages Publishing House, 1959.

Zavalishin, Viacheslav, *Early Soviet Writers*. New York: Published for Research Program on U.S.S.R. by Frederick A. Praeger, 1958.

Zenkovsky, Serge A., *Pan-Turkism and Islam in Russia*. Cambridge, Mass.: Harvard University Press, 1960.

Zirkle, Conway, ed., *Death of Science in Russia*. Philadelphia: University of Pennsylvania Press, 1949.

Zlatopolsky, D., *State System of the U.S.S.R.* Moscow: Foreign Languages Publishing House, 1960.

Zverev, Arsenii G., *The Soviet Standard of Living: Social Benefits*. New York: International Arts and Sciences Press, 1959.

INDEX

DATE DUE